DISTRIBUTED
SYSTEMS
SECOND EDITION

ACM PRESS BOOKS

Editor-in-Chief	**Peter Wegner**	Brown University
International Editor	**Dines Bjørner**	Technical University
(Europe)		of Denmark

SELECTED TITLES

Object-Oriented Reuse, Concurrency and Distribution
 Colin Atkinson

Advances in Database Programming Languages   *Francois Bançilhon
and Peter Buneman (Eds)*

Algebraic Specification   *J.A. Bergstra, J. Heering and P. Klint (Eds)*

Software Reusability (Volume 1: Concepts and Models)
 Ted Biggerstaff and Alan Perlis (Eds)

Software Reusability (Volume 2: Applications and Experience)
 Ted Biggerstaff and Alan Perlis (Eds)

Object-Oriented Software Engineering: A Use CASE Driven Approach
 *Ivar Jacobson, Magnus Christerson, Patrik Jonnson
 and Gunnar Övergaard*

Object-Oriented Concepts, Databases and Applications
 Won Kim and Frederick H. Lochovsky (Eds)

Computing: a Human Activity   *Peter Naur*

The Oberon System: User Guide and Programmer's Manual
 Martin Reiser

Programming in Oberon: Steps Beyond Pascal and Modula
 Martin Reiser and Niklaus Wirth

Project Oberon: The Design of an Operating System and Compiler
 Niklaus Wirth and Jürg Gutknecht

The Programmer's Apprentice   *Charles Rich and Richard C. Waters*

User Interface Design   *Harold Thimbleby*

Advanced Animation and Rendering Techniques
 Alan Watt and Mark Watt

DISTRIBUTED SYSTEMS ▼

SECOND EDITION

▲

Edited by

SAPE MULLENDER

University of Twente
The Netherlands

ACM Press New York,
New York

ADDISON-WESLEY
PUBLISHING
COMPANY

Wokingham, England · Reading, Massachusetts · Menlo Park, California · New York
Don Mills, Ontario · Amsterdam · Bonn · Sydney · Singapore
Tokyo · Madrid · San Juan · Milan · Paris · Mexico City · Seoul · Taipei

ACM Press Frontier Series

© 1993 by the ACM Press. A division of the Association for Computing Machinery, Inc. (ACM)

The programs in this book have been included for their instructional value. They have been tested with care but are not guaranteed for any particular purpose. The publisher does not offer any warranties or representations nor does it accept any liabilities with respect to the programs.

Many of the designations used by manufacturers and sellers to distinguish their products are claimed as trademarks. Addison-Wesley has made every attempt to supply trademark information about manufacturers and their products mentioned in this book. A list of the trademark designations and their owners appears below.

The cartoon *'Where Theory meets Practice'* on the cover was drawn by Jorge Stolfi while a computer scientist at the Digital Equipment Corporation's Systems Research Center in Palo Alto, California, and is reproduced here with their permission.
Cover designed by Chris Eley
and printed in the United States of America.
Camera-ready copy prepared by the editor.
Printed and bound in the United States of America.

First printed 1993. Reprinted 1994 and 1995.

ISBN 0–201–62427–3

British Library Cataloguing-in-Publication Data
A catalogue record for this book is available from the British Library.

Library of Congress Cataloguing-in-Publication Data is available

Trademark Notice
Ada is a trademark of the US DoD
Courier and Ethernet are trademarks of Xerox Corp.
MVS is a trademark of IBM
NCS is a trademark of HP Apollo
NFS is a trademark of SUN Microsystems
UNIX is a trademark of UNIX Systems Laboratories

Preface

This book collects the lecture notes used at the *Advanced Course on Distributed Systems* which has now been held five times — *Arctic'88* in Tromsø, Norway, *Fingerlakes'89* in Ithaca, NY, *Bologna '90* in Italy, *Karuizawa '91* in Japan and *Lisboa '92* in Portugal. Its inauguration will be at the sixth advanced course, *Seattle '93* in Seattle, WA.

The first edition was based on the lecture notes used at *Arctic'88* and *Fingerlakes'89*. Since then, the course has evolved and steadily improved: coordination between the lecturers has eliminated duplication of material; it has produced agreement on terminology; and the course now reflects a more balanced view of both 'theoretical' and 'practical' aspects of research in distributed systems.

As a consequence, the material in this second edition is almost entirely new. Only one chapter, in fact, has survived unscathed from the first edition. This book, I believe, has now become a coherent treatment of an increasingly important research area.

Distributed Systems is intended for people in universities and industry interested in distributed systems. Teachers can use this book to refresh their knowledge of distributed systems. Graduate students can use it to get acquainted with the field and as a reference to other work. Distributed systems designers and builders can use it as a source book when trying to solve problems they encounter in their work. It can be (and is, by some of the authors) used in post-graduate distributed systems courses. It is aimed at graduate students in computer science: the reader should have a good general knowledge of computer organization, computer networks, and operating systems.

The book can be roughly partitioned into seven parts — an introduction (Chapters 1–3), a part on theoretical foundations (Chapters 4–8), a part on communication (Chapters 9–11), a part on file systems and database systems (Chapters 12–14), a single chapter on kernel support (Chapter 15), a part on real-time systems (Chapters 16–19) and a part on security (Chapters 20 and 21).

In Chapter 1, Schroeder explains what distinguishes distributed systems from other systems, and he discusses properties of distributed systems and techniques for achieving them. Then, in Chapter 2, Schneider discusses the importance of making models of the behaviour of distributed systems and the failures that need to be masked by them. Chapter 3, by Weihl, introduces a specification method for concurrent systems and then derives specifications for the alternating-bit protocol, mutexes and condition variabes, remote procedure call, and a name service.

The second group of chapters covers theoretical foundations of distributed and fault-tolerant algorithms. Chapter 4, by Babaoğlu and Marzullo, describes how one can deduce, through the exchange of messages, what the state is of a distributed system. It introduces *consistent cuts* and *snapshots, causality, logical* and *vector clocks,* and characterizes *stable* and *unstable predicates.* Chapter 5, by Hadzilacos and Toueg, introduces various *broadcast* mechanisms. Using broadcasts, it is possible to provide to a set of cooperating processes a consistent view of a distributed computation. Broadcast protocols play an important rôle in the following three chapters. Chapter 6, by Babaoğlu and Toueg, gives protocols for *non-blocking atomic commitment,* Chapter 7, by Schneider, describes one well-known technique for turning a deterministic program running on a single computer into a distributed one running on a set of computers so that it becomes fault tolerant, and Chapter 8, by Budhiraja, Marzullo, Schneider and Toueg, shows another technique for transforming a program into a fault-tolerant one.

In Chapter 9, Mullender discusses practical aspects of protocol design for interprocess communication in distributed systems. Attention is given to achieving *at-most-once* behaviour of remote-invocation protocols in unreliable networks. *Remote procedure call* is also described in Chapter 9. Lampson applies the specification methods of Chapter 2 to the derivation of a protocol for *connection establishment* in Chapter 10. In Chapter 11, Rodeheffer and Schroeder examine a particular distributed application — building up the routing tables for a high-speed *switch-based local-area network.*

Needham discusses issues associated with *naming* in Chapter 12 and shows that building naming databases for very large systems is a far from trivial. Weihl describes the protocols used for implementing *atomic transactions* in distributed systems subject to processor and network failures in Chapter 13. And Satyanarayanan, in Chapter 14, shows how empirical data about how file systems are used can be used to advantage in the implementation of distributed file systems. One file system, *Coda,* is also decribed there in detail.

In Chapter 15, Mullender uses the design of the Amoeba distributed system to discuss issues of distributed system kernel design and discuss techniques for memory management and process management.

In Chapters 16–19, Kopetz and Veríssimo cover the subject of *real-time systems.* Chapter 16 introduces real time and the concept of *dependability.* Chapter 17 then covers communication in real-time systems, while Chapter 18 discusses *scheduling* of real-time processes. Two case studies, MARS and DELTA-4, are the subject of Chapter 19.

The final part of the book is about *security and cryptography.* Needham explains how cryptography is used to build *secure authenticated* communication channels in Chapter 20. In Chapter 21, Lampson unfolds a *security architecture* for distributed systems, in which he covers security aspects ranging from secure bootstrapping to authenticating a party on the other side of the planet.

Amsterdam, March, 1993
Sape J. Mullender, editor

Contents

Chapter 1

A State-of-the-Art Distributed System: Computing with BOB

Michael D. Schroeder

Distributed systems are a popular and powerful computing paradigm. Yet existing examples have serious short-comings as a base for general purpose computing. This chapter explores the characteristics, strengths, and weaknesses of distributed systems. It describes a model for a state-of-the-art distributed system that can do a better job of supporting general-purpose computing than existing systems. This model system combines the best features of centralized and networked systems, with improved availability and security. The chapter concludes by outlining the technical approaches that appear most promising for structuring such a system.

This chapter does not specifically discuss application-specific distributed systems, such as automated banking systems, control systems for roaming and tracking cellular telephones, and retail point-of-sales systems, although there are many economically important examples. The issues raised in the chapter do apply to such systems and the model system described here should be a suitable base for many of them. Some systems that are designed to support a narrow set of uses, however, may need to be structured in application-specific ways that can be simpler and more efficient for those uses. The extent to which special-purpose systems should be built on a general-purpose distributed base needs to be investigated further. This chapter also does not address real-time distributed systems, such as control systems for factories, aircraft, or automobiles, which face distinctive scheduling and resource utilization requirements.

1.1 Characteristics of Distributed Systems

A distributed system is several computers doing something together. Thus, a distributed system has three primary characteristics.

1

- *Multiple Computers* — A distributed system contains more than one physical computer, each consisting of CPUs, some local memory, possibly some stable storage like disks, and I/O paths to connect it with the environment.
- *Interconnections* — Some of the I/O paths will interconnect the computers. If they cannot talk to each other, then it is not going to be a very interesting distributed system.
- *Shared State* — The computers cooperate to maintain some shared state. Put another way, if the correct operation of the system is described in terms of some global invariants, then maintaining those invariants requires the correct and coordinated operation of multiple computers.

Building a system out of interconnected computers requires that four major issues be addressed.

- *Independent Failure* — Because there are several distinct computers involved, when one breaks others may keep going. Often we want the 'system' to keep working after one or more have failed.
- *Unreliable Communication* — Because, in most cases, the interconnections among computers are not confined to a carefully controlled environment, they will not work correctly all the time. Connections may be unavailable. Messages may be lost or garbled. One computer cannot count on being able to communicate clearly with another, even if both are working.
- *Insecure Communication* — The interconnections among the computers may be exposed to unauthorized eavesdropping and message modification.
- *Costly Communication* — The interconnections among the computers usually provide lower bandwidth, higher latency, and higher cost communication than that available between the independent processes within a single machine.

A centralized system that supports multiple processes and provides some form of interprocess communication, e.g. a UNIX timesharing system, can exhibit in virtual form the three primary characteristics of a distributed system. A centralized system may even manifest independent failure, e.g. the dæmon process for mail transport may crash without stopping interactive user processes on the same system. Thus, design and programming techniques associated with communicating sequential processes in centralized systems form part of the basic techniques in the distributed systems arena. However, centralized systems are usually successful without dealing with independent failure and usually do not confront unreliable, insecure, and costly communications. In a distributed system these issues must be addressed.

The canonical example of a general-purpose distributed system today is a networked system — a set of workstations/PCs and servers interconnected with a network.

1.2   Networked vs Centralized Systems

It is easy to understand why networked systems are popular. Such systems allow the sharing of information and resources over a wide geographic and organizational spread. They allow the use of small, cost-effective computers and get the computing cycles close to the data. They can grow in small increments over a large range of sizes. They allow a great deal of autonomy through separate component purchasing decisions, selection of multiple vendors, use of multiple software versions, and adoption of multiple management policies. Finally, they do not necessarily all crash at once. Thus, in the areas of sharing, cost, growth, and autonomy, networked systems are better than traditional centralized systems as exemplified, say, by timesharing.

On the other hand, centralized systems do some things better than today's networked systems. All information and resources in a centralized system are equally accessible. Functions work the same way and objects are named the same way everywhere in a centralized system. And a centralized system is easier to manage. So despite the advantages of networked systems, centralized systems are often easier to use because they are more accessible, coherent, and manageable.

In the areas of security and availability, the comparison between networked systems and centralized systems produces no clear-cut advantage for either.

1.2.1   Security

In usual practice to date, neither centralized nor networked systems offer real security, but for different reasons.

A centralized system has a single security domain under the control of a single authority. The trusted computing base is contained in a single operating system. That operating system executes on a single computer that can have a physically secure environment. With all the security eggs in one basket, so to speak, users understand the level of trust to assign to the system and who to speak to when problems arise. On the other hand, it is notoriously difficult to eliminate all the security flaws from an operating system or from the operating environment, and with a single security domain one such flaw can be exploited to break the security of the entire system.

Networked systems have multiple security domains and thus exhibit the inverse set of security properties. The trusted computing base is scattered among many components that operate in environments with varying degrees of physical security, differing security policies, and possibly under different authorities. The interconnections among the computers are physically insecure. It is hard to know what is being trusted and what can be trusted. But, because the system contains many computers, exploiting a security flaw in the software or environment of one computer does not automatically compromise the entire system.

1.2.2   Availability

A similar two-sided analysis applies to availability. A centralized system can have a controlled physical and operational environment. Since a high proportion of system failures are the result of operational and environmental factors, careful management of this single environment can produce good availability. But when something does go wrong the whole system goes down at once, stopping all users from getting work done.

In a networked system the various computers fail independently. However, it is often the case that several computers must be in operation simultaneously before a user can get work done, so the probability of the system failing is greater than the probability of one component failing. This increased probability of not working, compared to a centralized system, is the result of ignoring independent failure. The consequence is Leslie Lamport's definition of a distributed system: 'You know you have one when the crash of a computer you've never heard of stops you from getting any work done.'

On the other hand, independent failure in a distributed system can be exploited to increase availability and reliability. When independent failure is properly harnessed by replicating functions on independent components, multiple component failures are required before system availability and reliability suffer. The probability of the system failing thus can be less than the probability in a centralized system. Dealing with independent failure to avoid making availability worse, or even to make it better, is a major task for designers of distributed systems.

A distributed system also must cope with communication failures. Unreliable communication not only contributes to unavailability, it can lead to incorrect functioning. A computer cannot reliably distinguish a down neighbor from a disconnected neighbor and therefore can never be sure an unresponsive neighbor has actually stopped. Maintaining global state invariants in such circumstances is tricky. Careful design is required to actually achieve correct operation and high availability using replicated components.

1.2.3 A State-of-the-Art Distributed System

It seems feasible to develop a distributed system that combines the accessibility, coherence, and manageability advantages of centralized systems with the sharing, growth, cost, and autonomy advantages of networked systems. If real security and high availability were added to the mix, then we would have a state-of-the-art computing base for many purposes. Achieving this combination of features in a single system is the central challenge of supporting general-purpose computing well with a distributed system. No existing system fulfills this ideal.

1.3 The Properties and Services Model

We can describe this best-of-both-worlds (BOB) distributed computing base in terms of a model of its properties and services. This more technical description of the goals provides a structure that will help us to understand the mechanisms needed to achieve them.

The properties and services model defines BOB as:

- a heterogeneous set of hardware, software, and data components;
- whose size and geographic extent can vary over a large range;

- connected by a network;
- providing a uniform set of services (naming, remote invocation, user registration, time, files, etc);
- with certain global properties (names, access, security, management and
  availability).

Because we are talking about a base for general-purpose computing, the model
is defined in terms most appropriate to understanding by the programmers who
develop components that are part of the base and who develop the many different
applications that are to be built on top of it. But the fundamental coherence
provided by the model will show through such components and applications
(when they are correctly implemented) to provide a coherent system as viewed by
its human users too.

The coherence that makes BOB a system rather than a collection of computers
is a result of its uniform services and global properties. The services are available
in the same way to every part of the system and the properties allow every part
of the system to be viewed in the same way, regardless of system size. Designers
are well aware of the care that must be taken to produce implementations that can
support growth to very large sizes (thousands of nodes). A similar challenge exists
in making such expandable systems light-weight and simple enough to be suitable
for very small configurations too.

BOB's coherence does not mean that all the components of the system must be
the same The model applies to a heterogeneous collection of computers running
operating systems such as UNIX, VMS, MS-DOS, Windows NT, and others. In
short, all platforms can operate in this framework, even computers and systems
from multiple vendors. The underlying network can be a collection of local area
network segments, bridges, routers, gateways, and various types of long distance
services with connectivity provided by various transport protocols.

1.3.1   Properties

What do BOB's pervasive properties mean in more detail?

- *Global names* — the same names work everywhere. Machines, users, files,
  distribution lists, access control groups, and services have full names that
  mean the same thing regardless of where in the system the names are
  used. For instance, Butler Lampson's user name might be something like
  /com/dec/src/bwl throughout the system. He will operate under that
  name when using any computer. Global naming underlies the ability to
  share things.
- *Global access* — the same functions are usable everywhere with reasonable
  performance. If Butler sits down at a machine when visiting in California, he can do everything there that he can do when in his usual office in
  Massachusetts, with perhaps some performance degradations. For instance,
  from Palo Alto Butler could command the local printing facilities to print a
  file stored on his computer in Cambridge. Global access also includes the
  idea of data coherence. Suppose Butler is in Cambridge on the phone to

Mike Schroeder in Palo Alto and Butler makes a change to a file and writes it. Mike should be able to read the new version as soon as Butler thinks he has saved it. Neither Mike nor Butler should have to take any special action to make this possible.

- *Global security* — the same user authentication and access control work everywhere. For instance, Butler can authenticate himself to any computer in the system; he can arrange for data transfer secure from eavesdropping and modification between any two computers; and assuming that the access control policy permits it, Butler can use exactly the same mechanism to let the person next door and someone from another site read his files. All the facilities that require controlled access (logins, files, printers, management functions, etc.) use the same machinery to provide access control.
- *Global management* — the same person can manage components anywhere. Obviously one person will not manage all of a large system. But the system should not impose *a priori* constraints on which set of components a single person can manage. All of the components of the system provide a common interface to management tools. The tools allow a manager to perform the same action on large numbers of components at once. For instance, a single system manager can configure all the workstations in an organization without leaving his office.
- *Global availability* — the same services work even after some failures. System managers get to decide (and pay for) the level of replication for each service. As long as the failures do not exceed the redundancy provided, each service will go on working. For instance, a group might decide to duplicate its file servers but get by with one printer per floor. System-wide policy might dictate a higher level of replication for the underlying communication network. Mail does not have to fail between Palo Alto and Cambridge just because some machine goes down in Lafayette, Indiana.

1.3.2 Services

The standard services defined by BOB include the following fundamental facilities:

- *Names* — provides access to a replicated, distributed database of global names and associated values for machines, users, files, distribution lists, access control groups, and services. A name service is the key BOB component for providing global names, although most of the work involved in implementing global names is making all the other components of the distributed system, e.g., existing operating systems, use the name service in a consistent way.
- *Remote procedure call* — provides a standard way to define and securely invoke service interfaces. This allows service instances to be local or remote. The RPC mechanism can be organized to operate by dynamically choosing one of a variety of transport protocols. Choosing RPC for the standard service invocation mechanism does not force blocking call semantics on all programs. RPC defines a way to match response messages with request messages. It does not require that the calling program block to await a response. Meth-

ods for dealing with asynchrony inside a single program are a local option. Blocking on RPC calls is a good choice when the local environment provides multiple threads per address space.

- *User registrations* — allows users to be registered and authenticated and issues certificates permitting access to system resources and information.
- *Time* — distributes consistent and accurate time globally.
- *Files* — provides access to a replicated, distributed, global file system. Each component machine of BOB can make available the files it stores locally through this standard interface. The multiple file name spaces are connected by the name service. The file service specification should include standard presentations for the different VMS, UNIX, etc. file types. For example, all implementations should support a standard view of any file as an array of bytes.
- *Management* — provides access to the management data and operations of each component.

In addition to these base level facilities, BOB can provide other services appropriate to the intended applications, such as:

- *Records* — provides access to records, either sequentially or via indexes, with record locking to allow concurrent reading and writing, and journaling to preserve integrity after a failure.
- *Printers* — allows printing throughout the network of documents in standard formats such as Postscript and ANSI, including job control and scheduling.
- *Execution* — allows programs to be run on any machine (or set of machines) in the network, subject to access and resource controls, and efficiently schedules both interactive and batch jobs on available machines, taking account of priorities, quotas, deadlines, and failures. The exact configuration and utilization of cycle servers (as well as idle workstations that can be used for computing) fluctuates constantly, so users and applications need automatic help in picking the machines on which to run.
- *Mailboxes* — provides a transport service for electronic mail.
- *Terminals* — provides access to a windowing graphics terminal from a computation anywhere in the network.
- *Accounting* — provides access to a system-wide collection of data on resource usage which can be used for billing and monitoring.

In many cases adequate, widely accepted standards already exist for the definition of the base and additional services. Each service must be defined and implemented to provide the five pervasive properties.

1.3.3 Interfaces

Interfaces are the key to making BOB be a coherent and open system. Each of the services is defined by an interface specification that serves as a contract between the service and its clients. The interface defines the operations to be provided, the parameters of each, and the detailed semantics of each relative to a model of the state maintained by the service. The specification is normally represented as an RPC interface definition. Some characterizations of the performance of the operations must be provided (although it is not well understood how to provide precise performance characterizations for operations whose performance varies widely depending on the parameters and/or use history). A precisely defined interface enables interworking across models, versions, and vendors. Several implementations of each interface can exist and this variety allows the system to be heterogeneous in its components. In its interfaces, however, the system is homogeneous.

It is this homogeneity that makes it a system with predictable behavior rather than a collection of components that can communicate. If more than one interface exists for the same function, it is unavoidable that the function will work differently through the different interfaces. The system will consequently be more complicated and less reliable. Perhaps some components will not be able to use others at all because they have no interface in common. Certainly customers and salesmen will find it much more difficult to configure workable collections of components, and programmers will not know what services they can depend upon being present.

1.4   Achieving the Global Properties

Experience and research have suggested a set of models for achieving global naming, access, security, management, and availability. For each of these pervasive properties, we will consider the general approach that seems most promising.

1.4.1   Naming Model

Every user and every client program sees the entire system as the same tree of named objects. A global name is interpreted by following the named branches in this tree starting from the global root. Every node has a way to find a copy of the root of the global name tree.

A hierarchic name space is used because it is the only naming structure we know of that scales well, allows autonomy in the selection of names, and is sufficiently malleable to allow for a long lifetime. A global root for the name space is required to provide each object with a single name that will work from everywhere. Non-hierarchic links can be added where a richer naming structure is required.

For each object type there is some service, whose interface is defined by BOB, that provides operations to create and delete objects of that type and to read and change their state.

The top part of the naming tree is provided by the BOB name service and the objects near the root of the tree are implemented by the BOB name service. A node in the naming tree, however, can be a *junction* between the name service and some other service, for instance, a file service. A junction object contains:

- a set of servers for the named object
- rules for choosing a server name

- the service interface ID, e.g., 'BOB File Service 2.3'
- an object parameter, e.g., a volume identifier

To look up a name through a junction, choose a server and call the service interface there with the name and the object parameter. The server looks up the rest of the name.

The servers listed in a junction object are designated by global names. To call a service at a server the client must convert the server name to something more useful, like the network address of the server machine and information on which protocols to use in making the call. Looking up a server name in the global name tree produces a server object that contains:

- a machine name
- a set of communication protocol names

A final name lookup maps the (global) machine name into the network address that will be the destination for the actual RPC to the service.

The junction machinery can be used at several levels, as appropriate. The junction is a powerful technique for unifying multiple implementations of naming mechanisms within the same hierarchic name space.

Figure 1.1 gives an example of what the top parts of the global name space might look like, based on the naming scheme of the Internet Domain Name Service. An X.500 service could also provide this part of the name space (or both the Internet DNS and X.500 could be accommodated). An important part of implementing BOB is defining the actual name hierarchy to be used in top levels of the global name space.

Consider some of the objects named here. /com, /com/dec, and /com/-dec/src are directories implemented by the BOB name service. /com/dec/-src/adb is a registered user, also an object implemented by the name service. The object /com/dec/src/adb contains a suitably encrypted password, a set of mailbox sites, and other information that is associated with this system user.

/com/dec/src/staff is a group of global names. Group objects are provided by BOB's name service to implement things like distribution lists, access control lists, and sets of servers. /com/dec/src/bin is a file system volume. Note that this object is a junction to the BOB file service. The figure does not show the content of this junction object, but it contains a group naming the set of servers implementing this file volume and rules for choosing which one to use, e.g., the first that responds. To look up the name /com/dec/src/bin/ls, for example, the operating system on a client machine traverses the path /com/dec/src/bin using the name service. The result at that point is the content of the junction object, which then allows the client to contact a suitable file server to complete the lookup.

The local management autonomy provided by hierarchic names allows system implementors and administrators to build and use their systems without waiting for a planet-wide agreement to be reached about the structure of the first few levels of the global hierarchy. A local hierarchic name space can be constructed that is sufficient to the local need, treating the local root as a global root. Later, this local name space can be incorporated as a subtree in a larger name space. Using a

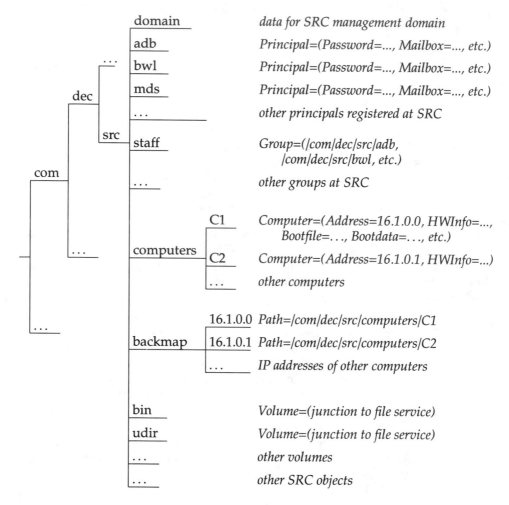

Figure 1.1. Global name-space hierarchy in BOB

variable to provide the name of the operational root (set to NIL at first) will ease the transition to the larger name space (and shorten the names that people actually use). Another technique is to initially name the local root with an identifier that is unlikely to appear in any future global root; then symbolic links in the global root, or special case code in the local name resolution machinery, can ease the transition.

1.4.2 Access Model

Global access means that a program can run anywhere in BOB (on a computer and operating system compatible with the program binary) and get the same result, although the performance may vary depending on the machine chosen. Thus, a program can be executed either on the user's workstation or on a fast cycle server in the machine room, while still accessing the same user files through the same names.

Achieving global access requires allowing all elements of the computing environment of a program to be remote from the computer where the program is executing. All services and objects required for a program to run need to be available to a program executing anywhere in the distributed system. For a particular user, 'anywhere' includes at least:

- on the user's own workstation;
- on public workstations or compute servers in the user's domain;
- on public workstations in another domain on the user's LAN;
- on public workstations across a low-bandwidth WAN.

Performance in the first three cases should be similar. Performance in the fourth case is fundamentally limited by the WAN characteristics, although use of caching can make the difference small in many cases.

In BOB, global naming and standard services exported via a uniform RPC mechanism provide the keys to achieving global access. All BOB services accept global names for the objects on which they operate. All BOB services are available to remote clients. Thus, any object whose global name is known can be accessed remotely.

In addition, programs must access their environments only by using the global names of objects. This last step will require a thorough examination of the computing environment provided by each existing operating system to identify all the ways in which programs can access their environment. For each way identified a mechanism must be designed to provide the global name of the desired object. For example, in UNIX systems that operate as part of BOB, the identities of the file system root directory, working directory, and the /tmp directory of a process must be specified by global names. Altering VMS, UNIX, and other operating systems to accept global names everywhere will be a major undertaking.

Another aspect of global access is making sure that BOB services have operation semantics that are location transparent. Without location transparency in the services it uses, a program will not get the same result when it runs on different computers. A service that allows read/write sharing of object state must provide a data coherence model. The model allows client programs to maintain correct object state and to behave in a manner that does not surprise users, no matter where clients and servers execute. Depending on the nature of the service, it is possible to trade off performance, availability, scale, and coherence.

In the name service, for example, it is appropriate to increase performance, availability, and scalability at the expense of coherence. A client update to the name service database can be made by contacting any server. After the client operation has completed, the server propagates the update to object replicas at other servers. Until propagation completes, different clients can read different values for the object. This lack of coherence produces several advantages: it increases performance by limiting the client's wait for update completion; it increases availability by allowing a client to perform an update when just one server is accessible; and it increases scale by making propagation latency separate from the visible latency of the client update operation. For the objects that the name service will store, this lack of coherence is deemed acceptable given the benefits it produces. The data coherence model for the name service defines the loose coherence invariants that programmers can depend upon, thereby meeting the requirement of a coherence model that is insensitive to client and server location.

On the other hand, the BOB file service needs to provide consistent write sharing, even at some cost in performance, scale, and availability. Many programs and users are accustomed to using the file system as a communication channel between programs. For example, a programmer may save a source file for a module from an editor and then trigger a recompilation and relinking on a remote cycle server. He will be annoyed if the program is rebuilt with an old version of the module because the cycle server retrieved an old, cached version of the file. File read/write coherence is also important among elements of distributed computations running, say, on multiple computers on the same LAN. The file system coherence model must cover file names and attributes as well as file data.

There is diversity of opinion among researchers about the best consistency model for a general-purpose distributed file system. Some feel that an open/close consistency model provides the best tradeoff. With this model changes made by one client are not propagated until that client closes the file and others (re)open it. Others feel that byte-level write sharing is feasible and desirable. With this model clients share the file as though all were accessing it in the same local memory. Successful systems have been built using variants of both models. BOB can be successful based on either model.

1.4.3   Security Model

Security is based on three notions:

- *Authentication* — for every request to do an operation, the name of the user or computer system making the request is known reliably. The source of a request is called a *principal*.
- *Access control* — for every resource (computer, printer, file, database, etc.) and every operation on that resource (read, write, delete, etc.), it is possible to specify the names of the principals allowed to do that operation on that resource. Every request for an operation is checked to ensure that its principal is allowed to do that operation.
- *Auditing* — every access to a resource can be logged if desired, as can the evidence used to authenticate every request. If trouble comes up, there is a record of exactly what happened.

To authenticate a request as coming from a particular principal, the system must determine that the principal originated the request, and that it was not modified on the way to its destination. We do the latter by establishing a *secure channel* between the system that originates the request and the one that carries it out. Practical security in a distributed system requires encryption to secure the communication channels. The encryption must not slow down communication, since in general it is too hard to be sure that a particular message does not need to be encrypted. So the security architecture should include methods of doing encryption and decryption on the fly, as data flows from computers into the network and back.

To determine who originated a request, it is necessary to know who is on the other end of the secure channel. Usually this is done by having the principal at the other end demonstrate that it knows some secret (such as a password), and then finding out in a reliable way the name of the principal that knows that secret. BOB's security architecture needs to specify how to do both these things. It is best if a principal can show that it knows the secret without giving it away, since otherwise the system can later impersonate the principal. Password-based schemes reveal the secret, but schemes based on encryption do not.

It is desirable to authenticate a user by his possession of a device which knows his secret and can demonstrate this by encryption. Such a device is called a *smart card*. An inferior alternative is for the user to type his password to a trusted agent. To authenticate a computer system, we need to be sure that it has been properly loaded with a good operating system image; BOB must specify methods to ensure this.

Security depends on naming, since access control identifies the principals that are allowed access by name. Practical security also depends on being able to have groups of principals e.g., the Executive Committee, or the system administrators for the cluster named 'Star'. Both these facilities must be provided by the name service. To ensure that the names and groups are defined reliably, digital signatures are used to certify information in the name service; the signatures are generated by a special *certification authority* which is engineered for high reliability and kept off-line, perhaps in a safe, when its services are not needed. Authentication depends only on the smallest sub-tree of the full naming tree that includes both the requesting principal and the resource; certification authorities that are more remote are assumed to be less trusted.

Security also depends on time. Authentication, access control, and secure channels require correct timestamps and clocks. The time service must distribute time securely.

1.4.4 Management Model

System management is the adjustment of system state by a human manager. Management is needed when satisfactory algorithmic adjustments cannot be provided — when human judgement is required. The problem in a large-scale distributed system is to provide each system manager with the means to monitor and adjust a fairly large collection of different types of geographically distributed components. Of the five persuasive properties of BOB, global management is the one we understand least well how to achieve. The facilities, however, are likely to be structured along the following lines.

The BOB management model is based on the concept of a *domain*. Every component in a distributed system is assigned to a domain. (A component is a piece of equipment or a piece of management-relevant object state.) Each domain has a responsible system manager. In the simple version of the model (that is probably adequate for most, perhaps all, systems) domains are disjoint and managers are disjoint, although more complex arrangements are possible, e.g., overlapping domains, a hierarchy of managers. Ideally a domain would not depend on any other domains for its correct operation.

There needs to be quite a bit of flexibility available for defining domains, as different arrangements will be effective in different installations. Example domains include:

- components used by a group of people with common goals;
- components that a group of users expects to find working;
- largest pile of components under one system manager;
- arbitrary pile of components that is not too big.

As a practical matter, customers will require guidelines for defining effective management domains.

BOB requires that each component define and export a management interface, using RPC if possible. Each component is managed via calls to this interface from interactive tools run by human managers. Some requirements for the management interface of a component are:

- *Remote access* — The management interface provides remote access to all management functions. Local error logs are maintained that can be read from the management interface. A secure channel is provided from management tools to the interface and the operations are subject to authentication and access control. No running around by the manager is required.
- *Program interface* — Each component's management interface is designed to be driven by a program, not a person. Actual invocation of management functions is by RPC calls from management tools. This allows a manager to do a lot with a little typing. A good management interface provides end-to-end checks to verify successful completion of a series of complex actions and provides operations that are independent of initial component state to make it easier to achieve the desired final state.
- *Relevance* — The management interface operates only on management-relevant state. In places where the flexibility is useful rather than just confusing, the management interface permits decentralized management by individual users.
- *Uniformity* — Different kinds of components should strive for uniformity in their management interfaces. This allows a single manager to retain intellectual control of a larger number of kinds of components.

The management interfaces and tools make it practical for one person to manage large domains. An interactive management tool can invoke the management interfaces of all components in a domain. It provides suitable ways to display and correlate the data, and to change the management-relevant state of components. Management tools are capable of making the same state change in a large set of similar components in a domain via iterative calls. To provide the flexibility to invent new management operations, some management tools support the construction of programs that call the management interfaces of domain components.

1.4.5   Availability Model

To achieve high availability of a service there must be multiple servers for that service. If these servers are structured to fail independently, then any desired degree of availability can be achieved by adjusting the degree of replication.

The most practical scheme for replication of the services in BOB is *primary/backup replication*, in which a client uses one server at a time and servers are arranged (as far as possible) to fail in a benign way, say by stopping. The alternative method, called *active replication*, has the client perform each operation at several servers. Active replication uses more resources than primary/backup but has no fail-over delays and can tolerate arbitrary failure behavior by servers.

To see how primary/backup works, recall from the naming model discussion that the object that represents a service includes a set of servers and some rules for choosing one. If the chosen server (the primary) fails, then the client can fail-over to another server (the backup) and repeat the operation. The client assumes failure if a response to an operation does not occur within a timeout period. The timeout should be as short as possible so that the latency of an operation that fails over is comparable to the usual latency. In practice, setting good timeouts is hard and fixed timeouts may not be adequate. If clients can do operations that change long-term state then the primary server must keep the backup servers up-to-date.

To achieve transparent fail-over from the point of view of client programs, knowledge of the multiple servers should be encapsulated in an agent on the client computer. In this chapter we refer to the agent as a *clerk*. The clerk can export a logically centralized, logically local service to the client program, even when the underlying service implementation is distributed, replicated, and remote. The clerk software can have many different structural relationships to its client. In simple cases it can be runtime libraries loaded into the client address space and be invoked with local procedure calls. Or it may operate in a separate address space on the same machine as the client and be invoked by same-machine IPC, same-machine RPC, or call-backs from the operating system. Or it can be in the operating system itself.

The clerk interface need not be the same as the server interface. Indeed, the server interface usually will be significantly more complex. In addition to implementing server selection and fail-over, a clerk may provide caching and write behind to improve performance, and can implement aggregate operations that read-modify-write server state. As simple examples of caching, a name service clerk might remember the results of recently looked up names and maintain open connections to frequently used name servers, or a file service clerk might cache the results of recent file directory and file data reads. Write-behind allows a clerk to batch several updates as a single server operation which can be done asynchronously, thus reducing the latency of operations at the clerk interface. Implementing a client's read-modify-write operation might require the clerk to use complex retry strategies involving several server operations when a fail-over occurs at some intermediate step.

As an example of how a clerk masks the existence of multiple servers, consider the actions involved in listing the contents of /com/dec/src/udir/bwl/-Mail/inbox, a BOB file system directory. The client program presents the entire path name to the file service clerk. The clerk locates a name server that stores the root directory and presents the complete name. That server may store the directories down to, say, `/com/dec`. The directory entry for `/com/dec/src` will indicate another set of servers. So the first lookup operation will return the new server set and the remaining unresolved path name. The clerk will then contact a server in the new set and present the unresolved path `src/udir/bwl/Mail/inbox`. This server discovers that `src/udir` is a junction to a file system volume, so returns the junction information and the unresolved path name `udir/bwl/Mail/inbox`. Finally, the clerk uses the junction information to contact a file server, which in this example actually stores the target directory and responds with the directory contents. What looks like a single operation to the client program actually involves RPCs to three different servers by the clerk.

This example of a name resolution would be completed with fewer or no operations at remote servers if the clerk has a cache that already contains the necessary information. In practice, caches are part of most clerk implementations and most operations are substantially speeded by the presence of cached data.

Other issues arise when implementing a high-availability service with long term state. The servers must cooperate to maintain consistent state among themselves, so a backup can take over reasonably quickly. Problems to be solved include arranging that no writes get lost during fail-over from one server to another and that a server that has been down can recover the current state when it is restarted. Combining these requirements with caching and write-behind to obtain good performance, without sacrificing consistent sharing, can make implementing a highly available service quite challenging.

1.5   Conclusion

This chapter covers the inherent strengths of centralized and networked computing systems. It outlines the structure and properties of BOB, a state-of-the-art distributed computing base for supporting general-purpose computing. This system combines the best features of centralized and networked systems with recent advances in security and availability to produce a powerful, cost-effective, easy-to-use computing environment.

Getting systems like BOB into widespread use will be hard. Given the state-of-the-art in distributed systems technology, building a prototype for proof of concept is certainly feasible. But the only practical method for getting widespread use of systems with these properties is to figure out ways to approach the goal by making incremental improvements to existing networked systems. This requires producing a sequence of useful, palatable changes that lead all the way to the goal.

Acknowledgements

The material in this chapter was jointly developed by Michael Schroeder, Butler Lampson, and Andrew Birrell. The ideas explored here aggregate many years of experience of the designers, builders, and users of distributed systems. Colleagues at SRC and fellow authors of this book have provided useful suggestions on the presentation.

Chapter 2

What Good are Models
and
What Models are Good?

Fred B. Schneider

2.1 Refining Intuition

Distributed systems are hard to design and understand because we lack intuition
for them. Perhaps this is because our lives are fundamentally sequential and
centralized. Perhaps not. In any event, distributed systems are being built. We
must develop an intuition, so that we can design distributed systems that perform
as we intend and so that we can understand existing distributed systems well
enough for modification as needs change.

Although developing an intuition for a new domain is difficult, it is a problem
that engineers and scientists have successfully dealt with before. We have acquired
intuition about flight, about nuclear physics, and about chaotic phenomena (like
turbulence). Two approaches are conventionally employed:

- **Experimental Observation**. We build things and observe how they behave
  in various settings. A body of experience accumulates about approaches that
  work. Even though we might not understand why something works, this
  body of experience enables us to build things for settings similar to those that
  have been studied.
- **Modeling and Analysis**. We formulate a model by simplifying the object of
  study and postulating a set of rules to define its behavior. We then analyze
  the model — using mathematics or logic — and infer consequences. If the
  model accurately characterizes reality, then it becomes a powerful mental
  tool.

Both of these approaches are illustrated in this text. Some chapters report experimental observation; others are more concerned with describing and analyzing models. Taken together, however, the chapters constitute a collective intuition for the design and analysis of distributed systems.

In a young discipline — like distributed systems — there is an inevitable tension between advocates for 'modeling and analysis' and those for 'experimental observation'. This tension masquerades as a dichotomy between 'theory' and 'practice'. Each side believes that theirs is the more effective way to refine intuition. Practitioners complain that they learn little from the theory. Theoreticians complain that practitioners are not addressing the right problems. A theoretician might simplify too much when defining a model; the analysis of such models will rarely enhance our intuition. A practitioner might incorrectly generalize from experience or concentrate on the wrong attributes of an object; our intuition does not profit from this, either. On the other hand, without experimental observation, we have no basis for trusting our models. And, without models, we have no hope of mastering the complexity that underlies distributed systems.

The remainder of this chapter is about models for distributed systems. We start by discussing useful properties of models. We then illustrate that simple distributed systems can be difficult to understand — our intuition is not well developed — and how models help. We next turn to two key attributes of a distributed system and discuss models for these attributes. The first concerns assumptions about process execution speeds and message delivery delays. The implications of such assumptions are pursued in greater detail in Chapter 4. The second attribute concerns failure modes. This material is fundamental for later chapters on implementing fault tolerance, Chapters 5 through 8. Finally, we argue that all of these models are useful and interesting, both to practitioners and theoreticians.

2.2   Good Models

For our purposes, a *model* for an object is a collection of attributes and a set of rules that govern how these attributes interact. There is no single correct model for an object. Answering different types of questions about an object usually requires that we employ different models, each with different attributes and/or rules. A model is *accurate* to the extent that analyzing it yields truths about the object of interest. A model is *tractable* if such an analysis is actually possible.

Defining an accurate model is not difficult; defining an accurate and tractable model is. An accurate and tractable model will include exactly those attributes that affect the phenomena of interest. Selecting these attributes requires taste and insight. Level of detail is a key issue.

In a tractable model, rules governing interactions of attributes will be in a form that supports analysis. For example, mathematical and logical formulas can be analyzed by uninterpreted symbolic manipulations. This makes these formalisms well suited for defining models. Computer simulations can also define models. While not as easy to analyze, a computer simulation is usually easier to analyze than the system it simulates.

In building models for distributed systems, we typically seek answers to two fundamental questions:

- **Feasibility**. What classes of problems can be solved?
- **Cost**. For those classes that can be solved, how expensive must the solution be?

Both questions have practical import as well as having theoretical value. First, being able to recognize an unsolvable problem lurking beneath a system's requirements can head off wasted effort in design, implementation, and testing. Second, knowing the cost implications of solving a particular problem allows us to avoid designs requiring protocols that are inherently slow or expensive. Finally, knowing the inherent cost of solving a particular problem provides a yardstick with which we can evaluate any solution that we devise.

By studying algorithms and computational complexity, most undergraduates learn about undecidable problems and about complexity classes, the two issues raised above. The study builds intuition for a particular model of computation — one that involves a single sequential process and a uniform access-time memory. Unfortunately, this is neither an accurate nor useful model for the systems that concern us. Distributed systems comprise multiple processes communicating over narrow-bandwidth, high-latency channels, with some processes and/or channels faulty. Having multiple processes provides more computational power but requires that they be coordinated. The channel bandwidth limitations help isolate the effects of failures but also mean that interprocess communication is a scarce system resource. In short, distributed systems raise new concerns and understanding these requires new models.

A Coordination Problem

In implementing distributed systems, process coordination and coping with failures are pervasive concerns. Here is an example of such a problem.

> **Coordination Problem**. Two processes, A and B, communicate by sending and receiving messages on a bidirectional channel. Neither process can fail. However, the channel can experience transient failures, resulting in the loss of a subset of the messages that have been sent. Devise a protocol where either of two actions α and β are possible, but (i) both processes take the same action and (ii) neither takes both actions. □

That this problem has no solution usually comes as a surprise. Here is the proof.

> Any protocol that solves this problem is equivalent to one in which there are rounds of message exchange: first A (say) sends to B, next B sends to A, then A sends to B, and so on. We show that in assuming the existence of a protocol to solve the problem, we are able to derive a contradiction. This establishes that no such protocol exists.
>
> Select the protocol that solves the problem using the fewest rounds. By assumption, such a protocol must exist and, by construction, no protocol

solving the problem using fewer rounds exists. Without loss of generality, suppose that m, the last message sent by either process, is sent by A.

Observe that the action ultimately taken by A cannot depend on whether m is received by B, because its receipt could never be learned by A (since this is the last message). Thus, A's choice of action α or β does not depend on m. Next, observe that the action ultimately taken by B cannot depend on whether m is received by B, because B must make the same choice of action α or β even if m is lost (due to a channel failure).

Having argued that the action chosen A and B does not depend on m, we conclude that m is superfluous. Thus, we can construct a new protocol in which one fewer message is sent. However, the existence of such a shorter protocol contradicts the assumption that our original protocol used the fewest number of rounds.   □

We established that the Coordination Problem could not be solved by building a simple, informal model. Two insights were used in this model:

1. All protocols between two processes are equivalent to a series of message exchanges.
2. Actions taken by a process depend only on the sequence of messages it has received.

Having defined the model and analyzed it, we have now refined our intuition. Notice that in so doing we not only learned about this particular problem but also about variations. For example, we might wonder whether coordination of two processes is possible if the channel never fails (so messages are never lost) or if the channel informs the sender whenever a message is lost. For each modification, we can determine whether the change invalidates some assertion being made in the analysis (i.e., the proof above) and thus we can determine whether the change invalidates the proof.

2.3   Synchronous versus Asynchronous Systems

When modeling distributed systems, it is useful to distinguish between *asynchronous* and *synchronous* systems. With an asynchronous system, we make no assumptions about process execution speeds and/or message delivery delays; with a synchronous system, we do make assumptions about these parameters. In particular, the relative speeds of processes in a synchronous system is assumed to be bounded, as are any delays associated with communications channels.

Postulating that a system is asynchronous is a non-assumption. Every system is asynchronous. Even a system in which processes run in lock step and message delivery is instantaneous satisfies the definition of an asynchronous system (as well as that of a synchronous system). Because all systems are asynchronous, a protocol designed for use in an asynchronous system can be used in any distributed system. This is a compelling argument for studying asynchronous systems.

In theory, any system that employs reasonable schedulers can be regarded as being synchronous, because there are then (trivial) bounds on the relative speeds of processes and channels. This, however, is not necessarily a useful way to view a distributed system. Protocols that assume the system is synchronous exhibit performance degradation as the ratios of the various process speeds and delivery delays increase. Reasonable throughput can be attained by these protocols only when processes execute at about the same speed and delivery delays are not too large. Thus, there is no value to considering a system as being synchronous unless the relative execution speeds of processes and channel delays are close.

In practice, then, postulating that a system is synchronous constrains how processes and communications channels are implemented. The scheduler that multiplexes processors must not violate the constraints on process execution speeds. If long-haul networks are employed for communications, then queuing delays, unpredictable routings, and retransmission due to errors must not be allowed to violate the constraints on channel delays. On the other hand, asserting that the relative speeds of processes is bounded is equivalent to assuming that all processors in the system have access to approximately rate-synchronized real-time clocks. This is because either one can be used to implement the other. Thus, timeouts and other time-based protocol techniques are possible only when a system is synchronous.

An Election Protocol

In asserting that a system is synchronous, we rule out certain system behaviors. This, in turn, enables us to employ simpler or cheaper protocols than would be required to solve the same problem in an asynchronous system (where these behaviors are possible). An example is the following election problem.

> **Election Problem.** A set of processes $P_1, P_2, \ldots, P_n$ must select a leader. Each process P_i has a unique identifier $uid(i)$. Devise a protocol so that all of the processes learn the identity of the leader. Assume all processes start executing at the same time and that all communicate using broadcasts that are reliable. □

Solving this problem in an asynchronous system is not difficult, but somewhat expensive. Each process P_i broadcasts $\langle i, uid(i) \rangle$. Every process will eventually receive these broadcasts, so each can independently 'elect' the P_i for which $uid(i)$ is smallest. Notice that n broadcasts are required for an election.

In a synchronous system, it is possible to solve the Election Problem with only a single broadcast. Let τ be a known constant bigger than the largest message delivery delay plus the largest difference that can be observed at any instant by reading clocks at two arbitrary processors. Now, it suffices for each process P_i to wait until either (i) it receives a broadcast or (ii) $\tau * uid(i)$ seconds elapse on its clock at which time it broadcasts $\langle i \rangle$. The first process that makes a broadcast is elected.

We have illustrated that by restricting consideration to synchronous systems, time can be used to good advantage in coordinating processes. The act of *not* sending a message can convey information to processes. This technique is used, for example, by processes in the synchronous election protocol above to infer values of $uid(i)$ that are held by no process.

2.4   Failure Models

A variety of failure models have been proposed in connection with distributed systems. All are based on assigning responsibility for faulty behavior to the system's components — processors and communications channels. It is faulty components that we count, not occurrences of faulty behavior. And, we speak of a system being t-fault tolerant when that system will continue satisfying its specification provided that no more than t of its components are faulty.

By way of contrast, in classical work on fault-tolerant computing systems, it is the occurrences of faulty behavior that are counted. Statistical measures of reliability and availability, like MTBF (mean-time-between-failures) and probability of failure over a given interval, are deduced from estimates of elapsed time between fault occurrences. Such characterizations are important to users of a system, but there are real advantages to describing the fault tolerance of a system in terms of the maximum number of faulty components that can be tolerated over some interval of interest. Asserting that a system is t-fault tolerant is a measure of the fault tolerance supported by the system's architecture, in contrast to fault tolerance achieved simply by using reliable components.

Fault tolerance of a system will depend on the reliability of the components used in constructing that system — in particular, the probability that there will be more than t failures during the operating interval of interest. Thus, once t has been chosen, it is not difficult to derive the more traditional statistical measures of reliability. We simply compute the probabilities of having various configurations of 0 through t faulty components. So, no expressive power is lost by counting faulty components — as we do — rather than counting fault occurrences.

Some care is required in defining failure models when it is the faulty components that are being counted. For example, consider a fault that leads to a message loss. We could attribute this fault to the sender, the receiver, or the channel. Message loss due to signal corruption from electrical noise should be blamed on the channel, but message loss due to buffer overflow at the receiver should be blamed on the receiver. Moreover, since replication is the only way to tolerate faulty components, the architecture and cost of implementing a t-fault tolerant system very much depends on exactly how fault occurrences are being attributed to components. Incorrect attribution leads to an inaccurate distributed system model; erroneous conclusions about system architecture are sure to follow.

A faulty component exhibits behavior consistent with some failure model being assumed. Failure models commonly found in the distributed systems literature include:

- **Failstop**. A processor fails by halting. Once it halts, the processor remains in that state. The fact that a processor has failed is detectable by other processors (Schneider [1984]).
- **Crash**. A processor fails by halting. Once it halts, the processor remains in that state. The fact that a processor has failed may not be detectable by other processors (Lamport and Fischer [1982]).

- **Crash+Link**. A processor fails by halting. Once it halts, the processor remains in that state. A link fails by losing some messages, but does not delay, duplicate, or corrupt messages (Budhiraja *et al.* [1992]).
- **Receive Omission**. A processor fails by receiving only a subset of the messages that have been sent to it or by halting and remaining halted (Perry and Toueg [1986]).
- **Send Omission**. A processor fails by transmitting only a subset of the messages that it actually attempts to send or by halting and remaining halted (Hadzilacos [1984]).
- **General Omission**. A processor fails by receiving only a subset of the messages that have been sent to it, by transmitting only a subset of the messages that it actually attempts send, and/or by halting and remaining halted (Perry and Toueg [1986]).
- **Byzantine Failures**. A processor fails by exhibiting arbitrary behavior (Lamport, Shostak and Pease [1982]).

Failstop failures are the least disruptive, because processors never perform erroneous actions and failures are detectable. Other processors can safely perform actions on behalf of a faulty failstop processor.

Unless the system is synchronous, it is not possible to distinguish between a processor that is executing very slowly and one that has halted due to a crash failure. Yet, the ability to make this distinction can be important. A processor that has crashed can take no further action, but a processor that is merely slow can. Other processors can safely perform actions on behalf of a crashed processor, but not on behalf of a slow one, because subsequent actions by the slow processor might not be consistent with actions performed on its behalf by others. Thus, crash failures in asynchronous systems are harder to deal with than failstop failures. In synchronous systems, however, the crash and failstop models are equivalent.

The next four failure models — Crash+Link, Receive Omission, Send-Omission, and General Omission — all deal with message loss, each modeling a different cause for the loss and attributing the loss to a different component. Finally, Byzantine failures are the most disruptive. A system that can tolerate Byzantine failures can tolerate anything.

The extremes of our spectrum of models — failstop and Byzantine — are not controversial, but there can be debate about the other models. Why not define a failure model corresponding to memory disruptions or misbehavior of the processor's arithmetic-logic unit (ALU)? The first reason brings us back to the two fundamental questions of Section 2.2. The feasibility and cost of solving certain fundamental problems is known to differ across the seven failure models enumerated above. (We return to this point below.) A second reason that these failure models are interesting is a matter of taste in abstractions. A reasonable abstraction for a processor in a distributed system is an object that sends and receives messages. The failure models given above concern ways that such an abstraction might be faulty. Failure models involving the contents of memory or the functioning of an ALU, for example, concern internal (and largely irrelevant) details of the processor abstraction. A good model encourages suppression of irrelevant details.

Fault Tolerance and Distributed Systems

As the size of a distributed system increases, so does the number of its components and, therefore, so does the probability that some component will fail. Thus, designers of distributed systems must be concerned from the outset with implementing fault tolerance. Protocols and system architectures that are not fault tolerant simply are not very useful in this setting.

The link between fault tolerance and distributed systems goes in the other direction as well. Implementing a distributed system is the only way to achieve fault tolerance. All methods for achieving fault tolerance employ replication of function using components that fail independently. In a distributed system, the physical separation and isolation of processors linked by a communications network ensures that components fail independently. Thus, achieving fault tolerance in a computing system can lead to solving problems traditionally associated with distributed computing systems.

Failures — be they hard or transient — can be detected only by replicating actions in failure-independent ways. One way to do this is by performing the action using components that are physically and electrically isolated; we call this *replication in space*. The validity of the approach follows from an empirically justified belief in the independence of failures at physically and electrically isolated devices. A second approach to replication is for a single device to repeatedly perform the action. We call this *replication in time*. Replication in time is valid only for transient failures.

If the results of performing a set of replicated actions disagree, a failure has occurred. Without making further assumptions, this is the strongest statement that can be made. In particular, if the results agree, we cannot assert that no component is faulty (and the results are correct). This is because if there are enough faulty components, all might be corrupted, yet still agree. For Byzantine failures, $t + 1$-fold replication permits t-fault tolerant failure detection but not masking. This is because when there is disagreement among $t + 1$ independently obtained results, one cannot assume that the majority value is correct. In order to implement t-fault tolerant masking, $2t + 1$-fold replication is needed, since then as many as t values can be faulty without causing the majority value to be faulty. At the other extreme of our failure models spectrum, for failstop failures a single component suffices for detection. And, $t + 1$-fold replication is sufficient for masking the failure of as many as t faulty components.

2.5   Which Model When?

Theoreticians have good reason to study all of the models we have discussed. The models each idealize some dimension of real systems, and it is useful to know how each system attribute affects the feasibility or cost of solving a problem. Theoreticians also may have reason to define new models. Identifying attributes that affect the problems that arise in distributed systems allows us to identify the key dimensions of the problems we face.

The dilemma faced by practitioners is that of deciding between models when building a system. Should we assume that processes are asynchronous or synchronous, failstop or Byzantine? The answer depends on how the model is being used. One way to regard a model is as an interface definition — a set of assumptions that programmers can make about the behavior of system components. Programs are written to work correctly assuming the actual system behaves as prescribed by the model. And, when system behavior is not consistent with the model, then no guarantees can be made.

For example, a system designed assuming that Byzantine failures are possible can tolerate anything. Assuming Byzantine failures is prudent in mission critical systems, because the cost of system failure is usually great, so there is considerable incentive to reduce the risk of a system failure. For most applications, however, it suffices to assume a more benign failure model. In those rare circumstances where the system does not satisfy the model, we must be prepared for the system to violate its specification.

Large systems, especially, are rarely constructed as single monolithic entities. Rather, the system is structured by implementing abstractions. Each abstraction builds on other abstractions, providing some added functionality. Here, having a collection of models can be used to good advantage. Among the abstractions that might be implemented are processors possessing the attributes discussed above. We might start by assuming our processors only exhibit crash failures. Failstop processors might then be approximated by using timeout based protocols. Finally, if we discover that processors do not only exhibit crash failures we might go back and add various sanity-tests to system code, causing processors to crash rather than behave in a way not permitted by the crash failure model.

Lastly, the various models can and should be regarded as limiting cases. The behavior of a real system is bounded by our models. Thus, understanding the feasibility and costs associated with solving problems in these models, can give us insight into the feasibility and cost of solving a problem in some given real system whose behavior lies between the models.

Acknowledgement

This material is based on work supported in part by the Office of Naval Research under contract N00014-91-J-1219, the National Science Foundation under Grant No. CCR-8701103, and DARPA/NSF Grant No. CCR-9014363. Any opinions, findings, and conclusions or recommendations expressed in this publication are those of the author and do not reflect the views of these agencies.

2.6 References

Budhiraja, N., Marzullo, K., Schneider, F. B. and Toueg, S. (1992), Primary-backup protocols: Lower bounds and optimal implementations, *Proceedings of the Third IFIP Working Conference on Dependable Computing*, Mondello, Italy, 187–198.

Hadzilacos, V. (1984), Issues of Fault Tolerance in Concurrent Computations, Harvard University, Ph.D. Dissertation.

Lamport, L. and Fischer, M. J. (1982), Byzantine Generals and Transaction Commit Protocols, SRI International, Technical Report 62.

Lamport, L., Shostak, R. and Pease, M. (1982), The Byzantine Generals Problem, *ACM Transactions on Programming Languages and Systems* 4(3), 382–401.

Perry, K. J. and Toueg, S. (1986), Distributed agreement in the presence of processor and communication faults, *IEEE Transactions on Software Engineering* SE-12(3), 477–482.

Schneider, F. B. (1984), Byzantine generals in action: Implementing fail-stop processors, *ACM Transactions on Computer Systems* 2(2), 145–154.

Chapter 3

Specifications of Concurrent and Distributed Systems

William E. Weihl

Specifications are at the core of modern modular programming methods for sequential as well as concurrent and distributed systems. In this chapter, we discuss the issues involved in writing specifications for concurrent and distributed systems. We present a simple method based on state machines and atomic actions, and show a number of examples illustrating the use of the method. We discuss techniques that can be used to prove the correctness of an implementation of a module; these techniques can be used quite rigorously, or as the basis of more informal reasoning about correctness. We include a number of hints for writing good specifications.

3.1 Abstraction and Specifications

Specifications form the basis of a system design methodology based on the Machiavellian principle of divide-and-conquer: a system is divided into modules, and each module's interface with other modules is described by a *specification*. By dividing the system into parts, we reduce the complex problem of implementing the entire system to a set of (one hopes) simpler problems of implementing the individual modules. Of course, these modules can be further divided.[1]

The specifications of the individual modules provide another vital advantage: they allow us to understand the system without having to understand all the details of its construction. In other words, they provide *abstraction*: they hide details of the implementation of one module that are not relevant to the workings of other modules. This is perhaps the most powerful technique we have available to us to reduce the complexity of large systems.

---

[1]This is not meant to imply that design should proceed as a strictly top-down process. In practice, the decomposition of a system into modules is best accomplished through a combination of top-down and bottom-up design, with some amount of iteration as later stages of the design make clear that some earlier decisions should be changed.

Specifications are used throughout engineering as a mechanism for abstraction. For example, in designing a bridge, a beam might be specified by its weight, strength, stiffness, and other factors, but typically not by the details of its composition or of the manufacturing process used to produce it. (Such details need to be specified at some point, but are not needed to decide whether the bridge will remain standing under the anticipated load.) In computer science, we might specify a *sort* routine by stating that it takes an array of records as an argument, and when it returns, the array has the same arguments as when it was called but they appear in ascending order according to their keys. There are many possible implementations of this specification, and they differ widely in running time, space required, use of external storage, and programming complexity.

So one of the key reasons for using specifications is to reduce complexity by suppressing irrelevant details. There is no *a priori* definition, however, of which details are relevant and which are irrelevant. This can only be determined by considering how the entity being specified is to be used. For example, the performance of a beam at sub-freezing temperatures might be relevant in Boston, but irrelevant in Tahiti. Similarly, some users of a *sort* routine might care that the sort be stable (i.e., preserve the order of elements with equal keys). Others might not care, and might prefer the option of using an implementation that is not stable because it has better time, space, or programming complexity.

One of the key attributes of a good specification is that it describes only those properties that are needed by its clients. In other words, it does not over-constrain the implementation. A good way to think about this is that a specification should describe *what* a module needs to do, not *how* it should do it. In the case of the *sort* routine above, the specification should describe what final states are acceptable, not what algorithm should be used to sort. For another example, consider a routine to compute the square root of a floating point number. Since floating point arithmetic is not exact, the routine must return an approximation to the square root, not the real square root. A good specification of this routine would characterize what approximations are acceptable (e.g., within some given ϵ of the real square root), rather than saying how to compute it (e.g., using Newton's method). Often many results are acceptable, yet most algorithms are deterministic; thus, using an algorithm as a specification will over-constrain the implementation, unless the algorithm is nondeterministic.

A specification can be thought of as a *contract* between the users of a module and its implementors. The implementors agree to provide the properties described in the specification; the users agree to rely only on those properties, and not on other properties that happen to be true of one particular implementation. The specification also provides documentation of what the module is supposed to do. As with a legal contract, the specification can cover many properties, including the functional behavior of a module, its performance (time and space used), other resource usage, programming cost, and fault-tolerance. In this chapter, we focus on using specifications to describe the functional behavior of a module.

As with a legal contract, a specification can be used as a basis for validation: testing whether a module or a system has the required properties. In the absence of a written specification, there is no way to develop a set of test cases, except by relying on people's intuition about what the module should do.[2] When a system fails some tests, the specifications of the modules in the system can be used to help narrow down which module is at fault.

As discussed above, the abstraction achieved through specifications provides useful *modularity*: only a module's specification needs to be examined to understand how it interacts with other modules, not its implementation. Another important advantage of using specifications is *modifiability*: a module's implementation can be modified without changing other modules that use it, as long as the new implementation meets the same specification. If the design is carefully planned, this allows one to follow an important principle of system construction: avoid premature optimization.[3] Rather than striving to make each module as efficient as possible, one can choose to use an inefficient, but simple, implementation of modules that are not known in advance to be performance bottlenecks. After the system is up and running, the performance can be evaluated, and effort can be focused on providing more efficient (and more complex) implementations for *only* those modules that are causing performance problems.

Specification techniques are fairly well understood for sequential systems (although they are probably not as widely or carefully used as they should be). Similar techniques apply to concurrent and distributed systems, but concurrency introduces subtleties that complicate things somewhat. In this chapter, we will describe one approach to specifying concurrent and distributed systems, and give a number of examples to illustrate the issues involved and how the technique can be used. At the end, we will briefly discuss other approaches.

One final note before we dive into technical issues: specifications can be either formal (i.e., written in some precise logical language) or informal (i.e., written in English or your favorite natural language). Informal specifications have the disadvantage that they are usually ambiguous and prone to misinterpretation — witness the immense amount of time spent in courtrooms arguing about the meaning of a law or a contract. Of course, an informal specification is better than none at all. Formal specifications have the advantage of being precise and unambiguous, but they can be hard to read and write. In this chapter, we will not concern ourselves with the details of a precise syntax for writing specifications, but we will use a precise semantics based on simple mathematics.

3.2   Issues

The subsections below discuss several important issues raised by concurrency and distribution.

3.2.1   Interfaces and Behavior

Modules in sequential systems have relatively simple interfaces and behavior. For example, a procedure has an interface that describes the types of its arguments

---

[2]Relying on people's intuition is an approach that is widely used, but is also one that almost always fails.

[3]See Lampson's paper on hints for computer system design for a discussion of this and many other principles (Lampson [1983]).

and results. In addition, the behavior of a procedure as seen by its caller can be described by an input-output relation, which specifies the possible outputs that can be produced for each input. (Procedures with side-effects can be modeled by viewing the initial state as an argument and the final state as a result.)

Modules in concurrent systems are more complex. For example, a procedure may interact with concurrent threads by reading and writing shared memory, or by exchanging messages. Thus, a simple input-output relation is not adequate for describing the behavior of a procedure, since its internal intermediate states may be visible to its client through other interactions. Another way of viewing this is that the procedure's interface is wider in a concurrent system: it includes not just the call and return points, but also the intermediate points at which it can interact with other concurrent threads. Modules in concurrent systems can also be active: they can have internal background threads, whose effects must somehow be modeled in a specification.

The greater complexity of concurrent systems has two important effects. First, the tools we use to specify modules in concurrent systems are slightly more complex than in sequential systems. Second, the modules themselves are more complex: for the same number of lines of code, concurrent programs tend to be much harder to understand. This complexity makes it even more important to try to write careful specifications about the behavior of modules in concurrent systems: if relying on one's intuition about what a relatively simple module does is unlikely to work, relying on intuition for very complex modules is virtually guaranteed not to work!

3.2.2 Safety vs. Liveness

In discussing specifications of concurrent systems, it is important to distinguish between *safety* and *liveness* properties. Informally, a safety property says that nothing bad ever happens. In other words, the system always remains in a good state (for some appropriate definition of 'good'). A liveness property, on the other hand, says that something good eventually happens (again for some appropriate definition of 'good'). These two kinds of properties are fundamentally different, and require different tools for specifying them and for reasoning about the correctness of implementations. In this chapter, we focus primarily on safety properties. However, in this subsection, we discuss the differences between the two kinds of properties and give informal examples of each.

A typical specification for a procedure in a sequential system combines both safety and liveness.[4] The safety property places constraints on the results that the procedure is allowed to return and the side-effects it is allowed to have. For example, a square root routine must return a result within ϵ of the positive square root of its argument, and a sort routine must rearrange the elements of its argument array so that they are sorted in ascending order by key. These properties state that the system never gets in the bad state in which the procedure has returned the

---

[4]In fact, it is a theorem that any specification that takes the form of a predicate on individual behaviors of a module can be decomposed into the conjunction of a pure safety property and a pure liveness property (Alpern and Schneider [1984]).

wrong result or has had a side-effect that is not permitted by the specification. Such properties are typically referred to as *partial correctness* specifications.

The liveness property in a procedure's specification in a sequential system is typically quite simple: it requires the procedure to terminate. The combination of this termination requirement with a partial correctness specification is called a *total correctness* specification. Termination is probably the most common liveness property used for sequential modules, but it is not the only one. For example, a data structure used to keep track of nodes to be visited in a search program might have a liveness requirement that every node inserted is eventually extracted (assuming that the client does not stop asking for nodes to be extracted).

Mutual exclusion is a good example of a safety property in a concurrent system: two threads are never in critical sections at the same time. Another example is FIFO servicing of requests: requests are serviced in the order in which they arrive. Liveness properties include various notions of fairness (of which there are several — for instance, see Francez [1986]), which require that no process be prevented from running forever. Another example of a liveness property is the requirement that every request to a service must eventually receive service (i.e., *starvation* cannot occur.)

The key difference between safety and liveness properties is that a violation of a safety property can be observed in finite time, while testing for violations of liveness properties requires looking at infinite executions. To prove safety properties, one uses the kinds of techniques discussed later in this chapter, which fundamentally boil down to proving invariants on the state. To prove liveness properties, one uses techniques similar to those used to prove that loops (or recursive programs) terminate.

3.2.3 Performance vs. Functionality

In designing a system, one often makes tradeoffs between performance and functionality: greater functionality tends to result in poorer performance, more complex code, etc. In concurrent and distributed systems, such tradeoffs seem to be more frequent and more difficult to handle. It often happens that a module in a concurrent or distributed system provides weaker guarantees to its clients than would a similar module in a sequential system. Later in this chapter, we show some examples of this kind of tradeoff.

3.2.4 Failures

Distributed systems, like concurrent systems, exhibit concurrency and all the problems that it entails. The major wrinkle added by distributed systems is the possibility of partial failure: part of the system may fail and recover while the rest of the system keeps running. This has a significant impact on the design of distributed systems, since one often wants to build distributed systems that continue to provide service even though some of the components are down. It also has an impact on the specifications that one writes, since in practice, the guarantees made by fault-tolerant distributed systems are often weaker than the guarantees one might expect from a similar system that fails as a single unit. This is another example of a tradeoff between performance and functionality; specific examples appear later in this chapter.

3.3   A Specification Method for Concurrent Systems

In this section we describe a method for specifying modules in concurrent systems. In later sections, we discuss how to prove implementations correct, give a number of additional examples, and discuss the additional complications introduced by distributed systems.

Our specification method involves describing the set of allowable behaviors for a module. The key issue in making the method precise is defining what constitutes a behavior; as is common in specification methods for concurrent systems, we view a behavior as a 'trace' of atomic actions. In Section 3.3.1 below, we define our notion of behavior and how it is used to define correctness. Then, in Section 3.3.2, we introduce *state machines*, which are a convenient mechanism for describing sets of traces. Finally, in Section 3.3.3, we present a simple example illustrating the definitions.

3.3.1   Behaviors and Correctness

When we write a specification, we are trying to constrain the behavior of a module as seen by its clients. To do this, we need a precise notion of the *interface* between the module and its clients. We view the interface as consisting of a collection of named *actions* that are shared by the clients and the module. For a module that exports a collection of procedures, these actions might be the invocations and returns of the procedures. For a network, the actions might correspond to a client on one machine presenting a message to be sent, and to a message being received by a client on another machine.

The simplest abstract view of a specification is that it defines a set of sequences of actions.[5] Each sequence of actions is a single *behavior* of the module. Thus, the specification can be thought of as specifying the allowable behaviors, and an implementation is considered *correct* if every behavior that it actually produces is in the set defined by the specification.

For example, a specification of a memory system might have actions corresponding to *read* and *write* operations (where the names of the actions include the addresses and the data involved in the operations). The behaviors in the specification have the property that the data returned in a *read* action for a given address is the last value written to that address by a *write* action, or is arbitrary if there is no preceding *write*. Thus, the following behavior is in the specification:

write(1,3)
read(2,843)
write(2,17)
read(1,3)
read(2,17)

---

[5]In this chapter, we consider only finite sequences. This is sufficient to handle safety properties; infinite sequences must be considered to handle liveness properties.

(The action *write*(1,3) means that the value 3 is written to the address 1; the action *read*(2,843) means that the value 843 is read from address 2.) The following behavior, however, is not:

write(1,3)
read(2,843)
write(2,17)
read(1,843)
read(2,12)

Similarly, a specification of a network might have *send* and *receive* actions (each including the message sent or received). Different networks have different characteristics; for example, some are FIFO, some can lose messages, some can duplicate messages, and some can corrupt messages. These differences might be important to clients of the networks, and thus are important to capture in specifications. For any of these kinds of networks, the following behavior is in the specification, since messages are not lost, corrupted, duplicated, or delivered out of order:

send(a)
send(b)
receive(a)
send(c)
receive(b)

(Since we are not considering liveness properties, the behaviors we consider correspond to all finite executions of a system, thus, the behavior above need not include the delivery of message c, since that might just not have happened yet.) The following behavior, however, is in the specifications of only those networks that can deliver messages out of order:

send(a)
send(b)
receive(b)
send(c)
receive(a)

Similarly, the following behavior is in the specification of only those networks that lose messages or that can deliver them out of order — it is not in the specification of a network that guarantees FIFO delivery of all messages:

send(a)
send(b)
receive(b)
send(c)
receive(c)

The next behavior is in the specification of networks that can duplicate messages:

send(a)
send(b)
receive(b)
send(c)
receive(b)

Finally, the following behavior is in the specification of only those networks that can corrupt messages:

send(a)
send(b)
receive(d)
send(c)
receive(b)

3.3.2 State Machines

The specification of a module is nicely captured by a set of behaviors, where each behavior is a trace of actions that occur at the interface between the module and its clients. This begs the question, however, of how one describes such sets. Enumerating them is not generally feasible. It is possible to write down a predicate that characterizes the behaviors in the set; for example, one might write the predicate corresponding to the constraint that a *read* returns the last value written by a *write*, or the predicate corresponding to guaranteed FIFO delivery of uncorrupted messages. Another approach, and the one we take here, is to describe a way of *generating* the behaviors in a specification. Viewing a set of behaviors as a language (a set of strings over some alphabet), this is a natural strategy.

We generate sets of behaviors using *state machines*. A state machine M consists of several components:

1. A set S of states.
2. A set I of initial states, which must be a subset of S.
3. A *signature*, which is a set of actions partitioned into *internal* and *external* actions.
4. A set T of state transitions of the form (s, a, s'), where s and s' are states in S and a is an action in the signature.

We distinguish between internal and external actions because it is often convenient to use 'extra' actions that are not part of a module's interface with its clients when describing a state machine that generates the allowable behaviors for the module.

A sequence of actions $a_1, a_2, \ldots, a_n$ is *generated* by a state machine M if there exists a sequence of states $s_0, s_1, \ldots, s_n$ such that $(s_{i-1}, a_i, s_i) \in T$ for $0 < i \le n$. Similarly, a *behavior* α (a sequence of external actions) is generated by a state machine M if there exists a sequence β of (internal and external) actions such that β is generated by M and α is the subsequence of β consisting of the external actions. The specification denoted by a state machine consists of all behaviors generated by the state machine.

The subsection below gives examples of state machines.

3.3.3 Examples

We adopt the following stylized form for writing descriptions of state machines. First, we declare a set of state variables; a state of the state machine is a tuple with one component for each state variable. We include in this declaration an

VAR m: A → D
ACTIONS
    read(a:A,d:D) ≡ d = m(a) ⇒ SKIP
    write(a:A,d:D) ≡ m(a) := d

Figure 3.1. SM — Specification of a simple memory

initialization of each state variable. (If no initialization is given, any value is acceptable as an initial state.) Second, we declare the actions, and give for each action a description of the transitions associated with that action. External actions are declared first, followed by the internal actions.

Each action description has the following form:

    name ≡ *guard* ⇒ *assignments*

where the *name* includes any 'parameters' (e.g., the address and data for a *write* action), the *guard* specifies those states *s* in which the action can cause a state transition, and the *assignments* give new values for the state variables that define the state change caused by the action when it happens.

Here are some examples of state machines. The first, in Figure 3.1, is a specification of a simple memory system; we call it *SM* (for 'simple memory'). In this specification, A and D are the types of the addresses and data for the memory system. The state of the memory system is represented in the specification by a function from addresses to data. A *read(a, d)* action can occur only when *d* is the value stored at address *a*, and does not change the state (SKIP is the assignment statement that does nothing). A *write* action changes the data stored at an address.

The reader can easily check the example behaviors given earlier in Section 3.3.1 to see that the ones that are in the specification of the memory system are generated by *SM*, and the ones that are not in the specification of the memory system are not generated by *SM*.

The second example, in Figure 3.2, is a specification of a network that does not lose, corrupt, or duplicate messages, or deliver them out of order. We call it *IN* (for 'ideal network'). The state of *IN* is represented as a sequence of messages (those that have been sent but not yet received), initially empty. The actions are written using several functions on sequences; the *send* action appends a new message to the state, and the receive action, which can occur only in states in which *msgs* is non-empty, removes the first message from the state.

In Figure 3.3 is a different network specification that allows messages to be duplicated and lost; it illustrates the use of internal actions. We call it *LN* (for 'lossy network'). In this specification, we have added an internal action *drop* that drops the first message from the state. In addition, the *receive* action does not change the

VAR msgs: SEQ[M] := ∅
ACTIONS
    send(m:M) ≡ msgs := append(msgs,m)
    receive(m:M) ≡ msgs ≠ ∅ ∧ m = first(msgs) ⇒ msgs := tail(msgs)

Figure 3.2. IN — Specification of an ideal network

VAR msgs: SEQ[M] := ∅
ACTIONS
    send(m:M) ≡ msgs := append(msgs,m)
    receive(m:M) ≡ msgs ≠ ∅ ∧ m = first(msgs) ⇒ SKIP
INTERNAL
    drop ≡ msgs ≠ ∅ ⇒ msgs := tail(msgs)

Figure 3.3. LN — Specification of a lossy network

state; it merely returns the first waiting message. Thus, the same message could be received several times before being dropped, or could be dropped without being received at all.

Again, the reader can easily check the example behaviors given earlier to see that these state machines generate the appropriate sets for the different network specifications.

It is important to realize that the internal *drop* action is not visible to clients of the network. The behaviors generated by *LN* are sequences of *send* and *receive* actions only. Internal actions such as *drop*, however, are convenient devices for specifying complex sets of behaviors. In addition, internal actions show up in descriptions of implementations; for example, to represent the effects of background processes.

3.4   Correctness

The definition of correctness given earlier in Section 3.3.1 is based on viewing both a specification and an implementation as a set of behaviors: an implementation is *correct* if it is a subset of the specification. In other words, the implementation never does anything that the specification disallows.

This 'subset' definition of correctness is simple, but it is difficult to use directly as a basis for proving the correctness of an implementation. If the specification and implementation are both described by state machines, however, it is easy to use standard proof techniques such as induction and case analysis. In the first subsection below, we describe the general technique, which is based on invariants and abstraction functions. We then present two examples illustrating the use of the technique. We conclude this section with a brief discussion.

3.4.1   Invariants and Abstraction Functions

Let $\mathcal{M}_S$ be the specification state machine, and let $\mathcal{M}_I$ be the implementation state machine. Throughout, we assume that the set of external actions of $\mathcal{M}_I$ is a subset of those of $\mathcal{M}_S$. Their state sets, initial states, internal actions, and transitions may differ arbitrarily, but $\mathcal{M}_I$ must not have any external actions other than those in $\mathcal{M}_S$.

The first step in a proof is typically to prove some *invariants* on the state of $\mathcal{M}_I$. An invariant is a property that is true of every state that the implementation ever enters. To prove that a property is an invariant, we use induction:

- First, prove that the property holds for the initial states of $\mathcal{M}_I$. (This is the basis of the induction.)
- Second, prove that each action a *preserves* the property — that is, that if a makes a state change from s to s' and the property holds for s, then the property holds for s'. (This is the inductive step.)

The second step in a proof is to show that $\mathcal{M}_I$ 'simulates' $\mathcal{M}_S$. The key to the simulation is an *abstraction function*, which is a function from the states of $\mathcal{M}_I$ to the states of $\mathcal{M}_S$; it explains how to interpret an implementation state in terms of the specification.

Given an abstraction function f and an invariant I on the state of $\mathcal{M}_I$, there are two conditions that must be shown to prove that $\mathcal{M}_I$ is correct. Before stating the conditions, we need some definitions. First, we say that a sequence α of actions of $\mathcal{M}_S$ is the same externally as an action u of $\mathcal{M}_I$ if they are the same after all internal actions are discarded. In other words, if a is external, then α must contain exactly one external action, which must be the same as a; if a is internal, then α must contain only internal actions. Second, we say that a sequence $a_1, ..., a_n$ of actions of a machine $\mathcal{M}$ *can take* $\mathcal{M}$ *from* s *to* s' if there exists a sequence $s_1, ..., s_{n-1}$ of states of $\mathcal{M}$ such that (s, a_1, s_1), (s_{n-1}, a_n, s'), and (s_{i-1}, a_i, s_i) for $1 < i < n$ are all transitions of $\mathcal{M}$.

Now we can state the conditions needed to show the correctness of $\mathcal{M}_I$:

- f maps initial states of $\mathcal{M}_I$ to initial states of $\mathcal{M}_S$.
- For each action a of $\mathcal{M}_I$ and each state s that satisfies I, if (s, a, s') is a transition of $\mathcal{M}_I$, then there exists a sequence α of actions of $\mathcal{M}_S$ that is the same externally as a and that can take $\mathcal{M}_S$ from $f(s)$ to $f(s')$.

If these two conditions hold, a straightforward induction shows that $\mathcal{M}_I$ implements $\mathcal{M}_S$: for any sequence of actions generated by $\mathcal{M}_I$, we can construct a sequence generated by $\mathcal{M}_S$ that is the same externally. Thus, any behavior of $\mathcal{M}_I$ is also a behavior of $\mathcal{M}_S$.

The second condition above is represented by the commutative diagram in Figure 3.4. The diagram is interpreted as saying that for each a and s (where s satisfies I), there exists an α that is externally the same as a such that the diagram commutes — that is, if a can take s to s', then α can take $f(s)$ to $f(s')$.

Another way of thinking about the second condition is that for each state transition of $\mathcal{M}_I$, there must be a way of explaining its effects in terms of the specification. In other words, there must be transitions allowed by the specification that can account for the effects of the implementation-level transition — and if the implementation transition is external, the same external action in the specification must be part of the explanation.

Some of the different cases are shown in the diagram in Figure 3.5, in which the external actions are the e_i, and the internal actions are the i_j^S and i_j^I. The external action e_1 is explained by the sequence consisting of i_1^S followed by e_1. The internal actions i_1^I and i_2^I are explained by empty sequences — that is, as far as the client can tell, they are no-ops. The internal action i_3^I is explained by the internal action i_2^S, and the external action e_2 is explained by itself.

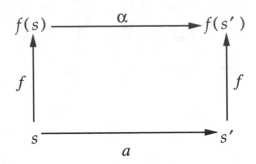

Figure 3.4. Requirements on abstraction functions

In practice, one rarely encounters cases like that shown in Figure 3.5 for e_1. Typically, an external action in the implementation corresponds to a sequence of length one containing that and only that action in the specification (as shown for e_2 in the figure), while an internal action in the implementation corresponds either to a single internal action in the specification (as shown for i_3^I), or to no state change at all in the specification (as shown for i_1^I and i_2^I).

3.4.2 Example: Write-Back Cache

We now turn to an example implementation, showing how to use the tools described above to prove it correct. The example is an implementation of the simple memory specification *SM*. The implementation, called *WBC*, uses a write-back cache; it is a somewhat abstract description of the operation of write-back caches in various memory systems, including processor memories, file systems, and virtual memory systems.

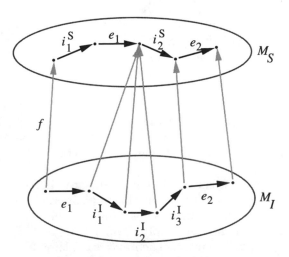

Figure 3.5. Example abstraction mappings

VAR
   m: $A \to D$
   c: $A \to (D + Null)$:= {*→nil}
ACTIONS
   read(a:A,d:D) ≡ $d = c(a) \Rightarrow$ SKIP
   write(a:A,d:D) ≡ $c(a) := d$
INTERNAL
   load(a:A) ≡ $c(a) = nil \Rightarrow c(a) := m(a)$
   write-back(a:A) ≡ $c(a) \ne nil \Rightarrow m(a) := c(a)$
   drop(a:A) ≡ $c(a) = m(a) \Rightarrow c(a) := nil$

Figure 3.6. WBC — A write-back cache implementation

WBC is described in Figure 3.6.   The cache is represented by the variable c, which maps an address to either a data value or *nil*; initially it maps all addresses to *nil*. The external actions deal only with the cache; a *read* action returns whatever is in the cache, and a *write* action simply updates the cache. The internal actions move data between the cache and the main memory. The *load* action loads the data for an address into the cache from main memory. The *write-back* action writes data from the cache back into main memory, while the *drop* action drops data from the cache (without writing it back). The *drop* action can occur only if the main memory already has the current data for that address — that is, if the cache and the main memory have the same data.

We claim that WBC is a correct implementation of SM. Recall that this requires that every behavior (sequence of external actions) generated by WBC must also be generated by SM. We could attempt to test this claim by examining different traces. For example, the following trace is generated by WBC, and corresponds to a behavior generated by SM (in fact, to the example given in Section 3.3.1):

   write(1,3)
   load(2)
   read(2,843)
   write(2,17)
   read(1,3)
   drop(1)
   write-back(2)
   read(2,17)

However, to prove the claim, we need to consider all possible traces. We can do this systematically using invariants and abstraction functions.

For this example, it turns out that we do not need to use an invariant on the state of WBC. We still need an abstraction function, however, because the state domains of WBC and SM are different. The abstraction function is quite simple; it maps the state (c_I, m_I) of WBC to the state m_S of SM defined as follows:

$m_S(a) = $ if $c_I(a) \ne nil$ then $c_I(a)$ else $m_I(a)$

Informally, this says that the cache has the current value for each address; if the cache has no data for a given address, then the current value can be found in the main memory.

To prove *WBC* correct, we must show that the abstraction function maps initial states to initial states, and that each action of *WBC* is explained by some sequence of actions of *SM* that is externally the same.

Denote the abstraction function by f. The first condition is easy; c_I is initially the constant function that maps every address to *nil*, so applying f to an initial state of *WBC* gives a value for m_S equal to m_I. The initial values for m_S and m_I are both arbitrary functions from addresses to data, so an initial state of *WBC* is mapped by f to an initial state for *SM*.

For the second condition, we use the following definition of the sequence α_a used to explain the effects of an action a of *WBC*: if a is external, then $\alpha_a = a$; if a is internal, then α_a is the empty sequence. Now we need to show, for each action a of *WBC*, if a can take s to s', then α_a can take $f(s)$ to $f(s')$. For the external actions, this is immediate from their definitions and the definition of f. For the internal actions, we must show that $f(s) = f(s')$ (since α_a is the empty sequence for the internal actions). The reader can easily check that this is the case.

3.4.3   Example: Alternating Bit Protocol

We now consider a different example that requires the use of an invariant in the proof. The example is the 'alternating bit protocol' (Bartlett, Scantlebury and Wilkinson [1969]), which is a simple protocol for implementing an ideal network on top of lossy (but FIFO) channels. It is not practical for some systems because its throughput is limited to $1/r$ where r is the round-trip time, but it is a simple example that has been widely used in the literature to illustrate different specification and verification techniques (e.g., see Halpern and Zuck [1987], Lamport [1983], Lynch [1989], among others). The implementation, which we call *ABP*, is in Figure 3.7. Comments are included in italics.

The alternating bit protocol works as follows. The sender and receiver are connected by two unreliable FIFO channels that can lose or duplicate messages, but cannot reorder them. The FIFO property is key; if messages could be reordered, this protocol would not work. When the sender is given a message to send, it is buffered in a local queue (*sbuf*). If the sender has a buffered message waiting to be sent, it pairs it with a tag and sends it over one of the channels (*s2r*) to the receiver; it retransmits the tagged message until it receives an acknowledgement that the message was received. Each tag is just a single bit, and the acknowledgement for a message is just the message's tag. The sender keeps track of the tag for the message at the front of its queue (*sflag*), and the receiver keeps track of the tag for the last message it received (*rflag*). The receiver ignores messages with tags equal to *rflag* (these are duplicates), and the sender ignores acknowledgements that are not equal to *sflag* (these are old acknowledgement). When the sender receives an acknowledgement for the current message, it deletes the first message in the queue and toggles *sflag* so the next message will be sent with a different tag. Similarly, when the receiver receives a new message from the sender, it buffers it (in *rbuf*) and toggles *rflag* to ensure that duplicate copies of the message will be ignored.

VAR
> *The state maintained by the sender:*
> sflag: Bool := false   % *tag of current message*
> sbuf: SEQ[M] := Ø   % *buffered messages to be sent*
> *The channel from the sender to the receiver; each packet*
> *has a message and a tag:*
> s2r: SEQ[{m:M,b:Bool}] := Ø
> *The state maintained by the receiver:*
> rflag: Bool := true   % *tag of last received message*
> rbuf: SEQ[M] := Ø   % *buffered messages already received*
> *The channel from the receiver to the sender:*
> r2s: SEQ[Bool] := Ø   % *each ack is just a tag*

ACTIONS
> send(m:M) ≡ sbuf := append(sbuf,m)
> receive(m:M) = rbuf ≠ Ø ∧ m = first(rbuf) ⇒ rbuf := tail(rbuf)

INTERNAL
> *Sender transmits; {m:= ..., b:= ...} is a record constructor*
> xmitM ≡ sbuf ≠ Ø
> ⇒ s2r := append(s2r, {m:= first(sbuf), b:= sflag})
> *Sender receives an ack for current message*
> getAck ≡ r2s ≠ Ø ∧ b = first(r2s) ∧ b = sflag
> ⇒ sbuf := tail(sbuf); sflag := ¬ sflag
> *Receiver gets a new message from channel*
> getM ≡ s2r ≠ Ø ∧ {m,b} = first(s2r) ∧ b = ¬ rflag
> ⇒ rbuf := append(rbuf,m); rflag := b
> *Receiver sends an ack*
> xmitAck ≡ r2s := append(r2s,rflag)
> *Message from sender to receiver is dropped*
> dropM ≡ s2r ≠ Ø ⇒ s2r := tail(s2r)
> *Ack from receiver to sender is dropped*
> dropAck ≡ r2s ≠ Ø ⇒ r2s := tail(r2s)

Figure 3.7. ABP — Alternating bit protocol

The implementation shown here has a lot of nondeterminism. For example, the sender could transmit many copies of a message, and the receiver could transmit many acknowledgements for each message received. In practice, the sender would retransmit only after a timeout expires, and the receiver might send an acknowledgement only in response to messages received from the sender. An implementation with these additional constraints is easily shown to implement the protocol shown here, since the only change is that the guards on actions have been strengthened. Since the 'implements' relation is transitive, the correctness of this more deterministic implementation follows from that of the one shown here.

One way of thinking about the operation of *ABP* is to view it as an optimization of a similar protocol that replaces the single-bit tags with unbounded sequence numbers. The single-bit tags in *ABP* are just the low-order bits of the sequence numbers. The protocol with unbounded sequence numbers has a critical invariant, namely that the sequence numbers present in the system (*sflag*, *rflag*, the tags in the messages in *s2r*, and the acknowledgements in *r2s*) differ by at most one. In addition, because the channels preserve order, there is at most one place (either in a channel, or between a channel and one of the flags) where adjacent numbers differ at all. Thus, if we look at the single-bit tags in *ABP* in the order they appear in the system, concatenating them starting with the first tags in *r2s*, then *rflag*, then the tags in messages in *s2r*, and then *sflag*, there can be at most one change from *true* to *false* or vice-versa in that sequence.

One other invariant is needed for the proof: if a packet in *s2r* has a tag that equals *sflag*, then the *m* component of the packet equals the first message in *sbuf*. Proving these invariants involves a straightforward induction.

The abstraction function *f* from *ABP* to *IN* maps a state of *ABP* to the state *msgs* of *IN* defined as follows:

msgs = if *sflag* = *rflag*
     then *concat(rbuf, tail(sbuf))*
     else *concat(rbuf, sbuf)*

The packets in the channels are irrelevant for the abstraction function, since the sender does not discard a message until the receiver has acknowledged receiving it (also, they can be lost). If the sender's and receiver's flags are different, that means that the first message in *sbuf* has not been delivered to the receiver and put in *rbuf*; if the flags are the same, then the first message in *sbuf* has been delivered to the receiver and put in *rbuf*. (It might no longer be in *rbuf*, since a *receive* action could have delivered it to the client.)

The proof of correctness is relatively straightforward. The sequence α_a that explains an action *a* is just as in the previous example: if *a* is external, then $\alpha_a = a$, and if *a* is internal, then $\alpha_a = \varnothing$. The first condition on *f*, that it map initial states to initial states, is immediate. For the second condition, we consider cases. The external actions are straightforward. The internal actions *xmitM*, *xmitAck*, *dropM*, and *dropAck* are also immediate, since they do not modify state variables that affect the value of the abstraction function. For the actions *getAck* and *getM*, we need to use the invariants described above.

The *getAck* action takes a state *s* in which *sflag* equals the first acknowledgement in *r2s*, and produces a state *s'* in which the first message in *sbuf* has been deleted, and *sflag* has been toggled. By the invariant, if *sflag* equals the received acknowledgement in *s*, then it must also equal *rflag* (since otherwise there would be two changes in the sequence of tags in the system). It follows that $f(s) = f(s')$.

The *getM* action is similar. It takes a state *s* in which the tag on the first packet in *s2r* is different from *rflag*, and produces a state *s'* in which the message from the first packet in *s2r* has been appended to *rbuf* and *rflag* has been toggled. By the invariant, if the tag on the first packet in *s2r* is different from *rflag*, *rflag* must be different from *sflag*, and the tag on the first packet must be the same as *sflag*. Thus, the message in the first packet must be the same as the first message in *sbuf*. Again, it follows that $f(s) = f(s')$.

3.4.4 Discussion

The verification technique described here based on abstraction functions and invariants is an adaptation of a standard technique used for verification of data abstractions in sequential systems (see Hoare [1972], Liskov and Guttag [1986]). The technique has been generalized slightly to deal with arbitrary atomic actions, but is almost identical to the original technique proposed by Hoare and others.

Given a verification technique, such as the one described above, an obvious question is whether the technique is complete; i.e., if an implementation is correct, whether it is always possible to prove it correct using the technique. In this case, the question comes down to whether one can always find an invariant and an abstraction function that satisfy the conditions given in Section 3.4.1. The answer to this question is rather subtle, but can be viewed as a somewhat qualified 'yes'. However, one may have to introduce 'history variables' and 'prophecy variables' in the implementation to make the proof work; see Abadí and Lamport [1991] for details.

In the presentation above, we have discussed invariants and abstraction functions primarily as tools for verifying implementations. The reader might get the impression that the invariant and abstraction function for an implementation are developed after the implementation is complete. In fact, it is much more effective to develop the invariant and abstraction function during the design of the implementation. Given the state variables of the implementation, the invariant, and the abstraction function, the details of the actions often follow almost mechanically. We do not have space here to give examples of this process, but several examples (for sequential systems) can be found in Liskov and Guttag [1986].

3.5 Example: Synchronization of Threads

In this section we present a specification of the synchronization primitives for a threads package, derived from the primitives provided in the Topaz operating system for the Firefly multiprocessor developed at DEC SRC (Birrell [1989]; Owicki [1989]). The specification, which is based on the one presented by Birrell *et al.* [1987], illustrates a common tradeoff between performance, complexity, and functionality, and shows how to handle such tradeoffs in writing specifications.

One of the key issues in writing a specification, particularly of a module in a concurrent system, is how much nondeterminism to allow. More nondeterminism provides the implementor with greater freedom, but provides weaker guarantees to the clients. Less nondeterminism provides the clients with more useful guarantees, but may force the implementor to use a less efficient or more complex implementation.

In the case of the threads package, the issue of nondeterminism shows up in the specification of the *signal* operation, which is used to wake up a thread that is waiting on a condition variable. From the client's point of view, the ideal specification would have *signal* wake up exactly one thread. In the Topaz system and many others, however, the designers have made the decision to allow *signal* to wake up more than one thread. (Most of the time it wakes up exactly one,

VAR
    A mutex:
  m: (Thread + Null) := nil
    A condition variable:
  c: SET[Thread] := $\varnothing$
  a: SET[Thread] := $\varnothing$
ACTIONS
  acquire(t:Thread) $\equiv$ m = nil $\Rightarrow$ m := t
  release(t:Thread) $\equiv$ m = t $\Rightarrow$ m := nil
  release(t:Thread) $\equiv$ m $\neq$ t $\Rightarrow$ HAVOC
  wait(t:Thread) $\equiv$ m = t $\Rightarrow$ m := nil; c := c $\cup$ {t}
  wait(t:Thread) $\equiv$ m $\neq$ t $\Rightarrow$ HAVOC
  resume(t:Thread) $\equiv$ t $\in$ a $\wedge$ m = nil $\Rightarrow$ m := t; a := a $-$ {t}
  signal $\equiv$ s $\subseteq$ c $\wedge$ (c = $\varnothing$ $\vee$ s $\neq$ $\varnothing$) $\Rightarrow$ c := c $-$ s; a := a $\cup$ s
  broadcast $\equiv$ a := a $\cup$ c; c := $\varnothing$

Figure 3.8. Specification of mutex and condition variable operations

but there are circumstances under which it can wake up several.) There are two reasons for allowing this behavior in *signal*. First, the implementation in many cases is simpler and more efficient. Second, unlike the condition variables in Hoare's monitors (Hoare [1974]), which ensure that the waiting thread awakened by a signal runs immediately after the signal, the condition variables in Topaz allow other threads to enter the monitor between the signal and the time the awakened thread runs. As a result, the awakened thread must already be prepared for the predicate it is waiting for to be invalidated by other threads, so allowing multiple threads to be awakened by a signal has minimal effect on client programs.

The specification, which is shown in Figure 3.8, allows *signal* to choose any set of waiting threads to awaken. The specification does not say anything about what should happen most of the time — that is, that *signal* should wake up exactly one thread — rather, it specifies only what is guaranteed. To use the interface effectively, a client needs to know what is likely, not just what is guaranteed. This is a defect in most approaches to specifications.

For simplicity, in Figure 3.8 we specify the behavior of a single mutex and condition variable only; a complete specification would include provisions for allocating new mutexes and condition variables. In the specification, a value of type *Thread* is a thread name. The state of the mutex is modeled as either the name of the thread holding the mutex or the distinguished value *nil*. The state of a condition variable is modeled as the set of names of threads waiting on the condition variable (the set *c*), plus the set of names of threads that have been signalled but not yet resumed (the set *a*).

The specification shows six kinds of atomic actions: *acquire, release, wait, resume, signal* and *broadcast*. The first two correspond to acquiring and releasing a mutex. The mutex can be acquired only when it is not held (i.e., its value is *nil*). Two cases are shown for *release*. In the first case, the thread attempting to release the mutex is the one that holds it; in this case, the mutex is released by setting it to *nil*. In the second case, the thread does not hold the mutex; in this case, anything is allowed to happen (denoted by the special term HAVOC).

The remaining actions deal with condition variables. The *wait* and *resume* actions occur as part of the operation called by a thread to wait on a condition variable in the Topaz interface. A thread must be holding the mutex when it waits on the condition variable (otherwise anything can happen). The *wait* action releases the mutex and records the thread as waiting (in the state variable *c*). The thread resumes running after the action *resume* has occurred. This can happen only if the mutex is available (since the thread needs the mutex when it starts running again) and if the thread has been awakened by a *signal* or *broadcast* (in which case it will be in the set *a* in the specification). The *resume* action marks the mutex as held by the thread and removes it from the set *a*.

The *broadcast* action is simple: it moves all the threads in *c* to *a*, indicating that they can resume one after another as the mutex is available. The *signal* action is more complex. It can awaken any subset of the set of waiting threads (except that it must wake up at least one if there are any waiting).

Similar issues of nondeterminism show up in many other concurrent and distributed systems. Concurrency sometimes requires expensive and complex synchronization to avoid race conditions; it may be better to accept a weaker specification that permits the race conditions. Similarly, the communication delays in a distributed system may result in unacceptable performance, but sometimes they can be hidden if a weaker specification is used. Examples of the latter are discussed in the next section.

We note that most specification methods have something similar to the HAVOC concept. Whenever there is a restriction on the client of a module that the module cannot easily check, the specification should state the restriction explicitly, and make clear to the client that the behavior of the module is undefined if the restriction is not met. For example, a *search* routine that expects its array argument to be sorted cannot easily check whether the array is sorted, since the reason for expecting it to be sorted is to use a search technique that takes time logarithmic in the length of the array. In the example above, many implementations of mutexes do not actually store the identity of the thread holding a mutex, so they cannot check whether the thread releasing the mutex is the current holder.

3.6   Distributed Systems

At this point the reader may be wondering what is special about distributed systems. One answer is not much. Distributed systems are concurrent, and the specification and verification techniques discussed above can be used for them, just as for other concurrent systems. Another answer, however, is that quite a bit is special. Distributed systems introduce the possibility of independent failures — individual components failing while others continue running — and also have much larger communication delays than most multiprocessors. These attributes of distributed systems do not require different techniques for specification and veri-

TYPE
>   *The operations requested by clients:*
>   Op = S → (S,V)

VAR
>   *The state of the server:*
>   s: S

ACTIONS
>   *Execute a request and return a result*
>   OpReturnV(v:V,op:Op) ≡ (s',v) = op(s) ⇒ s := s'
>
>   *Return "failed" from a request*
>   *The request does nothing*
>   OpReturnFail(op:Op) ≡ SKIP
>   *Execute a request but return "failed"*
>   OpReturnFail(op:Op) ≡ (s',v) = op(s) ⇒ s := s'

Figure 3.9. Specification of zero-or-once RPC

fication. However, the desire to tolerate failures and hide communication delays sometimes forces a system designer to provide weaker guarantees to the system's clients than would be provided by a single-site system. In addition, the behavior of the resulting system is often complex and difficult to describe abstractly.

In this section, we discuss two examples that illustrate the tradeoffs between performance and functionality. We also show how specifications can be written that provide a high-level yet useful description of a system's behavior to its clients. The key idea is to introduce nondeterminism in the specifications to model the uncertainty introduced by failures and by communication delays. In addition, special 'failure' actions can be introduced to constrain the system's behavior in the absence of failures.

3.6.1   Remote Procedure Call

Modern remote procedure call (RPC) systems often provide an 'at-most-once' semantics: a remote call might be executed zero times, partially, or once, but not more than once (Birrell and Nelson [1984]). With the use of atomic transactions, a 'zero-or-once' semantics can be achieved: a call is executed either completely or not at all. In both cases, however, if the caller receives an error response, he cannot tell whether or not the call occurred. (For example, the network might partition after the call is executed but before the reply is sent to the caller.)

We can use nondeterminism to model the caller's uncertainty about calls that return errors, as shown in Figure 3.9. In the specification, we model the state of the service and the operations requested by clients abstractly: an operation is just a function on the server state that returns a new state and a result value; the result value is returned to the client. When a value is actually returned, the operation is performed and the state is updated. When 'failed' is returned, the service can choose whether to perform the operation and update the state; the client is left uncertain.

The specification above raises two questions. First, it describes a 'zero-or-once' semantics; partial executions of requests are not allowed. So how can we model partial executions, as in at-most-once semantics? Second, it is very nondeterministic; for example, the system could choose to ignore requests and simply return 'failed' to every call. We expect a reasonable implementation to do this only when an actual failure occurs in the system — for example, a node crashes, or the network takes too long to deliver a message. How can we write the specification to prevent the implementation from returning 'failed' in the absence of actual failures?

At-most-once semantics can be modeled by including in the specification a mapping from an operation requested by a client to the sequences of atomic state changes that are allowed for an implementation. Performing an operation then involves choosing some prefix of the sequence of state changes and performing that prefix; a result can be returned only when the entire sequence is performed. This specification is more complicated than the one given above for zero-or-once semantics, but that is an artifact of the semantics of the system being described, not of the specification method or the specification itself.

Failures can be modeled more accurately by introducing new (external) atomic actions corresponding to failures and recoveries of the system. 'Failed' is then returned to a client only if the system was failed and not recovered at some time between the client's request and the reply to that request. Capturing this restriction requires introducing new actions to model the start and the end of a client's request, so that we can tell whether the system was in a failed state at some point during the execution of the request. Once these extra actions have been introduced, we can capture the desired behavior by keeping track of the number of failures and recoveries in the state; if the number of recoveries is less than the number of failures when a client makes a request, then the system is is in a failed state when the request starts, while if the number of failures when the reply is returned is greater than the number of failures when the client made the request, then the system failed at some point during the execution of the request.

Introducing failure and recovery actions makes sense only if we constrain how implementations are modeled. If the implementor is free to call any action a 'failure' action (e.g., a client request, or the tick of a clock), then the implementation has just as much freedom to return 'failed' as in the specification shown above. So in addition to the constraints discussed in the previous paragraph, we need to specify what actual implementation actions can be viewed as 'failure' and 'recovery' actions.

3.6.2   A Replicated Name Service

Our final example is a specification for a replicated name service, derived from Grapevine (Birrell *et al.* [1982]) and Digital's Global Name Service (GNS) (Lampson [1986]). Name services need to be highly available, so they are often replicated to ensure that clients can continue to perform operations even when parts of the network or some of the servers are down. To avoid long delays during client requests, many name services, including Grapevine and GNS, perform each client operation at a single replica and then propagate any updates resulting from the

TYPE
    Updates
   U = S → S
    Observers
   O = S → V
VAR
    The state of the service:
   us: SET[U] := ∅
ACTIONS
   update(u:U) ≡ us := us ∪ {u}
   observer(o:O,v:V) ≡ consistent(us,o,v)
Where consistent is a predicate defined as follows:
   consistent(us:SET[U],o:O,v:V) ≡ ∃ us' ⊆ us, s':S such that
     finalState(us',s') ∧ o(s') = v
and finalState is defined as follows (where s0 is
the initial state of the service):
   finalState(us:SET[U],s:S) ≡
     (us = ∅ ⇒ s = s0)
     ∧ (us ≠ ∅ ⇒ ∃ u ∈ us, s':S
       such that finalState(us−{u},s') ∧ u(s')=s)

Figure 3.10. Simplified specification of name service

operation to other replicas in the background. (Similar lazy replication schemes are used in many other applications, such as distributing password files, or updating installed software after a new release.) Such designs lead to good performance, but provide a significantly different semantics than one would expect from a single-site service. In this section we give a simple specification that captures some of the subtleties of this kind of behavior.

As in our specification of RPC in the previous section, we model the client operations abstractly. For simplicity of presentation, we distinguish between *updates*, which modify the state but do not return any information, and *observers*, which extract information from the state. We also ignore the possibility of a 'failed' response, which might occur when the client is unable to contact any of the servers.

In Figure 3.10 we show a simplified specification of a name service modeled on Grapevine. We model the state of the service as a set of updates. An observer determines a result by choosing some subset of the updates that have been performed so far, and basing its result on those updates only. The predicate *consistent(us, o, v)* tests whether there is a subset of *us* such that executing the updates in that subset in some order gives a state in which *o* returns *v*. The predicate *finalState(us, s)* tests whether there is an order in which the updates in *us* can be performed to give the state *s*.

Notice that the specification given above is very nondeterministic. For example, an observer could always choose the empty set of updates, and just base its result on the initial state *s0*. In general, an observer is allowed to choose an arbitrary subset of the updates that have occurred as the basis for its result. Such behavior is difficult for clients to cope with, and one might ask whether there is a better specification of the behavior of systems such as Grapevine. In fact, systems such as Grapevine can exhibit such behavior, although it is extremely unlikely that updates performed a long time before an observer is run will not be seen by the observer.

One could undoubtedly write a more accurate specification of Grapevine that does a better job of modeling the circumstances under which an observer will miss some updates. However, clients will still have to cope with occasional failure conditions in which a very old update is missed by an observer. More recent system designs, such as Digital's GNS, restrict the nondeterminism of systems such as Grapevine by periodically 'sweeping' all replicas to ensure that all updates recorded anywhere before the sweep are recorded everywhere after the sweep. This means that an observer can only miss seeing an update that was recorded after the start of the last sweep. In other words, clients are guaranteed that very old updates will be seen, but there is still some uncertainty about which recent updates will be seen.

We can capture the behavior of GNS by tagging each update in the state with a timestamp, and also keeping in the state the time of the last sweep. An internal action can advance the time of the last sweep, and the set of updates on which an observer bases its result must include every update whose timestamp is before the time of the last sweep.

3.7 Hints For Writing Specifications

There are several useful hints for writing better specifications for concurrent and distributed systems. The first and most basic for a specification of any kind of system is to avoid overspecification. A specification should describe *what* a module does, not *how* it should do it. Overspecification reduces the implementor's choices in designing the implementation of the module, and makes it difficult to modify the system later to meet changing requirements.

Second, 'coarser' atomic actions are simpler. For example, consider the specification of RPC given earlier. The specification shown treats each client request as a single atomic action. To model failures more accurately, however, we must introduce separate actions corresponding to the start and end of a client request. These actions are necessary to capture the desired constraints. Similarly, to model at-most-once instead of zero-or-once RPC, the execution of a single client request must be viewed as a sequence of atomic actions.

In general, the fewer actions in the specification, the easier it will be for clients (and designers) to understand. Sometimes greater complexity is needed to provide an accurate description of the behavior provided by the system. But sometimes a simpler specification will give the clients all the information they need. (For example, the specification of condition variables given earlier does not explain when *signal* can wake up more than one waiting thread; in this case, such information would probably not be useful to clients.)

Third, nondeterminism is very useful in writing high-level specifications. For example, *signal* can nondeterministically choose the set of waiting threads to be awakened. Similarly, the RPC system can nondeterministically decide whether the state is updated by a 'failed' request. Excessive nondeterminism is not good — but this is sometimes an indication that the system being specified needs to be redesigned to provide stronger guarantees.

Fourth, actions can be introduced into specifications to model the failures and recoveries of a system. This allows the specification to constrain the behavior allowed in the absence of failures while still covering all the possible behaviors that can occur.

Finally, we note that precise specifications can be hard to write, and there is a significant learning curve involved. At the same time, writing them is very often a worthwhile exercise. As discussed earlier, a good specification provides documentation to clients, and also serves the role of a contract. In addition, the act of writing a specification often leads to significantly enhanced understanding of what a system does, making it easier to evaluate whether the system is providing the right service to its clients. And while a precise formal specification is usually best, a carefully written informal specification is better than no specification at all.

3.8 Bibliographic Notes

These notes are not intended as a comprehensive survey of work on specification and verification techniques for concurrent and distributed systems. Rather, they give the reader an overview of work in the area, as well as pointers to papers that provide useful further references.

Virtually all methods for specifying and reasoning about concurrent and distributed systems are based on a model of computation that incorporates some notion of atomic actions. At the same time, there are a number of differences between approaches. For example, some approaches focus on specifying properties of the *states* of modules and the sequences of states that can occur — for instance, UNITY (Chandy and Misra [1988]), the State Transition Systems of Lam and Shankar [1984], and Lamport's temporal logic of actions (TLA) (Lamport [1989]; Lamport [1990]). Other approaches, such as Lynch and Tuttle's input-output automata (Lynch and Tuttle [1987]; Lynch and Tuttle [1989]), focus on the *events* that cause state changes and view the states as secondary. Similarly, different approaches have different notions of what constitutes a module's *interface*: some use events that are shared with other modules, while others use external variables that can be read and written. Finally, some approaches are almost purely model-theoretic, while others are proof-theoretic, providing a formal logic for proving properties of modules. Most proof-theoretic work has focused on some form of temporal logic; a good description can be found in Manna and Pnueli's book (Manna and Pnueli [1991]).

Abstraction functions first appeared in the 1970s in work on data abstraction (Hoare [1972]). They are useful whenever the state domain used in the specification differs from that used in the implementation. A number of researchers, including Lamport [1983] and Lynch [1986], recognized the importance of similar mapping techniques for concurrent and distributed systems in the late 1970s and early 1980s. Questions about the completeness of proof techniques based on abstraction functions have been addressed by a number of people, including Abadí and Lamport [1991] and Merritt [1989]. In addition, the techniques have been extended to handle timing properties; see Lynch and Vaandrager's work for one approach and a survey of others (Lynch and Vaandrager [1991]).

Many other examples of specifications and implementations of concurrent and distributed systems, together with abstraction functions and invariants, can be found in the collected notes for the course 'Principles of Computer Systems' taught by Professors Lampson and Weihl at MIT (Weihl, Lampson and Brewer [1992]).

Acknowledgements

William E. Weihl's work on this chapter was supported in part by the Advanced Research Projects Agency (ARPA) under Contract N00014-91-J-1698,[6] by grants from IBM and AT&T, and by an equipment grant from DEC.

3.9 References

Abadí, M. and Lamport, L. (1991), The Existence of Refinement Mappings, *Theoretical Computer Science* **2(82)**, 253–284.

Alpern, B. and Schneider, F. B. (1984), Defining Liveness, Cornell University Department of Computer Science, Technical Report 85-650, Revised February 1985.

Bartlett, K. A., Scantlebury, R. A. and Wilkinson, P. T. (1969), A Note on Reliable Full-Duplex Transmission Over Half-Duplex Links, *Communications of the ACM* **12**, 260–261.

Birrell, A. D. (1989), An Introduction to Programming with Threads, DEC Systems Research Center, SRC Report 35, 130 Lytton Ave., Palo Alto, CA 94301.

Birrell, A. D., Guttag, J., Horning, J. and Levin, R. (1987), Synchronization Primitives for a Multiprocessor: A Formal Specification, *Proceedings of the Eleventh Symposium on Operating Systems Principles*, Austin, TX, 94–102, In *ACM Operating Systems Review* **21(5)**.

Birrell, A. D., Levin, R., Needham, R. M. and Schroeder, M. D. (1982), Grapevine: An Exercise in Distributed Computing, *Communications of the ACM* **25**, 260–274.

Birrell, A. D. and Nelson, B. J. (1984), Implementing Remote Procedure Calls, *ACM Transactions on Computer Systems* **2**, 39–59.

Chandy, K. M. and Misra, J. (1988), *Parallel Program Design: A Foundation*, Addison-Wesley.

Francez, N. (1986), *Fairness*, Springer-Verlag, Berlin.

---

[6]The views and conclusions contained here are those of the author and should not be interpreted as representing the official policies, either expressed or implied, of the U.S. government.

Halpern, J. and Zuck, L. (1987), A Little Knowledge Goes a Long Way: Simple Knowledge-Based Derivations and Correctness Proofs for a Family of Protocols, *Proceedings of the Sixth ACM Annual Symposium on Principles of Distributed Computing*, Schneider, F. B., ed., Vancouver, BC, Canada, 269–290.

Hoare, C. A. R. (1972), Proof of Correctness of Data Representations, *Acta Informatica* **1**, 271–281.

Hoare, C. A. R. (1974), Monitors: an Operating System Structuring Concept, *Communications of the ACM* **17**(10), 549–557.

Lam, S. S. and Shankar, A. U. (1984), Protocol Verificiation via Projections, *IEEE Transactions on Software Engineering* **10**, 325–342.

Lamport, L. (1983), Specifying Concurrent Program Modules, *ACM Transactions on Programming Languages and Systems* **5**(2), 190–222.

Lamport, L. (1989), A Simple Approach to Specifying Concurrent Systems, *Communications of the ACM* **32**, 32–45.

Lamport, L. (1990), A Temporal Logic of Actions, DEC Systems Research Center, SRC Report 57, 130 Lytton Ave., Palo Alto, CA 94301.

Lampson, B. W. (1983), Hints for Computer System Design, *Proceedings of the Ninth Symposium on Operating Systems Principles*, Bretton Woods, NH, 33–48, In *ACM Operating Systems Review* **17**(5).

Lampson, B. W. (1986), Designing a Global Name Service, *Proceedings of the Fifth ACM Annual Symposium on Principles of Distributed Computing*, Calgary, Canada, 1–10.

Liskov, B. and Guttag, J. (1986), *Abstraction and Specification in Program Development*, MIT Press, Cambridge, MA.

Lynch, N. A. (1986), Concurrency Control for Resilient Nested Transactions, *Advances in Computing Research* **3**, 335–373.

Lynch, N. A. (1989), Multivalued Possibilities Mappings, *Proceedings of the REX Workshop on Stepwise Refinement*, Bakker, J. W. de, Roever, W. -P. de and Rozenberg, G., eds., Springer-Verlag, 519–543, published as Lecture Notes in Computer Science Number 430.

Lynch, N. A. and Tuttle, M. R. (1987), Hierarchical Correctness Proofs for Distributed Algorithms, *Proceedings of the Sixth ACM Annual Symposium on Principles of Distributed Computing*, Schneider, F. B., ed., Cambridge, MA, April 1987, 137–151, Expanded version available as Technical Report MIT/LCS/TR-387, MIT Laboratory for Computer Science.

Lynch, N. A. and Tuttle, M. R. (1989), An Introduction to Input/Output Automata, *CWI-Quarterly* **2**(3), 219–246, Also available as Technical Memo MIT/LCS/TM-373, MIT Laboratory for Computer Science.

Lynch, N. A. and Vaandrager, F. (1991), Forward and Backward Simulations for Timing-Based Systems, *Proceedings of the REX Workshop on Stepwise Refinement*, Springer-Verlag, Available as MIT/LCS/TM-458.

Manna, Z. and Pnueli, A. (1991), *The Temporal Logic of Reactive Systems*, Springer Verlag.

Merritt, M. (1989), Completeness Theorems for Automata, *Proceedings of the REX Workshop on Stepwise Refinement*, Bakker, J. W. de, Roever, W. -P. de and Rozenberg, G., eds., Springer-Verlag, 520–560, published as Lecture Notes in Computer Science Number 430.

Owicki, S. (1989), Experience with the Firefly Multiprocessor Workstation, DEC Systems Research Center, SRC Report 51, 130 Lytton Ave., Palo Alto, CA 94301.

Weihl, W. E., Lampson, B. W. and Brewer, E. (1992), 6.826 — Principles of Computer Systems: Lecture Notes and Handouts, MIT Laboratory for Computer Science, MIT/LCS/RSS 19, Cambridge, MA, Collected notes for the Fall 1991 course.

Chapter 4

Consistent Global States of Distributed Systems: Fundamental Concepts and Mechanisms

Özalp Babaoğlu and Keith Marzullo

Many important problems in distributed computing admit solutions that contain a phase where some global property needs to be detected. This subproblem can be seen as an instance of the *Global Predicate Evaluation* (GPE) problem where the objective is to establish the truth of a Boolean expression whose variables may refer to the global system state. Given the uncertainties in asynchronous distributed systems that arise from communication delays and relative speeds of computations, the formulation and solution of GPE reveal most of the subtleties in global reasoning with imperfect information. In this chapter, we use GPE as a canonical problem in order to survey concepts and mechanisms that are useful in understanding global states of distributed computations. We illustrate the utility of the developed techniques by examining distributed deadlock detection and distributed debugging as two instances of GPE.

4.1 Introduction

A large class of problems in distributed computing can be cast as executing some notification or reaction when the state of the system satisfies a particular condition. Examples of such problems include monitoring and debugging, detection of particular states such as deadlock and termination, and dynamic adaptation of a program's configuration such as for load balancing. Thus, the ability to construct a global state and evaluate a predicate over such a state constitutes the core of solutions to many problems in distributed computing.

The global state of a distributed system is the union of the states of the individual processes. Given that the processes of a distributed system do not share memory but instead communicate solely through the exchange of messages, a process that wishes to construct a global state must infer the remote components of that state through message exchanges. Thus, a fundamental problem in distributed computing is to ensure that a global state constructed in this manner is meaningful.

In asynchronous distributed systems, a global state obtained through remote observations could be obsolete, incomplete, or inconsistent. Informally, a global state is inconsistent if it could never have been constructed by an idealized observer that is external to the system. It should be clear that uncertainties in message delays and in relative speeds at which local computations proceed prevent a process from drawing conclusions about the instantaneous global state of the system to which it belongs. While simply increasing the frequency of communication may be effective in making local views of a global state more current and more complete, it is not sufficient for guaranteeing that the global state is consistent. Ensuring the consistency of a constructed global state requires us to reason about both the order in which messages are observed by a process as well as the information contained in the messages. For a large class of problems, consistency turns out to be an appropriate formalization of the notion that global reasoning with local information is 'meaningful'.

Another source of difficulty in distributed systems arises when separate processes independently construct global states. The variability in message delays could lead to these separate processes constructing different global states for the same computation. Even though each such global state may be consistent and the processes may be evaluating the same predicate, the different processes may execute conflicting reactions. This 'relativistic effect' is inherent to all distributed computations and limits the class of system properties that can be effectively detected.

In this chapter, we formalize and expand the above concepts in the context of an abstract problem called *Global Predicate Evaluation* (GPE). The goal of GPE is to determine whether the global state of the system satisfies some predicate Φ. Global predicates are constructed so as to encode system properties of interest in terms of state variables. Examples of distributed system problems where the relevant properties can be encoded as global predicates include deadlock detection, termination detection, token loss detection, unreachable storage (garbage) collection, checkpointing and restarting, debugging, and in general, monitoring and reconfiguration. In this sense, a solution to GPE can be seen as the core of a generic solution for all these problems; what remains to be done is the formulation of the appropriate predicate Φ and the construction of reactions or notifications to be executed when the predicate is satisfied.

We begin by defining a formal model for asynchronous distributed systems and distributed computations. We then examine two different strategies for solving GPE. The first strategy, introduced in Section 4.5, and refined in Section 4.13, is based on a monitor process that actively interrogates the rest of the system in order to construct the global state. In Section 4.6 we give a formal definition for consistency of global states. The alternative strategy, discussed in Section 4.7, has the monitor passively observe the system in order to construct its global states. Sections 4.8–4.13 introduce a series of concepts and mechanisms necessary for making the two strategies work efficiently. In Section 4.14 we identify properties that global predicates must satisfy in order to solve practical problems using GPE. In Section 4.15 we address the issue of multiple monitors observing the same computation. We illustrate the utility of the underlying concepts and mechanisms by applying them to deadlock detection and to debugging in distributed systems.

4.2   Asynchronous Distributed Systems

A distributed system is a collection of sequential *processes* $p_1, p_2, ..., p_n$ and a network capable of implementing unidirectional communication *channels* between pairs of processes for message exchange. Channels are reliable but may deliver messages out of order. We assume that every process can communicate with every other process, perhaps through intermediary processes. In other words, the communication network is assumed to be strongly connected (but not necessarily completely connected).

In defining the properties of a distributed system, we would like to make the weakest set of assumptions possible. Doing so will enable us to establish upper bounds on the costs of solving problems in distributed systems. More specifically, if there exists a solution to a problem in this weakest model with some cost γ, then there is a solution to the same problem with a cost no greater than γ in *any* distributed system.

The weakest possible model for a distributed system is called an *asynchronous system* and is characterized by the following properties: there exist no bounds on the relative speeds of processes and there exist no bounds on message delays. Asynchronous systems rule out the possibility of processes maintaining synchronized local clocks (Dolev, Halpern and Strong [1984]; Lamport and Melliar-Smith [1985]) or reasoning based on global real-time. Communication remains the only possible mechanism for synchronization in such systems.

In addition to their theoretical interest as noted above, asynchronous distributed systems may also be realistic models for actual systems. It is often the case that physical components from which we construct distributed systems are *synchronous*. In other words, the relative speeds of *processors* and message delays over network *links* making up a distributed system can be bounded. When, however, layers of software are introduced to multiplex these physical resources to create abstractions such as *processes* and (reliable) communication *channels*, the resulting system may be better characterized as asynchronous.

4.3   Distributed Computations

Informally, a distributed computation describes the execution of a distributed program by a collection of processes. The activity of each sequential process is modeled as executing a sequence of *events*. An event may be either internal to a process and cause only a local state change, or it may involve communication with another process. Without loss of generality, we assume that communication is accomplished through the events *send(m)* and *receive(m)* that match based on the message identifier m. In other words, even if several processes send the same data value to the same process, the messages themselves will be unique.[1] Informally, the event $send(m)$ enqueues message m on an outgoing channel for transmission to the destination process. The event $receive(m)$, on the other hand, corresponds to the act of dequeueing message m from an incoming channel at the destination process. Clearly, for event $receive(m)$ to occur at process p, message m must have arrived at p and p must have declared its willingness to receive a message. Otherwise, either the message is delayed (because the process is not ready) or the process is delayed (because the message has not arrived).

Note that this 'message passing' view of communication at the event level may be quite different from those of higher system layers. Remote communication at the programming language level may be accomplished through any number of paradigms including remote procedure calls (Chapter 9), broadcasts (Chapter 5), distributed transactions (Chapter 13), distributed objects (Levy and Tempero [1991])or distributed shared memory (Li and Hudak [1989]). At the level we observe distributed computations, however, all such high-level communication boil down to generating matching send and receive events at pairs of processes.

The *local history* of process p_i during the computation is a (possibly infinite) sequence of events $h_i = e_i^1 e_i^2 \ldots$. This labeling of the events of process p_i where e_i^1 is the first event executed, e_i^2 is the second event executed, etc. is called the *canonical enumeration* and corresponds to the total order imposed by the sequential execution on the local events. Let $h_i^k = e_i^1 e_i^2 \ldots e_i^k$ denote an initial prefix of local history h_i containing the first k events. We define h_i^0 to be the empty sequence. The *global history* of the computation is a set $H = h_1 \cup \cdots \cup h_n$ containing all of its events.[2]

Note that a global history does not specify any relative timing between events. In an asynchronous distributed system where no global time frame exists, events of a computation can be ordered only based on the notion of 'cause-and-effect'. In other words, two events are constrained to occur in a certain order only if the occurrence of the first may affect the outcome of the second. This in turn implies that information flows from the first event to the second. In an asynchronous system, information may flow from one event to another either because the two events are of the same process, and thus may access the same local state, or because the two events are of different processes and they correspond to the exchange of a message. We can formalize these ideas by defining a binary relation $\rightarrow$ defined over events such that (Lamport [1978]):

1. If $e_i^k, e_i^\ell \in h_i$ and $k < \ell$, then $e_i^k \rightarrow e_i^\ell$,
2. If $e_i = send(m)$ and $e_j = receive(m)$, then $e_i \rightarrow e_j$,
3. If $e \rightarrow e'$ and $e' \rightarrow e''$, then $e \rightarrow e''$.

---

[1] For finite computations, this can be easily accomplished by adding the process index and a sequence number to the data value to construct the message identifier.

[2] Sometimes we are interested in local histories as *sets* rather than *sequences* of events. Since all events of a computation have unique labels in the canonical enumeration, h_i as a set contains exactly the same events as h_i as a sequence. We use the same symbol to denote both when the appropriate interpretation is clear from context.

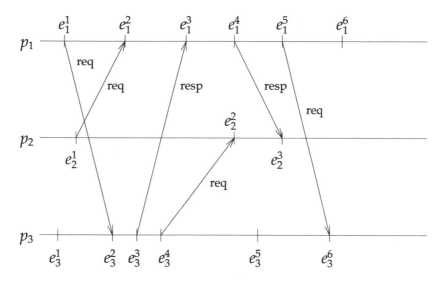

Figure 4.1. Space-time diagram representation of a distributed computation

As defined, this relation effectively captures our intuitive notion of 'cause-and-effect' in that $e{\rightarrow}e'$ if and only if e causally precedes e'.[3] Note that only in the case of matching send-receive events is the cause and-effect relationship certain. In general, the only conclusion that can be drawn from $e{\rightarrow}e'$ is that the mere occurrence of e' and its outcome *may* have been influenced by event e.

Certain events of the global history may be causally unrelated. In other words, it is possible that for some e and e', neither $e{\rightarrow}e'$ nor $e'{\rightarrow}e$. We call such events *concurrent* and write $e\|e'$.

Formally, a *distributed computation* is a partially ordered set (poset) defined by the pair $(H, \rightarrow)$. Note that all events are labeled with their canonical enumeration, and in the case of communication events, they also contain the unique message identifier. Thus, the total ordering of events for each process as well as the send-receive matchings are implicit in H.

It is common to depict distributed computations using an equivalent graphical representation called a *space-time diagram*. Figure 4.1 illustrates such a diagram where the horizontal lines represent execution of processes, with time progressing from left to right. An arrow from one process to another represents a message being sent, with the send event at the base of the arrow and the corresponding receive event at the head of the arrow. Internal events have no arrows associated with them. Given this graphical representation, it is easy to verify if two events are causally related: if a path can be traced from one event to the other proceeding left-to-right along the horizontal lines and in the sense of the arrows, then they are related; otherwise they are concurrent. For example, in the figure $e_2^1{\rightarrow}e_3^6$ but $e_2^2\|e_3^6$.

---

[3]While "e may causally affect e'," or "e' occurs in the causal context of e" (Peterson, Bucholz and Schlichting [1989]) are equivalent interpretations of this relation, we prefer not to interpret it as "e happens before e'," (Lamport [1978]) because of the real-time connotation.

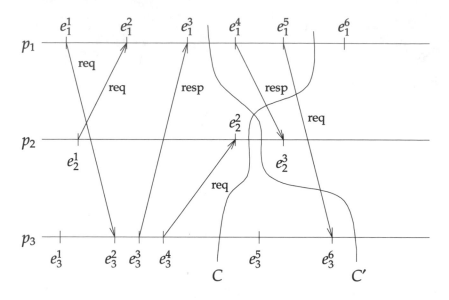

Figure 4.2. Cuts of a distributed computation

4.4 Global States, Cuts and Runs

Let σ_i^k denote the local state of process p_i immediately after having executed event e_i^k and let σ_i^0 be its initial state before any events are executed. In general, the local state of a process may include information such as the values of local variables and the sequences of messages sent and received over the various channels incident to the process. The *global state* of a distributed computation is an n-tuple of local states $\Sigma = (\sigma_1, \ldots, \sigma_n)$, one for each process.[4] A *cut* of a distributed computation is a subset C of its global history H and contains an initial prefix of each of the local histories. We can specify such a cut $C = h_1^{c_1} \cup \cdots \cup h_n^{c_n}$ through the tuple of natural numbers $(c_1, \ldots, c_n)$ corresponding to the index of the last event included for each process. The set of last events $(e_1^{c_1}, \ldots, e_n^{c_n})$ included in cut $(c_1, \ldots, c_n)$ is called the *frontier* of the cut. Clearly, each cut defined by $(c_1, \ldots, c_n)$ has a corresponding global state which is $(\sigma_1^{c_1}, \ldots, \sigma_n^{c_n})$.

As shown in Figure 4.2, a cut has a natural graphical interpretation as a partitioning of the space-time diagram along the time axis. The figure illustrates two cuts C and C' corresponding to the tuples $(5, 2, 4)$ and $(3, 2, 6)$, respectively.

Even though a distributed computation is a partially ordered set of events, in an actual execution, all events, including those at different processes, occur in some total order.[5] To be able to reason about executions in distributed systems, we

---

[4] We can define global states without referring to channel states since they can always be encoded as part of the process local states. We discuss explicit representation of channel states in Section 4.13.

[5] If two events actually *do* occur at the same real-time, we can arbitrarily say that the event of the process with the smaller index occurs before the event of the larger-index process.

introduce the notion of a *run*. A run of a distributed computation is total ordering R that includes all of the events in the global history and that is consistent with each local history. In other words, for each process p_i, the events of p_i appear in R in the same order that they appear in h_i. Note that a run need not correspond to any possible execution and a single distributed computation may have many runs, each corresponding to a different execution.

4.5   Monitoring Distributed Computations

Given the above notation and terminology, GPE can be stated as evaluating a predicate Φ that is a function of the global state Σ of a distributed system. For the time being, we will assume that a single process called the *monitor* is responsible for evaluating Φ. Let p_0 be this process which may be one of $p_1, \ldots, p_n$ or may be external to the computation (but not the system). In this special case, where there is a single monitor, solving GPE reduces to p_0 constructing a global state Σ of the computation (to which Φ is applied). For simplicity of exposition, we assume that events executed on behalf of monitoring are external to the underlying computation and do not alter the canonical enumeration of its events.

In the first strategy we pursue for constructing global states, the monitor p_0 takes on an active role and sends each process a 'state enquiry' message. Upon the receipt of such a message, p_i replies with its current local state σ_i. When all n processes have replied, p_0 can construct the global state $(\sigma_1, \ldots, \sigma_n)$. Note that the positions in the process local histories that state enquiry messages are received effectively defines a cut. The global state constructed by p_0 is the one corresponding to this cut.

Given that the monitor process is part of the distributed system and is subject to the same uncertainties as any other process, the simple-minded approach sketched above may lead to predicate values that are not meaningful. To illustrate the problems that can arise, consider a distributed system composed of *servers* providing remote services and *clients* that invoke them. In order to satisfy a request, a server may invoke other services (and thus act as a client). Clients and servers interact through *remote procedure calls*—after issuing a request for service, the client remains blocked until it receives the response from the server. The computation depicted in Figure 4.1 could correspond to this interaction if we interpret messages labeled *req* as requests for service and those labeled *resp* as responses. Clearly, such a system can deadlock. Thus, it is important to be able to detect when the state of this system includes deadlocked processes.

One possibility for detecting deadlocks in the above system is as follows. Server processes maintain local states containing the names of clients from which they received requests but to which they have not yet responded. The relevant aspects of the global state Σ of this system can be summarized through a *waits-for*[+] *graph* (WFG[+]) where the nodes correspond to processes and the edges model blocking. In this graph, an edge is drawn from node i to node j if p_j has received a request from p_i to which it has not yet responded. Note that WFG[+] can be constructed solely on the basis of local states. It is well known that a cycle in WFG[+] is a sufficient condition to characterize deadlock in this system (Gligor and Shattuck [1980]). The nodes of the cycle are exactly those processes involved in the deadlock. Thus, the predicate Φ = 'WFG$^+$ contains a cycle' is one possibility for deadlock detection.[6]

Let us see what might happen if process p_0 monitors the computation of Figure 4.1 as outlined above. Suppose that the state enquiry messages of p_0 are received by the three application processes at the points corresponding to cut C' of Figure 4.2. In other words, processes p_1, p_2 and p_3 report local states σ_1^3, σ_2^2 and σ_3^6, respectively. The WFG$^+$ constructed by p_0 for this global state will have edges $(1,3)$, $(2,1)$ and $(3,2)$ forming a cycle. Thus, p_0 will report a deadlock involving all three processes.

An omniscient external observer of the computation in Figure 4.1, on the other hand, would conclude that at no time is the system in a deadlock state. The condition detected by p_0 above is called a *ghost deadlock* in that it is fictitious. While every cut of a distributed computation corresponds to a global state, only certain cuts correspond to global states that *could* have taken place during a run. Cut C of Figure 4.2 represents such a global state. On the other hand, cut C' constructed by p_0 corresponds to a global state that could never occur since process p_3 is in a state reflecting the receipt of a request from process p_1 that p_1 has no record of having sent. Predicates applied to cuts such as C' can lead to incorrect conclusions about the system state.

We return to solving the GPE problem through active monitoring of distributed computations in Section 4.13 after understanding why the above approach failed.

4.6   Consistency

Causal precedence happens to be the appropriate formalism for distinguishing the two classes of cuts exemplified by C and C'. A cut C is *consistent* if for all events e and e'

$$(e \in C) \land (e' \rightarrow e) \Rightarrow e' \in C.$$

In other words, a consistent cut is left closed under the causal precedence relation. In its graphical representation, verifying the consistency of a cut becomes easy: if all arrows that intersect the cut have their bases to the left and heads to the right of it, then the cut is consistent; otherwise it is inconsistent. According to this definition, cut C of Figure 4.2 is consistent while cut C' is inconsistent. A *consistent global state* is one corresponding to a consistent cut. These definitions correspond exactly to the intuition that consistent global states are those that could occur during a run in the sense that they could be constructed by an idealized observer external to the system. We can now explain the ghost deadlock detected by p_0 in the previous section as resulting from the evaluation of Φ in an inconsistent global state.

Consistent cuts (and consistent global states) are fundamental towards understanding asynchronous distributed computing. Just as a scalar time value denotes a particular instant during a sequential computation, the frontier of a consistent

---

[6]Note that Φ defined as a cycle in WFG$^+$ characterizes a stronger condition than deadlock in the sense that Φ implies deadlock but not vice versa. If, however, processes can receive and record requests while being blocked, then a deadlocked system will eventually satisfy Φ.

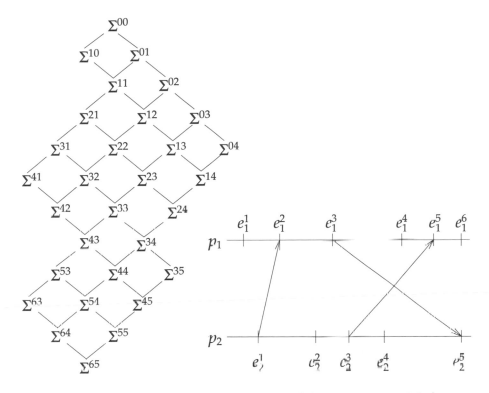

Figure 4.3 A distributed computation and the lattice of its global states

cut establishes an 'instant' during a distributed computation. Similarly, notions such as 'before' and 'after' that are defined with respect to a given time in sequential systems have to be interpreted with respect to consistent cuts in distributed system: an event e is *before* (*after*) a cut C if e is to the left (right) of the frontier of C.

Predicate values are meaningful only when evaluated in consistent global states since these characterize exactly the states that could have taken place during an execution. A run R is said to be *consistent* if for all events, $e \rightarrow e'$ implies that e appears before e' in R. In other words, the total order imposed by R on the events is an extension of the partial order defined by causal precedence. It is easy to see that a run $R = e^1 e^2 \ldots$ results in a sequence of global states $\Sigma^0 \Sigma^1 \Sigma^2 \ldots$ where Σ^0 denotes the initial global state $(\sigma_1^0, \ldots, \sigma_n^0)$. If the run is consistent, then the global states in the sequence will all be consistent as well. We will use the term 'run' to refer to both the sequence of events and the sequence of resulting global states. Each (consistent) global state Σ^i of the run is obtained from the previous state Σ^{i-1} by some process executing the single event e^i. For two such (consistent) global states of run R, we say that Σ^{i-1} *leads to* Σ^i in R. Let $\leadsto_R$ denote the transitive closure of the leads-to relation in a given run R. We say that Σ' is *reachable from* Σ *in run R* if and only if $\Sigma \leadsto_R \Sigma'$. We drop the run subscript if there exists *some* run in which Σ' is reachable from Σ.

The set of all consistent global states of a computation along with the leads-to relation defines a *lattice*. The lattice consists of n orthogonal axes, with one axis for each process. Let $\Sigma^{k_1\cdots k_n}$ be a shorthand for the global state $(\sigma_1^{k_1}, \ldots, \sigma_n^{k_n})$ and let $k_1 + \cdots + k_n$ be its *level*. Figure 4.3 illustrates a distributed computation of two processes and the corresponding global state lattice. Note that every global state is reachable from the initial global state Σ^{00}. A path in the lattice is a sequence of global states of increasing level (in the figure, downwards) where the level between any two successive elements differs by one. Each such path corresponds to a consistent run of the computation. The run is said to 'pass through' the global states included in the path. For the example illustrated in Figure 4.3, one possible run may pass through the sequence of global states

$$\Sigma^{00} \ \Sigma^{01} \ \Sigma^{11} \ \Sigma^{21} \ \Sigma^{31} \ \Sigma^{32} \ \Sigma^{42} \ \Sigma^{43} \ \Sigma^{44} \ \Sigma^{54} \ \Sigma^{64} \ \Sigma^{65}.$$

Note that one might be tempted to identify the run corresponding to the *actual* execution of the computation. As we argued earlier, in an asynchronous distributed system, this is impossible to achieve from within the system. Only an omniscient external observer will be able to identify the sequence of global states that the execution passed through.

4.7   Observing Distributed Computations

Let us consider an alternative strategy for the monitor process p_0 in constructing global states to be used in predicate evaluation based on a *reactive* architecture (Harel and Pnueli [1985]). In this approach, p_0 will assume a passive role in that it will not send any messages of its own. The application processes, however, will be modified slightly so that whenever they execute an event, they notify p_0 by sending it a message describing the event.[7] As before, we assume that monitoring does not generate any new events in that the send to p_0 for notification coincides with the event it is notifying. In this manner, the monitor process constructs an *observation* of the underlying distributed computation as the sequence of events corresponding to the order in which the notification messages arrive (Helary *et al.* [1986]).

We note certain properties of observations as constructed above. First, due to the variability of the notification message delays, a single run of a distributed computation may have different observations at different monitors. This is the so-called 'relativistic effect' of distributed computing to which we return in Section 4.15. Second, an observation can correspond to a consistent run, an inconsistent run or no run at all since events from the same process may be observed in an order different from their local history. A *consistent observation* is one that corresponds to

---

[7]In general, the application processes need to inform p_0 only when they execute an event that is relevant to Φ. A local event e_i^k is said to be *relevant* to predicate Φ if the value of Φ evaluated in a global state $(\ldots, \sigma_i^k, \ldots)$ could be different from that evaluated in $(\ldots, \sigma_i^{k-1}, \ldots)$. For example, in the client-server computation of Figure 4.1, the only events relevant to deadlock detection are the sending/receiving of request and response messages since only these can change the state of the WFG+.

a consistent run. To illustrate these points, consider the following (consistent) run of the computation in Figure 4.1:

$$R = e_3^1 \, e_1^1 \, e_3^2 \, e_2^1 \, e_3^3 \, e_3^4 \, e_2^2 \, e_1^2 \, e_3^5 \, e_1^3 \, e_1^4 \, e_1^5 \, e_3^6 \, e_2^3 \, e_1^6$$

All of the following are possible observations of R:

$$O_1 = e_2^1 \, e_1^1 \, e_1^1 \, e_3^2 \, e_3^4 \, e_1^2 \, e_2^2 \, e_3^3 \, e_1^3 \, e_1^4 \, e_3^5 \ldots$$
$$O_2 = e_1^1 \, e_3^1 \, e_2^1 \, e_3^2 \, e_1^2 \, e_3^3 \, e_3^4 \, e_1^3 \, e_2^2 \, e_3^5 \, e_3^6 \ldots$$
$$O_3 = e_3^1 \, e_2^1 \, e_1^1 \, e_1^2 \, e_3^2 \, e_3^3 \, e_1^3 \, e_3^4 \, e_1^4 \, e_2^2 \, e_1^5 \ldots$$

Given our asynchronous distributed system model where communication channels need not preserve message order, *any* permutation of run R is a possible observation of it. Not all observations, however, need be meaningful with respect to the run that produced them. For example, among those indicated above, observation O_1 does not even correspond to a run since events of process p_3 do not represent an initial prefix of its local history (e_3^4 appears before event e_3^3). Observation O_2, on the hand, corresponds to an inconsistent run. In fact, the global state constructed by p_0 at the end of observation O_2 would be $(\sigma_1^3, \sigma_2^2, \sigma_3^6)$, which is exactly the global state defined by cut C' of Figure 4.2 resulting in the detection of a ghost deadlock. Finally, O_3 is a consistent observation and leads to the same global state as that of cut C in Figure 4.2.

It is the possibility of messages being reordered by channels that leads to undesirable observations such as O_1. We can restore order to messages between pairs of processes by defining a *delivery rule* for deciding when received messages are to be presented to the application process. We call the primitive invoked by the application *deliver* to distinguish it from *receive*, which remains hidden within the delivery rule and does not appear in the local history of the process.

Communication from process p_i to p_j is said to satisfy *First-In First-Out (FIFO) delivery* if for all messages m and m'

FIFO Delivery: $send_i(m) \rightarrow send_i(m') \Rightarrow deliver_j(m) \rightarrow deliver_j(m')$.[8]

In other words, FIFO delivery prevents one message overtaking an earlier message sent by the *same* process. For each source-destination pair, FIFO delivery can be implemented over non-FIFO channels simply by having the source process add a sequence number to its messages and by using a delivery rule at the destination that presents messages in an order corresponding to the sequence numbers. While FIFO delivery is sufficient to guarantee that observations correspond to runs, it is not sufficient to guarantee consistent observations. To pursue this approach for solving the GPE problem where Φ is evaluated in global states constructed from observations, we need to devise a mechanism that ensures their consistency.

We proceed by devising a simple mechanism and refining it as we relax assumptions. Initially, assume that all processes have access to a global real-time clock and that all message delays are bounded by δ. This is clearly not an asynchronous system but will serve as a starting point. Let $RC(e)$ denote the value of the global

---

[8]Subscripts identify the process executing the event.

clock when event e is executed. When a process notifies p_0 of some local event e, it includes $RC(e)$ in the notification message as a *timestamp*. The delivery rule employed by p_0 is the following:

DR1: At time t, deliver all received messages with timestamps up to $t - \delta$ in increasing timestamp order.

To see why an observation O constructed by p_0 using DR1 is guaranteed to be consistent, first note that an event e is observed before event e' if and only if $RC(e) < RC(e')$.[9] This is true because messages are delivered in increasing timestamp order and delivering only messages with timestamps up to time $t - \delta$ ensures that no future message can arrive with a timestamp smaller than any of the messages already delivered. Since the observation coincides with the delivery order, O is consistent if and only if

$$\text{Clock Condition: } e{\rightarrow}e' \Rightarrow RC(e) < RC(e').$$

This condition is certainly satisfied when timestamps are generated using the global real-time clock. As it turns out, the clock condition can be satisfied without any assumptions—in an asynchronous system.

4.8   Logical Clocks

In an asynchronous system where no global real-time clock can exist, we can devise a simple clock mechanism for 'timing' such that event orderings based on increasing clock values are guaranteed to be consistent with causal precedence. In other words, the clock condition can be satisfied in an asynchronous system. For many applications, including the one above, any mechanism satisfying the clock condition can be shown to be sufficient for using the values produced by it as if they were produced by a global real-time clock (Neiger and Toueg [1987]).

The mechanism works as follows. Each process maintains a local variable LC called its *logical clock* that maps events to the positive natural numbers (Lamport [1978]). The value of the logical clock when event e_i is executed by process p_i is denoted $LC(e_i)$. We use LC to refer to the current logical clock value of a process that is implicit from context. Each message m that is sent contains a timestamp $TS(m)$ which is the logical clock value associated with the sending event. Before any events are executed, all processes initialize their logical clocks to zero. The following update rules define how the logical clock is modified by p_i with the occurrence of each new event e_i:

$$LC(e_i) := \begin{cases} LC + 1 & \text{if } e_i \text{ is an internal or send event} \\ \max\{LC, TS(m)\} + 1 & \text{if } e_i = receive(m) \end{cases}$$

In other words, when a receive event is executed, the logical clock is updated to be greater than both the previous local value and the timestamp of the incoming message. Otherwise (i.e., an internal or send event is executed), the logical clock is

---

[9] Again, we can break ties due to simultaneous events based on process indexes.

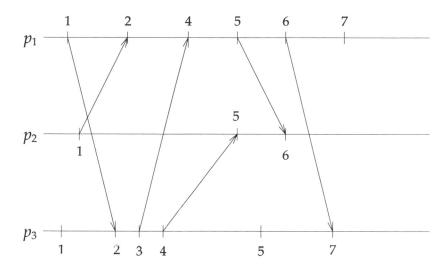

Figure 4.4. Logical clocks

simply incremented. Figure 4.4 illustrates the logical clock values that result when these rules are applied to the computation of Figure 4.1.

Note that the above construction produces logical clock values that are increasing with respect to causal precedence. It is easy to verify that for any two events where $e \rightarrow e'$, the logical clocks associated with them are such that $LC(e) < LC(e')$. Thus, logical clocks satisfy the clock condition of the previous section.[10]

Now let us return to the goal at hand, which is constructing consistent observations in asynchronous systems. In the previous section, we argued that delivery rule DR1 lead to consistent observations as long as timestamps satisfied the clock condition. We have just shown that logical clocks indeed satisfy the clock condition and are realizable in asynchronous systems. Thus, we should be able to use logical clocks to construct consistent observations in asynchronous systems. Uses of logical clocks in many other contexts are discussed in (Raynal [1992]).

Consider a delivery rule where those messages that are delivered, are delivered in increasing (logical clock) timestamp order, with ties being broken as usual based on process index. Applying this rule to the example of Figure 4.4, p_0 would construct the observation

$$ e_1^1 \; e_2^1 \; e_3^1 \; e_1^2 \; e_3^2 \; e_3^3 \; e_1^3 \; e_3^4 \; e_1^4 \; e_2^2 \; e_3^5 \; e_1^5 \; e_2^3 \; e_1^6 \; e_3^6 $$

which is indeed consistent. Unfortunately, the delivery rule as stated lacks liveness since, without a bound on message delays (and a real-time clock to measure it), no message will ever be delivered for fear of receiving a later message with a smaller timestamp. This is because logical clocks, when used as a timing mechanism, lack what we call the *gap-detection* property:

---

[10]Note that logical clocks would continue to satisfy the clock condition with any arbitrary positive integer (rather than one) as the increment value of the update rules.

Gap-Detection: Given two events e and e' along with their clock values $LC(e)$ and $LC(e')$ where $LC(e) < LC(e')$, determine whether some other event e'' exists such that $LC(e) < LC(e'') < LC(e')$.

It is this property that is needed to guarantee liveness for the delivery rule and can be achieved with logical clocks in an asynchronous system only if we exploit information in addition to the clock values. One possibility is based on using FIFO communication between all processes and p_0. As usual, all messages (including those sent to p_0) carry the logical clock value of the send event as a timestamp. Since each logical clock is monotone increasing and FIFO delivery preserves order among messages sent by a single process, when p_0 receives a message m from process p_i with timestamp $TS(m)$, it is certain that no other message m' can arrive from p_i such that $TS(m') \leq TS(m)$. A message m received by process p is called *stable* if no future messages with timestamps smaller than $TS(m)$ can be received by p. Given FIFO communication between all processes and p_0, stability of message m at p_0 can be guaranteed when p_0 has received at least one message from *all* other processes with a timestamp greater than $TS(m)$. This idea leads to the following delivery rule for constructing consistent observations when logical clocks are used for timestamps:

DR2: Deliver all received messages that are stable at p_0 in increasing timestamp order.[11]

Note that real-time clocks lack the gap-detection property as well. The assumption, however, that message delays are bounded by δ was sufficient to devise a simple stability check in delivery rule DR1: at time t, all received messages with timestamps smaller than $t - \delta$ are guaranteed to be stable.

4.9 Causal Delivery

Recall that FIFO delivery guarantees order to be preserved among messages sent by the *same* process. A more general abstraction extends this ordering to all messages that are causally related, even if they are sent by different processes. The resulting property is called *causal delivery* and can be stated as:

Causal Delivery (CD): $send_i(m) \rightarrow send_j(m') \Rightarrow deliver_k(m) \rightarrow deliver_k(m')$

for all messages m, m', sending processes p_i, p_j and destination process p_k. In other words, in a system respecting causal delivery, a process cannot know about the existence of a message (through intermediate messages) any earlier than the event corresponding to the delivery of that message (Sandoz and Schiper [1992]). Note that having FIFO delivery between all pairs of processes is not sufficient to

---

[11] Even this delivery rule may lack liveness if some processes do not communicate with p_0 after a certain point. Liveness can be obtained by the monitor p_0 requesting an acknowledgement from all processes to a periodic empty message (Lamport [1978]). These acknowledgements serve to 'flush out' messages that may have been in the channels.

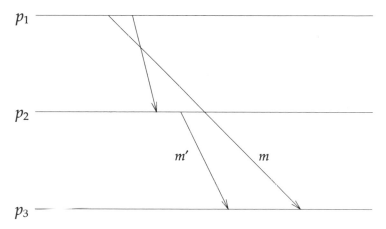

Figure 4.5. Message delivery that is FIFO but not causal

guarantee causal delivery. Figure 4.5 illustrates a computation where all deliveries (trivially) satisfy FIFO but those of p_3 violate CD.

The relevance of causal delivery to the construction of consistent observations is obvious: if p_0 uses a delivery rule satisfying CD, then all of its observations will be consistent. The correctness of this result is an immediate consequence of the definition of CD, which coincides with that of a consistent observation. In retrospect, the two delivery rules DR1 and DR2 we developed in the previous sections are instances of CD that work under certain assumptions. What we seek is an implementation for CD that makes no assumptions beyond those of asynchronous systems.

4.10   Constructing the Causal Precedence Relation

Note that we have stated the gap-detection property in terms of clock values. For implementing causal delivery efficiently, what is really needed is an effective procedure for deciding the following: given events e, e' that are causally related and their clock values, does there exist some other event e'' such that $e{\rightarrow}e''{\rightarrow}e'$ (i.e., e'' falls in the causal 'gap' between e and e')?

By delivering event notification messages in strict increasing timestamp order, rules DR1 and DR2 assume that $RC(e) < RC(e')$ (equivalently, $LC(e) < LC(e')$) implies $e{\rightarrow}e'$. This is a conservative assumption since timestamps generated using real-time or logical clocks only guarantee the clock condition, which is this implication in the opposite sense. Given $RC(e) < RC(e')$ (or $LC(e) < LC(e')$), it may be that e causally precedes e' or that they are concurrent. What is known for certain is that $\neg(e'{\rightarrow}e)$. Having just received the notification of event e', DR1 and DR2 could unnecessarily delay its delivery even if they could predict the timestamps of all notifications yet to be received. The delay would be unnecessary if there existed future notifications with smaller timestamps, but they all happened to be for events concurrent with e'.

The observations of the preceding two paragraphs suggest a timing mechanism TC whereby causal precedence relations between events can be deduced from their timestamps. We strengthen the clock condition by adding an implication in the other sense to obtain:

Strong Clock Condition: $e \rightarrow e' \equiv TC(e) < TC(e')$.

While real-time and logical clocks are consistent with causal precedence, timing mechanism TC is said to *characterize* causal precedence since the entire computation can be reconstructed from a single observation containing TC as timestamps (Fidge [1988]; Schwarz and Mattern [1992]). This is essential not only for efficient implementation of CD, but also for many other applications (e.g., distributed debugging discussed in Section 4.14.2) that require the entire global state lattice rather than a single path through it.

4.10.1   Causal Histories

A brute-force approach to satisfying the strong clock condition is to devise a timing mechanism that produces the set of all events that causally precede an event as its 'clock' value (Schwarz and Mattern [1992]). We define the *causal history* of event e in distributed computation $(H, \rightarrow)$ as the set

$$\theta(e) = \{e' \in H \mid e' \rightarrow e\} \cup \{e\}.$$

In other words, the causal history of event e is the smallest consistent cut that includes e. The projection of $\theta(e)$ on process p_i is the set $\theta_i(e) = \theta(e) \cap h_i$. Figure 4.6 graphically illustrates the causal history of event e_1^4 as the darkened segments of process local histories leading towards the event. From the figure, it is easy to see that $\theta(e_1^4) = \{e_1^1, e_1^2, e_1^3, e_1^4, e_2^1, e_3^1, e_3^2, e_3^3\}$.

In principle, maintaining causal histories is simple. Each process p_i initializes local variable θ to be the empty set. If e_i is the receive of message m by process p_i from p_j, then $\theta(e_i)$ is constructed as the union of e_i, the causal history of the previous local event of p_i and the causal history of the corresponding send event at p_j (included in message m as its timestamp). Otherwise (e_i is an internal or send event), $\theta(e_i)$ is the union of e_i and the causal history of the previous local event.

When causal histories are used as clock values, the strong clock condition can be satisfied if we interpret clock comparison as set inclusion. From the definition of causal histories, it follows that

$$e \rightarrow e' \equiv \theta(e) \subset \theta(e').$$

In case $e \neq e'$, the set inclusion above can be replaced by the simple set membership test $e \in \theta(e')$. The unfortunate property of causal histories that renders them impractical is that they grow rapidly.

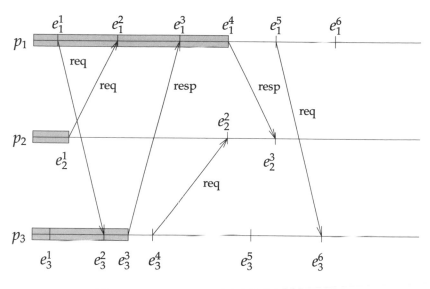

Figure 4.6. Causal history of event e_1^4

4.10.2 Vector Clocks

The causal history mechanism proposed in the previous section can be made practical by periodically pruning segments of history that are known to be common to all events (Peterson, Bucholz and Schlichting [1989]). Alternatively, the causal history can be represented as a fixed-dimensional vector rather than a set. The resulting growth rate will be logarithmic in the number of events rather than linear. In what follows, we pursue this approach.

First, note that the projection of causal history $\theta(e)$ on process p_i corresponds to an initial prefix of the local history of p_i. In other words, $\theta_i(e) = h_i^k$ for some unique k and, by the canonical enumeration of events, $e_i^\ell \in \theta_i(e)$ for all $\ell < k$. Thus, a single natural number is sufficient to represent the set $\theta_i(e)$. Since $\theta(e) = \theta_1(e) \cup \cdots \cup \theta_n(e)$, the entire causal history can be represented by an n-dimensional vector $VC(e)$ where for all $1 \leq i \leq n$, the ith component is defined as

$$VC(e)[i] = k, \quad \text{if and only if } \theta_i(e) = h_i^k.$$

The resulting mechanism is known as *vector clocks* and has been discovered independently by many researchers in many different contexts (see Schwarz and Mattern [1992] for a survey). In this scheme, each process p_i maintains a local vector VC of natural numbers where $VC(e_i)$ denotes the vector clock value of p_i when it executes event e_i. As with logical clocks, we use VC to refer to the current vector clock of a process that is implicit from context. Each process p_i initializes VC to contain all zeros. Each message m contains a timestamp $TS(m)$ which is the vector clock value of its send event. The following update rules define how the vector clock is modified by p_i with the occurrence of each new event e_i:

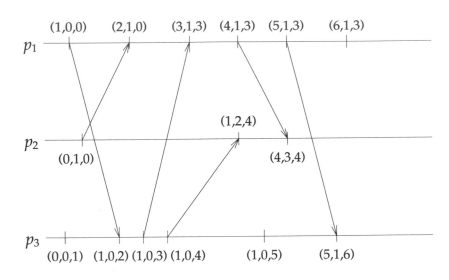

Figure 4.7. Vector clocks

$VC(e_i)[i] := VC[i] + 1$ if e_i is an internal or send event

$VC(e_i)\quad := \max\{VC, TS(m)\}$ if $e_i = receive(m)$
$VC(e_i)[i] := VC[i] + 1$

In other words, an internal or send event simply increments the local component of the vector clock. A receive event, on the other hand, first updates the vector clock to be greater than (on a component-by-component basis) both the previous value and the timestamp of the incoming message, and then increments the local component. Figure 4.7 illustrates the vector clocks associated with the events of the distributed computation displayed in Figure 4.1.

Given the above implementation, the jth component of the vector clock of process p_i has the following operational interpretation for all $j \neq i$:

$VC(e_i)[j] \equiv$ number of events of p_j that causally precede event e_i of p_i.

On the other hand, $VC(e_i)[i]$ counts the number of events p_i has executed up to and including e_i. Equivalently, $VC(e_i)[i]$ is the ordinal position of event e_i in the canonical enumeration of p_i's events.

From the definition of vector clocks, we can easily derive a collection of useful properties. Given two n-dimensional vectors V and V' of natural numbers, we define the 'less than' relation (written as <) between them as follows

$$V < V' \equiv (V \neq V') \wedge (\forall k : 1 \leq k \leq n : V[k] \leq V'[k]).$$

This allows us to express the strong clock condition in terms of vector clocks as

Property 1 *(Strong Clock Condition)*
$e{\rightarrow}e' \equiv VC(e) < VC(e')$.

Note that for the above test, it is not necessary to know on which processes the two events were executed. If this information is available, causal precedence between two events can be verified through a single scalar comparison.

Property 2 *(Simple Strong Clock Condition) Given event e_i of process p_i and event e_j of process p_j, where $i \neq j$*
$$e_i \rightarrow e_j \equiv VC(e_i)[i] \leq VC(e_j)[i].$$

Note that the condition $VC(e_i)[i] = VC(e_j)[i]$ is possible and represents the situation where e_i is the latest event of p_i that causally precedes e_j of p_j (thus e_i must be a send event).

Given this version of the strong clock condition, we obtain a simple test for concurrency between events that follows directly from its definition

Property 3 *(Concurrent) Given event e_i of process p_i and event e_j of process p_j*
$$e_i \| e_j = (VC(e_i)[i] > VC(e_j)[i]) \wedge (VC(e_j)[j] > VC(e_i)[j]).$$

Consistency of cuts of a distributed computation can also be easily verified in terms of vector clocks. Events e_i and e_j are said to be *pairwise inconsistent* if they cannot belong to the frontier of the same consistent cut. In terms of vector clocks, this can be expressed as

Property 4 *(Pairwise Inconsistent) Event c_i of process p_i is pairwise inconsistent with event c_j of process p_j, where $i \neq j$, if and only if*
$$(VC(e_i)[i] < VC(e_j)[i]) \vee (VC(e_j)[j] < VC(e_i)[j]).$$

The two disjuncts characterize exactly the two possibilities for the cut to include at least one receive event without including its corresponding send event (thus making it inconsistent). While this property might appear to be equivalent to $\neg(e_i \| e_j)$ at first sight, this is not the case; it is obviously possible for two events to be causally related and yet be pairwise consistent.

We can then characterize a cut as being consistent if its frontier contains no pairwise inconsistent events. Given the definition of a cut, it suffices to check pairwise inconsistency only for those events that are in the frontier of the cut. In terms of vector clocks, the property becomes

Property 5 *(Consistent Cut) A cut defined by $(c_1, \ldots, c_n)$ is consistent if and only if*
$$\forall i, j : 1 \leq i \leq n, 1 \leq j \leq n : VC(e_i^{c_i})[i] \geq VC(e_j^{c_j})[i].$$

Recall that, for all $j \neq i$, the vector clock component $VC(e_i)[j]$ can be interpreted as the number of events of p_j that causally precede event e_i of p_i. The component corresponding to the process itself, on the other hand, counts the total number of events executed by p_i up to and including e_i. Let $\#(e_i) = (\sum_{j=1}^{n} VC(e_i)[j]) - 1$. Thus, $\#(e_i)$ denotes exactly the number of events that causally precede e_i in the entire computation.

Property 6 *(Counting) Given event e_i of process p_i and its vector clock value $VC(e_i)$, the number of events e such that $e \rightarrow e_i$ (equivalently, $VC(e) < VC(e_i)$) is given by $\#(e_i)$.*

Finally, vector clocks supply a weak form of the gap-detection property that logical and real-time clocks do not. The following property follows directly from the vector clock update rules and the second form of the Strong Clock Condition. It can be used to determine if the causal 'gap' between two events admits a third event.

Property 7 *(Weak Gap-Detection) Given event e_i of process p_i and event e_j of process p_j, if $VC(e_i)[k] < VC(e_j)[k]$ for some $k \neq j$, then there exists an event e_k such that*
$$\neg(e_k \rightarrow e_i) \wedge (e_k \rightarrow e_j).$$

The property is 'weak' in the sense that, for arbitrary processes p_i, p_j and p_k, we cannot conclude if the three events form a causal chain $e_i \rightarrow e_k \rightarrow e_j$. For the special case $i = k$, however, the property indeed identifies the sufficient condition to make such a conclusion.

4.11   Implementing Causal Delivery with Vector Clocks

The weak gap-detection property of the previous section can be exploited to efficiently implement causal delivery using vector clocks. Assume that processes increment the local component of their vector clocks only for events that are notified to the monitor.[12] As usual, each message m carries a timestamp $TS(m)$ which is the vector clock value of the event being notified by m. All messages that have been received but not yet delivered by the monitor process p_0 are maintained in a set $\mathcal{M}$, initially empty.

A message $m \in \mathcal{M}$ from process p_j is deliverable as soon as p_0 can verify that there are no other messages (neither in $\mathcal{M}$ nor in the network) whose sending causally precede that of m. Let m' be the last message delivered from process p_k, where $k \neq j$. Before message m of process p_j can be delivered, p_0 must verify two conditions:

1. there is no earlier message from p_j that is undelivered, and
2. there is no undelivered message m'' from p_k such that
   $send(m') \rightarrow send(m'') \rightarrow send(m), \forall k \neq j$.

The first condition holds if exactly $TS(m)[j] - 1$ messages have already been delivered from p_j. To verify the second condition, we can use the special case of weak gap-detection where $i = k$ and $e_i = send_k(m')$, $e_k = send_k(m')$ and $e_j = send_j(m)$. Since the two events $send_k(m')$ and $send_k(m')$ both occur at process p_k, Property 7 can be written as

(Weak Gap-Detection) If $TS(m')[k] < TS(m)[k]$ for some $k \neq j$, then there exists event $send_k(m'')$ such that
$$send_k(m') \rightarrow send_k(m'') \rightarrow send_j(m).$$

---

[12]Equivalently, processes send a notification message to the monitor for *all* of their events.

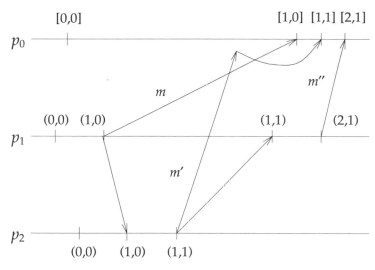

Figure 4.8. Causal delivery using vector clocks

Thus, no undelivered message m'' exists if $TS(m')[k] \geq TS(m)[k]$, for all k. These tests can be efficiently implemented if p_0 maintains an array $D[1 \ldots n]$ of counters, initially all zeros, such that counter $D[i]$ contains $TS(m_i)[i]$ where m_i is the last message that has been delivered from process p_i. The delivery rule then becomes:

DR3: (Causal Delivery) Deliver message m from process p_j as soon as both of the following conditions are satisfied

$$D[j] \;=\; TS(m)[j] - 1$$
$$D[k] \;\geq\; TS(m)[k], \forall k \neq j.$$

When p_0 delivers m, array D is updated by setting $D[j]$ to $TS(m)[j]$.

Figure 4.8 illustrates the application of this delivery rule by p_0 in a sample computation. The events of p_1 and p_2 are annotated with the vector clock values while those of p_0 indicate the values of array D. Note that the delivery of message m' is delayed until message m has been received and delivered. Message m'', on the other hand, can be delivered as soon as it is received since p_0 can verify that all causally preceding messages have been delivered.

At this point, we have a complete reactive-architecture solution to the GPE problem in asynchronous distributed systems based on passive observations. The steps are as follows. Processes notify the monitor p_0 of relevant events by sending it messages. The monitor uses a causal delivery rule for the notification messages to construct an observation that corresponds to a consistent run. The global predicate Φ can be applied to any one of the global states in the run since each is guaranteed to be consistent. An application of this solution to deadlock detection is given in Section 4.14.1.

Causal delivery can be implemented at any process rather than just at the monitor. If processes communicate exclusively through broadcasts (rather than point-

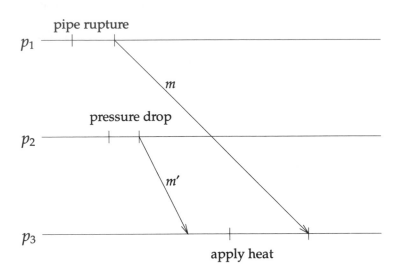

Figure 4.9. External environment as a hidden channel

to-point sends), then delivery rule DR3 remains the appropriate mechanism for achieving causal delivery at all destinations (Birman, Schiper and Stephenson [1991]). The resulting primitive, known as *causal broadcast* (c.f. Section 4.15, Chapter 5), has been recognized as an important abstraction for building distributed applications (Birman, Schiper and Stephenson [1991]; Kaashoek and Tanenbaum [1991]; Peterson, Bucholz and Schlichting [1989]). If, on the other hand, communication can take place through point-to-point sends, a delivery rule can be derived based on an extension of vector clocks where each message carries a timestamp composed of n vector clocks (i.e., an $n \times n$ matrix) (Raynal, Schiper and Toueg [1991]; Schiper, Eggli and Sandoz [1989]).

4.12 Causal Delivery and Hidden Channels

In general, causal delivery allows processes to reason globally about the system using only local information. For such conclusions to be meaningful, however, we need to restrict our attention to *closed* systems—those that constrain all communication to take place within the boundaries of the computing system. If global reasoning based on causal analysis is applied to systems that contain so-called *hidden channels*, incorrect conclusions may be drawn (Lamport [1978]).

To illustrate the problem, consider the example taken from Kopetz [1992] and shown in Figure 4.9. A physical process is being monitored and controlled by a distributed system consisting of p_1, p_2 and p_3. Process p_1 is monitoring the state of a steam pipe and detects its rupture. The event is notified to the controller process p_3 in message m. Process p_2 is monitoring the pressure of the same pipe, several meters downstream from p_1. A few seconds after the rupture of the pipe, p_2 detects a drop in the pressure and notifies p_3 of the event in message m'. Note that from the point of view of explicit communication, messages m and m' are concurrent. Message m' arrives at p_3 and is delivered without delay since there are no undelivered messages that causally precede it. As part of its control action, p_3 reacts to the pressure drop by applying more heat to increase the temperature. Some time later, message m arrives reporting the rupture of the pipe. The causal sequence observed by p_3 is ⟨*pressure drop, apply heat, pipe rupture*⟩ leading it to conclude that the pipe ruptured due to the increased temperature. In fact, the opposite is true.

The apparent anomaly is due to the steam pipe which acts as a communication channel external to the system. The rupture and pressure drop events are indeed causally related even though it is not captured by the → relation. When the pipe is included as a communication channel, the order in which messages are seen by p_3 violates causal delivery. In systems that are not closed, global reasoning has to be based on totally ordered observations derived from global real-time. Since this order is consistent with causal precedence, anomalous conclusions such as the one above will be avoided.

4.13 Distributed Snapshots

In Section 4.5 we presented a strategy for solving the GPE problem through active monitoring. In this strategy, p_0 requested the states of the other processes and then combined them into a global state. Such a strategy is often called a 'snapshot' protocol, since p_0 'takes pictures' of the individual process states. As we noted, this global state may not be consistent, and so the monitor may make an incorrect deduction about the system property encoded in the global predicate.

We will now develop a snapshot protocol that constructs only consistent global states. The protocol is due to Chandy and Lamport [1985], and the development described here is due to Morgan [1985]. For simplicity, we will assume that the channels implement FIFO delivery, and we omit details of how individual processes return their local states to p_0.

For this protocol, we will introduce the notion of a *channel state*. For each channel from p_i to p_j, its state $\chi_{i,j}$ are those messages that p_i has sent to p_j but p_j has not yet received. Channel states are only a convenience in that each $\chi_{i,j}$ can be inferred from just the local states σ_i and σ_j as the set difference between messages sent by p_i to p_j (encoded in σ_i) and messages received by p_j from p_i (encoded in σ_j). In many cases, however, explicit maintenance of channel state information can lead to more compact process local states and simpler encoding for the global predicate of interest. For example, when constructing the waits-for graph in deadlock detection, an edge is drawn from p_i to p_j if p_i is blocked due to p_j. This relation can be easily obtained from the local process states and channel states: process p_i is blocked on p_j if σ_i records the fact that there is an outstanding request to p_j, and $\chi_{j,i}$ contains no response messages.

Let IN_i be the set of processes that have channels connecting them directly to p_i and OUT_i be the set of processes to which p_i has a channel. Channels from $p_j \in IN_i$ to p_i are called *incoming* while channels from p_i to $p_j \in OUT_i$ are called *outgoing* with respect to p_i. For each execution of the snapshot protocol, a process p_i will record its local state σ_i and the states of its incoming channels ($\chi_{j,i}$, for all $p_j \in IN_i$).

4.13.1   Snapshot Protocols

We proceed as before by devising a simple protocol based on a strong set of assumptions and refining the protocol as we relax them. Initially, assume that all processes have access to a global real-time clock RC, that all message delays are bound by some known value, and that relative process speeds are bounded.

The first snapshot protocol is based on all processes recording their states at the same real-time. Process p_0 chooses a time t_{ss} far enough in the future in order to guarantee that a message sent now will be received by all other processes before t_{ss}.[13] To facilitate the recording of channel states, processes include a timestamp in each message indicating when the message's send event was executed.

Snapshot Protocol 1

1. Process p_0 sends the message 'take snapshot at t_{ss}' to all processes.[14]
2. When clock RC reads t_{ss}, each process p_i records its local state σ_i, sends an empty message over all of its outgoing channels, and starts recording messages received over each of its incoming channels. Recording the local state and sending empty messages are performed before any intervening events are executed on behalf of the underlying computation.
3. First time p_i receives a message from p_j with timestamp greater than or equal to t_{ss}, p_i stops recording messages for that channel and declares $\chi_{j,i}$ as those messages that have been recorded.

For each $p_j \in IN_i$, the channel state $\chi_{j,i}$ constructed by process p_i contains the set of messages sent by p_j before t_{ss} and received by p_i after t_{ss}. The empty messages in Step 2 are sent in order to guarantee liveness:[15] process p_i is guaranteed to eventually receive a message m from every incoming channel such that $TS(m) \geq t_{ss}$.

Being based on real-time, it is easy to see that this protocol constructs a consistent global state—it constructs a global state that did in fact occur and thus could have been observed by our idealized external observer. However, it is worth arguing this point a little more formally. Note that an event e is in the consistent cut C_{ss} associated with the constructed global state if and only if $RC(e) < t_{ss}$. Hence,

$$(e \in C_{ss}) \wedge (RC(e') < RC(e)) \Rightarrow (e' \in C_{ss}).$$

Since real-time clock RC satisfies the clock condition, the above equation implies that C_{ss} is a consistent cut. In fact, the clock condition is the only property of RC that is necessary for C_{ss} to be a consistent cut. Since logical clocks also satisfy the clock condition, we should be able to substitute logical clocks for real-time clocks in the above protocol.

There are, however, two other properties of synchronous systems used by Snapshot Protocol 1 that need to be supplied:

---

[13] Recall that there need not be a channel between all pairs of processes, and so t_{ss} must account for the possibility of messages being forwarded.

[14] For simplicity, we describe the protocols for a single initiation by process p_0. In fact, they can be initiated by any process, and as long as concurrent initiations can be distinguished, multiple initiations are possible.

[15] Our use of empty messages here is not unlike their use in distributed simulation for the purposes of advancing global virtual time (Misra [1986]).

- The programming construct 'when $LC = t$ do S' doesn't make sense in the context of logical clocks since the given value t need not be attained by a logical clock.[16] For example, in Figure 4.4 the logical clock of p_3 never attains the value 6, because the receipt of the message from p_1 forces it to jump from 5 to 7. Even if LC does attain a value of t, the programming construct is still problematic. Our rules for updating logical clocks are based on the occurrence of new events. Thus, at the point $LC = t$, the event that caused the clock update has been executed rather than the first event of S.

    We overcome this problem with the following rules. Suppose p_i contains the statement 'when $LC = t$ do S', where S generates only internal events or send events. Before executing an event e, process p_i makes the following test:
    - If e is an internal or send event and $LC = t - 2$, then p_i executes e and then starts executing S.
    - If $e = receive(m)$ where $TS(m) \geq t$ and $LC < t - 1$, then p_i puts the message back onto the channel, re-enables e for execution, sets LC to $t - 1$ and starts executing S.
- In Protocol 1, the monitor p_0 chooses t_{ss} such that the message 'take snapshot at t_{ss}' is received by all other processes before time t_{ss}. In an asynchronous system, p_0 cannot compute such a logical clock value. Instead, we assume that there is an integer value ω large enough that no logical clock can reach ω by using the update rules in Section 4.8.

Assuming the existence of such an ω requires us to bound both relative process speeds and message delays, and so we will have to relax it as well. Given the above considerations, we obtain Snapshot Protocol 2, which differs from Protocol 1 only in its use of logical clocks in place of the real-time clock.

Snapshot Protocol 2
1. Process p_0 sends 'take snapshot at ω' to all processes and then sets its logical clock to ω.
2. When its logical clock reads ω, process p_i records its local state σ_i, sends an empty message along each outgoing channel, and starts recording messages received over each of its incoming channels. Recording the local state and sending empty messages are performed before any intervening events are executed on behalf of the underlying computation.
3. First time p_i receives a message from p_j with timestamp greater than or equal to ω, p_i stops recording messages for that channel and declares $\chi_{j,i}$ as those messages that have been recorded.

Channel states are constructed just as in Protocol 1 with ω playing the role of t_{ss}. As soon as p_0 sets its logical clock to ω, it will immediately execute Step 2, and the empty messages sent by it will force the clocks of processes in OUT_0 to attain ω. Since the network is strongly connected, all of the clocks will eventually attain ω, and so the protocol is live.

---

[16]Note that this problem happens to be one aspect of the more general problem of simulating a synchronous system in an asynchronous one (Awerbuch [1985]).

We now remove the need for ω. Note that, with respect to the above protocol, a process does nothing between receiving the 'take snapshot at ω' message and receiving the first empty message that causes its clock to pass through ω. Thus, we can eliminate the message 'take snapshot at ω' and instead have a process record its state when it receives the first empty message. Since processes may send empty messages for other purposes, we will change the message from being empty to one containing a unique value, for example, 'take snapshot'. Furthermore, by making this message contain a unique value, we no longer need to include timestamps in messages—the message 'take snapshot' is the first message that any process sends after the snapshot time. Doing so removes the last reference to logical clocks, and so we can eliminate them from our protocol completely.

Snapshot Protocol 3 (Chandy and Lamport [1985])
1. Process p_0 starts the protocol by sending itself a 'take snapshot' message.
2. Let p_f be the process from which p_i receives the 'take snapshot' message for the first time. Upon receiving this message, p_i records its local state σ_i and relays the 'take snapshot' message along all of its outgoing channels. No intervening events on behalf of the underlying computation are executed between these steps. Channel state $\chi_{f,i}$ is set to empty and p_i starts recording messages received over each of its other incoming channels.
3. Let p_s be the process from which p_i receives the 'take snapshot' message beyond the first time. Process p_i stops recording messages along the channel from p_s and declares channel state $\chi_{s,i}$ as those messages that have been recorded.

Since a 'take snapshot' message is relayed only upon the first receipt and since the network is strongly connected, a 'take snapshot' message traverses each channel exactly once. When process p_i has received a 'take snapshot' message from all of its incoming channels, its contribution to the global state is complete and its participation in the snapshot protocol ends.

Note that the above protocols can be extended and improved in many ways including relaxation of the FIFO assumption (Mattern [1989]; Taylor [1989]) and reduction of the message complexity (Mattern [1993]; Sandoz and Schiper [1992]).

4.13.2   Properties of Snapshots

Let Σ^s be a global state constructed by the Chandy-Lamport distributed snapshot protocol. In the previous section, we argued that Σ^s is guaranteed to be consistent. Beyond that, however, the actual run that the system followed while executing the protocol may not even pass through Σ^s. In this section, we show that Σ^s is not an arbitrary consistent global state, but one that has useful properties with respect to the run that generated it.

Consider the application of Chandy-Lamport snapshot protocol to the distributed computation of Figure 4.3. The composite computation is shown in Figure 4.10 where solid arrows indicate messages sent by the underlying computation while dashed arrows indicate 'take snapshot' messages sent by the protocol. From the protocol description, the constructed global state is Σ^{23} with $\chi_{1,2}$ empty and $\chi_{2,1}$

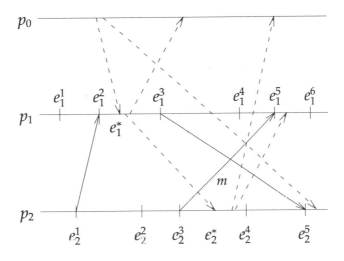

Figure 4.10. Application of the Chandy-Lamport snapshot protocol

containing message m. Let the run followed by processes p_1 and p_2 while executing the protocol be

$$r = e_2^1 \; e_1^1 \; e_1^2 \; e_1^3 \; e_2^2 \; e_1^4 \; e_2^3 \; e_2^4 \; e_1^5 \; e_2^5 \; e_1^6$$

or in terms of global states,

$$r = \Sigma^{00} \; \Sigma^{01} \; \Sigma^{11} \; \Sigma^{21} \; \Sigma^{31} \; \Sigma^{32} \; \Sigma^{42} \; \Sigma^{43} \; \Sigma^{44} \; \Sigma^{54} \; \Sigma^{55} \; \Sigma^{65}.$$

Let the global state of this run in which the protocol is initiated be Σ^{21} and the global state in which it terminates be Σ^{55}. Note that run r does not pass through the constructed global state Σ^{23}. As can be verified by the lattice of Figure 4.3, however, $\Sigma^{21} \leadsto \Sigma^{23} \leadsto \Sigma^{55}$ in this example. We now show that this relationship holds in general.

Let Σ^a be the global state in which the snapshot protocol is initiated, Σ^f be the global state in which the protocol terminates and Σ^s be the global state constructed. We will show that there exists a run R such that $\Sigma^a \leadsto_R \Sigma^s \leadsto_R \Sigma^f$. Let r be the actual run the system followed while executing the snapshot protocol, and let e_i^* denote the event when p_i receives 'take snapshot' for the first time, causing p_i to record its state. An event e_i of p_i is a *prerecording* event if $e_i \rightarrow e_i^*$; otherwise, it is a *post-recording* event.

Consider any two adjacent events $\langle e, e' \rangle$ of r such that e is a post-recording event and e' is a prerecording event.[17] We will show that $\neg(e \rightarrow e')$, and so the order of these two events can be swapped, thereby resulting in another consistent run. If we continue this process of swapping $\langle$post-recording, prerecording$\rangle$ event pairs, then we will eventually construct a consistent run in which no prerecording event follows a post-recording event. The global state associated with the last

---

[17] Adjacent event pairs $\langle e_1^3, e_2^2 \rangle$ and $\langle e_1^4, e_2^3 \rangle$ of run r are two such examples.

prerecording event is therefore reachable from Σ^a and the state Σ^f is reachable from it. Finally, we will show that this state is Σ^s, the state that the snapshot protocol constructs.

Consider the subsequence $\langle e, e' \rangle$ of run r where e is a post-recording event and e' a prerecording event. If $e \rightarrow e'$ then the two events cannot be swapped without resulting in an inconsistent run. For contradiction, assume that $e \rightarrow e'$. There are two cases to consider:

1. Both events e and e' are from the same process. If this were the case, however, then by definition e' would be a post-recording event.
2. Event e is a send event of p_i and e' is the corresponding receive event of p_j. If this were the case, however, then from the protocol p_i will have sent a 'take snapshot' message to p_j by the time e is executed, and since the channel is FIFO, e' will also be a post-recording event.

Hence, a post-recording event cannot causally precede a prerecording event and thus any $\langle$post-recording, prerecording$\rangle$ event pair can be swapped. Let R be the run derived from r by swapping such pairs until all post-recording events follow the prerecording events. We now argue that the global state after the execution of the last prerecording event e in R is Σ^s. By the protocol description and the definition of prerecording, post-recording events that record local states will record them at point e. Furthermore, by the protocol, the channel states that are recorded are those messages that were sent by prerecording events and received by post-recording events. By construction, these are exactly those messages in the channels after the execution of event e, and so Σ^s is the state recorded by the snapshot protocol. $\square$

4.14   Properties of Global Predicates

We have derived two methods for global predicate evaluation: one based on a monitor actively constructing snapshots and another one based on a monitor passively observing runs. The utility of either approach for solving practical distributed systems problems, however, depends in part on the properties of the predicate that is being evaluated. In this section, some of these properties are examined.

4.14.1   Stable Predicates

Let Σ^s be a consistent global state of a computation constructed through any feasible mechanism. Given that communication in a distributed system incurs delays, Σ^s can only reflect some past state of the system— by the time they are obtained, conclusions drawn about the system by evaluating predicate Φ in Σ^s may have no bearing to the present.

Many system properties one wishes to detect, however, have the characteristic that once they become true, they remain true. Such properties (and their predicates) are called *stable*. Examples of stable properties include deadlock, termination, the loss of all tokens, and unreachability of storage (garbage collection). If Φ is stable, then the monitor process can strengthen its knowledge about when Φ is satisfied.

```
process p(i): 1 ≤ i ≤ n
    var pending: queue of [message, integer] init empty;      % pending requests to p(i)
        working: boolean init false;                          % processing a request
        m: message; j: integer;
    while true do
        while working or (size(pending) = 0) do
            receive m from p(j);                              % m set to message, j to its source
            case m.type of
                request:
                    pending := pending + [m, j];
                response:
                    [m, j] := NextState(m, j);
                    working := (m.type = request);
                    send m to p(j);
            esac
        od ;
        while not working and (size(pending) > 0) do
            ⌊m, j⌋ := first(pending);
            pending := tail(pending);
            [m, j] := NextState(m, j);
            working := (m.type = request);
            send m to p(j)
        od
    od
end p(i);
```

Figure 4.11   Server process

As before, let Σ^a be the global state in which the global state construction protocol is initiated, Σ^f be the global state in which the protocol terminates and Σ^s be the global state it constructs. Since $\Sigma^a \leadsto \Sigma^s \leadsto \Sigma^f$, if Φ is stable, then the following conclusions are possible

(Φ is true in Σ^s) $\Rightarrow$ (Φ is true in Σ^f)

and

(Φ is false in Σ^s) $\Rightarrow$ (Φ is false in Σ^a).

As an example of detecting a stable property, we return to deadlock in the client-server system described in Section 4.5. We assume that there is a bidirectional communication channel between each pair of processes and each process when acting as a server runs the same program, shown in Figure 4.11. The behavior of a process as a client is much simpler: after sending a request to a server it blocks until the response is received. The server is modeled as a *state machine* (Chapter 7): it repeatedly receives a message, changes its state, and optionally sends one or more messages. The function NextState() computes the action a server next takes: given a message m from process p_j, the invocation NextState(m, j) changes the state of the server and returns the next message to send along with its destination. The resulting message may be a response to the client's request or it may be a further request whose response is needed to service the client's request. All requests received by a server, including those received while it is servicing an earlier request, are queued on the FIFO queue pending, and the server removes and

```
process p(i): 1 ≤ i ≤ n
    var pending: queue of [message, integer] init empty;        % pending requests to p(i)
        working: boolean init false;                            % processing a request
        blocking: array [1..n] of boolean init false;       % blocking[j] = 'p(j) is blocked on p(i)'
        m: message; j: integer; s: integer init 0;
    while true do
        while working or (size(pending) = 0) do
            receive m from p(j);                            % m set to message, j to its source
            case m.type of
                request:
                    blocking[j] := true;
                    pending := pending + [m, j];
                response:
                    [m, j] := NextState(m, j);
                    working := (m.type = request);
                    send m to p(j);
                    if (m.type = response) then blocking[j] := false;
                snapshot:
                    if s = 0 then
                            % this is the first snapshot message
                            send [type: snapshot, data: blocking] to p(0);
                            send [type: snapshot] to p(1),...,p(i−1),p(i+1),...,p(n)
                    s := (s + 1) mod n;
            esac
        od ;
        while not working and (size(pending) > 0) do
            [m, j] := head(pending);
            pending := tail(pending);
            [m, j] := NextState(m, j);
            working := (m.type = request);
            send m to p(j);
            if (m.type = response) then blocking[j] := false;
        od
    od
end p(i);
```

Figure 4.12. Deadlock detection through snapshots: Server side

begins servicing the first entry from pending after it finishes an earlier request by sending the response.

Figures 4.12 shows the server of Figure 4.11 with a snapshot protocol embedded in it. Each server maintains a boolean array blocking that indicates which processes have sent it requests to which it has not yet responded (this information is also stored in pending, but we duplicate it in blocking for clarity). When a server p_i first receives a snapshot message, it sends the contents of blocking to p_0 and relays the snapshot message to all other processes. Subsequent snapshot messages are ignored until p_i has received n such messages, one from each other process.[18]

The conventional definition of 'p_i waits-for p_j' is that p_i has sent a request to p_j and p_j has not yet responded. As in Section 4.5, we will instead use the weaker

---

[18]By the assumption that the network is completely connected, each invocation of the snapshot protocol will result in exactly n snapshot messages to be received by each of the processes.

```
process p(0):
    var wfg: array [1..n] of array [1..n] of boolean;          % wfg[i, j] = p(j) waits-for p(i)
        j, k: integer; m: message;
    while true do
        wait until deadlock is suspected;
        send [type: snapshot] to p(1), ..., p(n);
        for k := 1 to n do
            receive m from p(j);
            wfg[j] := m.data;
        if (cycle in wfg) then  system is deadlocked
    od
end p(0);
```

Figure 4.13. Deadlock detection through snapshots: Monitor side

definition p_i *waits-for*$^+$ p_j which holds when p_j has received a request from p_i to which it has not yet responded (Gligor and Shattuck [1980]). By structuring the server as a state machine, even requests sent to a deadlocked server will eventually be received and denoted in blocking. Hence, a system that contains a cycle in the conventional WFG will eventually contain a cycle in the WFG$^+$, and so a deadlock will be detected eventually. Furthermore, using the WFG$^+$ instead of the WFG has the advantage of referencing only the local process states, and so the embedded snapshot protocol need not record channel states.

Figure 4.13 shows the code run by the monitor p_0 acting as the deadlock detector. This process periodically starts a snapshot by sending a snapshot message to all other processes. Then, p_0 receives the arrays blocking from each of the processes and uses this data to test for a cycle in the WFG$^+$. This approach has the advantage of generating an additional message load only when deadlock is suspected. However, the approach also introduces a latency between the occurrence of the deadlock and detection that depends on how often the monitor starts a snapshot.

Figures 4.14 and 4.15 show the server and monitor code, respectively, of a reactive-architecture deadlock detector. This solution is much simpler than the snapshot-based version. In this case, p_i sends a message to p_0 whenever p_i receives a request or sends a response to a client. Monitor p_0 uses these notifications to update a WFG$^+$ in which it tests for a cycle. The simplicity of this solution is somewhat superficial, however, because the protocol requires all messages to p_0 to be sent using causal delivery order instead of FIFO order. The only latency between a deadlock's occurrence and its detection is due to the delay associated with a notification message, and thus, is typically shorter than that of the snapshot-based detector.

4.14.2   Nonstable Predicates

Unfortunately, not all predicates one wishes to detect are stable. For example, when debugging a system one may wish to monitor the lengths of two queues, and notify the user if the sum of the lengths is larger than some threshold. If both queues are dynamically changing, then the predicate corresponding to the desired condition is not stable. Detecting such predicates poses two serious problems.

```
process p(i): 1 ≤ i ≤ n
    var pending: queue of [message, integer] init empty;        % pending requests to p(i)
        working: boolean init false;                            % processing a request
        m: message; j: integer;
    while true do
        while working or (size(pending) = 0) do
            receive m from p(j);                                % m set to message, j to its source
            case m.type of
                request:
                    send [type: requested, of: i, by: j] to p(0);
                    pending := pending + [m, j];
                response:
                    [m, j] := NextState(m, j);
                    working := (m.type = request);
                    send m to p(j);
                    if (m.type = response) then
                            send [type: responded, to: j, by: i] to p(0);
            esac
        od ;
        while not working and (size(pending) > 0) do
            [m, j] := first(pending);
            pending := tail(pending);
            [m, j] := NextState(m, j);
            working := (m.type = request);
            send m to p(j);
            if (m.type = response) then
                    send [type: responded, to: j, by: i] to p(0)
        od
    od
end p(i);
```

Figure 4.14. Deadlock detection using reactive protocol: Server side

```
process p(0):
    var wfg: array [1..n, 1..n] of boolean init false;        % wfg[i, j] = 'p(j) waits-for p(i)'
        m: message; j: integer;
    while true do
        receive m from p(j);                                  % m set set to message, j to its source
        if (m.type = responded) then
            wfg[m.by, m.to] := false
        else
            wfg[m.of, m.by] := true;
        if (cycle in wfg) then  system is deadlocked
    od
end p(0);
```

Figure 4.15. Deadlock detection using reactive protocol: Monitor side

The first problem is that the condition encoded by the predicate may not persist long enough for it to be true when the predicate is evaluated. For example, consider the computation of Figure 4.16 in which variables x and y are being maintained by two processes p_1 and p_2, respectively. Suppose we are interested in monitoring the

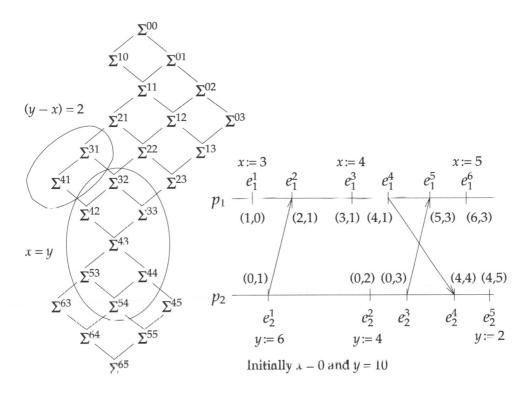

Figure 4.16. Global states satisfying predicates $(x = y)$ and $(y-x) = 2$

condition $(x = y)$. There are seven consistent global states in which the condition $(x = y)$ holds, yet if the monitor evaluates $(x = y)$ after state Σ^{54} then the condition will be found not to hold.

The second problem is more disturbing: if a predicate Φ is found to be true by the monitor, we do not know whether Φ *ever* held during the actual run. For example, suppose in the same computation the condition being monitored is $(y - x) = 2$. The only two global states of Figure 4.16 satisfying this condition are Σ^{31} and Σ^{41}. Let a snapshot protocol be initiated in state Σ^{11} of the run

$$\Sigma^{00}\ \Sigma^{01}\ \Sigma^{11}\ \Sigma^{12}\ \Sigma^{22}\ \Sigma^{32}\ \Sigma^{42}\ \Sigma^{43}\ \Sigma^{44}\ \Sigma^{45}\ \Sigma^{55}\ \Sigma^{65}.$$

From the result of Section 4.13.2, we know that the snapshot protocol could construct either global state Σ^{31} or Σ^{41} since both are reachable from Σ^{11}. Thus, the monitor could 'detect' $(y - x) = 2$ even though the actual run never goes through a state satisfying the condition.

It appears that there is very little value in using a snapshot protocol to detect a nonstable predicate—the predicate may have held even if it is not detected, and even if it is detected it may have never held. The same problems exist when nonstable predicates are evaluated over global states constructed from observations of runs: if a nonstable predicate holds at some state during a consistent observation, then the condition may or may not have held during the actual run that produced it.

With observations, however, we can extend nonstable global predicates such that they are meaningful in the face of uncertainty of the run actually followed by the computation. To do this, the extended predicates must apply to the entire distributed computation rather than to individual runs or global states of it. There are two choices for defining predicates over computations (Cooper and Marzullo [1991]; Marzullo and Neiger [1991]):

1. **Possibly**(Φ): There exists a consistent observation O of the computation such that Φ holds in a global state of O.
2. **Definitely**(Φ): For every consistent observation O of the computation, there exists a global state of O in which Φ holds.

The distributed computation of Figure 4.16 satisfies both predicates **Possibly**($(y - x) = 2$) and **Definitely**($x = y$). As with stable predicates, by the time they are detected, both of these predicates refer to some past state or states of a run. The predicate 'Φ currently holds' can also be detected, but to do so will introduce blocking of the underlying computation.

An application of these extended predicates is when a run is observed for purposes of debugging (Cooper and Marzullo [1991]). For instance, if Φ identifies some erroneous state of the computation, then **Possibly**(Φ) holding indicates a bug, even if it is not observed during an actual run. For example, if $(y - x) = 2$ denotes an erroneous state, then the computation of Figure 4.16 is incorrect, since there is no guarantee that the erroneous state will not occur in some run.

The intuitive meanings of **Possibly** and **Definitely** could lead one to believe that they are duals of each other: $\neg$**Definitely** (Φ) being equivalent to **Possibly**($\neg\Phi$) and $\neg$**Possibly** (Φ) being equivalent to **Definitely**($\neg\Phi$). This is not the case. For example, while it is true that $\neg$**Definitely**(Φ) holding through a computation does imply **Possibly**($\neg\Phi$) (there must be an observation O in which $\neg\Phi$ holds in all of its states), it is possible to have both **Possibly**($\neg\Phi$) and **Definitely**(Φ) hold. Figure 4.16 illustrates the latter: the computation satisfies both **Possibly**($x \neq y$) and **Definitely**($x = y$). Furthermore, if predicate Φ is stable, then **Possibly**(Φ) $\equiv$ **Definitely**(Φ). The inverse, however, is not true in general.

The choice between detecting whether Φ currently holds versus whether Φ possibly or definitely held in the past depends on which restrictions confound the debugging process more. Detecting a condition that occurred in the past may require program replay or reverse execution in order to recover the state of interest, which can be very expensive to provide. Hence, detection in the past is better suited to a *post-mortem* analysis of a computation. Detecting the fact that Φ currently holds, on the other hand, requires delaying the execution of processes, which can be a serious impediment to debugging. By blocking some processes when the predicate becomes potentially true, we may make the predicate either more or less likely to occur. For example, a predicate may be less likely to occur if processes 'communicate' using timeouts or some other uncontrolled

```
procedure Possibly(Φ);
    var current: set of global states;
        ℓ: integer;
    begin
        % Synchronize processes and distribute Φ
        send Φ to all processes;
        current := { Σ^{0...0} };
        release processes;
        ℓ := 0;
        % Invariant: current contains all states of level ℓ that are reachable from Σ^{0...0}
        while (no state in current satisfies Φ) do
            if (current = { final global state }) then return false
            ℓ := ℓ + 1;
            current := { states of level ℓ }
        od
        return true
    end
```

Figure 4.17. Algorithm for detecting **Possibly**(Φ)

form of communication. The latter is a particular problem when processes are multithreaded; that is, consisting of multiple, independently schedulable threads of control which may communicate through shared memory. In fact, it is rarely practical to monitor such communication when debugging without hardware or language support.

4.14.3 Detecting Possibly and Definitely Φ

The algorithms for detecting **Possibly**(Φ) and **Definitely**(Φ) are based on the lattice of consistent global states associated with the distributed computation. For every global state Σ in the lattice there exists at least one run that passes through Σ. Hence, if any global state in the lattice satisfies Φ, then **Possibly**(Φ) holds. For example, in the global state lattice of Figure 4.16 both Σ^{31} and Σ^{41} satisfy $(y - x) = 2$ meaning that **Possibly**($(y - x) = 2$) holds for the computation. The property **Definitely**(Φ) requires all possible runs to pass through a global state that satisfies Φ. In Figure 4.16 the global state Σ^{43} satisfies $(x = y)$. Since this is the only state of level 7, and all runs must contain a global state of each level, **Definitely**($x = y$) also holds for the computation.

Figure 4.17 is a high-level procedure for detecting **Possibly**(Φ). The procedure constructs the set of global states current with progressively increasing levels (denoted by ℓ). When a member of current satisfies Φ, then the procedure terminates indicating that **Possibly**(Φ) holds. If, however, the procedure constructs the final global state (the global state in which the computation terminates) and finds that this global state does not satisfy Φ, then the procedure returns ¬ **Possibly**(Φ).

In order to implement this procedure, the monitored processes send the portion of their local states that is referenced in Φ to the monitor p_0. Process p_0 maintains sequences of these local states, one sequence per process, and uses them to construct the global states of a given level. The basic operation used by the procedure is 'current := states of level ℓ', and so we must be able to determine when all of the global states of a given level can be assembled and must be able to effectively assemble them.

Let Q_i be the sequence of local states, stored in FIFO order, that p_0 maintains for process p_i, where each state σ_i^k in Q_i is labeled with the vector timestamp $VC(e_i^k)$. Define $\Sigma_{min}(\sigma_i^k)$ to be the global state with the smallest level containing σ_i^k and $\Sigma_{max}(\sigma_i^k)$ to be the global state with the largest level containing σ_i^k. For example, in Figure 4.16, $\Sigma_{min}(\sigma_1^3) = \Sigma^{31}$ and $\Sigma_{max}(\sigma_1^3) = \Sigma^{33}$. These states can be computed using Property 5 of vector clocks as follows:

$$\Sigma_{min}(\sigma_i^k) = (\sigma_1^{c_1}, \sigma_2^{c_2}, ..., \sigma_n^{c_n}): \forall j: VC(\sigma_j^{c_j})[j] = VC(\sigma_i^k)[j]$$

and

$$\Sigma_{max}(\sigma_i^k) = (\sigma_1^{c_1}, \sigma_2^{c_2}, ..., \sigma_n^{c_n}):$$

$$\forall j: (VC(\sigma_j^{c_j})[i] \le VC(\sigma_i^k)[i]) \wedge ((\sigma_j^{c_j} = \sigma_j^f) \vee (VC(\sigma_j^{c_j+1})[i] > VC(\sigma_i^k)[i]))$$

where σ_j^f is the state in which process p_j terminates.

Global states $\Sigma_{min}(\sigma_i^k)$ and $\Sigma_{max}(\sigma_i^k)$ bound the levels of the lattice in which σ_i^k occurs. The minimum level containing σ_i^k is particularly easy to compute: it is the sum of components of the vector timestamp $VC(\sigma_i^k)$. Thus, p_0 can construct the set of states with level ℓ when, for each sequence Q_i, the sum of the components of the vector timestamp of the last element of Q_i is at least ℓ. For example, if p_0 monitors the computation shown in Figure 4.16, then p_0 can start enumerating level 6 when it has received states σ_1^5 and σ_2^4 because any global state containing σ_1^5 must have a level of at least 8 (5 + 3) and any global state containing σ_2^4 must also have a level of at least 8 (4 + 4). Similarly, process p_0 can remove state σ_i^k from Q_i when ℓ is greater than the level of the global state $\Sigma_{max}(\sigma_i^k)$. For the example in Figure 4.16, $\Sigma_{max}(\sigma_1^2) = \Sigma^{23}$, and so p_0 can remove σ_1^2 from Q_1 once it has set ℓ to 6.

Given the set of states of some level ℓ, it is also straightforward (if somewhat costly) to construct the set of states of level $\ell + 1$: for each state $\Sigma^{i_1,i_2,...,i_n}$ of level ℓ, one constructs the n global states $\Sigma^{i_1+1,i_2,...,i_n}, ..., \Sigma^{i_1,i_2,...,i_n+1}$. Then, Property 5 of vector clocks can be used to determine which of these global states are consistent. One can be careful and avoid redundantly constructing the same global state of level $\ell + 1$ from different global states of level ℓ, but the computation can still be costly.

Figure 4.18 gives the high-level algorithm used by the monitoring process p_0 to detect **Definitely(Φ)**. This algorithm iteratively constructs the set of global states that have a level ℓ and are reachable from the initial global state without passing through a global state that satisfies Φ. If this set of states is empty, then **Definitely(Φ)** holds and if this set contains only the final global state then ¬ **Definitely(Φ)** holds. Note that, unlike detecting **Possibly(Φ)**, not all global states need be examined. For example, in Figure 4.16, suppose that when the global states of level 2 were constructed, it was determined that Σ^{02} satisfied Φ. When constructing the states of level 3, global state Σ^{03} need not be included since it is reachable only through Σ^{02}.

The two detection algorithms are linear in the number of global states, but unfortunately the number of global states is $O(k^n)$ where k is the maximum number events a monitored process has executed. There are techniques that can be used to limit the number of constructed global states. For example, a process p_i need only

```
procedure Definitely(Φ);
    var current, last: set of global states;
        ℓ: integer;
    begin
        % Synchronize processes and distribute Φ
        send Φ to all processes;
        last := { Σ⁰⋯⁰ };
        release processes;
        remove all states in last that satisfy Φ;
        ℓ := 1;
        % Invariant: last contains all states of level ℓ − 1 that are reachable
        % from Σ⁰⋯⁰ without passing through a state satisfying Φ
        while (last ≠ { }) do
            current := { states of level ℓ reachable from a state in last };
            remove all states in current that satisfy Φ;
            if (current = { final global state }) then return false
            ℓ := ℓ + 1;
            last := current
        od
        return true
    end ;
```

Figure 4.18. Algorithm for detecting **Definitely(Φ)**

send a message to p_0 when p_i potentially changes Φ or when p_i learns that p_j has potentially changed Φ. Another technique is for p_i to send an empty message to all other processes when p_i potentially changes Φ. These, and other techniques for limiting the number of global states are discussed in (Marzullo and Neiger [1991]). An alternative approach is to restrict the global predicate to one that can be efficiently detected, such as the conjunction and disjunction of local predicates (Garg and Waldecker [1992]).

4.15 Multiple Monitors

There are several good reasons for having multiple monitors observe the same computation for the purposes of evaluating the same predicate (Helary *et al.* [1986]). One such reason is increased performance—in a large system, interested parties may have the result of the predicate sooner by asking the monitor that is closest to them.[19] Another reason is increased reliability—if the predicate encodes the condition guarding a critical system action (e.g., shutdown of a chemical plant), then having multiple monitors will ensure the action despite a bounded number of failures.

The reactive-architecture solution to GPE based on passive observations can be easily extended to multiple monitors without modifying its general structure. The only change that is required is for the processes to use a causal broadcast communication primitive to notify the group of monitors (Chapter 5). In this manner, each monitor will construct a consistent, but not necessarily the same,

---

[19] In the limit, each process could act as a monitor such that the predicate could be evaluated locally.

observation of the computation. Each observation will correspond to a (possibly different) path through the global state lattice of the computation. Whether the results of evaluating predicate Φ by each monitor using local observations are meaningful depends on the properties of Φ. In particular, if Φ is stable and some monitor observes that it holds, then all monitors will eventually observe that it holds. For example, in the case of deadlock detection with multiple monitors, if any one of them detects a deadlock, eventually all of them will detect the same deadlock since deadlock is a stable property. They may, however, disagree on the identity of the process that is responsible for creating the deadlock (the one who issued the last request forming the cycle in the WFG$^+$).

Multiple observations for evaluating nonstable predicates create problems similar to those discussed in Section 4.14.2. There are essentially two possibilities for meaningfully evaluating nonstable predicates over multiple observations. First, the predicate can be extended using **Definitely** or **Possibly** such that it is made independent of the particular observation but becomes a function of the computation, which is the same for all monitors. Alternatively, the notification messages can be disseminated to the group of monitors in a manner such that they all construct the same observation. This can be achieved by using a *causal atomic broadcast* primitive that results in a unique total order consistent with causal precedence for all messages (even those that are concurrent) at all destinations (Cristian *et al.* [1985], Chapter 5). Note that the resulting structure is quite similar to that proposed in Chapter 7 for handling replicated state machines.

Now consider the case where the monitor is replicated for increased reliability. If communication or processes in a distributed system are subject to failures, then sending the same notification message to all monitor replicas using causal delivery is not sufficient for implementing a causal broadcast primitive. For example if channels are not reliable, some of the notification messages may be lost such that different monitors effectively observe different computations. Again, we can accommodate communication and processes failures in our reactive architecture by using a *reliable* version of causal broadcast as the communication primitive (Chapter 5). Informally, a reliable causal broadcast, in addition to preserving causal precedence among message send events, guarantees delivery of a message either to all or none of the destination processes.[20] A formal specification of reliable causal broadcast in the presence of failures has to be done with care and can be found in Chapter 5.

Note that in an asynchronous system subject to failures, reliable causal broadcast is the best one can hope for in that it is impossible to implement communication primitives that achieve totally-ordered delivery using deterministic algorithms. Furthermore, in an environment where processes may fail, and thus certain events never get observed, our notion of a consistent global state may need to be reexamined. For some global predicates, the outcome may be sensitive not only to the order in which events are observed, but also to the order in which failures are observed by the monitors. In such cases, it will be necessary to extend the

---

[20]Note that in Chapter 5, this primitive is called *casual broadcast* without the *reliable* qualifier since all broadcast primitives are specified in the presence of failures.

causal delivery abstraction to include not only actual messages but also failure notifications (as is done in systems such as ISIS (Birman [1993])).

4.16 Conclusions

We have used the GPE problem as a motivation for studying consistent global states of distributed systems. Since many distributed systems problems require recognizing certain global conditions, the construction of consistent global states and the evaluation of predicates over these states constitute fundamental primitives with which one can build such systems.

We derived two classes of solutions to the GPE problem: a snapshot based one, that constructs a consistent global state and a reactive-architecture based one, that constructs a consistent run of the system. To derive these two classes, we have developed a set of basic concepts and mechanisms for representing and reasoning about computations in asynchronous distributed systems. These concepts represent generalizations of the notion of *time* in order to capture the uncertainty that is inherent in the execution of such systems. Two kinds of clocks were presented: *logical clocks* that generalize real-time clocks, and *vector clocks* that are incomparable to real-time clocks but exactly capture the causal precedence relation between events.

We illustrated the practicality of our concepts and mechanisms by applying them to distributed deadlock detection and distributed debugging. Reactive-architecture solutions based on passive observations were shown to be more flexible because they capture a run instead of just a global state. In particular, these solutions can be easily adapted to deal with nonstable predicates, multiple observations and failures. Each extension can be easily accommodated by using an appropriate communication primitive for notifications, leaving the overall reactive architecture unchanged.

Acknowledgements

The material on distributed debugging is derived from joint work with Robert Cooper and Gil Neiger. We are grateful to them for consenting to its inclusion here. The presentation has benefited greatly from extensive comments by Friedemann Mattern, Michel Raynal and Fred Schneider on earlier drafts. Babaoğlu was supported in part by the Commission of the European Communities under ESPRIT Programme Basic Research Project 6360 (BROADCAST), Hewlett-Packard of Italy and the Italian Ministry of University, Research and Technology. Marzullo was supported in part by the Defense Advanced Research Projects Agency (DoD) under NASA Ames grant number NAG 2–593, and by grants from IBM and Siemens. The views, opinions, and findings contained in this report are those of the authors and should not be construed as an official Department of Defense position, policy, or decision.

4.17   References

Awerbuch, B. (1985), Complexity of Network Synchronization, *Journal of the ACM* **32(4)**, 804–823.

Birman, K. P. (1993), The process group approach to reliable distributed computing, Department of Computer Science, Cornell University, Technical Report TR91-1216, To appear in Communications of the ACM.

Birman, K. P., Schiper, A. and Stephenson, P. (1991), Lightweight causal and atomic group multicast, *ACM Transactions on Computer Systems* **9(3)**, 272–314.

Chandy, K. M. and Lamport, L. (1985), Distributed Snapshots: Determining Global States of Distributed Systems, *ACM Transactions on Computer Systems* **3(1)**, 63–75.

Cooper, R. and Marzullo, K. (1991), Consistent detection of global predicates, *Proceedings of the ACM/ONR Workshop on Parallel and Distributed Debugging*, Santa Cruz, CA, 163–173.

Cristian, F., Aghili, H., Strong, H. R. and Dolev, D. (1985), Atomic Broadcast: From Simple Message Diffusion to Byzantine Agreement, *Proceedings of the 15th International Symposium on Fault-Tolerant Computing*, Ann Arbor, MI, 200–206, A revised version appears as IBM Research Laboratory Technical Report RJ5244 (April 1989).

Dolev, D., Halpern, J. Y. and Strong, R. (1984), On the possibility and impossibility of achieving clock synchronization, *Proceedings of the ACM Symposium on the Theory of Computing*, 504–511.

Fidge, C. J. (1988), Timestamps in Message-Passing Systems that Preseve the Partial Ordering, *Proceedings of the Eleventh Australian Computer Science Conference*, University of Queensland, Australia, 55–66.

Garg, V. K. and Waldecker, B. (1992), Unstable predicate detection in distributed programs, Technical Report TR-92-07-82, University of Texas at Austin.

Gligor, V. and Shattuck, S. (1980), On deadlock detection in distributed systems, *IEEE Transactions on Software Engineering* **SE-6**, 435–440.

Harel, D. and Pnueli, A. (1985), On the development of reactive systems, in *Logics and Models of Concurrent Systems*, Apt, K. R., ed., NATO ASI, Springer-Verlag, 477–498.

Helary, J., Jard, C., Plouzeau, N. and Raynal, M. (1986), Detection of stable properties in distributed applications, *Proceedings of the Fifth ACM Annual Symposium on Principles of Distributed Computing*, Halpern, J., ed., Calgary, Alberta, Canada, 125–136.

Kaashoek, M. F. and Tanenbaum, A. S. (1991), Group communication in the Amoeba distributed operating system, *Proceedings of the Eleventh International Conference on Distributed Computer Systems*, Arlington, TX, IEEE Computer Society, 222–230.

Kopetz, H. (1992), Sparse Time versus Dense Time in Distributed Real-Time Systems, *Proceedings of the Twelfth International Conference on Distributed Computing Systems*, Yokohama, Japan, IEEE Computer Society Press, 460–467.

Lamport, L. (1978), Time, Clocks, and the Ordering of Events in a Distributed System, *Communications of the ACM* **21(7)**, 558–565.

Lamport, L. and Melliar-Smith, P. M. (1985), Synchronizing Clocks in the Presence of Faults, *Journal of the ACM* **32(1)**, 52–78.

Levy, H. M. and Tempero, E. D. (1991), Modules, objects, and distributed programming: Issues in rpc and remote object invocation, *Software—Practice & Experience* **21(1)**, 77–90.

Li, K. and Hudak, P. (1989), Memory coherence in shared virtual memory systems, *ACM Transactions on Computer Systems* **7(4)**, 321–359.

Marzullo, K. and Neiger, G. (1991), Detection of global state predicates, *Proceedings of the Fifth International Workshop on Distributed Algorithms (WDAG-91)*, Delphi, Greece, Springer-Verlag.

Mattern, F. (1989), Virtual time and global states of distributed systems, *Proceedings of the International Workshop on Parallel and Distributed Algorithms*, Cosnard, M., ed., North-Holland, 215–226.

Mattern, F. (1993), Efficient algorithms for distributed snapshots and global virtual time approximation, *Journal of Parallel and Distributed Computing*, To appear.

Misra, J. (1986), Distributed-discrete event simulation, *ACM Computing Surveys* **18(1)**, 39–65.

Morgan, C. (1985), Global and logical time in distributed algorithms, *Information Processing Letters* **20**, 189–194.

Neiger, G. and Toueg, S. (1987), Substituting for real time and common knowledge in asynchronous distributed systems, *Proceedings of the Sixth ACM Annual Symposium on Principles of Distributed Computing*, Schneider, F. B., ed., Vancouver, BC, Canada, 281–293.

Peterson, L. L., Bucholz, N. C. and Schlichting, R. D. (1989), Preserving and using context information in interprocess communication, *ACM Transactions on Computer Systems* **7(3)**, 217–246.

Raynal, M. (1992), About logical clocks for distributed systems, *ACM Operating System Review* **26(1)**, 41–48.

Raynal, M., Schiper, A. and Toueg, S. (1991), The causal ordering abstraction and a simple way to implement it, *Information Processing Letters* **39(6)**, 343–350.

Sandoz, A. and Schiper, A. (1992), A characterization of consistent distributed snapshots using causal order, Departement d'Informatique, Ecole Polytechnique Fédérale de Lausanne, Technical Report 92-14, Switzerland.

Schiper, A., Eggli, J. and Sandoz, A. (1989), A new algorithm to implement causal ordering, *Proceedings of the Third International Workshop on Distributed Algorithms*, Bermond, J. -C. and Raynal, M., eds., Nice, France, Springer-Verlag, 219–232.

Schwarz, R. and Mattern, F. (1992), Detecting causal relationships in distributed computations: In search of the Holy Grail, Department of Computer Science, University of Kaiserslautern, Technical Report SFB124-15/92, Kaiserslautern, Germany.

Taylor, K. (1989), The role of inhibition in asynchronous consistent-cut protocols, *Proceedings of the Third International Workshop on Distributed Algorithms*, Bermond, J. -C. and Raynal, M., eds., Nice, France, Springer-Verlag, 280–291.

Chapter 5

Fault-Tolerant Broadcasts and Related Problems

Vassos Hadzilacos and Sam Toueg

5.1   Introduction

The design and verification of fault-tolerant distributed applications is widely viewed as a complex endeavor. In recent years, several paradigms have been identified which simplify this task. Key among these are Consensus and several types of Reliable Broadcasts. Roughly speaking, Consensus allows processes to reach a common decision, which depends on their initial inputs, despite failures. Consensus algorithms can be used to solve many problems that arise in practice, such as electing a leader or agreeing on the value of a replicated sensor. In many applications processes must be able to reliably broadcast messages, so that they agree on the set of messages they deliver. Sometimes processes must also agree on the order of message deliveries. Reliable Broadcast and its variants are convenient tools to fulfill these requirements. Applications based on these paradigms include SIFT (Wensley *et al.* [1978]), State Machines (Lamport [1978a]; Schneider [1990]; and Chapter 7 of this book), Isis (Birman *et al.* [1990]; Birman and Joseph [1987]), Psync (Peterson, Bucholz and Schlichting [1989]), Amoeba (Kaashoek [1992]), Delta-4 (Veríssimo and Marques [1990]), Transis (Amir *et al.* [1992]), HAS (Cristian [1987]), FAA (Cristian, Dancey and Dehn [1990]), and Atomic Commitment (see Chapter 6).

Given their wide applicability, Consensus, Reliable Broadcast, and related problems have been extensively studied by both theoretical and experimental researchers for over a decade. This has resulted in a voluminous literature which, unfortunately, is not distinguished for its coherence. The differences in notation and the haphazard nature of the assumptions obfuscates the close relationship among these problems.

Our primary goal here is to organize this material in a coherent way so as to expose its intrinsic unity. We also strive to make it as simple as possible, without sacrificing precision or rigor. To accomplish this, we rely on two devices. First, we draw a sharp line between the *specification* of problems, and the *algorithms* that solve them. Second, we make extensive use of the well-known concept of *reduction* between problems — a concept that allows us to classify problems according to their difficulty. This enables us to present both specifications and algorithms in a highly modular fashion. Thus, the results are easier to understand and verify.

Given the vastness of the literature on this subject, and the space limitations, we do not attempt an encyclopedic presentation of the material. In particular, we do not address *multicasts*, a generalization of broadcasts where messages are targeted to specific groups rather than being delivered by all processes. We focus on failures that are the most common ones in practice, give only one algorithm for each type of broadcast, and omit all proofs. Furthermore, many important results are either mentioned in passing, or not at all. Similarly, the bibliographic references are extensive, but incomplete. A comprehensive treatment will be found in the forthcoming book by Hadzilacos, Jayanti and Toueg [1993].

The rest of this chapter is organized as follows. In Section 5.2, we describe the models of computation commonly used in fault-tolerant distributed computing. In Section 5.3, we specify Reliable Broadcast and its variants. Algorithms for these problems are given in Section 5.4. We specify Terminating Reliable Broadcast, a close relative of Reliable Broadcast, in Section 5.5, and Consensus in Section 5.6. In Section 5.7, we determine relationships among problems considered in this chapter. Consensus and some related problems cannot be solved with deterministic algorithms in asynchronous systems. This fundamental impossibility result, and various ways of circumventing it, are discussed in Section 5.8. The chapter concludes in Section 5.9 with a survey of key complexity results.

To enhance the readability of this chapter, many references, historical notes, and other tangential and potentially distracting material, are collected at the end of each section.

5.2   Models of Distributed Computation

Problems in fault-tolerant distributed computing have been studied in a variety of computational models. Such models fall into two broad categories, *message-passing* and *shared-memory*. In the former, processes communicate by sending and receiving messages over the links of a network; in the latter, they communicate by accessing shared objects, such as registers, queues, etc. In this chapter we focus on message-passing models. (In Hadzilacos, Jayanti and Toueg [1993] we also consider shared-memory models.) The following parameters determine a particular message-passing model: Synchrony of processes and communication, types of process failures, types of communication failures, network topology, and deterministic versus randomized processes.

5.2.1   Synchrony

Synchrony is an attribute of both processes and communication. We say that a system is *synchronous* if it satisfies the following properties:

- There is a known upper bound δ on message delay; this consists of the time it takes for sending, transporting, and receiving a message over a link.
- Every process p has a local clock C_p with known bounded rate of drift $\rho \geq 0$ with respect to real-time. That is, for all p and all $t > t'$,

$$(1 + \rho)^{-1} \leq \frac{C_p(t) - C_p(t')}{(t - t')} \leq (1 + \rho)$$

  where $C_p(t)$ is the reading of C_p at real-time t.
- There are known upper bounds on the time required by a process to execute a step.

In synchronous systems it is possible to measure message timeouts, and this provides a mechanism for failure detection (as illustrated in the next chapter of this book). Furthermore, it is possible to implement *approximately synchronized clocks*, i.e., clocks that, in addition to the bounded rate of drift property, also satisfy the following condition: there is an ϵ such that for all t, and any two processes p and q, $|C_p(t) - C_q(t)| \leq \epsilon$. In fact, such clocks can be implemented even in the presence of failures (for example see Lamport and Melliar-Smith [1985], Srikanth and Toueg [1987a], or Cristian [1989]).[1] Approximately synchronized clocks have many applications, for instance, real-time process control, file management, cache consistency, authentication, etc. (see Liskov [1991]).

For many problems, approximately synchronized clocks can also be used to simulate *perfectly* synchronized clocks, that is, clocks with $\epsilon = 0$, and this simplifies the design of distributed algorithms (Neiger and Toueg [1987]; Welch [1987]). Together with the bound δ on message delay, such clocks can implement the so-called synchronous round model, which has been widely used in theoretical work (see Section 5.9.2).

A system is *asynchronous* if there is no bound on message delay, clock drift, or the time necessary to execute a step. Thus, to say that a system is asynchronous is to make *no* timing assumptions whatsoever. This model is attractive and has recently gained much currency for several reasons: It has simple semantics; applications programmed on the basis of this model are easier to port than those incorporating specific timing assumptions; and in practice, variable or unexpected workloads are sources of asynchrony — thus synchrony assumptions are at best probabilistic.

The synchronous and asynchronous models are the two extremes of a spectrum of possible models. Many intermediate models have also been studied. For example, processes may have bounded speeds and perfectly synchronized clocks, but message delays may be unbounded (Dolev, Dwork and Stockmeyer [1987]). Or, message delays may be bounded but unknown (Dwork, Lynch and Stockmeyer [1988]).

---

[1]In general, a clock synchronization algorithm can approximately synchronize only the clocks of *correct* processes.

5.2.2   Process Failures

A process is *faulty* in an execution if its behavior deviates from that prescribed by the algorithm it is running; otherwise, it is *correct*. A *model of failure* specifies in what way a faulty process can deviate from its algorithm. The following is a list of models of failures that have been studied in the literature:

- *Crash*: A faulty process stops prematurely and does nothing from that point on. Before stopping, however, it behaves correctly.
- *Send omission*: A faulty process stops prematurely, or intermittently omits to send messages it was supposed to send, or both.
- *Receive omission*: A faulty process stops prematurely, or intermittently omits to receive messages sent to it, or both.
- *General omission*: A faulty process is subject to send or receive omission failures, or both.
- *Arbitrary* (sometimes called *Byzantine* or *malicious*): A faulty process can exhibit any behavior whatsoever. For example, it can change state arbitrarily.
- *Arbitrary with message authentication*: Faulty processes can exhibit arbitrary behavior but a mechanism for authenticating messages using *unforgeable signatures* is available. With arbitrary failures, a faulty process may claim to have received a particular message from a correct process, even though it never did. A message authentication mechanism allows the other correct processes to validate this claim.

These failure models can be classified in terms of 'severity'. Model A is *more severe* than model B if the set of faulty behaviors allowed by B is a proper subset of the set of those allowed by A. Thus, an algorithm that tolerates failures of type A, also tolerates those of type B. Arbitrary failures are the most severe failures, since they do not place any restrictions on the behavior of a faulty process. Crash failures are the least severe failures listed above. The classification of models is illustrated in Figure 5.1, where an arrow from type B to type A indicates that A is more severe than B.

The above models of failures are applicable to both synchronous and asynchronous systems. In contrast, timing failures is a model that is only pertinent to synchronous systems. Recall that in such systems there are bounds on clock drift and the time necessary to execute a step. A process subject to *timing failures* can fail in one or more of the following ways:

1. it commits general omission failures,
2. its local clock drift exceeds the specified bound (*a clock failure*),
3. it violates the bounds on the time required to execute a step (*a performance failure*).

When we consider systems with approximately synchronized clocks and processes subject to timing failures, we will assume that only the clocks of *correct* processes are at most ϵ apart.

Recall that in a synchronous system there is an upper bound δ on message delay. If processes are subject to timing failures, we assume that this bound applies only

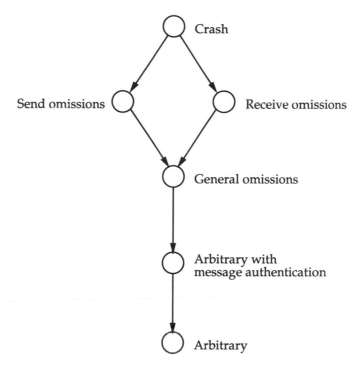

Figure 5.1. Classification of Failure Models

to messages over links between *correct* processes. This is because δ includes the time for the send and receive steps, and with performance failures these steps could take any amount of time.

In our classification of failures, timing failures are more severe than general omission but less severe than arbitrary failures with message authentication. In this classification, all failure types that are no more severe than timing failures are called *benign*. A process that suffers a benign failure does not arbitrarily change state, or send a message that is not prescribed by its algorithm according to its present state. Both of these faulty behaviors are possible with more severe failures. Because benign failures are the ones that arise most commonly in practice, in this chapter we focus almost exclusively on them.

5.2.3 Communication Failures

Communication links can be affected by the following types of failures:

- *Crash*: A faulty link stops transporting messages. Before stopping, however, it behaves correctly.
- *Omission*: A faulty link intermittently omits to transport messages sent through it.
- *Arbitrary* (sometimes called *Byzantine* or *malicious*): A faulty link can exhibit any behavior whatsoever. For example, it can generate spurious messages.

In the case of synchronous systems, we also have:

- *Timing failures*: A faulty link transports messages faster or slower than its specification.

Thus, in a synchronous system with process and link timing failures, we assume that the upper bound δ on message delay applies only to messages between *correct* processes over *correct* links. In such a system, only the subsystem consisting of correct processes and correct links is really synchronous.

5.2.4   Network Topology

The communications network can be modeled as a graph, where nodes are processes and edges are communication links between processes. This model encompasses point-to-point as well as broadcast networks, and most results in this chapter apply to both kinds of networks. The problems we consider are not solvable if failures result in a partition of the network. Thus, the underlying network must have sufficient connectivity to allow correct processes to communicate directly or indirectly despite process and communication failures. Precise assumptions on network topology will be made as needed, when we state specific results.

5.2.5   Determinism versus Randomization

The behavior of a process may be either *deterministic* or *randomized*. In general, a process can be modeled as a (possibly infinite) state automaton. Roughly speaking, the state transition relation of a deterministic process *uniquely* determines the state that results from the execution of each step on the current state. With a randomized process, the execution of a given step on the current state may result in one of several possible states, and each such transition has an associated probability. Informally, a process can 'toss coins' to determine which transition to take. As we will see, the solvability of many problems and the efficiency of solutions is dramatically affected by whether processes are restricted to use deterministic algorithms or not.

Bibliographic Notes

The synchronous round model of distributed systems was used to study the problems of fault-tolerant broadcast and Consensus in two seminal papers by Pease, Shostak and Lamport [1980] and Lamport, Shostak and Pease [1982]. The asynchronous model has been adopted by many systems, such as described in Birman and Joseph [1987], Peterson, Bucholz and Schlichting [1989] and Amir *et al.* [1992]. Theoretical investigation of this model was spurred by the surprising result of Fischer, Lynch and Paterson [1985], stating that Consensus cannot be solved deterministically in this model. A variety of models of partial synchrony are studied in Dolev, Dwork and Stockmeyer [1987] and Dwork, Lynch and Stockmeyer [1988]. Clock synchronization algorithms are given in Lamport [1978b], Halpern *et al.* [1984], Lamport and Melliar-Smith [1985], Cristian, Aghili and Strong [1986],

Dolev, Halpern and Strong [1986], Babaoğlu and Drummond [1987], Kopetz and Ochsenreiter [1987], Srikanth and Toueg [1987b], Welch and Lynch [1988] and Cristian [1989].

The original papers, Pease, Shostak and Lamport [1980] and Lamport, Shostak and Pease [1982], considered systems with arbitrary failures with and without message authentication. A precise definition of the properties of message authentication and a mechanism for providing them without digital signatures appears in Srikanth and Toueg [1987a]. Crash failures, in the context of broadcast and Consensus problems, were first considered by Lamport and Fischer [1982]. Schlichting and Schneider [1983] defined a more restricted type of process failure, referred to as *failstop*. A failstop process can only fail by crashing but, in addition, all correct processes are informed of the crash, and they have access to any information written by the faulty process in its stable storage before it crashed. Send omission failures were introduced by Hadzilacos [1984], general omission failures by Perry and Toueg [1986], and timing failures by Cristian *et al.* [1985].

There are methods for *automatically* increasing the fault-tolerance of algorithms. This is achieved by translations that transform any given algorithm tolerant of a certain type of failure into an algorithm that tolerates a more severe type of failure. Such translations are given by Bracha [1987], Coan [1987], Srikanth and Toueg [1987a], Neiger and Toueg [1990], Bazzi and Neiger [1991, 1992]. They can be used to transform any algorithm tolerant of crash failures into one tolerant of arbitrary failures, in both synchronous and asynchronous systems.

5.3   Broadcast Specifications

Consider a distributed system where processes communicate via broadcasts. If failures occur during a broadcast, it is conceivable that only a subset of the processes actually deliver the message that was broadcast. Such inconsistencies can compromise the integrity of the distributed system, and therefore *unreliable* broadcasts are not appropriate tools for building fault-tolerant applications. In this section, we give precise specifications for a collection of broadcast primitives with stronger semantics, which are much better suited to such applications.

Roughly speaking, *Reliable Broadcast* — the weakest type of broadcast that we consider — guarantees three properties: (1) all correct processes agree on the set of messages they deliver, (2) all messages broadcast by correct processes are delivered, and (3) no spurious messages are ever delivered. While these properties may be sufficient for some applications, Reliable Broadcast imposes no restriction on the *order* in which the messages are delivered. Sometimes this order is important. Thus, we define a collection of stronger broadcasts, differing in the guarantees they provide on message delivery order.

Informally, *FIFO Broadcast* is a Reliable Broadcast that guarantees that messages broadcast by the same sender are delivered in the order they were broadcast. *Causal Broadcast*, a strengthening of FIFO Broadcast, requires that messages be delivered according to the *causal precedence* relation, a fundamental concept in distributed systems (Lamport [1978b]). For example, if a process delivers a message m and later broadcasts m' (thus, the broadcast of m' may 'depend' on the previous delivery of m), then Causal Broadcast requires processes to deliver m before delivering m'. However, Causal Broadcast allows processes to deliver causally unrelated messages in different orders. This is prevented by *Atomic Broadcast*, a broadcast that requires processes to deliver all messages in the same order. *FIFO Atomic Broadcast* combines the requirements of FIFO Broadcast and Atomic Broadcast, and *Causal Atomic Broadcast* combines the requirements of Causal Broadcast and Atomic Broadcast.

In our definitions of the various types of broadcast, we assume that we are only dealing with benign failures. This not only simplifies the definitions, but also makes it possible to strengthen the properties of broadcasts in ways that are important in practice.

5.3.1   Reliable Broadcast

Informally, Reliable Broadcast requires that all correct processes deliver the same set of messages (Agreement), and that this set include all messages broadcast by correct processes (Validity), and no spurious messages (Integrity). Formally, Reliable Broadcast is defined in terms of two primitives: *broadcast(m)* and *deliver(m)*, where m is a message from a set $\mathcal{M}$ of possible messages. When a process invokes *broadcast(m)*, we say that it *broadcasts* m. Similarly, when a process executes *deliver(m)*, we say that it delivers m.

Since every process can broadcast several messages, it is important to be able to determine the identity of a message's sender, and to distinguish the different messages broadcast by a particular sender. Thus, we assume that every message m includes the following fields: the identity of its sender, denoted *sender(m)*, and a sequence number, denoted *seq#(m)*. If *sender(m)* = p and *seq#(m)* = i, then m is the ith message broadcast by p. These fields make every message unique.

Reliable Broadcast is a broadcast that satisfies the following three properties:

- *Validity*: If a correct process broadcasts a message m, then all correct processes eventually deliver m.
- *Agreement*: If a correct process delivers a message m, then all correct processes eventually deliver m.
- *Integrity*: For any message m, every correct process delivers m at most once, and only if m was previously broadcast by *sender(m)*.

It is important to realize that if a process p fails during the broadcast of a message, Reliable Broadcast allows two possible outcomes: either the message is delivered by all correct processes or by none. For example, if p invokes *broadcast(m)* and then immediately crashes, correct processes will never be aware of p's intention to broadcast that message, and thus cannot deliver anything. On the other hand, if p fails during the broadcast, but after having sent enough information, then correct processes may be able to deliver m. An example of a Reliable Broadcast algorithm is given in Section 5.4.1.

5.3.2 FIFO Broadcast

In general, each message has a context without which it may be misinterpreted. Such a message should not be delivered by a process that does not know its context. In some applications, the context of a message m consists of the messages previously broadcast by the sender of m. For example, in an airline reservation system, the context of a message cancelling a reservation consists of the message that previously established that reservation: the cancellation message should not be delivered at a site that has not yet 'seen' the reservation message. Such applications require the semantics of *FIFO Broadcast*, a Reliable Broadcast that satisfies the following requirement on message delivery:

- *FIFO Order*: If a process broadcasts a message m before it broadcasts a message m', then no correct process delivers m' unless it has previously delivered m

Our definition of FIFO Order is subtler than meets the eye. Some alternative formulations of FIFO Broadcast which have appeared in the literature have a similar flavor, but are ambiguous or do not fully capture the desirable property described above. For example, consider the following definition: 'all messages broadcast by the same process are delivered to all processes in the order they are sent.' Suppose process p broadcasts messages m_1, m_2, and m_3 in that order, and correct process q delivers m_1 and then m_3 (but never delivers m_2). This scenario could happen if p suffers a transient failure while broadcasting m_2. Note that m_3 was delivered without its proper context, namely m_2. This undesirable behavior is allowed by the alternative definition (since m_1 and m_3 are indeed delivered in the order they are broadcast), but not by our definition of FIFO Order.[2] A FIFO Broadcast algorithm is given in Section 5.4.4.

5.3.3 Causal Broadcast

FIFO Order is adequate when the context of a message m consists only of the messages that the sender of m broadcast before m. However, a message m may also depend on messages that the sender of m *delivered* before broadcasting m. In this case, the message delivery order guaranteed by FIFO Broadcast is not sufficient. For example, in a network news application, if users distribute their articles with FIFO Broadcast, the following undesirable scenario could occur. User A broadcasts an article. User B, at a different site, delivers that article and broadcasts a response that can only be understood by a user who has already seen the original article. User C delivers B's response before delivering the original article from A and so misinterprets the response. Causal Broadcast is a strengthening of FIFO Broadcast that prevents the above problem by generalizing the notion of a message 'depending' on another one, and ensuring that a message is not delivered until all the messages it depends on have been delivered.

---

[2]This alternative definition, taken from the literature, is also flawed in another way: it requires messages be delivered by *all* processes. Clearly, this is impossible, since a faulty process cannot be forced to deliver any message.

We formalize this more general notion of dependence as follows. An execution of a *broadcast* or *deliver* primitive by a process is called an *event*. We say that event e *causally precedes* event f, denoted $e \rightarrow f$, if and only if:

1. a process executes both e and f, in that order, or
2. e is the broadcast of some message m and f is the delivery of m, or
3. there is an event h, such that $e \rightarrow h$ and $h \rightarrow f$.

Since the delivery of a message m can only occur after the broadcast of m (in real-time), this causal precedence relation is acyclic. This relation between broadcast/delivery events is an adaptation of the 'happened before' relation between send/receive events, a fundamental concept in distributed systems (see Lamport [1978a] and the previous chapter of this book).

A *Causal Broadcast* is a Reliable Broadcast that satisfies the following requirement:

- *Causal Order*: If the broadcast of a message m causally precedes the broadcast of a message m', then no correct process delivers m' unless it has previously delivered m.

The following alternative formulation of Causal Order has appeared in the literature: if the broadcast of m causally precedes the broadcast of m', then every correct process that delivers both messages must deliver m before m'. In a system with failures, this definition of Causal Order is flawed. In fact, it allows the same non-FIFO execution described in the previous section, where a faulty process broadcasts m_1, m_2, and m_3, and a correct process delivers m_1 and then m_3. This alternative definition also allows the following undesirable scenario from our network news example. Faulty user A broadcasts an article; faulty user B, who is the only one to deliver that message, broadcasts a response. Correct user C delivers B's response, although it never delivers A's original article. It is easy to see that this scenario satisfies all the properties of Reliable Broadcast, namely Validity, Agreement and Integrity, as well as the alternative definition of Causal Order (but not our definition of Causal Order). Note that defining Causal Order as 'messages that are causally related are delivered in the causal order' is also flawed.

A Causal Broadcast algorithm is given in Section 5.4.5.

5.3.4   Atomic Broadcast

Causal Broadcast does not impose any delivery order on messages that are not causally related. Thus, two correct processes may deliver causally unrelated messages in different orders, and this creates problems in some applications. For example, consider a replicated database with two copies of a bank account x residing at different sites. Initially, x has a value of $100. A user deposits $20, triggering a broadcast of $m = $ [add $20 to x] to the two copies of x. At the same time, at a different site, the bank initiates a broadcast of the message $m' = $ [add 10% interest to x]. Because these two broadcasts are not causally related, Causal Broadcast allows the two copies of x to deliver these update messages in different orders. This results in the two copies of x having different values, creating an inconsistency in the database.

To prevent such problems, Atomic Broadcast requires that all correct processes deliver *all* messages in the same order. This total order on message delivery ensures that all correct processes have the same 'view' of the system; hence they can act consistently without any additional communication. Formally, an *Atomic Broadcast* is a Reliable Broadcast that satisfies the following requirement:

- *Total Order*: If correct processes p and q both deliver messages m and m', then p delivers m before m' if and only if q delivers m before m'.

The Agreement and Total Order requirements of Atomic Broadcast imply that correct processes eventually deliver the same *sequence* of messages. An Atomic Broadcast algorithm is given in Section 5.4.6.

5.3.5 FIFO Atomic Broadcast

Atomic Broadcast does *not* require that messages be delivered in FIFO Order. For example, Atomic Broadcast allows the following scenario: a process suffers a transient failure during the broadcast of a message m, and then broadcasts m', and correct processes only deliver m'. Thus, Atomic Broadcast is not stronger than FIFO Broadcast.

We therefore define FIFO Atomic Broadcast which is a Reliable Broadcast that satisfies both the FIFO and Total Order requirements. FIFO Atomic Broadcast is stronger than both Atomic Broadcast and FIFO Broadcast. A FIFO Atomic Broadcast algorithm is given in Section 5.4.7.

5.3.6 Causal Atomic Broadcast

FIFO Atomic Broadcast does *not* require that messages be delivered in Causal Order. Reconsider the earlier network news example, and suppose FIFO Atomic Broadcast is used to disseminate articles. The following undesirable scenario is possible. Faulty user A broadcasts an article; faulty user B, who is the only one to deliver that message, broadcasts a response and then immediately crashes (before delivering its own response). Correct user C delivers the response, although it never delivers the original article. Thus, FIFO Atomic Broadcast does not necessarily satisfy Causal Order.

We therefore define Causal Atomic Broadcast which is a Reliable Broadcast that satisfies both the Causal and Total Order requirements. Causal Atomic Broadcast is stronger than both FIFO Atomic Broadcast and Causal Broadcast. This type of broadcast is the key mechanism of the State Machine approach to fault-tolerance (cf. Lamport [1978a], Schneider [1990] and Chapter 7 of this book). A Causal Atomic Broadcast algorithm is given in Section 5.4.8.

5.3.7 Timed Broadcasts

Many applications require that if a message is delivered at all, it is delivered within a bounded time after it was broadcast. This property is called Δ-*Timeliness*. As usual, in a distributed environment elapsed time can be interpreted in two different ways: real time, as measured by an external observer, or local time, as measured by the local clocks of processes. This gives rise to two different ways of defining the Δ-Timeliness property. The one corresponding to real-time is:

- *(Real-Time) Δ-Timeliness*: There is a known constant Δ such that if the broadcast of m is initiated at real-time t, no correct process delivers m after real-time $t + \Delta$.

On the other hand, the definition of Δ-Timeliness in terms of local clocks bounds the difference between the local broadcasting time and the local delivery time. To formally specify such a bound, we assume that each message m contains a *timestamp* $ts(m)$ denoting the local time at which m was broadcast according to the sender's clock. That is, if a process p wishes to broadcast a message m when its local clock shows c, then p tags m with $ts(m) = c$. The definition of Δ-Timeliness that corresponds to local time is:

- *(Local-Time) Δ-Timeliness*: There is a known constant Δ such that no correct process p delivers a message m after local time $ts(m) + \Delta$ on p's clock.

A broadcast that satisfies either version of the Δ-Timeliness property is called a *Timed Broadcast*. For example, *Timed Reliable Broadcast* is a Reliable Broadcast that satisfies (Local- or Real-Time) Δ-Timeliness. When referring to a Timed Broadcast, one must explicitly state which of the two Timeliness properties is assumed. The parameter Δ is called the *latency* of the Timed Broadcast.

In asynchronous systems, no Reliable Broadcast algorithm can satisfy either Real- or Local-Time Δ-Timeliness; that is, Timed Reliable Broadcast is not implementable.[3] In synchronous systems, one can implement a Reliable Broadcast that satisfies the local-time version of Δ-Timeliness. In contrast, no Reliable Broadcast can satisfy the real-time version of Δ-Timeliness in a system with timing failures. Informally, this is because a set of faulty processes (whose local clocks are running fast) can withhold a message broadcast by one of them long ago, and then release it into the system as if it were a recent broadcast. To correct processes, this is indistinguishable from a scenario in which this is a recent broadcast from a correct process. Now correct processes are in a bind: if they don't deliver the message, they may be violating Validity; if they do deliver the message, they may be violating Δ-Timeliness. In spite of this limitation, the real-time version of Δ-Timeliness is the one needed by some applications. Such an application is described in the next chapter of this book. Some Timed Reliable Broadcast algorithms with both Local- and Real-Time Δ-Timeliness are given in Section 5.4.3.

5.3.8 Uniform Broadcasts

The Agreement, Integrity, Order, and Δ-Timeliness properties of the broadcasts defined so far place no restrictions on the messages delivered by faulty processes.

---

[3]The impossibility result for the local-time version requires some reasonable assumptions on the local clocks, for instance, that they are monotonically increasing (see Section 5.4.6).

Since we are dealing with benign failures, such restrictions are desirable and achievable. For example, the Agreement property allows a faulty process to deliver a message that is never delivered by the correct processes. This faulty behavior is undesirable in some applications, such as Atomic Commitment in distributed databases (Gray [1978]; Bernstein, Hadzilacos and Goodman [1987]; see also the next chapter of this book), and can be avoided if the failures are benign. For such failures, we can strengthen the Agreement property to:

- *Uniform Agreement*: If a process (whether correct or faulty) delivers a message *m*, then all correct processes eventually deliver *m*.

Similarly, Integrity allows a faulty process to deliver a message more than once, and to deliver messages 'out of thin air' (i.e., messages that were never broadcast by any processes). If failures are benign, this behavior can be avoided and we can strengthen the Integrity property as follows:

- *Uniform Integrity*: For any message *m*, every process (whether correct or faulty) delivers *m* at most once, and only if some process broadcast *m*.

We can also strengthen each version of the Δ-Timeliness property by requiring even faulty processes to respect the bound on the broadcast latency. For example:

- *Uniform Local-Time Δ-Timeliness*: There is a known constant Δ such that no process *p* (whether correct or faulty) delivers a message *m* after local time $ts(m) + \Delta$ on *p*'s clock.

Real-Time Δ-Timeliness also has an analogous Uniform counterpart. Likewise, we can strengthen each of the Order properties, by requiring that even faulty processes do not violate them. Specifically, we define:

- *Uniform FIFO Order*: If a process broadcasts a message *m* before it broadcasts a message *m'*, then no process (whether correct or faulty) delivers *m'* unless it has previously delivered *m*.
- *Uniform Causal Order*: If the broadcast of a message *m* causally precedes the broadcast of a message *m'*, then no process (whether correct or faulty) delivers *m'* unless it has previously delivered *m*.
- *Uniform Total Order*: If any processes *p* and *q* (whether correct or faulty) both deliver messages *m* and *m'*, then *p* delivers *m* before *m'* if and only if *q* delivers *m* before *m'*.

For each type of broadcast we define a Uniform counterpart, by replacing its Agreement, Integrity, Order, and Δ-Timeliness properties by the corresponding Uniform ones. For example, a *Uniform Timed Reliable Broadcast* satisfies Validity, Uniform Agreement, Uniform Integrity, and Uniform Δ-Timeliness. This type of broadcast is used to solve the Non-Blocking Atomic Commitment problem in the next chapter of this book. A Uniform Timed Reliable Broadcast algorithm is also given in Section 5.4.3.

5.3.9   Inconsistency and Contamination

Consider an application where processes communicate via fault-tolerant broadcasts. Assume that only benign failures may occur; thus, the current state of every process (whether correct or faulty) depends on the messages that it delivered so far. This state, and the application protocol that the process executes, determines whether it should broadcast a message, and if so, the contents of that message.

Suppose that a process p fails, say by omitting to deliver a message that is delivered by all the correct processes. The state of p may now be 'inconsistent' with respect to the state of correct processes. Suppose further that p continues to execute, and then, based on its inconsistent state, p broadcasts a message m that is delivered by all the correct processes. Note that m is 'corrupted', that is, its contents reflect p's erroneous state. Thus, by delivering m and changing state accordingly, the *correct* processes incorporate p's inconsistency into their own state — correct processes are now 'contaminated.' We come to the disconcerting conclusion that, even with benign failures, broadcasts can easily lead to the corruption of the *entire* system!

Unfortunately, the traditional specifications of most broadcasts, including Uniform broadcasts, allow the inconsistency of faulty processes, and the subsequent contamination of correct processes. For example, with Atomic Broadcast a faulty process may reach an inconsistent state in several ways: for instance, by omitting to deliver a message m that is delivered by all correct processes, or by delivering an extra message m that is not delivered by any correct process, or by delivering messages out-of-order. With Uniform Atomic Broadcast, inconsistency may only result from skipping a message that is delivered by all correct processes. Contamination can then follow. An example of inconsistency with respect to (Uniform) Atomic Broadcast is explained below.

A variable x with initial value 5 is replicated at three processes, p, q, and r. Process p atomically broadcasts an instruction to increment x, and q atomically broadcasts an instruction to double x. Processes p and q are correct, and they deliver the instructions to increment x and to double x, in that order. Their value of x is now 12. However, r is faulty: it first omits to deliver p's instruction to increment x, and then delivers q's instruction to double x. By skipping the increment x instruction, r becomes *inconsistent* — its new value of x (namely, 10) is now incorrect. Note that since r is faulty, this execution *does* indeed satisfy the usual specification of Atomic Broadcast. In fact, this particular execution can occur even with a Uniform Atomic Broadcast.

Once r is inconsistent, it can broadcast messages that are based on its erroneous state and thus contaminate all the correct processes. For example, suppose process r uses its new value of x to compute and broadcast the value of the replicated variable y, which is supposed to be $3x$ everywhere. Since r is inconsistent and has incorrectly computed x to be 10, r broadcasts $y := 30$, instead of the correct $y := 36$. When p and q deliver the message $y := 30$ and update their copies of y to be 30, they become contaminated.

Note that r becomes inconsistent by committing a simple 'benign' failure — just skipping the delivery of a single message. However, as a result of this undetected failure, r subsequently broadcasts an incorrect message, and this broadcast 'spreads' r's error to the rest of the system. At this point, it is almost as if r commits an 'arbitrary-like' failure, even though it only fails by omission. Worse yet, r's failure corrupts the whole system.

It should be clear that preventing the inconsistency of faulty processes, or at least the contamination of correct ones, is desirable in many situations. Fortunately, this is possible with all the broadcasts that we considered in this chapter, and for all benign failures. Intuitively, a process can prevent being contaminated by refusing to deliver messages from processes whose previous deliveries are not compatible with its own. The amount of information that each message should carry, so that every process can determine whether it is safe to deliver it, depends on the type of broadcast (e.g., FIFO Broadcast or Causal Atomic Broadcast), and on the failure assumptions. Preventing inconsistency is, however, more difficult and costly. Roughly speaking, it requires techniques that allow a faulty process to detect whether it is about to make a message delivery error, and, if so, to immediately stop.

A precise definition of inconsistency and contamination with respect to broadcasts is beyond the scope of this chapter. We also omit the description of algorithms that prevent inconsistency and/or contamination. For a more complete treatment of this subject the reader is referred to Gopal and Toueg [1991] or Gopal [1992].

5.3.10 Amplification of Failures

A fault-tolerant broadcast is usually implemented by a *broadcast algorithm* that uses lower-level communication primitives, such as point-to-point message *sends* and *receives* (Figure 5.2). With such a broadcast algorithm, the *broadcast* or *delivery* of a message requires the execution of several instructions, and may include several sends and receives.

The models of failures commonly considered in the literature are defined in terms of failures that occur at the level of send and receive primitives, for instance, omissions to receive messages (Section 5.2.2). How do these failures affect the execution of higher-level primitives, such as broadcasts and deliveries? In particular, can we assume that if a process suffers a certain type of failure at the send/receive level, then it will always suffer the same type of failure at the broadcast/delivery level? For example, if a faulty process omits to receive messages, will it simply omit to deliver messages? Unfortunately, this is not always so. In general a broadcast algorithm is likely to *amplify* the severity of failures that occur at the low level. For example, there are Atomic Broadcast algorithms where the omission to receive messages causes a faulty process to deliver messages in the wrong order (Gopal [1992]).

But what if processes are only subject to *crash* failures? Can we assume that the message deliveries that a process makes before crashing are always 'correct' (i.e., consistent with those of correct processes)? Intuitively, this seems very reasonable, since *by definition* a process that crashes executes perfectly until the moment it crashes. In other words, it seems impossible for such a process to make 'mistakes' in its message deliveries before crashing. However, this intuition *is* wrong. We

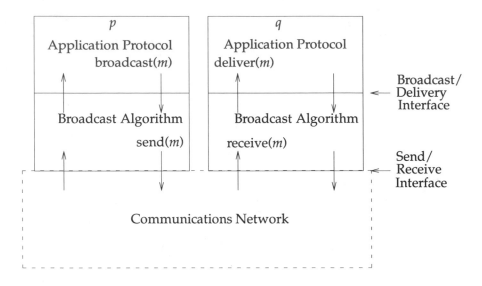

Figure 5.2. Application/Broadcast Layering

illustrate this by a coordinator-based Atomic Broadcast algorithm that exhibits a surprising behavior: *even if a faulty process behaves correctly until it crashes, it may still deliver messages out-of-order before it crashes!* This algorithm, which satisfies the specification of Atomic Broadcast, is sketched below.

When a process intends to broadcast a message m, it first sends m to a *coordinator*. The coordinator delivers messages in the order in which it receives them, and periodically informs the other processes of this message delivery order. Other processes deliver messages according to this order. If the coordinator crashes, another process takes over as coordinator. Now, suppose a coordinator delivers m before m', and then crashes before informing any other process that m should be delivered before m'. The new coordinator cannot determine the order chosen by the faulty coordinator, and may decide that m' should be delivered before m. In this scenario, all correct processes follow the new coordinator and deliver m' before m. Thus, the faulty coordinator delivered messages out-of-order before crashing, even though it executed its protocol perfectly until it crashed.

The above example shows that even if a process is only subject to crash failures, it may become inconsistent *before* crashing. In other words, crash failures just by themselves do *not* guarantee reasonable behavior at the broadcast/delivery level. Furthermore, from the time that such a process becomes inconsistent to the time that it crashes, it may broadcast messages and thus contaminate all correct processes. Thus, even if processes can only fail by crashing, inconsistency and contamination can occur.[4]

These observations have subtle but important consequences. In particular, consider the State Machine approach to fault-tolerance (cf. Lamport [1984], Schneider

---

[4]Of course, the prevention of inconsistency and contamination is much easier with crash failures, than with omission or timing failures.

[1990] and Chapter 7 of this book). This is a client/server system, where the server is replicated, and clients broadcast their requests to servers using Causal Atomic Broadcast. Thus, all *correct* servers deliver the same set of requests, in the same causal order, and so they have identical state. When a server delivers a request from a client, it computes the appropriate reply to that request, and sends it to the client. Suppose that up to f servers are subject to general omission failures. Clearly, the state of such a server can be erroneous, and so it may send incorrect replies. To how many servers should a client broadcast its request, in order to determine the correct reply? It is easy to see that $2f + 1$ servers are sufficient: the client is guaranteed to receive at least $f+1$ identical replies (a majority) from correct servers. This scheme works even when servers are subject to arbitrary failures. However, requiring $2f + 1$ servers and computing the majority reply is expensive. Can a client get by with fewer servers and replies if failures are less severe?

In particular, suppose that servers are subject to *crash failures only*. Since a faulty server executes correctly until it crashes, it is tempting to conclude that if *any* server sends a reply, that reply must be correct. Can the client indeed assume that any reply is correct? (If this was true, the client could broadcast its request to only $f + 1$ servers: at least one of them would reply, and any reply would do.) Unfortunately, the answer is negative. A reply may originate from a server s that will later crash. As we saw in our previous example, the particular Causal Atomic Broadcast algorithm used to broadcast requests may be such that s delivers requests out-of-order before crashing. In other words, s could be in an inconsistent state and send the wrong reply before crashing! A single reply is guaranteed to be correct *if and only if* the Causal Atomic Broadcast used is specifically designed to prevent inconsistency, as discussed in the previous section.

5.3.11 Summary of Broadcast Specifications

All our broadcasts have the following three properties of Reliable Broadcast:

- *Validity*: If a correct process broadcasts a message m, then all correct processes eventually deliver m.
- *Agreement*: If a correct process delivers a message m, then all correct processes eventually deliver m.
- *Integrity*: For any message m, every correct process delivers m at most once, and only if m was previously broadcast by *sender*(m).

They only differ by the strength of their message delivery order requirements. There are three such requirements:

- *FIFO Order*: If a process broadcasts a message m before it broadcasts a message m', then no correct process delivers m' unless it has previously delivered m.
- *Causal Order*: If the broadcast of a message m causally precedes the broadcast of a message m', then no correct process delivers m' unless it has previously delivered m.

- *Total Order*: If correct processes p and q both deliver messages m and m', then p delivers m before m' if and only if q delivers m before m'.

Thus:

- Reliable Broadcast = Validity + Agreement + Integrity
- FIFO Broadcast = Reliable Broadcast + FIFO Order
- Causal Broadcast = Reliable Broadcast + Causal Order
- Atomic Broadcast = Reliable Broadcast + Total Order
- FIFO Atomic Broadcast = Reliable Broadcast + FIFO Order + Total Order
- Causal Atomic Broadcast = Reliable Broadcast + Causal Order + Total Order

The relation between these six types of broadcasts, in term of their Order properties, is illustrated in Figure 5.3.

The above broadcasts do not bound the latency of a broadcast. Such a bound can be required by adding one of the following two Δ-Timeliness requirements:

- *(Real-Time) Δ-Timeliness*: There is a known constant Δ such that if the broadcast of m is initiated at real-time t, no correct process delivers m after real-time $t + \Delta$.
- *(Local-Time) Δ-Timeliness*: There is a known constant Δ such that no correct process p delivers a message m after local time $ts(m) + \Delta$ on p's clock.

A broadcast with Δ-Timeliness is called a *Timed* broadcast. We also defined *Uniform* versions of Agreement, Integrity, FIFO Order, Causal Order, Total Order, and Δ-Timeliness, by imposing the corresponding requirement even on messages delivered by faulty processes. A broadcast is *Uniform* if all its properties are Uniform. Finally, we observed that the specifications of most broadcasts allow a faulty process to become *inconsistent* (e.g., by failing with respect to the delivery of a message), and then *contaminate* correct processes (e.g., by broadcasting a message whose content reflects its previous incorrect delivery).

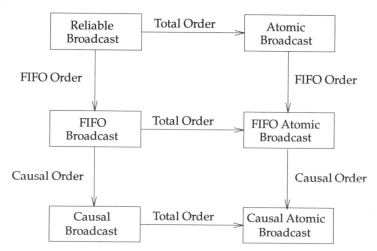

Figure 5.3. Relationship among Broadcast Primitives

Bibliographic Notes

The specification of the various types of broadcasts given in this section was designed by the authors with the help of Ajei Gopal. Similar specifications have appeared in the literature, but we have found them wanting (for example, the Integrity property is not explicitly stated). Our specifications are modular, they remove ambiguities and unify the problems. They also enable us to unify the broadcast algorithms, as will be seen in the next section. The roots of FIFO Broadcast and Causal Broadcast are in the Isis system (Birman and Joseph [1987]), although many systems now provide such primitives, including Psync (Peterson, Bucholz and Schlichting [1989]) and Transis (Amir *et al.* [1992]). Atomic Broadcast goes back to the early work of Lamport on the State Machine approach to fault-tolerance (Lamport [1978a]); the name was coined by Cristian *et al.* [1985].

The notion of Uniformity was introduced with respect to the Agreement property by Neiger and Toueg [1987]. It was extended to the other properties by the authors. The problems of inconsistency, contamination, and failure amplification, were first defined and studied by Gopal and Toueg [1991] and Gopal [1992].

5.4   Broadcast Algorithms

In the following sections, we describe a broadcast algorithm for each one of the broadcast specifications that we considered in Section 5.3. In particular, we give algorithms for Reliable Broadcast, FIFO Broadcast, Causal Broadcast, Atomic Broadcast, FIFO Atomic Broadcast, and Causal Atomic Broadcast. For each one of these broadcasts, we also consider their Timed and Uniform counterparts. Our Reliable Broadcast, FIFO Broadcast, and Causal Broadcast algorithms work in both synchronous and asynchronous systems. In contrast, Atomic Broadcast, FIFO Atomic Broadcast, and Causal Atomic Broadcast cannot be solved with deterministic algorithms in asynchronous systems; accordingly, our algorithms require a synchronous system.

The broadcast algorithms presented here are built in a highly modular and 'layered' fashion, in a way that closely follows their hierarchical specifications. Starting with an implementation of the weakest broadcast in this hierarchy (Reliable Broadcast), we show how to build stronger and stronger broadcasts 'on top of' the weaker broadcasts that are already implemented.

We first give a simple Reliable Broadcast algorithm. We then show how to transform *any* Reliable Broadcast algorithm (not necessarily the one that we present here) into a FIFO Broadcast algorithm. Similarly, we show how to convert any FIFO Broadcast into a Causal Broadcast. By combining these two transformations in sequence, we can convert any Reliable Broadcast algorithm into a Causal Broadcast algorithm.

These transformations also preserve Δ-Timeliness and Uniformity, that is, if the underlying Reliable Broadcast is Timed and/or Uniform, so are the derived FIFO and Causal Broadcasts. Under some assumptions about the synchrony and the failures of the underlying system, our Reliable Broadcast algorithm is indeed

Timed and/or Uniform. Thus, under the same assumptions, the derived FIFO Broadcast and Causal Broadcast will also be Timed and/or Uniform.

We also build Atomic Broadcast algorithms from weaker broadcast primitives by showing how to transform: (i) any Timed Reliable Broadcast into an Atomic Broadcast, (ii) any Atomic Broadcast into a FIFO Atomic Broadcast, (iii) any FIFO Atomic Broadcast into a Causal Atomic Broadcast, and (iv) any Timed Causal Broadcast into a Timed Causal Atomic Broadcast.

Taken together, our set of transformations can be used to take any implementation of (Timed) Reliable Broadcast, the weakest broadcast, and convert it (in many possible ways) into an implementation for any of the broadcasts that we consider. This modular approach has several advantages. The broadcast algorithms are developed incrementally, and so they are smaller, simpler, and easier to understand. The techniques required to achieve each one of the three possible order properties (FIFO, Causal, and Total Order) are shown separately. The proofs are also modular, easier, and 'safer': a broadcast algorithm that invokes a weaker broadcast primitive as a 'black box' can only rely on the *specification* of that 'box', so its proof cannot erroneously rely on a property that is only true for a *particular implementation*.

A hierarchical implementation of stronger broadcasts in terms of weaker ones also increases the portability of the broadcast software. In this section, *only* the algorithms for Reliable Broadcast and Timed Reliable Broadcast rely on specific features of the underlying communications network, such as the particular topology and synchrony. For example, both were designed assuming a point-to-point topology. Thus, these algorithms cannot be 'ported' to other topologies, such as redundant broadcast networks, without significant modifications.

In sharp contrast, *all* the other broadcast algorithms that we describe (from FIFO Broadcast to Causal Atomic Broadcast) do *not* depend on topology or synchrony: they can be ported and executed 'as is' on any system where Reliable Broadcast or Timed Reliable Broadcast are implemented. In other words, if we consider our set of algorithms to be a software package for fault-tolerant broadcasts, the layered construction allows us to port this package from one system to another by reimplementing and fine-tuning only the two lower-level broadcasts, namely Reliable Broadcast (used for FIFO Broadcast and Causal Broadcast), and Timed Reliable Broadcast (used for Atomic Broadcast, FIFO Atomic Broadcast, and Causal Atomic Broadcast). Improving the performance of these two lower-level broadcasts (e.g., by using a better algorithm or hardware support) immediately improves the performance of all the broadcasts that are built 'on top' of them. However, layered implementations may lead to a decrease in efficiency, because they hide specific features of the underlying communications network that may be exploited by certain algorithms.

In this section, we consider only systems with benign failures. In such systems, it is possible to implement broadcast algorithms that satisfy the Uniform versions of the usual properties (as defined in Section 5.3.8). In particular, all the broadcasts that we describe here satisfy the *Uniform* version of Integrity. This is important to our layered approach because to build stronger broadcast primitives from weaker ones, the latter are often required to satisfy Uniform Integrity. For the sake of brevity, for the rest of this section, when we mention a type of broadcast we always assume that it satisfies Uniform Integrity without explicitly saying so.

Given the space limitations, we give only one implementation for each broadcast (usually the simplest, but not necessarily the most efficient one), and we omit all proofs of correctness. Even though our implementations have optimizations that are quite important in practice, their descriptions are omitted or only briefly mentioned here. For a more complete treatment of broadcast algorithms, including other transformations, various optimizations, extensions to severe types of failures, and proofs of correctness, the reader is referred to the forthcoming book by Hadzilacos, Jayanti and Toueg [1993].

Since we build our broadcast primitives in a layered fashion, it is typical for a higher-level broadcast primitive to invoke a lower-level one as a procedure. To disambiguate between the different broadcast primitives used in an algorithm, we introduce the following notation. We first define a short-hand notation for the *type* T of a broadcast. In particular, R stands for Reliable Broadcast, F for FIFO Broadcast, and C for Causal Broadcast. Similarly, A stands for Atomic Broadcast, FA for FIFO Atomic Broadcast, and CA for Causal Atomic Broadcast. We denote by **broadcast**(T, m) and **deliver**(T, m), the two primitives corresponding to a broadcast of type T. Moreover, if a process invokes **broadcast**(T, m), we say that it *T-broadcasts* m; if it executes **deliver**(T, m), we say that it *T-delivers* m. For example, **broadcast**(R, m) is the broadcast primitive for Reliable Broadcast, and if a process invokes **broadcast**(R, m), we say that it R-broadcasts m. Similarly, **deliver**(CA, m) is the delivery primitive for Causal Atomic Broadcast, and if a process executes **deliver**(CA, m), we say that it CA-delivers m. Finally, type T^Δ corresponds to the Timed version of the broadcast of type T, where the superscript Δ denotes the latency. For example, **broadcast**(R^Δ, m) is the broadcast primitive for Timed Reliable Broadcast.

5.4.1   Reliable Broadcast

Reliable Broadcast can be easily implemented in asynchronous systems with benign process and link failures, provided that the underlying communications network does not partition the correct processes. The implementation that we give here is based on a very simple idea. To R-broadcast a message, a process sends it to all its neighbors in the network (including itself). When a process receives a message for the first time, it relays the message to all its neighbors, and then R-delivers it. This 'message diffusion' algorithm is shown in Figure 5.4. Some obvious optimizations are possible (e.g., if p receives m from q, it does not need to relay m to q), but we do not consider such details here.

We assume that the **send**(m) and **receive**(m) primitives used to transmit a message m over a link (say, from process p to process q) satisfy the following two properties:

- *Validity*: If p sends m to q, and both p and q and the link between them are correct, then q eventually receives m.
- *Uniform Integrity*: For any message m, q receives m at most once from p, and only if p previously sent m to q.

Every process p executes the following:
To execute **broadcast**(R, m):
      tag m with *sender*(m) and *seq#*(m)   /* *These tags make m unique* */
      send(m) **to** all neighbors including p

deliver(R, m) *occurs as follows*:
    upon receive(m) **do**
        if p has not previously executed **deliver**(R, m)
        then
            if *sender*(m) ≠ p **then send**(m) **to** all neighbors
            deliver(R, m)

Figure 5.4. Reliable Broadcast using Send and Receive (by message diffusion)

Theorem 1 *Consider an asynchronous system where every two correct processes are connected via a path of processes and links that never fail. The algorithm in Figure 5.4 is a Reliable Broadcast for such a system.*

If we make stronger assumptions about the underlying system, the algorithm in Figure 5.4 satisfies additional properties, such as Uniform Agreement and Δ-Timeliness. This is shown in the next two sections.

5.4.2   Uniform Reliable Broadcast

Under stronger assumptions about process and communication failures, the algorithm in Figure 5.4 satisfies Uniform Agreement. This is because a process always relays a message to all its neighbors *before* delivering it. More precisely:

Theorem 2 *Consider an asynchronous system where processes only fail by receive omission failures, and every process (whether correct or faulty) is connected to every correct process via a path of processes and links that never fail. The algorithm in Figure 5.4 is a Uniform Reliable Broadcast for such a system.*

It is interesting to note that for send omission or more severe failures this algorithm does not guarantee Uniform Agreement. More sophisticated algorithms are required to achieve Uniform Agreement with such failures (Neiger and Toueg [1990]).

5.4.3   Timed Reliable Broadcast

Under some failure and synchrony assumptions about the underlying system, the algorithm in Figure 5.4 satisfies Δ-Timeliness. In particular, assume that the underlying network satisfies the following properties:

1. At most f processes can fail.
2. Every two correct processes are connected via a path of length at most d, consisting entirely of correct processes and links.
3. There is a known upper bound δ on message delay.
4. The time to execute a local step is taken to be zero.[5]

Real-Time Timeliness

Under these assumptions, and *provided there are no timing failures*, there is a known constant Δ such that if the broadcast of m is initiated at real-time t, no correct process delivers m after real-time $t + \Delta$. Thus:

Theorem 3 *With general omission failures and assumptions 1–4, the algorithm in Figure 5.4 is a (Real-Time) Timed Reliable Broadcast with $\Delta = (f + d)\delta$.*

For receive omission failures, the algorithm in Figure 5.4 is actually a *Uniform* (Real-Time) Timed Reliable Broadcast, provided we strengthen Assumption 2 as follows: Every process (correct or faulty) is connected to every correct process via a path of length at most d, consisting entirely of correct processes and links.

Local-Time Timeliness

Now suppose that processes and links *are* subject to timing failures. In this case, no Reliable Broadcast algorithm can guarantee *Real-Time* Δ-Timeliness (see Section 5.3.7). However, we can modify the algorithm in Figure 5.4 so that it satisfies *Local-Time* Δ-Timeliness, provided that some additional assumptions hold. First note that because of timing failures, the upper bound δ applies only to messages between correct processes over correct links (see Section 5.2.3). Now assume that:

5. Clocks of correct processes are approximately synchronized to within ϵ of each other, and their drift with respect to real time is bounded by ρ.

With this assumption, we can now modify the algorithm in Figure 5.4 so that it guarantees Local-Time Δ-Timeliness. When a process wishes to broadcast a message, it tags it with the sending time, according to its clock, and then sends it to all its neighbors. A message also contains a counter that indicates how many links it has traversed so far. When a process p receives a message m that traversed k links, p checks whether the receipt time, according to its clock, minus the sending time (included in m) is greater than $k(\delta(1 + \rho) + \epsilon)$. If so, p simply discards m. Otherwise, p relays m to all neighbors and then delivers it, as in the original algorithm. It can be shown that this modified message-diffusion algorithm is a Timed Reliable Broadcast that satisfies Local-Time Δ-Timeliness.

Theorem 4 *With timing failures and assumptions 1–5, the algorithm in Figure 5.4 as modified above is a (Local-Time) Timed Reliable Broadcast with $\Delta = (f + d)\delta(1 + \rho) + (f + 1)\epsilon$.*

---

[5]For the type of algorithms that we are considering, this assumption is reasonable because the overall local processing time is negligible compared to the message delay δ. Thus, local processing can be absorbed in δ.

Every process p executes the following:
Initialization:

$msgBag := \varnothing$ /* set of messages that p R-delivered
                                                       but not yet F-delivered */

$next[q] := 1$ for all q /* sequence number of next message from q
                                                    that p will F-deliver */

To execute **broadcast**(F, m):
   broadcast(R, m)

deliver(F, m) *occurs as follows*:
   upon deliver(R, m) **do**
      $q := sender(m)$
      $msgBag := msgBag \cup \{m\}$
      while $(\exists\, m' \in msgBag : sender(m') = q$ **and** $seq\#(m') = next[q])$ **do**
         deliver(F, m')
         $next[q] := next[q] + 1$
         $msgBag := msgBag - \{m'\}$

Figure 5.5. Using Reliable Broadcast to build FIFO Broadcast

5.4.4   FIFO Broadcast

It is easy to use Reliable Broadcast to build a FIFO Broadcast algorithm that satisfies Uniform FIFO Order. To F-broadcast a message m, a process q simply R-broadcasts m. Recall that if m is the ith message F-broadcast by q, then m is tagged with $sender(m) = q$ and $seq\#(m) = i$. For each q, every process p maintains a counter $next[q]$ that indicates the sequence number of the next F-broadcast from q that p is willing to F-deliver. When a process p R-delivers m, it puts m in a $msgBag$, and F-delivers all the messages in that set that can now be delivered in FIFO Order. For example, suppose p already F-delivered messages tagged 1 and 2 from q (i.e., $next[q] = 3$), and p's $msgBag$ contains messages tagged 4, 5, and 8 from q. If p R-delivers message m with $sender(m) = q$ and $seq\#(m) = 3$, p F-delivers m and then messages tagged 4 and 5 from q. This algorithm, which ensures Uniform FIFO Order, is given in Figure 5.5. Several obvious optimizations, such as keeping a separate $msgBag$ for each sender, can be made.

It is important to note that this FIFO Broadcast algorithm relies only on the correctness of the Reliable Broadcast primitive that it invokes. Thus, it requires *no* assumptions on the network topology, the synchrony of the system, or the type or number of benign failures.

Theorem 5 *Given a Reliable Broadcast algorithm, the algorithm in Figure 5.5 is a FIFO Broadcast that satisfies Uniform FIFO Order. Furthermore, if the Reliable Broadcast satisfies Uniform Agreement or Δ-Timeliness, then so does the derived FIFO Broadcast.*[6]

---

[6]The preservation of Local-Time Δ-Timeliness requires local clocks that are monotonically increasing.

Every process p executes the following:
Initialization:
     $prevDlvrs := \perp$ */* sequence of messages that p C-delivered since its previous C-broadcast */*

To execute **broadcast(C, m):**
     broadcast(F, $\langle prevDlvrs \parallel m \rangle$)
     $prevDlvrs := \perp$

deliver(C, m) *occurs as follows:*
    upon deliver(F, $\langle m_1, m_2, \ldots, m_l \rangle$) *for some l* **do**
        for $i := 1 .. l$ **do**
            if p has not previously executed **deliver**(C, m_i)
            then
                deliver(C, m_i)
                $prevDlvrs := prevDlvrs \parallel m_i$

Figure 5.6. Causal Broadcast using FIFO Broadcast (with Uniform FIFO Order)

5.4.5 Causal Broadcast

In Figure 5.6, we use FIFO Broadcast to construct a Causal Broadcast algorithm. This algorithm works as follows. To C-broadcast a message m, a process p uses the given FIFO Broadcast algorithm to F-broadcast the sequence of messages $prevDlvrs \parallel m$, where $prevDlvrs$ is the sequence of messages that p C-delivered since its previous C-broadcast ('$\parallel$' is the concatenation operator). When a process q F-delivers such a sequence, q C-delivers all the messages in the sequence that it did not previously C-deliver. The correctness of this algorithm requires that the given FIFO Broadcast algorithm satisfies *Uniform* FIFO Order.

This Causal Broadcast algorithm relies only on the properties of the FIFO Broadcast algorithm that it uses. In particular, it makes no assumptions about system synchrony or network topology, and it works for any type and number of benign failures.

Theorem 6 *Given a FIFO Broadcast algorithm that satisfies Uniform FIFO Order, the algorithm in Figure 5.6 is a Causal Broadcast that satisfies Uniform Causal Order. Furthermore, if the given FIFO Broadcast satisfies Uniform Agreement or Δ-Timeliness, then so does the derived Causal Broadcast.*

5.4.6 Atomic Broadcast

As we saw in the previous sections, Reliable Broadcast, FIFO Broadcast, and Causal Broadcast can be implemented in asynchronous systems with benign failures. In sharp contrast, there are no deterministic Atomic Broadcast algorithms for asynchronous systems, even if we assume that at most one process may fail, and that

Every process p executes the following:
To execute **broadcast**(A^{Δ}, m):
    broadcast(R^{Δ}, m)

deliver(A^{Δ}, m) *occurs as follows*:
    upon deliver(R^{Δ}, m) **do**
        schedule deliver(A^{Δ}, m) **at time** $ts(m) + \Delta$

Figure 5.7. Timed Atomic Broadcast using Timed Reliable Broadcast

it can only fail by crashing. This is because Consensus can be reduced to Atomic Broadcast (see Section 5.7.2), and it is well-known that there are no deterministic algorithms for Consensus in such systems (see Section 5.8). However, Atomic Broadcast can be implemented in synchronous systems, and we give one such implementation below.

In Figure 5.7, we show how to use any Timed Reliable Broadcast (that satisfies Local-Time Δ-Timeliness) to construct a Timed Atomic Broadcast. If p wishes to A-broadcast m, it simply R-broadcasts m. When a process R-delivers m, it schedules its A-delivery at local time $ts(m) + \Delta$ (recall that $ts(m)$ is the sending time of m according to the sender's clock, and Δ is the Timeliness bound on message latency guaranteed by the given Timed Reliable Broadcast). If two or more messages are scheduled to be A-delivered at the same local time then they are A-delivered in an *a priori* agreed order, for instance, in increasing order of the senders' ids. If a process R-delivers m after local time $ts(m) + \Delta$, then it never A-delivers m.

We assume that the local clocks of all processes are monotonically increasing, and given any T, each local clock eventually reaches time T.[6] The Timed Atomic Broadcast algorithm relies solely on this assumption and on the correctness of the Timed Reliable Broadcast primitive that it invokes. No other assumptions (e.g., network topology, synchrony, or the type or number of benign failures) are necessary.

Theorem 7 *Given a (Local-Time) Timed Reliable Broadcast algorithm in a system with clocks that satisfy the monotonicity assumption, the algorithm in Figure 5.7 is a (Local-Time) Timed Atomic Broadcast.*

Two observations are now in order. First, it is easy to implement a (Local-Time) Timed Reliable Broadcast algorithm in synchronous systems with approximately synchronized clocks (cf. Section 5.2.1). In fact, we described one such implementation for a system with timing failures at the end of Section 5.4.3. Moreover, most clock synchronization algorithms give approximately synchronized clocks that satisfy the monotonicity assumption required by the algorithm in Figure 5.7.

---

[6]The clock of a process that crashes is only required to monotonically increase until the crash occurs.

We conclude that this algorithm can be used to implement a Timed Atomic Broadcast in synchronous systems. Our second observation is that (Local-Time) Timed Reliable Broadcast *cannot* be implemented in an *asynchronous* system where local clocks satisfy the monotonicity assumption: Figure 5.7 would transform this implementation into an Atomic Broadcast algorithm for asynchronous systems, and, as we noted before, such an algorithm does not exist.

The Timed Atomic Broadcast obtained by the reduction in Figure 5.7 actually satisfies the *Uniform* versions of Δ-Timeliness and Total Order. Thus, if we 'plug in' a Timed Reliable Broadcast that satisfies *Uniform* Agreement, then we obtain a Uniform Timed Atomic Broadcast.

5.4.7   FIFO Atomic Broadcast

The algorithm in Figure 5.7 does *not* satisfy FIFO Order, as the following scenario shows. A process broadcasts m_1, but fails during that broadcast and no process delivers m_1. It then broadcasts m_2, and behaves correctly during that broadcast: all correct processes now could deliver m_2 — thereby violating FIFO Order. However, it is easy to transform any Atomic Broadcast into a FIFO Atomic Broadcast by using sequence numbers to A-deliver messages in the order in which they were A-broadcast by each sender. This is exactly the same technique that we used in Section 5.4.4 to transform any Reliable Broadcast into a FIFO Broadcast, and we omit the details here.

5.4.8   Causal Atomic Broadcast

We give two Causal Atomic Broadcast algorithms: one is built from Timed Causal Broadcast, and the other from FIFO Atomic Broadcast.

From Timed Causal Broadcast

The transformation used in Section 5.4.6 to convert a Timed Reliable Broadcast into a Timed Atomic Broadcast can also transform any Timed Causal Broadcast into a Timed Causal Atomic Broadcast. This Timed Causal Atomic Broadcast algorithm, shown in Figure 5.8, requires no assumptions other than the monotonicity of local clocks as given in Section 5.4.6. In particular, it works for any type and number of benign failures.

Theorem 8 *Given a (Local-Time) Timed Causal Broadcast algorithm in a system with clocks that satisfy the monotonicity assumption, the algorithm in Figure 5.8 is a (Local-Time) Timed Causal Atomic Broadcast. Furthermore, if the Timed Causal Broadcast is Uniform, then so is the derived Timed Causal Atomic Broadcast.*

From FIFO Atomic Broadcast

In Figure 5.9, we use FIFO Atomic Broadcast to construct a Causal Atomic Broadcast algorithm. This algorithm works as follows. Each process keeps track of two sets: the set of messages that it has CA-delivered since its previous CA-broadcast, called

Every process p executes the following:
To execute **broadcast**(CA$^\Delta$, *m*):
    broadcast(C$^\Delta$, *m*)

deliver(CA$^\Delta$, *m*) *occurs as follows*:
    upon deliver(C$^\Delta$, *m*) **do**
        schedule deliver(CA$^\Delta$, *m*) **at time** *ts*(*m*) + Δ

Figure 5.8. Timed Causal Atomic Broadcast using Timed Causal Broadcast

prevDlvrs, and the set of processes it suspects of being faulty. To CA-broadcast a message *m*, a process uses the given FIFO Atomic Broadcast algorithm to FA-broadcast *m* together with *prevDlvrs*. When a process *p* FA-delivers a message *m* with the associated *D* (*D* is the value of the sender's *prevDlvrs* variable at the time it CA-broadcast *m*), *p* checks that the sender of *m* is not in its set of suspects, and that it has previously CA-delivered all the messages in *D*. If so, *p* CA-delivers *m*; otherwise, *p* adds the sender of *m* to its set of suspects.

This Causal Atomic Broadcast algorithm works for any type and number of benign failures. In fact, it relies only on the properties of the FIFO Atomic Broadcast algorithm that it uses. In particular, it makes no assumptions about system synchrony or network topology.

Theorem 9 *Given a FIFO Atomic Broadcast algorithm, the algorithm in Figure 5.9 is a Causal Atomic Broadcast. Furthermore, if the FIFO Atomic Broadcast satisfies Uniform Agreement or Δ-Timeliness, then so does the derived Causal Atomic Broadcast.*

Several optimizations can be made. For example, the algorithm in Figure 5.9 requires a process *p* to 'piggyback' on each broadcast the set *prevDlvrs* of all messages that *p* CA-delivered since its previous CA-broadcast. We can modify the algorithm so that *p* piggybacks only a vector of integers that indicates how many messages *p* CA-delivered from each process since its last CA-broadcast. These and other optimizations are described in Hadzilacos, Jayanti and Toueg [1993].

Bibliographic Notes

The algorithm for Timed Reliable Broadcast with timing failures (see Theorem 4 in Section 5.4.3), and the Timed Atomic Broadcast algorithm in Figure 5.7 are based on Cristian *et al.* [1985]. The remaining algorithms are novel, as is the methodology of building more powerful broadcast primitives by using simpler ones as 'black boxes'. Many other broadcast algorithms are known, including those described by Chang and Maxemchuk [1984], Babaoğlu and Drummond [1985], Birman and Joseph [1987], Peterson, Bucholz and Schlichting [1989], Gopal *et al.* [1990], Veríssimo and Marques [1990], Birman, Schiper and Stephenson [1991], Garcia-Molina and Spauster [1991] and Amir *et al.* [1992].

Every process p executes the following:
Initialization:
    $prevDlvrs := \emptyset$ /* *set of messages that p CA-delivered*
                                                       since its previous CA-broadcast */
    $suspects := \emptyset$ /* *processes that p suspects to be faulty* */

To execute **broadcast**(CA, *m*):
    broadcast(FA, $\langle m, prevDlvrs \rangle$)
    $prevDlvrs := \emptyset$

deliver(CA, *m*) *occurs as follows*:
    upon deliver(FA, $\langle m, D \rangle$) **do**
        if *sender(m)* $\notin$ *suspects* **and**
            p has previously executed **deliver**(CA, *m′*) for all $m' \in D$
        then
            deliver(CA, *m*)
            $prevDlvrs := prevDlvrs \cup \{m\}$
        else   /* *either p or sender(m) is faulty* */
            discard *m*
            $suspects := suspects \cup \{sender(m)\}$

Figure 5.9. Causal Atomic Broadcast using FIFO Atomic Broadcast

5.5 Terminating Reliable Broadcast

Recall that with Reliable Broadcast, any process is allowed to broadcast any message, from a set $\mathcal{M}$ of possible messages, at any time. In particular, processes have no *a priori* knowledge of the impending broadcasts. Thus, as we noted before, if a process *p* fails immediately after invoking the broadcast primitive, the correct processes cannot be expected to deliver any message, as they were not even aware of *p*'s intention to broadcast before it crashed.

In contrast, in some applications we can assume that there is a single sender that wishes to broadcast a single message. Furthermore, we can also assume that processes know the sender's identity and its intention to broadcast some message. For example, a real-time distributed control system may have a temperature sensor process that is supposed to reliably broadcast the temperature at known times, say every minute, to three monitoring processes. Each such broadcast can be considered to be an independent instance of Terminating Reliable Broadcast, a type of broadcast that requires correct processes to *always* deliver a message — even if the sender is faulty and, say, crashes before the broadcast. The message delivered could be the special message SF $\notin$ $\mathcal{M}$ indicating that the sender is faulty. Thus, the set of messages that can be delivered is $\mathcal{M} \cup \{$SF$\}$.

The specification of Terminating Reliable Broadcast is very similar to that of Reliable Broadcast, except that it has the additional property that correct processes always deliver a message (*Termination*). Also, the Integrity requirement is slightly weakened, to allow processes to deliver SF, a message that is never actually broadcast. Thus, *Terminating Reliable Broadcast* is specified as follows:

- *Termination*: Every correct process eventually delivers some message.
- *Validity*: If the sender is correct and broadcasts a message m, then all correct processes eventually deliver m.
- *Agreement*: If a correct process delivers a message m, then all correct processes eventually deliver m.
- *Integrity*: Every correct process delivers at most one message, and if it delivers $m \neq$ SF then the sender must have broadcast m.

Terminating Reliable Broadcast has been studied extensively in the case of arbitrary failures under the name of *Byzantine Agreement* or *Byzantine Generals' Problem*. With such failures, the second clause of Integrity is problematic: since the sender may be subject to arbitrary failures during broadcasts, the meaning of 'the sender must have broadcast m' is not always clear. Even if the sender invokes *broadcast*(m), the external behavior of this invocation may look like an invocation of *broadcast*(m') to some or all other processes, and vice-versa. Thus, in the case of arbitrary failures, the second clause of Integrity is dropped from the requirement.[7]

The reader should verify that the specification of Terminating Reliable Broadcast implies that a correct process delivers SF only if the sender is faulty. We can define *Timed Terminating Reliable Broadcast*, and, for benign failures, *Uniform Terminating Reliable Broadcast*, just as we did with Reliable Broadcast.

5.6   Consensus

In Terminating Reliable Broadcast, a single process is supposed to broadcast a message, and all correct processes must agree on that message. In the Consensus problem, all correct processes propose a value, and must agree on some value related to the proposed values. We define the Consensus problem in terms of two primitives, *propose*(v) and *decide*(v), where v is a value. When a process invokes *propose*(v), we say that it *proposes* v; similarly, when a process executes *decide*(v), we say that it *decides* v.[8] We denote by $\mathcal{V}$ the set of all values that may be proposed. The set of all values that may be decided is $\mathcal{V} \cup \{\text{NU}\}$, where NU $\notin \mathcal{V}$ is a special value indicating that not all processes proposed the same value ('NU' stands for 'no unanimity'). The *Consensus* problem is specified as follows:

- *Termination*: Every correct process eventually decides some value.
- *Validity*: If all processes that propose a value, propose v, then all correct processes eventually decide v.
- *Agreement*: If a correct process decides v, then all correct processes eventually decide v.

---

[7]Equivalently, we could adopt the convention that, with arbitrary failures, if a process p is faulty then the statement "p broadcasts m" is true for *all* $m \in \mathcal{M}$: With this convention, the above formulation of Terminating Reliable Broadcast holds for all types of failures.

[8]As with the broadcast problem, in the case of arbitrary failures, we adopt the following convention: if p is faulty, the statement "p proposes v" is true for all $v \in \mathcal{V}$.

- *Integrity*: Every correct process decides at most one value, and if it decides $v \neq$ NU then some process must have proposed v.

Validity dictates the decision when there is unanimity in the proposed values. If the proposed values are not the same, the second clause of Integrity ensures that the decision value is not created 'out of thin air'. Validity and Integrity, together with the fact that no process can propose NU, imply that a correct process decides NU only if there are two processes that proposed different values.

In some cases, it is useful to require the following stronger version of Validity:

- *Strong Validity*: If all *correct* processes propose v, then all correct processes eventually decide v.

Similarly, the following stronger version of Integrity is sometimes needed (e.g., see Section 5.7.2):

- *Strong Integrity*: Every correct process decides at most one value, and if it decides v then some process must have proposed v.

With this property, correct processes never have the option of deciding NU, even if there is no unanimity in the proposed values. In the case of benign failures, we can also define Uniform versions of Agreement, Integrity and Strong Integrity in a straightforward manner. When we use Consensus with one of these stronger properties we shall explicitly say so.

5.7 Relations among Problems

In this section we examine the relation between Consensus and Terminating Reliable Broadcast, and between Consensus and Atomic Broadcast. In each case, we shall see that the two problems are, under certain conditions, equivalent to each other. The technical tool that allows us to show equivalence between problems is the notion of *reduction*.

Generally speaking, we say that a problem $\mathcal{B}$ *reduces to* problem $\mathcal{A}$ if there is an algorithm $T_{\mathcal{A} \to \mathcal{B}}$ which transforms *any* algorithm for $\mathcal{A}$ into an algorithm for $\mathcal{B}$. We have already seen several such reductions in Section 5.4. For example, Figure 5.6 shows an algorithm that transforms any algorithm for FIFO Broadcast into one for Causal Broadcast. This is just a reduction of Causal Broadcast to FIFO Broadcast. Informally, a reduction of $\mathcal{B}$ to $\mathcal{A}$, sometimes written $\mathcal{B} \preceq \mathcal{A}$, shows that $\mathcal{B}$ is 'no harder' than $\mathcal{A}$. Two problems are *equivalent* if each is reducible to the other.

The correctness of a reduction algorithm $T_{\mathcal{A} \to \mathcal{B}}$ may rely on some assumptions about the system model, such as synchrony, network topology, the type and number of failures that may occur, etc. If we 'plug-in' a particular algorithm A for $\mathcal{A}$ into this reduction, we get an algorithm B for $\mathcal{B}$ that, in general, is only guaranteed to work in those systems that satisfy all the assumptions that algorithms A and $T_{\mathcal{A} \to \mathcal{B}}$ require. For example, suppose that algorithm A works in any system where fewer than a third of the processes fail, and that it tolerates arbitrary failures. Furthermore, suppose that the reduction algorithm $T_{\mathcal{A} \to \mathcal{B}}$ requires a synchronous system, that it works with any number of failures, and it assumes that all failures are benign. In general, the algorithm B that results from A by this reduction is only guaranteed to work in synchronous systems where fewer than a third of the processes fail and only benign failures occur.

In the next two sections we consider reductions between Consensus on one hand, and Terminating Reliable Broadcast and Atomic Broadcast on the other. These reductions are only informally described here. For a detailed treatment the reader is referred to Hadzilacos, Jayanti and Toueg [1993].

5.7.1 Relating Consensus and Terminating Reliable Broadcast

First consider the reduction of Consensus to Terminating Reliable Broadcast (abbreviated to TRB in this section). To solve Consensus, each process first uses TRB to broadcast the value it wishes to propose. When a process delivers a value from a process q, it inserts that value into entry $V[q]$ of a vector V that has one entry per process. Once all the entries of V have been filled, the process decides the first non-SF value in V.

This reduction works in any system where only benign failures occur. In particular, it makes no assumptions on the system synchrony or topology, or the number of process and link failures that may occur. With a simple modification, it can be made to tolerate even arbitrary failures, provided that a majority of the processes are correct.

Now consider the reduction of TRB to Consensus. In contrast to the above reduction of Consensus to TRB, it requires a synchronous system, and *a priori* knowledge of the time t_0 at which the sender is supposed to broadcast. Furthermore, it assumes a completely connected network, and no link failures.

To broadcast a message m, the sender sends m to all processes at the designated time t_0. Recall that δ is the bound on message transmission time over a link. If a process receives m within the expected time, $t_0 + \delta$, it uses the given Consensus algorithm to propose m, otherwise it proposes SF. To deliver a message, a process waits for the decision of the Consensus algorithm: if the decision value is other than NU, it delivers that value; otherwise it delivers SF.

This reduction tolerates any number of sending omission failures, but it does not work with receive omission failures. However, if the given Consensus algorithm satisfies Strong Validity, then the reduction works even for arbitrary failures.

From these two reductions we conclude the following:

- In *synchronous* systems, Consensus is *equivalent* to TRB. This allows us to translate both positive and negative results proven for one problem, to the other. For example, the transformation from Consensus to TRB is message- and time-efficient. In particular, it can convert any constant-time randomized Consensus algorithm (such as the one in Feldman and Micali [1990]), into a constant-time randomized TRB algorithm.
- In *asynchronous* systems, these two problems are not equivalent: Consensus is reducible to TRB, but the converse does not hold. This is because Consensus is solvable with randomization, while we can show that TRB is not solvable even with randomization.

5.7.2   Relating Consensus and Atomic Broadcast

Consensus can be easily reduced to Atomic Broadcast as follows. To propose a value, a process A-broadcasts it. To decide a value, a process picks the value of the first message that it A-delivers. By Total Order of Atomic Broadcast, all correct processes choose the same value; hence Agreement of Consensus is satisfied. The other properties of Consensus are also easy to verify. This reduction makes no assumptions on the system synchrony or topology, and it tolerates any number of benign failures.

It is also possible to reduce Atomic Broadcast to Consensus in systems with crash failures (Chandra and Toueg [1991]). This reduction is beyond the scope of this chapter. Here we only remark that it makes no assumptions on the system synchrony or topology, and it tolerates any number of crash failures. However, it requires that Reliable Broadcast be solvable in the system, and that the given Consensus algorithm satisfy Strong Integrity.

Thus, these two reductions imply that Consensus and Atomic Broadcast are equivalent in *asynchronous* systems with crash failures. This equivalence has important consequences regarding the solvability of Atomic Broadcast in such systems:

1. Atomic Broadcast *cannot* be solved with a deterministic algorithm in asynchronous systems, even if we assume that at most one process may fail, and it can only fail by crashing. This is because Consensus has no deterministic solution in such systems.
2. Atomic Broadcast can be solved using *randomization* or *failure detectors* in asynchronous systems. This is because Consensus is solvable with these techniques in such systems.

This matter is discussed in more detail in the following section.

5.8   Consensus and Atomic Broadcast in Asynchronous Systems

One of the fundamental results about fault-tolerant distributed computing is the impossibility of Consensus in asynchronous systems (Fischer, Lynch and Paterson [1985]). More precisely, this result asserts that there is no deterministic algorithm that solves Consensus in an asynchronous system and tolerates *even a single crash failure*. Furthermore, this results holds even if the communication network is completely connected and reliable. That is, a message sent by a process will eventually be received, provided that the recipient keeps trying to receive it.

This result has many important theoretical and practical implications. The asynchronous model of computation is especially popular in practice because it is easy to support and has straightforward semantics, and because unpredictable workloads are sources of asynchrony in many real systems — thereby rendering any synchrony assumptions valid only probabilistically. Thus, the impossibility of achieving Consensus reveals a serious limitation of this model for fault-tolerant applications. Because Consensus is such a fundamental problem, researchers have investigated various ways of circumventing the impossibility result. We now briefly present some of the fruits of these studies.

The impossibility result only rules out *deterministic* algorithms for Consensus. Soon after the result was published, it was established that one way of avoiding it is by using randomization. This is a dramatic illustration of the power of randomization in distributed algorithms.

Another direction of research that was motivated by the impossibility of Consensus in asynchronous systems was the investigation of various models of *partial* synchrony. The starting point here is the recognition that asynchrony has a variety of causes: processes may take steps asynchronously; messages may be reordered; or the message delay may be unbounded. Still other possibilities exist: the maximum message delay may be bounded, but the bound may be unknown; or the bound may be known, but messages may be subject to longer delays for some initial period of unknown duration. These considerations have led to a detailed study of several models of partial synchrony, and a precise demarcation of the boundary between those models in which Consensus is solvable, and those in which it is not.

In an asynchronous system, a process that has crashed cannot be distinguished by the other processes from one that is extremely slow. The inability of correct processes to accurately determine which processes are really faulty is at the heart of the impossibility of reaching Consensus. This observation led to another way of getting around the impossibility of Consensus; namely, by extending the asynchronous model of computation with unreliable *failure detectors*. Informally, a failure detector is a distributed 'oracle' that gives (possibly incorrect) hints about which processes may have crashed so far. Each process has access to a local *failure detector module* that monitors other processes in the system, and maintains a set of ones that it currently suspects to have crashed. Each process periodically consults its failure detector module and can use the set of suspects returned in solving Consensus.

A failure detector module can make mistakes by erroneously adding processes to its set of suspects: that is, it can suspect that a process p has crashed even though p is still running. If it later believes that suspecting p was a mistake, it can remove p from its set of suspects. Thus, each module may repeatedly add and remove processes from its set of suspects. Furthermore, at any given time the failure detector modules at two different processes may have different sets of suspects. It is important to note that the mistakes made by a failure detector should not prevent any correct process from behaving according to specification. It turns out that Consensus can be solved even with failure detectors that are very weak — for instance, even with ones that can make an infinite number of mistakes!

Because of the equivalence between Consensus and Atomic Broadcast in asynchronous systems, both the impossibility of Consensus and the ways of circumventing it also apply to Atomic Broadcast. Since Consensus is reducible to Atomic Broadcast, the impossibility of Consensus immediately implies the impossibility of Atomic Broadcast: there is no deterministic algorithm for Atomic Broadcast — even one that tolerates a single crash failure. Note that this is *not* true for Reliable Broadcast, FIFO Broadcast or Causal Broadcast. All these types of broadcasts *can* be implemented deterministically in asynchronous systems subject to benign failures. In fact, such algorithms were given in Section 5.4.

On the other hand, as mentioned in Section 5.7.2, Atomic Broadcast is reducible to Consensus in any system (subject to crash failures) where Reliable Broadcast can be solved. Thus, Atomic Broadcast can be implemented in asynchronous systems by using randomized algorithms, or by using failure detectors, or in partially synchronous models where Consensus is solvable. As an example, take any randomized algorithm for Consensus that works in asynchronous systems, such as the one described in (Ben-Or [1983]). By 'plugging' this into the generic algorithm that transforms Consensus to Atomic Broadcast, we obtain a randomized algorithm for Atomic Broadcast. The same transformation can be used by 'plugging in' Consensus algorithms that rely on failure detectors or on partial synchrony.

The impossibility of Atomic Broadcast in asynchronous systems seems paradoxical since this primitive is a basic service provided by many practical systems which, on the face of it, appear to be asynchronous. (Such systems include Isis (Birman et al. [1990]; Birman and Joseph [1987]), Psync (Peterson, Bucholz and Schlichting [1989]), Amoeba (Kaashoek [1992]), Delta-4 (Veríssimo and Marques [1990]), and Transis (Amir et al. [1992]).) There is no contradiction here. What this indicates is that such systems, at some level, explicitly or implicitly make use of one of the mechanisms previously mentioned for circumventing the impossibility result. For example, the Isis Atomic Broadcast algorithm uses a failure detector based on timeouts. This means that it relies, at some level, on synchrony assumptions.

Another way of dealing with the impossibility result is to consider weaker problems that are solvable (deterministically) in asynchronous systems. One such problem is *Approximate Consensus*, a weaker variant of Consensus. Intuitively, it requires that correct processes decide on values that are within ϵ of each other, where $\epsilon > 0$ is a pre-specified tolerance, within the range of the proposed values.

We close this section with a word of caution against confusing the impossibility of Consensus in asynchronous systems with a seemingly similar but, in fact, quite different impossibility result in fault tolerant distributed computing, sometimes known as *the generals' paradox* (Gray [1978]). This concerns a problem, technically known as Non-Blocking Atomic Commitment,[9] that is similar to Consensus, but in a model of computation which makes very weak assumptions about communication. More precisely, in this model it is possible for the network to partition into two or more components, so that no messages can be exchanged between processes in different components. Under these assumptions, Non-Blocking Atomic Commitment (as well as Consensus) is not solvable. However, the reason underlying this unsolvability result is the possibility of a partition — not asynchrony. In fact, this result works even in synchronous systems, where each message is either delivered within a known bound or not at all. In contrast, the impossibility of Consensus is due to the asynchrony of the system, and works even if communication is guaranteed to be reliable. The difference in the reasons underlying these two impossibility results is reflected in their proofs, which are based on entirely different ideas.

---

[9] This problem arises in transaction processing in distributed databases. For related papers, in addition to Gray [1978], see Skeen [1982], Halpern and Moses [1990] and Chapter 6.

Bibliographic Notes

Fischer, Lynch and Paterson [1985] proved the basic result that Consensus is not solvable deterministically in asynchronous systems. Soon after this result was first published, it was shown that Consensus can be solved with randomized algorithms in asynchronous systems. Such algorithms include Ben-Or [1983], Rabin [1983], Bracha [1987], and are surveyed by Chor and Dwork [1989].

The key papers on partial synchrony are Dolev, Dwork and Stockmeyer [1987] and Dwork, Lynch and Stockmeyer [1988]. The former considers a space of 32 models of partially synchrony based on five key operational characteristics of a distributed system, and determines in which models Consensus is solvable deterministically and in which it is not. The latter deals with partial synchrony as a result of timing uncertainty.

Unreliable failure detectors were introduced by Chandra and Toueg [1991], who gave Consensus algorithms based on failure detectors of varying strength. Chandra, Hadzilacos and Toueg [1992] determines the weakest failure detector that can be used to solve Consensus. Ricciardi and Birman [1991] consider failure detectors in the context of the Group-Membership problem.

Approximate Consensus was first considered by Dolev *et al.* [1986], and subsequently by Fekete [1990, 1993]. Other fault-tolerant agreement-like problems that are solvable in asynchronous systems are described in Attiya *et al.* [1987] and Bridgland and Watro [1987]. Biran, Moran and Zaks [1988] gives a graph-theoretic characterization of the problems that can be solved (deterministically) in asynchronous systems with one crash failure.

5.9 Complexity Results

There is a variety of complexity measures that we may be interested in when judging the efficiency of a distributed algorithm. Key among these are the amount of *time* and the number of *messages* required by the algorithm. When considering a fault-tolerant algorithm, in particular, another criterion of efficacy is its *robustness*, or *fault-tolerance*, which can be measured as the fraction of faulty processes that the algorithm can tolerate, or as the connectivity of the network that it requires. In this section we present some results about the complexity and robustness of the problems we have been discussing.

As before, let n be the number of processes in the system and f, $1 \leq f \leq n$, be a parameter that indicates the *maximum* number of faulty processes that we wish to tolerate.

5.9.1 Fault-Tolerance

In this section we consider the fault-tolerance of Terminating Reliable Broadcast and Consensus algorithms. It turns out that this attribute is not affected by randomization. That is, the lower bounds on fault-tolerance that we mention hold even if we allow randomized algorithms; while the upper bounds can be achieved with deterministic algorithms. Thus, we ignore the issue of randomization in this section.

In the case of *arbitrary failures*, there is a limit to the fraction of faulty processes that any Terminating Reliable Broadcast or Consensus algorithm can tolerate. More specifically, if $n \leq 3f$, there is no algorithm that tolerates arbitrary failures for either one of these problems. This is so even if the system is synchronous, the network is fully connected, and no link failures occur. This bound on robustness is quite sensitive to the type of failure. It does not hold for more restricted types of failures than arbitrary ones. In particular, even for arbitrary failures with message authentication (and, *a fortiori*, for benign failures), both problems are solvable with any number of faulty processes. This result is tight, since there are algorithms that can solve these problems in synchronous systems, if $n > 3f$.

Another bound on fault-tolerance concerns the connectivity of the communications network[10] that is required for solving Terminating Reliable Broadcast and Consensus. These problems cannot be solved in a system subject to *arbitrary failures*, if the underlying network has connectivity $\kappa \leq 2f$. This is true even if the system is synchronous, and there are no link failures. In the case of benign failures, the problems are unsolvable if the network has connectivity $\kappa \leq f$. For both types of failures, the bounds are tight: the problems can be solved in synchronous systems if $\kappa > 2f$ for arbitrary failures, and if $\kappa > f$ for benign failures.

Another interesting lower bound on fault-tolerance concerns Reliable Broadcast, Terminating Reliable Broadcast and Consensus with Uniform Agreement. These problems cannot be solved if $n \leq 2f$ in the case of *general omission* (or more severe) failures. This is so even if the system is synchronous, the network is fully connected, and there are no link failures. This result is also tight: if $n > 2f$, all three problems can be solved in the case of general omission failures. Therefore, for general omission failures, there is a cost associated with achieving Uniform Agreement: to tolerate f faulty processes we need a system with more than $2f$ processes. In contrast, the Uniform counterparts of Integrity, Timeliness, and the various Order properties, can be achieved without a majority of correct processes.

5.9.2 Time Complexity

In this section we consider the time complexity of the problems we have been discussing. In asynchronous systems it is not clear what is an appropriate measure of time. Although several definitions have been proposed, it is a matter of controversy which, if any, is the 'right' one. We sidestep this issue by only considering synchronous systems when discussing time complexity.

To study time complexity it is convenient to introduce a particular model of synchrony, called the *synchronous round* model. In this model, we assume that all clocks are perfectly synchronized and tick at discrete instants $0, 1, 2, \ldots$ The time interval between ticks $i - 1$ and i is called the *ith round*. During a round, each process takes the following actions in the specified order:

---

[10]The connectivity of a network is the smallest number of nodes whose removal disconnects the network.

1. It sends messages to (some subset of) its neighbors.
2. It receives messages sent to it by its neighbors at the beginning of *that* round.
3. It changes its local state on the basis of its present state and the messages it received.

Frequently, the synchronous round model is used in conjunction with the assumptions that the communication network is completely connected, and that no link failures occur. In this case, any pair of correct processes can exchange messages in one round. In this section we also adopt these assumptions except when we explicitly disavow them.

First consider Terminating Reliable Broadcast and Consensus in this model. In a Terminating Reliable Broadcast algorithm we assume that the sender (if it is correct) broadcasts its message in round 1. We say that an execution of the algorithm *terminates* at the earliest round by which *all* correct processes have delivered their message. Similarly, in Consensus we assume that all correct processes propose their values in round 1, and say that an execution of the algorithm terminates at the earliest round by which *all* correct processes have reached their decision. Thus, a natural way of formulating the question of time complexity for such algorithms is in terms of the number of rounds required for termination.

The results on time complexity are identical for both Terminating Reliable Broadcast and Consensus since there are round-preserving mutual reductions between the two problems. Therefore, we shall use the word 'algorithm' to mean 'algorithm for Terminating Reliable Broadcast or Consensus' until, later in the section, we turn our attention to other problems.

The first result is that, in the worst-case execution, at least $f + 1$ rounds are required, even for crash failures. More precisely, for any algorithm that tolerates crash failures, there is an execution in which at most f processes fail and termination does not occur before round $f + 1$. Of course, this lower bounds applies, *a fortiori*, to more severe types of failures. Furthermore, this bound is tight: for each type of failure there are algorithms that terminate by round $f + 1$ in any execution with at most f faulty processes.

It is important to understand that the $f + 1$ bound on the round complexity is a *worst-case* bound. It does not imply that this delay must be incurred in *every* execution; only that it cannot be avoided in *some* execution. In particular, this result does not rule out the possibility of so-called early-stopping algorithms. Informally, these guarantee faster termination in executions where fewer failures occur. More precisely, an algorithm is *early-stopping* if termination occurs in time proportional to the number of processes that *actually* fail — rather than the *maximum* number of process failures that the algorithm was designed to tolerate.

The philosophy underlying early-stopping algorithms is that, to the extent possible, the cost of tolerating failures should be incurred only when failures occur; and then only to a degree that depends on the actual number of failures. Since, in practice, it is very rare that many processes fail during the course of a single execution, early-stopping algorithms are especially significant. The worst-case lower bound immediately implies that for any early-stopping algorithm there is some execution in which f' processes actually fail and termination does not occur before round $f' + 1$, for any $0 \le f' \le f$. In addition, it is possible to show that there is such an execution in which correct processes do not *halt* before round $f' + 2$. (A process cannot necessarily halt immediately after delivering a message; its participation in the algorithm may still be required to assist other processes to deliver that message.) More precisely, it can be shown that there is some execution in which f' processes actually fail, but correct processes do not halt before round $\min(f' + 2, f + 1)$. This bound holds even for crash failures (and *a fortiori* for more severe ones) and is tight.

The previously mentioned bounds on the number of rounds apply only to *deterministic* algorithms. With *randomized* algorithms, Terminating Reliable Broadcast and Consensus can be achieved in *constant expected* number of rounds, even for arbitrary failures. Note that the expected termination time for such algorithms is independent of the maximum and even the actual number of failures! This is another illustration of the power of randomization in distributed computing.

We now turn our attention to Timed Reliable Broadcast. Recall that the specification of this problem includes the Δ-Timeliness property, where the latency Δ is the maximum delay that a message can experience, if it is delivered at all. For this problem, the most natural way of defining time complexity is in terms of latency: what is the minimum latency that a Timed Reliable Broadcast algorithm can guarantee? Consider the synchronous round model first, and assume, as before, that the network is completely connected and there are no link failures. Then the lower bound of $f + 1$ rounds for Terminating Reliable Broadcast also implies that the latency of Timed Reliable Broadcast is at least $f + 1$ rounds in the worst case, even for crash failures.

Now consider a more general setting, where the network need not be completely connected, and suppose that, in addition to f processes, up to k links may fail. We assume that the network topology and the parameters f and k are such that the removal of any set of f (faulty) processes and k (faulty) links leaves the remaining (correct) processes connected by paths of at most d links. If d is chosen to be as small as possible for the given network topology and the parameters f and k, it can be shown that in such a network the latency of Reliable Broadcast is at least $f + d$ rounds, even for crash failures.

Finally, consider the model of synchrony we used in Section 5.4.3, where all processes have perfectly synchronized clocks and a message sent between correct processes over a correct link is received within δ time units after it is sent. In this model, it can be shown that the lower bound on the latency of Reliable Broadcast is $(f + d)\delta$. This matches the latency achieved by the Timed Reliable Broadcast algorithm described in Section 5.4.3, and hence that algorithm is optimal in this respect.

5.9.3 Message complexity

In this section we present some results on the message complexity of the problems we have been discussing. For all these results we shall assume the synchronous round model, a completely connected network, no link failures, and deterministic algorithms. For concreteness we concentrate on Terminating Reliable Broadcast.

Similar results apply for Consensus. Like fault-tolerance, and unlike time complexity, message complexity is quite sensitive to the failure model.

First, consider the number of messages necessary in the worst-case execution. In the case of arbitrary failures $\Omega(nf)$ messages are necessary. This bound is asymptotically tight, since algorithms that only require $O(nf)$ messages are known. For general omission failures, the lower bound is $\Omega(n + f^2)$, and this bound is also asymptotically tight. For sending omission failures and crash failures, the best lower bound known is the trivial one: $\Omega(n)$ messages are necessary. However, this is not known to be tight. In the case of sending omission failures, the best known algorithm requires $O(n + f^2)$ messages in the worst case. For crash failures, the best known algorithm requires $O(n + f \log f)$ messages.

Another set of results concerns the number of messages needed in the failure-free executions of Terminating Reliable Broadcast algorithms. Here, although we consider algorithms that are designed to tolerate failures, we are only interested in the number of messages used in the failure-free executions. This is an interesting measure because in most systems it is expected that in the overwhelming majority of executions no failures actually occur. It is therefore important to design algorithms that are optimized for the no-failure case. The simplest and most interesting results on the message complexity of failure-free executions concern the important special case of *Binary* Terminating Reliable Broadcast, where the set of messages that the sender may broadcast consists of only two messages.[11] For this problem, in the case of arbitrary failures, exactly $\lceil nf / 4 \rceil$ messages are necessary and sufficient in failure-free executions. For arbitrary failures with message authentication, exactly $\lceil (n + 2f - 1) / 2 \rceil$ messages are necessary and sufficient in failure-free executions. Finally, for benign failures exactly $\lceil (n + f - 1) / 2 \rceil$ messages are necessary and sufficient in failure-free executions.

Focusing on the message complexity of the failure-free executions reflects a philosophy similar to early-stopping algorithms. Namely, that the cost of tolerating failures should be borne only when failures do, in fact, occur. The difference is that in the case of early-stopping algorithms the performance of the algorithm is required to degrade gracefully as the number of faulty processes increases. When we focus only on the complexity of failure-free runs, we admit the possibility of a precipitous performance degradation as soon as a single process fails. For general omission (and less severe) failures there are algorithms whose performance, in terms of *both* messages and time, decreases gracefully with the number of processes that actually fail. Specifically, these algorithms guarantee termination in $O(f')$ rounds using only $O(nf')$ messages in any execution where at most $f' \leq f$ processes actually fail. That is, each additional failure introduces an overhead of a (small) constant number of rounds, and of a (small) constant number of extra messages per process.

---

[11]For example, in the Uniform Timed Reliable Broadcast algorithms used to implement Atomic Commitment in the next chapter of this book only two values — 'commit' and 'abort' — can be broadcast.

Bibliographic Notes

Fault-Tolerance

The fact that Terminating Reliable Broadcast and Consensus require $n > 3f$ for arbitrary failures was proved in the seminal papers on fault-tolerant agreement: Pease, Shostak and Lamport [1980] and Lamport, Shostak and Pease [1982]. An alternative proof is given in Fischer, Lynch and Merritt [1986]. Pease, Shostak and Lamport [1980] and Lamport, Shostak and Pease [1982] also give algorithms that work when $n > 3f$; these algorithms have optimal worst-case round complexity $(f + 1)$, but require exponentially long messages. Srikanth and Toueg [1987a] describes a simple algorithm that works when $n > 3f$, requires messages of small size (logarithmic in n and the size of the set of possible messages $\mathcal{M}$), but requires $2(f+1)$ rounds in the worst-case execution. Other algorithms that tolerate arbitrary failures for $n > 3f$ include Berman, Garay and Perry [1989], Coan and Welch [1992] and Garay and Moses [1993].

The results on connectivity requirements for Terminating Reliable Broadcast with arbitrary failures are from Dolev [1982]. An alternative proof of the lower bound is given by Fischer, Lynch and Merritt [1986]. The connectivity requirements for benign failures are discussed by Hadzilacos [1987], which also considers link failures. The results on Uniform Agreement are from Neiger and Toueg [1990].

Time Complexity

The lower bound of $f + 1$ rounds on the worst-case execution was first proved for arbitrary failures by Fischer and Lynch [1982]. It was later extended to arbitrary failures with message authentication by Dolev and Strong [1983]; this proof applies verbatim to sending omission failures. Lamport and Fischer [1982] and Hadzilacos [1984] further extended the result to crash failures. An alternative proof by Dwork and Moses [1990], based on knowledge theory, is particularly insightful.

Early-stopping algorithms were introduced by Dolev, Reischuk and Strong [1990], who also proved the related lower bounds, and gave an early-stopping algorithm for arbitrary failures that is round-optimal. Other early-stopping algorithms for arbitrary failures include those of Moses and Waarts [1988], Toueg, Perry and Srikanth [1987] and Burns and Neiger [1992]. A simple and round-optimal early-stopping algorithm for general omission failures is given in Perry and Toueg [1986].

A randomized Consensus algorithm for arbitrary failures that works when $n > 3f$ and terminates after an expected constant number of rounds is given in Feldman and Micali [1990].

Message Complexity

Dolev and Reischuk [1985] give tight bounds on the message complexity of the worst-case execution of Terminating Reliable Broadcast algorithms in the case of arbitrary failures, arbitrary failures with message authentication, and (implicitly) general omission failures. The Terminating Reliable Broadcast algorithm for crash failures with worst-case message complexity $O(n + f \log f)$ is from Dwork, Halpern and Waarts [1992].

The message complexity of failure-free executions of Terminating Reliable Broadcast algorithms is discussed by Amdur, Weber and Hadzilacos [1992] and Hadzilacos and Halpern [1993]. Chandra and Toueg [1990] give Terminating Reliable Broadcast algorithms for general omission failures and crash failures whose time and message performance degrades gracefully with the number of processes that actually fail in the execution.

Acknowledgements

We are indebted to a large number of colleagues for extremely useful discussions and comments on a draft of this chapter: Navin Budhiraja, Tushar Chandra, David Cooper, Prasad Jayanti, Mike Reiter and King Tan. Ajei Gopal helped us formulate the properties of broadcast problems. Over the past few years we have received invaluable feedback on this material from students of CS 444 and CS 618 at Cornell, and CSC 2221 at the University of Toronto.

This work was supported by a grant from the Natural Sciences and Engineering Research Council of Canada, by NSF grants CCR-8901780 and CCR-9102231 and by a grant from IBM Endicott Programming Laboratory.

5.10   References

Amdur, E., Weber, S. and Hadzilacos, V. (1992), On the Message Complexity of Binary Byzantine Agreement under Crash Failures, *Distributed Computing* 5(2), 175–186.

Amir, Y., Dolev, D., Kramer, S. and Malki, D. (1992), Transis: A Communication Sub-System for High Availability, *Proceedings of the 22nd International Symposium on Fault-Tolerant Computing*, IEEE Computer Society Press, 76–84.

Attiya, H., Bar-Noy, A., Dolev, D., Koller, D., Peleg, D. and Reischuk, R. (1987), Achievable Cases in an Asynchronous Environment, *Proceedings of the 28th Annual Symposium on Foundations of Computer Science*, Chandra, A., ed., Los Angeles, CA, IEEE Computer Society Press, 337–346.

Babaoğlu, Ö. and Drummond, R. (1985), Streets of Byzantium: Network Architectures for Fast Reliable Broadcasts, *IEEE Transactions on Software Engineering* 11(6), 546–554.

Babaoğlu, Ö. and Drummond, R. (1987), (Almost) No Cost Clock Synchronization, *Proceedings of the 17th International Symposium on Fault-Tolerant Computing*, Cristian, F. and Goldberg, J., eds., Pittsburgh, PA, IEEE Computer Society Press, 42–47.

Bazzi, R. and Neiger, G. (1991), Optimally Simulating Crash Failures in a Byzantine Environment, *Proceedings of the Fifth International Workshop on Distributed Algorithms*, Toueg, S., Spirakis, P. G. and Kirousis, L., eds., Delphi, Greece, Springer Verlag, 108–128.

Bazzi, R. and Neiger, G. (1992), Simulating Crash Failures with Many Faulty Processors, *Proceedings of the Sixth International Workshop on Distributed Algorithms*, Segal, A. and Zaks, S., eds., Haifa, Israel, Springer Verlag, 166–184.

Ben-Or, M. (1983), Another advantage of free choice: Completely asynchronous agreement protocols, *Proceedings of the Second ACM Annual Symposium on Principles of Distributed Computing*, Lynch, N. A., ed., Montreal, Canada, 27–30.

Berman, P., Garay, J. A. and Perry, K. J. (1989), Towards Optimal Distributed Consensus, *Proceedings of the 30th Annual Symposium on Foundations of Computer Science*, Galil, Z., ed., Research Triangle Park, NC, IEEE Computer Society Press, 410–415.

Bernstein, P. A., Hadzilacos, V. and Goodman, N. (1987), *Concurrency Control and Recovery in Database Systems*, Addison-Wesley, Reading, MA.

Biran, O., Moran, S. and Zaks, S. (1988), A combinatorial characterization of the distributed tasks that are solvable in the presence of one faulty processor, *Proceedings of the Seventh ACM Annual Symposium on Principles of Distributed Computing*, Dolev, D., ed., Toronto, Ontario, Canada, 263–275.

Birman, K. P., Cooper, R., Joseph, T. A., Kane, K. P. and Schmuck, F. B. (1990), Isis — A Distributed Programming Environment.

Birman, K. P. and Joseph, T. A. (1987), Reliable Communication in the Presence of Failures, *ACM Transactions on Computer Systems* 5(1), 47–76.

Birman, K. P., Schiper, A. and Stephenson, P. (1991), Lightweight Causal and Atomic Group Multicast, *ACM Transactions on Computer Systems* 9(3), 272–314.

Bracha, G. (1987), Asynchronous Byzantine Agreement Protocols, *Information and Computation* 75(2), 130–143.

Bridgland, M. F. and Watro, R. J. (1987), Fault-tolerant Decision Making in Totally Asynchronous Distributed Systems, *Proceedings of the Sixth ACM Annual Symposium on Principles of Distributed Computing*, Schneider, F. B., ed., Vancouver, BC, Canada, 52–63.

Burns, J. E. and Neiger, G. (1992), Fast and Simple Byzantine Agreement, College of Computing, Georgia Institute of Technology, Technical Report 92/12.

Chandra, T. D., Hadzilacos, V. and Toueg, S. (1992), The Weakest Failure Detector for Solving Consensus, *Proceedings of the Eleventh ACM Annual Symposium on Principles of Distributed Computing*, Herlihy, M., ed., Vancouver, British Columbia, 147–158.

Chandra, T. D. and Toueg, S. (1990), Time and Message Efficient Reliable Broadcasts, *Proceedings of the Fourth International Workshop on Distributed Algorithms*, van Leeuwen, J. and Santoro, N., eds., Bari, Italy, Springer Verlag.

Chandra, T. D. and Toueg, S. (1991), Unreliable Failure Detectors for Asynchronous Systems (Preliminary Version), *Proceedings of the Tenth ACM Annual Symposium on Principles of Distributed Computing*, Ladner, R., ed., Montreal, Québec, ACM Press, 325–340.

Chang, J-M. and Maxemchuk, N. F. (1984), Reliable broadcast protocols, *ACM Transactions on Computer Systems* **2(3)**, 251–273.

Chor, B. and Dwork, C. (1989), Randomization in Byzantine Agreement, *Advances in Computer Research* **5**, 443–497.

Coan, B. A. (1987), Achieving Consensus in Fault-Tolerant Distributed Computer Systems: Protocols, Lower Bounds, and Simulations, Massachusetts Institute of Technology, Ph.D. Dissertation.

Coan, B. A. and Welch, J. L. (1992), Modular Construction of a Byzantine Agreement Protocol with Optimal Message Bit Complexity, *Information and Computation* **97(1)**, 61–85.

Cristian, F. (1987), Issues in the Design of Highly Available Computing Services, *Proceedings of the Annual Symposium of the Canadian Information Processing Society*, 9–16, Also IBM Research Report RJ5856 July 1987.

Cristian, F. (1989), Probabilistic Clock Synchronization, *Distributed Computing* **3**, 146–158.

Cristian, F., Aghili, H. and Strong, H. R. (1986), Approximate Clock Synchronization despite Omission and Performance Faults and Processor Joins, *Proceedings of the 16th International Symposium on Fault-Tolerant Computing*, Vienna, Austria.

Cristian, F., Aghili, H., Strong, H. R. and Dolev, D. (1985), Atomic Broadcast: From Simple Message Diffusion to Byzantine Agreement, *Proceedings of the 15th International Symposium on Fault-Tolerant Computing*, Ann Arbor, MI, 200–206, A revised version appears as IBM Research Laboratory Technical Report RJ5244 (April 1989).

Cristian, F., Dancey, R. D. and Dehn, J. (1990), Fault-Tolerance in the Advanced Automation System, IBM Research Laboratory, Technical Report RJ 7424.

Dolev, D. (1982), The Byzantine Generals Strike Again, *Journal of Algorithms* **3(1)**, 14–30.

Dolev, D., Dwork, C. and Stockmeyer, L. (1987), On the Minimal Synchronism Needed for Distributed Consensus, *Journal of the ACM* **34(1)**, 77–97.

Dolev, D., Halpern, J. Y. and Strong, H. R. (1986), On the Possibility and Impossibility of Achieving Clock Synchronization, *Journal of Computer and System Sciences* **22(2)**, 230–250.

Dolev, D., Lynch, N. A., Pinter, S. S., Stark, E. W. and Weihl, W. E. (1986), Reaching Approximate Agreement in the Presence of Faults, *Journal of the ACM* **33(3)**, 499–516.

Dolev, D. and Reischuk, R. (1985), Bounds on Information Exchange for Byzantine Agreement, *Journal of the ACM* **32(1)**, 191–204.

Dolev, D., Reischuk, R. and Strong, H. R. (1990), Early Stopping in Byzantine Agreement, *Journal of the ACM* **37(4)**, 720–741.

Dolev, D. and Strong, H. R. (1983), Authenticated Algorithms for Byzantine Agreement, *Siam Journal on Computing* **12(4)**, 656–666.

Dwork, C., Halpern, J. Y. and Waarts, O. (1992), Performing Work Efficiently in the Presence of Faults, *Proceedings of the Eleventh ACM Annual Symposium on Principles of Distributed Computing*, Herlihy, M., ed., Vancouver, British Columbia, 91–102.

Dwork, C., Lynch, N. A. and Stockmeyer, L. (1988), Consensus in the Presence of Partial Synchrony, *Journal of the ACM* **35(2)**, 288–323.

Dwork, C. and Moses, Y. (1990), Knowledge and Common Knowledge in a Byzantine Environment: Crash Failures, *Information and Computation* **88(2)**, 156–186.

Fekete, A. D. (1990), Asymptotically Optimal Algorithms for Approximate Agreement, *Distributed Computing* **4(1)**, 9–30.

Fekete, A. D. (1993), Asynchronous Approximate Agreement, *Information and Computation*, To appear.

Feldman, P. and Micali, S. (1990), An Optimal Algorithm for Synchronous Byzantine Agreement, MIT Laboratory for Computer Science, Technical Report MIT/-LCS/TM-425, Cambridge, MA.

Fischer, M. J. and Lynch, N. A. (1982), A Lower Bound for the Time to Assure Interactive Consistency, *Information Processing Letters* **14**, 183–186.

Fischer, M. J., Lynch, N. A. and Merritt, M. (1986), Easy Impossibility Proofs for Distributed Consensus Problems, *Distributed Computing* **1**, 26–39.

Fischer, M. J., Lynch, N. A. and Paterson, M. S. (1985), Impossibility of Distributed Consensus with One Faulty Process, *Journal of the ACM* **32**(**2**), 374–382.

Garay, J. and Moses, Y. (1993), Fully Polynomial Byzantine Agreement in $t + 1$ rounds, To appear.

Garcia-Molina, H. and Spauster, A. (1991), Ordered and Reliable Multicast Communication, *ACM Transactions on Computer Systems* **9**(**3**), 242–271.

Gopal, A. (1992), Fault-Tolerant Broadcasts and Multicasts: The Problem of Inconsistency and Contamination, Cornell University, Ph.D. Dissertation.

Gopal, A., Strong, R., Toueg, S. and Cristian, F. (1990), Early-Delivery Atomic Broadcast, *Proceedings of the Ninth ACM Annual Symposium on Principles of Distributed Computing*, Dwork, C., ed., Québec City, Québec, 297–310.

Gopal, A. and Toueg, S. (1991), Inconsistency and Contamination, *Proceedings of the Tenth ACM Annual Symposium on Principles of Distributed Computing*, Ladner, R., ed., Montreal, Québec, ACM Press, 257–272.

Gray, J. N. (1978), Notes on database operating systems, in *Operating Systems — An Advanced Course*, Bayer, R., Graham, R. M. and Seegmuller, G., eds., Lecture Notes on Computer Science, vol. **66**, springer, 393–481, Also available as Technical Report RJ2188, IBM Research Laboratory, San Jose, California, 1978.

Hadzilacos, V. (1984), Issues of Fault Tolerance in Concurrent Computations, Harvard University, Ph.D. Dissertation, Department of Computer Science Technical Report 11-84.

Hadzilacos, V. (1987), Connectivity Requirements for Byzantine Agreement under Restricted Types of Failures, *Distributed Computing* **2**(**2**), 95–103.

Hadzilacos, V. and Halpern, J. Y. (1993), Message and Bit-Optimal Protocol for Byzantine Agreement, *Mathematics Systems Theory* **26**(**1**), 41–102.

Hadzilacos, V., Jayanti, P. and Toueg, S. (1993), Fundamentals of Fault-Tolerant Distributed Computing, Forthcoming.

Halpern, J. Y. and Moses, Y. (1990), Knowledge and Common Knowledge in a Distributed Environment, *Journal of the ACM* **37**(**3**), 549–587.

Halpern, J. Y., Simons, B., Strong, R. and Dolev, D. (1984), Fault-Tolerant Clock Synchronization, *Proceedings of the Third ACM Annual Symposium on Principles of Distributed Computing*, Misra, J., ed., Vancouver, BC, Canada, 89–102.

Kaashoek, M. F. (1992), Group Communication in Distributed Computer Systems, Vrije Universiteit, Ph.D. Dissertation, Amsterdam.

Kopetz, H. and Ochsenreiter, W. (1987), Clock Synchronization in Distributed Real-Time Systems, *IEEE Transactions on Computers* **C-36(8)**, 933–940.

Lamport, L. (1978a), The Implementation of Reliable Distributed Multiprocess Systems, *Computer Networks* **2**, 95–114.

Lamport, L. (1978b), Time, Clocks, and the Ordering of Events in a Distributed System, *Communications of the ACM* **21(7)**, 558–565.

Lamport, L. (1984), Using Time Instead of Timeout for Fault-Tolerant Distributed Systems, *ACM Transactions on Programming Languages and Systems* **6(2)**, 254–280.

Lamport, L. and Fischer, M. J. (1982), Byzantine Generals and Transaction Commit Protocols, SRI International, Technical Report 62.

Lamport, L. and Melliar-Smith, P. M. (1985), Synchronizing Clocks in the Presence of Faults, *Journal of the ACM* **32(1)**, 52–78.

Lamport, L., Shostak, R. and Pease, M. (1982), The Byzantine Generals Problem, *ACM Transactions on Programming Languages and Systems* **4(3)**, 382–401.

Liskov, B. (1991), Practical Uses of Synchronized Clocks in Distributed Systems, *Proceedings of the Tenth ACM Annual Symposium on Principles of Distributed Computing*, Ladner, R., ed., Montreal, Québec, ACM Press, 1–9.

Moses, Y. and Waarts, O. (1988), Coordinated Traversal: $(t + 1)$-Round Byzantine Agreement in Polynomial Time, *Proceedings of the 29th Annual Symposium on Foundations of Computer Science*, Kozen, D., ed., White Plains, NY, IEEE Computer Society Press, 246–255.

Neiger, G. and Toueg, S. (1987), Substituting for Real Time and Common Knowledge in Asynchronous Distributed Systems (preliminary version), *Proceedings of the Sixth ACM Annual Symposium on Principles of Distributed Computing*, Schneider, F. B., ed., Vancouver, BC, Canada, 281–293, A revised and expanded version appears as Georgia Institute of Technology School of Information and Computer Science Technical Report 90/05. To appear in the *Journal of the ACM*.

Neiger, G. and Toueg, S. (1990), Automatically Increasing the Fault-Tolerance of Distributed Algorithms, *Journal of Algorithms* **11(3)**, 374–419.

Pease, M., Shostak, R. and Lamport, L. (1980), Reaching Agreement in the Presence of Faults, *Journal of the ACM* **27(2)**, 228–234.

Perry, K. J. and Toueg, S. (1986), Distributed agreement in the presence of processor and communication faults, *IEEE Transactions on Software Engineering* **SE-12(3)**, 477–482.

Peterson, L. L., Bucholz, N. C. and Schlichting, R. D. (1989), Preserving and using context information in interprocess communication, *ACM Transactions on Computer Systems* **7(3)**, 217–246.

Rabin, M. (1983), Randomized Byzantine Generals, *Proceedings of the 24th Annual Symposium on Foundations of Computer Science*, Snyder, L., ed., Tucson, Arizona, IEEE Computer Society Press, 403–409.

Ricciardi, A. and Birman, K. (1991), Using Process Groups to Implement Failure Detection in Asynchronous Environments, *Proceedings of the Tenth ACM Annual Symposium on Principles of Distributed Computing*, Ladner, R., ed., Montreal, Québec, ACM Press, 341–351.

Schlichting, R. D. and Schneider, F. B. (1983), Fail-Stop Processors: an Approach to Designing Fault-Tolerant Computing Systems, *ACM Transactions on Computer Systems* **1(3)**, 222–238.

Schneider, F. B. (1990), Implementing Fault-Tolerant Services Using the State Machine Approach: A Tutorial, *ACM Computing Surveys* **22(4)**, 299–319.

Skeen, D. (1982), Crash Recovery in a Distributed Database System, University of California, Berkeley, Department of EECS, Ph.D. Dissertation.

Srikanth, T. K. and Toueg, S. (1987a), Simulating Authenticated Broadcasts to Derive Simple Fault-Tolerant Algorithms, *Distributed Computing* **2(2)**, 80–94.

Srikanth, T. K. and Toueg, S. (1987b), Optimal Clock Synchronization, *Journal of the ACM* **34(3)**, 626–645.

Toueg, S., Perry, K. J. and Srikanth, T. K. (1987), Fast Distributed Agreement, *Siam Journal on Computing* **16(3)**, 445–457.

Veríssimo, P. and Marques, J. A. (1990), Reliable Broadcast for Fault-Tolerance on Local Computer Networks, *Proceedings of the Ninth Symposium on Reliable Distributed Systems*, Huntsville, AL, IEEE.

Welch, J. L. (1987), Simulating Synchronous Processors, *Information and Computation* **74(2)**, 159–171.

Welch, J. L. and Lynch, N. A. (1988), A New Fault-Tolerant Algorithm for Clock Synchronization, *Information and Computation* **77(1)**, 1–36.

Wensley, J. H., Lamport, L., Goldberg, J., Green, M. W., Levitt, K. N., Melliar-Smith, P. M., Shostak, R. E. and Weinstock, C. B. (1978), SIFT: Design and Analysis of a Fault-Tolerant Computer for Aircraft Control, *Proceedings of the IEEE* **66(10)**, 1240–1255.

Chapter 6

Non-Blocking Atomic Commitment

Özalp Babaoğlu and Sam Toueg

In distributed database systems, an *atomic commitment protocol* ensures that transactions terminate consistently at all participating sites even in the presence of failures. An atomic commitment protocol is said to be *non-blocking* if it permits transaction termination to proceed at correct participants despite failures of others. Protocols that have this property are desirable since they limit the time intervals during which transactions may be holding valuable resources. In this chapter, we show how non-blocking atomic commitment protocols can be obtained through slight modifications of the well-known Two-Phase Commit (2PC) protocol, which is known to be blocking. Our approach is modular in the sense that both the protocols and their proofs of correctness are obtained by plugging in the appropriate reliable broadcast algorithms as the basic communication primitives in the original 2PC protocol. The resulting protocols are not only conceptually simple, they are also efficient in terms of time and message complexity.

6.1 Introduction

There are two principal reasons for structuring a data management system as a distributed system rather than a centralized one. First, the data being managed may be inherently distributed, as in the customer accounts database of a bank with multiple branches. Second, the data may be distributed to achieve failure independence for increased availability, as in a replicated file system.

When transactions update data in a distributed system, partial failures can lead to inconsistent results. For instance, in the banking example above, a transaction to transfer money between two accounts at different branches may result in the credit operation without performing the corresponding debit. In the replicated file system, a write operation may cause two replicas of the same file to diverge. It is clear that termination of a transaction that updates distributed data has to be coordinated among its participants if data consistency is to be preserved even in the presence of failures. The coordination that is required is specified by the *atomic commitment problem* (Hadzilacos [1990]).

Among the solutions proposed for this problem, perhaps the best known is the Two-Phase Commit (2PC) protocol (Gray [1978]; Lampson [1981]). While 2PC indeed solves the atomic commitment problem, it may result in *blocking* executions where a correct participant is prevented from terminating the transaction due to inopportune failures in other parts of the system (Bernstein, Hadzilacos and Goodman [1987]). During these blocking periods, correct participants will also be prevented from relinquishing valuable system resources that they may have acquired for exclusive use on behalf of the transaction. Thus, it is desirable to devise *non-blocking* solutions to atomic commitment that permit correct participants to proceed and terminate the transaction under as many failure scenarios as possible.

It is well known that distributed systems with unreliable communication do not admit non-blocking solutions to atomic commitment (Gray [1978]; Halpern and Moses [1990]; Skeen [1982]). If communication failures are excluded, non-blocking protocols do exist (Dolev and Strong [1982]; Dwork and Skeen [1983]; Hadzilacos [1984]; Lamport and Fischer [1982]; Skeen [1982]) and are typified by the Three-Phase Commit (3PC) protocol of Skeen (Skeen [1982]). These non-blocking protocols are not only inherently more costly (in time) than their blocking counterparts (Dwork and Skeen [1983]), they are also much more complex to program and understand. For example, to prevent blocking, correct participants may need to communicate with each other and consider a large number of possible system states in order to proceed with the correct decision towards termination. Furthermore, protocols such as 3PC invoke sub-protocols for electing a leader (Garcia-Molina [1982]) and determining the last process to fail (Skeen [1985]), which themselves are complex and costly.

In this chapter, we develop a family of non-blocking protocols to solve the atomic commitment problem. All of our protocols share the basic structure of 2PC and differ only in the details of the communication primitive they use to broadcast certain messages. By exploiting the properties of these broadcast primitives, we are able to achieve non-blocking without adding any complexity beyond that of 2PC. We complete this 'compositional methodology' of protocol design by demonstrating algorithms that achieve the properties of the hypothesized broadcast primitives. These algorithms turn out to be variants of *uniform reliable broadcast* (Chandra and Toueg [1990]; Neiger and Toueg [1990]). The modular approach we advocate results in non-blocking atomic commitment protocols that are easy to prove and understand. This conceptual economy is obtained without any performance penalties — the best of our protocols is as efficient as 2PC. Furthermore, our solutions are complete in the sense that no additional sub-protocols are needed to put them to practice.

In the next two sections, we define the distributed system model and the context for distributed transaction execution. Within this environment, the requirement of global consistency despite failures is formally specified as the atomic commitment problem in Section 6.4. A generic atomic commitment protocol is described in Section 6.5 and serves as the generator for our future protocols. The first of a series of broadcast primitives we consider is defined through a set of properties given in Section 6.6. In the same section, we illustrate a simple algorithm that achieves the required properties. Plugging in this algorithm to the generic protocol of the previous section results in the classical implementation of 2PC, which is proven correct in Section 6.7. In Section 6.8, we consider the issue of blocking and refine the atomic commitment problem specification to include the non-blocking property. This section contains the key result of the chapter where we show that if the simple broadcast primitive specification of Section 6.6 is extended to include a *uniform agreement* property, then any algorithm that achieves this broadcast can be plugged into the generic protocol to obtain a non-blocking atomic commitment protocol. An algorithm that indeed achieves this broadcast is given in Section 6.10. The issue of recovery from failures is the subject of Section 6.11. The performance analysis carried out in Section 6.12 of our basic non-blocking protocol leads to several improvements discussed in Sections 6.13.1 and 6.13.2. Communication failures, imperfect clocks and related work are discussed in Sections 6.14 and 6.15 before concluding the chapter.

6.2   System Model

We follow closely the model and terminology used in Bernstein, Hadzilacos and Goodman [1987]. The distributed system consists of a set of sites interconnected through a communication network. Sites support computation in the form of processes that communicate with each other by exchanging messages. We assume a *synchronous* model of computation in the sense that bounds exists (and are known) for both relative speeds of processes and message delays.

At any given time, a process may be either *operational* or *down*. While operational, it follows exactly the actions specified by the program it is executing. Failures may cause operational processes to go down, after which they take no actions at all. This operational-to-down transition due to failures is called a *crash*. It is also possible for a process that is down to become operational again after executing a *recovery protocol*. When a process crashes, all of its local state is lost except for what it wrote in *stable storage* (Lampson [1981]). During recovery, the only information available to a process is the contents of this stable storage. A process is *correct* if it has never crashed; otherwise it is *faulty*.[1]

While processes may crash, we assume that communication is reliable. Furthermore, each message is received within δ time units (as measured in real-time) after being sent. This parameter δ includes not only the time required to transport the message by the network, but also the delays incurred in processing it at the sending and receiving processes. For the sake of exposition, we initially assume that every process has a local clock that advances at the same rate as real-time. As discussed in Section 6.14, our results can be easily extended to systems where local clocks are not perfect but their rate of drift from real-time is bounded. Each local clock is only used to measure time intervals. Thus, we do not need to assume that clocks are synchronized with each other (Lamport and Melliar-Smith [1985]).

Given the above model and the assumption that communication is failure free, timeouts can be used to detect process failures. In particular, if a process does

---

[1]The periods of interest for these definitions are the duration of the atomic commitment protocol execution.

```
    % Some participant (the invoker) executes:
1       send [T_START: transaction, Δc, participants] to all participants

    % All participants (including the invoker) execute:
2       upon (receipt of [T_START: transaction, Δc, participants])
3           Cknow := local_clock
4           % Perform operations requested by transaction
5           if (willing and able to make updates permanent) then
6               vote := YES
7           else vote := NO
            % Decide commit or abort for the transaction
8           atomic_commitment(transaction, participants)
```

Figure 6.1. Distributed transaction execution schema

not receive a response to a message within 2δ time units (as measured on its local clock) after sending it, it can conclude that the destination process is faulty (i.e., it has crashed at least once).

6.3 Distributed Transactions

Informally, a distributed transaction (henceforth called a 'transaction') is the execution of a program accessing shared data at multiple sites (Lampson [1981]). The isolated execution of a transaction in the absence of failures is assumed to transform the data from one consistent state to another. Logical isolation in the presence of concurrent transactions is typically formalized as a *serializable execution* (Papadimitriou [1979]) and is achieved through a *concurrency control protocol* (Bernstein and Goodman [1981]). In this chapter, we focus on *failure atomicity* — preserving data consistency in the presence of failures — which is orthogonal to serializability.

For each transaction, the set of processes that perform updates on its behalf are called *participants*. Each participant updates data that are local to it. To conclude the transaction, participants must coordinate their actions so that either all or none of the updates to the data are made permanent. We consider only the so-called centralized version of this coordination where one of the participants acts as the *coordinator* in order to orchestrate the actions. We assume that each transaction is assigned a unique global identifier. For sake of simplicity, we will consider only one transaction at a time and omit explicit transaction identifiers from our notation. Obviously, in a system with multiple concurrent transactions, all messages and variables will have to be tagged with identifiers so as to be able to distinguish between multiple instances.

Figure 6.1 illustrates the schema governing distributed transaction execution. It will serve as the context for specifying and solving the atomic commitment problem. The transaction begins at a single participant called the *invoker*. The invoker distributes the transaction to its participants by sending them T_START messages containing a description of the transaction operations and the full list of participants. As soon as a participant receives a T_START message (in Line 2 of Figure 6.1) it is said to 'know' about the transaction. The local time at which this event happens is recorded in the variable C_{know} for future use. The invoker computes an upper bound for the interval of time that may elapse from the instant any participant knows about the transaction to the time the coordinator (not necessarily the same participant as the invoker) actively begins concluding it. This interval, denoted Δ_c, is also included in the T_START message.

After a participant performs the operations requested by the transaction, it uses a variable *vote* to indicate whether it can install the updates. A YES vote indicates that the local execution was successful and that the participant is willing and able to make the updates to the data permanent. In other words, the updates have been written to stable storage so that they can be installed as the new data values even if there are future failures. A NO vote indicates that for some reason (e.g., storage failure, deadlock, concurrency control conflict, etc.) the participant is unable to install the results of the transaction as the new permanent data values. Finally, participants engage in the coordination step to decide the outcome of the transaction by executing an atomic commitment protocol.

We are not interested in the details of how a participant is chosen to become the coordinator of a transaction. All we require is that each transaction is assigned a coordinator in a manner satisfying the following three axioms:

AX1: At most one participant will assume the role of coordinator.

AX2: If no failures occur, one participant will assume the role of coordinator.

AX3: There exists a constant Δ_c such that no participant assumes the role of coordinator more than Δ_c real-time units after the beginning of the transaction.

Axioms AX1 and AX2 are simply statements about the syntactic well-formedness of transactions — the program should guarantee that no more than one participant ever reaches the code for the coordinator and, in the absence of failures, indeed one participant should execute this code. Axiom AX3 allows us to bound the duration of a transaction even when its coordinator crashes before taking any steps.

At this point, we describe the programming notation used in this chapter. As can be seen in Figure 6.1, we use a pseudo-Pascal syntax with the usual sequential control flow structures. We denote concurrent activities as tasks separated by '//' enclosed within **cobegin** and **coend**. Communication is accomplished through the **send** and **receive** statements by supplying the message and the destination/source process name. In our protocols, all messages carry type identifiers, written in SMALL-CAPS, within the message body. We use '**send** m **to** $\mathcal{G}$' as a shorthand for sending message m one at a time to each process that is a member of the set $\mathcal{G}$. Note that we make no assumptions about the indivisibility of this operation. In particular, the sender may crash after having sent to some but not all members of the destination set. The receiver of a message may synchronize its execution with the receipt of a message in one of two ways. The **wait-for** statement is used to block the receiver until the receipt of a particular message. If the message may arrive at unspecified times and should be received without blocking the receiver, then the **upon** statement is appropriate. Actually, both the **wait-for** and **upon** statements can be applied to arbitrary asynchronous events and not just to message receipts.

When the specified event occurs, execution proceeds with the body of the respective statement. In case of a blocking wait, an optional timeout may be set to trigger at a particular (local) time using the **set-timeout-to** statement. The timeout value in effect is that set by the most recent **set-timeout-to** before the execution of a **wait-for** statement. If the event being waited for does not occur by the specified time, then the **on-timeout** clause of the **wait-for** statement is executed rather than its body. The body and the timeout clause of **wait-for** are mutually exclusive.

6.4   The Atomic Commitment Problem

The *atomic commitment problem* is concerned with bringing a transaction to a globally consistent conclusion despite failures. For each participant, its goal is to select among two possible decision values — **commit** and **abort**. Deciding **commit** indicates that all participants will make the transaction's updates permanent, while deciding **abort** indicates that none will. The individual decisions taken are irreversible. A **commit** decision is based on unanimity of YES votes among the participants.

We formalize these notions as a set of properties that, together, define the atomic commitment problem:

AC1: All participants that decide reach the same decision.
AC2: If any participant decides **commit**, then all participants must have voted YES.
AC3: If all participants vote YES and no failures occur, then all participants decide **commit**.
AC4: Each participant decides at most once (that is, a decision is irreversible).

A protocol that satisfies all four of the above properties is called an *atomic commitment protocol*.

6.5   A Generic Atomic Commitment Protocol

Figure 6.2 illustrates a generic atomic commitment protocol, called ACP, that has the same structure as 2PC. It is generic in the sense that the details of **broadcast** used by the coordinator to disseminate the decision have not been specified. We will use this protocol to obtain others (including 2PC) by plugging in appropriate instances of the broadcast primitive.

The protocol consists of two concurrent tasks, one executed only by the coordinator (task 1) and the other executed by all participants, including the coordinator (task 2). The coordinator starts out by collecting the votes of participants by sending them VOTE_REQUEST messages. When a participant receives such a message, it 'votes' by sending the value of local variable *vote* to the coordinator. Phase 1 ends when the coordinator has votes from all participants. If a YES vote was received from all participants, then the decision is **commit**; otherwise it is **abort**. In Phase 2, the coordinator disseminates the decision to all participants. If a participant voted NO in Phase 1, it can unilaterally decide **abort**. Otherwise it has to wait for

```
procedure atomic_commitment(transaction, participants)
    cobegin
    % Task 1: Executed by the coordinator
1       send [VOTE_REQUEST] to all participants              % Including the coordinator
2       set-timeout-to local_clock + 2δ
3       wait-for (receipt of [vote: vote] messages from all participants)
4           if (all votes are YES) then
5               broadcast (commit, participants)
6           else broadcast (abort, participants)
7       on-timeout
8           broadcast (abort, participants)

    //

9   % Task 2: Executed by all participants (including the coordinator)
10      set-timeout-to C_{know} + Δ_c + δ
11      wait-for (receipt of [VOTE_REQUEST] from coordinator)
12          send [vote: vote] to coordinator
13          if (vote = NO) then
14              decide abort
15          else
16              set-timeout-to C_{know} + Δ_c + 2δ + Δ_b
17              wait-for (delivery of decision message)
18                  if (decision message is abort) then
19                      decide abort
20                  else decide commit
21              on-timeout
22                  decide according to termination_protocol()
23      on-timeout
24          decide abort
    coend
end
```

Figure 6.2. ACP: A Generic Atomic Commitment Protocol

the decision to arrive from the coordinator. If no decision arrives at a participant from the coordinator, it engages in a termination protocol in an attempt to conclude the transaction with the help of others. If a participant has not received a VOTE_REQUEST by the appropriate time, it can safely assume that the coordinator has crashed and unilaterally decide **abort**. The choice of the timeout periods will be discussed when we prove the correctness of specific instances of this generic protocol.

6.6   A Simple Broadcast Primitive: SB

A key step in the generic protocol ACP of Figure 6.2 is the dissemination of the decision value to all participants by the coordinator in Phase 2. We call the primitive to achieve this dissemination a **broadcast** which has a corresponding action at the destination called **deliver**. It is clear that **broadcast** and **deliver** will be implemented using multiple **send** and **receive** operations that the network provides.

```
procedure broadcast(m, G)

% Broadcaster executes:
    send [DLV: m] to all processes in G
    deliver m

% Process p ≠ broadcaster in G executes:
    upon (receipt of [DLV: m])
        deliver m
end
```

Figure 6.3. SB1: A Simple Broadcast Algorithm

The simplest way for a process p to broadcast a message m to the members of a set G is for p to sequentially send m to each process in G. When a process in G receives such a message, it just delivers it.

It is easy to see that this simple broadcast algorithm, called SB1 (Figure 6.3), satisfies the following properties (with $\Delta_b = \delta$):

B1 (Validity): If a correct process broadcasts a message m, then all correct processes in G eventually deliver m.

B2 (Integrity): For any message m, each process in G delivers m at most once, and only if some process actually broadcasts m.

B3 (Δ_b-Timeliness): There exists a known constant Δ_b such that if the broadcast of m is initiated at real-time t, no process in G delivers m after real-time $t + \Delta_b$.[2]

We assume that each broadcast message m is unique. This can be easily achieved by tagging messages with the name of the broadcaster and a sequence number.

Any broadcast primitive that satisfies the above three properties is called a *Simple Broadcast* (SB). The primitive allows any process to broadcast any message at any time. In other words, there is no *a priori* knowledge of the broadcast times or of the identity of the broadcasters. Note that SB is not reliable — if the broadcaster crashes in the middle of a Simple Broadcast, it is possible for some correct processes to deliver the broadcaster's message while other correct processes never do so.

6.7   The Two-Phase Commit Protocol: ACP-SB

Let us first consider an instantiation of the generic protocol ACP obtained by plugging in any SB algorithm (such as SB1) as the broadcast primitive in Figure 6.2. The resulting protocol is called ACP-SB and corresponds exactly to the classical Two-Phase Commit (2PC) protocol. Since this protocol forms the basis for all others to come, we give a detailed proof of its correctness. Large portions of this proof will remain valid also for other protocols we develop based on ACP.

---

[2]Note that Integrity prevents even *faulty* processes from delivering a message more than once or 'out of thin air'. Similarly, Timeliness prevents *faulty* processes from delivering m after real-time $t + \Delta_b$. Since these two properties impose restrictions on message deliveries not only by correct processes, but also by faulty ones, they are called '*Uniform* Integrity and *Uniform* Δ_b-Timeliness' in the terminology of Chapter 5. In what follows, we omit the qualifier 'Uniform' for the sake of brevity.

For the purposes of this proof, we assume that the termination protocol, which is invoked if a timeout occurs while waiting for the decision from the coordinator, simply 'blocks' the participant. We do this without any loss of generality since the protocols developed later will be able to decide unilaterally without needing a termination protocol.

Theorem 10 *Protocol ACP-SB achieves properties AC1–AC4 of the atomic commitment problem.*

Proof: We prove the properties in the order AC2, AC3, AC4 and AC1.

AC2: If any participant decides **commit***, then all participants must have voted* YES.

Assume some participant decides **commit**. This can only occur in Line 20, and the participant must have delivered a **commit** message in Line 17. By the Integrity property of the broadcast, **commit** was broadcast by some participant. This can only occur at Line 5. Thus the coordinator must have received votes from all participants and all these votes were YES.

AC3: If all participants vote YES *and no failures occur, then all participants decide* **commit**.

Suppose all participants vote YES and no failures occur. Let t_{start} be the real-time at which the transaction begins (this is the time at which some participant sends a T_START message). From AX2 and AX3, one participant assumes the role of coordinator by real-time $t_{start} + \Delta_c$. This coordinator immediately sends VOTE_REQUEST messages which arrive by $t_{start} + \Delta_c + \delta$. Note that in Line 11 each participant waits for this VOTE_REQUEST, with a timeout set to trigger $\Delta_c + \delta$ time units after the real-time, t_{know}, at which it first learned about the transaction (in Line 2 of Figure 6.1).[3] In other words, this timeout is set to trigger at real-time $t_{know} + \Delta_c + \delta$. Since $t_{start} \leq t_{know}$, each participant receives the VOTE_REQUEST message it was waiting for, before the timeout is ever triggered. Thus, all participants send their YES votes to the coordinator. These votes arrive at the coordinator within 2δ time units of its sending the VOTE_REQUEST. Therefore, the timeout associated with the coordinator's wait for votes in Line 3 never triggers. So, the coordinator receives YES votes from all participants and broadcasts a **commit** message to all participants by real-time $t_{start} + \Delta_c + 2\delta$. Note that in Line 17, all correct participants are waiting for the delivery of this decision message, with a timeout set to trigger at real-time $t_{know} + \Delta_c + 2\delta + \Delta_b$. By the Validity and Δ_b-Timeliness properties of the broadcast, every participant delivers the **commit** message by real-time $t_{start} + \Delta_c + 2\delta + \Delta_b$, before this timeout is triggered. Thus all participants decide **commit**.

AC4: Each participant decides at most once.

From the structure of protocol ACP-SB, each participant decides at most once while executing Task 2.

AC1: All participants that decide reach the same decision.

For contradiction, suppose participant p decides **commit** and participant q decides **abort**. By AC4, $p \neq q$. Participant q can decide **abort** only in Lines 14, 19 and 24. By the proof of AC2, since p decides **commit**, the coordinator must have received votes from all participants, including q, and all these votes were YES. Since q sent a YES vote, it could not have decided **abort** in Lines 14 or 24. So it must

---

[3]Note that the variable C_{know} records the local time at which this event occurs.

have decided **abort** in Line 19, following the delivery of an **abort** message. By the Integrity property of the broadcast, some participant c' must have broadcast this message. From the protocol it is clear that c' assumed the role of coordinator. Since by the protocol, a coordinator may broadcast at most one decision message, c must be different from c'. This contradicts axiom AX1, stipulating that each transaction has at most one coordinator.   □

6.8   The Non-Blocking Atomic Commitment Problem

Recall that in protocol ACP-SB, if a participant times out waiting for the decision from the coordinator, it invokes a termination protocol. Informally, this protocol will try to contact some other participant that has already decided or one that has not yet voted. If it succeeds, this will lead to a decision. There will, however, be failure scenarios for which no termination protocol can lead to a decision (Gray [1978]; Skeen [1982]).

For example, consider a ACP-SB execution where the coordinator crashes during the broadcast of the decision (in Phase 2 of Task 1). Suppose that:

- all faulty participants deliver the decision and then crash, and
- all correct participants have previously voted YES (in Phase 1 of Task 1), and they do not deliver the decision.

If faulty participants do not recover, no termination protocol can lead correct participants to decide: Any such decision may contradict the decision made by a participant that crashed. We say that an atomic commitment protocol is *blocking* if it admits executions in which *correct* participants cannot decide. The scenario above shows that ACP-SB is blocking.

As we have argued in the Introduction, blocking atomic commitment protocols are undesirable since they result in poor system resource utilization. An atomic commitment protocol is said to be *non-blocking* if it satisfies the following property in addition to AC1–AC4:

AC5: Every correct participant that executes the atomic commitment protocol eventually decides.

Note that the non-blocking property of atomic commitment protocol is stated in terms of *correct* and not *operational* participants. This is because an operational participant may have crashed and then recovered, in which case, decision is to be achieved through the recovery protocol rather than the commitment protocol. Furthermore, the property requires only those participants that execute the atomic commitment protocol to eventually decide. From the distributed transaction execution schema of Figure 6.1, there may be others that do not execute the protocol because they do not know about the transaction. For them, we do not insist on a decision since they are not holding any resources on behalf of the transaction.

6.9   The Non-Blocking Atomic Commitment Protocol: ACP-UTRB

We now show that protocol ACP-SB can be made non-blocking by replacing SB with a stronger broadcast primitive. Recall that ACP-SB leads to blocking only if the coordinator crashes while broadcasting a decision and this decision is delivered only by participants that later crash. Thus blocking can occur because SB (the broadcast used to disseminate the decision) allows faulty processes to deliver a message that is never delivered by correct processes. This undesirable scenario is prevented by using *Uniform Timed Reliable Broadcast (UTRB)*, a broadcast primitive that requires

B4 (Uniform Agreement): If any process (correct or not) in G delivers a message m, then all correct processes in G eventually deliver m

in addition to the Validity, Integrity, and Δ_b-Timeliness of SB.[4] Note that with respect to message delivery, property B4 requires agreement among all processes, and not just those that are correct. It is this *uniformity* aspect of agreement that makes blocking scenarios impossible.

Figure 6.4 illustrates ACP-UTRB, a non-blocking atomic commitment protocol based on UTRB. This non-blocking protocol is obtained from ACP as follows:

- the coordinator uses UTRB (rather than SB) to broadcast the decision in Lines 5, 6 and 8, and
- If a participant times out while waiting to deliver this decision, it simply decides **abort** (rather than invoking a termination protocol) in Line 22.

Removing the termination protocol, the only source of indefinite wait in ACP-SB, eliminates blocking.

Theorem 11 *Protocol ACP-UTRB achieves properties AC1–AC4 of the atomic commitment problem.*

Proof: The proofs of AC2, AC3 and AC4 remain exactly the same as with ACP-SB. This is because UTRB has the Validity, Integrity and Δ_b-Timeliness properties of SB, and the modifications made to ACP in obtaining ACP-UTRB do not affect these proofs. The proof of AC1, however, is modified as follows.

The proof is by contradiction. Suppose participant p decides **commit** and participant q decides **abort**. By AC4, $p \neq q$. Participant q can decide **abort** only in Lines 14, 19, 22 and 24. The proof that q cannot decide **abort** in Lines 14, 19 and 24 is exactly as before. Suppose that q decides **abort** at Line 22, that is after timing out while waiting for the delivery of the decision message. Note that this timeout occurs at real-time $t_{know} + \Delta_c + 2\delta + \Delta_b$. From the first part of the proof, a coordinator must have broadcast a **commit** message which was delivered by p. By AX3 and the protocol, this broadcast occurred by real-time $t_{start} + \Delta_c + 2\delta$. Since p delivered **commit**, by the Uniform Agreement property of the broadcast, q eventually delivers **commit** as well. By the Δ_b-Timeliness property of the broadcast, q does so by

---

[4]Thus, UTRB is a strengthening of SB.

```
procedure atomic_commitment(transaction, participants)
    cobegin
    % Task 1: Executed by the coordinator
1       send [VOTE_REQUEST] to all participants          % Including the coordinator
2       set-timeout-to local_clock + 2δ
3       wait-for (receipt of [vote: vote] messages from all participants)
4           if (all votes are YES) then
5               broadcast (commit, participants)          % Using a UTRB
6           else broadcast (abort, participants)          % Using a UTRB
7           on-timeout
8               broadcast (abort, participants)           % Using a UTRB

    //

9       % Task 2: Executed by all participants (including the coordinator)
10          set-timeout-to C_{know} + Δ_c + δ
11          wait-for (receipt of [VOTE_REQUEST] from coordinator)
12              send [vote: vote] to coordinator
13              if (vote = NO) then
14                  decide abort
15              else
16                  set-timeout-to C_{know} + Δ_c + 2δ + Δ_b
17                  wait-for (delivery of decision message)
18                      if (decision message is abort) then
19                          decide abort
20                      else decide commit
21                  on-timeout
22                      decide abort                      % Replaces termination protocol
23          on-timeout
24              decide abort
    coend
end
```

Figure 6.4. ACP-UTRB: A Non-Blocking Atomic Commitment Protocol Based on UTRB

real-time $t_{start} + \Delta_c + 2\delta + \Delta_b$. Since $t_{start} \leq t_{know}$, q must have delivered **commit** before timing out. This, however, contradicts the semantics of the **wait-for** statement. □

We now prove that ACP-UTRB is indeed non-blocking by showing that it satisfies AC5.

Theorem 12 *Every correct participant that executes ACP-UTRB eventually decides.*

Proof: In ACP-SB, a correct participant could be prevented from reaching a decision only by executing the termination protocol of Line 22. This is because each **wait-for** statement has an associated timeout clause that makes indefinite waiting elsewhere impossible. In ACP-UTRB, we substituted the termination protocol with a unilateral **abort** decision, thus eliminating the only potential source of blocking. So, every correct participant that executes ACP-UTRB eventually decides.   □

```
procedure broadcast(m, G)

% Broadcaster executes:
    send [DLV: m] to all processes in G
    deliver m

% Process p ≠ broadcaster in G executes:
    upon (first receipt of [DLV: m])
        send [DLV: m] to all processes in G
        deliver m
end
```

Figure 6.5. UTRB1: A Simple UTRB Algorithm

6.10   A Simple UTRB Algorithm

In Figure 6.5 we show UTRB1, a simple UTRB algorithm obtained from SB1 as follows. First, each process relays every message it receives to all others (so, if any correct process receives a message, then all correct processes also receive it, even if the broadcaster crashes). Second, a process does not deliver a message it has received until it has completed relaying it (thus, all correct processes receive and deliver the message even if the relayer subsequently crashes).

Theorem 13 *Algorithm UTRB1 achieves broadcast properties B1–B4.*

Proof: The proofs that UTRB1 satisfies B1 and B2 (Validity, Integrity) are trivial. We now prove B3 and B4.

B3 (Δ_b-*Timeliness*): Let F denote the maximum number of processes that may crash during the execution of the atomic commitment protocol. Suppose the broadcast of message m is initiated at real-time t_b and some process, say p, delivers m. We show that there exists a constant delay $\Delta_b = (F + 1)\delta$ by which this delivery must occur. Let $p_1, p_2, \ldots, p_i$ be the sequence of processes that relayed m from the broadcaster on its way to p, where $p_1 = broadcaster$ and $p_i = p$. Since a process never sends the same message more than once, these processes are all distinct. Note that for all j, $1 \leq j \leq i$, message m traverses $j - 1$ links before it is delivered by a process p_j. So p_j delivers m by real-time $t_b + (j - 1)\delta$. There are two cases to consider:

1. ($i \leq F + 1$) Process $p = p_i$ delivers m by time $t_b + F\delta$, that is within Δ_b of the broadcast.
2. ($i > F + 1$) Consider processes $p_1, p_2, \ldots, p_{F+1}$. Since they are all distinct, one of them, say p_j for some $j \leq F + 1$, must be correct. Note that p_j delivers and relays m by time $t_b + (j - 1)\delta$. Since p_j is correct, p will receive m from p_j at most δ time units later, that is by time $t_b + j\delta$. Since $j \leq F + 1$, p_j delivers m by time $t_b + (F + 1)\delta$, that is within Δ_b of the broadcast.

B4 *(Uniform Agreement)*: To show that UTRB1 satisfies B4, note that a process does not deliver a message unless it has previously relayed that message to all. So, if any process delivers a message, this message will eventually be received and delivered by all correct processes.   □

6.11   Recovery from Failures

To complete our discussion of non-blocking atomic commitment, we need to consider the possibility of a participant that was down becoming operational after
being repaired. Such a participant returns to the operational state by executing
a *recovery protocol*. This protocol first restores the participant's local state using a
distributed transaction log (DT-log) that the participant maintains in stable storage.
The protocol then tries to conclude all the transactions that were in progress at the
participant at the time of the crash. Our recovery protocol and DT-log management
scheme are very similar to those of 2PC with cooperative termination (Bernstein,
Hadzilacos and Goodman [1987]).

We consider the possibility of recovery by adding the following requirement to
the specification of the atomic commit problem:

AC6: If all participants that know about the transaction remain operational long
enough, then they all decide.

The recovery protocol consists of two components — the actions performed
by the recovering participant and the actions performed by other participants in
response to requests for help. For each transaction that was active at the time of
the crash, the recovering participant first tries to decide unilaterally based on the
DT-log. If it cannot, it send out requests for help from the other participants until it
either receives a decision from some participant, or it receives 'don't know' replies
from all participants. When this protocol is used for recovery together with our
non-blocking ACP-UTRB, we can prove the following property (which is stronger
than AC6):

Theorem 14 *(AC6′) If a participant that knows about the transaction recovers, it will
eventually decide provided that either (i) there was no total failure, or (ii) there was a total
failure but all participants recover and stay operational long enough.*

The details of the protocol along with its proof of correctness can be found in
Babaoğlu and Toueg [1993].

6.12   Performance of ACP-UTRB

Just as its development and proof of correctness, the performance of the non-
blocking atomic commitment protocol ACP-UTRB can be analyzed in a modular
fashion. Both the time delay and message complexity of ACP-UTRB can be expressed as the sum of the cost of ACP and the cost of the particular instance of
UTRB used.

Let n denote the number of participants for the transaction. Recall that F is
the maximum number of participants that may crash during the protocol execution. Let $T_{ACP-UTRB}$ and $M_{ACP-UTRB}$ denote the time delay and message complexity, respectively, of ACP-UTRB. From the structure of ACP-UTRB, it is clear that
$T_{ACP-UTRB} = 2\delta + \Delta_b$ and $M_{ACP-UTRB} = 2n + \mu_b$, where Δ_b and μ_b denote the timeliness

and message complexity, respectively, of the particular UTRB algorithm used. The additive terms 2δ and $2n$ are the time and message costs due to ACP.

We now consider the performance of ACP-UTRB when UTRB1 is used as the broadcast algorithm. In UTRB1, each process relays each message to all other participants, so the message complexity of UTRB1 is n^2. The proof of Theorem 13 shows that the timeliness of UTRB1 is $(F+1)\delta$. Thus, the performance of ACP-UTRB using UTRB1 is $T_{ACP-UTRB1} = (F+3)\delta$ and $M_{ACP-UTRB1} = 2n + n^2$.

6.13 Optimizations

As we saw in the previous section, the performance of ACP-UTRB depends on the performance of the particular implementation of UTRB that is used. The implementation that we gave so far, UTRB1, is very simple but requires a quadratic number of messages. In the next two sections, we present more efficient implementations of UTRB. We first describe UTRB2, an algorithm that requires only a linear number of messages. We then give UTRB3, a message-efficient algorithm that improves on the timeliness of UTRB2.

6.13.1 A Message-Efficient UTRB Algorithm

The message complexity of algorithm UTRB1 can be reduced from quadratic to linear using the idea of *rotating coordinators* (Chandra and Toueg [1990]). Rather than having each process relay every message to all other processes under all circumstances, we arrange for a process to assume the role of the initial broadcaster only in case of failures. The resulting algorithm is called UTRB2 and is displayed in Figure 6.6. The algorithm relies on the FIFO property of the communication channels.

The algorithm uses three types of messages: MSG announces the initial message, DLV causes a delivery, and REQ is used to request help. The initial broadcaster constructs a list of processes called *cohorts* that will cooperate in performing the broadcast. The first process on this cohort list is the broadcaster itself. To tolerate the failure of up to F processes, the cohort list contains $F+1$ distinct process names. This list, along with the index of the current cohort is included in MSG and REQ messages.

Recall that Δ_b, the timeliness of UTRB, is the maximum time that may elapse between the broadcast and delivery of a message. In other words, *if* a message is delivered, it is delivered within Δ_b time units after the broadcast (but it is possible for a message broadcast by a faulty process not to be delivered by any process). Let f denote the number of processes that *actually* crash just during the execution of the broadcast algorithm. Clearly $f \leq F$, since F denotes the *maximum* number of processes that may crash during the entire atomic commitment protocol execution. We now derive expressions for Δ_b, and the message complexity of UTRB2, as a function of f.

The broadcaster sends a MSG message immediately followed by a DLV message to all. We assume that τ time units elapse between these two **send to all** operations.

```
     procedure broadcast(m, G)

     % Broadcaster executes:
1        send [MSG: m, cohorts, 1] to all processes in G
2        send [DLV: m] to all processes in G

     % Process p in G executes:
3        upon (first receipt of [MSG: m, cohorts, index])
4            i := index
5            first_timeout := local_clock + (δ + τ)
6            for k := 0, 1, ... do
7                set-timeout-to first_timeout + k(2δ + τ)
8                wait-for (receipt of [DLV: m])
9                    deliver m
10                   exit loop
11               on-timeout
12                   if (i < F+ 1) then
13                       i := i + 1
14                       send [REQ: m, cohorts, i] to cohorts[i]
15                   else exit loop                    % More than F cohorts have failed
             od

16       upon (first receipt of [REQ: m, cohorts, index])
17           send [MSG: m, cohorts, index] to all processes in G
18           send [DLV: m] to all processes in G
     end
```

Figure 6.6. UTRB2: A Message-Efficient UTRB Algorithm

This time accounts only for the processing delays and does not include network transport delays.[5] If there are no failures ($f = 0$), each process will receive this DLV message within $\delta + \tau$ time units from the time MSG was broadcast. This scenario results in a total of $2n$ messages.

Now consider the case $f = 1$ and the broadcaster is faulty. The worst-case delay occurs if at least one process receives the broadcaster's MSG message but not all receive the DLV. The initial MSG message could take up to δ time units to arrive. Those processes that receive MSG but do not receive DLV will wait an additional $\delta + \tau$ time units from the time they received MSG before timing out and requesting help from the next cohort. The cohort receives this request at most δ time units later. This cohort has to be correct (since $f = 1$) and sends MSG followed by DLV at most τ time units after it received the request. This DLV is received at most δ time units later. Thus, the maximum total elapsed time before delivery becomes $\delta + (\delta + \tau) + \delta + \tau + \delta = 4\delta + 2\tau$. As for messages, note that only those processes that did not receive DLV send REQ messages to the next cohort. Thus, the number of MSG and DLV messages sent by the broadcaster and the REQ messages sent by processes to the next cohort sum to $2n$. The cohort behaves just like the original broadcaster and sends $2n$ additional messages, resulting in $4n$ total messages.

In general, worst-case performance results when each additional failure is that

---

[5]In systems where the communication subsystem buffers messages such that send operations do not block a process, τ should be negligible compared to δ.

Number of Faulty Processes	Timeliness (Δ_b)	Messages
$f = 0$	$\delta + \tau$	$2n$
$1 \le f \le F$	$(f + 1)(2\delta + \tau)$	$(f + 1)2n$

Table 6.1. Performance of algorithm UTRB2

of a different cohort. The loop with a $2\delta + \tau$ timeout period is repeated until either a DLV message arrives (and causes delivery), or there are no more cohorts to ask for help (i.e., more than F processes crash). Thus, each new failure beyond the first results in $2\delta + \tau$ additional time units and $2n$ additional messages. These results are summarized in Table 6.1. The proof of correctness of algorithm UTRB2 can be found in Babaoğlu and Toueg [1993].

6.13.2   A Message- and Time-Efficient UTRB Algorithm

We can modify UTRB2 to improve timeliness while maintaining a linear number of messages. The basic idea is to overlap sending of REQ messages to the next cohort with the (possible) arrival of DLV messages from the previous cohort. By being pessimistic and asking for help before the full round-trip message delay ($2\delta + \tau$), a process can reduce the time to deliver a message. The resulting algorithm, called UTRB3, is essentially UTRB2 with the timeout period for the request loop reduced from $2\delta + \tau$ to δ. Note that this modification may result in increased message traffic if the pessimism is unwarranted in the sense that the previous cohort was correct but REQ messages were sent before waiting long enough for the arrival of its DLV messages. In case of no failures, UTRB3 behaves exactly like UTRB2 and has the same timeliness and message complexity. In the general case, we can show that the timeliness of UTRB3 is $3\delta + 2\tau + f\delta$ and its message complexity is $8n + 2fn$.

Recall that the time performance of ACP-UTRB is given by the expression $2\delta + \Delta_b$ where Δ_b is the timeliness of the particular instance of UTRB that is used. As we have seen with UTRB2, in executions that actually deliver a message, some UTRB algorithms can exhibit 'early stopping' in the sense that Δ_b is proportional to f, the number of processes that actually crash. However, when Δ_b is used to set a timeout for the delivery of a decision, it has to be instantiated using F rather than f to obtain the worst-case delay. Thus, when an **abort** decision occurs due to a timeout because no decision message was delivered, the delay is proportional to F. In other words, there may be executions were a single failure occurs (the coordinator crashes before sending any messages) yet no participant can decide before waiting for a time proportional to F.

The observation that participants gain knowledge about the imminent broadcast of a decision value during the voting phase can be exploited to expedite decisions that normally would have waited for the timeout period to expire in ACP-UTRB. In particular, a participant that received a VOTE_REQUEST message knows that a broadcast (of the decision) is supposed to be performed by the coordinator within 2δ time units. We can use this knowledge to obtain a 'Terminating' version Uniform Timed Reliable Broadcast, called UTTRB, that is able to detect that the broadcaster is faulty without having to wait for a time proportional to F. Formal specifications of UTTRB, an algorithm that achieves them and an atomic commitment protocol based on UTTRB can be found in Babaoğlu and Toueg [1993].

6.14   Communication Failures and Imperfect Clocks

As stated earlier, distributed systems with unreliable communication do not admit non-blocking solutions to the atomic commitment problem. Our protocols are no exception — if communication is not reliable, they have to block in order not to violate property AC1. The same blocking scenario of Section 6.8 where participants are partitioned into two groups may result through communication failures even if no participant crashes. In this case, undecided correct participants cannot proceed because the other group is disconnected due to communication failures rather than its participants being down. In terms of our modular construction, the possibility of blocking can be explained by noting that communication failures render the Uniform Agreement property (B4) of UTRB broadcast impossible to achieve. Given the impossibility result, the best we can hope for is to extend our protocols such that participants in a majority partition are able to proceed towards a decision while others remain blocked (Lamport [1989]).

Up to now, we have assumed that local clocks of processes are perfect in that they run exactly at the same rate as real-time. In practice, local clocks only guarantee a bounded drift rate with respect to real-time. In other words, there exists a parameter $\rho > 0$ such that for all $t_2 \geq t_1$,

$$(1 + \rho)^{-1}(t_2 - t_1) \leq C_i(t_2) - C_i(t_1) \leq (1 + \rho)(t_2 - t_1)$$

where $C_i(t)$ is the reading of the local clock of process p_i at real-time t. Thus, local clocks are within a linear envelope of real-time. We assume that parameter ρ is common to all of the clocks.

In our protocols, clocks are used only to measure the passage of local time intervals in implementing the timeouts associated with various wait events at a process. In particular, they are never used in a manner where the clock value of process p_i is interpreted in the context of another process p_j. Thus, local clocks need not be synchronized with each other.

Since all of the parameters used by our protocols (e.g., δ, τ, Δ_c and Δ_b) are given in terms of real-time, we need to convert timeout periods specified in terms of real-time to local clock time. We also need to be able to convert a time interval measured by one process into an interval measured at another process. Note that these modifications are not exclusive to our protocols — *any* protocol that bases its actions on the passage of real-time must be modified in a similar manner in order to function correctly with realistic clocks. All of the algorithms and protocols we have developed remain valid if the timeout values are corrected by factors derived from the following observations:

- To guarantee that at least T seconds of real-time elapse, $T(1 + \rho)$ ticks must elapse on a local clock,
- To guarantee that at least X ticks elapse on the local clock of process p_i, $X(1 + \rho)^2$ ticks must elapse on the local clock of process p_j.

6.15   Related Work

The role of reliable broadcast (or other formulations including Byzantine Agreement (Lamport, Shostak and Pease [1982])) in distributed database transaction processing has been the subject of numerous works (Coan and Lundelius [1986]; Garcia-Molina, Pittelli and Davidson [1984]; Gray [1990]; Hadzilacos [1990]; Lamport and Fischer [1982]; Mohan, Strong and Finkelstein [1983]). Most of these studies have tried to relate the atomic commitment problem of transaction processing to various formulations of the Byzantine Agreement (BA) problem. In others, BA has been proposed as a way to relax the synchronous system assumptions or permit failures that are more general than the crash model. For instance, in Coan and Lundelius [1986], the transaction commitment problem is formulated in an 'almost asynchronous' system and solved using a randomized BA protocol (Ben-Or [1983]). It is well known that in such a system, no deterministic solution to the atomic commitment problem exists that can tolerate even a single crash failure (Fischer, Lynch and Paterson [1985]). In Garcia-Molina, Pittelli and Davidson [1984] BA is used to cope with data storage nodes that may fail in an arbitrary and malicious manner.

Perhaps the work that is most similar in spirit is (Mohan, Strong and Finkelstein [1983]) where BA is is used to replace the second phase of 2PC. The motivation for the work, however, is to reduce recovery time at the cost of increased message traffic and longer delays for deciding. Moreover, no formal specifications are given for either the atomic commitment problem or the BA used in the protocol.

6.16   Conclusions

We have described a solution to the non-blocking atomic commitment problem that is as easy to understand and prove as the well-known Two-Phase Commit protocol, a protocol that may lead to blocking (Gray [1978]; Lampson [1981]). Furthermore, our solution is *complete*: it does not require any additional protocols that other solutions typically require (e.g., the Three-Phase Commit Protocol requires a fault-tolerant leader election protocol (Skeen [1982])).

This solution was derived by focusing on the *properties* of the broadcast primitive used to disseminate the decision values. Indeed, it was obtained just by strengthening the broadcast used in the second phase of the Two-Phase Commit protocol.

Our non-blocking atomic commitment protocol, ACP-UTRB, was given modularly: a generic ACP protocol that relies on the properties of the UTRB broadcast. To demonstrate the practicality of ACP-UTRB, we have given several implementations of UTRB, each improving some performance measure. The performance of the resulting ACP-UTRB implementations are comparable to 2PC, yet they are non-blocking.

Acknowledgments

We are grateful to Tushar Chandra for his comments on an early draft of this chapter. Babaoğlu was supported in part by the Commission of European Communities under ESPRIT Programme Basic Research Project Number 6360 (BROADCAST), the United States Office of Naval Research under contract N00014-91-J-1219, IBM Corporation, Hewlett-Packard of Italy and the Italian Ministry of University, Research and Technology. Toueg was supported in part by the National Science Foundation under Grant Number CCR-9102231, IBM Corporation (Endicott Programming Laboratory) and the Italian National Research Council (CNR-GNIM) through a Visiting Professor Grant.

6.17   References

Babaoğlu, Ö. and Toueg, S. (1993), Understanding Non-Blocking Atomic Commitment, University of Bologna, Laboratory for Computer Science Technical Report UBLCS-93-2, Italy.

Ben-Or, M. (1983), Another advantage of free choice: Completely asynchronous agreement protocols, *Proceedings of the Second ACM Annual Symposium on Principles of Distributed Computing*, Lynch, N. A., ed., Montreal, Canada, 27–30.

Bernstein, P. A. and Goodman, N. (1981), Concurrency Control in Distributed Database Systems, *ACM Computing Surveys* **13(2)**, 185–222.

Bernstein, P. A., Hadzilacos, V. and Goodman, N. (1987), *Concurrency Control and Recovery in Database Systems*, Addison-Wesley, Reading, MA.

Chandra, T. D. and Toueg, S. (1990), Time and Message Efficient Reliable Broadcast, in *Proceedings of the Fourth International Workshop on Distributed Algorithms*, Leeuwen, J. van and Santoro, N., eds., Lecture Notes in Computer Science, vol. **486**, Springer-Verlag, Bari, Italy, 289–300, Full version available as Cornell Technical Report, TR 90-1094, May 1990.

Coan, B. A. and Lundelius, J. (1986), Transaction Commit in a Realistic Fault Model, *Proceedings of the Fifth ACM Annual Symposium on Principles of Distributed Computing*, Halpern, J., ed., Calgary, Alberta, Canada, 40–51.

Dolev, D. and Strong, H. R. (1982), Distributed Commit with Bounded Waiting, *Proceedings of the Second Symposium on Reliability in Distributed Software*, 53–60.

Dwork, C. and Skeen, D. (1983), The Inherent Cost of Nonblocking Commitment, *Proceedings of the Second ACM Annual Symposium on Principles of Distributed Computing*, Lynch, N. A., ed., Montreal, Canada, 1–11.

Fischer, M. J., Lynch, N. A. and Paterson, M. S. (1985), Impossibility of Distributed Consensus with One Faulty Process, *Journal of the ACM* **32(2)**, 374–382.

Garcia-Molina, H. (1982), Elections in a Distributed Computing System, *IEEETC* **C-31(1)**, 48–59.

Garcia-Molina, H., Pittelli, F. and Davidson, S. B. (1984), Applications of Byzantine Agreement in Database Systems, Princeton University, Princeton, NJ, Technical Report TR 316.

Gray, J. N. (1990), A Comparison of the Byzantine Agreement Problem and the Transaction, in *Fault-Tolerant Distributed Computing*, Simons, B. and Spector, A. Z., eds., Lecture Notes in Computer Science, vol. **448**, Springer-Verlag, New York, 10–17. $Q A \; 76 \cdot 6 \; O6$

Gray, J. N. (1978), Notes on database operating systems, in *Operating Systems — An Advanced Course*, Bayer, R., Graham, R. M. and Seegmuller, G., eds., Lecture Notes on Computer Science, vol. **66**, springer, 393–481, Also available as Technical Report RJ2188, IBM Research Laboratory, San Jose, California, 1978.

Hadzilacos, V. (1984), Issues of Fault Tolerance in Concurrent Computations, Harvard University, Ph.D. Dissertation, Department of Computer Science Technical Report 11-84.

Hadzilacos, V. (1990), On the Relationship Between the Atomic Commitment and Consensus Problems, in *Fault-Tolerant Distributed Computing*, Simons, B. and Spector, A. Z., eds., Lecture Notes in Computer Science, vol. **448**, Springer-Verlag, New York, 201–208.

Halpern, J. Y. and Moses, Y. (1990), Knowledge and Common Knowledge in a Distributed Environment, *Journal of the ACM* **37**(3), 549–587.

Lamport, L. (1989), The Part-Time Parliament, DEC Systems Research Center, Technical Report 49, Palo Alto, California.

Lamport, L. and Fischer, M. J. (1982), Byzantine Generals and Transaction Commit Protocols, SRI International, Technical Report 62.

Lamport, L. and Melliar-Smith, P. M. (1985), Synchronizing Clocks in the Presence of Faults, *Journal of the ACM* **32**(1), 52–78.

Lamport, L., Shostak, R. and Pease, M. (1982), The Byzantine Generals Problem, *ACM Transactions on Programming Languages and Systems* **4**(3), 382–401.

Lampson, B. W. (1981), Atomic Transactions, in *Distributed Systems — Architecture and Implementation:*, Lampson, B., Paul, M. and Siegert, H., eds., Lecture Notes in Computer Science, vol. **105**, Springer-Verlag, 246–265.

Mohan, C. K., Strong, R. and Finkelstein, S. (1983), Methods for Distributed Transaction Commit and Recovery Using Byzantine Agreement within Clusters of Processors, *Proceedings of the Second ACM Annual Symposium on Principles of Distributed Computing*, Lynch, N. A., ed., Montreal, Canada, 89–103.

Neiger, G. and Toueg, S. (1990), Automatically Increasing the Fault-Tolerance of Distributed Algorithms, *Journal of Algorithms* **11**(3), 374–419.

Papadimitriou, C. H. (1979), The Serializability of Concurrent Database Updates, *Journal of the ACM* **26**(4), 631–653.

Skeen, D. (1982), Crash Recovery in a Distributed Database System, University of California, Berkeley, Ph.D. dissertation.

Skeen, D. (1985), Determining the Last Process to Fail, *ACM Transactions on Computer Systems* **3**(1), 15–30.

Chapter 7

Replication Management using the State-Machine Approach

Fred B. Schneider

This chapter reprints my paper 'Implementing Fault-tolerant Services using the State-Machine Approach: A Tutorial' *which orginally appeared in* ACM Computing Surveys **22** *(Dec. 1990). The paper has been reformatted, but otherwise remains unchanged.*

Most distributed systems employ replicated services in one form or another. By replicating a service, we can support fault-tolerance as well as improving overall throughput by placing server replicas at sites where the service is needed. Protocols for replication management can be divided into two general classes. The first, called 'the state-machine approach' or 'active replication', has no centralized control. This class is the subject of this chapter. The second class of protocols is called the 'primary-backup approach', and it is discussed in Chapter 8.

The state-machine approach ties together a number of the fundamental problems that have been discussed in previous chapters. Chapter 2 should be consulted to put in perspective the distributed systems models of this chapter. Chapter 4 discusses the logical clocks used here to order client requests. And Chapter 5 discusses semantics for various communications primitives that support the state-machine approach.

7.1   Introduction

Distributed software is often structured in terms of *clients* and *services*. Each service comprises one or more *servers* and exports *operations* which clients invoke by making *requests*. Although using a single, centralized, server is the simplest way to implement a service, the resulting service can only be as fault-tolerant as the processor executing that server. If this level of fault tolerance is unacceptable, then multiple servers that fail independently must be employed. Usually, replicas of a single server are executed on separate processors of a distributed system, and protocols are employed to coordinate client interactions with these replicas. The physical and electrical isolation of processors in a distributed system ensures that server failures are independent, as required.

The *state-machine approach* is a general method for implementing a fault-tolerant service by replicating servers and coordinating client interactions with server replicas.[1] The approach also provides a framework for understanding and designing replication management protocols. Many protocols that involve replication of data or software — be it for masking failures or simply to facilitate cooperation without centralized control — can be derived using the state-machine approach. Although few of these protocols actually were obtained in this manner, viewing them in terms of state machines helps in understanding how and why they work.

This chapter is a tutorial on the state-machine approach. It describes the approach and its implementation for two representative environments. Small examples suffice to illustrate the points. However, the approach has been successfully applied to larger examples; some of these are mentioned in Section 7.9. Section 7.2 describes how a system can be viewed in terms of a state machine, clients, and output devices. Coping with failures is the subject of Sections 7.3 through 7.6. An important class of optimizations — based on the use of time — is discussed in Section 7.7. Section 7.8 describes dynamic reconfiguration. The history of the approach and related work is discussed in Section 7.9.

7.2   State Machines

Services, servers, and most programming language structures for supporting modularity define *state machines*. A *state machine* consists of *state variables*, which encode its state, and *commands*, which transform its state. Each command is implemented by a deterministic program; execution of the command is atomic with respect to other commands and modifies the state variables and/or produces some output. A *client* of the state machine makes a *request* to execute a command. The request names a state machine, names the command to be performed, and contains any information needed by the command. Output from request processing can be to an actuator (e.g. in a process-control system), to some other peripheral device (e.g. a disk or terminal), or to clients awaiting responses from prior requests.

In this chapter, we will describe a state machine simply by listing its state variables and commands. As an example, state-machine *memory* of Figure 7.1 implements a time-varying mapping from locations to values. A *read* command permits a client to determine the value currently associated with a location, and a *write* command associates a new value with a location.

For generality, our descriptions of state machines deliberately do not specify how command invocation is implemented. Commands might be implemented

- using a collection of procedures that share data and are invoked by a **call**, as in a monitor,

---

[1]The term 'state machine' is a poor one but, nevertheless, is the one used in the literature.

```
memory : state_machine
        var store : array [0..n] of word
        read :  command (loc : 0 .. n)
                send store[loc] to client
                end read;
        write :command(loc : 0..n, value : word)
                store[loc] := value
                end write
        end memory
```

Figure 7.1. A memory

- using a single process that awaits messages containing requests and performs the actions they specify, as in a server, or
- using a collection of interrupt handlers, in which case a request is made by causing an interrupt, as in an operating system kernel. (Disabling interrupts permits each command to be executed to completion before the next is started.)

For example, the state machine of Figure 7.2 implements commands to ensure that at all times at most one client has been granted access to some resource. In it, $x \diamond y$ denotes the result of appending y to the end of list x, $head(x)$ denotes the first element of list x, and $tail(x)$ denotes the list obtained by deleting the first element of list x. This state machine would probably be implemented as part of the supervisor-call handler of an operating system kernel.

Requests are processed by a state machine one at a time, in an order that is consistent with potential causality. Therefore, clients of a state machine can make the following assumptions about the order in which requests are processed:

O1: Requests issued by a single client to a given state machine sm are processed by sm in the order they were issued.

O2: If the fact that request r was made to a state machine sm by client c could have caused a request r' to be made by a client c' to sm, then sm processes r before r'.

Note that due to communications network delays, O1 and O2 do not imply that a state machine will process requests in the order made or in the order received.

To keep our presentation independent of the interprocess communication mechanism used to transmit requests to state machines, we will program client requests as tuples of the form ⟨*state_machine.command, arguments*⟩ and postulate that any results from processing a request are returned using messages. For example, a client might execute

⟨*memory.write*, 100, 16.2;⟩
⟨*memory.read*, 100⟩;
⟨**receive** *v* **from** *memory*⟩

to set the value of location 100 to 16.2, request the value of location 100, and await that value, setting v to it upon receipt.

mutex : **state_machine**
    var *user* : **client_id init** $\varnothing$;
        waiting : **list of client_id init** $\varnothing$
    acquire : **command**
        if *user* = $\varnothing$ $\rightarrow$ **send** *OK* **to** *client*;
                           user := *client*

        $\Box$ *user* $\neq$ $\varnothing$ $\rightarrow$ *waiting* := *waiting* $\diamond$ *client*
        fi
        end *acquire*
    release : **command**
        if *waiting* = $\varnothing$ $\rightarrow$ *user* := $\varnothing$

        $\Box$ *waiting* $\neq$ $\varnothing$ $\rightarrow$ **send** *OK* **to** *head*(*waiting*);
                                  user := *head*(*waiting*);
                                  waiting := *tail*(*waiting*)
        fi
        end *release*
    end *mutex*

Figure 7.2. A resource allocator

The defining characteristic of a state machine is not its syntax, but that it specifies a deterministic computation that reads a stream of requests and processes each, occasionally producing output:

Semantic Characterization of a State Machine. Outputs of a state machine are completely determined by the sequence of requests it processes, independent of time and any other activity in a system.

Not all collections of commands necessarily satisfy this characterization. Consider the following program to solve a simple process-control problem in which an actuator is adjusted repeatedly based on the value of a sensor. Periodically, a client reads a sensor, communicates the value read to state machine *pc*, and delays approximately *D* seconds:

monitor : **process**
    do *true* $\rightarrow$ *val* := **sensor**;
              $\langle$*pc.adjust, val;*$\rangle$
              delay *D*
    od
    end *monitor*

State machine *pc* adjusts an actuator based on past adjustments saved in state variable *q*, the sensor reading, and a control function *F*.

```
pc : state_machine
    var q : real;
    adjust : command(sensor_val : real)
             q := F(q, sensor_val);
             send q to actuator
             end adjust
    end pc
```

Although it is tempting to structure *pc* as a single command that loops — reading from the sensor, evaluating *F*, and writing to *actuator* — if the value of the sensor is time-varying, then the result would not satisfy the semantic characterization given above and therefore would not be a state machine. This is because values sent to *actuator* (the output of the state machine) would not depend solely on the requests made to the state machine but would, in addition, depend on the execution speed of the loop. In the structure used above, this problem has been avoided by moving the loop into *monitor*.

In practice, having to structure a system in terms of state machines and clients does not constitute a real restriction. Anything that can be structured in terms of procedures and procedure calls can also be structured using state machines and clients — a state machine implements the procedure, and requests implement the procedure calls. In fact, state machines permit more flexibility in system structure than is usually available with procedure calls. With state machines, a client making a request is not delayed until that request is processed, and the output of a request can be sent someplace other than to the client making the request. We have not yet encountered an application that could not be programmed cleanly in terms of state machines and clients.

7.3 Fault Tolerance

Before turning to the implementation of fault-tolerant state machines, we must introduce some terminology concerning failures. A component is considered *faulty* once its behavior is no longer consistent with its specification. In this chapter, we consider two representative classes of faulty behavior:

- **Byzantine Failures**. The component can exhibit arbitrary and malicious behavior, perhaps involving collusion with other faulty components (Lamport, Shostak and Pease [1982]).
- **Failstop Failures**. In response to a failure, the component changes to a state that permits other components to detect that a failure has occurred and then stops (Schneider [1984]).

Byzantine failures can be the most disruptive, and there is anecdotal evidence that such failures do occur in practice. Allowing Byzantine failures is the weakest possible assumption that could be made about the effects of a failure. Since a design based on assumptions about the behavior of faulty components runs the risk of failing if these assumptions are not satisfied, it is prudent that life-critical systems tolerate Byzantine failures. However, for most applications, it suffices to assume failstop failures.

A system consisting of a set of distinct components is *t-fault-tolerant* if it satisfies its specification provided that no more than t of those components become faulty during some interval of interest.[2] Fault-tolerance traditionally has been specified in terms of MTBF (mean-time-between-failures), probability of failure over a given interval, and other statistical measures (Siewiorek and Swarz [1982]). While it is clear that such characterizations are important to the users of a system, there are advantages in describing fault tolerance of a system in terms of the maximum number of component failures that can be tolerated over some interval of interest. Asserting that a system is t fault-tolerant makes explicit the assumptions required for correct operation; MTBF and other statistical measures do not. Moreover, t fault-tolerance is unrelated to the reliability of the components that make up the system and therefore is a measure of the fault tolerance supported by the system architecture, in contrast to fault tolerance achieved simply by using reliable components. MTBF and other statistical reliability measures of a t fault-tolerant system can be derived from statistical reliability measures for the components used in constructing that system — in particular, the probability that there will be t or more failures during the operating interval of interest. Thus, t is typically chosen based on statistical measures of component reliability.

7.4   Fault-tolerant State Machines

A t fault-tolerant version of a state machine can be implemented by replicating that state machine and running a replica on each of the processors in a distributed system. Provided each replica being run by a non-faulty processor starts in the same initial state and executes the same requests in the same order, then each will do the same thing and produce the same output. Thus, if we assume that each failure can affect at most one processor, hence one state-machine replica, then by combining the output of the state-machine replicas of this *ensemble*, we can obtain the output for the t fault-tolerant state machine.

When processors can experience Byzantine failures, an ensemble implementing a t fault-tolerant state machine must have at least $2t + 1$ replicas, and the output of the ensemble is the output produced by the majority of the replicas. This is because with $2t+1$ replicas, the majority of the outputs remain correct even after as many as t failures. If processors experience only failstop failures, then an ensemble containing $t + 1$ replicas suffices, and the output of the ensemble can be the output produced by any of its members. This is because only correct outputs are produced by failstop processors, and after t failures one non-faulty replica will remain among the $t + 1$ replicas.

The key, then, for implementing an t fault-tolerant state machine is to ensure

---

[2] A t-fault-tolerant system might continue to operate correctly if more than t failures occur, but correct operation cannot be guaranteed.

Replica Coordination. All replicas receive and process the same sequence of requests.

This can be decomposed into two requirements concerning dissemination of requests to replicas in an ensemble.

Agreement. Every non-faulty state-machine replica receives every request.
Order. Every non-faulty state-machine replica processes the requests it receives in the same relative order.

Notice that Agreement governs the behavior of a client in interacting with state-machine replicas and that Order governs the behavior of a state-machine replica with respect to requests from various clients. Thus, while Replica Coordination could be partitioned in other ways, the Agreement-Order partitioning is a natural choice because it corresponds to the existing separation of the client from the state-machine replicas.

Implementations of Agreement and Order are discussed in Sections 7.1 and 7.2. These implementations make no assumptions about clients or commands. While this generality is useful, knowledge of commands allows Replica Coordination, hence Agreement and Order, to be weakened, and thus allows cheaper protocols to be employed for managing the replicas in an ensemble. Examples of two common weakenings follow.

First, Agreement can be relaxed for read-only requests when failstop processors are being assumed. When processors are failstop, a request r whose processing does not modify state variables need only be sent to a single non-faulty state-machine replica. This is because the response from this replica is — by definition — guaranteed to be correct and, because r changes no state variables, the state of the replica that processes r will remain identical to the states of replicas that do not.

Second, Order can be relaxed for requests that commute. Two requests r and r' commute in a state machine sm if the sequence of outputs and final state of sm that would result from processing r followed by r' is the same as would result from processing r' followed by r. An example of a state machine where Order can be relaxed appears in Figure 7.3. State machine $tally$ determines the first from among a set of alternatives to receive at least MAJ votes and sends this choice to SYSTEM.

If clients cannot vote more than once and the number of clients Cno satisfies $2\text{MAJ} > Cno$, then every request commutes with every other. Thus, implementing Order would be unnecessary — different replicas of the state machine will produce the same outputs even if they process requests in different orders. On the other hand, if clients can vote more than once or $2\text{MAJ} \leq Cno$, then reordering requests might change the outcome of the election.

Theories for constructing state-machine ensembles that do not satisfy Replica Coordination are proposed in Aizikowitz [1989] and Mancini and Pappalardo [1988]. Both theories are based on proving that an ensemble of state machines implements the same specification as a single replica does. The approach taken by Aizikowitz [1989] uses temporal logic descriptions of state sequences, while the approach of Mancini and Pappalardo [1988] uses an algebra of actions sequences. A detailed description of this work is beyond the scope of this chapter.

tally : **state_machine**
　　　var *votes* : **array**[*candidate*] **of integer init** 0
　　　cast_vote : **command**(*choice* : *candidate*)
　　　　　　　votes[*choice*] := *votes*[*choice*] + 1;
　　　　　　　if *votes*[*choice*] ≥ MAJ → **send** *choice* **to** SYSTEM;
　　　　　　　　　　　　　　　　　　　　　halt

　　　　　　　[] *votes*[*choice*] < MAJ → **skip**
　　　　　　fi
　　　　　　end *cast_vote*
　　end *tally*

Figure 7.3. Election

7.4.1　Agreement

The Agreement requirement can be satisfied by using any protocol that allows a designated processor, called the *transmitter*, to disseminate a value to some other processors in such a way that:

IC1:　All non-faulty processors agree on the same value.
IC2:　If the transmitter is non-faulty, then all non-faulty processors use its value as the one on which they agree.

　Protocols to establish IC1 and IC2 have received considerable attention in the literature and are sometimes called *Byzantine Agreement* protocols, *reliable broadcast protocols*, or simply *agreement* protocols. The hard part in designing such protocols is coping with a transmitter that fails part way through an execution. See Strong and Dolev [1983] for protocols that can tolerate Byzantine processor failures and Schneider, Gries and Schlichting [1984] for a (significantly cheaper) protocol that can tolerate (only) failstop processor failures.

　If requests are distributed to all state-machine replicas by using a protocol that satisfies IC1 and IC2, then the Agreement requirement is satisfied. Either the client can serve as the transmitter or the client can send its request to a single state-machine replica and let that replica serve as the transmitter. When the client does not itself serve as the transmitter, however, the client must ensure that its request is not lost or corrupted by the transmitter before the request is disseminated to the state-machine replicas. One way to monitor for such corruption is by having the client be among the processors that receive the request from the transmitter.

7.4.2　Order and Stability

The Order requirement can be satisfied by assigning unique identifiers to requests and having state-machine replicas process requests according to a total ordering relation on these unique identifiers. This is equivalent to requiring the following, where a request is defined to be *stable* at sm_i once no request from a correct client and bearing a lower unique identifier can be subsequently delivered to state-machine replica sm_i:

> **Order Implementation.** A replica next processes the stable request with smallest unique identifier.

Further refinement of Order Implementation requires selecting a method for assigning unique identifiers to requests and devising a stability test for that assignment method. Note that any method for assigning unique identifiers is constrained by O1 and O2 of Section 7.2, which imply that if request r_i could have caused request r_j to be made then $uid(r_i) < uid(r_j)$ holds, where $uid(r)$ is the unique identifier assigned to a request r.

In the subsections that follow, we give three refinements of the Order Implementation. Two are based on the the use of clocks; a third uses an ordering defined by the replicas of the ensemble.

Using Logical Clocks

A *logical clock* (Lamport [1978b]) is a mapping $\hat{T}$ from events to the integers. $\hat{T}(e)$, the 'time' assigned to an event e by logical clock $\hat{T}$, is an integer such that for any two distinct events e and e', either $\hat{T}(e) < \hat{T}(e')$ or $\hat{T}(e') < \hat{T}(e)$, and if e might be responsible for causing e' then $\hat{T}(e) < \hat{T}(e')$. It is a simple matter to implement logical clocks in a distributed system. Associated with each process p is a counter $\hat{T}_p$. In addition, a *timestamp* is included in each message sent by p. This timestamp is the value of $\hat{T}_p$ when that message is sent. $\hat{T}_p$ is updated according to:

LC1: $\hat{T}_p$ is incremented after each event at p.

LC2: Upon receipt of a message with timestamp τ, process p resets $\hat{T}_p$:
$$\hat{T}_p := \max(\hat{T}_p, \tau) + 1.$$

The value of $\hat{T}(e)$ for an event e that occurs at processor p is constructed by appending a fixed-length bit string that uniquely identifies p to the value of $\hat{T}_p$ when e occurs.

Figure 7.4 illustrates the use of this scheme for implementing logical clocks in a system of three processors, p, q and r. Events are depicted by dots and an arrow is drawn between events e and e' if e might be responsible for causing event e'. For example, an arrow between events in different processes starts from the event corresponding to the sending of a message and ends at the event corresponding to the receipt of that message. The value of $\hat{T}_p(e)$ for each event e is written above that event.

If $\hat{T}(e)$ is used as the unique identifier associated with a request whose issuance corresponds to event e, the result is a total ordering on the unique identifiers that satisfies O1 and O2. Thus, a logical clock can be used as the basis of an Order Implementation if we can formulate a way to determine when a request is stable at a state-machine replica.

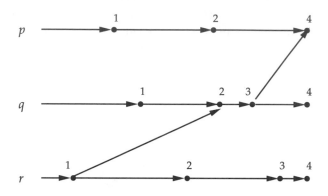

Figure 7.4. Logical Clock Example

It is pointless to implement a stability test in a system where Byzantine failures are possible and a process or message can be delayed for an arbitrary length of time without being considered faulty. This is because no deterministic protocol can implement agreement under these conditions (Fischer, Lynch and Paterson [1985]).[3] Since it is impossible to satisfy the Agreement requirement, there is no point in satisfying the Order requirement. The case where relative speeds of non-faulty processors and messages is bounded is equivalent to assuming that they have synchronized real-time clocks, and will be considered shortly. This leaves the case where failstop failures are possible and a process or message can be delayed for an arbitrary length of time without being considered faulty. Thus, we now turn to devising a stability test for that environment.

By attaching sequence numbers to the messages between every pair of processors, it is trivial to ensure that the following property holds of communications channels.

> **FIFO Channels.** Messages between a pair of processors are delivered in the order sent.

For failstop processors, we can also assume:

> **Failure Detection Assumption.** A processor p detects that a failstop processor q has failed only after p has received q's last message sent to p.

The Failure Detection Assumption is consistent with FIFO Channels, since the failure event for a failstop processor necessarily happens after the last message sent by that processor and, therefore, should be received after all other messages.

Under these two assumptions, the following stability test can be used.

> **Logical Clock Stability Test Tolerating Failstop Failures.** Every client periodically makes some — possibly null — request to the state machine. A

---

[3]The result of Fischer, Lynch and Paterson [1985] is actually stronger than this. It states that IC1 and IC2 cannot be achieved by a deterministic protocol in an asynchronous system with a single processor that fails in an even less restrictive manner — by simply halting.

request is stable at replica sm_i if a request with larger timestamp has been received by sm_i from every client running on a non-faulty processor.

To see why this stability test works, we show that once a request r is stable at sm_i, no request with smaller unique identifier (timestamp) will be received. First, consider clients that sm_i does not detect as being faulty. Because logical clocks are used to generate unique identifiers, any request made by a client c must have a larger unique identifier than was assigned to any previous request made by c. Therefore, from the FIFO Channels assumption, we conclude that once a request from a non-faulty client c is received by sm_i, no request from c with smaller unique identifier than $uid(r)$ can be received by sm_i. This means that once requests with larger unique identifiers than $uid(r)$ have been received from every non-faulty client, it is not possible to receive a request with a smaller unique identifier than $uid(r)$ from these clients. Next, for a client c that sm_i detects as faulty, the Failure Detection Assumption implies that no request from c will be received by sm_i. Thus, once a request r is stable at sm_i, no request with smaller timestamp can be received from a client — faulty or non-faulty.

Synchronized Real-Time Clocks

A second way to produce unique request identifiers satisfying O1 and O2 is by using approximately synchronized real-time clocks.[4] Define $T_p(e)$ to be the value of the real-time clock at processor p when event e occurs. We can use $T_p(e)$ followed by a fixed-length bit string that uniquely identifies p as the unique identifier associated with a request made as event e by a client running on a processor p. To ensure that O1 and O2 (of Section 7.2) hold for unique identifiers generated in this manner, two restrictions are required. O1 follows provided no client makes two or more requests between successive clock ticks. Thus, if processor clocks have a resolution of R seconds, then each client can make at most one request every R seconds. O2 follows provided the degree of clock synchronization is better than the minimum message delivery time. In particular, if clocks on different processors are synchronized to within δ seconds, then it must take more than δ seconds for a message from one client to reach another; otherwise, O2 would be violated because a request r made by one client could have a unique identifier that was smaller than a request r' made by another, even though r was caused by a message sent after r' was made.

When unique request identifiers are obtained from synchronized real-time clocks, a stability test can be implemented by exploiting these clocks and the bounds on message delivery delays. Define Δ to be constant such that a request r with unique identifier $uid(r)$ will be received by every correct processor no later than time $uid(r) + \Delta$ according to the local clock at the receiving processor. Such a Δ must

---

[4]A number of protocols to achieve clock synchronization while tolerating Byzantine failures have been proposed (Halpern et al. [1984]; Lamport and Melliar-Smith [1984]). See Schneider [1986] for a survey. The protocols all require that known bounds exist for the execution speed and clock rates of non-faulty processors and for message delivery delays along non-faulty communications links. In practice, these requirements do not constitute a restriction. Clock synchronization achieved by the protocols is proportional to the variance in message delivery delay, making it possible to satisfy the restriction — necessary to ensure O2 — that message delivery delay exceeds clock synchronization.

exist if requests are disseminated using a protocol that employs a fixed number of rounds, like the ones cited above for establishing IC1 and IC2.[5] By definition, once the clock on a processor p reaches time τ, p cannot subsequently receive a request r such that $uid(r) < \tau - \Delta$. Therefore, we have the following stability test.

> **Real-time Clock Stability Test Tolerating Byzantine Failures I**. A request r is stable at a state-machine replica sm_i being executed by processor p if the local clock at p reads τ and $uid(r) < \tau - \Delta$.

One disadvantage of this stability test is that it forces the state machine to lag behind its clients by Δ, where Δ is proportional to the worst-case message delivery delay. This disadvantage can be avoided. Due to property O1 of the total ordering on request identifiers, if communications channels satisfy FIFO Channels, then a state-machine replica that has received a request r from a client c can subsequently receive from c only requests with unique identifiers greater than $uid(r)$. Thus, a request r is also stable at a state-machine replica provided a request with larger unique identifier has been received from every client.

> **Real-time Clock Stability Test Tolerating Byzantine Failures II**. A request r is stable at a state-machine replica sm_i if a request with larger unique identifier has been received from every client.

This second stability test is never passed if a (faulty) processor refuses to make requests. However, by combining the first and second test, so that a request is considered stable when it satisfies either test, a stability test results that lags clients by Δ only when faulty processors or network delays force it.

Using Replica-Generated Identifiers

In the previous two refinements of the Order Implementation, clients determine the order in which requests are processed — the unique identifier $uid(r)$ for a request r is assigned by the client making that request. In the following refinement of the Order Implementation, the state-machine replicas determine this order. Unique identifiers are computed in two phases. In the first phase, which can be part of the agreement protocol used to satisfy the Agreement requirement, state-machine replicas propose candidate unique identifiers for a request. Then, in the second phase, one of these candidates is selected and it becomes the unique identifier for that request.

The advantage of this approach to computing unique identifiers is that communications between all processors in the system is not necessary. When logical clocks or synchronized real-time clocks are used in computing unique request identifiers, all processors hosting clients or state-machine replicas must communicate. In the case of logical clocks, this communication is needed in order for requests to become stable; in the case of synchronized real-time clocks, this communication is needed

---

[5]In general, Δ will be a function of the variance in message delivery delay, the maximum message delivery delay, and the degree of clock synchronization. See Cristian *et al.* [1985] for a detailed derivation for Δ in a variety of environments.

in order to keep the clocks synchronized.[6] In the replica-generated identifier approach of this subsection, the only communication required is among processors running the client and state-machine replicas.

By constraining the possible candidates proposed in phase 1 for a request's unique identifier, it is possible to obtain a simple stability test. To describe this stability test, some terminology is first required. We say that a state-machine replica sm_i has *seen* a request r once sm_i has received r and proposed a candidate unique identifier for r; and we say that sm_i has *accepted* r once that replica knows the ultimate choice of unique identifier for r. Define $cuid(sm_i, r)$ to be the candidate unique identifier proposed by replica sm_i for request r. Two constraints that lead to a simple stability test are:

UID1: $cuid(sm_i, r) \leq uid(r)$
UID2: If a request r' is seen by replica sm_i after r has been accepted by sm_i then $uid(r) < cuid(sm_i, r')$.

If these constraints hold throughout execution, then the following test can be used to determine whether a request is stable at a state-machine replica.

> **Replica-Generated Identifiers Stability Test.** A request r that has been accepted by sm_i is stable provided there is no request r' that has (i) been seen by sm_i, (ii) not been accepted by sm_i, and (iii) for which $cuid(sm_i, r') \leq uid(r)$ holds.

To prove that this stability test works, we must show that once an accepted request r is deemed stable at sm_i, no request with smaller unique identifier will be subsequently accepted at sm_i. Let r be a request that, according to the Replica-Generated Identifiers Stability Test, is stable at replica sm_i. Due to UID2, for any request r' that has not been seen by sm_i, $uid(r) < cuid(sm_i, r')$ holds. Thus, by transitivity using UID1, $uid(r) < uid(r')$ holds, and we conclude that r' cannot have a smaller unique identifier than r. Now consider the case where request r' has been seen but not accepted by sm_i and — because the stability test for r is satisfied — $uid(r) < cuid(sm_i, r')$ holds. Due to UID1, we conclude that $uid(r) < uid(r')$ holds and, therefore, r' does not have a smaller unique identifier than r. Thus, we have shown that once a request r satisfies the Replica-Generated Identifiers Stability Test at sm_i, any request r' that is accepted by sm_i will satisfy $uid(r) < uid(r')$, as desired.

Unlike clock-generated unique identifiers for requests, replica-generated ones do not necessarily satisfy O1 and O2 of Section 7.2. Without further restrictions, it is possible for a client to make a request r, send a message to another client causing request r' to be issued, yet have $uid(r') < uid(r)$. However, O1 and O2 will hold provided that once a client starts disseminating a request to the state-machine replicas, the client performs no other communication until every state-machine replica has accepted that request. To see why this works, consider a request r being

---

[6]This illustrates an advantage of having a client forward its request to a single state-machine replica that then serves as the transmitter for disseminating the request. In effect, that state-machine replica becomes the client of the state machine, and so communication need only involve those processors running state-machine replicas.

made by some client and suppose some request r' was influenced by r. The delay ensures that r is accepted by every state-machine replica sm_j before r' is seen. Thus, from UID2 we conclude $uid(r) < cuid(sm_i, r')$ and, by transitivity with UID1, that $uid(r) < uid(r')$, as required.

To complete this Order Implementation, we have only to devise protocols for computing unique identifiers and candidate unique identifiers such that:

- UID1 and UID2 are satisfied.   (7.1)
- $r \neq r' \Rightarrow uid(r) \neq uid(r')$.   (7.2)
- Every request that is seen eventually becomes accepted.   (7.3)

One simple solution for a system of failstop processors is the following.

Replica-generated Unique Identifiers. Each state-machine replica sm_i maintains two variables:
$SEEN_i$ is the largest $cuid(sm_i, r)$ assigned to any request r so far seen by sm_i, and
$ACCEPT_i$ is the largest $uid(r)$ assigned to any request r so far accepted by sm_i.

Upon receipt of a request r, each replica sm_i computes
$$cuid(sm_i, r) := \max(\lfloor SEEN_i \rfloor, \lfloor ACCEPT_i \rfloor) + 1 + i \qquad (7.4)$$
(Notice, this means that all candidate unique identifiers are themselves unique.) The replica then disseminates — using an agreement protocol — $cuid(sm_i, r)$ to all other replicas and awaits receipt of a candidate unique identifier for r from every non-faulty replica, participating in the agreement protocol for that value as well. Let NF be the set of replicas from which candidate unique identifiers were received. Finally, the replica computes
$$uid(r) := \max_{sm_j \in NF}(cuid(sm_j, r)) \qquad (7.5)$$
and accepts r.

We prove that this protocol satisfies (7.1)–(7.3) as follows. UID1 follows from using assignment (7.5) to compute $uid(r)$, and UID2 follows from assignment (7.4) to compute $cuid(sm_i, r)$. To conclude that (7.2) holds, we argue as follows. Because an agreement protocol is used to disseminate candidate unique identifiers, all replicas receive the same values from the same replicas. Thus, all replicas will execute the same assignment statement (7.5) and all will compute the same value for $uid(r)$. To establish that the these $uid(r)$ values are unique for each request, it suffices to observe that maximums of disjoint subsets of a collection of unique values — the candidate unique identifiers — are also unique. Finally, in order to establish (7.3), that every request that is seen is eventually accepted, we must prove that for each replica sm_j, a replica sm_i eventually learns $cuid(sm_j, r)$ or learns that sm_j has failed. This follows trivially from the use of an agreement protocol to distribute the $cuid(sm_j, r)$ and the definition of a failstop processor.

An optimization of our Replica-generated Unique Identifiers protocol is the basis for the ABCAST protocol in the ISIS Toolkit (Birman and Joseph [1987]) developed at Cornell. In this optimization, candidate unique identifiers are returned to the client instead of being disseminated to the other state-machine replicas. The client then executes assignment (7.5) to compute $uid(r)$. Finally, an agreement protocol is used by the client in disseminating $uid(r)$ to the state-machine replicas. Some unique replica takes over for the client if the client fails.

It is possible to modify our Replica-generated Unique Identifiers protocol for use in systems where processors can exhibit Byzantine failures, have synchronized real-time clocks, and communications channels have bounded message-delivery delays — the same environment as was assumed for using synchronized real-time clocks to generate unique identifiers. The following changes are required. First, each replica sm_i uses timeouts so that sm_i cannot be forever delayed waiting to receive and participate in the agreement protocol for disseminating a candidate unique identifier from a faulty replica sm_j. Second, if sm_i does determine that sm_j has timed-out, sm_i disseminates 'sm_j timeout' to all replicas (by using an agreement protocol). Finally, NF is the set of replicas in the ensemble less any sm_j for which 'sm_j timeout' has been received from $t + 1$ or more replicas. Notice, Byzantine failures that cause faulty replicas to propose candidate unique identifiers not produced by (7.4) do not cause difficulty. This is because candidate unique identifiers that are too small have no effect on the outcome of (7.5) at non faulty replicas and those that are too large will satisfy UID1 and UID2.

7.5   Tolerating Faulty Output Devices

It is not possible to implement a t-fault tolerant system by using a single voter to combine the outputs of an ensemble of state-machine replicas into one output. This is because a single failure — of the voter — can prevent the system from producing the correct output. Solutions to this problem depend on whether the output of the state machine implemented by the ensemble is to be used within the system or outside the system.

Outputs Used Outside the System

If the output of the state machine is sent to an output device, then that device is already a single component whose failure cannot be tolerated. Thus, being able to tolerate a faulty voter is not sufficient — the system must also be able to tolerate a faulty output device. The usual solution to this problem is to replicate the output device and voter. Each voter combines the output of each state-machine replica, producing a signal that drives one output device. Whatever reads the outputs of the system is assumed to combine the outputs of the replicated devices. This reader, which is not considered part of the computing system, implements the critical voter.

If output devices can exhibit Byzantine failures, then by taking the output produced by the majority of the devices, $2t + 1$-fold replication permits up to t faulty output devices to be tolerated. For example, a flap on an airplane wing might be designed so that when the $2t + 1$ actuators that control it do not agree, the flap always moves in the direction of the majority (rather than twisting). If output devices exhibit only failstop failures, then only $t + 1$-fold replication is necessary to tolerate t failures because any output produced by a failstop output device can be assumed correct. For example, video display terminals usually present information with enough redundancy so that they can be treated as failstop — failure detection is implemented by the viewer. With such an output device, a human user can look at a one of $t + 1$ devices, decide whether the output is faulty, and only if it is faulty, look at another, and so on.

Outputs Used Inside the System

If the output of the state machine is to a client, then the client itself can combine the outputs of state-machine replicas in the ensemble. Here, the voter — a part of the client — is faulty exactly when the client is, so the fact that an incorrect output is read by the client due to a faulty voter is irrelevant. When Byzantine failures are possible, the client waits until it has received $t + 1$ identical responses, each from a different member of the ensemble, and takes that as the response from the t fault-tolerant state machine. When only failstop failures are possible, the client can proceed as soon as it has received a response from any member of the ensemble, since any output produced by a replica must be correct.

When the client is executed on the same processor as one of the state-machine replicas, optimization of client-implemented voting is possible.[7] This is because correctness of the processor implies that both the state-machine replica and client will be correct. Therefore, the response produced by the state-machine replica running locally can be used as that client's response from the t fault-tolerant state machine. And, if the processor is faulty, then we are entitled to view the client as being faulty, so it does not matter what state machine responses the client receives. Summarizing, we have:

> **Dependent-Failures Output Optimization.** If a client and a state-machine replica run on the same processor, then even when Byzantine failures are possible, the client need not gather a majority of responses to its requests to the state machine. It can use the single response produced locally.

7.6   Tolerating Faulty Clients

Implementing a t-fault-tolerant state machine is not sufficient for implementing a t-fault-tolerant system. Faults might result in clients making requests that cause the state machine to produce erroneous output or that corrupt the state machine so that subsequent requests from non-faulty clients are incorrectly processed. Therefore, in this section, we discuss various methods for insulating the state machine from faults that affect clients.

---

[7]Care must be exercised when analyzing the fault-tolerance of such a system because a single processor failure can now cause two system components to fail. Implicit in most of our discussions is that system components fail independently. It is not always possible to transform a t fault-tolerant system in which clients and state-machine replicas have independent failures to one in which they share processors.

7.6.1   Replicating the Client

One way to avoid having faults affect a client is by replicating the client and running each replica on hardware that fails independently. However, this replication also requires changes to state machines that handle requests from that client. This is because after a client has been replicated N-fold, any state machine it interacts with will receive N requests — one from each client replica — when it formerly received a single request. Moreover, corresponding requests from different client replicas will not necessarily be identical. First, they will differ in their unique identifiers. Second, unless the original client is itself a state machine and the methods of Section 7.4 are used to coordinate the replicas, corresponding requests from different replicas can also differ in their content. For example, if a client makes requests based on the value of some time-varying sensor, then its replicas will each read their sensors at slightly different times and, therefore, make different requests.

We first consider modifications to a state machine sm for the case where requests from different client replicas are known to differ only in their unique identifiers. For this case, modifications are needed for coping with receiving N requests instead of a single one. These modifications involve changing each command so that instead of processing every request received, requests are buffered until enough[8] have been received; only then is the corresponding command performed (a single time). In effect, a voter is being added to sm to control invocation of its commands. Client replication can be made invisible to the designer of a state machine by including such a voter in the support software that receives requests, tests for stability, and orders stable requests by unique identifier.

Modifying the state machine for the case where requests from different client replicas can also differ in their content typically requires exploiting knowledge of the application. As before, the idea is to transform multiple requests into a single one. For example, in a t fault-tolerant system, if $2t + 1$ different requests are received, each containing the value of a sensor, then a single request containing the median of those values might be constructed and processed by the state machine. (Given at most t Byzantine faults, the median of $2t + 1$ values is a reasonable one to use because it is bounded from above and below by a non-faulty value.) A general method for transforming multiple requests containing sensor values into a single request is discussed in Marzullo [1989]. That method is based on viewing a sensor value as an interval that includes the actual value being measured; a single interval (sensor) is computed from a set of intervals by using a fault-tolerant intersection algorithm.

7.6.2   Defensive Programming

Sometimes a client cannot be made fault-tolerant by using replication. In some circumstances, due to the unavailability of sensors or processors, it simply might

---

[8]If Byzantine failures are possible then a t-fault-tolerant client requires $2t + 1$-fold replication and a command is performed after $t + 1$ requests have been received; if failures are restricted to failstop, then $t + 1$-fold replication will suffice and a command can be performed after a single request has been received.

release : **command**
    if *user* ≠ *client* → **skip**
    ⬚ *waiting* = ∅ ∧ *user* = *client* → *user* := ∅
    ⬚ *waiting* ≠ ∅ ∧ *user* = *client* → **send** *OK* **to** *head(waiting)*;
                                            user := *head(waiting)*;
                                            waiting := *tail(waiting)*
    fi
    end *release*

Figure 7.5. Modified *release* in *mutex*

not be possible to replicate the client. In other circumstances, the application semantics might not afford a reasonable way to transform multiple requests from client replicas into the single request needed by the state machine. In all of these circumstances, careful design of state machines can limit the effects of requests from faulty clients. For example, *memory* (Figure 7.1) permits any client to write to any location. Therefore, a faulty client can overwrite all locations, destroying information. This problem could be prevented by restricting write requests from each client to only certain memory locations — the state machine can enforce this.

Including tests in commands is another way to design a state machine that cannot be corrupted by requests from faulty clients. For example, *mutex* as specified in Figure 7.2, will execute a *release* command made by any client — even one that does not have access to the resource. Consequently, a faulty client could issue such a request and cause *mutex* to grant a second client access to the resource before the first has relinquished access. A better formulation of *mutex* ignores *release* commands from all but the client to which exclusive access has been granted. This is implemented by changing the *release* in *mutex* as shown in Figure 7.5.

Sometimes, a faulty client *not* making a request can be just as catastrophic as one making an erroneous request. For example, if a client of *mutex* failed and stopped while it had exclusive access to the resource, then no client could be granted access to the resource. Of course, unless we are prepared to bound the length of time that a correctly functioning process can retain exclusive access to the resource, there is little we can do about this problem. This is because there is no way for a state machine to distinguish between a client that has stopped executing because it has failed and one that is executing very slowly. However, given an upper bound B on the interval between an *acquire* and the following *release*, the *acquire* command of *mutex* can automatically schedule *release* on behalf of a client.

We use the notation

schedule *REQUEST* **for** +τ

to specify scheduling *REQUEST* with a unique identifier at least τ greater than the identifier on the request being processed. Such a request is called a *timeout request* and becomes stable at some time in the future, according to the stability test being

acquire : **command**
　　if *user* = ∅ → **send** *OK* **to** *client*;
　　　　　　　　user := *client*;
　　　　　　　　time_granted := *TIME*;
　　　　　　　　schedule *mutex.timeout, time_granted* **for** +B

　　▯ *user* ≠ ∅ → *waiting* := *waiting* ◇ *client*
　　fi
　　end *acquire*

timeout :**command**(*when_granted* : **integer**)
　　if *when_granted* ≠ *time_granted* → **skip**

　　▯ *waiting* = ∅ ∧ *when_granted* = *time_granted* → *user* := ∅

　　▯ *waiting* ≠ ∅ ∧ *when_granted* = *time_granted* →
　　　　　　　　send *OK* **to** *head*(*waiting*);
　　　　　　　　user := *head*(*waiting*);
　　　　　　　　time_granted := *TIME*;
　　　　　　　　waiting := *tail*(*waiting*)

　　fi
　　end *timeout*

Figure 7.6. Defensive version of *acquire* and *release*

used for client-generated requests. Unlike requests from clients, requests that result from executing **schedule** need not be distributed to all state-machine replicas of the ensemble. This is because each state-machine replica will independently **schedule** its own (identical) copy of the request.

We can now modify *acquire* so that a *release* operation is automatically scheduled (Figure 7.6). In the code that follows, *TIME* is assumed to be a function that evaluates to the current time. Note that *mutex* might now process two *release* commands on behalf of a client that has acquired access to the resource: one command from the client itself and one generated by its *acquire* request. However, the new state variable *time_granted* ensures that superfluous *release* commands are ignored.

7.7　Using Time to Make Requests

A client need not explicitly send a message to make a request. Not receiving a request can trigger execution of a command — in effect, allowing the passage of time to transmit a request from client to state machine (Lamport [1984]). Transmitting a request using time instead of messages can be advantageous because protocols that implement IC1 and IC2 can be costly both in total number of messages exchanged and in delay. Unfortunately, using time to transmit requests has only limited applicability, since the client cannot specify parameter values.

The use of time to transmit a request was employed in Section 7.6 when we revised the *acquire* command of *mutex* to foil clients that failed to release the resource. There, a *release* request was automatically scheduled by *acquire* on behalf of a client being granted the resource. A client transmits a *release* request to *mutex* simply by permitting B (logical clock or real-time clock) time units to pass. It is only to increase utilization of the shared resource that a client might use messages to transmit a *release* request to *mutex* before B time units have passed.

A more dramatic example of using time to transmit a request is illustrated in connection with *tally* of Figure 7.3. Assume that

- all clients and state-machine replicas have (logical or real time) clocks synchronized to within Γ and
- the election starts at time *Strt* and this is known to all clients and state-machine replicas.

Using time, a client can cast a vote for a *default* by doing nothing; only when a client casts a vote different from its default do we require that it actually transmit a request message. Thus, we have:

> **Transmitting a Default Vote**. If client has not made a request by time *Strt* $+\Gamma$, then a request with that client's default vote has been made.

Notice that the default need not be fixed nor even known at the time a vote is cast. For example, the default vote could be 'vote for the first client that any client casts a non-default vote for'. In that case, the entire election can be conducted as long as one client casts a vote by using actual messages.[9]

7.8   Reconfiguration

An ensemble of state-machine replicas can tolerate more than t faults if it is possible to remove state-machine replicas running on faulty processors from the ensemble and add replicas running on repaired processors. (A similar argument can be made for being able to add and remove copies of clients and output devices.) Let $P(\tau)$ be the total number of processors at time τ that are executing replicas of some state machine of interest, and let $F(\tau)$ be the number of them that are faulty. In order for the ensemble to produce the correct output, we must have

> **Combining Condition**: $P(\tau) - F(\tau) > \textit{Enuf}$ for all $0 \le \tau$.

$$\text{where } \textit{Enuf} \equiv \begin{cases} P(\tau)/2 & \text{if Byzantine failures are possible.} \\ 0 & \text{if only failstop failures are possible.} \end{cases}$$

A processor failure may cause the Combining Condition to be violated by increasing $F(\tau)$, thereby decreasing $P(\tau) - F(\tau)$. When Byzantine failures are possible, if a faulty processor can be identified, then removing it from the ensemble decreases *Enuf* without further decreasing $P(\tau) - F(\tau)$; this can keep the Combining

---

[9]Observe that if Byzantine failures are possible, then a faulty client can be elected. Such problems are always possible when voters do not have detailed knowledge about the candidates in an election.

Condition from being violated. When only failstop failures are possible, increasing the number of non-faulty processors — by adding one that has been repaired — is the only way to keep the Combining Condition from being violated because increasing $P(\tau)$ is the only way to ensure that $P(\tau) - F(\tau) > 0$ holds. Therefore, provided the following conditions hold, it may be possible to maintain the Combining Condition forever and thus tolerate an unbounded total number of faults over the life of the system.

F1: If Byzantine failures are possible, then state-machine replicas being executed by faulty processors are identified and removed from the ensemble before the Combining Condition is violated by subsequent processor failures.

F2: State-machine replicas running on repaired processors are added to the ensemble before the Combining Condition is violated by subsequent processor failures.

F1 and F2 constrain the rates at which failures and repairs occur.

Removing faulty processors from an ensemble of state machines can also improve system performance. This is because the number of messages that must be sent to achieve agreement is usually proportional to the number of state-machine replicas that must agree on the contents of a request. In addition, some protocols to implement agreement execute in time proportional to the number of processors that are faulty. Removing faulty processors clearly reduces both the message complexity and time complexity of such protocols.

Adding or removing a client from the system is simply a matter of changing the state machine so that henceforth it responds to or ignores requests from that client. Adding an output device is also straightforward — the state machine starts sending output to that device. Removing an output device from a system is achieved by *disabling* the device. This is done by putting the device in a state that prevents it from affecting the environment. For example, a CRT terminal can be disabled by turning off the brightness so that the screen can no longer be read; a hydraulic actuator controlling the flap on an airplane wing can be disabled by opening a cutoff valve so that the actuator exerts no presure on that control surface. However, as suggested by these examples, it is not always possible to disable a faulty output device: turning off the brightness might have no effect on the screen and the cutoff valve might not work. Thus, there are systems in which no more than a total of t actuator faults can be tolerated because faulty actuators cannot be disabled.

The *configuration* of a system structured in terms of a state machine and clients can be described using three sets: the clients C, the state-machine replicas S, and the output devices O. S is used by the agreement protocol and therefore must be known to clients and state-machine replicas. It can also be used by an output device to determine which **send** operations made by state-machine replicas should be ignored. C and O are used by state-machine replicas to determine from which clients requests should be processed and to which devices output should be sent. Therefore, C and O must be available to all state-machine replicas.

Two problems must be solved to support changing the system configuration. First, the values of C, S, and O must be available when required. Second, whenever a client, state-machine replica, or output device is added to the configuration, the state of that *element* must be updated to reflect the current state of the system. These problems are considered in the following two subsections.

7.8.1   Managing the Configuration

The configuration of a system can be managed using the state machine in that system. Sets C, S, and O are stored in state variables and changed by commands. Each configuration is *valid* for a collection of requests — those requests r such that $uid(r)$ is in the range defined by two successive configuration-change requests. Thus, whenever a client, state-machine replica, or output device performs an action connected with processing r, it uses the configuration that is valid for r. This means that a configuration-change request must schedule the new configuration for some point far enough in the future so that clients, state-machine replicas, and output devices all find out about the new configuration before it actually comes into effect.

There are various ways to make configuration information available to the clients and output devices of a system. (The information is already available to the state machine.) One is for clients and output devices to query the state machine periodically for information about relevant pending configuration changes. Obviously, communication costs for this scheme are reduced if clients and output devices share processors with state-machine replicas. Another way to make configuration information available is for the state machine to include information about configuration changes in messages it sends to clients and output devices in the course of normal processing. Doing this requires periodic communication between the state machine and clients and between the state machine and output devices.

Requests to change the configuration of the system are made by a failure/recovery detection mechanism. It is convenient to think of this mechanism as a collection of clients, one for each element of C, S, or O. Each of these *configurators* is responsible for detecting the failure or repair of the single object it manages and, when such an event is detected, for making a request to alter the configuration. A configurator is likely to be part of an existing client or state-machine replica and might be implemented in a variety of ways.

When elements are failstop, a configurator need only check the failure-detection mechanism of that element. When elements can exhibit Byzantine failures, detecting failures is not always possible. When it is possible, a higher degree of fault tolerance can be achieved by reconfiguration. A non-faulty configurator satisfies two safety properties.

C1: Only a faulty element is removed from the configuration.
C2: Only a non-faulty element is added to the configuration.

However, a configurator that does nothing satisfies C1 and C2. Changing the configuration enhances fault-tolerance only if F1 and F2 also hold. For F1 and F2 to hold, a configurator must also (1) detect faults and cause elements to be removed and (2) detect repairs and cause elements to be added. Thus, the degree to which a configurator enhances fault tolerance is directly related to the degree to which (1) and (2) are achieved. Here, the semantics of the application can be helpful. For example, to infer that a client is faulty, a state machine can compare requests made by different clients or by the same client over a period of time. To determine that a processor executing a state-machine replica is faulty, the state machine can monitor messages sent by other state-machine replicas during execution of an agreement protocol. And, by monitoring aspects of the environment being controlled by actuators, a state-machine replica might be able to determine that an output device is faulty. Some elements, such as processors, have internal failure-detection circuitry that can be read to determine whether that element is faulty or has been repaired and restarted. A configurator for such an element can be implemented by having the state machine periodically poll this circuitry.

In order to analyze the fault-tolerance of a system that uses configurators, failure of a configurator can be considered equivalent to the failure of the element that the configurator manages. This is because with respect to the Combining Condition, removal of a non-faulty element from the system or addition of a faulty one is the same as that element failing. Thus, in a t-fault-tolerant system, the sum of the number of faulty configurators that manage non-faulty elements and the number of faulty components with non-faulty configurators must be bounded by t.

7.8.2 Integrating a Repaired Object

Not only must an element being added to a configuration be non-faulty, it also must have the correct state so that its actions will be consistent with those of rest of the system. Define $e[r_i]$ to be the state that a non-faulty system element e should be in after processing requests r_0 through r_i. An element e joining the configuration immediately after request r_{join} must be in state $e[r_{join}]$ before it can participate in the running system.

An element is *self-stabilizing* (Dijkstra [1974]) if its current state is completely defined by the previous k inputs it has processed, for some fixed k. Obviously, running such an element long enough to ensure that it has processed k inputs is all that is required to put it in state $e[r_{join}]$. Unfortunately, the design of self-stabilizing state machines is not always possible.

When elements are not self-stabilizing, processors are failstop, and logical clocks are implemented, cooperation of a single state-machine replica sm_i is sufficient to integrate a new element e into the system. This is because state information obtained from any state-machine replica sm_i must be correct. In order to integrate e at request r_{join}, replica sm_i must have access to enough state information so that $e[r_{join}]$ can be assembled and forwarded to e.

- When e is an output device, $e[r_{join}]$ is likely to be only a small amount of device-specific set-up information — information that changes infrequently and can be stored in state variables of sm_i.
- When e is a client, the information needed for $e[r_{join}]$ is frequently based on recent sensor values read and can therefore be determined by using information provided to sm_i by other clients.

- And, when e is a state-machine replica, the information needed for $e[r_{join}]$ is stored in the state variables and pending requests at sm_i.

The protocol for integrating a client or output device e is simple — $e[r_{join}]$ is sent to e before the output produced by processing any request with a unique identifier larger than $uid(r_{join})$. The protocol for integrating a state-machine replica sm_{new} is a bit more complex. It is not sufficient for replica sm_i simply to send the values of all its state variables and copies of any pending requests to sm_{new}. This is because some client request might be received by sm_i after sending $e[r_{join}]$ but delivered to sm_{new} before its repair. Such a request would neither be reflected in the state information forwarded by sm_i to sm_{new} nor received by sm_{new} directly. Thus, sm_i must, for a time, relay to sm_{new} requests received from clients.[10] Since requests from a given client are received by sm_{new} in the order sent and in ascending order by request identifier, once sm_{new} has received a request directly (i.e., not relayed) from a client c, there is no need for requests from c with larger identifiers to be relayed to sm_{new}. If sm_{new} informs sm_i of the identifier on a request received directly from each client c, then sm_i can know when to stop relaying to sm_{new} requests from c.

The complete integration protocol is summarized in the following.

Integration with Failstop Processors and Logical Clocks. A state-machine replica sm_i can integrate an element e at request r_{join} into a running system as follows.

If e is a client or output device, sm_i sends the relevant portions of its state variables to e and does so before sending any output produced by requests with unique identifiers larger than the one on r_{join}.

If e is a state-machine replica sm_{new}, then sm_i

1. sends the values of its state variables and copies of any pending requests to sm_{new},
2. sends to sm_{new} every subsequent request r received from each client c such that $uid(r) < uid(r_c)$, where r_c is the first request sm_{new} received directly from c after being restarted.

The existence of synchronized real-time clocks permits this protocol to be simplified because sm_i can determine when to stop relaying messages based on the passage of time. Suppose, as in Section 7.4 there exists a constant Δ such that a request r with unique identifier $uid(r)$ will be received by every (correct) state-machine replica no later than time $uid(r) + \Delta$ according to the local clock at the receiving processor. Let sm_{new} join the configuration at time τ_{join}. By definition, sm_{new} is guaranteed to receive every request that was made after time τ_{join} on the requesting client's clock. Since unique identifiers are obtained from the real-time clock of the client making the request, sm_{new} is guaranteed to receive every request r such that $uid(r) \geq \tau_{join}$. The first such a request r must be received by sm_i by time $\tau_{join} + \Delta$ according to its clock. Therefore, every request received by sm_i after $\tau_{join} + \Delta$ must also be received directly by sm_{new}. Clearly, sm_i need not relay such requests, and we have the following protocol.

---

[10]Duplicate copies of some requests might be received by sm_{new}.

Integration with Failstop Processors and Real-time Clocks. A state-machine replica sm_i can integrate an element e at request r_{join} into a running system as follows.

If e is a client or output device, then sm_i sends the relevant portions of its state variables to e and does so before sending any output produced by requests with unique identifiers larger than the one on r_{join}.

If e is a state-machine replica sm_{new} then sm_i

1. sends the values of its state variables and copies of any pending requests to sm_{new},
2. sends to sm_{new} every request received during the next interval of duration Δ.

When processors can exhibit Byzantine failures, a single state-machine replica sm_i is not sufficient for integrating a new element into the system. This is because state information furnished by sm_i might not be correct — sm_i might be executing on a faulty processor. To tolerate t failures in a system with $2t + 1$ state-machine replicas, $t + 1$ identical copies of the state information and $t + 1$ identical copies of relayed messages must be obtained. Otherwise, the protocol is as described above for real-time clocks.

Stability Revisited

The stability tests of Section 7.4 do not work when requests made by a client can be received from two sources — the client and via a relay. During the interval that messages are being relayed, sm_{new}, the state-machine replica being integrated, might receive a request r directly from c but later receive r', another request from c, with $uid(r) > uid(r')$, because r' was relayed by sm_i. The solution to this problem is for sm_{new} to consider requests received directly from c stable only after no relayed requests from c can arrive. Thus, the stability test must be changed:

> **Stability Test During Restart**. A request r received directly from a client c by a restarting state machine replica sm_{new} is stable only after the last request from c relayed by another processor has been received by sm_{new}.

An obvious way to implement this is for a message to be sent to sm_{new} when no further requests from c will be relayed.

7.9   Related Work

The state-machine approach was first described in Lamport [1978b] for environments in which failures could not occur. It was generalized to handle failstop failures in Schneider [1982], a class of failures between failstop and Byzantine failures in Lamport [1978a], and full Byzantine failures in Lamport [1984]. These various state-machine implementations were first characterized using the Agreement and Order requirements and a stability test in Schneider [1985].

The state-machine approach has been used in the design of significant fault-tolerant process control applications (Wensley *et al.* [1978]). It has also been used in the design of distributed synchronization — including read/write locks and distributed semaphores (Schneider [1980]), input/output guards for CSP and conditional Ada SELECT statements (Schneider [1982]) — and in the design of a failstop processor approximation using processors that can exhibit arbitrary behavior in response to a failure (Schlichting and Schneider [1983]; Schneider [1984]). A stable storage implementation described in (Bernstein [1985]) exploits properties of a synchronous broadcast network to avoid explicit protocols for Agreement and Order and employs Transmitting a Default Vote (as described in Section 7.7). The notion of Δ common storage, suggested in Cristian *et al.* [1985], is a state-machine implementation of memory that uses the Real-time Clock Stability Test. The decentralized commit protocol of Skeen [1982] can be viewed as a straightforward application of the state-machine approach, while the 2 phase commit protocol described in Gray [1978] can be obtained from decentralized commit simply by making restrictive assumptions about failures and performing optimizations based on these assumptions. The Paxon Synod commit protocol (Lamport [1989]) also can be understood in terms of the state-machine approach. It is similar to, but cheaper to execute, than the standard 3 phase commit protocol. Finally, the method of implementing highly available distributed services in Liskov and Ladin. [1986] uses the state-machine approach, with clever optimizations of the stability test and agreement protocol that are possible due to the semantics of the application and the use of failstop processors.

A critique of the state-machine approach for transaction management in database systems appears in Garcia-Molina, Pittelli and Davidson [1984]. Experiments evaluating the performance of various of the stability tests in a network of SUN Workstations are reported in Pittelli and Garcia-Molina [1989]. That study also reports on the performance of request batching, which is possible when requests describe database transactions, and the use of null requests in the Logical Clock Stability Test Tolerating Failstop Failures of Section 7.4.

Primitives to support the Agreement and Order requirements for Replica Coordination have been included in two operating systems toolkits. The ISIS Toolkit (Birman [1985]) provides ABCAST and CBCAST for allowing an applications programmer to control the delivery order of messages to the members of a process group (i.e. collection of state-machine replicas). ABCAST ensures that all state-machine replicas process requests in the same order; CBCAST allows more flexibility in message ordering and ensures that causally related requests are delivered in the correct relative order. ISIS has been used to implement a number of prototype applications. One example is the RNFS (replicated NFS) file system, a network file system that is tolerant to failstop failures and runs on top of NFS, that was designed using the state-machine approach (Marzullo and Schmuck. [1988]).

The Psync primitive (Peterson, Bucholz and Schlichting [1989]), which has been implemented in the x-kernel (Hutchinson and Peterson [1988]), is similar to the CBCAST of ISIS. Psync, however, makes available to the programmer the graph of the message 'potential causality' relation, while CBCAST does not. Psync is intended to be a low-level protocol that can be used to implement protocols like

ABCAST and CBCAST; the ISIS primitives are intended for use by applications programmers and, therefore, hide the 'potential causality' relation while at the same time including support for group management and failure reporting.

Acknowledgements

Discussions with Ö. Babaoğlu, K. Birman, and L. Lamport over the past 5 years have helped me to formulate these ideas. Useful comments on drafts of this paper were provided by J. Aizikowitz, Ö. Babaoğlu, A. Bernstein, K. Birman, R. Brown, D. Gries, K. Marzullo, and B. Simons. I am also very grateful to Sal March, managing editor of *ACM Computing Surveys*, for his thorough reading of this paper and many helpful comments.

This material is based on work supported in part by the Office of Naval Research under contract N00014-91-J-1219, the National Science Foundation under Grant No. CCR-8701103, and DARPA/NSF Grant No. CCR-9014363. Any opinions, findings, and conclusions or recommendations expressed in this publication are those of the author and do not reflect the views of these agencies.

7.10   References

Aizikowitz, J. (1989), Designing Distributed Services Using Refinement Mappings, Computer Science Department, Cornell University, Ph.D. Dissertation, Ithaca, New York. Also available as technical report TR 89-1040.

Bernstein, A. J. (1985), A loosely coupled system for reliably storing data, *IEEE Transactions on Software Engineering* **SE-11**(5), 446–454.

Birman, K. P. (1985), Replication and fault tolerance in the ISIS system, *Proceedings of the Tenth Symposium on Operating Systems Principles*, Orcas Island, WA, 79–86, In *ACM Operating Systems Review* **19**(5).

Birman, K. P. and Joseph, T. A. (1987), Reliable Communication in the Presence of Failures, *ACM Transactions on Computer Systems* **5**(1), 47–76.

Cristian, F., Aghili, H., Strong, H. R. and Dolev, D. (1985), Atomic Broadcast: From Simple Message Diffusion to Byzantine Agreement, *Proceedings of the 15th International Symposium on Fault-Tolerant Computing*, Ann Arbor, MI, 200–206, A revised version appears as IBM Research Laboratory Technical Report RJ5244 (April 1989).

Dijkstra, E. W. (1974), Self-Stabilizing Systems in Spite of Distributed Control, *Communications of the ACM* **17**(11), 643–644.

Fischer, M. J., Lynch, N. A. and Paterson, M. S. (1985), Impossibility of Distributed Consensus with One Faulty Process, *Journal of the ACM* **32**(2), 374–382.

Garcia-Molina, H., Pittelli, F. and Davidson, S. B. (1984), Applications of Byzantine Agreement in Database Systems, Princeton University, Princeton, NJ, Technical Report TR 316.

Gray, J. N. (1978), Notes on database operating systems, in *Operating Systems — An Advanced Course*, Bayer, R., Graham, R. M. and Seegmuller, G., eds., Lecture Notes on Computer Science, vol. **66**, springer, 393–481, Also available as Technical Report RJ2188, IBM Research Laboratory, San Jose, California, 1978.

Halpern, J., Simons, B., Strong, R. and Dolev, D. (1984), Fault-tolerant clock synchronization, *Proceedings of the Third ACM Annual Symposium on Principles of Distributed Computing*, Misra, J., ed., Vancouver, BC, Canada, 89–102.

Hutchinson, N. and Peterson, L. (1988), Design of the x-kernel, *Proceedings of the of SIGCOMM '88 — Symposium on Communication Architectures and*, Stanford, CA, 65–75.

Lamport, L. (1978a), The implementation of reliable distributed multiprocess systems, *Computer Networks* **2**, 95–114.

Lamport, L. (1978b), Time, Clocks, and the Ordering of Events in a Distributed System, *Communications of the ACM* **21(7)**, 558–565.

Lamport, L. (1984), Using Time Instead of Timeout for Fault-Tolerant Distributed Systems, *ACM Transactions on Programming Languages and Systems* **6(2)**, 254–280.

Lamport, L. (1989), The Part-Time Parliament, DEC Systems Research Center, Technical Report 49, Palo Alto, California.

Lamport, L. and Melliar-Smith, P. M. (1984), Byzantine clock synchronization, *Proceedings of the Third ACM Annual Symposium on Principles of Distributed Computing*, Misra, J., ed., Vancouver, BC, Canada, 68–74.

Lamport, L., Shostak, R. and Pease, M. (1982), The Byzantine Generals Problem, *ACM Transactions on Programming Languages and Systems* **4(3)**, 382–401.

Liskov, B. and Ladin., R. (1986), Highly-available distributed services and fault-tolerant distributed, *Proceedings of the Fifth ACM Annual Symposium on Principles of Distributed Computing*, Halpern, J., ed., Calgary, Alberta, Canada, 29–39.

Mancini, L. and Pappalardo, G. (1988), Towards a theory of replicated processing, in *Formal Techniques in Real-time and Fault-tolerant Systems*, Lecture Notes in Computer Science, Vol. 331, Springer-Verlag, New York, 175–192.

Marzullo, K. (1989), Implementing fault-tolerant sensors, Computer Science Department, Cornell University, Technical Report TR 89-997, Ithaca, NY.

Marzullo, K. and Schmuck., F. (1988), Supplying high availability with a standard network file system, *Proceedings of the Eighth International Conference on Distributed Computing Systems*, San Jose, CA, IEEE Computer Society Press, 447–455.

Peterson, L. L., Bucholz, N. C. and Schlichting, R. D. (1989), Preserving and using context information in interprocess communication, *ACM Transactions on Computer Systems* 7(3), 217–246.

Pittelli, F. and Garcia-Molina, H. (1989), Reliable Scheduling in a TMR database System, *ACM Transactions on Computer Systems* 7(1), 25–60.

Schlichting, R. D. and Schneider, F. B. (1983), Fail-Stop Processors: an Approach to Designing Fault-Tolerant Computing Systems, *ACM Transactions on Computer Systems* 1(3), 222–238.

Schneider, F. B. (1980), Ensuring Consistency on a Distributed Database System by Use of, *Proceedings of the International Symposium on Distributed Data Bases*, Paris, France, 183–189.

Schneider, F. B. (1982), Synchronization in distributed programs, *ACM Transactions on Programming Languages and Systems* 4(2), 125–148.

Schneider, F. B. (1984), Byzantine generals in action: Implementing fail-stop processors, *ACM Transactions on Computer Systems* 2(2), 145–154.

Schneider, F. B. (1985), Paradigms for distributed programs, in *Distributed Systems — Methods and Tools for Specification*, Lecture Notes in Computer Science, Vol. 190, Springer-Verlag, New York, NY, 343–430.

Schneider, F. B. (1986), A Paradigm for Reliable Clock Synchronization, *Proceedings of the Advanced Seminar on Real-Time Local Area Networks, Bandol, France*.

Schneider, F. B., Gries, D. and Schlichting, R. D. (1984), Fault-Tolerant Broadcasts, *Science of Computer Programming* 4(1), 1–15.

Siewiorek, D. P. and Swarz, R. S. (1982), *The Theory and Practice of Reliable System Design*, Digital Press, Bedford, Mass.

Skeen, D. (1982), Crash Recovery in a Distributed Database System, University of California, Berkeley, Ph.D. dissertation.

Strong, H. R. and Dolev, D. (1983), Byzantine agreement, *Proceedings of the Intellectual Leverage for the Information Society*, IEEE Computer Society, 77–82.

Wensley, J. H., Lamport, L., Goldberg, J., Green, M. W., Levitt, K. N., Melliar-Smith, P. M., Shostak, R. E., Weinstock, C. B. and Bersow, D. (1978), SIFT: Design and analysis of a fault-tolerant computer for aircraft control, *Proceedings of the IEEE* 10(6), 1240–1255.

Chapter 8

The Primary–Backup Approach

Navin Budhiraja, Keith Marzullo, Fred B. Schneider and
Sam Toueg

8.1   Introduction

One way to implement a fault-tolerant service is by using multiple servers that fail
independently. The state of the service is replicated and distributed among these
servers, and updates are coordinated so that even when a subset of servers fail, the
service remains available.

Such fault-tolerant services are generally structured in one of two ways. One
approach is to replicate the service state at all servers and to present the client
requests, in the same order, to all non-faulty servers. This service architecture
is commonly called *active replication* or *the state-machine approach* and is discussed
in Chapter 7. The other approach is to designate one server as the *primary* and
all the others as *backups*. Clients make requests by sending messages only to
the primary. If the primary fails, then a *failover* occurs and one of the backups
takes over. This service architecture is commonly called the *primary–backup* or
the *primary–copy* approach (Alsberg and Day [1976]) and has been widely used in
commercial fault-tolerant systems.

With both the state-machine approach and the primary–backup approach, the
goal is to provide clients with the illusion of a service that is implemented by a
single server. The approaches differ in how each handles failures. With the state-
machine approach, the effects of failures are completely masked by voting, and
the resulting service is indistinguishable from a single non-faulty server. With the
primary–backup approach, a request can be lost — additional protocols must be
employed to retry such lost requests. The primary–backup approach, however,
involves less redundant processing, is less costly, and therefore is more prevalent
in practice.

In this chapter, we discuss some fundamental costs that arise in connection with building fault-tolerant services using the primary–backup approach. Here are three key cost metrics of any primary–backup protocol:

- *Degree of Replication:* The number of servers used to implement the service.
- *Blocking Time:* The worst-case period between a request and its response in any failure–free execution.
- *Failover Time:* The worst-case period during which requests can be lost because there is no primary.

The fundamental question, then, is:

> Given that no more than f components can fail, what are the smallest possible values of the the degree of replication, the blocking time and the failover time?

An answer to this question defines lower bounds for the degree of replication, the blocking time and the failover time of primary–backup protocols, where a *lower bound* defines a necessary cost that any protocol purporting to solve a problem must incur. Nobody will ever design a protocol with lower cost than the lower bound. Knowing lower bounds for a problem, therefore, gives a basis to evaluate the quality of a protocol.

The existence of a lower bound does not imply the existence of a protocol having this cost, however. Every problem has a trivial lower bound (*viz* 0). We desire lower bounds that are tight — lower bounds that are actually achieved by some protocol. The cost of running any protocol defines an *upper bound* for the problem that protocol solves. If this upper bound is the same as the lower bound, then the lower bound is *tight* and the protocol is *optimal*. (The lower bound implies that a cheaper protocol cannot exist.) Thus, given a problem, we strive to identify tight lower bounds and optimal protocols.

In this chapter, we present and discuss lower and upper bounds for the above three questions. However, deriving these bounds requires a precise specification of the problem solved by a primary–backup protocol. We give this in Sections 8.2 and 8.3. Section 8.4 contains our lower bounds and Section 8.5 contains our upper bounds. Finally, in Section 8.6 we discuss some existing primary–backup protocols in terms of our specification, model, and bounds.

8.2   Specification of Primary–Backup

Informally, a service that is implemented using the primary–backup approach consists of a set of servers, of which no more than one is the *primary* at any time. A client sends a request to the service by sending it to the server it believes to be the primary. A client learns from the service when the primary changes and directs future requests accordingly. We assume that a client can send any request to the service at any time.

More precisely, we require that to be a primary–backup protocol four properties must be satisfied. The first property states that no more than one server can be the primary at any time.

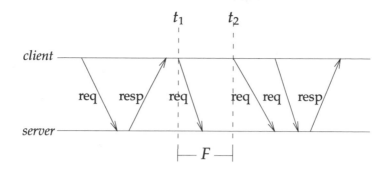

Figure 8.1. Service Outages

Pb1: There exists a local predicate $Prmy_s$ on the state of each server s. At any time, there is at most one server s whose state satisfies $Prmy_s$.

For brevity, whenever we say that 's is the primary (at time t)' we mean that the state of s satisfies $Prmy_s$ (at time t). We can now formally define the *failover time* of a primary–backup service to be the longest period of time during which $Prmy_s$ is not true for any s.

Property Pb2 distinguishes the primary–backup approach from the state-machine approach. In the latter, each client broadcasts its request to all the servers (at considerable cost).

Pb2: Each client i maintains a server identity $Dest_i$ such that to make a request, client i sends a message to $Dest_i$.

We assume that requests sent to a server s are enqueued in a *message queue* at s. Property Pb3 says that requests that arrive at a backup are ignored.

Pb3: If a client request arrives at a server that is not the current primary, then that request is not enqueued (and therefore is not processed).

It may appear that Pb1 and Pb3 eliminate the need for Pb2. This is not the case. Pb1–Pb3 ensure that no more than one server can enqueue each client request. Eliminating Pb2 would allow protocols in which this could be violated. In such a protocol, a client would send its request to multiple servers. And, if this request were sent while the identity of the primary is changing, then the request could get enqueued at more than one server. Some of our lower bounds do not hold for such protocols.

Properties Pb1–Pb3 specify a protocol for client interactions with a service but not the obligations of the service. For example, Pb1–Pb3 do not rule out a primary that ignores all requests. We now give a fourth property that precludes such trivial implementations.

For simplicity, we assume that every request requires a response to be sent. Consider a service that is implemented by a single server. Define a *server outage* to occur at time t in this service if some correct client sends a request at time t to

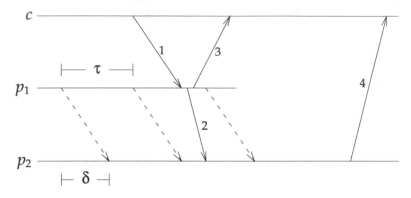

Figure 8.2. A Simple Primary–Backup Protocol

the service but does not receive a response. The above server is called a (k, Δ)–*bofo server* (bounded outages, finitely often) if all server outages can be grouped into at most k intervals of time, with each interval having length at most Δ. For example, the computation shown in Figure 8.1 shows two server outages at times t_1 and t_2 respectively. If the length of this outage period is F and if this is the only such period, then the server is $(1, F)$–bofo.

Thus, even though some requests made to a (k, Δ)–bofo server can be lost, the number of such requests is bounded. The fourth property states that a group of servers implementing a service using the primary–backup approach behave as a single bofo server implementing the same service:

Pb4: There exist fixed values k and Δ such that the service behaves like a single (k, Δ)–bofo server.

Pb4 implies that primary–backup protocols can be used only to implement services that tolerate a bounded number of failures over their lifetime. In practice, we can implement a service that tolerates an unbounded number of failures by partitioning its operation into periods. Only a bounded number of failures occur in each period, and repaired servers are reintegrated at period boundaries. Pb4 need only hold throughout each period. We do not discuss reintegration in this chapter.

8.2.1   A Simple Primary–Backup Protocol

As an example of a primary–backup protocol, here is one that tolerates the crash of a single server. Assume that all communication is over point-to-point non-faulty links and that each link has an upper bound δ on message delivery time. An execution of this protocol is shown in Figure 8.2.

There exists a primary server p_1 and a backup server p_2 connected by a communications link. A client c initially sends a request to p_1 (indicated by the arrow labeled 1 in the figure). Whenever p_1 receives a request, it

- Processes the request and updates its state accordingly.
- Sends information about the update to p_2 (message 2 in the figure). We call such a message a *state update* message.
- Without waiting for an acknowledgement from p_2, sends a response to the client (message 3 in the figure).

The order in which messages 2 and 3 are sent is important because it guarantees that, given our assumption about failures, if the client receives a response, then either p_2 will eventually receive the state update message or p_2 will crash.

Server p_2 updates its state upon receiving a state update message from p_1. In addition, p_1 sends dummy messages to p_2 every τ seconds (shown by the dashed arrows in the figure). If p_2 does not receive such a message for $\tau + \delta$ seconds, then p_2 becomes the primary. Once p_2 has become the primary, it informs the clients (message 4 in the figure) and begins processing subsequent requests from the clients.

We now show that this protocol satisfies our characterization of a primary–backup protocol. Property Pb1 requires that there never be two primaries. This is satisfied by the following definitions of *Prmy*:

$$Prmy_{p_1} \overset{\text{def}}{=} p_1 \text{ has not crashed}$$

$$Prmy_{p_2} \overset{\text{def}}{=} p_2 \text{ has not received a message from } p_1 \text{ for } \tau + \delta$$

Predicate $Prmy_{p_1} \wedge Prmy_{p_2}$ is always false in a system executing our protocol, hence Pb1 is satisfied. The failover time is the longest interval during which $\neg Prmy_{p_1} \wedge \neg Prmy_{p_2}$ can hold. In this protocol, this interval occurs when p_1 crashes immediately after sending a message to p_2 which takes δ to arrive, and so the failover time is $\tau + 2\delta$ seconds.

Property Pb2 follows trivially from the description of the protocol, and Pb3 holds because requests are not sent to p_2 until after p_1 has failed.

Finally, Pb4 requires that the protocol implement a single (k, Δ)–bofo server. To implement a single server, we require that if the primary updates its state and sends a response to a client, then any backup that might later become the primary knows about this state update. In our protocol, this is ensured since p_1 sends the state update message to the backup before it sends any response. To compute k, note that there is at most one switch of the primary, so there is at most one outage period: $k = 1$. To compute Δ, it suffices to compute the longest interval during which a client request may not elicit a response. Assume that p_1 crashes at time t_c. Thus any client request sent to p_1 at $t_c - \delta$ or later may be lost. Furthermore, p_2 may not learn about p_1's crash until $t_c + \tau + 2\delta$, and clients may not learn that p_2 is the primary for another δ. So, the total period during which a request may not elicit a response is $t_c - \delta$ through $t_c + \tau + 3\delta$; the protocol implements a single $(1, \tau + 4\delta)$–bofo server.

8.3   System Model

Consider a system consisting of n servers and a set of clients, where server clocks are synchronized arbitrarily close to real time. We assume that clients and servers communicate by exchanging messages through a completely connected point-to-point network and that there is exactly one FIFO link between any two processes. Messages are enqueued in a message queue maintained by the receiving process, and the receiver accesses this queue by executing a **receive** statement. Furthermore, we assume that there is a known constant δ such that if processes p_i and p_j are connected by a (non-faulty) link, then a message sent from p_i to p_j at time t will be enqueued in p_j's queue at or before $t + \delta$.

For computing lower bounds on protocol execution, it is best to assume that a server can compute the response to a request in an arbitrarily short time. While not realistic, the resulting bounds reflect only the cost of the primary–backup protocols. And that is what we seek.

Execution of a system is modeled by a *run*, which is a sequence of events involving clients, servers, and message queues (see Chapter 4). These events are timestamped with the real time that each event occurs. The events include: sending a message, enqueuing a message, receiving a message, and computation at a process. Two runs σ_1 and σ_2 of the system are defined to be *indistinguishable* to a process p if the same sequence of events (with the same timestamps) occur at p in both σ_1 and σ_2.

We assume that servers are deterministic: if two runs σ_1 and σ_2 are indistinguishable to p and p has the same initial state in both runs, then at any time t the state of p at t in σ_1 is the same as the state of p at t in σ_2. We make this assumption in order to simplify the discussion — our results hold for non-deterministic servers as well.

We assume that server and link failures occur independently and consider the following hierarchy of failure models introduced inChapter 2:

Crash failures: A server may fail by halting prematurely. Until it halts, the server behaves correctly; once it halts, it never recovers (Lamport and Fischer [1982]).[1]

Crash+Link failures: A server may crash or a link may lose messages (but links do not delay, duplicate or corrupt messages).

Receive-Omission failures: A server may fail not only by crashing, but also by omitting to receive some of the messages directed to it over a non-faulty link (Perry and Toueg [1986]).

Send-Omission failures: A server may fail not only by crashing, but also by omitting to send some messages over a non-faulty link (Hadzilacos [1984]).

General-Omission failures: A server may exhibit send-omission and receive-omission failures (Perry and Toueg [1986]).

A protocol tolerates f failures of a given model if it works correctly despite faulty behavior (as prescribed by that model) of up to f components.

---

[1]The lower bounds for crash failures also hold for failstop failures (Schlichting and Schneider [1983])except for the bound on failover time. The lower bound on failover time depends on the maximum interval between when a server fails and when this failure is recognized by the other servers.

Failure Model	Degree of Replication
crash	$n > f$
crash+link	$n > f + 1$
receive-omission	$n > \lfloor \frac{3f}{2} \rfloor$
send-omission	$n > f$
general-omission	$n > 2f$

Table 8.1. Lower bounds on the degree of replication

Note that crash+link failures and the various classes of omission failures are quite different. All admit loss of messages, but each class is handled by a different masking technique: link failures are tolerated by replicating links and omission failures are tolerated by replicating servers. Receive-omission failures model problems at a server, such as the failure to receive messages from the network due to high transfer rates or insufficient buffers. When such problems occur, sending messages using multiple links is not a remedy. Link failures, on the other hand, model problems in the network, such as congestion at a bridge or problems with the physical medium itself. Sending messages over multiple independent links is an effective way to remedy such problems.

8.4 Lower Bounds

For each failure model, we now give the lower bounds on the degree of replication, blocking time, and failover time for any primary–backup protocol.

8.4.1 Bounds on Replication

Table 8.1 summarizes the lower bounds on the degree of replication. Recall, n is the total number of servers and f is the maximum number of faulty components to be tolerated.

For crash failures and send-omission failures, the lower bound is $n > f$. In fact, this is a lower bound for all failure models, since if $n \leq f$ failures could occur, then all of the servers could crash, leaving no primary. A system that has no primary violates Pb4 since a primary is required for the service to behave like a single (k, Δ)–bofo server. For the other failure models, however, $n > f$ is not sufficient as no protocol can achieve this lower bound. As argued below, in the absence of further replication under these failure models, the servers can be divided into mutual non-communicating partitions. Neither partition can tell if the servers in the other partitions have crashed or not. Thus, each partition must eventually contain a primary so that Pb4 is not violated. Yet, if the other partitions have not crashed, then Pb1 will be violated.

The lower bounds on replication for crash+link failures and receive-omission failures are based a further (reasonable) assumption about primary–backup protocols. Let Γ be the maximum time that can elapse between any two successive requests from non-faulty clients. Let D bound the time it takes for a client to learn

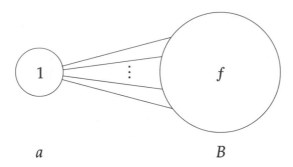

Figure 8.3. Crash+Link Failures

the identity of a new server, so if some server s becomes the primary at time t_0 and remains the primary through time $t \geq t_0 + D$ when a correct client c_i sends a request, then $Dest_i = s$ at time t. For example, in the protocol of Section 8.2.1, $D = \delta$. For deriving our lower bounds, we assume that if Γ is bounded then $D < \Gamma$, which implies that the service must be able to detect the failure of a primary and disseminate the new primary's identity to the clients without using messages from the clients. If one assumes that Γ is bounded and $D \geq \Gamma$, then protocols that require less replication can be constructed.[2]

We now informally derive the lower bounds for crash+link failures, receive-omission failures and general-omission failures. The arguments are not rigorous; for example, the assumption regarding D and Γ is apparently not needed. However, the structure of our detailed formal proofs for the lower bounds in Budhiraja *et al.* [1992a] parallel the arguments below.

For crash+link failures, the need for an additional server (*i.e.*, $n > f + 1$) is illustrated by the counterexample shown in Figure 8.3.

Assume that $n = f + 1$ and divide the n servers into a single server a and set B containing f servers. If, in some run, all of the servers in B crash, then a must eventually be the primary since otherwise there would be no primary. Similarly, if a crashes in some run, then a server in B must eventually become the primary. However, there are only f links between a and the servers in B, so all of the links can fail. If this occurs in some run, then to a this run is indistinguishable from the run in which all the servers in B crashed, and to B this run is indistinguishable from the run in which server a crashed. Hence, a will eventually become the primary and some process in B will eventually become a primary, violating Pb1. Note that this counterexample is not possible if $n > f + 1$, because then at least one link between a and B must remain non-faulty. *I.e.* with $n > f + 1$, two servers are always connected through some path of non-faulty links and servers, so no partition can occur.

The need for still more replication (*i.e.*, $n > \lfloor 3f/2 \rfloor$) in the face of receive-omission failures is illustrated in Figure 8.4.

Assume that $n = \lfloor 3f/2 \rfloor$, the servers are divided into sets A and B that each

---

[2]When $D \geq \Gamma$, there is a primary–backup protocol that tolerates a single crash+link failure using only two servers. In this protocol, when the backup stops receiving messages from the primary, it uses the client requests to distinguish between the primary having crashed and the link having failed.

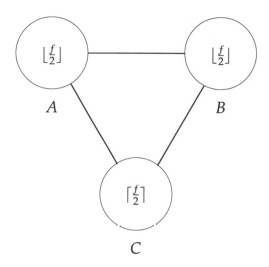

Figure 8.4. Receive-Omission Failures

contain $\lfloor f / 2 \rfloor$ servers, and a set C contains $\lceil f / 2 \rceil$ servers. If all the servers in sets A and C crash in some run, then eventually a server in B will become the primary. Similarly, if in some run all the servers in B and C crash, then eventually a server in A will be the primary. However, if in some run all of the servers in A and B commit receive-omission failures for messages sent from outside their respective partitions, then this run is indistinguishable from the first run to the servers in B and is indistinguishable from the second run to the servers in A. Hence, there will eventually be a primary in A and a primary in B, violating Pb1.

Finally, the need for replication degree $n > 2f$ to tolerate general-omission failures is illustrated in Figure 8.5. Assume that $n = 2f$ and the servers are divided into sets A and B, each containing f servers. If all the servers in A crash in some run, then eventually a server in B will become the primary, and similarly if the servers in B crash in some run, then eventually a server in A will become the primary. However, if the servers in A commit general-omission failures for messages

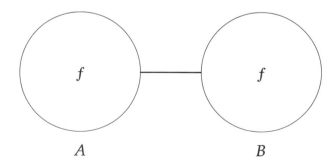

Figure 8.5. General-Omission Failures

Failure Model	Blocking Time
crash	0
crash+link	0
receive-omission	δ when $f = 1$ and $n = 2$ 2δ when $f > 1$ and $n \leq 2f$ 0 when $n > 2f$
send-omission	δ when $f = 1$ 2δ when $f > 1$
general-omission	δ when $f = 1$ 2δ when $f > 1$

Table 8.2. Lower bounds on the blocking times

exchanged with servers in B (*i.e.*, they omit to send messages or receive messages from severs in B), then this run is indistinguishable from the first run to the servers in B, and is also indistinguishable from the second run to the servers in A. Hence, there will eventually be a primary in A and a primary in B, violating Pb1.

8.4.2   Bounds on Blocking Time

Table 8.2 summarizes our lower bounds on the blocking time.

Recall that blocking time is the worst-case elapsed time between the receipt of a request *req* and the sending of the associated response *resp* in a run that contains no failures. As can be seen from the table, the values of the lower bounds for blocking time are 0, δ, or 2δ depending on the failure model, f and n. A value of 0 means that the primary can immediately respond to the client. We call such protocols *non-blocking* (Budhiraja *et al.* [1992a]). The simple protocol discussed in Section 8.2.1 is an example of a non-blocking protocol. Non-blocking protocols exist that tolerate crash failures and crash+link failures because in such systems there is always at least one non-faulty path from the primary to the other servers. Once the primary sends a state update message, it can reply to the client immediately because it knows that this message will eventually be received.

In contrast, non-blocking protocols cannot be built for send-omission failures, general-omission failures, and receive-omission failures where $n \leq 2f$. For these failure models, the blocking time is at least δ. For example, with send-omission failures, a primary cannot immediately send the response to a request after sending the state update message, because the primary may commit a send-omission failure in sending that message. Protocols for which the blocking time is δ can be built by making a backup send the response to the client. The primary sends the state update message to a backup b. Once b receives this message, it sends the response to the client. Such δ blocking protocols can, however, tolerate only a single failure ($f = 1$).

If more than one failure can occur ($f > 1$), then both the responding backup and the primary may crash after the response is sent, and because of the failure model being assumed (send-omission, general-omission or receive-omission with $n \leq 2f$), the state update messages may never be received by the other servers.

Failure Model	Failover Time
crash	$f\delta$
crash+link	$2f\delta$
receive-omission	$2f\delta$
send-omission	$2f\delta$
general-omission	$2f\delta$

Table 8.3. Lower bounds on failover time

These protocols have a blocking time of at least 2δ — further communication from the backups is needed prior to sending a response to the client. This ensures that the state update message has been received by the other backups as well.

8.4.3 Bounds on Failover Time

Table 8.3 summarizes lower bounds on failover time.

For crash failures, a backup can detect the failure of a primary by the absence of an expected message from the primary. For example, if clocks are synchronized then the primary can send a 'I am alive: $\ell\tau$' message to the backups at time $\ell\tau$ for $\ell = 0, 1, 2, \ldots$. If a backup does not receive this message by time $\ell\tau + \delta$, then the primary crashed at some time t_x in the range $(\ell - 1)\tau \leq t_x \leq \ell\tau$. In this case, the failover time, given a single failure, is at most $\tau + \delta$ and it approaches δ as τ becomes small. Similarly, if the backup that next becomes the primary crashes just before $t_x + \tau + \delta$, then there may not be a primary until $t_x + 2(\tau + \delta)$, and so on. Thus, for crash failures, the failover time can be $f\delta$ (as τ approaches zero). However, to show that this is also a lower bound, a fifth property about primary–backup protocols must be assumed:

Pb5: A correct server that is the primary remains so until there is a failure of *some* server or link.

Pb5 is not a very restrictive, and all existing primary–backup protocols satisfy it. However, if the identity of the primary changes rapidly enough — even when there are no failures — then there exist crash-resilient protocols with failover times that violate the $f\delta$ lower bound.[3]

8.5 Upper Bounds

There exist protocols that establish that all but two of our lower bounds are tight. In this section, we describe these protocols informally. The material here summarizes Budhiraja *et al.* [1992b].

For crash failures, one can modify the simple protocol given in Section 8.2.1 to use 'I am alive: $\ell\tau$' messages for failure detection (see Section 8.4.3). We can

---

[3]By violating Pb5, it is possible to construct a protocol where the passage of time, rather than the absence of a message, is used to transfer the role of primary from one server to another. Having pre-agreed times for transfering the role of primary can, under assumptions (which are rarely satisfied in practice) allow smaller failover times.

then extend that in a straightforward manner to tolerate f failures: whenever the primary receives a request from the client, it processes that request, sends the state update message to all the backups, and then sends a response to the client. In case the primary fails, one of the backups becomes the primary using an *a priori* defined order. This protocol uses $f + 1$ servers, so the lower bound on the degree of replication is tight. Furthermore, it is non-blocking and has failover time $f(\delta + \tau)$ for arbitrarily small and positive τ— the lower bounds on blocking time and failover time are tight as well.

According to our lower bounds for replication, in order for any primary–backup protocol to tolerate crash+link failures, an additional server is required. The additional server ensures that even in the presence of f failures, there is at least one non-faulty path between any two servers, where such a path contains zero or more intermediate servers. The protocol for crash failures outlined above can now be modified to tolerate crash+link failures by ensuring that any state update or 'I am alive: $\ell\tau'$ message that a backup receives is forwarded to the other backups. The forwarding of the messages ensures that at least one copy of a message will get to all the intended receivers, since there is at least one non-faulty path between the sender and the receivers. Thus the protocol masks link failures by sending messages over multiple, independent links. This protocol uses $f + 2$ servers, so our lower bound on the degree of replication is tight. Furthermore, the protocol is non-blocking and has failover time $f(2\delta + \tau)$ for arbitrarily small and positive τ, so the lower bounds on blocking time and failover time are also tight.

Most of the protocols for the various kinds of omission failures can be obtained by applying translation techniques (Neiger and Toueg [1988]) to the protocol for crash failures outlined above. These techniques re-implement the message send and receive routines in such a way that a faulty server can detect its failure to send or receive a message and halt. All of the omission–failure protocols obtained in this fashion have failover time $f(2\delta + \tau)$. Thus, our lower bounds on failover times are tight. The protocol for send-omission failures uses $f + 1$ servers and is $2\delta + \tau$–blocking. Furthermore, a send-omission protocol for $f = 1$ that is δ–blocking has been constructed. Thus, the lower bounds on the degree of replication and blocking time are also tight for send-omission failures. Finally, the protocol for general-omission failures obtained by translation uses $2f + 1$ servers and is 2δ–blocking, so the lower bounds on the degree of replication and blocking time are tight for general-omission failures as well.

For receive-omission failures, it is not known whether our lower bounds are tight for degree of replication or for blocking time when $n \leq 2f$ and $f > 1$. The protocol for this failure model obtained by translation uses $2f + 1$ servers, but the lower bound is $n > \lfloor \frac{3f}{2} \rfloor$. Individual protocols for $n = 2, f = 1$ and $n = 4, f = 2$ have been constructed, but have not been generalized. However, the protocol for $n = 2$, $f = 1$ is δ–blocking, so the lower bound on blocking time when $n = f$ and $f = 1$ is tight.

Table 8.4 summarizes the lower bounds and indicates which of these lower bounds are known to be tight.

Failure Model	Degree of Replication	Blocking Time		Failover Time
crash	$n > f$	0		$f\delta$
crash+link	$n > f + 1$ [†]	0		$2f\delta$
receive-omission	$n > \lfloor \frac{3f}{2} \rfloor$ [* †]	δ 2δ 0	when $n \leq 2f$ and $f = 1$ [†] when $n \leq 2f$ and $f > 1$ [* †] when $n > 2f$	$2f\delta$
send-omission	$n > f$	δ 2δ	when $f = 1$ when $f > 1$	$2f\delta$
general-omission	$n > 2f$	δ 2δ	when $f = 1$ when $f > 1$	$2f\delta$

[*] Bound not known to be tight.
[†] $D < \Gamma$ assumed.

Table 8.4. Summary of the lower bounds

8.6   Existing Primary–Backup Protocols

We now discuss some existing primary–backup protocols: the Alsberg and Day (Alsberg and Day [1976]) protocol, the Tandem protocol (Bartlett [1981]), HA–NFS (Bhide, Elnozahy and Morgan [1991]) and an experimental non-blocking protocol Budhiraja and Marzullo [1992].

8.6.1   The Alsberg and Day Protocol

We believe this protocol to be the earliest primary–backup protocol appearing in the literature. It employs two servers and tolerates a single crash failure.[4]

In this protocol, a client sends a request to the service and then blocks waiting for either a response from the service or a timeout.

- If the request arrives at the primary, then the primary performs the requested update, sends a state update message to the backup, and blocks. The backup, upon receiving the state update message, updates its state, sends the response to the client, and finally sends an acknowledgement to the primary saying that it performed the update. On receiving the acknowledgement, a primary can unblock and process the next pending request.
- If the request arrives at the backup, then the backup forwards the request to the primary. The primary, upon receiving the forwarded request, performs the update, sends the response to the client, and finally sends a state update message to the backup (which then updates its state and discards the request).

Failures are detected by lost acknowledgement messages. In addition, failures are also detected by sending periodic 'Are you alive' messages. In case the primary fails, the backup takes over as the new primary. And, when a primary has no

---

[4]The authors also claim that the protocol tolerates network partitions. However, during partitions the primary and the erstwhile backup can diverge, violating Pb4. In the analysis that follows, we assume that partitions do not occur.

backup (either because the backup crashed or the backup becomes the primary), the primary uses another protocol to recruit another server to become the backup.

The above protocol requires two servers to tolerate a single server crash and has a blocking time of δ. Note that the protocol does not satisfy Pb3. However, for crash failures, our lower bound results do not depend on Pb3, so the protocol is optimal for degree of replication and not optimal for blocking time. The suboptimal blocking time is the result of allowing the backup to send a response. The paper is not clear why the authors chose to allow this. One can hypothesize that they were concerned with *transient* link failures. In particular, suppose the protocol were changed so that the primary sent the response to the client after queueing the state update message to be sent to the backup. Now if the primary crashes before the state update message is sent to the backup, then a client has received a response to a request that was never received by the backup. This would violate Pb4. By having the backup send the response, as done in the protocol, if a partition does not occur, then both the primary and the backup will update their state with respect to any request.

The failover time depends on the frequency that 'Are you alive' message are sent. If we assume that the period between 'Are you alive' messages is τ, then the failover time for this protocol is $\tau + 2\delta$. The protocol does not, however, use synchronized clocks. Our upper bounds on failover times do assume synchronized clocks. Thus, our upper bounds on failover time are incomparable. We do not know whether this protocol achieves optimal failover time.

8.6.2   The Tandem Protocol

This protocol is designed to tolerate a single crash+link failure. Any Tandem system consists of multiple nodes connected by a network. Each of these nodes consists of multiple processor and I/O controller modules interconnected by redundant buses. Each processor in the node can support concurrent processes (system or application), and the goal of the system is to make these processes fault–tolerant.

Processes are made fault–tolerant by using *process–pairs*. Process pairs are implemented by replicating each process on two different processors in the node, with one process being the primary and the other being the backup. Requests are sent to the primary of such a pair. The primary then sends a state update message to the backup over one of the redundant busses. Once an acknowledgement is received from the backup, the response is sent to the client. If an acknowledgement is not received for some time (one second in the protocol), then the underlying message mechanism resends the state update message over the second bus. Sequence numbers are used in order to prevent duplicates.

The backup process becomes the primary when it detects that the processor on which the primary resided has crashed, as follows. Every processor in the node periodically sends an 'I am alive' message to all other processors, over all the redundant buses. If such a message is not received from a processor, then that processor is declared crashed and any backup whose primary was on that processor becomes the primary.

The above protocol uses two servers to tolerate a single crash failure, and two links to tolerate a single link failure. Since there are two links between the two servers, and only one of these links can fail, our crash failure bounds apply to this protocol.[5] The protocol, therefore, has optimal degree of replication. The blocking time for this protocol is 2δ, and this is not optimal. However, using our optimal protocol would increase message traffic, which Tandem might not want to do. Finally, because this protocol does not assume synchronized clocks, the optimality of its failover time remains an open question.

8.6.3 HA-NFS

The goal of this protocol is to provide a highly available network file server (HA-NFS) under crash-link failures. The protocol tolerates a single crash failure by using two servers. One server is the primary, the other is the backup. The servers are connected to a dual-ported disk (in reality, there could be multiple disks). Only one server (the current primary) has access to the disk at any time. Disk failures are tolerated by mirroring the disk, and link failures are tolerated by replicating the network between the clients and the servers. The dual-ported disk is used as an additional communications link between the two servers.

During normal operation, client requests are sent to the primary, which writes the updates to the disk and then replies to the client. The primary does not inform the backup of the update, because the disk is dual-ported and the backup can access the disk when it takes over as the primary. The only communication between the two servers during normal operation is to exchange periodic 'Are you alive' messages that must be acknowledged.

In case the backup does not receive an acknowledgement after repeated 'Are you alive' messages, then either the primary has crashed or the link between the primary and the backup has failed. In order to maintain Pb1, before it becomes the primary the backup tries to communicate with the primary using the dual-ported disk hardware. If the backup finds that it cannot communicate with the primary even over this redundant link, then it becomes the new primary and takes over control of the dual-ported disk.

As with the Tandem protocol, our lower bounds for crash failures apply because only one of the communication channels between the servers can fail. The HA-NFS protocol requires two servers to tolerate a single failure, and has a blocking time of zero. Thus the protocol has optimal degree of replication and optimal blocking time. The failover time depends on the interval between successive 'Are you alive' messages, the number of times it is sent before detecting a failure, and the time needed to communicate using the disk as a channel. This time is at least 2δ. The optimality of its failover time remains an open question because this protocol does not assume synchronized clocks (and our bounds do).

---

[5]We assumed that there is exactly one link between any two processes. In Tandem's protocol, it is assumed that no more than one of the two links can be faulty. If this is the case, then any message can be simultaneously sent over both the links, thus guaranteeing that at most one copy of the message can be lost due to link failures. All our bounds that hold in the absence of link failures can be applied to protocols, like Tandem's, that utilize multiple links.

8.6.4   Non-Blocking Protocol

Non-blocking protocols are of practical interest because they can achieve the fastest possible response times. To see how the response time for these protocols compares with conventional blocking protocols, a non-blocking protocol tolerating receive-omission failures was built (Budhiraja and Marzullo [1992]).

An argument can be made that a receive-omission failure model is the most appropriate one for many environments. A primary–backup system should have all servers on a single local area network.   This is because the time required between the failure of a primary and the takeover by a backup is determined by the bandwidth between the primary and the backups. Furthermore, using a single local area network makes partitions that separate the servers unlikely. The kinds of message losses that are expected to occur on this network are restricted and correspond to our receive-omission failure model. According to Amir et al. [1992], as technology improves and newer, faster networks such as FDDI are used, the following will be the dominant causes for message losses on a local area network:

- Failure to intercept messages from the network at high transfer rates due to interrupt misses.
- Buffer overflows at the receiver.

This set of failures corresponds to receive-omission failure model, and one can construct a non-blocking primary–backup protocol for this model when $n > 2f$.

We now briefly describe our non-blocking protocol tolerating receive-omission failures. The protocol consists of $2f+1$ servers, one of which is the primary, and the rest of which are backups. When the current primary receives a client request, it sends the state update message to all the backups and then immediately responds to the client. A backup, upon receiving this message, updates its state. However, it is possible that some backup might experience a receive-omission fault and not receive the state update message. The protocol, therefore, must ensure that this faulty backup does not later become the primary with an out-of-date state. This is achieved by a failure detection scheme in which a faulty server detects its own failure to receive a message and halts. This technique requires $n > 2f$.

All the servers periodically exchange 'I am alive: $\ell\tau$' messages to detect server crashes. The backups are ranked, and if the primary crashes then the backup with the lowest rank takes over as the new primary.

This protocol has failover time $f(2\delta + \tau)$, which is optimal as τ approaches zero, and optimal blocking time of zero. Furthermore, it also has the optimal degree of replication for non–blocking protocols.

When we implemented this protocol on a local area network, we were surprised to find that blocking time is not the dominant factor in determining response time as seen by clients. In particular, our non-blocking protocol generated $O(n^2)$ messages to implement the failure detection. When client requests are made with high frequency, this message traffic led to high contention on our local area network. This bandwidth saturation was the key factor in determining the response time seen by clients.

8.7 Conclusions

In this chapter, we have given a precise characterization for primary–backup protocols in a system with synchronized clocks and bounded message delays. We then presented lower bounds on the degree of replication, the blocking time, and the failover time under various kinds of server and link failures. We also outlined a set of primary–backup protocols that show which of our lower bounds are tight.

We have attempted to give a characterization of primary–backup that is broad enough to include most synchronous protocols that are considered to be instances of the approach. As we have seen, there are protocols that are incomparable to the class of protocols we analyzed. Some protocols do not assume synchronized clocks; some protocols do not even assume a synchronous system. Possible characterizations for a primary–backup protocol in an asynchronous system is an area under active investigation.

Acknowledgements

The work on this chapter was supported in part by grants from the IBM T. J. Watson Research Center, the IBM Endicott Programming Laboratory, an IBM Graduate Fellowship, by Xerox Webster Research Center and Siemens, by the Defense Advanced Research Projects Agency (DoD) under NASA Ames grant number NAG 2-593, by the Office of Naval Research under contract N00014 91-J-1219, and by DARPA/NSF grants CCR-8701103, CCR-9014363, CCR-8901780 and CCR-9102231. The views, opinions, and findings contained in this chapter are those of the authors and should not be construed as an official Department of Defense position, policy, or decision.

8.8 References

Alsberg, P. A. and Day, J. D. (1976), A Principle for Resilient Sharing of Distributed Resources, *Proceedings of the Second International Conference on Software Engineering*, San Fancisco, CA, 562–570.

Amir, Y., Dolev, D., Kramer, S. and Malki, D. (1992), Transis: A Communication Sub-System for High Availability, *Proceedings of the 22nd International Symposium on Fault-Tolerant Computing*, IEEE Computer Society Press, 76–84.

Bartlett, J. F. (1981), A NonStop Kernel, *Proceedings of the Eighth Symposium on Operating Systems Principles*, In *ACM Operating Systems Review* **15**(5).

Bhide, A., Elnozahy, E. N. and Morgan, S. P. (1991), A highly available network file server, *Proceedings of the of USENIX*, 199–205.

Budhiraja, N. and Marzullo, K. (1992), Tradeoffs in implementing primary–backup protocols, Department of Computer Science, Cornell University, Technical Report TR 92-1307, Ithaca, NY.

Budhiraja, N., Marzullo, K., Schneider, F. B. and Toueg, S. (1992a), Primary-backup protocols: Lower bounds and optimal implementations, *Proceedings of the Third IFIP Working Conference on Dependable Computing*, Mondello, Italy, 187–198.

Budhiraja, N., Marzullo, K., Schneider, F. B. and Toueg, S. (1992b), Optimal primary–backup protocols, *Proceedings of the Sixth International Workshop on Distributed Algorithms*, Haifa, Israel, 362–378.

Hadzilacos, V. (1984), Issues of Fault Tolerance in Concurrent Computations, Harvard University, Ph.D. Dissertation, Department of Computer Science Technical Report 11-84.

Lamport, L. and Fischer, M. J. (1982), Byzantine Generals and Transaction Commit Protocols, SRI International, Technical Report 62.

Neiger, G. and Toueg, S. (1988), Providing Design Abstractions in Distributed Systems, *Proceedings of the International Workshop on Parallel and Distributed Algorithms*, Cosnard, M., Quinton, P., Robert, Y. and Raynal, M., eds., Château de Bonas, Gers, France, North-Holland, 227–242.

Perry, K. J. and Toueg, S. (1986), Distributed agreement in the presence of processor and communication faults, *IEEE Transactions on Software Engineering* **SE-12(3)**, 477–482.

Schlichting, R. D. and Schneider, F. B. (1983), Fail-Stop Processors: an Approach to Designing Fault-Tolerant Computing Systems, *ACM Transactions on Computer Systems* **1(3)**, 222–238.

Chapter 9

Interprocess Communication

Sape J. Mullender

9.1   Introduction

One of the fundamental characteristics of a distributed system is that it has multiple processing elements which may fail independently. Interprocess communication mechanisms are not merely there to allow the processes in a distributed system to communicate; they are also there to provide a mechanism that shields one process from failures of another. A vital function of communication mechanisms is the prevention of crashes in one process bringing down another.

Interprocess communication mechanisms provide a small and comprehensive set of interaction possibilities between processes which, if used exclusively for the interaction between them, forces clean and simple interfaces between processes.

In centralized multiprocessing systems, processes can communicate via shared memory, or UNIX pipes, or even RAM files. There is advantage in making use of the same mechanisms for interaction between processes on one processor, a shared-memory multiprocessor, and a distributed system. It allows redistribution of processes over processors and porting multiprocess applications between centralized and distributed systems.

Interprocess communication mechanisms thus serve four important functions in distributed systems:

1. they allow communication between separate processes over a computer network,
2. they provide *firewalls* against failures, and provide the means to cross protection boundaries,
3. they enforce clean and simple interfaces, thus providing a natural aid for modular structuring of large distributed applications, and
4. they hide the distinction between *local* and *remote* communication, thus allowing static or dynamic reconfiguration.

217

Interprocess communication mechanisms must be as unobtrusive as possible. This means that they must be easy to use and that they provide the performance that allows them to be used anywhere. One of the easiest and simplest communication interfaces is *remote procedure call*. It has already become one of the most popular in distributed systems research and appears to make its way slowly into commercial distributed and networked systems. Later in this chapter, we shall look in detail at how remote procedure call works.

When machine or protection boundaries must be crossed, interprocess communication mechanisms necessarily incur the performance penalties of operating system interfaces, the hardware mechanisms that need to be invoked — network and network interfaces, memory management — protocol machinery that deals with host, network and process failures, and the inefficiencies associated with making interprocess communication interfaces uniform.

Interprocess communication services should deliver information with *minimum latency, maximum throughput* and, in the case of continuous media (audio and video), they should also *minimize jitter*, the irregularities in the latency. Interprocess communication should be *authenticated* (receiver knows who sends it) and *secure* (sender knows who receives it). When communicating over a network, the interprocess communication mechanism should also hide as many failures in the communication medium as possible. Finally, failures that cannot be hidden should be reported as accurately as the system allows.

Error recovery and failure detection play a fundamental rôle in interprocess communication and we shall often return to this theme throughout this chapter.

9.2   Computer Networks

A computer network delivers data between *nodes*. Nodes can be uniprocessors or multiprocessors. We assume that nodes can *fail independently*. The interconnection between the processors of a shared-memory multiprocessor — usually a bus — connects entities that do not fail independently, so we shall not view it as a computer network.

Computer networks differ in the area they serve (a building, a campus, a city, a country, a continent), in the interconnection topology they offer (regular or irregular point-to-point topology, or a broadcast medium), in the transmission speeds, and the way in which data is packaged.

In practically all networks, there is a non-negligible probability that data received are different from those sent. Sometimes, just one bit is flipped, sometimes hundreds of bits in a row are lost. To catch such errors, data is bundled and transmitted as *packets* of bits; attached to each packet is redundancy that allows *error detection* and sometimes even *error correction*.

Error detection requires less redundancy than error correction. Which is better depends on the error rate, the number of bits in error as a percentage of the total number sent. Usually, the error rate is very low (e.g., for local-area networks, one faulty bit in 10^{12} is not unusual) and then the overhead of error detection and retransmission is much less than that of an error-correcting code.

Data packets are typically between a hundred and a few thousand bytes in size and they have a *checksum* as error-detecting redundancy attached to the end. The checksum is computed using an algorithm that catches most 'typical' errors and that can be computed in real time. *Cyclic redundancy checksums* (CRC) are most popular.

In some circumstances, however, an error-correcting code is the best solution. Communication between a deep-space probe and an earth station, for instance, has a high error rate, combined with a tremendous end-to-end latency (several hours) and then an error-correcting code works better than error detection and retransmission.

Another, closer to home example of data transmission where error detection and retransmission is not a good idea is in interactive continuous media. The maximum acceptable end-to-end latency in audio or audio/visual person-to-person interaction is a few tens of milliseconds. Over large distances, retransmission would just cost too much time — in continuous media, late data is useless data. Fortunately, the human ear and eye have some error correction built in: If there are small gaps in the data stream, the ear or eye won't notice. In audio, the gap can be a few milliseconds, in video, a few tens of milliseconds. Audio and video are usually transmitted without any error detection or error correction at all.

As early as in 1974, Hasler AG, now part of ASCOM, used a register-insertion ring network called SILK that carried data in very small fixed-sized packets in order to use it for digital telephony. The idea never caught on at the time. Now, with the advent of fibre-optical networks for long-haul data transport, phone companies are looking for networks that can carry all types of data — digital audio and video as well as data. As a result of this, networks that switch small fixed-size packets (called *cells*) are rapidly gaining popularity under the surprising name *Asynchronous Transfer Mode* (ATM) networks.

ATM networks carry cells of a fixed size with a small header (e.g., 5 bytes in Broadband ISDN (B-ISDN)) and 48 bytes of data. The header of a cell contains a *virtual circuit identifier* which is used to transport cells along previously created virtual circuits through the network. Individual cells do not have checksums on the data they carry, so a higher level of protocol has to detect damaged cells.

Error detection and, if necessary, error correction is done at the end points of the virtual circuits. Here, cells are collected into larger data units, packets. In the header of each cell is a bit that can be used to indicate the end of a logical message. Several virtual circuits may lead to one host, so the host must demultiplex packets from different virtual circuits into the correct packet buffers. The layer responsible for the demultiplexing and the packet-level error detection (with a per-packet checksum) is the *ATM Adaptation Layer* (AAL). The AAL is used for data connections which have to be error free. Audio or video connections, which need no error detection (and thus no packetization) only make use of the demultiplexing function.

ATM has good properties for low-latency continuous media transmission. The access time to the network for high-priority traffic is one cell time. Also, the latency caused by the time it takes to fill up a cell is small. For telephone-grade audio, which uses 8-bit samples at a frequency of 8 KHz, one cell represents 6 ms of audio.

The loss of a single such cell is barely detectable by the human ear.

Most networks today make use of physical connections, such as cables, wires, or optical fibres. Telephone companies also make use of microwave or satellite links, but they offer only point-to-point communication to customers. Wireless networks have been used in unusual environments. The University of Hawaii, for instance, which is scattered over a number of islands, already used the ALOHA *packet radio* network in the early seventies to interconnect pieces of the universities (Abramson [1970]).

But wireless communication will gain in importance now that fairly powerful portable work stations — lap-top, notebook and palm-top computers — are becoming common. People will want to be connected to the rest of the world even when on the road. The next generation of cellular telephone technology will no doubt be digital and therefore be usable to connect travelling computer users to the network.

Since one antenna can only support a moderate aggregate bandwidth, high point-to-point bandwidth can only be realized by keeping the number of connections per antenna low. This implies that one antenna should only cover a small geographical area. Cellular telephone systems today use cells (not to be confused with ATM cells) of a few kilometres in diameter. High-bandwidth wireless computer networks for buildings (where the number of users per square metre is large) may use cells of only a few metres in diameter. Such small cells offer the additional benefit that the portable computer devices using it do not have to have powerful — and thus heavy — batteries.

Wireless networks, as well as broadcast cable networks (e.g., Ethernet), are particularly vulnerable to unauthorized eavesdropping, modification or insertion of network traffic. In such networks, especially, authentication and privacy must be ensured by the use of encryption.

The weak spot in most computer networks is where they connect to the computer. The design of today's *network interfaces* appears to be inspired primarily by that of disk controllers: linked lists of I/O descriptors that indicate buffers for receiving (reading) or sending (writing) using DMA. The controller works down the list doing the indicated work. For network controllers, two such queues are usually maintained, one for sending and one for receiving.

Packets may arrive for several receiving processes in one host, and it would be desirable to receive data directly in the receiving process' address space. Most network controllers put received packets in the first available buffer on the queue, without interpreting the packet contents. The demultiplexing of the incoming packet stream, therefore, has to be done by protocol software and copying packet data to the appropriate location in the receiving process' address space is usually unavoidable.

In networks with bandwidths around 10 Mbps and 10 MIPS processors the latency increases by around 10%. If network bandwidths become ten times higher, the penalty would increase to between 50% and 100% (Schroeder and Burrows [1989]).

With the advent of ATM networks, host interfaces will have to start doing the demultiplexing of the incoming cell stream. The cells arrive at a rate where the demultiplexing cannot be done realistically in software. For operating system designers this is good news, because now it will be possible to program any ATM host interface of reasonable design to receive data from each virtual circuit into its own set of buffers. These buffers can then be allocated directly in the desired location in the receiving process' address space.

9.3   Protocol Organization

The physical medium is almost never error free. It corrupts bits, sometimes to the extent that packet boundaries are no longer recognized. Packets usually have a *checksum* that allows packets with bit errors in them to be detected and discarded. Checksums allow us to view the physical medium as one where packets are occasionally lost, or where communication may fail altogether, but where no other errors occur.

Media errors can be corrected by what the ISO [1981] OSI Basic Reference Model calls a *data-link-layer* protocol. Such a protocol uses timeout, acknowledgements (*acks*) and retransmission to detect and correct packet loss. As a consequence, packets are not always received in the same order as that in which they were sent. The data link layer may or may not restore order before delivering packets to the next layer. Order is restored, however, at the cost of a higher latency — correctly received packets may have to wait for the delivery of earlier packets that need to be retransmitted.

In point-to-point networks, packets may have to travel several *hops* before reaching their destination. *Network-layer* protocols, are responsible for *routing* packets through the network. They can make routing decisions for every individual packet, so that packets are delivered independently of other packets. We call this a *datagram* or *connectionless* service. They can also make routing decisions once for a long string of packets. All packets in a *connection* then follow the same route through the network and it is then a simple matter to detect and correct packet loss and maintain packet order within the connection. We call this a *virtual-circuit* or *connection-oriented* service. ATM networks are always based on virtual-circuits because packets arrive to rapidly to make routing decisions on a per-packet basis.

A connectionless network-layer service never guarantees that packets are delivered in the order sent. If it gives a reliable service, it will depend on the underlying data-link-layer protocols to do so. It is unlikely, though, that failures of intermediate network nodes are masked to the extent that no packets are ever lost.

A connection-oriented network-layer service usually does guarantee that packets are delivered in the order sent and that no packets are lost, but not always, as, for instance, in the case of ATM. Here also, intermediate-node failures are usually not masked. Virtual circuits break when such a failure occurs and it is up to higher layers of protocol to create another virtual circuit that avoids the crashed intermediate node.

Network-layer protocols deliver data between hosts. The real senders and recipients of data, however, are usually processes running on those hosts, so many independent data streams may exist between hosts. The protocol that is responsible for delivering data end-to-end between processes in the network is the *Transport Layer Protocol*. If the combination of the services of the underlying protocols — Physical, Data Link and Network — does not provide the desired reliability, then the Transport Layer Protocols must do it.

Transport protocols may run over connection-oriented or connectionless network layer services. One would expect that a transport protocol running over an underlying connection-oriented service would be simpler, because much of the work is done in lower-level protocols, but this is not really the case. Network connections may break and then the transport protocol must create new ones. In ATM networks, cells are only assembled into packets at the communication endpoints, so it is only there that transmission errors can be detected and corrected.

Transport protocols can offer a variety of services. The most common are a reliable stream of packets, a reliable byte stream, or a reliable stream of logical *messages*. Some transport protocols offer reliable pairs of *request* and *reply* messages for use in remote operations or remote procedure call.

9.4 Fundamental Properties of Protocols

We have seen that networks exhibit failures that manifest themselves as lost packets. As long as there is some communication — that is, not *all* packets are lost — these failures can be corrected using feedback in the form of acknowledgements and timeouts. When all packets are lost, such as when a cable breaks or a connector becomes unstuck, hosts can become disconnected altogether. If the processes that form the communication endpoints can crash, communication protocols cannot be made completely reliable.

If a client[1] process sends a request message to a remote server process via a network that can lose packets and, in spite of numerous retransmissions, no response ever comes back from the server, then the network may have broken, or the server may have crashed. As long as the fault is not repaired, the client has no way of finding out what happened.

The client cannot distinguish a server that went down from one that has become disconnected. By itself, this is no great problem; the real problem here is that the client has no way of finding out whether or not the server has received the request and has started carrying out the requested work. As shown in Figure 9.1, it is of no help to the client that the server sends an ack upon reception of the request. The server may crash before it has a chance to start the actual work, or the network may break while the server is doing the work so that the reply cannot be sent back.

The client will be left in the same sort of uncertainty if the network were completely reliable. The server could crash just before it starts the work, or just after it finishes, but before it can communicate this fact. When communication is reliable, but processes are not, at least clients know that a server crash has occurred when

---

[1] I will use the terms *client* and *server* here to distinguish the two communicating processes. The discussion here applies equally well to processes communicating in different rôles.

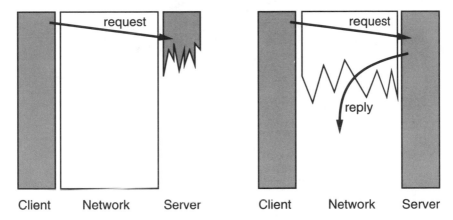

Figure 9.1. The impossibility of distinguishing down from disconnected. The two figures represent *space/time* diagrams — space
is represented horizontally, time vertically. Arrows indicate messages, narrow grey rectangles represent processes and a big white
one the network. Jagged edges represent crashes

no reply comes back. This uncertainty is easier to bear than that of not knowing
whether the server has crashed or the network has become disconnected.

When a server comes back up after a crash, its client can resume communication
with it by retransmitting the last — unanswered — request. But the server may
have carried out that request once already. If the server remembers this fact, it
could recompute the reply and send that to the client. But if the server suffers
total amnesia in a crash and forgets what it did when it crashed, the server will
not be able to distinguish between new requests and requests that have already
been carried out. Knowing that the request is a retransmission does not really
help. It can only serve to warn a server that it may have carried out the request in
a previous incarnation.

In this chapter, we discuss protocols where processor crashes are always *amnesia
failures*. Protocols also exist that use *stable storage* to write information to that
must survive crashes. These protocols are discussed in Chapter 13. In an amnesia
failure, a process suddenly stops and forgets all its state. It then resumes operation
from the initial state — it reboots. This failure model represents a large class of
failures of processors and processes in actual systems. Within this model, *exactly-
once* message delivery, a desirable property of communication protocols, cannot be
achieved. One can aim for either *at-least-once* or *at-most-once* message delivery.

At-least-once protocols deliver messages exactly once in the absence of failures,
but may deliver messages more than once when failures occur. Such protocols
work when requests are *idempotent*; that is, when carrying them out once has
the same effect as carrying them out several times. Most operations on files are
idempotent: Reading a block once has the same effect as reading it three times and
the same is true for writing. Creating or deleting files is almost idempotent: The

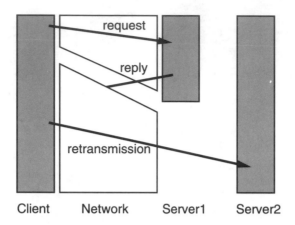

Figure 9.2. A client process, using functional addressing sends a request to one instance of a service, then retransmits to another

first try will do the work, subsequent tries will fail. SUN's Network File System (SUN NFS) uses an at-least-once protocol (SUN RPC) for its file operations and, for that purpose, this is perfectly reasonable. NFS servers are, for purposes of the communication protocol, *stateless*, so there is no state to forget when the server crashes.

At-least-once message delivery hides communication failures and server failures and this only works in a very restricted set of circumstances. In most interactions between processes, losing the communication state is a serious failure and, although we have seen that it cannot be prevented, it certainly should not go unnoticed. At-most-once message delivery protocols detect the fact that the network, or one of the communicating processes has failed and report this fact.

At-most-once protocols operate in the context of a *session* — an association between two processes during which both maintain protocol state. Whenever state is lost, either as a consequence of a crash, a network failure, or because the state was deliberately discarded, the session is terminated. The communicating parties must agree on what is the current session, so that no messages sent in one session are received in another. To do this, sessions have unique names.

Generating unique names for sessions is not quite as easy as it appears. Remember that, when processes crash, they forget everything, including the name of the current session. If only one party crashes, the other can choose a new session identifier, but if both crash, this doesn't work.

A good way to choose session identifiers is to use timestamps as part of the identifier. Most modern processors have a battery-operated clock whose value survives crashes. Even if they don't, they can ask a network time service for the time when they come up. Another way is to use random numbers and hope that the random number generation is good enough to make the probability of re-using session identifiers sufficiently small.

Session identifiers must belong to an association of two processes. Some distributed systems use a form of *functional addressing* where a client sends a request for a remote operation to some generic service. An association between a client process and some generic service will not do, unless the service is stateless. Figure 9.2 illustrates what can happen if functional addressing is used injudiciously. Here, a client process sends a request to an abstract service which happens to be a replicated one with two server processes. The request goes to one of them and is carried out there. The response is lost, for instance, because the server crashes, and the client retransmits. The second server receives the retransmission and carries the request out for the second time, clearly violating the at-most-once principle. In Chapter 10, a specification is given of a protocol that establishes shared state.

Amoeba (Mullender *et al.* [1990]; Tanenbaum *et al.* [1990]) is an example of a distributed system using functional addressing. Client applications send requests to a *service* rather than to a specific *server* process. The name of a service is called a *port* in Amoeba. The client application's operating system kernel, which runs the communication protocol, always finds out a unique name for a specific process implementing the service before sending the request addressed to that specific process. Amoeba's session identifiers consist of the concatenation of the client and server process' unique names.

We have now seen that there is fundamental uncertainty in case of a crash. It is not possible for a client, in every circumstance, to tell whether or not a service has crashed and, if it has crashed, whether that was before or after doing the requested work. Crashes, however, are rare occurrences and protocol designers should design for the normal case to behave optimally. This means that, in the normal case — that is when there is no crash — a client should get to know that a request has been carried out correctly. That this is possible is illustrated in Figure 9.3.

In Figure 9.3a, we see that a response sent to the client after the complete execution of a request is a positive indication that the request was carried out without failure. But we cannot achieve the reverse at the same time. It is not possible, even with an elaborate protocol, to get a result that is fundamentally better than the one shown in Figure 9.3b: when the client does not get a response, it does not know whether the request was executed correctly or perhaps not executed at all.

But we can do a little bit better. It is possible to provide useful feedback to a client in many situations. For instance, it is possible that a client is informed that the network is broken, or that the server has crashed, or that the request could not be delivered. But note that only in the last example — notification of not being able to deliver a request — a client gets positive information that the request was not executed.

A response from a server to a request sent by a client is the only way in which a client process can know that a request has been carried out correctly by a server. (We are still assuming only amnesia crashes and communication failures. As stated before, if servers retain (part of) their memory, the situation is different, as discussed in Chapter 13.) Acknowledgements of messages received or messages not received can be useful to enhance performance, but they never tell a client what it really needs to know: whether the server carried out the work.

Responses, in a sense, are acknowledgements at the application level. A commu-

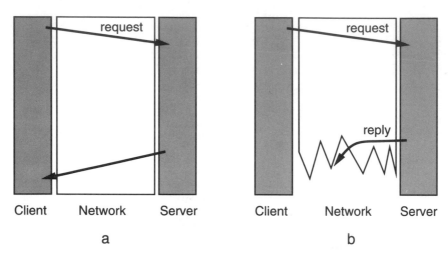

Figure 9.3. (a) The correct reception of the response to a request tells the client there were no failures during its execution. (b) The reverse does not hold. When a request is executed without failure it is still possible that the response does not make it back to the client

nication protocol cannot decide to send a response. The server application must do it. Whatever machinery communication protocols invoke to make communication more reliable, there must always be an application-level protocol for the true end-to-end checking that all went correctly. Saltzer, Reed and Clark [1984] called this the *end-to-end argument*. A good interpretation of the argument is: 'Look, we need an application-level end-to-end protocol to make things reliable anyway, so why not integrate this end-to-end machinery with the rest of the protocol machinery for reliable message delivery.'

Many request/response protocols have been created that do this exactly and some of the implementations have shown that this can benefit both the usefulness of the protocols as the performance.

To sum up: Communication between processes exhibiting amnesia crashes over networks exhibiting omission failures can be made perfectly reliable except for fundamental uncertainty about the delivery of the last message in a session that is broken off by a failure. Sessions mark a period during which the communicating parties maintain mutual state. Sessions can be terminated gracefully and then there need be no uncertainty about outstanding messages, or it can be terminated abruptly by a crash. Positive feedback about the delivery and processing of messages can only be provided by an end-to-end application-level acknowledgement

9.5   Types of Data Transport

Transport protocols in distributed systems are often tailored for a specific class of applications. The diversity of communication requirements prohibits the use of a single protocol that is useful under all circumstances. We can distinguish between four broad classes of communication protocols:

- *Remote Operations,*
- *Bulk Data Transfer,*
- *One-to-Many Communication,* and
- *Continuous Media.*

A remote operation is the most basic form of communication in distributed systems. One process sends a message to another, asking it to do some work. The other process carries out the work and returns a message with the result. The first process is referred to as the *client* process and the second as the *server* process, but note that these terms only refer to the rôles these processes play during the remote operation. One process may simultaneously be a client and a server. Note also that the return message need be nothing more than an acknowledgement that the work has been carried out or merely that the request has been received.[2]

Remote operations are often made to look like procedure or function calls. *Remote procedure calls* are, in fact, remote operations with an extra layer of software that packages procedure arguments in request and response messages. Remote procedure call today forms an essential item in the distributed system designer's toolbox. Section 9.7 is completely devoted to the issues of RPC.

Remote operations are often referred to by other names. Common names are *remote invocation*, *client/server* communication, and *request/response* communication. Sometimes the term RPC is misused to indicate only remote operations.

Remote operations are used for communication between user processes and system services, but also between processes within a single distributed application. The current trend in operating system development towards the use of microkernels and user-level servers has made remote operations an essential ingredient of modern distributed system interfaces.

Bulk data transfer protocols specialize in transferring very large bodies of data efficiently. They are often used as part of file-transfer protocols, such as FTAM, an ISO standard. Bulk data transfer can be viewed as a special form of remote operation, since it is seldom the case that the data does not either come from or go to the client process (the process instigating the transfer). When data goes to the client, the operation can be viewed as a *read* operation and when data comes from the client process, a *write* operation.

There is no reason why transport protocols for remote operations should not be designed to be able to carry very large request or response messages, so that bulk data transfer can be done just as efficiently using request/response protocols as bulk-data-transfer protocols. In fact, the end-to-end argument of the previous

---

[2]*Cf.* end-to-end argument in the previous section.

section argues that having a bulk-data-transfer protocol as a separate protocol function still requires an additional application-level protocol for end-to-end feedback. The combination of the two is just a request/response protocol that happens to be capable of transporting very large messages.

Services that use replication to tolerate failures need large amounts on internal communication to keep the replicas consistent. It is important that this communication reaches all of the replicas in a well-defined order and that agreement exists on which replicas are up and which are down. For such communication an extensive variety of *broadcast* protocols have been established during the last decade. Chapter 5 contains a classification of broadcast protocols in terms of reliability and atomicity properties and it gives the principles of their implementations.

Protocol designers tend to distinguish between *broadcast* and *multicast* . Broadcast means sending to all hosts on the network; multicast means sending to a selected subset of hosts. In practice, replication protocols are always multicast protocols. The designers of such protocols, however, usually reason from a universe that only contains the members of the multicast group, so for them it makes sense to call them broadcast protocols.

When making a practical implementation of a broadcast protocol, attention must be paid to avoiding unintentionally synchronized messages. In a protocol that makes use of the hardware broadcast facility of an Ethernet, for instance, it would not be a good idea for all the recipients of a broadcast message to return an acknowledgement immediately; the acks would result in one big collision on the Ethernet that would take some time to sort out. One host, receiving large numbers of packets simultaneously, may lose some due to overload of its network controller.

Several protocols for various forms of broadcast exist. One of the earliest systems containing reliable broadcast protocols with a variety of ordering properties (causal order, total order within a group, global order) was ISIS, a system developed at Cornell University (Birman and Joseph [1987]). In recent years, protocols have also been developed for Amoeba (Kaashoek and Tanenbaum [1991]) and there appears to be a trend to include multicast protocols in many other systems as well.

Networks for digital telephony have been in existence for a long time now. These networks are monomedia networks, of course, but telephone companies have nonetheless built up a great body of expertise delivering data at a constant rate with very small latencies. All telephony uses virtual circuits which can only be established if the necessary network bandwidth and switch capacity can be guaranteed. Since all circuits require equal bandwidth, this is not unreasonably difficult. The difficulties of managing telephone networks do not stem from the complexity of its data, but from the gigantic size of the network.

Multimedia networks have to combine continuous media transport, which requires low-latency and constant-rate data transport and 'normal' data traffic which is very bursty and also requires low-latency delivery. ATM networks appear to be good at allowing the mixture of these data types.

Opinions differ wildly, however, when it comes to guaranteeing the constant latency of the continuous-media traffic. One school of thought maintains that the capacity of the network should be so large that one type of traffic does not interfere with another. Another spends large amounts of thought on prioritizing network traffic and bandwidth-reservation algorithms that guarantee the timely delivery of continuous-media traffic even at high network loads.

The truth, as usual, is probably somewhere in the middle. Taking data networks as an example, we see that early on similar battles were fought over fair allocation of bandwidth to the various customers. Today, local networks do not implement any access restrictions — the network has enough bandwidth to satisfy all traffic during normal operation. Long-haul networks are exploited on a commercial basis, so there is accounting of its use. In high-speed long-haul networks, this by itself may be enough to keep customers from monopolizing the network. In low-speed long-haul networks, such as the ones covering most of Europe, PTTs do have bandwidth-reservation schemes in place, but customers complain bitterly about the service just the same.

9.6   Transport Protocols for Remote Operations

In the previous sections, some of the desirable properties of transport protocols were discussed. We list them here.

- at-most-once behaviour,
- positive feedback when no failures occur,
- error report when there may have been failures,
- low end-to-end latency, and
- support for very large request and reply messages.

In this section, we investigate how such protocols can be built and what design aspects contribute to low overhead and high performance.

Achieving at-most-once behaviour requires that the client and server maintain state which allows the client to generate requests in such a way that the server can always tell requests that it has processed already from those that are new. Doing this requires setting up a session between client and server. As discussed before, requests and responses must be labelled with the session identifier and the session identifier must be distinguishable from all previous session identifiers used.

Many transport protocols are very careless about establishing new and unique session identifiers and trust that all old packets will have disappeared by the time a new session starts. Those protocols that do the job properly obey the specification of session-establishment protocols discussed in Chapter 10. Two examples are given there of correct session-establishment protocols but many others exist.

Amoeba (Mullender *et al.* [1990]) uses session identifiers made up of the unique ports of the client and server processes. Unique ports, for purposes of this discussion, are random numbers drawn carefully enough from a large enough set that the probability of session identifiers clashing is small enough to be ignored.

An interesting protocol for session establishment is the ΔT protocol designed by Fletcher and Watson [1978]. This protocol makes use of the assumption that packets have a maximum lifetime in the network, ΔT, which is composed of the transmission delay through the network, the maximum number of retransmissions of a packet, and the time interval between retransmissions.[3] The protocol dictates that when there is no communication, or no successful communication, for longer than ΔT, the current session automatically terminates and a new one starts. Since packets have a maximum lifetime of ΔT, no packets from a previous session can arrive in the new one.

In the ΔT protocol, no session identifiers are necessary, obviating the need for random number generators, stable storage, or battery-backed-up clock. There is no connection setup, the protocol just starts numbering packets from zero at the start of a new session. The price paid is that there is a time-out between sessions, but new sessions are only started when there was no communication for a time greater than ΔT anyway, or when a host has crashed. After a host comes back up, it enforces the timeout by waiting for a time ΔT before accepting or sending messages.

Each remote operation must be part of a session. Request and reply messages must be distinguishable so that it is possible to tell new messages from retransmissions of already accepted ones. There are several ways of doing this.

1. Packets can be numbered separately for each direction, independently of the actual remote operations.
2. Messages can be numbered and a subnumbering scheme can be used for the packets within a message.
3. Remote operations can be numbered and *message types* and packet subnumbering can be used for distinguishing packets within a remote operation.

The third method is the most practical for high-performance remote-operations transport protocols for reasons explained below.

In Figure 9.4, a protocol is shown that acknowledges each message. The protocol sends a request (for the time being, we assume messages fit in a single packet) which is acknowledged before the server starts processing it. When the server finishes it sends a reply which is also acknowledged. In order to detect server crashes, the client, after receiving the initial ack, periodically sends a *keep-alive* message which the server acks.

Most requests are serviced quickly so that no keep-alives are actually sent. In fact, very many requests are serviced so quickly that the response message actually has to wait in the transmission queue for the ack to the request to go out. Similarly, clients often send several requests in a row sufficiently quickly for the next request to have to wait for the ack to the previous reply.

This suggests another protocol, optimized for 'fast operations', illustrated in Figure 9.5. A reply doubles as an ack for the associated request and the client's next request doubles as an ack for the previous reply.

It is obvious how this protocol would work when there are not failures and no messages are lost, and when the supply of requests never ends. But what if these conditions are not fulfilled? If messages are lost, they can be retransmitted and

---

[3]The time between retransmissions must, of course, be longer than the time it normally takes for an ack to come back.

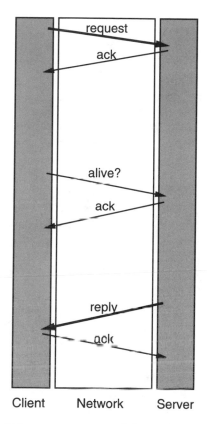

Client   Network   Server

Figure 9.4. A full transport protocol for remote operations; each message is acknowledged and keep-alives are used for detecting server crashes

the protocol would still work (request and reply sequence numbers would be used to distinguish originals from duplicates). But the client could never distinguish between a server that just takes extraordinarily long to compute its answer and one that has crashed — no feedback is generated by a server until processing is complete.

As an aside, note that numbering remote operations, rather than messages or packets, makes it easy to couple replies to requests and requests to previous replies. This is why message-numbering scheme 3 above is the preferred one.

Wouldn't it be nice if we could design a protocol that would work as the protocol of Figure 9.5 in the normal case and that — in the worst case — would turn into something like the protocol of Figure 9.4 whenever messages are lost or the server takes a long time to compute a reply? As it turns out, this is quite possible, as shown next.

In the normal case, a request should be acknowledged by its reply, so requests should not be acknowledged immediately. Acks can be postponed using a piggy-

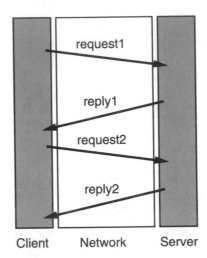

Figure 9.5. A minimal transport protocol for remote operations of short duration; each request is acknowledged by its reply and each reply by the following request.

back timer, a technique that is well known in the networking world. But this means that both the client and the server have to maintain timers — the client needs a retransmission timer and the server a piggyback timer. In networks that lose very few messages, another technique is even simpler.

The client maintains a retransmission timer and retransmits a request when the timer expires. The server does not maintain a timer, but acknowledges any request it receives *for the second time*. In the most common case — no messages are lost and the server sends a reply within the retransmission period — this obviously works with a minimum number of messages. In the next common case — no messages are lost and the server takes longer than the retransmission period — the client retransmits the request when its timer expires and the server responds with an ack. The client then knows that the request has arrived and that the server is working on it.

For reply messages the same technique can be used with the rôles of client and server reversed: When the client receives a reply for the first time, it does not send an ack. If it has a new request, it sends it to the server and the server interprets that as an ack for the previous reply. If the client has no new request, the server times out and retransmits the reply; the client acknowledges the retransmission.

There is one sticky detail here. Not infrequently, a client invokes a remote operation, receives the reply and exits before the server's retransmission timer expires. The server will then retransmit into the void. Does this matter? Not really. The server cannot distinguish between a client that crashed just before receiving the reply and one that crashed just after receiving the reply anyway. But the time spent retransmitting is, of course, a waste of resources. A simple solution is to let clients, when they terminate, send acknowledgements for all replies that have not been followed up by another request.

One detail still needs to be addressed — detecting server crashes. This can be done as follows. The client state is extended with an *'ack-received'* flag, which is set to *false* when a request is transmitted. When the client receives an ack it sets the flag to *true* and it increases the retransmission timeout period. When the retransmission timer expires, the client checks the flag. If it is *false* it retransmits the request. If it is *true* it retransmits only the header of the request, but not the data. When the server receives a request, it checks the header to see if it had received that request already. If this is the case, it ignores the data portion and returns an ack.

The complete protocol is illustrated in Figure 9.6 for the case of a remote operation of long duration. Timers are indicated by vertical lines with a black arrow head when the timer expires and an open arrow head when the timer is stopped because of the arrival of the expected message. Messages are indicated by the usual diagonal arrows, messages containing data by thick ones, header-only messages by thin ones. Three state variables are indicated, *seq* is the operation sequence number, *timer* is the retransmission timer value (which can be set to *long* or *short* and also affects running timers), and *gotack* is the ack-received flag.

So far, one-packet requests and replies have been assumed. Now we shall look at the transmission of very large request and reply messages. Not all remote-operation transport protocols implement large messages. The protocol used in Topaz (Schroeder and Burrows [1989]) specializes in one-packet messages. In Topaz, large entities are sent by having several parallel threads simultaneously doing multiple remote operations.

Normally, however, transport protocols for remote operations handle large messages. An obvious technique from the connection-oriented-protocol world is to use a *sliding-window* protocol for large messages. But sliding-window protocols are complicated and impractical for small messages.

A protocol that has become rather popular is the *packet-blast* or *netblit* protocol. An early implementation of such a protocol can be found in VMTP (Nordmark and Cheriton [1989]). The idea is that some fixed number of packets — a *packet blast* — is sent and acknowledged as one unit. When the sender gets the ack, it can send the next packet blast. If packets are two kilobytes in size, and a blast is 32 packets, then a megabyte message is 16 blasts.

Packet blasts can easily be incorporated in our one-packet-message remote-operations protocol. Let us assume a request is n blasts in size ($B_1, B_2, \ldots, B_n$; $n >= 0$). For $i = 1$ to n, the client

1. sends B_i,
2. starts a retransmission timer, and
3. waits for expiration of the timer or reception of an ack;
4. if the retransmission timer expires, the client goes back to step 1,
5. if an ack is received, the client cancels the timer and iterates.

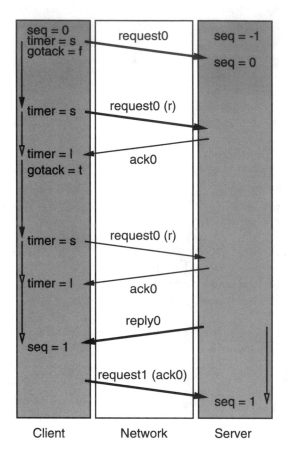

Figure 9.6. A remote-operations transport protocol that uses just two messages per operation in the normal case, tolerates message loss and detects server crashes

The last blast, B_n may be a 'partial blast', when the size of the message is not a multiple of the blast size. The total size of the message should be sent as part of the header, so that the server knows when to start work.

All blasts but the last are acknowledged immediately by the server. The last blast is treated just like the request message in the previous protocol: it is acknowledged by the reply, or, if it is received for the second time, by an ack. The same strategy is used by the response message.

Figure 9.7 shows the protocol for a large request message, a quick response, and a small reply message.

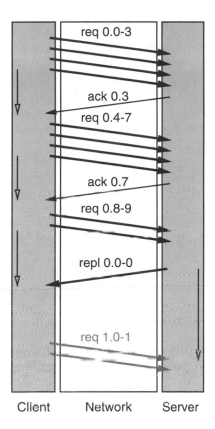

req 0.0-3

ack 0.3

req 0.4-7

ack 0.7

req 0.8-9

repl 0.0-0

req 1.0-1

Client   Network   Server

Figure 9.7. The packet-blast protocol integrated in the remote-operations protocol. Shown is a large request message, followed by a quick and short reply

9.7 Remote Procedure Call

An overwhelming proportion of interactions between processes in a distributed system are remote operations — one process sends a message to another with a request of some kind and the other process returns a reply or an acknowledgement.

Interactions of this kind can also be found in centralized systems. System calls can be viewed as operations invoked by a process and carried out by the operating system.

Remote operations have much the same structure as ordinary procedure calls. In making a procedure call, the caller relinquishes control to the called procedure and gets it back when the procedure returns its result. System calls are, in fact, almost always 'encapsulated' in procedure calls. For a Unix programmer, there is little syntactic difference between a call to *read* and one to *strlen* — one is a system call, the other is a library routine.

There is much to be said for using the syntax of procedure calls to invoke remote operations. Every programmer is thoroughly familiar with the concept of

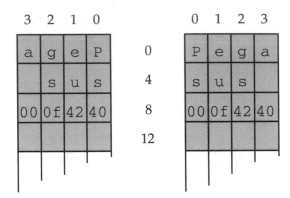

Figure 9.8. Representation of a string and an integer in a little-endian architecture (left) and a big-endian one (right)

procedure calls and it is nice to have the details of sending and receiving request and reply messages hidden behind the facade of an elegant procedural interface.

Remote procedure call is just that: remote operations in the guise of a procedural interface. In this section we shall discuss how remote procedures work, what the difference is between ordinary procedure calls and remote procedure calls and we shall look at some examples of remote procedure call systems. But in the following section, we shall first show that remote procedure call is not merely syntactic sugar, but that, in many systems, it would be very hard to do without.

9.7.1 The Problems of Heterogeneity

It is a sad fact of life that different processor types and different programming languages use different representations for the data they manipulate. When a message is sent from one process, written in one programming language and running on one processor type, to another, written in another language and running on another processor type, the contents of the message will no be understood unless there has been prior agreement on the representation of data in the message.

Let us illustrate the problem by an example, shown in Figure 9.8. In this figure, two data structures are shown containing the same data in the representations of two different processor architectures. The first data item is a string of eight characters, representing the string 'Pegasus'. The second data item is a 32-bit integer containing the number one million (shown in its hexadecimal representation). The processor on the left has a *little-endian* architecture: the least-significant byte of an integer has the lowest address — 8, in the example shown. The processor on the right has a *big-endian* architecture: the least-significant byte of an integer has the highest address — 11, in the example.

When the data structure shown is sent from a little-endian machine to a big-endian one as a byte array, the n'th byte in the little-endian representation will end up as the n'th byte of the big-endian one. The string 'Pegasus' will arrive correctly, but the number one million with hexadecimal representation 00-0f-42-40 will arrive as $40-42-0f-00$ which is quite a different number. If, on the other hand, the data structure is sent as a 32-bit-word array, the number one million will go across correctly, but the string 'Pegasus' will end up looking like 'ageP sus' which can't be right.

The point being made here is this: When transmitting data from a machine with one data representation to one with another, one must know the structure of that data. A transport protocol, therefore, can only present data in the representation of the receiving machine if it knows the exact structure of the data.

Most transport protocols execute in the operating system, but carry user-defined data structures, so they cannot be used to do data conversion. Note, that the interpretation of protocol headers does not present a problem, because the protocol knows the exact lay out of the header. It is the data portion of a message that is the problem.

Similar problems occur when process written in different programming languages communicate data structures. Even programs compiled using different compilers for the same programming language can give problems. The size of integers may be different, for instance, or the way in which data items are aligned to byte, word, or long-word boundaries.

9.7.2 RPC Structure

The notion of Remote Procedure Call was introduced by Birrell and Nelson [1984] to deal with the problems of heterogeneity discussed in the previous section and to provide a pleasant interface to program to.

The components of a remote procedure call mechanism are illustrated in Figure 9.9. An application which we shall call the *client* calls a subroutine which is executed in another application, the *server*. If the client and the server applications were one and the same, the client would call the subroutine directly. Here, however, the client calls another subroutine, called the *client stub*. This subroutine has exactly the same interface as the server's subroutine, but it is implemented by code that asks the server to execute the subroutine and returns to the client the values it gets back from the server.

The client stub copies the parameters from the stack into a request message. It then calls on a transport protocol to ship the request message to the server. At the server end it is received by another special piece of code, the *server stub*. The server stub takes the call parameters out of the request message, pushes them onto the stack and calls the actual remote subroutine. When it returns, the whole procedure repeats itself in the reverse direction: The server stub puts the result parameters in a reply message, and invokes the transport protocol to ship the message back to the client stub. The client stub takes the result parameters and passes the back to the client. For the client code the whole thing looks exactly like a normal local procedure call.

Let us go over this mechanism again by looking at an example.

Assume that we want to use an RPC interface between a time server and its clients. It has an interface consisting of two calls as shown in Figure 9.10.

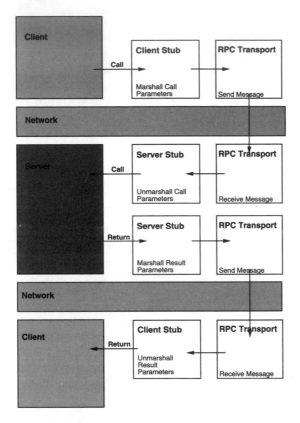

Figure 9.9. Structure of remote procedure call

The client stub, in this case, would consist of two subroutines with the same interface as the remote-procedure one. The one for settime could look like the code of Figure 9.11.

The client stub shown declares a message buffer and fills it with a code that identifies the call to be made and its parameter: the contents of the struct t ime. It

```
struct time{
    int seconds;
    int minutes;
    int hours;
    int day;
    int month;
    int year;
    char timezone[4];
}
int gettime(t); struct time *t;
int settime(t); struct time *t;
```

Figure 9.10. The time server interface uses a data structure called t ime which is passed in the two calls gettime and settime

```
int settime(t); struct time *t; {
    char *p,*message[32];
    int stat;

    p = message;
    p = put_int(p, SETTIME);
    p = put_int(p, t->seconds);
    p = put_int(p, t->minutes);
    p = put_int(p, t->hours);
    p = put_int(p, t->day);
    p = put_int(p, t->month);
    p = put_int(p, t->year);
    p = put_string(p, t->timezone, 4);
    stat = do_operation("time_server", message, 28);
    if (stat == SUCCESS) get_int(message, &stat);
    return(stat);
}
```

Figure 9.11. A possible implementation of the client stub for settime

then sends the request message using the transport protocol's do_operation call.
When the transport protocol returns the constant SUCCESS the call succeeded and
the reply message will have been put in the buffer message. From this buffer it
retrieves a code that indicates whether or not the call succeeded which is returned.

Let us now look at the code for the client stub in more detail. The first thing
to note is that the client stub is written using knowledge of the semantics of the
settime call: The contents of the struct time pointed to by the parameter t is
copied into the request message, but not copied back from the reply message.
The implementor of the stub used the knowledge that settime sets the time and
does not read the time. Settime returns an integer indicating whether setting the
time succeeded. The implementor uses this knowledge and has written code that
retrieves this status code and returns it to the caller.

The second thing to notice is that specific calls to routines called put_int,
put_string, and get_int are made to copy integers and strings into and out of
messages. These routines are *marshalling routines* and their task is to convert data
types from the machine's representation into a standard *network representation*. We
shall see more about marshalling and network representations in a later section.

Finally, the client stub calls on a transport-protocol function do_operation that
sends a request message from client to server and returns a reply message from
the server (in the same buffer, in our example). Do_operation returns a status
code that indicates whether the remote invocation of the server succeeded. In this
example, we have overloaded the error indications of the transport mechanism
with those of the settime call itself. This only works if the implementors of
settime use a disjoint set of error codes (e.g., zero for success, negative values for
transport errors and positive values for error in calls to settime).

Now, let us look at a possible implementation of the server stub code, shown in
Figure 9.12.

```
void main_loop() {
    char *p,*message[32];
    int len, op_code;
    struct time t;

    for (;;) {
        len = receive_request(message, 28);
        if (len < 4) {
            /* error handling code */
        }
        p = message;
        p = get_int(p, op_code);
        switch(op_code) {
        case SETTIME:
            if (len < 32) {
                /* error handling code */
            }
            p = get_int(p, &t.seconds);
            p = get_int(p, &t.minutes);
            p = get_int(p, &t.hours);
            p = get_int(p, &t.day);
            p = get_int(p, &t.month);
            p = get_int(p, &t.year);
            p = get_string(p, &t.timezone, 4);
            len = settime(&t);
            put_int(message, len);
            len = 4;
            break;
        case GETTIME:
            /* code for marshalling and calling
             * gettime
             */
        }
        send_reply(message, len);
    }
}
```

Figure 9.12. A possible implementation of the server stub for the time server

The server stub has a very different structure from the client stub. The client stub is a subroutine that is called by the client to handle a specific call (settime in our example). The server stub is really a *process* that receives calls from all sorts of clients, figures out which subroutine in the RPC interface must be called and calls them, doing the marshalling in the process.

Our example server consists of an infinite loop, each iteration of the loop handling one RPC call. At the top of the loop we find a call to the transport protocol's receive_request function. At the bottom we find a call to send_reply. In between, the RPC is carried out. First, the operation code is picked out of the message and a *case statement* selects the marshalling code for a specific call in the interface. We only show the marshalling code for settime in the example.

After marshalling the arguments of settime into a local struct time t, the actual settime routine is called. Settime does not modify its arguments, so they need no be marshalled again for the reply message. The return code from settime is marshalled, however, and sent back to the client.

Now that we have seen how remote procedure call works, we shall go into several aspects of RPC in more detail. The next section will describe the difference between normal procedure calls and remote ones. Section 9.7.4 will look at marshalling in more detail. In Section 9.7.5 the automatic generation of stubs from a description of the RPC interface is explained. These descriptions are called *interface definition languages* and they are discussed in Section 9.7.5.

9.7.3 Procedure Call vs. Remote Procedure Call

The important thing to know about about remote procedure call is that it is not the same as ordinary procedure call. There are fundamental differences. They all have to do with the fact that the caller of the procedure and the called procedure execute in different domains.

The most important difference is perhaps that client and server can fail independently. The server may crash while the client does not. As a consequence an RPC may fail. When a crash occurs during the execution of a normal procedure call, the caller crashes also, so no code needs to be written to deal with server crashes. In the remote-procedure-call case, such code will have to be present. If the programming language into which RPC is embedded has an exception-handling mechanism, such as in the case of Modula-2, extra exceptions can be declared for the case of communication or server failures. In other languages, such as, for example, C, the failure codes are usually overloaded on the return values from the remote procedures themselves. Obviously, this restricts the value space of return types.

Client and server do not execute in the same address space, so global variables and pointers cannot be used across the interface. The set of global variables of the client is not accessible from a remote procedure. Pointer passing is useless too. A pointer has meaning only in one address space. In some cases, instead of a pointer, one can pass the data pointed to, as we did in the settime example of the previous section. But this does not always work. If a pointer is passed to an element in the middle of a singly-linked list, should one marshal one element in the linked list, the whole linked list, or just the tail of the list starting at the element pointed to? It depends on what the remote procedure does.

Passing functions as arguments to a procedure is normally implemented by passing a pointer to the function. In an RPC interface, function-passing is close to impossible. One could try to pass the whole function, but this can only work in very favourable circumstances indeed — homogeneous hardware, position-independent code, no dependencies on global variables, and probably quite a few more.

9.7.4 Marshalling

Marshalling is the technical term for transferring data structures used in remote procedure calls from one address space to another. Marshalling is needed to achieve two goals. One is linearizing the data structures for transport in messages and reconstructing the original data structures at the far end. The other is converting data structures from the data representation on the calling process to that of the called process.

When linearizing data structures, the most complicated problem is to recognize when a structure pointed to has already been marshalled. It is possible that first a pointer to a character is encountered and later a pointer to the string containing that character. It is these complications that make marshalling complex data structures in such a way that they can be reconstructed at the other end quite difficult.

One way of dealing with pointers is not to marshal the data pointed to, but instead to generate a *call-back handle*. The idea is that the called procedure, when it runs into a pointer, is made to make an RPC back to the caller to retrieve the data pointed to. This approach avoids unnecessary copying of data across the interface and is therefore particularly suitable when passing pointers into very large data structures. However, multiple pointers into the same data will usually go unrecognized with this method.

The marshalling code at the sending and receiving side must use an agreed representation for the data passed in messages between them. This representation is usually identical or nearly identical to the data representation of one of the participating machines (e.g., big-endian, ASCII and IEEE floating point representation) and languages (e.g., integers are four bytes, booleans one bytes, etc.). Sometimes several different representations are allowed to avoid unnecessary translations.

Note that it is unnecessary to use a network standard representation that is *self-describing*; that is, a representation such as ASN.1 where each character, integer, string, etc. is labelled with its type. The stubs at both ends do not require this information since their code was derived from a common interface definition. In the examples of Figures 9.11 and 9.12 this can be observed. `Get_int` and `get_string` are called in the appropriate places without first looking into the message to see what data type comes next.

Variable-length, or variable-structure data types must be self-describing to some extent. Variable-length arrays must be accompanied by the number of elements, unions by a discriminator. Sometimes fixed-length buffers are used for variable-length data. An input routine, such as `get_line`, for example may be called with a buffer of 256 characters which will usually be only partly filled with data. It can be useful to use specialized marshalling code for cases like this and save network bandwidth.

9.7.5 Stub Generation

Stubs as shown in Figures 9.11 and 9.12 can simply be hand-crafted from the header declaration of Figure 9.10 and a little bit of knowledge of what the procedures in the interface do.

It is an attractive notion to generate these stubs purely mechanically from the interface description, but descriptions such as that of Figure 9.10 do not carry sufficient information to do that.

Specialized languages are used to define remote procedure call interfaces and provide the information that existing programming languages do not provide. From an interface definition in such a language, client stubs and server stubs can be generated automatically by a *stub compiler*.

The language in which a remote procedure call interface is described is usually referred to as an *Interface Definition Language* or IDL. They tend to be derived from existing programming languages and sometimes the extra information needed for stub generation for the IDL is made to look like a series of comments in the original programming language.

Essential extra information an IDL should provide is the direction in which parameters travel (*in*, *out*, or *in/out*), discriminators for unions, and information about the length of arrays passed as parameters.

Sometimes, a single server implements multiple interfaces. It is therefore a sensible precaution to make the identifier of the subroutine to be called a global one, for instance by the concatenation of a global *interface identifier* and an identifier for the function to be called in the interface.

In a combination of a well-designed IDL and a carefully implemented stub compiler, the marshalling code can be very nearly optimal. Examples of IDLs are HP/Apollo's NCS which is now part of the Distributed Computing Environment of OSF, SUN RPC (Sun Microsystems [1985]), Mercury (Liskov *et al.* [1987]), Flume (Birrell, Lazowska and Wobber [1984]), Courier (Xerox Corporation [1981]), and AIL (van Rossum [1989]).

9.8   Systems Issues

If one technology has influenced research in distributed systems, it is the Ethernet. This 10 Mbps local-area network has been the principal interconnection network for work stations and servers for two decades and, as a result, most well-known distributed systems were based on it: Amoeba, Emerald, Sprite, Topaz, V, and many more.

When RPC emerged as the communication paradigm of choice in distributed systems researchers set out to build high-performance transport protocols for RPC and many papers were published in which competed for the best round-trip latency or throughput for any protocol reported (Nordmark and Cheriton [1989]; Ousterhout *et al.* [1988]; van Renesse, van Staveren and Tanenbaum [1988]; Schroeder and Burrows [1989]). As a result, we now understand how to implement efficient RPC transport protocols for medium-speed networks quite well.

But now, a new generation of much faster networks is emerging and, at the same time, new applications place new demands on transport protocols. Building local networks operating at 100 Mbps has long ago ceased to be a technological challenge (Leslie and McAuley [1991]; Ross [1989]) and networks operating at one Gbps now work in various laboratories. Building communication protocols that exploit these speeds still *is* a challenge.

New applications are also making new demands on protocol designers. One such demand is that for authenticated, secure communication. Therefore, authentication protocols and key-establishment protocols must be integrated with transport protocols in an efficient manner.

But the most profound change in protocol design is being brought about by the integration of multimedia communication into distributed systems. The transport of digital audio and video data requires *timely* communication with very low end-to-end latencies — a requirement that never used to be deemed very important before. At the same time, the bandwidth requirements for digital video are quite considerable and often beyond what conventional transport protocols can offer. Digital audio and video transmission can tolerate moderate data loss, however, but conventional transport protocols have no way of exploiting this.

All this is rapidly changing the way we think about designing computer networks and protocols for communication in distributed systems.

9.8.1   ATM Networks

Let us briefly look into the requirements for networks that must carry both data and digital audio and video (contiguous media). The structure of such networks is, to a large extent, dictated by the maximum permissible end-to-end latency for interactive communication using audio and video. Experience has shown that latencies of more than a tenth of a second become noticeable and even irritating. Anyone who has conducted a telephone conversation across an ocean via satellite has noticed the irritating communication latency caused by the distance of the satellite.

To keep the end-to-end latency low, data packets containing digital audio or video must be placed on the network and forwarded at intermediate nodes within a few milliseconds from being offered. This puts a maximum size on *all* network packets — when a contiguous-media packet is ready for transmission, any communication going on at the time must finish within 10 ms; at 100 Mbps, one millisecond corresponds to 12.5 Kbyte. It also puts a maximum size on audio and video packets themselves.

Telephone-quality audio is sampled at 8000 Hz, using 8-bit samples. The PTTs have chosen to send a packet every six milliseconds which thus contain 48 bytes of audio each. This gives the telephone network an end-to-end latency of six milliseconds, plus the extra latency encountered at each forwarding node, plus the latency caused by the length of the cable. With 48-byte cells, the loss of a single cell is barely audible at the receiving end.

In general, smaller packets give better end-to-end latency, but the packet header takes up a greater fraction of the available bandwidth. For the efficient transmission of small packets, it is therefore necessary to minimize the size of the header and to minimize the amount of processing per packet.

ATM networks have been designed to handle small, 48-byte packets efficiently. These packets are called *cells*. The name ATM comes from *Asynchronous Transfer Mode* which must be contrasted with *Synchronous Transfer Mode* or STM. STM is time-division multiplexing in which each virtual circuit is assigned a fixed slot position within a *frame*, giving a fixed and constant bandwidth to each virtual circuit for its duration. In ATM, slots are not grouped into frames and outgoing cells for all virtual circuits are queued for the available slots. Prioritized queues are sometimes used to guarantee bandwidth.

In a 1 Gbps ATM network, a cell can be transmitted every 400 ns. ATM networks are therefore virtual-circuit oriented, because the time available for switching cells is not sufficient for making per-cell routing decisions. Each cell belongs to a virtual circuit and, on a link between two switches, cells are identified by a *virtual-circuit identifier* (VCI). A virtual circuit from one host to another is made up of the concatenation of a number of per-link virtual circuits — the concatenation is administrated by routing tables in the ATM switches. For each incoming virtual circuit, the table gives the outgoing link and VCI.

At the sending end of a virtual circuit, the ATM-device handler will typically receive a buffer and a VCI from an application which will then be divided into cells in hardware. At the receiving end, the ATM hardware can be equipped with a VCI table containing references to receive buffers, one for each active virtual circuit. The demultiplexing of virtual circuits and the reassembly of cells into larger units can thus be done in hardware and data can be received in memory where it has to go.

This last statement seems obvious, but isn't. In datagram-oriented networks (such as Ethernet and token ring), *medium-access-control-level* or MAC-level packet headers do not contain any information that allows the network controller to do demultiplexing. These networks use a pool of packet receive buffers and let higher levels of protocol do further demultiplexing (in software). This usually implies that packet data must be copied to its final destination. An exception to this is Topaz which has a pool of packet buffers shared by all processes — Topaz trades security for performance here and this is fine, because the machines on which Topaz runs are single-user work stations.

Individual ATM cells have no checksum to protect the data. The cells in a virtual circuit are therefore grouped together — at the end points — into larger units called packets. These packets can have a checksum for detecting transmission errors; they are the unit of retransmission. The packets can be delimited by a bit, reserved for the purpose in the header of the ATM cells. This bit allows the cell-management hardware of an ATM controller to invoke hardware or software for packet handling. The logical layer that defines and handles packets in ATM networks is the *ATM Adaptation Layer*, or AAL.

9.8.2   Encryption

In Chapter 20, Roger Needham explains how secure channels between communicating principals can be set up. For this discussion, the following is relevant:

- Before a connection can be established, the parties (called *principals* in the jargon of authentication protocols) must authenticate each other and agree on an encryption key to use for encrypting the data on the connection.

- The authentication process may require exchanging messages with an *authentication (server)* (usually only one of the parties needs to do this) or it may be carried out using cached authentication information.
- The encryption algorithms for authentication and data transmission can be different — the former is often a public-key algorithm such as RSA, while the latter is usually a shared-key algorithm such as DES. Public key for authentication makes key management simpler. Shared-key algorithms, such as DES, can be implemented in hardware at network speeds.
- The (shared) key used for encrypting the data on the connection between two (authenticated) principals is referred to as the *session key*. These keys should be used for a limited period, such as a single session, only.

An important issue in the design of transport protocols is where to place the mechanisms that achieve authentication and carry out encryption. The ISO [1981] OSI basic reference model places both in the Presentation Layer, above the protocols that provide reliable transmission and above all of the multiplexing of end-to-end connections over transport connections.

This implies that an end-to-end connection must be established between principals before authentication can take place and that encryption and decryption must be carried out above the transport and session protocols. As a result, transport-protocol headers will not be encrypted so that an active intruder can inject packets into the connection that will be accepted by the transport protocol as genuine; the *real* packets will subsequently be rejected by the transport protocol (e.g., as superfluous retransmissions). On decryption the injected packets will also be rejected. An active intruder can thus cause complete denial of service, even if all of the proper protocol packets do reach their destination.

If the encryption-protocol layer were placed below the protocol layers that create reliable data transport (by timeout and retransmission, typically), then the encryption-protocol layer would filter out all of the intruder's data, leaving an untampered stream of packets for the transport protocol to create a reliable data stream with.

A protocol layering with the encryption protocol at the bottom has the added advantage that hardware-encryption support on the network controller can be used efficiently. On transmission, the network device driver can provide the controller with a packet and a key; the controller will then send the packet, encrypting it on-the-fly with the key. Doing reception this way is more difficult, because received packets must be examined in order to decide which key to use for decryption — one host usually has many connections in use simultaneously. This makes it much harder to use hardware decryption support than encryption support.

Butler Lampson suggested an elegant mechanism for making use of decryption hardware without having to enlist the help of protocol software to decide which key to use. The key that decrypts the packet is simply sent along with every packet. To prevent intruders from decrypting the packet, the key itself is also encrypted, but with a different key; let us call this key the *master key*.

Every network controller is given a master key, for instance, upon bootstrap. When an authentication handshake is made and a session key established, an extra step is carried out: The session key is encrypted with the master key and sent over the channel. It cannot be decrypted at the other end. It is simply stored and sent along with every packet encrypted with the session key going the other way.

A network controller receiving an encrypted packet first decrypts the session key in the packet header with the master key, then encrypts the rest of the packet with the session key. No protocol software need be invoked until the packet is ready for higher layers.

9.8.3 Demultiplexing

A network is a shared resource. Many processes on many machines communicate in various patterns. One process can communicate with many others simultaneously. As a result, on one machine, many connections between processes, sometimes using different protocol stacks, must be multiplexed over a single network interface.

Multiplexing the outgoing data streams is straightforward. The sending process invokes the upper part of the protocol stack in its own address space, sometimes it then invokes a middle part of the protocol stack in a protocol-server process on the same machine, and finally the rest of the protocol stack is invoked in the operating system kernel. Each protocol-processing entity adds layers of encapsulation to the data to be transmitted and passes the data down the protocol stack. The actual multiplexing usually happens when the data reaches the network device driver's queue of outgoing packets. Essentially, a single thread of control traverses the protocol stack all the way down to the level of the device driver. No scheduling decisions are necessary and this makes the downward multiplexing efficient.

Demultiplexing the incoming data stream efficiently is much harder. The problem is that the identity of the application thread awaiting the received data is not know until most of the demultiplexing has been done and most of the protocol layers have been traversed in an upward direction. The ISO [1981] OSI Basic Reference Model allows multiplexing and demultiplexing in six of its seven layers.

A network device interrupt routine can only do the most minimal protocol processing before it must wake up some process' thread to continue the processing and demultiplexing. At this point, however, it is not yet known which thread is the ultimate receiver of the data, so there will have to be another level of thread-awakening, placing two scheduler decisions in the path of incoming messages.

Distributed systems claiming low-latency communication are — without exception, I believe — essentially single-protocol systems with a minimum number of demultiplexing points which do all the multiplexing in the interrupt routine. Schroeder and Burrows [1989] give a very clear exposition of this mechanism.

In networks that use virtual circuits at the MAC level, an opportunity exists to place all multiplexing at that level by using a different virtual circuit for every end-to-end connection. It is then possible to place arbitrary protocol stacks on top of the MAC-level virtual circuits, but the multiplexing functions of these protocols can remain unused. Since each virtual circuit can be coupled to an application thread, the issue of waking up the correct thread is easily resolved.

McAuley [1989] proposes a protocol architecture called the Multi-Service Network Architecture or MSNA that concentrates multiplexing and demultiplexing in the MAC level. To build high-performance ATM network protocols, an architecture such as MSNA is a requirement.

9.8.4   Conclusions

When networks run at Ethernet speeds, high-performance communication can only be achieved through extreme frugality with the numbers of packet exchanges. Transport protocols for distributed systems in local networks tended to be connectionless, although some protocols cached protocol-state information to get better performance in sequences of remote operations.

Today, there are several good reasons to construct transport protocols in distributed systems along connection-oriented lines. Connection orientation is necessary at the level of authenticated and encrypted communication and, as we have seen, encryption is best done at the lowest protocol levels. Connection-orientation is also necessary for multimedia communication. Continuous-media connections need timely delivery of large amounts of data and, to do this, bandwidth reservation and an efficient path through the operating systems at both ends is a must.

Connection orientation, combined with a single point of multiplexing at the root of the tree formed by the collection of protocol stacks helps to avoid copying of packet data and allows a single thread invocation of only the receiving application thread.

For good performance, a fast path through the protocol stack is needed. Protocols need to be able to invoke higher- and lower-layer protocols efficiently. Specialized implementations of protocols can often be used in specialized circumstances. For example, when running TCP/IP over an ATM network in which each end-to-end connection uses its own virtual circuit, the multiplexing code in IP and TCP can be eliminated allowing considerable speedup.

Hutchinson *et al.* [1989] built the x-kernel to demonstrate a very efficient mechanism for building protocol stacks. Their mechanism also allows the use of simplified versions of protocols in special environments, such as described in the previous paragraph.

Distributed systems will have to support multimedia communication as well as group-communication protocols. This will obviously lead to a diversity of protocols in simultaneous use. The days of getting just RPC to go fast are over, but, fortunately, we have a reasonably good idea how transport protocols can be made to run just as fast while offering much more functionality.

9.9   References

Abramson, N. (1970), The ALOHA system — Another alternative for computer communications, *Proceedings of the Fall Joint Computer Conference* **37**, 281–285.

Birman, K. P. and Joseph, T. A. (1987), Exploiting Virtual Synchrony in Distributed Systems, in *Proceedings of the Eleventh Symposium on Operating Systems Principles*, Austin, TX, 123–138, In *ACM Operating Systems Review* **21**(5).

Birrell, A. D., Lazowska, E. D. and Wobber, E. (1984), Flume — Remote Procedure Call Stub Generator for Modula-2+, Topaz manpage.

Birrell, A. D. and Nelson, B. J. (1984), Implementing Remote Procedure Calls, *ACM Transactions on Computer Systems* **2**, 39–59.

Fletcher, J. G. and Watson, R. W. (1978), Mechanisms for a Reliable Timer Based Protocol, *Computer Networks* **2**, 271–290.

Hutchinson, N. C., Peterson, L. L., Abbott, M. B. and O'Malley, S. (1989), RPC in the x-Kernel: Evaluating New Design Techniques, *Proceedings of the Twelfth Symposium on Operating Systems Principles* **23**(5), 91–101, In *ACM Operating Systems Review* **23**(5).

ISO (1981), ISO Open Systems Interconnection Basic Reference Model, *SIGCOMM* **11**(2), 15–65.

Kaashoek, M. F. and Tanenbaum, A. S. (1991), Group communication in the Amoeba distributed operating system, *Proceedings of the Eleventh International Conference on Distributed Computer Systems*, Arlington, TX, IEEE Computer Society, 222–230.

Leslie, I. M. and McAuley, D. R. (1991), Fairisle: An ATM Network for the Local Area, *ACM Computer Communication Review* **21**(4).

Liskov, B., Bloom, T., Gifford, D., Scheifler, R. and Weihl, W. E. (1987), Communication in the Mercury System, MIT LCS, Programming Methodology Group Memo 59-1, Cambridge, Ma 02139.

McAuley, D. R. (1989), Protocol Design for High-Speed Networks, University of Cambridge Computer Laboratory, Ph.D. Dissertation, Cambridge CB2 3QG, United Kingdom, Also available as University of Cambridge Computer Laboratory Technical Report No. 186, January 1990.

Mullender, S. J., van Rossum, G., Tanenbaum, A. S., van Renesse, R. and van Staveren, J. M. (1990), Amoeba — A Distributed Operating System for the 1990s, *IEEE Computer* **23**(5).

Nordmark, E. and Cheriton, D. R. (1989), Experiences from VMTP: How to Achieve Low Response Time, *Proceedings of the IFIP WG6.1/WG6.4 International Workshop on Protocols for High-Speed Networks*, Rudin, H. and Williamson, R., eds., Zürich, Switzerland.

Ousterhout, J. K., Cherenson, A. R., Douglis, F., Nelson, M. N. and Welch, B. B. (1988), The Sprite Network Operating System, *IEEE Computer* **21**(2), 23–35.

van Renesse, R., van Staveren, H. and Tanenbaum, A. S. (1988), Performance of the World's Fastest Distributed Operating System, *Operating System Review* **22**(4), 25–34.

Ross, F. (1989), An Overview of FDDI: The Fiber Distributed Data Interface, *IEEE Journal on Selected Areas in Communication* **7**(7).

van Rossum, G. (1989), AIL – A Class-Oriented Stub Generator for Amoeba, *Workshop on Progress in Distributed Operating Systems and Distributed Systems Management* **433**.

Saltzer, J. H., Reed, D. P. and Clark, D. D. (1984), End-to-End Arguments in System Design, *ACM Transactions on Computer Systems* **2**, 277–278.

Schroeder, M. D. and Burrows, M. (1989), Performance of Firefly RPC, *Proceedings of the Twelfth Symposium on Operating Systems Principles* **23**(5), 83–90, In *ACM Operating Systems Review* **23**(5).

Sun Microsystems (1985), Remote Procedure Call Protocol Specification, Sun Microsystems, Inc.

Tanenbaum, A. S., van Renesse, R., van Staveren, J. M., Sharp, G. J., Mullender, S. J., Jansen, A. J. and van Rossum, G. (1990), Experiences with the Amoeba Distributed Operating System, *Communications of the ACM*.

Xerox Corporation (1981), Courier: The Remote Procedure Call Protocol, Xerox System Integration Standard XSIS-038112, Stamford, Connecticut.

Chapter 10

Reliable Messages and Connection Establishment

Butler W. Lampson

10.1   Introduction

Given an unreliable network, we would like to reliably deliver messages from a sender to a receiver. This is the function of the transport layer of the ISO seven-layer cake. It uses the network layer, which provides unreliable message delivery, as a channel for communication between the sender and the receiver.

Ideally we would like to ensure that

- messages are delivered in the order they are sent,
- every message sent is delivered exactly once, and
- an acknowledgement is returned for each delivered message.

Unfortunately, it's expensive to achieve the second and third goals in spite of crashes and an unreliable network. In particular, it's not possible to achieve them without making some change to stable state (state that survives a crash) every time a message is received. Why? When we receive a message after a crash, we have to be able to tell whether it has already been delivered. But if delivering the message doesn't change any state that survives the crash, then we can't tell.

So if we want a cheap deliver operation which doesn't require writing stable state, we have to choose between delivering some messages more than once and losing some messages entirely when the receiver crashes. If the effect of a message is idempotent, of course, then duplications are harmless and we will choose

---

The material in this chapter is the result of joint work with Nancy Lynch and Jørgen Søgaard-Andersen.

the first alternative. But this is rare, and the latter choice is usually the lesser of two evils. It is called 'at-most-once' message delivery. Usually the sender also wants an acknowledgement that the message has been delivered, or in case the receiver crashes, an indication that it might have been lost. At-most-once messages with acknowledgements are called 'reliable' messages.

There are various ways to implement reliable messages. An implementation is called a 'protocol', and we will look at several of them. All are based on the idea of tagging a message with an identifier and transmitting it repeatedly to overcome the unreliability of the channel. The receiver keeps a stock of *good* identifiers that it has never accepted before; when it sees a message tagged with a good identifier, it accepts it, delivers it, and removes that identifier from the good set. Otherwise, the receiver just discards the message, perhaps after acknowledging it. In order for the sender to be sure that its message will be delivered rather than discarded, it must tag the message with a good identifer.

What makes the implementations tricky is that we expect to lose some state when there is a crash. In particular, the receiver will be keeping track of at least some of its good identifiers in volatile variables, so these identifiers will become bad at the crash. But the sender doesn't know about the crash, so it will go on using the bad identifiers and thus send messages that the receiver will reject. Different protocols use different methods to keep the sender and the receiver more or less in sync about what identifiers to use.

In practice reliable messages are most often implemented in the form of 'connections'. The idea is that a connection is 'established', any amount of information is sent on the connection, and then the connection is 'closed'. You can think of this as the sending of a single large message, or as sending the first message using one of the protocols we discuss, and then sending later messages with increasing sequence numbers. Usually connections are full-duplex, so that either end can send independently, and it is often cheaper to establish both directions at the same time. We ignore all these complications in order to concentrate on the essential logic of the protocols.

What we mean by a crash is not simply a failure and restart of a node. In practice, protocols for reliable messages have limits, called 'timeouts', on the length of time for which they will wait to deliver a message or get an ack. We model the expiration of a timeout as a crash: the protocol abandons its normal operation and reports failure, even though in general it's possible that the message in fact has been or will be delivered.

We begin by writing a careful specification S for reliable messages. Then we present a 'lower-level' spec D in which the non-determinism associated with losing messages when there is a crash is moved to a place that is more convenient for implementations. We explain why D implements S but don't give a proof, since that requires techniques beyond the scope of this chapter. With this groundwork, we present a generic protocol G and a proof that it implements D. Then we describe two protocols that are used in practice, the handshake protocol H and the clock-based protocol C, and show how both implement G. Finally, we explain how to modify our protocols to work with finite sets of message identifiers, and summarize our results.

The goals of this chapter are to:

- Give a simple, clear, and precise specification of reliable message delivery in the presence of crashes.

- Explain the standard handshake protocol for reliable messages that is used in TCP, ISO TP4, and many other widespread communication systems, as well as a newer clock-based protocol.

- Show that both protocols can be best understood as special cases of a simpler, more general protocol for using identifiers to tag messages and acknowledgements for reliable delivery.

- Use the method of abstraction functions and invariants to help in understanding these three subtle concurrent and fault-tolerant algorithms, and in the process present all the hard parts of correctness proofs for all of them.

- Take advantage of the generic protocol to simplify the analysis and the arguments.

10.1.1   Methods

We use the definition of 'implements' and the abstraction function proof method explained in Chapter 3. Here is a brief summary of this material.

Suppose that X and Y are state machines with named transitions called *actions*; think of X as a specification and Y as an implementation. We partition the actions of X and Y into *external* and *internal* actions. A *behavior* of a machine M is a sequence of actions that M can take starting in an initial state, and an *external behavior* of M is the subsequence of a behavior that contains only the external actions. We say Y *implements* X iff every external behavior of Y is an external behavior of X.[1] This expresses the idea that what it means for Y to implement X is that from the outside you don't see Y doing anything that X couldn't do.

The set of all external behaviors is a rather complicated object and difficult to reason about. Fortunately, there is a general method for proving that Y implements X without reasoning explicitly about behaviors in each case. It works as follows. First, define an *abstraction function f* from the state of Y to the state of X. Then show that Y *simulates* X:

1. *f* maps an initial state of Y to an initial state of X.

2. For each Y-action and each reachable state *y* there is a sequence of X-actions (perhaps empty) that is the same externally, such that the following diagram commutes.

---

[1] Actually this definition only deals with the implementation of *safety* properties. Roughly speaking, a safety property is an assertion that nothing bad happens; it is a generalization of the notion of partial correctness for sequential programs. A system that does nothing implements any safety property. Specifications may also include *liveness* properties, which roughly assert that something good eventually happens; these generalize the notion of termination for sequential programs. A full treatment of liveness is beyond the scope of this chapter, but we do explain informally why the protocols make progress.

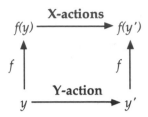

A sequence of X-actions is the same externally as a Y-action if they are the same after all internal actions are discarded. So if the Y-action is internal, all the X-actions must be internal (perhaps none at all). If the Y-action is external, all the X-actions must be internal except one, which must be the same as the Y-action.

A straightforward induction shows that Y implements X: For any Y-behavior we can construct an X-behavior that is the same externally, by using (2) to map each Y-action into a sequence of X-actions that is the same externally. Then the sequence of X-actions will be the same externally as the original sequence of Y-actions.

In order to prove that Y simulates X we usually need to know what the reachable states of Y are, because it won't be true that every action of Y from an arbitrary state of Y simulates a sequence of X-actions; in fact, the abstraction function might not even be defined on an arbitrary state of Y. The most convenient way to characterize the reachable states of Y is by an *invariant*, a predicate that is true of every reachable state. Often it's helpful to write the invariant as a conjunction, and to call each conjunct an invariant. It's common to need a stronger invariant than the simulation requires; the extra strength is a stronger induction hypothesis that makes it possible to establish what the simulation does require.

So the structure of a proof goes like this:

- Establish invariants to characterize the reachable states, by showing that each action maintains the invariants.

- Define an abstraction function.

- Establish the simulation, by showing that each Y-action simulates a sequence of X-actions that is the same externally.

This method works only with actions and does not require any reasoning about behaviors. Furthermore, it deals with each action independently. Only the invariants connect the actions. So if we change (or add) an action of Y, we only need to verify that the new action maintains the invariants and simulates a sequence of X-actions that is the same externally. We exploit this remarkable fact in Section 10.9 to extend our protocols so that they use finite, rather than infinite, sets of identifiers.

In what follows we give abstraction functions and invariants for each protocol. The actual proofs that the invariants hold and that each Y-action simulates a suitable sequence of X-actions are routine, so we give proofs only for a few sample actions.

10.1.2   Types and Notation

We use a type M for the messages being delivered. We assume nothing about M.

All the protocols except S and D use a type I of identifiers for messages. In general we assume only that Is can be compared for equality; C assumes a total ordering. If x is a multiset whose elements have a first I component, we write $ids(x)$ for the multiset of Is that appear first in the elements of x.

We write $\langle \cdots \rangle$ for a sequence with the indicated elements and $+$ for concatenation of sequences. We view a sequence as a multiset in the obvious way. We write $x = (y, *)$ to mean that x is a pair whose first component is y and whose second component can be anything, and similarly for $x = (*, y)$.

We define an action by giving its name, a *guard* that must be true for the action to occur, and an *effect* described by a set of assignments to state variables. We encode parameters by defining a whole family of actions with related names; for instance, $get(m)$ is a different action for each possible m. Actions are atomic; each action completes before the next one is started.

To express concurrency we introduce more actions. Some of these actions may be internal, that is, they may not involve any interaction with the client of the protocol. Internal actions usually make the state machine non-deterministic, since they can happen whenever their guards are satisfied, not just when there is an interaction with the environment. We mark external actions with *s, two for an input action and one for an output action. Actions without *s are internal.

It's convenient to present the sender actions on the left and the receiver actions on the right. Some actions are not so easy to categorize, and we usually put them on the left.

10.2   The Specification S

The specification S for reliable messages is a slight extension of the spec for a FIFO queue. Figure 10.1 shows the external actions and some examples of its transitions. The basic state of S is the FIFO queue q of messages, with $put(m)$ and $get(m)$ actions. In addition, the *status* variable records whether the most recently sent message has been delivered. The sender can use $getAck(a)$ to get this information; after that it may be forgotten by setting *status* to *lost*, so that the sender doesn't have to remember it forever. Both sender and receiver can crash and recover. In the absence of crashes, every message put is delivered by *get* in the same order and is positively acknowledged. If there is a crash, any message still in the queue may be lost at any time between the crash and the recovery, and its ack may be lost as well.

The $getAck(a)$ action reports on the message most recently put, as follows. If there has been no crash since it was put there are two possibilities:

- the message is still in q and *getAck* cannot occur;
- the message was delivered by $get(m)$ and $getAck(OK)$ occurs.

If there have been crashes, there are two additional possibilities:

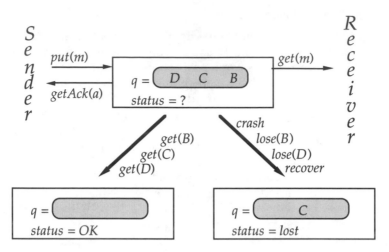

Figure 10.1. Some states and transitions for S

- the message was lost and *getAck(lost)* occurs;
- the message was delivered or is still in *q* but *getAck(lost)* occurs anyway.

The ack makes the most sense when the sender alternates *put(m)* and *getAck(a)* actions. Note that what is being acknowledged is delivery of the message to the client, not its receipt by some part of the implementation, so this is an end-to-end ack. In other words, the *get* should be thought of as including client processing of the message, and the ack might include some result returned by the client such as the result of a remote procedure call. This could be expressed precisely by adding an *ack* action for the client. We won't do that because it would clutter up the presentation without improving our understanding of how reliable messages work.

To define S we introduce the types *A* (for acknowledgement) with values in {*OK, lost*} and *Status* with values in {*OK, lost, ?*}. Table 10.1 gives the state and actions of S. Note that it says nothing about channels; they are part of the implementation and have nothing to do with the spec.

Why do we have both *crash* and *recover* actions, as opposed to just a *crash* action? A spec which only allows messages to be lost at the time of a *crash* is not implemented by a protocol like C in which the sender accepts a message with *put* and sends it without verifying that the receiver is running normally. In this case the message is lost even though it wasn't in the system at the time of the crash. This is why we have a separate *recover_r* action which allows the receiver to declare the point after a crash when messages are again guaranteed not to be lost. There seems to be no need for a *recover_s* action, but we have one for symmetry.

A spec which only allows messages to be lost at the time of a *recover* is not implemented by any protocol that can have two messages in the network at the same time, because after a *crash_s* and before the following *recover_s* it's possible for the second message in the network to be delivered, which means that the first one must be lost to preserve the FIFO property.

	Sender			Receiver	
Name	**Guard**	**Effect**	**Name**	**Guard**	**Effect**
**$put(m)$	$rec_s = false$	append m to q, status := ?	*$get(m)$	$rec_r = false$, m is first on q	remove head of q, if $q = empty$ and $status$ = ? then $status$:= OK
*$getAck(a)$	$rec_s = false$, $status = a$	optionally $status$:= $lost$			
**$crash_s$		rec_s := $true$	**$crash_r$		rec_r := $true$
*$recover_s$	rec_s	rec_s := $false$	*$recover_r$	rec_r	rec_r := $false$
$lose$	rec_s or rec_r	delete some element from q; if it's the last then $status$:= $lost$, or $status$:= $lost$			

$$
\begin{array}{lll}
q & : \text{sequence}[M] & := \langle\,\rangle \\
status & : Status & := lost \\
rec_s & : \text{Boolean} & := false \ \ (rec \text{ is short for 'recovering'}) \\
rec_r & : \text{Boolean} & := false
\end{array}
$$

Table 10.1. State and actions of S

The simplest spec which covers both these cases can lose a message at any time between a *crash* and its following *recover*, and we have adopted this alternative.

10.3   The Delayed-Decision Specification D

Next we introduce an implementation of S, called the delayed-decision specification D, that is more non-deterministic about when messages are lost. The reason for D is to simplify the proofs of the protocols: with more freedom in D, it's easier to prove that a protocol simulates D than to prove that it simulates S. A typical protocol transmits messages from the sender to the receiver over some kind of channel which can lose messages; to compensate for these losses, the sender retransmits. If the sender crashes with a message in the channel it stops retransmitting, but whether the receiver gets the message depends on whether the channel loses it. This may not be decided until after the sender has recovered. So the protocol doesn't decide whether the message is lost until after the sender has recovered. D has this freedom, but S does not.

D is the same as S except that the decisions about which messages to lose at recovery, and whether to lose the ack, are made by asynchronous *drop* actions that can occur after recovery. Each message in q, as well as the *status* variable, is augmented by an extra component of type *Mark* which is normally + but may become # between crash and recovery because of a *mark* action. At any time an *unmark* action can change a mark from # back to +, a message marked # can be lost by *drop*, or a *status* marked # can be set to *lost* by *drop*. Figure 10.2 gives an example of the transitions of D; the + marks are omitted.

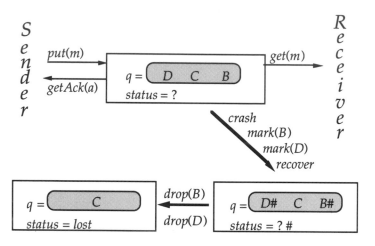

Figure 10.2. Some states and transitions of D

	Sender			**Receiver**	
Name	**Guard**	**Effect**	**Name**	**Guard**	**Effect**
**$put(m)$	$rec_S = false$	append $(m, +)$ to q, $status := (?, +)$	*$get(m)$	$rec_r = false$, $(m, *)$ first on q	remove head of q, if $q = empty$ and $status = (?, x)$ then $status := (OK, x)$
*$getAck(a)$	$rec_S = false$, $status = (a, *)$	$status := (a, +)$ or $status := (lost, +)$			
**$crash_S$		$rec_S := true$	**$crash_r$		$rec_r := true$
*$recover_S$	rec_S	$rec_S := false$	*$recover_r$	rec_r	$rec_r := false$
$mark$	rec_S or rec_r	for some element of q or for $status$, $mark := \#$	$unmark$		for some element of q or for $status$, $mark := +$

$drop$ delete an element of q with $mark = \#$;
         if it was the last element, $status := (lost, +)$
    or   if $status = (*, \#)$, $status := (lost, +)$

q	: sequence$[(M, Mark)]$	$:= \langle \rangle$
$status$	: $(Status, Mark)$	$:= (lost, +)$
rec_S	: Boolean	$:= false$
rec_r	: Boolean	$:= false$

Table 10.2. State and actions of D

Name	Guard	Effect	Name	Guard	Effect
$send_{sr}(p)$		add some number of copies of p to sr	**$send_{rs}(p)$**		add some number of copies of p to rs
*$rcv_{sr}(p)$	$p \in sr$	remove one p from sr	$rcv_{rs}(p)$	$p \in rs$	remove one p from rs
$lose_{sr}(p)$	$p \in sr$	remove one p from sr	$lose_{rs}(p)$	$p \in rs$	remove one p from rs

Table 10.3. Actions of the channels

To define D we introduce the type *Mark* which has values in the set $\{+, \#\}$. Table 10.2 gives the state and actions of D.

10.3.1 Proof that D Implements S

We do not give this proof, since to do it using abstraction functions we would have to introduce 'prophecy variables', also known as 'multi-valued mappings' or 'backward simulations' (Abadi and Lamport [1991], Lynch and Vaandrager [1993]). If you work out some examples, however, you will probably see why the two specs S and D have the same external behavior.

10.4 Channels

All our protocols use the same *channel* abstraction to transfer information between the sender and the receiver. We use the name 'packet' for the messages sent over a channel, to distinguish them from reliable messages. A channel can freely drop and reorder packets, and it can duplicate a packet any finite number of times when it's sent;[2] the only thing it isn't allowed to do is deliver a packet that wasn't sent. The reason for using such a weak specification is to ensure that the reliable message protocol will work over any bit-moving mechanism that happens to be available. With a stronger channel spec, for instance one that doesn't reorder packets, it's possible to have somewhat simpler or more efficient implementations.

There are two channels *sr* and *rs*, one from sender to receiver and one from receiver to sender, each a multiset of packets initially empty. The nature of a packet varies from one protocol to another. Table 10.3 gives the channel actions.

Protocols interact with the channels through the external actions *send*(...) and *rcv*(...) which have the same names in the channel and in the protocol. One of these actions occurs if both its pre-conditions are true, and the effect is both the effects. This always makes sense because the states are disjoint.

---

[2] You might think it would be more natural and closer to the actual implementation of a channel to allow a packet already in the channel to be duplicated. Unfortunately, if a packet can be duplicated any number of times it's possible that a protocol like H (see section 10.8) will not make any progress.

10.5   The Generic Protocol G

The generic protocol G generalizes two practical protocols described later, H and C; in other words, both of them implement G. This protocol can't be implemented directly because it has some 'magic' actions that use state from both sender and receiver. But both real protocols implement these actions, each in its own way.

The basic idea is derived from the simplest possible distributed implementation of S, which we call the stable protocol SB. In SB all the state is stable (that is, nothing is lost when there is a crash), and each end keeps a set g_s or g_r of good identifiers, that is, identifiers that have not yet been used. Initially $g_s \subseteq g_r$, and the protocol maintains this as an invariant. To send a message the sender chooses a good identifier i from g_s, attaches i to the message, moves i from g_s to a $last_s$ variable, and repeatedly sends the message. When the receiver gets a message with a good identifier it accepts the message, moves the identifier from g_r to a $last_r$ variable, and returns an ack packet for the identifier after the message has been delivered by get. When the receiver gets a message with an identifier that isn't good, it returns a positive ack if the identifier equals $last_r$ and the message has been delivered. The sender waits to receive an ack for $last_s$ before doing $getAck(OK)$. There are never any negative acks, since nothing is ever lost.

This protocol satisfies the requirements of S; indeed, it does better since it never loses anything.

1. It provides at-most-once delivery because the sender never uses the same identifier for more than one message, and the receiver accepts an identifier and its message only once.

2. It provides FIFO ordering because at most one message is in transit at a time.

3. It delivers all the messages because the sender's good set is a subset of the receiver's.

4. It acks every message because the sender keeps retransmitting until it gets the ack.

The SB protocol is widely used in practice, under names that resemble 'queuing system'. It isn't used to establish connections because the cost of a stable storage write for each message is too great.

In G we have the same structure of good sets and $last$ variables. However, they are not stable in G because we have to update them for every message, and we don't want to do a stable write for every message. Instead, there are operations to grow and shrink the good sets; these operations maintain the invariant $g_s \subseteq g_r$ as long as there is no receiver crash. When there is a crash, messages and acks can be lost, but S and D allow this. Figure 10.3 shows the state and some possible transitions of G in simplified form. The names in outline font are state variables of D, and the corresponding values are the values of the abstraction function in that state.

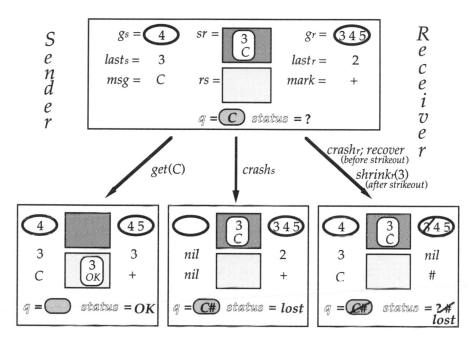

Figure 10.3. Some states and transitions of G

Figure 10.4 shows the state of G, the most important actions, and the S-shaped flow of information. The *new* variables in the figure are the complement of the *used* variables in the code. The heavy lines show the flow of a new identifier from the receiver to the sender, back to the receiver along with the message, and then back again to the sender along with the acknowledgement.

G also satisfies the requirements of S, but not quite in the same way as SB.

1. At-most-once delivery is the same as in SB.

2. The sender may send a message after a crash without checking that a previous outstanding message has actually been received. Thus more than one message can be in transit at a time, so there must be a total ordering on the identifiers in transit to maintain FIFO ordering of the messages. In G this ordering is defined by the order in which the sender chooses identifiers.

3. Complete delivery is the same as in SB as long as there is no receiver crash. When the receiver crashes $g_s \subseteq g_r$ may cease to hold, with the effect that messages that the sender handles during the receiver crash may be assigned identifiers that are not in g_r and hence may be lost. The protocol ensures that this can't happen to messages whose *put* happens after the receiver has recovered. When the sender crashes, it stops retransmitting the current message, which may be lost as a result.

4. As in SB, the sender keeps retransmitting until it gets an ack, but since messages can be lost, there must be negative as well as positive acks. When the receiver sees a message with an identifier that is not in g_r and not equal to

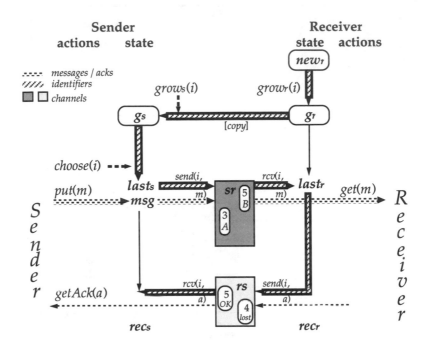

Figure 10.4. State, main actions, and information flow of G

$last_r$ it optionally returns a negative ack. There is no point in doing this for a message with $i < last_r$ because the sender only cares about the ack for $last_s$, and the protocol maintains the invariant $last_r \le last_s$. If $i > last_r$, however, the receiver must sometimes send a negative ack in response so that the sender can find out that the message may have been lost.

G is organized into a set of implementable actions that also appear, with very minor variations, in both H and C, plus the magic *grow*, *shrink*, and *cleanup* actions that are simulated quite differently in H and in C.

When there are no crashes, the sender and receiver each go through a cycle of modes, the sender perhaps one mode ahead. In one cycle one message is sent and acknowledged. For the sender, the modes are *idle*, [*needI*], *send*; for the receiver, they are *idle* and *ack*. An agent that is not idle is busy. The bracketed mode is 'internal': it's possible to advance to the next mode without receiving another message. The modes are not explicit state variables, but instead are derived from the values of the *msg* and *last* variables, as follows:

$mode_s = idle$ iff $msg = nil$ $mode_r = idle$ iff $last_r = nil$
$mode_s = needI$ iff $msg \ne nil$ and $last_s = nil$
$mode_s = send$ iff $msg \ne nil$ and $last_s \ne nil$ $mode_r = ack$ iff $last_r \ne nil$

To define G we introduce the types:

I, an infinite set of identifiers.

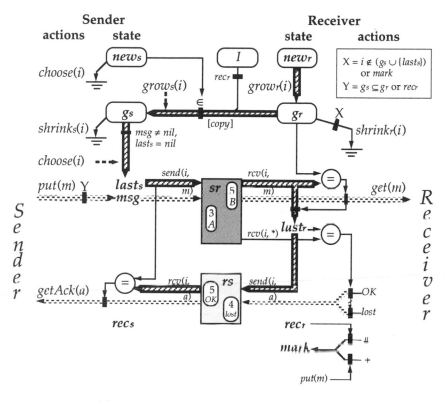

Figure 10.5. Details of actions and information flow in G

P (packet), a pair (I, M or A).

The sender sends (I, M) packets to the receiver, which sends (I, A) packets back. The I is there to identify the packet for the destination. We define a partial order on I by the rule that $i < i'$ iff i precedes i' in the sequence $used_s$.

The G we give is a somewhat simplified version, because the actions are not as atomic as they should be. In particular, some actions have two external inter-actions, sometimes one with a channel and one with the client, sometimes two with channels. However, the simplified version differs from one with the proper atomicity only in unimportant details. The appendix gives a version of G with all the fussy details in place. We don't give these details for the C and H protocols that follow, but content ourselves with the simplified versions in order to empha-size the important features of the protocols.

Figure 10.5 is a more detailed version of Figure 10.4, which shows all the actions and the flow of information between the sender and the receiver. State variables are given in bold, and the black guards on the transitions give the pre-conditions. The *mark* variable can be # when the receiver has recovered since a message was put; it reflects the fact that the message may be dropped.

Table 10.4 gives the state and actions of G. The magic parts, that is, those that touch non-local state, are boxed. The conjunct ¬ *recs* has been omitted from the

Name	Guard	Effect	Name	Guard	Effect
**put(m)$	$msg = nil$, $\boxed{g_s \subseteq g_r \text{ or } rec_r}$	$msg := m$, $\boxed{mark := +}$			
choose(i)	$msg \neq nil$, $last_s = nil$, $i \in g_s$	$g_s -:= \{j \mid j \leq i\}$, $last_s := i$, $used_s +:= \langle i \rangle$	*get(m)	exists i such that $rcv_{sr}(i,m)$, $i \in g_r$	$g_r -:= \{j \mid j \leq i\}$, $last_r := i$, $send_{rs}(i, OK)$
send	$last_s \neq nil$	$send_{sr}(last_s, msg)$			
*getAck(a)	$rcv_{rs}(last_s, a)$	$last_s := nil$, $msg := nil$	sendAck	exists i such that $rcv_{sr}(i,*)$, $i \notin g_r$	optionally $send_{rs}$ $(i$, if $i = last_r$ then OK else $lost)$
**crash$_s$		$rec_s := true$	**crash$_r$		$rec_r := true$
*recover$_s$	rec_s	$last_s := nil$, $msg := nil$, $rec_s := false$	*recover$_r$	rec_r, $\boxed{used_r \supseteq g_s \cup used_s}$	$last_r := nil$, $mark := \#$, $rec_r := false$
shrink$_s$(i)		$g_s -:= \{i\}$	shrink$_r$(i)	$\boxed{i \notin g_s, i \neq last_s}$ or $mark = \#$	$g_r -:= \{i\}$
grow$_s$(i)	$i \notin used_s$, $\boxed{i \in g_r \text{ or } rec_r}$	$g_s +:= \{i\}$	grow$_r$(i)	$i \notin used_r$	$g_r +:= \{i\}$, $used_r +:= \{i\}$
grow-used$_s$(i)	$i \notin used_s \cup g_s$, $\boxed{i \in used_r \text{ or } rec_r}$	$used_s +:= \{i\}$	cleanup	$\boxed{last_r \neq last_s}$	$last_r := nil$
			unmark	$\boxed{g_s \subseteq g_r, last_s \in g_r \cup \{last_r, nil\}}$	$mark := +$

$used_s$	: sequence[I]	$:= \langle \rangle$ (stable)		$used_r$	: set[I]	$:= \{\}$ (stable)
g_s	: set[I]	$:= \{\}$		g_r	: set[I]	$:= \{\}$
$last_s$	: I or nil	$:= nil$		$last_r$	: I or nil	$:= nil$
msg	: M or nil	$:= nil$		$mark$	: $Mark$	$:= \#$
rec_s	: Boolean	$:= false$		rec_r	: Boolean	$:= false$

Table 10.4. State and actions of G

guards of all the sender actions except $recover_s$, and likewise for $\neg rec_r$ and the receiver actions.

In addition to meeting the spec S, this protocol has some other important properties:

- It makes progress: regardless of prior crashes, provided both ends stay up and the channels don't always lose messages, then if there's a message to send it is eventually sent, and otherwise both parties eventually become idle, the sender because it gets an ack, the receiver because eventually *cleanup* makes *mode = idle*. Progress depends on doing enough *grow* actions, and in particular on completing the sequence $grow_r(i)$, $grow_s(i)$, $choose(i)$.

- It's not necessary to do a stable storage operation for each message. Instead, the cost of a stable storage operation can be amortized over as many messages as you like. G has only two stable variables: $used_s$ and $used_r$. Different implementations of G handle $used_s$ differently. To reduce the number of stable updates to $used_r$, refine G to divide $used_r$ into the union of a stable $used_r$-s and a volatile $used_r$-v. Move a set of Is from $used_r$-s to $used_r$-v with a single stable update. The $used_r$-v becomes empty in $recover_r$; simulate this with $grow_r(i)$ followed immediately by $shrink_r(i)$ for every i in $used_r$-v.

- The only state required for an idle agent is the stable variable $used$. All the other (volatile) state is the same at the end of a message transmission as at the beginning. The sender forgets its state in *getAck*, the receiver in *cleanup*, and both in *recover*. The *shrink* actions make it possible for both parties to forget the good sets. This is important because agents may need to communicate with many other agents between crashes, and it isn't practical to require that an agent maintain some state for everyone with whom it has ever communicated.

- An idle sender doesn't send any packets. An idle receiver doesn't send any packets unless it receives one, because it sends an acknowledgement only in response to a packet. This is important because the channel resources shouldn't be wasted.

We have constructed G with as much non-determinism as possible in order to make it easy to prove that different practical protocols implement G. We could have simplified it, for instance by eliminating *unmark*, but then it would be more difficult to construct an abstraction function from some other protocol to G, since the abstraction function would have to account for the fact that after a $recover_r$ the *mark* variable is # until the next *put*. With *unmark*, an implementation of G is free to set *mark* back to + whenever the guard is true.

10.5.1   Abstraction Function to D

The abstraction function is an essential tool for proving that the protocol implements the spec. But it is also an important aid to understanding what is going on. By studying what happens to the value of the abstraction function during each action of G, we can learn what the actions are doing and why they work.

Definitions

cur-q = $\{(msg, mark)\}$ if $msg \neq nil$ and ($last_s = nil$ or $last_s \in g_r$)
         $\{\}$ otherwise
$inflight_{sr}$ = $\{(i, m) \in ids(sr) \mid i \in g_r$ and $i \neq last_s\}$,
         sorted by i to make a sequence
old-q = the sequence of $(M, Mark)$'s gotten by turning
         each (i, m) in $inflight_{sr}$ into $(m, \#)$
$inflight_{rs}$ = $\{last_s\}$ if $(last_s, OK) \in rs$ and $last_s \neq last_r$
         $\{\}$ otherwise.

Note that the *inflight*s exclude elements that might still be retransmitted as well as elements that are not of interest to the destination. This is so the abstraction function can pair them with the # mark.

Abstraction function

q	$old\text{-}q + cur\text{-}q$		
$status$	$(?, mark)$	if $cur\text{-}q \neq \{\}$	(a)
	$(OK, +)$	if $mode_s = send$ and $last_s = last_r$	(b)
	$(OK, \#)$	if $mode_s = send$ and $last_s \in inflight_{rs}$	(c)
	$(lost, +)$	if $mode_s = send$ and $last_s \notin (g_r \cup \{last_r\} \cup inflight_{rs})$	(d)
	$(lost, +)$	if $mode_s = idle$	(e)
$rec_{s/r}$	$rec_{s/r}$		

The cases of *status* are exhaustive. Note that we do *not* want $(msg, +)$ in q if $mode_s = send$ and $last_{ss} \notin g_r$, because in this case *msg* has been delivered or lost.

We see that G simulates the q of D using $old\text{-}q + cur\text{-}q$, and that $old\text{-}q$ is the left-over messages in the channel that are still good but haven't been delivered, while $cur\text{-}q$ is the message the sender is currently working on, as long as its identifier is not yet assigned or still good. Similarly, *status* has a different value for each step in the delivery process: still sending the message (a), normal ack (b), ack after a receiver crash (c), lost ack (d), or delivered ack (e).

10.5.2   Invariants

Like the abstraction function, the invariants are both essential to the proof and an important aid to understanding. They express a great deal of information about how the protocol is supposed to work. It's especially instructive to see how the parts of the state that have to do with crashes ($rec_{s/r}$ and *mark*) affect them.

The first few invariants establish some simple facts about the *used* sets and their relation to other variables. (G2) reflects that fact that identifers move from g_s to $used_s$ one by one, (G3) the fact that unless the receiver is recovering, identifiers must enter $used_r$ before they can appear anywhere else (G4) the fact that they must enter $used_s$ before they can appear in *last* variables or channels.

If $msg = nil$ then $last_s = nil$	(G1)
$g_s \cap used_s = \{\}$	(G2a)
All elements of $used_s$ are distinct.	(G2b)
$used_r \supseteq g_r$	(G3a)
If $\neg rec_r$ then $used_r \supseteq g_s \cup used_s$	(G3b)
$used_s \supseteq \{last_s, last_r\} - \{nil\} \cup \text{ids}(sr) \cup \text{ids}(rs)$	(G4)

The next invariants deal with the flow of identifiers during delivery. (G5) says that each identifier tags at most one message. (G6) says that if all is well, g_s and $last_s$ are such that a message will be delivered and acknowledged properly. (G7) says that an identifier for a message being acknowledged can't be good.

$\{m \mid (i = last_s$ and $m = msg)$ or $(i, m) \in sr\}$ has 0 or 1 elements $\qquad$ (G5)

If $mark = +$ and $\neg rec_s$ and $\neg rec_r$ then $g_s \subseteq g_r$ and $last_s \in g_r \cup \{last_r, nil\}$ $\quad$ (G6)

$g_r \cap (\{last_r\} \cup ids(rs)) = \{\}$ $\qquad$ (G7)

Finally, some facts about the identifier $last_s$ for the message the sender is trying to deliver. It comes later in the identifier ordering than any other identifier in sr (G8a). If it's been delivered and is getting a positive ack, then neither it nor any other identifier in sr is in g_r, but they are all in $used_r$ (G8b). If it's getting a negative ack then it won't get a later positive one (G8c).

If $last_s \neq nil$ then

$$ids(sr) \leq last_s \qquad (G8a)$$

and $\quad$ if $last_s = last_r$ or $(last_s, OK) \in rs$ then $\quad (\{last_s\} \cup ids(sr)) \cap g_r = \{\}$ $\quad$ (G8b)

and $(\{last_s\} \cup ids(sr)) \subseteq used_r$

and $\quad$ if $(last_s, lost) \in ids(rs)$ then $last_s \neq last_r$ $\qquad$ (G8c)

10.5.3   Proof that G Implements D

This requires showing that every action of G simulates some sequence of actions of D which is the same externally. Since G has quite a few actions, the proof is somewhat tedious. A few examples give the flavor.

—$recover_s$: Mark msg and drop it unless it moves to old-q; mark and drop $status$.

—$get(m)$: For the change to q, first drop everything in old-q less than i. Then m is first on q since either i is the smallest I in old-q, or $i = last_s$ and old-q is empty by (G8a). So D's $get(m)$ does the rest of what G's does. Everything in old-$q + cur$-q that was $\leq i$ is gone, so the corresponding M's are gone from q as required.

We do $status$ by the abstraction function's cases on its old value. D says it should change to (OK, x) iff q becomes empty and it was $(?, x)$. In cases (c-e) $status$ isn't $(?, x)$ and it doesn't change. In case (b) the guard $i \in g_r$ of get is false by (G8b). In case (a) either $i = last_s$ or not. If not, then cur-q remains unchanged by (G8a), so $status$ does also and q remains non-empty. If so, then cur-q and q both become empty and $status$ changes to case (b). Simulate this by umarking $status$ if necessary; then D's $get(m)$ does the rest.

—$getAck(a)$: The q is unchanged because $last_s = i \in ids(rs)$, so $last_s \notin g_r$ by (G7) and hence cur-q is empty, so changing msg to nil keeps it empty. Because old-q doesn't change, q doesn't either. We end up with $status = (lost, +)$ according to case (e), as required by D. Finally, we must show that a agrees with the old value of $status$. We do this by the cases of $status$ as we did for get:

(a) Impossible, because it requires $last_s \in g_r$, but we know $last_s \in ids(rs)$, which excludes $last_s \in g_r$ by (G7).

(b) In this case $last_s = last_r$, so (G8c) ensures $a \neq lost$, so $a = OK$.

(c) If $a = OK$ we are fine. If $a = lost$ drop $status$ first.

(d) Since $last_s \notin inflight_{rs}$, only $(last_s, lost) \in rs$ is possible, so $a = lost$.

(e) Impossible because $last_s \neq nil$.

—*shrink$_r$*: If *rec$_r$* then *msg* may be lost from q; simulate this by marking and dropping it, and likewise for *status*. If *mark* = # then *msg* may be lost from q, but it is marked, so simulate this by dropping it, and likewise for *status*. Otherwise the precondition ensures that *last$_s$* ∈ g_r doesn't change, so *cur-q* and *status* don't. *Inflight$_{sr}$*, and hence *old-q*, can lose an element; simulate this by dropping the corresponding element of q, which is possible since it is marked #.

10.6   How C and H Implement G

We now proceed to give two practical protocols, the clock-based protocol C and the handshake protocol H. Each implements G, but they handle the good sets quite differently.

In C the good sets are maintained using time; to make this possible the sender and receiver clocks must be roughly synchronized, and there must be an upper bound on the time required to transmit a packet. The sender's current time *time$_s$* is the only member of g_s; if the sender has already used *time$_s$* then g_s is empty. The receiver accepts any message with an identifier in the range (*time$_r$* − 2ε − δ, *time$_r$* + 2ε), where ε is the maximum clock skew from real time and δ the maximum packet transmission time, as long as it hasn't already accepted a message with a later identifier.

In H the sender asks the receiver for a good identifier; the receiver's obligation is to keep the identifier good until it crashes or receives the message, or learns from the sender that the identifier will never be equal to *last$_s$*.

We begin by giving the abstraction functions from C and H to G, and a sketch of how each implements the magic actions of G, to help the reader in comparing the protocols. Careful study of these should make it clear exactly how each protocol implements G's magic actions in a properly distributed fashion.

Then for each protocol we give a figure that shows the flow of packets, followed by a formal description of the state and the actions. The portion of the figures that shows messages being sent and acks returned is exactly the same as the bottom half of Figure 10.4 for G; all three protocols handle messages and acks identically. They differ in how the sender obtains good identifiers, shown in the top of the figures, and in how the receiver cleans up its state. In the figures for C and H we show the abstraction function to G in outline font.

Note that G allows either good set to grow or shrink by any number of *I*s through repeated *grow* or *shrink* actions as long as the invariants $g_s \subseteq g_r$ and *last$_s$* ∈ $g_r \cup \{last_r\}$ are maintained in the absence of crashes. For C the *increase* actions simulate occurrences of several *grow$_r$* and *shrink$_r$* actions, one for each i in the set defined in the table. Likewise *rcv$_{rs}$*(j_s, i) in H may simulate several *shrink$_s$* actions.

Abstraction functions to G

G	C	H
$used_s$	$\{i \mid 0 \leq i < time_s\} \cup \{sent\} - \{nil\}$	$used_s$ (history)
$used_r$	$\{i \mid 0 \leq i < high\}$	$used_r$
g_s	$\{time_s\} - \{sent\}$	$\{i \mid (j_s, i) \in rs\}$
g_r	$\{i \mid low < i \text{ and } i < high\}$	$\{i_r\} - \{nil\}$
mark	# if $last_s \in g_r$ and *deadline* = *nil*	# if $mode_s = needI$ and $g_s \not\subseteq g_r$
	+ otherwise	+ otherwise

msg, $last_{s/r}$, and $rec_{s/r}$ are the same in G, C, and H

sr	*sr*	thc (I, M) messages in *sr*
rs	*rs*	the (I, A) messages in *rs*

Sketch of implementations

G	C	H
$grow_s(i)$	$tick(i)$	$send_{rs}(j_s, i)$
$shrink_s(i)$	$tick(i'), i \in \{time_s\} - \{sent\}$	$lose_{rs}(j_s, i)$ if thc last copy is lost
		or $rcv_{rs}(j_s, i')$, for each $i \in g_s - \{i'\}$
$grow_r(i)$	*increase-high*(i'), for each	$mode = idle$ and $rcv_{sr}(needI, *)$
	$i \in \{i \mid high < i < i'\}$	
$shrink_r(i)$	*increase-low*(i'), for each	$rcv_{sr}(i_r, done)$
	$i \in \{i \mid low < i \leq i'\}$	
cleanup	*cleanup*	$rcv_{sr}(last_r, done)$

10.7   The Clock-Based Protocol C

This protocol is due to Liskov, Shrira, and Wroclawski [1991]. Figure 10.6 shows the state and the flow of information. Compare it with Figure 10.4 for G, and note that there is no flow of new identifiers from receiver to sender. In C the passage of time supplies the sender with new identifiers, and is also allows the receiver to clean up its state.

The idea behind C is to use loosely synchronized clocks to provide the identifiers for messages. The sender uses its current *time* for the next identifier. The receiver keeps track of *low*, the biggest clock value for which it has accepted a message: bigger values than this are good. The receiver also keeps a stable bound *high* on the biggest value it will accept, chosen to be larger than the receiver s clock plus the maximum clock skew. After a crash the receiver sets *low* := *high*; this ensures that no messages are accepted twice.

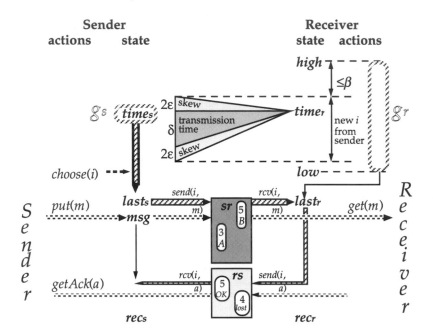

Figure 10.6. The flow of information in C

The sender's clock advances, which ensures that it will get new identifiers and also ensures that it will eventually get past *low* and start sending messages that will be accepted after a receiver crash.

It's also possible for the receiver to advance *low* spontaneously (by *increase-low*) if it hasn't received a message for a long time, as long as *low* stays smaller than the current time − 2ε − δ, where ε is the maximum clock skew from real time and δ is the maximum packet transmission time. This is good because it gives the receiver a chance to run several copies of the protocol (one for each of several senders), and make the values of *low* the same for all the idle senders. Then the receiver only needs to keep track of a single *low* for all the idle senders, plus one for each active sender. Together with C's *cleanup* action this ensures that the receiver needs no storage for idle senders.

If the assumptions about clock skew and maximum packet transmission time are violated, C still provides at-most-once delivery, but it may lose messages (because *low* is advanced too soon or the sender's clock is later than *high*) or acknowledgements (because *cleanup* happens too soon).

Modes, types, packets, and the pattern of messages are the same as in G, except that the *I* set has a total ordering. The *deadline* variable expresses the assumption about maximum packet delivery time: real time doesn't advance (by *progress*) past the deadline for delivering a packet. In a real implementation, of course, there will be some other properties of the channel from which the constraint imposed by *deadline* can be deduced. These are usually probabilistic; we deal with this by declaring a *crash* whenever the channel fails to meet its deadline.

Name	Guard	Effect	Name	Guard	Effect
**$put(m)$	$msg = nil$	$msg := m$			
$choose(i)$	$msg \neq nil$, $last_s = nil$, $i=time_s$, $i \neq sent$	$sent := i$, $last_s := i$, $deadline := now+\delta$	*$get(m)$	exists i such that $rcv_{sr}(i, m)$, $i \in (low..high)$	$low := i$, $last_r := i$, $deadline := nil$, $send_{rs}(i, OK)$
$send$	$last_s \neq nil$	$send_{sr}(last_s, msg)$			
*$getAck(a)$	$rcv_{rs}(last_s, a)$	$last_s := nil$, $msg := nil$	$sendAck$	exists i such that $rcv_{sr}(i, *)$, $i \notin (low..high)$	$low := \max(low, i)$, $send_{rs}(i,$ if $i = last_r$ then OK else $lost$) if $i = last_s$ then $deadline := nil$
**$crash_s$		$rec_s := true$, $deadline:= nil$	**$crash_r$		$rec_r := true$, $deadline:= nil$
*$recover_s$	rec_s	$last_s := nil$, $msg := nil$, $rec_s := false$	*$recover_r$	rec_r, $high < time_r - 2\varepsilon$	$last_r := nil$, $low := high$, $high := time_r + 2\varepsilon + \beta$, $rec_r := false$
			$increase\text{-}low(i)$	$low < i \leq time_r - 2\varepsilon - \delta$	$low := i$
			$increase\text{-}high(i)$	$high < i \leq time_r + 2\varepsilon + \beta$	$high := i$
$cleanup$	$sent \neq time_s$	$sent := nil$	$cleanup$	$last_r < time_r - 2\varepsilon - 2\delta$	$last_r := nil$
$tick(i)$	$time_s < i$, $\| now - i \| < \varepsilon$	$time_s := i$	$tick(i)$	$time_r < i$, $\| now - i \| < \varepsilon$, $i + 2\varepsilon < high$ or rec_r	$time_r := i$
$progress(i)$	$now < i$, $\| i - time_{s/r} \| < \varepsilon$, $i < deadline$ or $deadline=nil$	$now := i$			

$time_s$	$: I$	$:= 0$ (stable)	$time_r$	$: I$	$:= 0$ (stable)
$sent$	$: I$ or nil	$:= nil$	low	$: I$	$:= 0$
			$high$	$: I$	$:= \beta$ (stable)
$last_s$	$: I$ or nil	$:= nil$	$last_r$	$: I$ or nil	$:= nil$
msg	$: M$ or nil	$:= nil$			
rec_s	$:$ Boolean	$:= false$	rec_r	$:$ Boolean$:= false$	
	$deadline : I$ or $nil := nil$				
	now $: I$ $:= 0$				

Table 10.5. State and actions of C. Actions below the thick line handle the passage of time.

Table 10.5 gives the state and actions of C. The conjunct $\neg\ rec_s$ has been omitted from the guards of all the sender actions except $recover_s$, and likewise for $\neg\ rec_r$ and the receiver actions.

Note that like G, this version of C sends an ack only in response to a message. This is unlike H, which has continuous transmission of the ack and pays the price of a *done* message to stop it. Another possibility is to make timing assumptions about *rs* and time out the ack; some assumptions are needed anyway to make *cleanup* possible. This would be less practical but more like H.

Note that $time_s$ and $time_r$ differ from real time (*now*) by at most ε, and hence $time_s$ and $time_r$ can differ from each other by as much as 2ε. Note also that the deadline is enforced by the *progress* action, which doesn't allow real time to advance past the deadline unless someone is recovering. Both $crash_s$ and $crash_r$ cancel the deadline.

About the parameters of C

The protocol is parameterized by three constants:

- δ = maximum time to deliver a packet
- β = amount beyond $time_r$ + 2ε to increase *high*
- ε = maximum of $|\,now - time_{r/s}\,|$

These parameters must satisfy two constraints:

- δ > ε so that $mode_s$ = *send* implies $last_s$ < *deadline*.
- β > 0 so *increase-high* can be enabled. Aside from this constraint the choice of β is just a tradeoff between the frequency of stable storage writes (at least one every β, so a bigger β means fewer writes) and the delay imposed on $recover_r$ to ensure that messages put after $recover_r$ don't get dropped (as much as 4ε + β, because *high* can be as big as $time_r$ + 2ε + β at the time of the crash because of (e), and $time_r$ − 2ε has to get past this via $tick_r$ before $recover_r$ can happen, so a bigger β means a longer delay).

10.7.1   Invariants

Mostly these are facts about the ordering of various time variables; a lot of $x \neq nil$ conjuncts have been omitted. Nothing being sent is later than $time_s$ (C1). Nothing being acknowledged is later than *low*, which is no later than *high*, which in turn is big enough (C2). Nothing being sent or acknowledged is later than $last_s$ (C3). The sender's time is later than *low*, hence good unless equal to *sent* (C4).

$$last_s \leq time_s \tag{C1}$$

$$last_r \leq low \leq high \tag{C2a}$$

$$ids(rs) \leq low \tag{C2b}$$

$$\text{If } \neg\ rec_r \text{ then } time_r + 2\varepsilon \leq high \tag{C2c}$$

$$ids(sr) \leq last_s \tag{C3a}$$

$$last_r \leq last_s \tag{C3b}$$

$$\{i \mid (i, OK) \in rs\} \leq last_s \qquad \text{(C3c)}$$

$$low \leq time_s \qquad \text{(C4)}$$

$$low < time_s \text{ if } last_s \neq time_s$$

If a message is being sent but hasn't been delivered, and there hasn't been a crash, then *deadline* gives the deadline for delivering the packet containing the message (based on the maximum time for a packet that is being retransmitted to get through *sr*), and it isn't too late for it to be accepted (C5).

If *deadline* ≠ *nil* then

$$now < last_s + \varepsilon + \delta \qquad \text{(C5a)}$$

$$low < last_s \qquad \text{(C5b)}$$

An identifier getting a positive ack is no later than *low*, hence no longer good (C6). If it's getting a negative ack, it must be later than the last one accepted (C7).

If $(last_s, OK) \in rs$ then $last_s \leq low$ $\qquad$ (C6)

If $(last_s, lost) \in rs$ then $last_r < last_s$ $\qquad$ (C7)

10.8   The Handshake Protocol H

This is the standard protocol for setting up network connections, used in TCP, ISO TP-4, and many other transport protocols. It is usually called three-way handshake, because only three packets are needed to get the data delivered, but five packets are required to get it acknowledged and all the state cleaned up (Belsnes [1976]).

As in the generic protocol, when there are no crashes the sender and receiver each go through a cycle of modes, the sender perhaps one ahead. For the sender, the modes are *idle*, *needI*, *send*; for the receiver, they are *idle*, *accept*, and *ack*. In one cycle one message is sent and acknowledged by sending three packets from sender to receiver and two from receiver to sender, for a total of five packets. Table 10.6 summarizes the modes and the packets that are sent.

The modes are derived from the values of the state variables j and *last*:

$mode_s = idle$	iff $j_s = last_s = nil$		$mode_r = idle$	iff $j_r = last_r = nil$
$mode_s = needI$	iff $j_s \neq nil$		$mode_r = accept$	iff $j_r \neq nil$
$mode_s = send$	iff $last_s \neq nil$		$mode_r = ack$	iff $last_r \neq nil$

Figure 10.7 shows the state, the flow of identifiers from the receiver to the sender at the top, and the flow of *done* information back to the receiver at the bottom so that it can clean up. These are sandwiched between the standard exchange of message and ack, which is the same as in G (see Figure 10.4).

Intuitively, the reason there are five packets is that:

- One round-trip (two packets) is needed for the sender to get from the receiver an I (namely i_r) that both know has not been used.

- One round-trip (two packets) is then needed to send and ack the message.

	Sender			Receiver		
mode	send	advance on	packet	advance on	send	mode
idle	see idle below	put, to needI			(i, lost) when (i, m) arrives[3]	idle
needI	(needI, j_s) repeatedly		(needI, j) →	(needI, j) arrives, to accept		
		(j_s, i) arrives, to send	(j, i) ←		(j_r, i_r) repeatedly	accept
send	($last_s$, m) repeatedly		(i, m) →	(i_r, m) arrives, to ack; (i_r, done) arrives, to idle		
		($last_s$, a) arrives, to idle	(i, a) ←		($last_r$, OK) repeatedly[4]	ack
idle	(i, done) when (i, a) arrives		(i, done) →	($last_r$, done) arrives, to idle		
needI or send	(i, done) when (j ≠ j_s, i) or (i, OK) arrives, to force receiver to idle					

Table 10.6. Exchange of messages in H

- A final *done* packet from the sender informs the receiver that the sender has gotten the ack. The receiver needs this information in order to stop retransmitting the ack and discard its state. If the receiver discards its "I got the message" state before it knows that the sender got the ack, then if the channel loses the ack the sender won't be able to find out that the message was actually received, even though there was no crash. This is contrary to the spec S. The *done* packet itself needs no ack, because the sender will also send it when idle and hence can become *idle* as soon as it sees the *ack*.

We introduce a new type:

J, an infinite set of identifiers that can be compared for equality.

The sender and receiver send packets to each other. An *I* or *J* in the first component is there to identify the packet for the destination. Some packets also have an *I* or *J* as the second component, but it does not identify anything; rather it is being communicated to the destination for later use. The (i, a) and (i, done) packets are both often called 'close' packets in the literature.

---

[3] (i, lost) is a negative acknowledgement; it means that one of two things has happened:

— The receiver has forgotten about i because it has learned that the sender has gotten a positive ack for i, but then the receiver has gotten a duplicate (i, m), to which it responds with the negative ack, which the sender will ignore.

— The receiver has crashed since it assigned i, and i's message may have been delivered to *get* or may have been lost.

[4] (i, OK) is a positive acknowledgement; it means i's message was delivered to *get*.

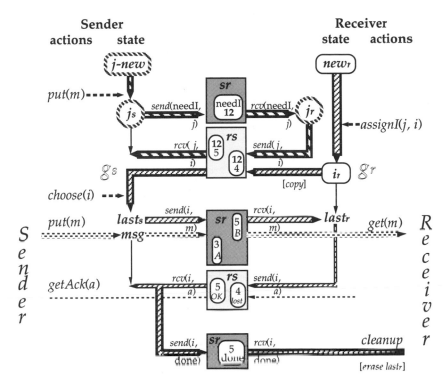

Figure 10.7. The flow of information in H

The H protocol has the same progress and efficiency properties as G, and in addition, although the protocol as given does assume an infinite supply of *I*s, it does not assume anything about clocks.

It's necessary for a busy agent to send something repeatedly, because the other end might be idle and therefore not sending anything that would get the busy agent back to idle. An agent also has a set of expected packets, and it wants to receive one of these in order to advance normally to the next mode. To ensure that the protocol is self-stabilizing after a crash, both ends respond to an unexpected packet containing the identifier *i* by sending an acknowledgement: (*i*, *lost*) or (*i*, *done*). Whenever the receiver gets *done* for its current *I*, it becomes idle. Once the receiver is idle, the sender advances normally until it too becomes idle.

Table 10.7 gives the state and actions of H. The conjunct $\neg\ rec_s$ has been omitted from the guards of all the sender actions except $recover_s$, and likewise for $\neg\ rec_r$ and the receiver actions.

10.8.1   Invariants

Recall that ids(*c*) is {*i* | (*i*, *) ∈ *c*}. We also define jds(*c*) = {*j* | (*j*, *) ∈ *c* or (*, *j*) ∈ *c*}.

Most of H's invariants are boring facts about the progress of *I*'s and *J*'s from *used* sets through $i/j_{s/r}$ to $last_{s/r}$. We need the history variables $used_s$ and *seen* to

Name	Guard	Effect	Name	Guard	Effect
**put(m)	$msg = nil$,	$msg := m$,			
requestI	exists j such that $j \notin j\text{-}used$, $j_s \neq nil$, $last_s = nil$	$j_s := j$, $j\text{-}used\ +:= \{j\}$ $send_{sr}(needI, j_s)$	assignI(j,i)	$rcv_{sr}(needI, j)$, $i_r = last_r = nil$, $i \notin used_r$	$j_r := j,\ i_r := i$, $used_r\ +:= i$, $seen\ +:= \{(j, i)\}$
choose(i)	$last_s = nil$, $rcv_{rs}(j_s, i)$	$j_s := nil,\ last_s := i$, $used_s\ +:= \langle i \rangle$	sendI	$j_r \neq nil$	$send_{rs}(j_r, i_r)$
send	$last_s \neq nil$	$send_{sr}(last_s, msg)$	*get(m)	exists i such that $rcv_{sr}(i, m)$, $i = i_r$	$j_r := i_r := nil$, $last_r := i$, $send_{rs}(i, OK)$
			sendAck	$last_r \neq nil$	$send_{rs}(last_r, OK)$
*getAck(a)	$rcv_{rs}(last_s, a)$	if $a = OK$ then $send_{sr}(last_s, done)$ $msg := last_s := nil$	bounce	exists i such that $rcv_{sr}(i, *)$, $i \neq i_r,\ i \neq last_r$	$send_{rs}(i, lost)$
bounce (j, i)	$rcv_{rs}(j, i)$, $j \neq j_s,\ i \neq last_s$ or $rcv_{rs}(i, OK)$	$send_{sr}(i, done)$	cleanup(i)	$rcv_{sr}(i, done)$, $i = i_r$ or $i = last_r$	$j_r := i_r := nil$, $last_r := nil$
**crash$_s$		$rec_s := true$	**crash$_r$		$rec_r := true$
*recover$_s$	rec_s	$msg := nil$, $j_s := last_s := nil$, $rec_s := false$	*recover$_r$	rec_r	$j_r := i_r := nil$, $last_r := nil$, $rec_r := false$
grow-j-used(j)		$j\text{-}used\ +:= \{j\}$	grow-used(i)		$used_r\ +:= \{i\}$

$used_s$	: sequence[I]	:= $\langle \rangle$ (history)	$used_r$	: set[I]	:= { } (stable)
$j\text{-}used$	: set[J]	:= { } (stable)	$seen$	: set[(J, I)]	:= { } (history)
j_s	: J or nil	:= nil	j_r	: J or nil	:= nil
msg	: M or nil	:= nil	i_r	: I or nil	:= nil
$last_s$	: I or nil	:= nil	$last_r$	: I or nil	:= nil
rec_s	: Boolean	:= $false$	rec_r	: Boolean	:= $false$

Table 10.7. State and actions of H. Heavy black lines outline additions to G

express some of them. (H6) says that there's at most one J (from a $needI$ packet) that gets assigned a given I. (H8) says that as long as the sender is still in mode $needI$, nothing involving i_r has made it into the channels.

$$j\text{-}used \supseteq \{j_s, j_r\} - \{nil\} \cup jds(sr) \cup jds(rs) \tag{H1}$$

$$used_r \supseteq \{i_r, last_r\} - \{nil\} \cup used_s \cup \{i \mid (*, i) \in rs\} \cup ids(sr) \cup ids(rs) \tag{H2}$$

$$used_s \supseteq \{last_s, last_r\} - \{nil\} \cup ids(sr) \cup ids(rs) \tag{H3}$$

$$\text{If } (i, done) \in sr \text{ then } i \neq last_s \tag{H4}$$

$$\text{If } i_r \neq nil \text{ then } (j_r, i_r) \in seen \tag{H5}$$

If $(j, i) \in seen$ and $(j', i) \in seen$ then $j = j'$ $\qquad$ (H6)

If $(j, i) \in rs$ then $(j, i) \in seen$ $\qquad$ (H7)

If $j_s = j_r \neq nil$ then $(i_r, *) \notin sr$ and $(i_r, done) \notin rs$ $\qquad$ (H8)

10.8.2   Progress

We consider first what happens without failures, and then how the protocol recovers from failures.

If neither partner fails, then both advance in sync through the cycle of modes. The only thing that derails progress is for some party to change *mode* without advancing through the full cycle of modes that transmits a message. This can only happen when the receiver is in *accept* mode and gets $(i_r, done)$, as you can see from Table 10.6. This can only happen if the sender got a packet containing i_r. But if the receiver is in *accept*, the sender must be in *needI* or *send*, and the only thing that's been sent with i_r is (j_s, i_r). The sender goes to or stays in *send* and doesn't make *done* when it gets (j_s, i_r) in either of these modes, so the cycling through the modes is never disrupted as long as there's no crash.

If either partner fails and then recovers, the other becomes idle rather than getting stuck; in other words, the protocol is self-stabilizing. Why? When the receiver isn't idle it always sends something, and if that isn't what the sender wants, the sender responds *done*, which forces the receiver to become idle. When the sender isn't idle it's either in *needI*, in which case it will eventually get what it wants, or it's in *send* and will get a negative ack and become idle. In more detail:

The receiver bails out when the sender crashes because

- the sender forgets i_s and j_s when it crashes,
- if the receiver isn't idle, it keeps sending (j_r, i_r) or $(last_r, OK)$,
- the sender responds with $(i_r/last_r, done)$ whenever it sees either of these, and
- the receiver ends up in *idle* whenever it receives this.

The sender bails out or makes progress when the receiver crashes because

- If the sender is in *needI*, either
  —it gets $(j_s, i \neq i_r)$ from the pre-crash receiver, advances to *send*, and bails out as below, or
  —it gets (j_s, i_r) from the post-crash receiver and proceeds normally.
- If the sender is in *send* it keeps sending $(last_s, msg)$,
  —the receiver has $last_r = nil \neq last_s$, so it responds $(last_s, lost)$, and
  —when the sender gets this it becomes *idle*.

An idle receiver might see an old $(needI, j)$ with $j \neq j_s$ and go into *accept* with $j_r \neq j_s$, but the sender will respond to the resulting (j_r, i_r) packets with $(i_r, done)$, which will force the receiver back to *idle*. Eventually all the old *needI* packets will drain out. This is the reason that it's necessary to prevent a channel from delivering an unbounded number of copies of a packet.

Name	Guard	Effect
recycle(i) for G	$i \notin g_s \cup g_r \cup \{last_s, last_r\}$ $\cup$ ids(sr) $\cup$ ids(rs)	$used_s$ −:= {i}, $used_r$ −:= {i}
recycle(i) for H	$i \notin \{last_s, i_r, last_r\}$ $\cup \{i \mid (*, i) \in rs\} \cup$ ids(sr) $\cup$ ids(rs)	$used_s$ −:= {i}, $used_r$ −:= {i}, $seen$ −:= {j $\mid$ (j, i) ∈ seen $\mid$ (j, i)}
recycle-j(j) for H	$j \notin \{j_s, j_r\} \cup$ jds(sr) $\cup$ jds(rs)	$used\text{-}j$ −:= {j}, $seen$ −:= {i $\mid$ (j, i) ∈ seen $\mid$ (j, i)}

Table 10.8. Actions to recycle identifiers

10.9   Finite Identifiers

So far we have assumed that the identifier sets I and J are infinite. Practical proto-cols use sets that are finite and often quite small. We can easily extend G to use finite sets by adding a new action *recycle(i)* that removes an identifier from $used_s$ and $used_r$ so that it can be added to g_r again. As we saw in Section 10.1, when we add a new action the only change we need in the proof is to show that it main-tains the invariants and simulates something in the spec. The latter is simple: *recycle* simulates no change in the spec. The former is also simple: we put a strong enough guard on *recycle* to ensure that all the invariants still hold. To find out what this guard is we need only find all the invariants that mention $used_s$ or $used_r$, since those are the only variables that *recycle* changes. Intuitively, the result is that an identifier can be recycled if it doesn't appear anywhere else in the variables or channels.

Similar observations apply to H, with some minor complications to keep the history variable *seen* up to date, and a similar *recycle-j* action. Table 10.8 gives the *recycle* actions for G and H.

How can we implement the guards on the *recycle* actions? The tricky part is ensuring that i is not still in a channel, since standard methods can ensure that it isn't in a variable at the other end. There are three schemes that are used in practice:

- Use a FIFO channel. Then a simple convention ensures that if you don't send any i_1's after you send i_2, then when you get back the ack for i_2 there aren't any i_1's left in either channel.

- Assume that packets in the channel have a maximum lifetime once they have been sent, and wait longer than that time after you stop sending packets containing i.

- Encrypt packets on the channel, and change the encryption key. Once the receiver acknowledges the change it will no longer accept packets encrypt-ed with the old key, so these packets are in effect no longer in the channel.

For C we can recycle identifiers by using time modulo some period as the identifier, rather than unadorned time. Similar ideas apply; we omit the details.

10.10 Conclusions

We have given a precise specification S of reliable at-most-once message delivery with acknowledgements. We have also presented precise descriptions of two practical protocols (C and H) that implement S, and the essential elements of proofs that they do so; the handshake protocol H is used for connection establishment in most computer networking. Our proofs are organized into three levels: we refine S first into another specification D that delays some of the decisions of S and then into a generic implementation G, and finally we show that C and H both implement G. Most of the work is in the proof that G implements D.

In addition to complete expositions of the protocols and their correctness, we have also given an extended example of how to use abstraction functions and invariants to understand and verify subtle distributed algorithms of some practical importance. The example shows that the proofs are not too difficult and that the invariants, and especially the abstraction functions, give a great deal of insight into how the implementations work and why they satisfy the specifications. It also illustrates how to divide a complicated problem into parts that make sense individually and can be attacked one at a time.

References

Abadi, M. and Lamport, L. (1991), The Existence of Refinement Mappings, *Theoretical Computer Science* **82** (2), 253-284.

Belsnes, D. (1976), Single Message Communication, IEEE *Trans. Communications* **COM-24**, 2.

Lampson, B., Lynch, N., and Søgaard-Andersen, J. (1993), Reliable At-Most-Once Message Delivery Protocols, Technical Report, MIT Laboratory for Computer Science, to appear.

Liskov, B., Shrira, L., and Wroclawski, J. (1991), Efficient At-Most-Once Messages Based on Synchronized Clocks, ACM *Trans. Computer Systems* **9** (2), 125-142.

Lynch, N. and Vaandrager, F. (1993), Forward and Backward Simulations, Part I: Untimed Systems, Technical Report, MIT Laboratory for Computer Science, to appear.

Appendix

For reference we give the complete protocol for G, with every action as atomic as it should be. This requires separating the getting and putting of messages, the sending and receiving of packets, the sending and receiving of acks, and the getting of acks. As a result, we have to add buffer queues $buf_{s/r}$ for messages at both ends, a buffer variable ack for the ack at the sender, and a $send\text{-}ack$ flag for positive acks and a buffer $nack\text{-}buf$ for negative acks at the receiver.

The state of the full G is:

$used_s$	: sequence[I]	$:= \langle \rangle$ (stable)		$used_r$	: set[I]	$:= \{ \}$ (stable)
g_s	: set[I]	$:= \{ \}$		g_r	: set[I]	$:= \{ \}$
$last_s$	: I or nil	$:= nil$		$last_r$	: I or nil	$:= nil$
buf_s	: sequence[M]	$:= \langle \rangle$		buf_r	: sequence[M]	$:= \langle \rangle$
msg	: M or nil	$:= nil$		$mark$	: $+$ or $\#$	$:= +$
ack	: A	$:= lost$		$send\text{-}ack$	: Boolean	$:= false$
				$nack\text{-}buf$	: sequence[I]	$:= \langle \rangle$
rec_s	: Boolean	$:= false$		rec_r	: Boolean	$:= false$

The abstraction function to D is:

q the elements of buf_r paired with $+$
        $+$ $old\text{-}q$ $+$ $cur\text{-}q$
        $+$ the elements of buf_s paired with $+$

$status$	$(?, +)$	if $buf_s \neq empty$	
	else $(?, mark)$	if $cur\text{-}q \neq \{ \}$	(a)
	$(?, +)$	if $mode_s = send$, $last_s = last_r$, $buf_r \neq \{ \}$	(b)
	$(OK, +)$	if $mode_s = send$, $last_s = last_r$, $buf_r = \{ \}$	(c)
	$(OK, \#)$	if $mode_s = send$ and $last_s \in inflight_{rs}$	(d)
	$(lost, +)$	if $mode_s = send$	(e)
		and $last_s \notin (g_r \cup \{last_r\} \cup inflight_{rs})$	
	$(ack, +)$	if $mode_s = idle$	(f)

$rec_{s/r}$ $rec_{s/r}$

Name	Guard	Effect	Name	Guard	Effect
**put(m)		append m to bufs			
prepare(m)	msg = nil, m first on bufs, $\boxed{g_s \subseteq g_r \text{ or } rec_r}$	bufs:=tail (bufs), msg := m, $\boxed{\text{mark} := +}$			
choose(i)	msg ≠ nil, lasts = nil, i ∈ gs	$g_s -:= \{j \mid j \le i\}$, lasts := i, useds +:= ⟨i⟩			
sendsr(i, m)	i = lasts ≠ nil, m = msg		rcvsr(i, m)		if i ∈ gr then append m to bufr, sendAck := false, $g_r -:= \{j \mid j \le i\}$, lastr := i, else if i ∉ gr ∪ {lastr} then optionally nack-buf +:= ⟨i⟩ else if i = lastr then sendAck :=true
			*get(m)	m first on bufr	if bufr = ⟨m⟩ then sendAck := true, bufr :=tail (bufr)
rcvrs(i, a)		if i – lasts then ack := a, msg := nil, lasts := nil	sendrs (i, OK)	i = lastr, sendAck	optionally sendAck := false
			sendru (i, lost)	i first on nack-buf	nack-buf := tail (nack-buf)
*getAck(a)	msg = nil, bufs = empty, ack = a	ack := lost			
**crashs		recs := true	**crashr		recr := true
*recovers	recs	lasts := nil, msg := nil, bufs := ⟨ ⟩, ack := lost, recs := false	*recoverr	recr, $\boxed{used_r \supseteq g_s \cup used_s}$	lastr := nil, mark := #, bufr:=⟨ ⟩, nack-buf:=⟨ ⟩, recr:=false
shrinks(i)		gs −:= {i}	shrinkr(i)	$\boxed{i \notin g_s, i \neq last_s}$ or mark = #	gr −:= {i}
grows(i)	i ∉ used, $\boxed{i \in g_r \text{ or } rec_r}$	gs +:= {i}	growr(i)	i ∉ usedr	gr +:= {i}, used +:= {i}
grow-useds(i)	i ∉ used ∪ gs, $\boxed{i \in used_r \text{ or } rec_r}$	used +:= {i}	cleanup	lastr ≠ lasts	lastr := nil
			unmark	$\boxed{g_s \subseteq g_r, last_s \in g_r \cup \{last_r, nil\}}$	mark := +

Table 10.9. G with honest atomic actions

Chapter 11

A Case Study: Automatic Reconfiguration in Autonet

Thomas L. Rodeheffer and Michael D. Schroeder

This chapter reprints the paper 'Automatic Reconfiguration in Autonet'[1] as a case study in distributed computing. Local area networks (LANs) are one of the reasons that distributed systems are so popular. Inexpensive networking with Ethernet and PC LANs has enabled workstations and PC's to communicate easily and quickly, allowing networked systems to become a prevalent way to compute. In this case study, however, we are not interested in a distributed system that uses the network, but a distributed system that is inside it.

Autonet is a switch-based LAN. In an Autonet installation a set of multiported switches is interconnected in an arbitrary pattern using point-to-point links, as illustrated in Figure 11.1. Additional links connect each host computer to two switches. Packets from a source host contain the address of the destination host and are forwarded through the network from switch to switch along a predetermined route. The distributed system in Autonet is the automatic reconfiguration mechanism, implemented by the switches, that monitors the configuration and adjusts the packet routes to provide maximum connectivity and to make effective use of the available switches and links.

The purpose of Autonet's reconfiguration mechanism is to provide high availability by exploiting redundancy in the physical configuration. When any switch detects a change in the set of neighboring links or switches that are working it triggers a distributed algorithm with which the switches discover the new topology and recalculate the best routes. This reconfiguration is done fast enough that it does not disrupt high-level communication protocols. Thus, Autonet continues to provide communication service to the hosts that are connected by the working components. The paper gives a glimpse into the surprisingly subtle mechanisms

---

[1]'Automatic Reconfiguration in Autonet', *Proceedings of the 13th ACM Symposium on Operating Systems Principles*, Operating Systems Review **25**(5), October 1991, pp 183–197

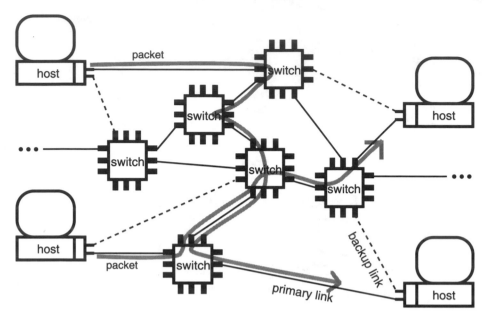

Figure 11.1. Portion of an Autonet showing two packets in transit

required to exploit redundancy and independent failure so that the resulting system surpasses the reliability of its components.

The monitoring, topology acquisition and topology distribution mechanisms described in the paper are a complex example of primary/backup replication. The service that is being replicated is communication between each pair of switches in the network (and thus communication between the hosts connected to those switches). Autonet also contains a much simpler example of primary/backup replication that the paper does not describe. As shown in Figure 11.1, a host attached to an Autonet can have links to two different switches. Low level communication software in the host functions as a clerk module for the communication service provided by the network. This clerk sends and arranges to receive all packets through one of the links (the primary) until there is evidence that it is not working. Evidence comes from hardware link status indicators as well as periodic packet exchanges with the nearest switch. If the active link stops working the clerk fails-over to the other link (the backup). Thus, a host loses network service only if both of its connections fail. The combination of replicated host connections and automatic reconfiguration of the switch-to-switch forwarding routes produces a high-availability LAN.

Given the close attention paid to availability in Autonet it is reasonable to ask whether the network is viewed by its customers as being continuously available. To answer this question we should first distinguish between reliability and availability. Reliability in the case of a LAN refers to the probability that a packet is delivered correctly to its destination. In Autonet, as in any LAN, each packet is delivered correctly with high probability, but not with probability one. Network reconfigurations and environmentally triggered transmission errors on links occasionally corrupt or lose packets. So customers must (and do) take these reliability characteristics into account when they design communication protocols. The typical method for dealing with occasional packet loss is to use acknowledgments, timeouts and retransmissions. Availability, on the other hand, concerns outages that are long enough to disrupt protocols or to be noticed by users.

In service use our Autonet is more available than the other (product) LANs in the building, but it has not been continuously available. Autonet outages have come from two sources: environment and software. The major environmental cause of outages has been power failures, usually building-wide, that affect enough switches to overcome the redundancy in the installation. A second order environmental cause has been disruptive experimentation with the service network. The power failures, however, usually take out all the hosts along with the network, so are not perceived as network outages. And in a service system serious about availability managers would carefully control experimentation.

Of more concern are the software-caused outages – bugs and design flaws in the switch software that disrupt service for noticeable periods of time. Software flaws that occasionally crash a single switch (an independent failure) do not cause network outages: the other switches remove the crashed one from the network and continue to provide service; the crashed switch later reboots itself and rejoins the network. The flaws of concern are distributed bugs that take out most or all switches (a coordinated failure). Will such distributed bugs disappear as the network matures or will they always be a source of outages? My opinion is that a mature system would have a very low probability of an outage due to a software failure. The Autonet approach to high availability can produce a network that will run for years without such an outage. It is imprudent, however, to ever assume it cannot happen, even in a mature system. Something may change about the way the network is managed or used that will discover a new bug.

A third potential cause for apparent outages is unnoticed increases in load. As use grows some links may become overloaded. The result can be performance so bad that it appears to be an outage to some customers. The usual scenario is for the increasing load slowly to use up the capacity of the redundant links so that eventually a failure produces a diminished configuration that is paralyzed by the load. The only remedy for this problem is tools for monitoring network load, periodic management attention to analyzing the load measurements, and addition of capacity as necessary. Whenever spare capacity is provided for availability reasons, it is essential to make sure that it stays spare and does not get used up as load grows.

Automatic Reconfiguration in Autonet

Thomas L. Rodeheffer and Michael D. Schroeder

Abstract

Autonet is a switch-based local area network using 100 Mbit/s full-duplex point-to-point links. Crossbar switches are interconnected to other switches and to host controllers in an arbitrary pattern. Switch hardware uses the destination address in each packet to determine the proper outgoing link for the next step in the path from source to destination. Autonet automatically recalculates these forwarding paths in response to failures and additions of network components. This automatic reconfiguration allows the network to continue normal operation without need of human intervention. Reconfiguration occurs quickly enough that higher-level protocols are not disrupted. This paper has been reprinted from the *Proceedings of the 13th ACM Symposium on Operating Systems Principles*, Operating Systems Review 25(5), October 1991, pp 183–197. It describes the fault monitoring and topology acquisition mechanisms that are central to automatic reconfiguration in Autonet.

11.1 Introduction

Autonet is a switch-based local area network. In an Autonet, 12-by-12 crossbar switches are interconnected to other switches and to host controllers with 100 Mbit/s full-duplex links in an arbitrary pattern. In normal operation each packet follows a precomputed link-to-link path from source to destination. At each switch, hardware uses the destination address in each packet as the lookup index in a forwarding table to determine the proper outgoing link for the next step in the path. An earlier paper (Schroeder *et al.* [1990]) provides an overview of the Autonet design. In the present paper we concentrate on automatic reconfiguration in Autonet.

Automatic operation and high availability are important objectives for Autonet. Our goal was to make Autonet look to host communications software like a fast, high-capacity Ethernet segment that never failed permanently. To provide automatic operation and high availability an Autonet automatically reconfigures itself to use the available topology of switches and links. A processor in each switch monitors the directly connected links and neighboring switches. Whenever this monitor notices a change in what is working (either additions or removals), it triggers a distributed algorithm on all switch processors that determines and distributes the new network topology to all switches. Once each switch knows the new topology, it recalculates routing information and reloads its forwarding table to permit operation with the new topology. This automatic reconfiguration is fast enough that high level communication protocols are not permanently disrupted, even though client packets may be lost while reconfiguration is in process.

When an Autonet is installed with a redundant topology, automatic reconfiguration allows it to continue to provide full interconnection of all hosts as components fail or are removed from service. If there are so many failures that connectivity is lost, the Autonet will partition, but service will continue within each connected portion. When components are repaired, or the topology is extended with new switches or links, automatic reconfiguration incorporates the added components in the operational network.

Autonet has been the service LAN for our research center since February of 1990, with 31 switches providing service to over 100 hosts. Operational experience has allowed (forced) us to improve the sensitivity, stability, and performance of the automatic reconfiguration mechanisms. So this paper, in addition to giving a more detailed description of reconfiguration than previously published, also highlights the important changes that were dictated by our experience.

The paper is organized as follows. Section 11.2 compares Autonet with other networks with automatic reconfiguration. Section 11.3 gives the overall structure of reconfiguration in Autonet. Section 11.4 discusses monitoring and Section 11.5 topology acquisition. Section 11.6 presents conclusions.

11.2   Reconfiguration in Other Networks

The standard example of automatic reconfiguration in a computer network is the ARPANET (McQuillan, Richer and Rosen [1980]; McQuillan and Walden [1977]). The principle differences between ARPANET and Autonet relate to the fact that ARPANET is designed as a wide-area, moderate-speed network while Autonet is designed as a local-area, high-speed network. The ARPANET performs store-and-forward routing based on topology descriptions maintained at each switch (IMP), and tolerates temporary forwarding loops by discarding packets if necessary. Each switch regularly broadcasts updates of the status of its local links.

The Autonet switch hardware processes packets first-come-first-served from each link and uses cut-through in order to decrease the expected delay through the switch. This design was chosen because it provided the best light-load performance for the simplest hardware. However as a consequence, transient forwarding loops might result in deadlock and thus cannot be tolerated. (We have efficient means neither to detect a deadlock nor to clear one.) We took the simplest approach of rapidly recalculating the entire topology whenever it changes and expunging all old forwarding tables before installing any new ones. This global-recalculation design is simpler than incremental approaches and represents an appropriate engineering tradeoff for a moderate-sized network of several dozen switches.

Another network that provides automatic topology maintenance is PARIS (Awerbuch et al. [1990]). Like ARPANET, PARIS uses the strategy of maintaining a topology description at each switch via regular broadcasts of local link status updates. PARIS is designed more as a fast connection network than a packet switching network. Packets travel on explicit source routes that are determined at connection setup by examining a description of the current topology. Topology changes have no effect on existing connections, except that a link failure kills all of the connections using that link. Reliable and very high bandwidth link update broadcasts are provided by hardware flooding over a software-managed spanning tree. The software tree management is very careful not to introduce inconsistencies into the tree. In contrast to PARIS, Autonet routes each new packet independently and thus automatically maintains ongoing conversations by routing around link failures and exploiting link recoveries.

Bridged Ethernet (Perlman [1985]) is another network that provides automatic reconfiguration. The principle difference from Autonet is that a bridged Ethernet supports multiple-access links with no way to distinguish forwarded packets from originals. A bridged Ethernet carefully maintains a loop-free forwarding tree so that each bridge can deduce what to do with each packet. Although the time constants required to maintain consistency in the forwarding tree are on the order of several seconds, a bridged Ethernet does eventually adapt to any topology change. In contrast, Autonet has an implicit addressing structure induced by its point to-point links. An arriving packet is always known to be intended for the recipient, at least as an intermediate hop. We also designed a packet encapsulation using network-assigned destination addresses, in order to make forwarding easier (much like Cypress (Comer and Narten [1988])). As a consequence, Autonet uses more forwarding paths and reconfigures much faster than a bridged Ethernet.

11.3   Overall Structure of Automatic Reconfiguration Mechanism

Automatic reconfiguration in Autonet involves three main tasks: monitoring, topology acquisition and routing. Monitoring involves watching the neighborhood of each switch to determine when the network topology changes. Topology acquisition involves collecting and distributing the description of the network topology. Routing involves recalculating the forwarding table at each switch.

Monitoring determines which links are useful for carrying client packets from one switch to another. From the point of view of reconfiguration, a link is useful if and only if it has an acceptable error rate in both directions, the nodes at each end are distinct, operational switches and each switch knows the identity of the other. (A switch is identified by a 48-bit unique identifier stored in a ROM.) Topology acquisition and route recalculation is triggered whenever the set of useful links changes. Of course, host-to-switch links also carry client packets, but changes in the state of such links never trigger topology acquisition and route recalculations. At most, changes in the host links to a particular switch cause locally calculated changes in that switch's forwarding table. So, from the point of view of network reconfiguration, we largely ignore such links.

Monitoring guarantees that topology acquisition (and client) packets will not travel over a link unless both switches agree the link is useful. Because there are two switches involved there will always be transient disagreement whenever the link is changing state, but the monitoring task makes the period of disagreement as brief as possible. A monitor runs independently for each link in each switch and is always active. It will trigger topology acquisition whenever its link changes from useful to not useful or vice versa. The monitors guarantee that, eventually, links remain stable in one state or the other long enough that topology acquisition and routing can finish.

Topology acquisition is responsible for discovering the network topology and delivering a description of it to every switch that is currently part of the network. This task runs in an artificial environment in which changes in link state do not occur. When two switches disagree about the state of a link, the task does not complete. The artificial environment is implemented on top of the monitoring layer by means of an epoch mechanism: any change or inconsistency triggers a new epoch corresponding to a new stable environment. Topology acquisition is a distributed computation that spreads to all switches from the one where a link monitor triggered it.

Routing, the final task of reconfiguration, uses the topology description to compute the forwarding tables for each switch. Because each switch knows the entire topology, each can calculate its own forwarding table. In this paper we are not concerned with the algorithm for constructing the forwarding tables. During topology acquisition and routing, the switch discards client packets. Once the forwarding table has been recalculated, a switch is able to forward any client packets it receives. The reason for discarding client packets during reconfiguration is to prevent deadlock.

The remainder of the paper concentrates on monitoring and topology acquisition. In considering these topics in more detail we can model the Autonet as a collection of nodes (switches) with numbered ports. Nodes may be interconnected in an arbitrary pattern by full-duplex, port-to-port links. Each node is a computer that can send and receive packets on each attached link that works. Each node has a predetermined unique identifier. From now on we will largely ignore links to hosts, the hosts themselves, forwarding of host packets and even the forwarding tables in the switches.

The neighborhood of a node N is the set of all useful switch-to-switch links that have N as one endpoint. The neighborhood of a set of nodes is the union of the neighborhoods of the members. Autonet reconfiguration can be characterized in terms of these neighborhoods. The monitoring task on node N is responsible for knowing the current neighborhood of N and for initiating a topology task whenever the neighborhood changes. Topology acquisition works by building a spanning tree, merging neighborhoods of larger and larger subtrees until the root has the neighborhood of the entire graph and then flooding the topology down the spanning tree to all nodes.

We are now ready to describe monitoring and topology acquisition in more detail. In this discussion, *packet* and *signal* refer to information passing between separate nodes over a connecting link. Packets are regular data packets whereas signals are transported in link protocols below the level of packet traffic. Message refers to information passing between software components in a single node.

11.4 Monitoring

The monitoring task imposes a model that allows only two types of changes in a node's neighborhood: link failure, which removes a connection from the network topology and link recovery, which adds a connection. All changes in network interconnection result in some combination of these two types of neighborhood change. For example, if a technician powers off a switch, all of the adjacent nodes see link failures on their links to the dead node.

The monitoring task responds rapidly to link failures and less rapidly to link recoveries. Link failure, especially abrupt failure, must be detected and reported quickly, because failure can disrupt ongoing client communication. It is not so urgent to rush back into service a link that recently gave problems. Although it is true that link recovery might heal a network partition or increase network capacity, repairing or adding a link usually takes quite a bit of time, so clients usually will not notice a small additional delay. Many networks, for example, the ARPANET, have a delay before placing links back in service (Heart *et al.* [1970]). By delaying longer as a link proves its reliability, we achieve network stability despite intermittent failures.

A useful link is one that allows bi-directional packet transfer with acceptably low error rates between two distinct nodes. The only way this condition can be verified, of course, is for the two nodes to periodically exchange packets and this is what the monitoring task does. This strategy has the strength that it is an end-to-end check (Saltzer, Reed and Clark [1984]). It has the disadvantage that failure detection may not be very prompt, because it depends on a time-out whose minimum value is bounded by processing overhead. In order to give prompt detection of expected modes of link failure, the monitoring task also treats certain hardware error status conditions as indicating failure. For example, if more than three link coding violations are detected in a ten millisecond interval, the monitoring task immediately assumes that the link has failed.

The monitoring task is organized as two layers: a transmission layer and a connectivity layer. The transmission layer deals with proper transmission and reception of data on the link as seen by the hardware. It makes sure that problems on this link do not interfere with other links and it responds promptly to expected modes of link failure. The connectivity layer, which rests on top of the transmission layer, deals with exchanging packets with the remote node and agreeing on the state of the link. Both of these layers make use of a method for defending against intermittent operation called the skeptic. We describe the skeptic and then the two layers of the monitoring task in detail.

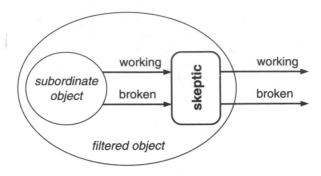

Figure 11.2. Concept of the skeptic

11.4.1   The Skeptic

The skeptic limits the failure rate of a link by delaying its recovery if it has a bad history. Without the skeptic, an intermittent link could cause an unlimited amount of disruption: we are especially concerned with limiting the frequency of reconfigurations. There are four requirements in the design of the skeptic: 1) A link with a good history must be allowed to fail and recover several times without significant penalty. 2) In the worst case, a link's average long-term failure rate must not be allowed to exceed some low rate. 3) Common behaviors shown by bad links should result in exceedingly low average long-term failure rates. 4) A link that stops being bad must eventually be forgiven its bad history. (Note: failure rate here means the number of transitions a link undergoes from working to broken per unit of time.)

Requirement 3 distinguishes the skeptic from typical fault isolation and for-giveness methods such as the auto restart mechanism in Hydra (Wulf, Levin and Harbison [1981]). The typical method to meet requirements 1, 2 and 4 sets a quota of say, ten failures per hour and refuses to recover any link that is over quota. We have observed a common pattern of intermittent behavior in which a link fails again soon after being recovered, in spite of its passing all diagnostics performed in the interim. With the quota method, this pattern would produce a long-term average failure rate of ten failures per hour. This kind of error pattern may not be uncommon, for example Lin and Siewiorek observed a clustering pattern of transient errors in the VICE file system (Lin and Siewiorek [1990]).

The skeptic can be used with any object whose status may change intermittently: it provides a 'filtered object' whose rate of status change is limited. As seen by the skeptic, an object is an abstraction that emits a series of messages, each of which says either 'working' or 'broken'. The skeptic in turn sends out a filtered version of these messages to the next higher level of abstraction. See Figure 11.2.

The skeptic is a state machine with auxiliary variables, timers, and policy param-eters. See Figure 11.3. Dead state means that the subordinate object is broken, wait state means that the object is working but the skeptic is delaying for a while before passing on that information, and good state means that the object is working and the skeptic has concurred.

Three of the state transitions are caused by messages from the subordinate object.

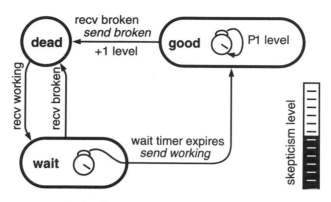

Figure 11.3. Internals of the skeptic

When the skeptic is in wait state or good state and it receives a 'broken' message, it moves to dead state. When the skeptic is in dead state and it receives a 'working' message, it moves to wait state. Otherwise the messages have no effect. The only other transition in the state machine happens when the wait timer expires; in this case the skeptic moves from wait state to good state.

When the skeptic moves from wait to good, it sends a 'working' message to the next higher level of abstraction. When the skeptic moves from good to dead, it sends a 'broken' message. Hence, in the filtered view provided by the skeptic, the object appears to be working only when the skeptic is in good. If the subordinate object fails intermittently, the skeptic alternates between dead and wait without ever reaching good.

When the skeptic enters wait state, it sets and starts the wait timer. The duration set on this timer is calculated by a formula described below. If the skeptic returns to dead before the timer expires, the timer is stopped. Otherwise, when the timer expires, the skeptic moves to good. This is the only way the skeptic can get to good state.

The skeptic responds to intermittent failures by maintaining a level of skepticism about the subordinate object. The skepticism level is kept in an auxiliary variable. Every time the skeptic leaves good state it increments the level. The skepticism level is used in computing wtime, the duration set on the wait timer, according to the formula

$$wtime = wbase + wmult * 2^{level}$$

where wbase and wmult are policy parameters and level is the skepticism level. A policy parameter maxlevel establishes an upper limit on skepticism.

The skeptic forgives old failures by decrementing the skepticism level occasionally. When the skeptic enters good state, it sets and starts the good timer. When the good timer expires, the skeptic decrements the skepticism level and sets and starts the good timer again. The good timer is always running as long as the skeptic is in good state. When the skeptic leaves good state, the good timer is stopped. The formula used to compute gtime, the duration set on the good timer, is identical to the formula used for the wait timer, except that it uses different policy parameters, gbase and gmult. The skepticism level never decrements below zero.

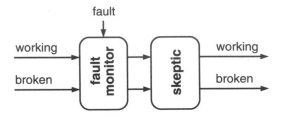

Figure 11.4. Skeptic with fault monitor

Skeptics are used in both the transmission layer and the connectivity layer. Each of these layers has mechanisms to decide when a significant error has occurred. A significant error is called a fault. Faults feed into the skeptic though a mechanism called the *fault monitor*. See Figure 11.4. The fault monitor relays the state of the subordinate object to the skeptic. Whenever the fault monitor receives a 'fault' message and the subordinate object is working, the fault monitor presents an interruption to the skeptic by sending it 'broken' immediately followed by 'working'. This causes the skeptic to notice the fault and enter wait state. If the subordinate object was already broken, the fault monitor takes no action on a 'fault' message.

In the actual implementation, the fault monitor and the skeptic are combined as one unit. Procedure calls are used for the messages.

Figure 11.5 shows an example of how the skeptic timers work, using the transmission layer policy parameters. Observe that for low skepticism levels, say those below 10, the wait time is approximately constant at 5 seconds. For high levels, say those above 12, the wait time doubles with each additional level. The interplay between wbase and wmult establishes the crossover point between low and high levels of skepticism. Policy parameters for all skeptics are given in Table 1.

A few examples of how the transmission layer skeptic responds to common problems will illustrate its utility. One common link failure mode we have observed, especially in newly installed hardware, is that the link transceiver hardware continuously detects coding violations. In this case the transmission layer will declare a fault about once every 170 milliseconds. Because this is much less than the five

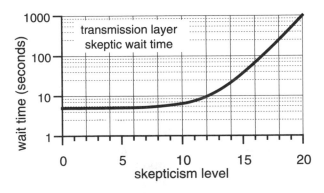

Figure 11.5. Skepticism level vs. wait time

	transmission skeptic	connectivity skeptic
wbase	5 sec	1 sec
wmult	0.001 sec	0.1 sec
gbase	600 sec	600 sec
gmult	0.01 sec	0.1 sec
maxlevel	20	20

Table 11.1. Skeptic policy parameters

second minimum wait time, the skeptic never lets the link recover. To higher levels of abstraction, the link appears permanently broken.

Another common link failure mode occurs when a technician screws in a link cable. As the metal components scrape past each other, the link transceiver hardware detects bursts of coding violations that the transmission layer quite reliably evaluates as faults. Unfortunately, the cable connectors we use are quite difficult to thread correctly, and often several tries and some wiggling are needed before the cable allows itself to be properly screwed in. Each additional wiggle tends to generate more faults. The five second minimum wait time in the skeptic causes all of these faults to be reflected as only one failure.

A third common failure mode occurs on marginal links. In our experience, the error rate on a marginal link is very data dependent: it is much higher when the link is carrying packets than when it is idle. This results in such a link failing soon after it recovers, but then having no further faults until it recovers again. The skepticism level on such a link increases over time. Eventually the transmission layer skepticism level reaches its maximum value of 20, at which point the wait time is about 17 minutes. If the link is part of the switch-to-switch topology, so that failures and recoveries cause network-wide reconfigurations, the connectivity layer skeptic gets involved and its policy parameters produce a maximum wait time of about 28 hours.

Now let us consider how the skeptic fulfills the design requirements. 1) A good history is represented by a low skepticism level. In this case, the skeptic delays a minimum time in wait state and consequently the filtered object recovers soon after the subordinate object recovers. 2) The worst case long-term average failure rate of the filtered object results when the skeptic spends the minimum time in good state required to forgive the lowest level of skepticism. The bound can be proved using a counting argument on the number of failures and observing that at sufficiently high skepticism levels the wait time exceeds the lowest level time to forgive. 3) A subordinate object that tends to fail again soon after the filtered object recovers will tend to increase the skepticism level. 4) If the subordinate object remains working, eventually all skepticism will be forgiven.

There is one more feature in the skeptic, which is that the duration set on the wait timer actually varies as a random fraction between one and two times the value calculated for wtime. This random variation causes different skeptics to disperse their wait timer expirations. If the network is running with several intermittent links, this randomness reduces the possibility of getting caught in some systematic pattern.

We chose the skeptic parameters as follows. The transmission layer skeptic deals with physical phenomena, so several of its parameters derive from maintenance needs. Five seconds is the shortest minimum wait time that will cover the process of screwing in a link cable. A technician often recables a host controller several times during testing, so we allow about eight levels before the increase in wait time becomes perceptible. Twenty minutes is the longest maximum wait time that a technician will bear to see if an attempted hardware repair has any effect on the system. Ten minutes seems like a reasonable interval for the minimum good time.

We expect problems in the connectivity layer to be unusual except when induced by the transmission layer, so we set its minimum wait time smaller, at one second and its crossover point lower, at level four. Because connectivity layer failures cause network-wide reconfigurations, the maximum wait time should be as long as possible. We chose 28 hours because we did not want the system to hold off much more than a day on its own authority.

Many networks contain a mechanism for discriminating against unreliable links. For example, PARIS (Awerbuch *et al.* [1990]) increments an (un)reliability counter with each link failure. The current value of a link's unreliability counter forms the most significant component of a link's weight, which is broadcast in regular link status updates. Connection setup and the tree manager shy away from links with high weight and thus unreliable links will tend not to get used unless necessary. The value in a link's unreliability counter decays over time so that information about old failures expires eventually (Awerbuch [1991]). However, PARIS does not have a backoff strategy, so if the unreliable link is the only connection between two parts of the network, PARIS will suffer repeated topology changes rather than permit the network to remain partitioned.

Jacobson observes that a network closely approximates a linear system and speculates that consequently its stability may be ensured by adding exponential damping to its primary excitation (Jacobsen [1988]). This speculation supports the exponential increase in wait time at high skepticism levels.

11.4.2 Transmission Layer

The transmission layer contains a skeptic with fault monitor, three error detectors and a round-trip verifier. See Figure 11.6. The transmission layer watches the error indicators in the link hardware and determines if the link appears to be successful at sending and receiving data. It passes its conclusion up to the connectivity layer. The transmission layer does not care where the data might be going to or coming from — it is the responsibility of the connectivity layer to determine that. If the transmission layer determines that the link is broken, it sets the switch hardware to discard all incoming and outgoing packets, isolating the link. No packets can be sent or received over an isolated link. The reason for isolating a broken link is to prevent it from interfering with the rest of the network.

The fault monitor here at the lowest level of the system really has no subordinate object, so it is connected to a dummy object that is always working. 'Working'

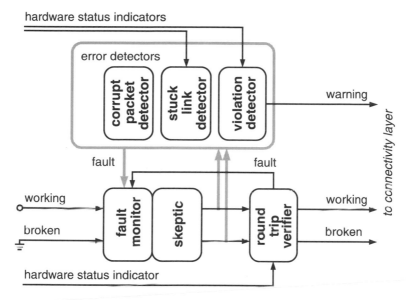

Figure 11.6. Diagram of the transmission layer

and 'broken' are abstractions that are synthesized based on the hardware status indicators, as interpreted by the error detectors and round trip verifier. The round-trip verifier filters the output of the skeptic by delaying 'working' messages until it believes that the transmission layer skeptic on the other end of the link also believes the link is working.

Each error detector analyzes and responds to a different type of error indication available in the switch hardware.

Corrupt packet detector

The corrupt packet detector examines all packets received by the switch control processor and declares a fault when CRC errors or impermissible packet lengths are seen too frequently. It is possible for packets to be corrupted without any detectable coding violations, when a data error happens inside the crossbar at some switch. Such an error is eventually detected as a CRC error at the packet's ultimate destination. It would be better if each link verified the CRC of all incoming packets, but this feature was omitted from the hardware. We achieve some protection against corruption by checking all of the packets destined for the local switch control processor.

An isolated corrupt packet might be the result of a random glitch, so it should be forgiven. Corrupt packets become a significant error if they happen too frequently. The corrupt packet detector imposes a quota on how often it forgives corrupt packets by using a leaky bucket mechanism (Turner [1986]). Every time it encounters a corrupt packet, it puts a token in the bucket. One token leaks out of the bucket every ten minutes. Whenever adding a token to the bucket causes the bucket to hold more than five tokens, the corrupt packet detector declares a fault.

Because the transmission layer isolates a broken link so that it can neither send nor receive packets, no further corrupt packets will arrive from the link until the skeptic recovers it.

Stuck link detector

In Autonet, certain problems cause a link to become stuck in a state that prevents any data transmission. Typically this is due to some corruption of flow control commands. If a link has been trying to transmit a packet, but has made no progress for several milliseconds, something is wrong on the link. At this point it is necessary to dump the stuck packet and free up its resources.

This recovery is bound to be disruptive, although in our switches it is perhaps more disruptive than absolutely necessary, since our only mechanism for dumping a packet is to reinitialize the entire switch. This destroys all packets in the switch. Fortunately, reinitializing only takes about ten microseconds. Isolating a broken link removes the opportunity for it to cause further switch reinitializations.

Although a stuck link should not happen in normal operation, links can appear to be stuck as a result of mistransmission of a single flow-control or packet framing command code. Thus the stuck link detector must be willing to forgive an isolated occurrence. The detector samples its hardware indicators every 100 milliseconds and, if the link is stuck, responds by reinitializing the switch. The stuck link detector imposes a quota on how often it forgives by using a leaky bucket mechanism to declare faults, exactly like the corrupt packet detector.

Violation detector

The violation detector analyzes and responds to coding and format violations received on the link. A coding violation usually means that the link receiver heard a piece of static on the line. For example, coding violations result from connecting or disconnecting the link cable, from a cable that is too long for good transmission, or from a nearby heavy-duty electric motor. Although connecting or disconnecting a link generates a burst of coding violations tens of milliseconds long, even the best links in our system pick up one or two isolated coding violations per week. A format violation means that the link receiver did not hear proper packet framing or flow-control where it expected. Static can cause isolated format violations, as can occasional activity such as reinitializing the switch. Hence a burst of violations is a significant error, but isolated violations should be ignored.

The violation detector samples link hardware status registers once every 1.3 milliseconds and accumulates the results for a block of 128 samples. At the end of each block, the violation detector checks the number of violations and, if there are too many it declares a fault. The permitted number of violations depends on whether the skeptic says the link is working or broken, which is why Figure 11.6 shows the error detectors receiving the 'working' and 'broken' messages from the skeptic. If the link is working, three errors are permitted in a block, but if the link is broken no errors are permitted. The more strict rule for broken links insures that no link will recover unless it can pass the entire skeptic recovery time without a single violation, while occasional violations on working links are ignored.

If a broken link continues to have violations, the violation detector continues to declare a fault at the end of each block. The transmission layer skeptic always spends at least five seconds in wait state, so it will keep believing that the link is broken.

In order promptly to detect the bursts of violations that result from the anticipated activity of plugging and unplugging link cables, the violation detector examines subblocks of eight samples. If a subblock contains more than three violations, the violation detector immediately declares a fault. In order to eliminate the processing overhead of declaring faults every subblock, subblock checking applies only to working links.

Our method of ignoring occasional problems by declaring a fault only when more than three violations occur in 128 samples is known as the k out of n method. This method is used in testing neighbor reachability in EGP (Mills [1984]) and in Cypress (Comer and Narten [1988]). For simplicity, we test k out of n only at the end of n samples, rather than continuously. EGP also shares our idea of using different threshold parameters depending on the current state of the link.

Round-trip verifier

Now let us consider the problem of getting the transmission layers in two adjacent nodes to agree about the state of a connecting link. The solution is a protocol in which each node indicates to its peer whether it thinks the link should be working or not. When a node knows both from itself and from its peer that the link should be working, then it declares the link to be working. Otherwise, the link is broken. This function is implemented by the round-trip verifier.

The round-trip verifier contains a state machine with three states: dead, test and good. See Figure 11.7. Because it supports the same structure of interactions between subordinate object and filtered object as the skeptic, the state machine resembles that of the skeptic (see Figure 11.3). Dead state means that the underlying skeptic declares that the link is broken, test state that the skeptic declares the link is working but the remote node does not yet concur and good state that both agree the link is working.

The round-trip verifier uses the flow-control channel on a link to send a signal to the other node. The flow-control channel is a dedicated time slot in which the link's transmitter normally sends flow-control command codes. Under software control, the transmitter fills this slot instead with a distinguished command code called *idhy*, which stands for 'I Don't Hear You'. The round-trip verifier uses *idhy* to send a 'bad' signal and uses the absence of *idhy* to send an 'okay' signal. The verifier receives these signals by decoding hardware status indicators using the same sampling system of blocks and subblocks as the violation detector.

The round-trip verifier continually sends 'bad' to its peer in dead state and 'okay' in test state and good state. Because the link transports these signals below the level of packet traffic, the nodes can exchange this information even when the link is isolated. The verifier remains in test state until it detects an 'okay' signal, at

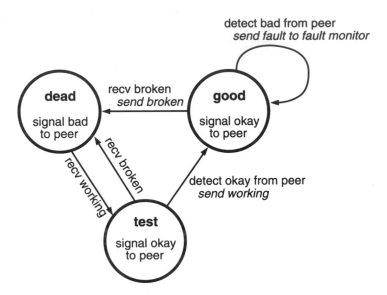

Figure 11.7. Round-trip verifier state machine

which point it moves to good. When the verifier is in good state, it immediately declares a fault if it ever detects a 'bad' signal. The fault causes the underlying skeptic to declare the link broken which results in the verifier moving back to dead state. The verifier sends and receives 'working' and 'broken' messages from adjacent software layers just like the skeptic does.

Notice the effect of the round-trip verifier on a link that works well in only one direction, say from node A to node B. The error detector in node B has no cause for complaint and its skeptic declares that the link is working. The error detector in node A is upset and its skeptic declares that the link is broken. The round-trip verifier in node A is signaling 'bad', which tells the round-trip verifier in node B that A is upset. Consequently, the transmission layers in both nodes agree that the link is broken. The verifier in A is in dead state and the verifier in B is in test state.

Now suppose that the link is repaired and the error detector in node A is now happy. After the skeptic recovery delay, the round-trip verifier in node A moves to test state and begins signaling 'okay'. It detects 'okay' from B, which is in test state and moves to good state. The round-trip verifier in node B soon detects the 'okay' from A and moves to good state. Both nodes now believe that the link is working. The transmission layer always brings a link up with this handshake.

One other task of the round-trip verifier is to filter out links that connect to host controllers. A host controller uses different command codes than a switch and this difference is reflected in the link's hardware status. The round-trip verifier classifies a link as a host link or a switch link based on an examination of this status and it declares a fault whenever the classification changes. A link that connects to a host has no effect on switch-to-switch connectivity and therefore is considered as broken for the purpose of reconfiguration, but assuming that the skeptic and

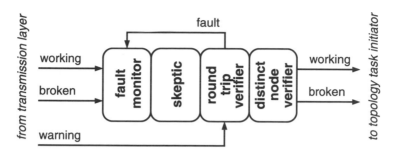

Figure 11.8. Diagram of the connectivity layer

verifier are otherwise happy, the link is taken out of isolation so that packets can pass across it to the host.

As we have seen, the transmission layer filters out links with error conditions and links that connect to host controllers. It is the job of the connectivity layer to filter out links that do not connect anywhere or that connect back to the same switch.

11.4.3   Connectivity Layer

The connectivity layer comes into action once the transmission layer has declared that a link is working. The connectivity layer sends packets back and forth across the link to determine if link is a useful node-to-node connection. When the connectivity layer declares that a link is useful, it also provides the identity of the remote node. The union of the results of the connectivity layers for the links at a node comprises the current state of the neighborhood monitoring task at that node.

The connectivity layer contains a skeptic with fault monitor, a round trip verifier and a distinct node verifier. See Figure 11.8. The fault monitor receives the messages from the transmission layer about whether the link is working or broken. The round-trip verifier filters the output of the skeptic by delaying 'working' messages until it has exchanged packets over the link and has determined the identity of the remote node. The distinct node verifier filters the output of the round-trip verifier by checking that the remote node is indeed different from the local node. Whenever the connectivity layer generates either a 'working' or 'broken' message, topology acquisition is initiated.

The design of the round-trip verifier satisfies several goals. 1) A link is tested vigorously whenever there is reason to believe that the testing might change the link's state. 2) A link is always regularly retested. 3) Retesting a stable link occurs at a rate low enough to impose little overhead. By adjusting the testing effort according to a hint of how interesting the test result might be, we achieve prompt detection of common changes while incurring little overhead on average. The testing effort never falls below a certain minimum to guarantee that any change is detected eventually. A more detailed description follows.

The round-trip verifier exchanges connectivity packets with its peer on the remote end of the link, with the purpose of determining the identity of its peer.

Peer identity (id) has two components: a 48-bit unique node identifier and a 4-bit port number within the node. To insure that an identity is current, we create a sequenced identity (s-id) by attaching a 32-bit sequence number. The round-trip verifier knows its own local s-id and it maintains a current estimate of the s-id of its remote peer. A connectivity packet carries the local and remote s-ids from the transmitter as source and destination s-ids.

The connectivity round-trip verifier has a state machine similar to that of the transmission round-trip verifier. In place of detecting 'okay' and 'bad' signals, the connectivity round-trip verifier checks the result of a round-trip exchange of connectivity packets.

Some connectivity packets are requests and others are replies. The only difference is that the receiver must send back a connectivity packet in response to a request, whereas a reply does not need a response. Requests and replies are distinguished by a flag in the packet header.

When the round-trip verifier enters test state, it begins sending request packets, waiting for a matching packet to be received. A matching packet contains a destination s-id equal to the local s-id. When it receives a matching packet, the verifier moves to good state and declares that the link is working. In any case, the receiver saves the source s-id of any received packet as its estimate of the remote s-id. This causes any subsequent packet sent back to be seen as a matching packet at the other end. The verifier retransmits very frequently at first but backs off exponentially if no matching packet is forthcoming.

The round-trip verifier continues sending request packets in good state, waiting for confirming packets to be received. A confirming packet contains a destination s-id equal to the local s-id and a source id equal to the remote id. (It is not necessary to inspect the remote sequence number to insure that the packet exchange is current.) We save the source s-id as the estimate of the remote s-id and increment the local sequence number. A packet that would be confirming except that the destination and local sequence numbers fail to match is ignored. Any other received connectivity packet causes an immediate fault (causing the skeptic to declare the link broken causing the verifier to move to dead state). The verifier transmits requests very frequently at first but backs off exponentially as confirming packets are received. When confirming packets fail to be received within five times the transmission interval, the interval is decreased by half and another five transmissions are attempted. A fault is declared if the interval had already attained its minimum value.

Whenever the skeptic declares that the link is broken, the round trip verifier passes on the declaration and enters dead state. In dead state, the round-trip verifier sends no requests. If any requests are received during dead state, they are answered with replies that good state treats as contradictory and test state ignores.

The effect of the round-trip verifier is as follows. Suppose that the link appears healthy to the transmission layer but connects to a node that does not answer. The round-trip verifier will be in test state and exponentially back off until the transmission rate is one request packet every ten seconds. Now suppose that the remote node begins responding. With the first matching reply, the round-trip verifier moves to good state with the minimum transmission interval. As confirmations arrive, the transmission interval increases to its maximum, at which point the round-trip verifier will be sending one request packet every ten seconds to continue verifying that the link is still working.

The exponential backoff in the round-trip verifier transmission interval allows a gradual transition between the vigorous testing regime and the background testing regime. Occasional losses or delays in responding to the round-trip protocol do not significantly alter the regime, while a reasonable response time is still provided in the case of complete autism.

The distinct node verifier filters the output of the round-trip verifier by comparing the remote node identity with the local node identity. If they are equal, the distinct node verifier does not pass on the declaration that the link is working. Links that connect back to the same node are not useful node-to-node connections even though they may carry packets perfectly. Whenever the distinct node verifier changes a link from working to broken or back, the neighborhood monitoring task declares a change in the neighborhood, which causes the topology task to recompute the network topology. The topology task is discussed in detail later.

In addition to the actions described above, the round-trip verifier also responds to warnings issued by the transmission layer error detector. The violation error detector issues an immediate warning whenever it detects one or more violations in a subblock, assuming the condition is not serious enough to warrant declaring a fault. The connectivity layer round-trip verifier responds to a warning in good state by resetting its transmission interval to the minimum. This results in rapid transmission of round-trip request packets and a fault if no confirmation is soon received. Warnings are ignored in dead state and test state.

All packets sent by the topology task, to be described in Section 5, have a header that contains the source id. These values are checked against the remote id and any mismatch results in a connectivity fault just like receiving a contradictory connectivity packet. If the distinct node verifier says that the link is broken, any topology packets received will be discarded.

11.4.4   Development History and Experience

In our original implementation we had a much simpler filter in place of the skeptic: the simple filter just refrained from recovering the link more than once every ten seconds. We had not realized how perverse malfunctioning hardware could be. As more and more hardware was deployed we soon had several marginal links that each cycled through failure and recovery once a minute or so. The problem was that the rate of errors on a marginal link depended on the data pattern being sent on the link and links that were in service tended to provoke a lot more errors than links that were being tested. At that time the topology task took about five seconds to complete, so the network was completely unusable. The skeptic fixed the problem by effectively removing marginal links from the network.

We encountered another difficulty due to a malfunctioning host controller that sent incorrect flow control commands. This caused the adjacent node to get stuck when it attempted to send the host a packet. We had not realized how important it would be to detect stuck links. The stuck node could not respond to connectivity requests from its neighbors, so after ten seconds they gave up and reconfigured. The stuck node also reconfigured into a partition by itself. Part of reconfiguration involves reinitializing the crossbar switch, which has the side effect of unsticking a stuck node. The node would then join back with its neighbors and everyone would reconfigure again. Soon the node would attempt to send the host another packet, and the process would repeat. Once we implemented the skeptic it defended against this problem by effectively partitioning the stuck node out of the network, which at least saved the network from collapse. Implementing stuck link detection allowed specific problem links to be identified and isolated, without partitioning the network.

We added the warnings when we observed an unexpectedly disruptive link failure mode that was not being detected promptly. The failure produced one or two error samples in the transmission layer error detector (not enough to declare a fault), but no other indications until the next time the connectivity layer round-trip verifier performed its end-to-end check, which would occur on average five seconds later. The failure mode was provoked by turning off the power of the remote node, which was quite frequent in the early days. The way the hardware is implemented, a powered-off node reflects data perfectly. A link watching its remote node power-off sees the line change from node-to-node to reflecting. In some cases, this change would be so clean that it dependably provoked only a single error sample. We needed to detect this failure promptly. If the link to the powered off node was on the broadcast distribution tree, outgoing broadcast packets would reflect back into the network and continuously regenerate, causing network collapse. This was unexpected. Users were unhappy. Implementing the warnings caused the end-to-end check to detect the failure promptly and fixed the problem.

One excellent success of the connectivity layer occurred when a node's crossbar switch started acting erratically. The crossbar began switching occasional packets to the wrong output link. The neighboring nodes would detect a connectivity violation and break their links, but the links would then seem to work fine in test state so they would recover for a while before breaking again. Eventually the skeptics partitioned the malfunctioning node out of the network.

One scenario that exercises most mechanisms in the monitoring task is the powering-on of a switch. Let A be a switch that is about to be powered-on. As mentioned above, a powered-off switch reflects data perfectly. Therefore, while A is powered-off, all of its neighbors B, C and D see links that work fine at the transmission layer and at the connectivity layer, except that the distinct node verifier refuses to pass on the working declaration. The connectivity layer round-trip verifiers are in good state at maximum back-off level. Now a technician powers on A. The software initializes all the state machines in dead state, which causes A's transmission layer round trip verifiers to send *idhy*. B, C and D probably hear enough static during the power-on to declare faults, but if not then their transmission layer round-trip verifiers will do so when the *idhy* from A starts arriving. At this point everything pauses at least five seconds for transmission layer skeptics to finish their wait time-outs. Whenever both transmission layer skeptics on a link concur, the transmission layers pass on working declarations to the connectivity layers, which then start the connectivity layer skeptic time-outs. Finally, both connectivity layer skeptics concur, a round-trip packet exchange verifies the connectivity of the link and the topology task performs a reconfiguration. Because of the random wait timer adjustment, this happens at different times on different links. In this example, we would probably have three separate reconfigurations as each of B, C and D established its connection to A.

11.5   Topology Acquisition

The monitoring task provides each node N with a description of its neighborhood. In this description the links that do not work or that connect from N back to N have been eliminated. The responsibility of the topology acquisition task is to provide each node with a description of the current topology of the entire network.

We first describe the basic method of the topology task assuming a very simple scenario: some single node initiates the task (for an unknown reason) and the task runs to completion without any confusion from topology changes (which are assumed never to happen). Then we describe how to extend the basic method to deal with multiple initiators and with topology changes.

11.5.1   Basic Method

Let us consider a single instance of topology acquisition as if it were the only thing that ever happened in the network. The basic method presumes that the network is quiet, some single node spontaneously initiates the topology task, it runs for a while and then the network is quiet forever after. Note that, even in this simple case, it is possible that two nodes may disagree about the state of their connecting link. In this circumstance it is required that the topology task never claim to produce a complete topology description.

The topology acquisition task consists of three phases: 1) propagation, which constructs a rooted spanning tree over the set of all reachable nodes; 2) collection, which merges descriptions of larger and larger subtree neighborhoods; and 3) distribution, which sends the complete description from the root back down the spanning tree to all nodes.

The propagation phase consists of a wave of packets that spreads across all links through the network starting from the initiating node. The initiating node becomes the root of the spanning tree, and each other node joins the spanning tree by designating as its parent link the link on which it is first contacted. This is called a propagation order spanning tree. Generally one would expect the depth of a propagation order spanning tree not to exceed by more than a small factor the minimum possible depth of a spanning tree rooted at the initiating node and experience in our network supports this intuition.

During the propagation phase, each node N in the spanning tree contacts each of its neighbors, M, to offer M the opportunity to join the spanning tree as a child of N. If M has not yet joined the spanning tree, it accepts the offer and joins. M then contacts each of its neighbors, in turn. Otherwise, M is already in the tree and it refuses the offer. M sends back a reply to N so that N knows whether M accepted or refused. In this way each node comes to know its parent and its children in the spanning tree.

During the propagation phase each node conducts a query-reply exchange with each of its neighbors. The neighborhood monitoring task guarantees that topology-task packets will pass only if both end nodes agree that the link is useful. Suppose there is disagreement about the state of a link between nodes P and Q: P considers the link to be useful but Q does not. Then the propagation phase will get stuck when it arrives at P, because P will not be able to get a reply from Q. Therefore the propagation phase will manage to finish building a spanning tree only if all nodes agree about the state of their connecting links.

The propagation phase dies out when all nodes have been contacted and a spanning tree has been formed. This is a global condition, however and no individual node knows when it has been attained. Instead, there is a rolling transition from the propagation phase to the collection phase that begins at the leaves of the spanning tree. A node knows that it is a leaf in the spanning tree when it has contacted all of its neighbors and they have all refused to be children.

The collection phase begins at the leaves of the spanning tree and rises up to the root. When a node M accepts a propagation-phase offer to be a child of N, it also commits to sending up to N a description of the neighborhood of M's subtree. If M is a leaf in the spanning tree, this is easy, because the link monitoring task provides each node with a description of its neighborhood. Otherwise, M has children. In this case, M waits for subtree neighborhood descriptions from all of its children, merges them with the description of its own neighborhood and then sends the result on up to N.

Eventually the collection phase reaches the point at which the root — just like any other node — has merged a description of its neighborhood with descriptions from all of its children to produce a description of its subtree neighborhood. But, in the case of the root, this is a description of the entire network. At this point the collection phase ends and the distribution phase begins. The root sends to each of its children the full network description. The children in turn send it to their children and so on, until every node in the network possesses the full network description.

11.5.2   Multiple Initiators

The basic method assumes that exactly one node initiates the topology task. Now we extend the method to deal with multiple initiators. Multiple initiators cause confusion because more than one node is claiming to be the root of the spanning tree. The confusion is solved by separating the activity into distinct instances of the topology task based on the initiator. Each initiator creates a new, distinct instance of the topology task, which runs independently of all other instances. All state records and packets are labeled with the unique identifier of the initiator in order to keep things straight.

For the purposes of both time and space efficiency, we do not want to run multiple instances of the topology task to completion. Also, the topology task is supposed to come to a single definite conclusion in each node. The solution is to conduct a competition during the propagation phase, so that exactly one instance wins and completes the phase, while all the others die out. Observe that the propagation phase spreads over the entire network, so if multiple instances do get started, they will come into competition with each other. Because the propagation phase has no definite end but instead rolls into the collection phase, no node knows which instance wins the competition until the end of the collection phase.

We conduct the competition as follows. Each node is allowed to belong to at most one instance of the topology task at a time. When the propagation phase of instance I first arrives at a node, the node can be in one of two states. If the node does not yet belong to any instance, it responds by joining instance I and then within that instance it joins the spanning tree in the normal way. Otherwise the node already belongs to some other instance J. In this case the node must decide whether to ignore I and remain in J, or discard J and join I. The node makes this decision by comparing the unique identifier labels of the instances. The instance with the lower unique identifier wins.

With the further proviso that only those nodes that do not yet belong to an instance may initiate instances, this competition assures us that exactly one instance will manage to complete the propagation phase — it will be the instance whose initiator has the lowest unique identifier over all initiators. All other instances will die out, as their nodes get taken over by the winning instance.

11.5.3 Topology Changes

We have extended the basic method to deal with multiple initiators. Now we further extend the method to deal with topology changes. Topology changes cause confusion because the method depends on running in a network whose topology is stable. So we simulate a stable topology by using an epoch mechanism. Each node maintains an *epoch number* that identifies the epoch in which its topology task is running, and this epoch number is included in all topology task packets. When a node's neighborhood monitoring task reports a change in the neighborhood, the node forgets all of its old topology task state, increments its epoch number and initiates a topology task in the new epoch. Whenever a node receives a topology task packet, it compares the epoch number in the packet to its own epoch number. If the packet has an old epoch number it is ignored, if it has the current epoch number it is processed, and if it has a new epoch number, the node forgets all its old topology task state, adopts the new epoch number and then processes the packet. In this latter case, the only possible packet is an offer to join the spanning tree.

One way to think of epochs is as competing instances of the topology task. (Of course, these are the multiple-initiator method tasks that have their own sub-instances based on initiators.) Each node is always trying to promulgate the newest epoch it has heard about. We optimize the competition by having a node keep track of the state of the topology task only for the newest epoch.

If any instance of the topology task runs to completion, it must have appeared that the network topology was consistent and stable. This is because a node effectively locks its current neighborhood into the epoch at the moment it adopts the epoch number. If any changes occur in the node's neighborhood, the neighborhood monitoring task reports it and the node advances to the next epoch. If there are nodes with inconsistent neighborhoods, which is a possible transient state of the network, the neighborhood monitoring task rapidly eliminates these inconsistencies and reports neighborhood changes in at least one of the affected nodes, which causes new epochs to be created.

11.5.4 Development History

An initial version of our terminating distributed spanning tree algorithm was invented in 1987 by Leslie Lamport and K. Mani Chandy. The current topology task method differs principally in constructing a propagation-order spanning tree with the initiator as the root. Lamport and Chandy's version constructs a unique minimum-depth spanning tree with the node of globally lowest unique identification as the root. In fact, we still use the Lamport-Chandy tree as our broadcast distribution tree, but each node computes it from the topology description rather than during reconfiguration. The current method also provides for retransmission and acknowledgment to deal with lost packets.

Although experience has not revealed problems with the basic algorithm, considerable work has gone into tuning the implementation. Initially, we had 27 switches in our network and the goal was reconfiguration in less than 200 milliseconds. The original implementation took about five seconds to run the topology task. We soon discovered that a major obstacle was that each node generated a voluminous debugging log. Code for logging events was optimized for flexibility, not speed, since its purpose was to help locate correctness bugs, which it did. Removing most of the debugging log events reduced the run time to about 1360 milliseconds. All of these times are for the topology task. Additionally, it takes about 20 milliseconds for the monitoring task to notice a link failure.

In order to speed up the topology task, we had to find performance bugs. We added code to each node to keep a trace log of interesting events such as packet arrival and departure and we added fields to topology packets to carry clock exchange information. This code was optimized for speed so that it would reveal rather than create performance bugs. Then we wrote a diagnostic program to extract trace logs from all the nodes, correlate them by computing clock synchronization, and then print out the result as a single, global event trace of all of the activity during a reconfiguration. This tool was essential in locating and fixing performance bugs. We ran many experiments and looked long and hard at the resulting traces.

We saved about 470 milliseconds by cranking down retransmission timers: in the propagation phase from 500 to 20 milliseconds and in the collection phase from 100 to 10 milliseconds. The event trace revealed that one or two retransmissions were always showing up in the critical path. After studying the situation, we concluded that these critical path retransmissions were unavoidable. During the propagation phase, each contacted node clears its forwarding table in order to purge old client traffic, during which the node is deaf for about 15 milliseconds. If the nodes do not purge old client traffic, forwarding cycles may arise during reconfiguration and cause deadlock or regenerative broadcasts. We tried doing without the purge and sure enough, we occasionally got regenerative broadcasts which, due to a bug in the host controller microcode, tended to crash the hosts. Because the original switch software for retransmission had too much overhead to permit the desired small timer values, we had to reimplement it as part of this improvement.

We saved about 420 milliseconds when we discovered that each node copied its forwarding table into its debugging log. The debugging log is flexible, but very slow. We thought these printings were not on the critical path, but it turned out that some were. The simplest solution was just to delete the printings.

We saved about 100 milliseconds when we replaced our software CRC algorithm with a software checksum for topology packets. There is no hardware support in the switches for CRC, so it had to be performed in software.

At this point we saw that the majority of the run time went into the topology distribution phase. We completely reimplemented this phase and saved about 170 milliseconds. The original implementation unmarshaled the topology description packets into an internal data structure and then for each child remarshaled the data structure back into packets to send. The redesigned implementation marshals the data structure once at the root, distributes the packets from generation to generation as quickly as possible and then unmarshals the data structure in all nodes in parallel.

At various times we made changes guided by intuition about what would speed things up, rather than by study of the trace log. The resulting improvements were uniformly disappointing. Changing from the Lamport-Chandy tree to an early version of the propagation order tree made the code much simpler but saved only 26 milliseconds. A later simplification saved an additional 14 milliseconds. Polishing all the code in the collection and distribution phases saved a total of 2 milliseconds. Changes guided by the performance trace were much more effective at speeding things up.

The result of performance tuning was a system that ran the topology task in 154 milliseconds on the 27-switch network. Our network has since expanded to 31 switches on which the topology task runs in 179 milliseconds. Based on trials using different subsets of our network, the formula
$$time = 58 + 3.34 * d + 1.36 * n + 0.315 * d * n$$
where d is the diameter of the network and n is the number of switches, gives a fairly reasonable approximation to the reconfiguration time in milliseconds. Extrapolating using this formula, a 100-switch network arranged in a diameter 10 torus would have a reconfiguration time of 542 milliseconds. Such a reconfiguration time would perhaps just barely be acceptable. The time would of course be less given a faster switch control processor.

11.5.5   Related Work

Topology acquisition based on computing a spanning tree was described by Perlman [1985] for Ethernet bridges. Her version of the spanning tree algorithm reaches steady state without any explicit termination.

The propagation and collection phases of topology acquisition in Autonet are an example of termination detection in a diffusing computation as described by Dijkstra and Scholten [1980].

The propagation-order tree used for coordinating the topology task represents an engineering tradeoff in favor of average-case performance for our network. Although in the worst case the propagation-order tree might be linear, the trees constructed in our network are almost always no more than one level deeper than a minimum depth tree. Distributed algorithms for constructing minimum depth trees with good asymptotic worst-case performance are known (Awerbuch and Gallager [1987]; Gallager [1982]), but they are considerably more complicated than the propagation-order method and are not nearly as efficient for moderate-sized networks.

11.6   Conclusions

The automatic reconfiguration of Autonet has succeeded in eliminating human management from day-to-day operation of the network. Our experience over the past year has been that the network runs itself. Reconfiguration runs quickly enough that the occasional network outages indeed are covered by normal retransmission in higher-level protocols.

Currently our Autonet installation experiences about ten reconfigurations per week, usually due to one of the 'usual suspects' – a small number of occasionally flaky switch-to-switch links that have not been worth trying to fix. A recent spell of hot weather provoked hundreds of isolated reconfigurations due to intermittent malfunctions in a few overheated switch crossbars, but in spite of the many brief disruptions the Autonet was almost always available and no user noticed an outage. Experimental hardware has the advantage of providing tests like this. Occasional reconfigurations also result from demonstrations to visiting dignitaries.

Redundancy is exploited to work around failed components as well as to facilitate repair. For most of the past year, several percent of our installed hardware link interfaces did not work at any given time. Because our Autonet had redundancy and automatically reconfigured itself around these failures, there was no urgency about getting them fixed. When a technician did finally get around to repairing a failure, it could be accomplished by powering-off the problem switch, replacing the faulty components and then powering the switch back on. Normal network operation continued during the repair because network redundancy and automatic reconfiguration covered for the missing switch. A similar scenario applies to downloading (compatible) new versions of the switch control program.

The skeptic mechanism has succeeded in defending the network against unreliable hardware, while still allowing quick recovery from isolated failures. An advantage of the skeptic structure is that none of the error detectors ever have to figure out what to do to recover from an error: all they have to do is declare a fault. We have found it much easier to figure out how to detect possible errors than to worry about how to respond to each one individually.

Our Autonet would be completely unusable without these automatic mechanisms.

It might be noted that the description of the monitoring task in this paper is much more lengthy than the description of the topology task. The reason is that the monitoring task bridges an enormous gulf between idiosyncratic hardware functionality and the abstraction of node neighborhoods, whereas the topology task builds upon a simple abstraction using well-understood concepts. The monitoring task has to get many details right in order to work acceptably. The topology task only has to work fast. In our implementation, the monitoring task contains about twice as many lines of code as the topology task.

As is usual in robust systems of this sort, it is important to report component status through a management interface so that timely repairs may be effected. Several times we have been surprised to discover that some section had only a single connection to the rest of the network, usually due to the combination of poor interconnection and multiple link failures. We are still working on management functions.

Two examples of needed improvements in reconfiguration are suppression of multiple reconfigurations during switch booting and provision to command a timely response to an attempted link repair.

Booting a switch causes separate reconfigurations as each of its switch-to-switch links is discovered. It would be less disruptive if all the links could be brought up using only one reconfiguration. Our idea to accomplish this would be to add a delay between declaring a link as working in the monitoring task and initiating the topology task. During this delay, any attempt to perform an action that depends on the state of the link would cancel the remainder of the delay. Such actions are receiving a topology message and running the topology task (either an old one or a new one started by some other link).

Because the skeptics may have attained a high level of skepticism and refuse to respond to a bad link, a technician may have difficulty determining if the link has indeed been repaired. The maximum wait time of the transmission skeptic is 17 to 34 minutes and of the connectivity skeptic is 28 to 56 hours. Our technicians have adopted two strategies: one is to come back the next day and the other is to reboot a switch. Unfortunately the technician may have to go to another floor to get to the necessary switch. There should be a more convenient mechanism that a technician could use to instruct the network that a link repair has been attempted.

Acknowledgements

Autonet was designed and built by Andrew Birrell, Michael Burrows, Butler Lampson, Hal Murray, Roger Needham, Tom Rodeheffer, Ed Satterthwaite, Michael Schroeder and Charles Thacker.

11.7 References

Awerbuch, B. (1991), Private Communication.

Awerbuch, B., Cidon, I., Gopal, I., Kaplan, M. and Kutten, S. (1990), Distributed control for PARIS, *Proceedings of the Ninth ACM Annual Symposium on Principles of Distributed Computing*, Dwork, C., ed., Québec City, Québec, 145–159.

Awerbuch, B. and Gallager, R. G. (1987), A New Distributed Algorithm to Find Breadth-First Search Trees, *IEEE Transactions on Information Theory* **33(3)**, 315–322.

Comer, D. and Narten, T. (1988), UNIX Systems as Cypress Implets, *USENIX 88 Winter Conference*, 55–62.

Dijkstra, E. W. and Scholten, C. S. (1980), Termination Detection for Diffusing Computations, *Information Processing Letters* **11(1)**, 1–4.

Gallager, R. G. (1982), Distributed Minimum Hop Algorithms, Massachusetts Institute of Technology, Technical Report LIDS-P-1175, Cambridge, MA.

Heart, F. E., Kahn, R. E., Ornstein, S. M., Crowther, W. R. and Walden, D. C. (1970), The interface message processor for the ARPA computer network, *AFIPS 1970 Spring Joint Computer Conference*, 551–567.

Jacobsen, V. (1988), Congestion Avoidance and Control, *ACM SIGCOMM Communications Architectures and Protocols*, 314–329.

Lin, T. Y. and Siewiorek, D. P. (1990), Error log analysis: Statistical modeling and heuristic trend analysis, *IEEE Transactions on Reliability* **39(4)**, 419–432.

McQuillan, J. M., Richer, I. and Rosen, E. C. (1980), The New Routing Algorithm for the ARPANET, *IEEE Transactions on Communication* **COM-28**, 711–719.

McQuillan, J. M. and Walden, D. C. (1977), The ARPA Network Design Decisions, *Computer Networks* **1**, 243–289.

Mills, D. L. (1984), Exterior gateway protocol formal specification, Network Information Center, Request for Comments 904, Menlo Park, CA.

Perlman, R. (1985), An Algorithm for Distributed Computation of a Spanning Tree, *Proceedings of the Ninth Data Communications Symposium*, ACM, 44–53.

Saltzer, J. H., Reed, D. P. and Clark, D. D. (1984), End-to-End Arguments in System Design, *ACM Transactions on Computer Systems* **2**, 277–278.

Schroeder, M. D., Birrell, A. D., Burrows, M., Murray, H., Needham, R. M., Rodeheffer, T. L., Satterthwaite, E. H. and Thacker, C. P. (1990), Autonet: A High-speed, Self-configuring Local Area Network Using Point-to-point Links, Digital Systems Research Center, Research Report 59, Palo Alto, CA, Also available in *IEEE Journal on Selected Areas in Communications*, **9**(8), October 1991, pp. 1318–1335.

Turner, J. S. (1986), New directions in communications (or which way to the information age?), *IEEE Communications Magazine* **24**(10), 8–15.

Wulf, W. A., Levin, R. and Harbison, S. P. (1981), *Hydra/C.mmp: An Experimental Computer System*, McGraw-Hill, NYC.

Chapter 12

Names

Roger M. Needham

What's special about naming in distributed systems? If you read Saltzer [1979] on naming and binding there doesn't seem to be very much that depends on the system being centralized, and there doesn't seem to be very much either that needs adding to that excellent exposition. The material that has to be stored to do with naming is of course not all in the same place in a distributed context, but there is a separate subject called distributed database and, on the face of it, that handles all we need to do. In fact, it is worth talking about naming in distributed systems, because it isn't really that simple.

12.1 Naming in General

Names have several purposes in computer systems. One is to facilitate sharing. If various computations want to act upon the same object, they are enabled to do so by each containing a name for the object. When such a name comes to be resolved, so that the shared object may be used, it has to be arranged that the names themselves and the contexts used to resolve them all give the same result. It is not at all necessary that the same name be used in all instances, though it will often turn out that way. This is because names are frequently used for communication about objects; if they are to achieve this correctly then they must either be valid in a universal context, or they must be accompanied by a representation of the context in which they are to be resolved, or it must be certain that the context will turn out to be identical wherever the names are to be resolved. The fact that names are used to refer to objects does not mean that names are bound whenever they are found. It is a perfectly legitimate use of names to arrange that several computations will, when executed, share an object, although we do not yet know which object that is. One must distinguish here between the use of names which have been bound to an object of as yet unknown value — typically a container which will at the appropriate time have some bits put in it — and names which have not been bound at all.

Another use of names is exemplified by unique identifiers, which are usually particular members of some large set, such as the integers up to $2^{128} - 1$. It is arranged that names of this form are never reused, so that a particular 128 bit pattern refers either to nothing or, if it refers to anything, to the same thing at all times. In practice, such names are never found unbound, and their function is largely to provide location independence. If we wish to have the flexibility to move the representation of an object from one place to another and still have it satisfactorily shared between computations, the names used by these computations must be, or resolve into, a form of name that is location independent and which can itself be resolved to find the current physical location information. Names of this form are sometimes used for a security-related purpose. If the proportion of possible names in a name space that actually refer to objects is sufficiently small, and if there is no general way of predicting which names will be used, then the names may be used as tickets of permission to access the objects. A computation that presents a valid name may be assumed to have been given it deliberately rather than to have guessed or invented it. This is an example of the use of protected names or capabilities, one of the classical approaches to access control management.

The last paragraph has implicitly referred to another distinction relevant to names. This is between human-sensible names such as

    rmn/animals/pig

and names intended for internal use only such as

    #257A 9B3F CD45 B1C8.

This distinction is often made, and it is not a particularly helpful one (except, of course, if you have to remember the names or type them in). A more serious distinction is between pure names and other names. A pure name is nothing but a bit-pattern that is an identifier, and is only useful for comparing for identity with other such bit-patterns — which includes looking up in tables in order to find other information. The intended contrast is with names which yield information by examination of the names themselves, whether by reading the text of the names or otherwise. For example, a human-sensible name like rmn/animals/pig may, in a suitable context, be interpretable to say that if it is a valid name at all, there is a directory called rmn and it contains an entry for a sub-directory called animals. Something that is less obviously penetrable like #257A 9B3F CD45 B1C8 may, if it is the unique identifier of a file from the Cambridge File Server (Needham and Herbert [1982]), be known to contain the identity of the disc pack on which the file resides.

Such impure names all carry commitments of one sort or another which have to be honoured if the names are to retain their validity. Looking at the previous examples, the former commits one to having, among other things, a directory called rmn, and the latter commits one not to move the file from one disc pack to another. Pure names are very attractive because they commit one to nothing. Of course, like most good things in computer science, pure names help by putting in a extra stage of indirection; but they are not much use for anything else.

12.2 Naming in Distributed Systems

What's different about distributed systems? That they are not centralized. If, in a system, there is anywhere that has global information about all instances of anything, then it isn't a real distributed system but a centralized one made of funny components. This rather gross statement has to be interpreted; we should really have said 'anywhere that *necessarily has to have* global information,' otherwise one could stop a system being distributed by storing a list of its components on a disc somewhere. We also have to be careful in principle about the definition of 'having global information'. In some distributed systems, one may approach any instance of a service to perform a task the correct execution of which requires that information from in a general way anywhere must be used. We do not deny that Grapevine (Birrell *et al.* [1982]), in which one may send a message anywhere from any message server, is distributed on these grounds. To pursue this point further would take us out of technology and into philosophy.

We must first consider some characteristics and consequences of distribution.

12.2.1 Bindings

A first and obvious consequence of distribution is that there is, in some sense, more naming because there is more binding. By this I mean that, by comparison with centralized systems, there is more that can change — consider

- binding machines to addresses
- binding services to machines

neither of which has a very obvious analogue in a centralized system. It is the conventional wisdom of distributed computing that in any cases of this sort early binding is extremely wicked, and every opportunity must be taken to allow for variability. To describe a system designer as the kind of person who would embed machine addresses in his code is considered to be not merely critical but downright offensive. In practice, the conventional wisdom is rarely followed as well as it should be, because of the practice of programmers of omitting code that they think they do not need. In order to preserve efficiency of operation it is necessary to cache bindings that are frequently required, and in many cases these bindings change very rarely indeed. The Cambridge File Servers had ring addresses 1B and 6C from their inception and retained these until they were abandoned. It is extremely likely that many programs which made use of them did not include reconsultation of the name server in their outermost retry loop, which, strictly speaking, they should have done. If someone had changed these numbers at three o'clock one morning, and updated the name server accordingly, it may confidently be expected that parts of the distributed world would have been found not to be working by nine. Clients of the file service would have behaved as if it were down. This in fact corresponds to behaviour in other aspects of life; if I call a friend on the telephone and get 'number unobtainable' I tend to assume that his phone is broken, not that he has moved. Eventually, though, I shall call enquiries just in case.

12.2.2   Interpreting Names

As was made clear in an earlier section, the purpose of names is to identify values, usually by being looked up in collections of names to yield the values from a table. In a distributed system complications arise. The lookup tables, or directories as they are often called, are frequently replicated for a variety of reasons including system robustness and, often more importantly, ease of access in the sense of being able to find an instance of desired material geographically close by. Replication, however, has its own complexities to do with distribution of updates. (Phone books are an everyday example of replication for easy access.) Also, given a name to look up, it is necessary to be able to find the directory to use, which may not be obvious. (Consider what it would be like to find a phone number for J. W. Tailcheck, 19 Gossamer Gardens, which is quite likely a unique identification — or to establish that such a person did not exist.)

This last point indicates why pure names are not much good in distributed systems, the point being that you don't know where to look them up, and pure names have to be looked up to be of any use at all. The nearest you can get to pure naming, in practice, is to accompany the name with a hint as to where abouts it may profitably be used; if the hint fails, global search may, in principle, be needed. How disastrous this is depends on the size of the network, how likely the need for such a search is, how good broadcast facilities there are, and how clever network components such as gateways are. The Amoeba system seeks to tackle this problem (Mullender *et al.* [1990]).

12.2.3   Consistency — Immediate

A common objective of distributed database technology is to arrange that when a request for the value associated with some name or definite description is put to some manifestation of a database, the reply, should one be forthcoming, will be correct in the sense that it reflects the most recent information that there is (anywhere). Systems that achieve goals of this type do so at a cost, incurring one or both of two penalties:

1. One can't do an update because insufficient of the places at which it must be made are accessible
2. One can't do a read because the material to be read isn't stable yet, or because insufficient replicates are accessible.

The bodies of data representing name lookup tables are sufficiently fundamental to practical distributed computing that it usually believed that there should be no compromise about accessibility. It is more important to get an answer than to be guaranteed to get the absolutely latest answer. It would not be considered tolerable for me to be unable to look up someone at MIT to find their mailbox because not all the replicates of the relevant directory in South America were known to be up to date. This attitude depends for its justification on a selection of assumptions, each of which is capable of discussion and argument:

1. Naming data doesn't change very fast, so inconsistencies will be rare
2. You will find that something doesn't work if you try to use obsolete naming data, so you can attend to it
3. Even if you don't find out, and use obsolete data, it doesn't matter much *sub specie æternitatis.*

The first assumption seems to be fairly true. A great bulk of the contents of a naming database concerns people, who do not change their names very often, who do not change their organisational affiliations on a daily basis, who do not change their passwords or their mailbox sites all that often. There is in fact not a great deal of solid evidence for this assumption; people who maintain naming databases have in general not kept many statistics. In the vicinity of Cambridge, UK, it seems that something like a quarter of the entries in the telephone book change each year, or, more precisely, that there are about 5000 changes a week to a database of about a million entries. However, it is easy to assume too much. The Grapevine Registration Servers started off in life as repositories for the information needed to translate between people's names and mailbox sites. They were also used for translating the names of distribution lists,[1] that is, for recording the contents of the lists. The assumption of slow change, at any rate, was not true for some of the distribution lists, and algorithmic changes needed to be made because of the resulting inconvenience. If a naming implementation has been designed on the assumption of low update traffic one must beware of adding applications which break the assumption.

The second assumption is fairly true too, with, interestingly, a cognate exception to the first. In many contexts the use of out-of-date naming data is self-detecting. You can't log in with a new password if the system at the other end only knows an old one for you, you can't connect to a service which is now on a different machine from where you thought it was, and you can't connect to a machine which is now at a different network address. If this property applied universally, a very attractive implementation technique comes at once to mind. Anyone may keep copies of parts (or the whole) of a naming database. Perhaps it is circulated on a CD-ROM from time to time. Certainly no attempt is made to propagate changes to it by pushing from the centre. Use of obsolete data will be detected, authority consulted, and the newer data cached for use until the next updated edition appears. The reader will recognize the technique adopted by the world's phone companies. The authority for consultation may logically be regarded as centralized though it would certainly have a distributed implementation; the point about it is that its implementation is orders of magnitude smaller than the naming database as a whole, and it may perfectly well be susceptible to standard methods of treatment such as quorum-consensus. Unfortunately, using an obsolete value of a list isn't that easily detected. It may only become apparent for reasons outside the system and after a long time. It certainly is not a basis for a visit to central authority and

---

[1]A distribution list contains a list of destinations for distributing information. Distribution lists are common in electronic-mail systems for distributing messages to a distributed group of subscribers.

the caching of a new value; distribution lists are, in a way, the Achilles' heel of the second assumption as well as of the first.

The third assumption is of a rather different status. If it is the case that, in almost all circumstances, changes to the naming data propagate very quickly to all stations, then one can argue that a use made of the data in place A at about the same time as it was being changed in place B has an essentially indeterminate result; as long as a half-changed state is never seen then all is as well as may reasonably be hoped for. After all, the user of the data might have asked for it a second or so sooner. Independent and unsynchronized activities are going to give indeterminate results and we should not futilely complain about this rather obvious fact. This may even be believed if propagation time is long. It is clearly deplorable for avoidable error to be made, but having people killed in battle in eighteenth century India because it was impossible for the British or French to tell the combatants instantly when they kissed and made up for a few years wasn't avoidable.

A point that is most naturally made in the context of consistency is that the issue may be fudged to some extent if what the naming system is used for is predominantly convergent. Grapevine is again our example, since its naming scheme was designed explicitly to support message delivery. The case in point is the translation from names to mailbox sites. If, because of the lack of propagation of an update in that system, a message is sent to the wrong message server, it is forwarded rather than rejected. Out-of-dateness is transformed from a correctness issue to a performance issue. Evidently, not every application can be expressed in a convergent way; it is not clear what characterizes the set of applications that can be so expressed. At any rate, there is here a prime example of making the substrate simpler by taking advantage of certain properties of an application.

Another consequence of the abandonment of transactional consistency for naming databases worth mentioning has to do with client blunders. If an attempt is made to look up an erroneous name, that is, something to which no entry corresponds, the answer should strictly be 'Either the name you have presented is wrong or it is as yet unknown to this instance of the service which is only guaranteed up-to-date to time t'. We are, once again, familiar with this topic from the world of the phone book. If I fail to find an entry for a company that I believe to have existed for some years, I shall look for an ad or a letterhead to check how they spell themselves rather than call enquiries and ask about new listings. I am not aware of any experience of this sort with computer name services.

12.2.4   Consistency — Long-Term

While there may be room for argument about how much effort should be devoted to obtaining very rapid consistency of an updated naming database, there is no room for argument about the desirability of avoiding long-term inconsistencies developing among what are supposed to be replicates of a single directory. This topic falls into two parts, one of which is germane to our present subject-matter and one of which is not. The latter, concerned with how one propagates updates among replicates of a naming database, whether it should be done by deterministic methods or by stochastic methods for example, is a fascinating subject in itself but cannot really be covered here. See Lampson [1986] and Demers and Sturgis [1987] for details of two very different approaches. The former part concerns the representation of values and updates in a naming database, and is directly relevant to us here.

A naming database is the aggregate effect of the changes or updates that were made to an initially empty state. In a centralized system, without replication and with all changes being entered at a common place, there is little conceptual difficulty in deciding what the database ought to contain at a particular time. One way of defining it would be as the result of taking a journal of all keystrokes at the origination site of the update and applying it to an empty state. In a distributed system things are not so straightforward for the reasons discussed in the last section, and no simple conceptual model like replaying journalized keystrokes will do. All the quirks and glitches that occurred in the network would have to be updated, which is not possible.

Updates are distributed by sending messages containing them to sites which are believed to be interested. The message delivery mechanism is never completely reliable, and it may have a deliberate element of randomness in its application. The result of this is that messages about differing or conflicting updates to the same value may arrive at a site in an arbitrary order, and it is essential that this does not affect the final result. We have to be a little careful about how we specify the desirable property since the most obvious way of doing it involves a counterfactual conditional:

> If the supply of updates stopped, then there would eventually be a glorious uniformity

where there is no reason to suppose that the supply would ever stop for long enough for the assertion to be tested. Attempts to deal with this are treated in some detail in Lampson's paper referenced above.

12.2.5 Scaling

In a centralized system there is usually some *a priori* idea about how large the set of names to be dealt with is liable to get. In many, if not in most, distributed systems this is not true, and it is good design to assume that it never is. Our image should rather be of an indefinite number of machines each providing some part of a name lookup service of indefinite size which is managed by a great number of more or less autonomous administrators. The whole business should never have to be subject to radical redesign simply because it has grown. The relevant topic here is the management of the name space rather than the avoidance of scale disasters in the implementation, and a prominent feature is the use of measures to avoid confusion resulting from accidental non-uniqueness of naming. Of course, it is easy enough to generate unique names as, for example, by prepending the time from a wall-clock to the serial number of the machine on which the name is being generated. Such names are not quite as useless as pure names are, because they do contain a reference to one machine, but we would not usually want to give the creating machine so special a status as would be implied by that approach, or to have to keep a machine in existence as long as all objects it had ever named. (There is a slightly arcane point here to do with trust. We could be trusting machines to use their own serial numbers rather than someone else's.)

The more customary way to control uniqueness is the use of hierarchy. Most reasonable suggestions for distributed naming make use of a hierarchic division of a name-space leading to the use of multi-part names reminiscent of (and thus to be carefully distinguished from) the familiar names for files in a garden variety operating system such as UNIX. If people are responsible for a small part of a hierarchic name-space they have no difficulty in maintaining uniqueness, which is only required within a directory. In real life the account just given is a little glib, and there is a buried issue that ought to be exposed. Early in these notes it was emphasized how many uses of naming there were in distributed systems. It has implicitly been assumed that these can and should all be catered to by the same naming structure and probably by a common naming mechanism. This is far from necessarily so, and the point warrants discussion.

That a certain machine is being prepared to offer a particular service by RPC, may very well be indicated by an entry in a name server relating the name of the service offered to the name or to the address of the offering machine. At some level, this is identical to the operation that relates the name of a user to his mailbox site, but, at another level, it is very different. One way of seeing this is to compare it with a different form of electronic mail, namely fax. It is, in principle, perfectly capable of integration into a workstation world, in which context I would have on my screen something like

John Evans, Nocturnal Aviation Ltd, Cambridge Science Park, 0223 234567 *

and would copy the appropriate number into the destination field. Assume that, in a very slight update of current fax practice, a digitally coded line is sent so that the whole line marked * appears at the destination machine-readably. It is reasonable to expect that a computer at the receiving end routes the material to Evans, or, if his screen won't produce it, prints it and tells him, or, if the matter isn't resolved, passes the decision as to what to do to a (human) clerk.

The foregoing is very like the way paper mail is dealt with in an organization such as the Computer Laboratory where I work, and is also very like the way Telex communications were handled in a place where I worked some years ago. It is very unsuitable, of course, for RPC binding and things like that, but is arguably more suitable for mail than the presently customary methods. Generality has its price, which is often much higher than one first thinks. In the present instance, the final name used — the phone number — is managed in a much flatter way than is usual with computer names, and is also administered in a much less intelligent manner, which is a good thing, since the less we rely on intelligence the better.

12.3   Examples

In conclusion, two examples are presented of approaches to naming, where rather different emphases occur.

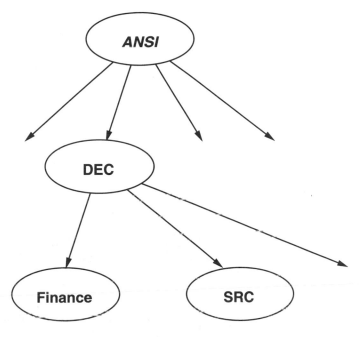

Figure 12.1.

12.3.1 The DEC Global Name Service

The following discussion is based on the system described in Lampson [1986], of which the author was one of the design group. Here we concern ourselves not with the mechanism for handling distribution but with the structure an interpretation of the naming system itself. Those of its goals relevant to the present discussion are:

- Long life, during which many changes will occur in the organization of the name space and the components that implement the service
- Large size, to handle an essentially arbitrary number of names and serve an arbitrary number of administrative organizations.

Hierarchy is used to manage name-creation and the user sees a multipart name looking much like a file-name in an ordinary operating systems such as UNIX. The purpose of the name service is to map names to values and values themselves may be structured. Suppose (and the examples are in the main taken from Lampson's paper) that there is a hierarchical directory structure rooted in a node called *ANSI*[2] and a substructure of values within a directory, as illustrated in Figure 12.1.

---

[2]The paper avoids the common American view that the US is the root of everything and does not itself need a name. This will be seen also in electronic mail systems, where there are domains such as UK, FR, and so on but not one called US. This has the odd consequence that UK domains have to be given different names from American ones, despite the apparent hierarchic structure. This is why US names for businesses begin COM and UK names for businesses begin CO.

Directories have unique identifiers known as DIs and the directory tree is stuck together by giving in a directory the DIs of its juniors; an arc labelled with a DI is a *directory reference* (DR). In this design there is a concept of *full name*, which has to be distinguished from a similar notion in filing systems. In a filing system we may consider a full name as starting from a well-known and unique *root*. A full path name will resolve correctly in any environment where the root is correct. In the present context a full name is any name starting with a DI. Such a name will resolve correctly wherever it is encountered; pedantically one might say that it will never resolve incorrectly, since inability to find the directory with the given DI will prevent resolution occurring at all. In the examples given above, the head node ANSI was put in italics to make a distinction which can now be appreciated: the string *ANSI* refers to the DI of the *ANSI* directory. If the DI of the directory *ANSI*/DEC/SRC is #783, then #783/Lampson is as good a full name as is *ANSI*/DEC/SRC/Lampson.

We may thus see that it is as if there were two trees among directories: one based on their text names as full names starting from a root such as ANSI, and another very flat one with a hypothetical super-root, which consists simply of a list of all the DIs.

Why should one go to all this complication? It is in order to be able to grow and combine pieces of name-space in response to organizational needs. There is no problem if a name service grows downwards and outwards from a fixed root; the manager of any directory may create entries in it for individuals or for new directories without having to engage in any outside consultation, and the best sort of full names will start with the local root. Suppose however that it is required to bring together under a common root the trees for DEC and IBM, wherein full names *DEC*/SRC/x or *IBM*/TJW/y. Notice first that these names will still work correctly, being full names the first component of which is a DI, provided that one can physically find the directory with the required DI. In order to get help with this, it is possible to place in the common root directory an entry of a different kind. Suppose the common root is *ANSI* = #999, *DEC* = #311, *IBM* = #552. We may then place in the ANSI directory translation entries for well-known directories such as DEC and IBM, of the form '#311 → #999/DEC,' and similarly '#552 → #999/IBM.' It will thus be possible to go to the new root ANSI with an old name DEC/SRC/x and have the correct result. The process is illustrated by Figure 12.2.

It should be emphasized that these devices are not required in order to maintain the correctness of the naming system. They are there to make it possible to use names in contexts where they would formerly not have worked because of the unavailability of a root directory, or perhaps one should say of the first directory in a full name.

Similar manœuvres can occur if the change is one of subsumption, for instance, if DEC buys IBM. Names of the form ANSI/IBM/X/Y will *prima facie* no longer work, because IBM is no longer an immediate child of ANSI. It is only necessary to insert in ANSI an entry of the form 'IBM → #999/DEC/IBM' and all will be well.

It is perhaps worth mentioning that it is not compulsory for a client of this naming service to utter nothing but full names. The standard helpful but confusing devices, familiar from filing systems, in which working directories, local roots, and

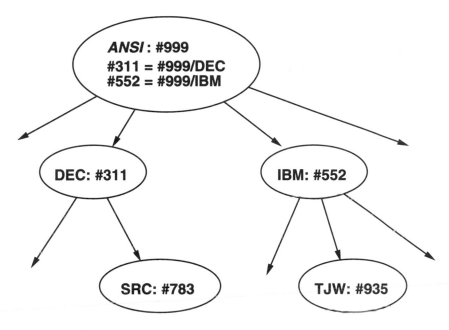

Figure 12.2.

what have you, are all available. They are nothing more than syntactic devices for prepending standard material to a quoted name; they have the effect of permitting a user to type less at the cost of having more hidden context, change to which may hamper correct name resolution in other places or at other times.

12.3.2   The Stanford Design

This approach (Cheriton and Mann [1989]), is characterized by a strong desire to avoid location problems having anything to do with the structure of a naming facility. They deal in objects managed by managers — to cause an operation to be performed on an object one sends a request to the manager and, subject to access controls and so on, the manager does the required work. An object's name determines its manager, and the primary task is to discover where physically the manager of a given object is. An object has a multi-part name with the same resemblance to a file name as in the system described earlier, but a name of that form is bound directly to the object; it is not bound to some internal name or unique identifier that is itself bound to the object (see the DIs in the last example). Indeed, the contrast goes further. Suppose there are names A/B/C, A/B/D, A/B/E, A/B/F, and so on. In the earlier system this would have presupposed the existence of a directory object A/B with a DI of its own, being a first-class member of the progeny of the hypothetical super-root. In the Stanford system there is no such implication. It may be, and indeed is, useful to be aware of clusters of names like the example, but there is no ontological commitment. An outline of the mechanisms follows.

It is assumed that there is a single root, and that any named object has an absolute name depending on that single root. The manager of any object will know the name of any object managed, and it is up to a client that depends upon an object to know where its manager is. It is envisaged that clients will typically have extensive caches of object names and their managers, and that if cache lookup fails, either because there is no entry or because no response is received from what is presumably an obsolete manager address then a new attempt is made by multicast (or even broadcast) to find a manager. Since it is certain that any attempt to have an object managed by an agency other than the manager will fail, there is no need to inform all clients which may have cached information about a manager's location that the manager has moved.

It is legitimate to record what Cheriton and Mann refer to as a context, and to use it as a hint in looking up a name. A context is the result of a partial lookup; for example to look up A/B/C/D we may look up C/D in the context provided by having antecedently looked up A/B. A context is rather a low-level notion, such as a process identifier and some numbers. It was said earlier that the existence of a number of objects of the form A/B/X/Y where X and Y vary does not presuppose that there is an object A/B which we should think of as a directory. The use of contexts does not violate this, because a context is just a hint. If on reference to a cache a client needing to interpret A/B/C/D finds a context for A/B, then it is quite legitimate for it to send to the appropriate place the context and C/D. If the operation does not succeed, then one multicasts with A/B/C/D.

As one would expect, there are arrangements for handling 'current contexts' which have no surprising properties.

12.3.3 Commentary

The two approaches outlined differ markedly. In the Stanford approach the path-name from the root is the only canonical name for an object, which makes for a level less of organization and some simplicity. A Stanford name as presented relative to a context may look very like a DEC name presented relative to a DI — they may even be bitwise identical, but the DI is the frozen truth and the context is just a hint. Accordingly, the Stanford design lacks the features which facilitate gross restructuring of the name-space by punning the use of DIs. These questions of gross readjustment are not yet the subject of reported experience.

This chapter has attempted to study naming in distributed systems as a function to be provided rather than to consider in detail how, in particular, replication is effected.

12.4   References

Birrell, A. D., Levin, R., Needham, R. M. and Schroeder, M. D. (1982), Grapevine: An Exercise in Distributed Computing, *Communications of the ACM* **25**, 260–274.

Cheriton, D. R. and Mann, T. P. (1989), Decentralizing a Global Naming Service for Efficient Fault-tolerant Access, *ACM Transactions on Computer Systems* **7(2)**, Also available as Stanford Report STAN-CS-86-1098.

Demers, A. and Sturgis, H. (1987), Epidemic Algorithms for replicated Database Maintenence, *Proceedings of the Sixth ACM Annual Symposium on Principles of Distributed Computing*.

Lampson, B. W. (1986), Designing a Global Name Service, *Proceedings of the Fifth ACM Annual Symposium on Principles of Distributed Computing*, Calgary, Canada, 1–10.

Mullender, S. J., van Rossum, G., Tanenbaum, A. S., van Renesse, R. and van Staveren, J. M. (1990), Amoeba — A Distributed Operating System for the 1990s, *IEEE Computer* **23(5)**.

Needham, R. M. and Herbert, A. J. (1982), *The Cambridge Distributed Computing System*, Addison-Wesley, Reading, MA.

Saltzer, J. H. (1979), Notes on Database Operating Systems, in *Operating Systems — An Advanced Course*, Bayer, R., Graham, R. M. and Seegmuller, G., eds., vol. **60**, Springer-Verlag, Lecture Notes in Computer Science.

Chapter 13

Transaction-Processing Techniques

William E. Weihl

Distributed systems are difficult to build in part because of failures: part of the system can fail while the rest keeps running. In addition, the concurrency in distributed systems can require complex synchronization to ensure correct behavior. The combination of concurrency with failures makes the problems even more difficult. In this chapter, we describe techniques that provide simple systematic solutions to the problems caused by failures and concurrency. The techniques are not a panacea — they impose restrictions that may be inappropriate for some applications — but in many cases they solve the problems simply and efficiently.

The techniques are based on what are called *atomic transactions*. Informally, an atomic transaction appears to occur indivisibly (with respect to failures and to other concurrent transactions). This means that the programmer can view an atomic transaction as a sequential program, even though it runs concurrently with other transactions and failures can occur while it is running.

We begin by describing in more detail the problems addressed by transactions. Then we explain more precisely what a transaction system is — i.e., we give a specification of the behavior allowed for a transaction system. The bulk of the chapter — Sections 13.3 through 13.8 — is devoted to a presentation of the key algorithms required to implement a transaction system. Following the description of these algorithms, we discuss extensions to the basic algorithms to support nested transactions. We conclude with a brief discussion, followed by a history of the area and a summary of papers and books on transaction-processing techniques.

13.1 Problems Addressed

Transactions help solve two kinds of problems. The first involves concurrency, and is illustrated by the following example. Consider a simple banking database in which each account includes a field with the current balance. Suppose that two people are both trying to deposit money to the same account simultaneously. The action of depositing money into an account is likely to be implemented by a long sequence of machine instructions that perform the following steps (among others):

1. Read the current balance in the account.
2. Compute the new balance.
3. Update the database to record the new balance.

If two of these actions run concurrently, both might execute step (1) before either executes step (3); the result will be that one of the updates is lost. Needless to say, this is bad for business. Some sort of synchronization is needed to prevent this kind of race condition from occurring.

The second kind of problem involves failures. Consider a simple replicated version of the database discussed above that stores a copy of each account on two sites. The action of depositing money must now be implemented so that it updates both copies of the account record. Suppose, however, that the system fails after only one of the copies has been updated. The system is now in an inconsistent state, and incorrect results could be obtained by later operations that examine only the copy that was not updated.

In general, failures are a problem whenever the actions in the system need to preserve an invariant that involves several data items, and where it is not directly possible to update all the data items atomically (i.e., where a failure in the middle could leave the system in a state in which some but not all of the data items have been updated). This kind of problem occurs in single-site systems, in which the typical atomic update is a single disk write, and in distributed systems, in which data items at different sites cannot be updated in a single atomic action.

13.2   What Are Transactions?

Transactions were developed to solve the kinds of problems illustrated in the previous section. Transactions have what are sometimes called the ACID properties: they are *Atomic, Consistent, Isolated,* and *Durable.* Consistency is a property of the specific functions performed by the individual transactions; the other properties are typically viewed as the responsibility of the underlying transaction-processing system, which isolates the application programmer from the details of synchronization and recovery. Consistency means that each transaction, when executed alone and to completion, preserves whatever invariants have been defined on the system state. In other words, the application programs for each transaction do not violate the consistency of the data.

Atomicity, sometimes called failure atomicity or recoverability, means that each transaction appears indivisible with respect to crashes. In other words, each transaction appears to occur either completely or not at all; partial effects cannot be seen. Transactions that complete successfully are said to *commit*; those that fail (and appear not to have happened at all) are said to *abort*. We will usually use the term *recoverability* for this property.

Isolation, sometimes called serializability or concurrency atomicity, means that transactions appear indivisible to each other: if a group of transactions is executed concurrently, the effect is the same as if they were executed sequentially in some order. We will usually use the term *serializability* for this property.

Durability, sometimes called permanence, means that the effects of committed transactions are very likely to survive subsequent failures. We cannot guarantee that they will survive all subsequent failures, since a catastrophic failure of all the data storage devices in the system would wipe out everything, including the effects of committed transactions.

The ACID properties are useful because they make it easier to think about complex systems. Rather than having to worry about all the ways in which concurrent transactions can interleave, or all the possible states that could result from a failure in the middle of some transaction, the programmer can view each transaction as a sequential program that always executes to completion. Another way of thinking about this is that the granularity of the atomic actions that the programmer must work with is no longer the individual machine instructions, but is instead the individual transactions. In fact, transactions *do* execute concurrently, and failures *can* occur in the middle of a transaction — *but* the programmer need not worry about this in trying to design his program or convince himself (or someone else) that it is correct.

For example, suppose that the system state has some invariants defined on it — e.g., an employee never makes more than his manager, or the net assets recorded for the bank equal the sum of all the account balances — and the programmer would like to be sure that these invariants are always true. Using transactions, it is enough to check that the initial state is consistent, and that each transaction, when run alone and to completion, preserves consistency.[1] Without transactions, one would need to do a similar check for every atomic action in the system — and each transaction might be composed of a very large number of atomic actions. Also, in the absence of transactions, the invariants could not be as simple as we have illustrated at the beginning of this paragraph. For example, it is not always the case that the net assets equal the sum of all the account balances, since any transaction that changes an account balance must also change the net assets, and these two updates can probably not be done in a single machine instruction. As a result, the invariant would need to be more complicated, stating that the net assets equal the sum of the accounts, except when some transaction has updated one and not the other, in which case some more complex relation holds.

In the remainder of this section, we give a more precise specification of the recoverability, serializability, and durability properties. We present the specification in two stages, first describing the desired behavior in the absence of concurrency, and then giving a specification that covers both concurrency and failures. The specifications are written in the style of Chapter 3: we give a set of state variables that models the abstract state of the system, and then describe a set of atomic actions that represents the allowable state transitions.

---

[1] By 'preserves consistency' we mean that if a transaction starts in a consistent system state, when it ends the state is again consistent. However, consistency can be violated in the middle of the transaction.

The type of client operations
TYPE Op = S → (S,V)
VAR
      Stable state; s0 is the initial state
   ss: S := s0
      Volatile state
   vs: S := s0
ACTIONS
   doOp(o:Op,v:V) ≡ (s,v)=o(vs) ⇒ vs := s
   commit ≡ ss := vs
   abort ≡ vs := ss
   fail ≡ vs := ss

Figure 13.1. Specification of sequential transactions

13.2.1 Sequential Specification

Our goal in this subsection is to specify the behavior of a sequential transaction system; failures are allowed, but concurrency is not. We assume that there is a single client that executes a sequence of transactions, each of which consists of a sequence of operations. When the client is done with all the operations in a transaction, it calls the *commit* operation. If the system fails while a transaction is active, the transaction aborts. The client can also ask for a transaction to be aborted.

In the specification, which is in Figure 13.1, we model the state of the system and the operations executed by transactions abstractly: each operation is just a function that takes a state and returns a new state and a result value.

The specification models the state of the system with two state variables, *ss* (for 'stable state') and *vs* (for 'volatile state'). While a transaction is running, any operations it requests are executed by updating the volatile state. When a transaction commits, the stable state is updated to whatever is currently recorded in the volatile state. If a transaction aborts or the system fails, the current volatile state is discarded and is replaced with whatever is in the stable state (which was updated the last time a transaction committed).

This specification captures the informal idea that each transaction appears to execute either to completion or not at all. If the client executes a *commit* action, then all the transaction's operations have been done and recorded in the volatile state, and the *commit* action installs them in the stable state. If a failure occurs, the partial effects recorded in the volatile state are discarded.

13.2.2 Concurrent Specification

In this subsection, we give a specification that covers serializability, recoverability, and durability. Recall that serializability means that the effect of executing a group of transactions concurrently is the same as executing them sequentially in some order. In fact, one usually wants an additional constraint, which is called *external consistency*: the apparent serial order must respect the real-time order of transactions, in the sense that if one transaction finishes before another starts, the second must not occur before the first in the apparent serial order.

Our specification captures the serializability and external consistency constraints by requiring there to be a total order of the committed transactions with two properties:

- Doing the operations of the committed transactions in the total order would yield the same result from each operation as actually obtained.
- The total order is consistent with the real-time order: if t_1 committed before t_2 started, then t_1 comes before t_2 in the total order.

The recoverability constraint is captured by considering only the committed transactions in the first property above: there must be a way of explaining what the committed transactions did without considering aborted and active transactions; i.e., aborted and active transactions have no apparent effect on the committed transactions. The durability constraint is captured because the total order includes all committed transactions, even if there have been failures since they committed.

The specification is shown in Figure 13.2. As with the previous specification, we treat the client operations abstractly.

In this specification, however, we go a step further; rather than recording the new state resulting from each operation, we simply record the history of operations executed by each transaction together with the result values returned for each operation. To distinguish between operations executed by different concurrent transactions, we introduce identifiers for transactions; these identifiers are assigned when transactions are started, and are not reused.

The specifications of the *abort* and *fail* actions are simple: they just mark the affected transactions as aborted (by moving them from the set *active* to the set *aborted*). The *doOp* action is also (deceptively) simple: it just records the operation done by the transaction with its result value. (Notice that this means that any result can be returned; we discuss this issue further below.) The real content of the specification is embedded in the *commit* action.

The specification of the *commit* action formalizes the two properties discussed above. A transaction is allowed to commit only if doing so would maintain the invariant that the committed transactions are serializable in an externally consistent order. If this invariant is maintained, the *commit* action simply marks the transaction as committed by moving it from *active* to *committed*. The invariant is checked by the predicate *serializable(t)*, which checks that there is a total order on the committed transactions plus t that is consistent with *rto* and such that doing the operations recorded for those transactions in the given total order starting in the initial state yields the same results as were obtained in *doOp*.

Notice that the specification places no constraints on the results of operations executed by uncommitted (active or aborted) transactions. Operationally, this means that an active transaction will be unable to commit if one of its operations returns a result that is not consistent with some ordering of it and the committed transactions. Worse yet, it means that the programmer must be prepared for arbitrary results to be returned by operations while a transaction is running.

TYPE
>   *The type of transaction identifiers*
> Tid
>   *The type of client operations*
> Op = S → (S,V)
>   *Events recorded for transactions*
> Event = {op:Op,v:V}

VAR
>   *Operations executed by transactions, together with their result values*
> ops: Tid → SEQ[Event] := {*→ ∅}
>   *Sets of transaction ids that have been used at all,*
>   *have committed, have aborted, or are still active*
> used: SET[Tid] := ∅
> committed: SET[Tid] := ∅
> aborted: SET[Tid] := ∅
> active: SET[Tid] := ∅
>   *Real-time order on transactions; rto(t1,t2) is true if*
>   *and only if t1 commits before t2 starts*
> rto: (Tid,Tid) → Bool := {*→false}

ACTIONS
>   *Choose an unused id and make it active*
> beginT(t:Tid) ≡ t ∉ used
>> ⇒ used := used ∪ {t}; active := active ∪ {t};
>>> for all t′ ∈ committed, rto(t′,t) := true
>
>   *DoOp simply records the operation and the result; the actual*
>   *check that the result is reasonable happens in Commit*
> doOp(t:Tid,o:Op,v:V) ≡ t ∈ active ⇒ ops(t) := concat(ops(t),{op:=o,v:=v})
>   *Commit can occur only if the transaction is active and the committed*
>   *transactions would still be serializable if it committed*
> commit(t:Tid) ≡ t∈ active ∧ serializable(t)
>> ⇒ committed := committed ∪ {t}; active := active − {t}
>
>   *Just mark it aborted*
> abort(t:Tid) ≡ t∈ active
>> ⇒ aborted := aborted ∪ {t}; active := active − {t}
>
>   *Abort all active transactions*
> fail ≡ for all t∈ active,
>> aborted := aborted ∪ {t}; active := active − {t}

Figure 13.2. Specification of concurrent transactions (Part I)

It might seem that returning arbitrary results to operations is okay, since transactions that receive arbitrary results will not be allowed to commit, so they will have no apparent effect on the state of the system. In practice, however, this is not satisfactory, since programs that receive arbitrary (and unexpected) results may crash, loop, wipe out the file system, dispense all the cash in the cash machine, or

Where serializable(t) *is the following predicate:*
  serializable(t) ≡ ∃ a total order T on committed∪{t}
    such that consistent(T,rto)
      ∧ valid(flatten(ops,T,committed∪{t}),s0)
And consistent, flatten, *and* valid *are the following functions:*
  consistent(T,rto) → Bool ≡
    ∀ t,t':Tid, rto(t,t') ⇒ t is before t' in T
  flatten(ops,T,tidSet) → SEQ[Event] ≡
    if tidSet = ∅ then ∅
      else append(ops(t),flatten(ops,T,tidSet−{t})),
        where t is the first Tid in tidSet according to T
  valid(events:SEQ[Event],s:S) → Bool ≡
    if events = ∅ then true
      else ∃ s':S such that first(events).op(s) = (s',first(events).v)
        ∧ valid(tail(events),s')

Figure 13.2(cont.). Specification of concurrent transactions (Part II).

otherwise behave badly in a way that affects the world outside the scope of the
transaction system. In practice, most transaction systems do *not* return arbitrary
results to active transactions; rather, the results are computed in a natural and
reasonable way from the current state of the system based on what the committed
transactions have done. We do not state constraints on the active transactions in
the specification, however, because it is difficult to do so in a way that encompasses
all (or even most) reasonable implementations. For example, some systems (e.g.,
those using two-phase locking — see Section 13.3) guarantee that the results seen
by active transactions are such that any given transaction can always commit without violating the invariant; others (using 'optimistic' concurrency control methods
— see Section 13.6) return results based on the committed transactions, but those
results may be invalidated when some other transaction commits.

Notice that our specification also does not constrain when an *abort* action can
happen. A transaction might be aborted because the client program requests it,
or because the transaction system decides to abort it (e.g., it has held locks too
long, or is deadlocked). It is difficult to specify in a general way the reasons
why a transaction might be aborted; different concurrency control methods abort
transactions for different reasons.

13.3   Concurrency Control

In the next few sections, we discuss the algorithms that can be used to implement
the specification given in the previous section. We begin in this section by describing *two-phase locking*, which is the most common synchronization method used in
transaction-processing systems. We focus here on a single-site system. In subsequent sections we describe recovery techniques and other concurrency control
methods, as well as the complications introduced by distributed systems.

Two-phase locking ensures that a transaction can always commit without violating the serializability invariant on committed transactions. This is done by acquiring locks on data so that the operations of different active transactions commute, and performing an operation in a state reflecting the effects of all the operations of committed and active (but not aborted) transactions. Thus, when a transaction commits, we can always serialize it after all the other committed transactions, since we can commute its operations over those of any other active transaction. This means that the serialization order is the commit order.

The locks must be associated with the data so that if two operations do not commute, they require conflicting locks. To be concrete, if the operations are reads and writes, we can use read/write locks, with the usual rule that read locks do not conflict with each other, but a write lock conflicts with both read locks and write locks. In other words, readers can run concurrently, but only one transaction can write a data item at a time, and while it is writing no other transaction can read. This works because reads commute with each other.

The term 'two-phase locking' is used because each transaction is required to consist of two phases. In the first phase, a transaction acquires locks, and in the second phase, a transaction releases locks. Thus, once a transaction has released any lock, it cannot acquire any more locks. In addition, when a transaction executes an operation, the locks it holds must be strong enough to ensure that the operation commutes with all operations executed by other active transactions.

In most systems that use two-phase locking, the locks acquired by a transaction are held until it commits or aborts; this is called *strict two-phase locking*. There are two reasons for holding locks until the end of a transaction. First, if the locks needed by the transaction are data-dependent, it may be impossible to tell when the first phase is over; only when the transaction finishes its last operation is it clear that no more locks are required. Thus, if locks were released before the end, the two-phase property would be violated. Second, if locks were released early, the data modified by a transaction could be seen by another transaction; if the first transaction aborted, the second would also have to be aborted (a process known as *cascading aborts*). If the second transaction finished first, it would also have to delay its commit until the first transaction committed. Some systems allow cascading aborts, but it can be expensive (and complicated) to keep track of the dependencies between transactions needed to cascade aborts, and the benefits of allowing cascading aborts are typically small.

One of the major drawbacks of two-phase locking is that there can be deadlocks. As always, there are three possible solutions: prevention, avoidance, and detection. Prevention involves ordering the locks, and requiring each transaction to acquire its locks in the specified order. This prevents a cycle of transactions, each waiting on the next, from forming. However, it may force some transactions to hold some locks longer than is required just by the two-phase locking rules; in some systems this can reduce concurrency sufficiently to cause performance problems. In addition, ordering locks does not work well when the locks needed are data-dependent, unless there is a natural order to the data being accessed (e.g., the data is structured as an acyclic graph).

Avoidance involves aborting transactions when they might be involved in a deadlock. For example, a simple timeout can be used to limit how long a transaction can wait for a lock; if there is a deadlock, the timeout will expire, and at least one of the transactions involved in the deadlock will be aborted. Alternatively, an ordering can be placed on the transactions, and a transaction allowed to wait for a lock only if it is held by a transaction that is earlier in the ordering. As with prevention methods, this prevents a cycle from forming. Avoidance techniques are simple to implement; however, they have the problem that they may abort transactions even when there is no deadlock.

Detection involves keeping track of the 'waits for' relationship among transactions, and looking for cycles of transactions, each waiting for the next in the cycle; a deadlock exists if and only if such a cycle exists. When a cycle is found, one or more of the transactions in the cycle is aborted to break the deadlock. Detection has the advantage that it aborts transactions only when there really is a deadlock. It has the disadvantage that it can be expensive, particularly in distributed systems in which the information needed to construct the 'waits for' relation is spread over multiple sites.

Read/write locks are simple, but the level of concurrency permitted by them may be too low in some cases. Some applications have 'hot spots' — data items that are updated by most or all transactions — and read/write locking reduces to exclusive locking for such data items. If more is known about the semantics of the operations on the data items, more concurrency can be allowed. For example, if the operations involve incrementing and decrementing a counter, the locks for them need not conflict, because increments and decrements commute. However, a more sophisticated recovery system is required for concurrent transactions to be able to update the same data item. This is discussed in more detail in Section 13.4.4.

13.4 Single-site Recovery

We now turn our attention to recovery; for now, we consider only a single site. As with any fault-tolerant system, we need a clear idea of the kinds of failures we wish to tolerate before we can discuss how to recover from them. We begin by characterizing the failures, and then discuss how to recover from each kind.

A typical transaction-processing system has a structure similar to that shown in Figure 13.3. Memory is divided into 3 classes: main memory (also called volatile memory), nonvolatile storage (e.g., disk), and stable storage (e.g., mirrored disks). We consider the following four kinds of failures:

- *Transaction abort*, in which the operations performed by a transaction need to be undone. (This is typically not caused by a hardware failure, but may be caused by a 'failure' of synchronization that leads to a deadlock, or may be requested by the client.)
- *System crash*, in which the main memory and active processes of the system are lost, but the nonvolatile storage and stable storage remain intact.
- *Media failure*, in which some or all of the nonvolatile storage is lost.
- *Catastrophe*, in which the stable and nonvolatile storage are both lost.

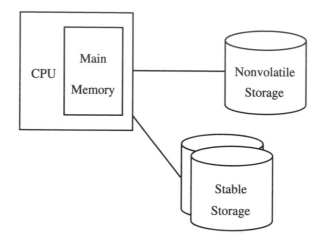

Figure 13.3. Transaction-processing system structure

In the sections below, we discuss how to recover from each of these kinds of failures. We do not discuss catastrophes, from which we cannot recover (as their name suggests). We ignore concurrency while presenting the recovery techniques; at the end we discuss how they interact with concurrency.

13.4.1   Abort Recovery

In this section we discuss how to recover from aborts. We assume that other failures do not occur. Note: we will typically use the term 'database' to refer to the system state; this should not be construed as implying that databases are the only applications that can use transactions.

There are two basic methods that can be used to recover from transaction aborts: *update-in-place* and *deferred-update*. Update-in-place involves updating the database as a transaction runs and undoing the updates if the transaction aborts; deferred-update involves saving a transaction's updates while it runs, and using the saved updates to update the database when the transaction commits.

To be more precise, there are four kinds of actions that might be performed by a transaction: updates (that read and modify the database), reads (that only read the database), commits, and aborts. (We consider reads and updates separately because implementations typically treat them quite differently.) For update-in-place, these actions are implemented as follows:

- *Update*: Record an undo record (e.g., the old value of the item being updated) in an undo log, and update the database.
- *Read*: Simply read the desired data from the database.
- *Commit*: Discard the transaction's undo log.
- *Abort*: Use the undo records in the transaction's undo log to back out the transaction's updates, by backing out the operations in the reverse of the order in which they were originally done.

For deferred-update, the actions are implemented slightly differently:

- *Update*: Record a redo record (e.g., the new value of the item being updated) in a redo log (also called an *intentions list*).
- *Read*: Combine the redo log and the database to determine the desired data.
- *Commit*: Update the database by applying the redo log in order (starting with the first operation done by the transaction).
- *Abort*: Discard the transaction's redo log.

To read data using deferred-update, one needs to use the redo log as well as the database because an earlier update by the same transaction might have modified the data item being read.

Update-in-place is the most commonly used method, largely for performance reasons. If we compare the costs of the various actions under the two schemes, we find that read and commit are cheaper under update-in-place than under deferred-update, while abort is cheaper under deferred-update than under update-in-place. In most database systems, read operations are much more common than update operations, so optimizing their performance is a good idea. In addition, one hopes that commits are much more common than aborts (since aborted transactions represent wasted work), so optimizing the performance of commits is better than optimizing the performance of aborts. However, there might be other reasons for choosing deferred-update instead of update-in-place. For example, these two recovery methods place slightly different constraints on concurrency control (see Weihl [1993]), and for a particular application deferred-update might permit more useful concurrency than update-in-place.

13.4.2 Crash Recovery

In this section we describe how a transaction-processing system can recover from system crashes. Recall the system structure described in Figure 13.3. Typically, the primary copy of the database is stored on nonvolatile storage, and some of it is cached in main memory (similar to virtual memory). The stable storage is used to store recovery information for recovering from media failure.

The first problem we need to solve is that the only atomic actions supported by a disk are to read and write a single disk block, but a single transaction might update data stored in many different blocks. Somehow we need to make the entire transaction appear atomic. The typical mechanism for accomplishing this is a *log*. Updates are recorded in entries in the log, as are transaction commits and aborts. After a crash, the commit and abort records can be used to tell which updates belong on disk and which do not. Of course, there are some subtleties involved in recovering from a crash; we discuss these shortly.

The second problem we need to solve is to make efficient use of the storage devices. Main memory is typically much faster than disk. However, some of the delays involved in writing to disk can be masked by doing the writes asynchronously, in part because then the application does not wait for them to complete, and in part because it may be possible to accumulate several updates to a single block before writing the block to disk. In addition, sequential writes to disk of large blocks are much faster than random writes of small blocks. Thus, it is important to avoid synchronous writes to disk, and to make most of the writes large and sequential.

There are many different recovery strategies in use in systems today. We describe one that is both simple and efficient. It is based on the method used in the ARIES system (Mohan *et al.* [1992]).

As mentioned above, the strategy is based on recording recovery data in a sequential log. The log is kept on disk along with the database. (For performance, the log and the database will be on separate disks to avoid contention.) The log is written to disk asynchronously; recently written records are buffered in main memory. Records include update records, which contain both undo and redo information, and transaction status records, which record the commits and aborts of transactions.

Transaction aborts are handled using update-in-place. In addition, records are written to the log as each operation is undone during the abort of a transaction to record the change to the state of the database that was performed to undo the operation. These records are called *compensation log records* in ARIES.

After a crash, we treat any transaction that does not have a commit record in the log on disk as aborted. Thus, when a transaction commits, we need to make sure that its commit record is in the log on disk. This is done by appending a commit record for the transaction to the log buffer and then *forcing* the log — i.e., writing the buffered log records to disk. (In fact, the commit does not really happen until the commit record reaches disk, and the transaction system should not acknowledge the commit request to the application until after this point.) The requirement that the log be forced when a transaction commits is sometimes called the *redo rule*.

The log forces can be a bottleneck that limits the throughput of the system (in transactions per second). This problem can be alleviated using 'group commit': when a transaction requests to commit, the system appends a commit record to the log buffer and then waits a short while; if the load on the system is high, other transactions are likely to request to commit soon, so several commits can be accomplished with a single log force. (Ideally, the system would wait only until the head of the log on disk is coming under the read/write head, and then write out whatever is in the log buffer at that point.) In addition, the bandwidth of the log can be increased by spreading it over multiple disks, either by striping or by partitioning.

The log is used to repair the disk copy of the database after a crash. Recall that the database is cached in primary memory. After a crash, the disk copy may be incorrect: some blocks may have uncommitted data, and others may be missing committed updates. The undo records in the log for active and aborted transactions are used to undo the uncommitted updates, and the redo records for the committed transactions are used to install the missing committed updates.

Some synchronization is needed between writing cached disk blocks back to disk and writing buffered log records to disk. In the absence of any synchronization, we could end up with uncommitted data on disk without the appropriate undo records in the log to be able to undo it. For example, suppose a transaction updates a disk block in the cache, recording an update record in the log buffer. If the disk block is written back to disk, and a crash happens before the log buffer is written to disk, we cannot reconstruct the committed value of the disk block.

To ensure that uncommitted updates can be undone, we impose the following constraint, known as the *write-ahead log rule* or *undo rule*: before an update to a disk block is written to disk, an undo record for that update must be recorded in the log on disk. This, combined with the rule that the log must be forced as part of committing a transaction, allows us to recover after a crash.

The crash recovery process is relatively simple. The first step, the *redo phase*, is to redo all the updates in the log — including the updates that were done to undo operations of aborted transactions. The second step, the *undo phase*, is to abort all transactions that have no commit or abort record in the log, using the standard abort mechanism. Once the abort record for a transaction is in the log on disk, disk blocks updated as part of the abort process for the transaction can be written back to disk asynchronously (as with any other dirty block). If another crash happens before such a block is written back, its state is recovered during the redo phase of recovery using the compensation log records written during the abort.

The crash recovery process outlined above relies on one important constraint: redo must be restartable. If a crash occurs during the redo phase of crash recovery, the same recovery process must work. For this to work, the redo part of the log must be what is sometimes called *idempotent*: if we start with some disk state and redo part of the log, and then redo the same part again, we must get the same result as redoing it once. From this it follows that we can redo any prefix of the log, followed by any other prefix, and so on, and as long as we end with the entire log, the effect will be the same as if we redid the entire log once.

If all the updates in redo records are simple writes (i.e., the new values to be recorded for some disk locations), we automatically get log idempotence. If some of the updates are not simple writes (e.g., an operation to be run to compute the new state, such as 'increment a field by 10'), then we can get log idempotence by recording a log sequence number (LSN) in each disk block. When a transaction updates a disk block, it updates the LSN in the block to the LSN of the log record with the redo information for the operation. During recovery, the LSN can be used to determine whether a given log record needs to be redone: if the LSN of the log record is less than or equal to the LSN on the block that it affects, then the block already reflects the update and it does not need to be redone. The LSNs also allow us to avoid doing some unnecessary work during recovery: if an update does not need to be redone, we do not have to update the page again or write it back later.

Notice that the only constraints we have imposed on when blocks must be written to disk are the redo rule and the write-ahead log rule. A synchronous write is required at commit to ensure the durability property of transactions. The write-ahead log rule constrains when blocks in the cache can be written back to disk (by delaying the writes until certain log records are on disk), but otherwise the cache manager is free to write blocks back however it pleases. This gives the cache manager considerable freedom to choose a good order for the writes that optimizes the use of the disk. For example, one good strategy is to sweep back and forth across the disk slowly, writing out dirty blocks from each successive cylinder. This reduces the cost of disk seeks, and also allows each block to accumulate several updates before being written back.

There is one problem hiding in the presentation above that we still need to solve. As described so far, the log grows forever, which means that the time for crash recovery (or at least the redo phase) grows as the system keeps running. We need a mechanism for reclaiming storage used for log records, since the actual storage is finite, and we would like to reduce the time required for crash recovery. A record in the log can be discarded if either the transaction involved is committed and the disk block involved has been updated on disk since the log record was written (so the redo information is no longer needed) or the transaction is aborted and a compensation log record is in the log for the update (so the undo information in the update record is no longer needed).

The typical approach is to discard a prefix of the log, using a mechanism called a *checkpoint*. Periodically, the system stops all activity and appends a *checkpoint record* to the log containing a list of the active transactions and the dirty pages in the cache. The checkpoint record also contains the LSN of the first log record for each active transaction, and the LSN when each dirty block was first updated since it was last fetched from or written back to disk. (The LSNs for the blocks can be maintained easily by the cache manager.) After a crash, the latest checkpoint record can be used to find the point in the log where the redo phase must begin. (Any records before the minimum LSN recorded for a block are unnecessary for redo.) In addition, any records in the log before the minimum LSN recorded for an active transaction are unnecessary for undo. Thus, all records before the minimum of all the LSNs in the checkpoint record are no longer needed, and the prefix of the log before that point can be discarded and the space reclaimed.

The write-ahead-log rule can be implemented in the cache manager by recording, for each block, the LSN of the latest log record containing an update for that block. Before writing a dirty block back to disk, the cache manager must ensure that the latest log record for it is on disk. If the log record is still buffered in main memory, the cache manager could force the log, or it could just wait a while for the log buffer to be written out. Waiting will work for most blocks, but for hot spots it may be necessary periodically to force the log and then write the block back.

13.4.3   Recovery from Media Failure

The final kind of failure we consider involves a failure of nonvolatile storage: some data on the disk is lost, either by being corrupted during a crash, or by random decay, or by a permanent failure such as a head crash. When this happens, we need another copy of the data. We get it from stable storage, which is typically implemented to be very unlikely to fail (e.g., mirrored disks, or copies at different locations on a network). As mentioned earlier, the probability of a catastrophe can be reduced by keeping more copies or working harder to make the failures of the copies independent, but catastrophes cannot be completely eliminated. The likelihood of a catastrophe depends on how much one is willing to pay to avoid them, both in hardware cost (for the storage of multiple copies) and in runtime cost (for writing more copies or more distant copies).

The data stored on stable storage consists of an archive copy of the database, together with an archive log. The archive log contains redo information only;

records in it for uncommitted transactions are ignored. If the disk copy of the database fails, it can be recovered by installing the archive copy, and then redoing the updates in the archive log for the committed transactions. If only a part of the disk fails, it is not necessary to rebuild the entire database from the archive copy; only the failed part needs to be reconstructed.

Getting a consistent archive copy is difficult, since doing so involves stopping all transactions while the archive copy is recorded. However, it is possible to use a technique known as a 'fuzzy dump', in which the archive copy is recorded asynchronously while normal transaction activity continues.

13.4.4   Discussion

So far we have presented recovery and concurrency control independently. In fact, they interact, and the choice of a recovery method may influence how much concurrency can be allowed. One way of thinking about the interactions for two-phase locking is that the lock obtained for an update must be strong enough to allow the recovery operations for the update. In other words, the recovery operations must also commute with the updates (and the recovery operations) of other active transactions. If the recovery method involves update-in-place, then the undo operation must commute with the operations of other active transactions; if the recovery method involves deferred-update, then the redo operation must commute.

For example, suppose that the undo and redo information in a log record for an update is just the old and new values for the locations updated by the update operation. Installing the old value does not commute with any other operation, so the undo operation for this update requires an exclusive lock on the locations of the database that will be updated if the old value is restored. Another way of thinking about this is that the granularity of locking must be at least as large as the granularity of recovery: the lock obtained for an update operation must cover the data that will be modified during recovery for the operation.

If we want to allow concurrent transactions to update the same data item — for example, if both want to increment a counter — then the undo information for their updates cannot be just the old value. Instead, the log record needs to contain an operation that can reverse the effect of the update. This is sometimes referred to as 'logical recovery', and locking that allows concurrent updates is sometimes referred to as 'logical locking'. For an increment operation, the reverse operation would simply be a decrement. For an operation that inserts an element into a set, the reverse operation would delete the element. (The set might be a database relation, and inserting the element might involve updating many disk blocks, including indices and other data structures.)

13.5   Distributed Recovery

Our discussion of recovery up to this point has been for a single site. We now turn our attention to distributed systems. The key issue in a distributed transaction system is to ensure that all the sites involved in a transaction reach a consistent decision about whether to commit or abort the transaction. It is not acceptable for some sites to commit and some to abort the transaction; they must agree. In addition, the transaction should be committed only if all sites are able to satisfy the redo rule. Chapter 6 discusses this *atomic commitment problem* in more detail. In this section, we present the basic idea and discuss interactions with the log-based recovery method discussed earlier in this chapter.

The most common solution to the atomic commitment problem is the *two-phase commit protocol*. (Not to be confused with two-phase locking!) In this protocol, we designate one of the sites involved in a transaction as the *coordinator; the rest are referred to as* participants. (The coordinator also acts as a participant.) The protocol operates in two phases. In the first phase, the coordinator sends *prepare* messages to each participant, asking each whether it believes it is okay to commit the transaction. If each participant responds positively, the coordinator decides to commit, and in the second phase sends the decision to all the participants.

The commit decision must be forced to the log at the coordinator before any of the participants are informed. In addition, before a participant responds positively to a *prepare* message, it must force a *prepare* record to the log recording that the transaction is 'prepared'. Once a participant prepares a transaction, it cannot commit or abort the transaction on its own: it must wait to hear the final decision from the coordinator. If the participant crashes after preparing a transaction, it must restore the transaction's locks during crash recovery to ensure that the transaction can be aborted later if necessary.

When a participant receives the decision from the coordinator, it writes the decision to the log, and then sends an acknowledgement to the coordinator after the decision is in the log on disk. When the coordinator has received acknowledgements from all the participants, it can delete its record of the decision. (This complicates the checkpointing mechanism discussed earlier for reclaiming storage used for the log: the decision records must be retained until all participants have acknowledged receiving the decision.)

One important issue about the description above is how a participant decides whether to respond positively or negatively to a *prepare* message. The goal of the first phase is to ensure that the redo rule is satisfied everywhere; i.e., all of the transaction's update records should be recorded in the logs on disk at all the participants along with *prepare* records. So if a participant has crashed since the transaction visited it and has lost some of the transaction's update records, then the participant must respond negatively.

A simple technique that allows participants to determine the correct response to *prepare* messages is to record *crash counts* (also known as *incarnation numbers*) at each site. The crash counts must be stored on stable storage. During recovery from a crash at a site, the crash count for the site is incremented and written back to stable storage. As a transaction visits sites, it collects the crash counts. If a transaction visits a site for a second time and sees a different crash count from the first time, then there must have been a crash between the two visits, and the transaction should abort. If the two crash counts are the same, then no crash has occurred. The coordinator includes the crash count for a participant in the *prepare* message sent to that participant; the participant can determine its response to the *prepare* by comparing its current crash count with the one sent to it by the coordinator; if they are the same, then no crash has occurred and a positive response can be sent, and otherwise a negative response should be sent.

The protocol described above can be optimized somewhat to eliminate some of the acknowledgements sent by the participants in the second phase. It is possible to eliminate the acknowledgements for either the commit decisions or the abort decisions, but not both. Since one hopes that more transactions commit than abort, it would be better to optimize the commit case. However, the standard way of doing so requires an additional log force by the coordinator at the start of the protocol (Mohan and Lindsay [1983]); as a result, most systems optimize the abort case. Recently, however, Lampson and Lomet have developed a way of eliminating this log force, which may make it practical to optimize the commit case.

It is also possible to eliminate the second phase completely for a read-only participant (one at which the transaction performs no updates). The first phase is still needed to check that the locks are still held (otherwise the two-phase locking rule would be violated). The second phase is not needed, however, since the participant will do the same thing regardless of whether the transaction commits or aborts: release the locks.

The two-phase commit protocol is vulnerable to crashes of the coordinator and to network partitions: if a participant has responded positively to a *prepare* message and then is unable to communicate with the coordinator, it cannot commit or abort the prepared transaction. In Chapter 6, protocols are discussed that can tolerate crashes without blocking. It is impossible, however, to avoid blocking at some sites when a network partition occurs.

13.6   Other Concurrency Control Methods

Two-phase locking is one of the first concurrency control methods developed for transaction systems and is widely used, but there are many other techniques. For example, timestamp-based techniques assign timestamps to transactions (e.g., when they begin), and then process read and write operations to ensure that transactions appear to run in timestamp order. Multi-version methods allow readers to read old versions while a writer is updating the current version; the first such method was developed by Reed [1978], and relies on timestamps. Hybrid techniques combine locking with timestamps to let read-only transactions run without interfering with update transactions, but use locking to synchronize the updates with each other (Herlihy and Weihl [1991]; Weihl [1987]). Optimistic methods (e.g., see Herlihy [1990] for a recent technique and a survey of others) allow transactions to run without synchronization until they attempt to commit; at that point a validation procedure is run to decide whether to commit the transaction by checking whether the transaction encountered any conflicts while it was running. In addition, a number of researchers have explored the idea of using the semantics of an application to permit more concurrency; see Weihl [1989] for one approach and a discussion of other work.

Given the vast number of concurrency control methods that have been proposed, an obvious question is which is best? Unfortunately, there is no simple answer to this question. All methods degrade under high load, but the peak performance achieved and the point at which performance starts to degrade depend heavily on the application. The best method for a general setting seems to be a hybrid approach, using two-phase locking for update transactions and a timestamp-based multi-version method for read-only transactions, with type-specific methods used for hot spots. However, the performance of such methods has not been thoroughly tested in real systems, most of which use simple two-phase locking (with read/write locks) with some type-specific methods for hot-spots. For an in-depth discussion of the performance issues, see the excellent paper by Agrawal, Carey and Livny [1987].

13.7   Distributed Concurrency Control

Concurrency control techniques such as two-phase locking also work in distributed systems: if every site uses two-phase locking, everything works fine. In general, however, one cannot use one concurrency control method at one site and a different method at some other site. The key issue is that the sites must coordinate to ensure that they agree on a serialization order for the committed transactions. This issue is important in heterogeneous distributed systems, in which the different sites might be implemented by different vendors; there needs to be an agreed-upon standard for the specification used by the different vendors. (Notice that this is an issue of modularity, not of distribution; the different systems could all be running on the same site.)

Weihl has invented the notion of a *local atomicity property*, which is a specification of the behavior permitted by an individual site in a multi-site transaction system (Weihl [1989]). One of these local properties, *dynamic atomicity*, specifies the behavior of concurrency control methods that serialize transactions in commit order (as do two-phase locking and many others). Others specify the behavior of methods that serialize in timestamp order, or that use hybrid techniques. No single standard has yet been agreed upon, although any standard is likely to include commit-order techniques simply because of the widespread use of two-phase locking.

13.8   Nested Transactions

An important extension to the basic notion of atomic transactions discussed above is the idea of *nested transactions*. The idea is to allow each transaction to have subtransactions; subtransactions can run concurrently, in which case siblings are serializable as part of their parent, and can fail. However, the failure of a subtransaction does not force the parent to fail. Thus, subtransactions provide a limited kind of firewall against failures. For example, subtransactions can be used to implement a zero-or-once semantics for RPC, in which each remote call is done either zero or one times, and where the caller knows whether or not the call was done.

Implementing nested transactions requires some extensions to the techniques described earlier. Two-phase locking is modified to allow a transaction to acquire a lock only if all conflicting locks are currently held by ancestors. In other words, no concurrent active transaction holds a conflicting lock at any level of the transaction tree. When a subtransaction commits, its locks are 'inherited' by its parent; when it aborts, its locks are discarded.

For abort recovery, we view each data item as conceptually having a stack of versions. When a transaction first updates a data item, it copies the version at the top of the data item's stack, and pushes the new version onto the stack. The update (and later updates by the same transaction) are then done on the new version at the top of the stack. When a subtransaction commits, its version (if any) at the top of the stack replaces its parent's version; if its parent already has a version on the stack, that version is discarded. When a subtransaction aborts, its version (if any) at the top of the stack is discarded.

This approach to abort recovery can be implemented fairly directly (as in the Argus system (Liskov and Scheifler [1983])) or by updating data items in place and keeping the rest of the versions in an undo log. The latter approach integrates nicely with crash recovery, which can use the same two phases discussed earlier (a redo phase, following by an undo phase).

One important note: the effects of a subtransaction are not permanent until the top-level ancestor of the subtransaction commits. If a transaction aborts, all effects of its descendents are undone, even if they had committed (i.e., commitment is relative to the parent's commit). This means that a full two-phase commit protocol is not needed when a subtransaction commits; instead, a subtransaction can make a local commit decision, even if it did work at other sites. The redo rule needs to be checked eventually for the transaction, but all that is necessary is to ensure that before a top-level transaction commits, the redo rule is satisfied at all sites for all of its descendents. This can be done in the first phase of two-phase commit for a top-level transaction.

13.9 Discussion

Atomicity is one of the fundamental concepts in concurrent and fault-tolerant systems. A machine typically provides some set of primitive atomic actions; much of the game of building a concurrent or fault-tolerant system involves building 'larger' atomic actions out of simpler ones. The techniques discussed in this chapter provide a systematic set of solutions to this problem.

It is not necessary to adopt all of the mechanisms associated with a transaction system to obtain some of the benefits. For example, some modern file systems are using logs to obtain nicer behavior when the system crashes, and also to improve the performance of writes by using the sequential nature of the log to make better use of the disk (Rosenblum and Ousterhout [1991]). Similarly, all of the concurrency control methods discussed in this chapter have been used in non-fault-tolerant concurrent systems. Locking is widespread, optimistic methods are sometimes used to avoid deadlock, and 'transactional' techniques are being explored as the basis for multiprocessor synchronization (Herlihy and Moss [1992]).

Transactions provide a very nice set of solutions to the problems caused by concurrency and failures. However, it is important to realize that atomic transactions are not a panacea that solves all such problems. Indeed, transactions have a reputation for being too constraining or performing poorly. However, this reputation is only partly deserved. In fact, transactions are quite flexible: the system designer can choose whatever granularity for transactions meets the needs of the system. In doing so, several competing concerns need to be addressed. On the one hand, a coarse granularity of transactions is likely to make the system simpler and easier to understand. On the other hand, a coarse granularity may result in relatively low concurrency, which may cause poor performance; thus, a finer granularity may be preferable. At the same time, a coarser granularity may result in lower overhead, since fewer transactions will be created or need to commit. In general, it is probably worth choosing the coarsest granularity that meets the performance goals of the system.

In addition, the reputation for poor performance is largely due to the high overheads of early transaction systems. Modern high-performance systems perform remarkably well, and are a far cry from early systems. The poor performance of early systems derived from two sources: high I/O overhead, and low levels of concurrency. The former has been solved in modern systems by using recovery methods similar to that described in this chapter; almost all synchronous I/O has been eliminated, and most writes to disk are sequential. The latter problem can often be solved by using clever concurrency control techniques that use knowledge of the semantics of operations to allow some updates to run concurrently.

We do not have space to give detailed examples of using transactions in distributed applications. Examples of the use of transactions can be found in the previous edition of this book, in papers by Liskov [1988] on Argus, and in papers on other transaction systems such as Avalon (Herlihy and Wing [1987]). In addition, transactions are the method of choice in most database systems today, and are also used in fault-tolerant systems such as Tandem's NonStop system as part of a systematic solution to the problem of ensuring reliable operation in the presence of failures. It is reasonable to expect that as hardware becomes faster and cheaper, memory systems such as nonvolatile RAM become more widespread, and well engineered transaction systems become more widely available, the performance of transaction systems will be adequate for an increasing range of applications, and more people will discover that they can solve their problems more easily, quickly, and reliably using transactions.

13.10   Bibliographic and Historical Notes

As mentioned above, transactions were first developed in database systems as a way of maintaining the integrity of data in the face of crashes and concurrent access. One of the earliest database systems to provide systematic support for transactions was System R, developed at IBM's San Jose Research Laboratory (Eswaran *et al.* [1976]; Gray *et al.* [1981]) in the early 1970s. The ideas for transactions grew out of early work on atomic actions (Davies [1973]; Davies [1978]). In the late 1970s, research began on distributed databases. One of the important early distributed database systems was R*, again developed at IBM's San Jose Lab (Lindsay *et al.* [1984]).

Around the same time as the work on R*, several research groups experimented with using transactions in distributed file systems. Notions of atomicity were also being explored at the University of Newcastle upon Tyne in their work on recovery blocks and extensions to accommodate concurrency (Anderson, Lee and Shrivastava [1978]; Randell [1975]). Concurrently, Lampson [1981] at Xerox PARC developed techniques for implementing atomic actions in distributed systems. Also starting in the late 1970s and early 1980s, a number of research groups began exploring atomic transactions as the basis for structuring distributed systems and applications; out of this work came several languages and systems that incorporate transactions, including Argus at MIT (Liskov and Scheifler [1983]), TABS, Camelot, and Avalon at CMU (Eppinger, Mummert and Spector [1991]; Herlihy and Wing [1987]; Spector *et al.* [1985]), and Clouds at Georgia Tech (McKendry [1984]). More recently, projects such as the Quicksilver project at IBM's Almaden Research Center have explored generalizing the mechanisms in transaction systems to support a wider range of applications and to make it easier for an application to use only those parts of the transaction system that are useful to it (Haskin *et al.* [1987]).

Nested transactions were invented by Reed [1978] at MIT, but were really an outgrowth of the work by Davies [1973], Davies [1978] and the work at Newcastle (Anderson, Lee and Shrivastava [1978]; Randell [1975]). Reed's formulation of nested transactions was based on a multi-version timestamping approach to concurrency control and recovery; Eliot Moss generalized the concept and showed how to extend standard two-phase locking methods to accommodate nested transactions (Moss [1981]). Based on Moss's work, nested transactions were used in Argus (Liskov and Scheifler [1983]). An in-depth analysis of a large number of algorithms for nested transaction systems can be found in the book by Lynch *et al.* [1993].

As mentioned earlier, the recovery method described in this chapter is based on that designed for the ARIES project at IBM Almaden (Mohan *et al.* [1992]). A (somewhat old) survey of recovery methods can be found in Haerder and Reuter [1983]. Recent work has focused on recovery in distributed and multi-disk systems (e.g., (Lomet [1990])) and on multi-level systems that support many levels of logical locking and logical logging (e.g., (Lomet [1992]; Weikum [1986]; Weikum and Schek [1984])).

A great deal has been written on transactions over the last decade and a half. Three books are of particular note. The book by Bernstein, Hadzilacos and Goodman [1987] provides a good survey of a wide range of concurrency control methods and a somewhat informal discussion of correctness issues. The book by Gray and Reuter [1992] gives an in-depth description of many techniques, and is an excellent reference. The book by Lynch *et al.* [1993] provides a careful rigorous treatment of correctness issues, showing how a wide variety of transaction-processing techniques can be analyzed in a single common framework. It also provides a rigorous model for describing and analyzing algorithms for implementing nested transactions.

Another useful source of information about transaction systems is the collected lecture notes for the course 'Principles of Computer Systems' taught by Profs. Lampson and Weihl at MIT (Weihl, Lampson and Brewer [1992]). The notes include a detailed description and analysis of the correctness of recovery methods, using the methods discussed in Chapter 3 of this book.

Acknowledgements

William E. Weihl's work on this chapter was supported in part by the Advanced Research Projects Agency (ARPA) under Contract N00014-91-J-1698,[2] by grants from IBM and AT&T, and by an equipment grant from DEC.

13.11   References

Agrawal, R., Carey, M. and Livny, M. (1987), Concurrency control performance modeling: alternatives and implications, *ACM Transactions on Database Systems* **12(4)**.

Anderson, T., Lee, P. and Shrivastava, S. (1978), A Model of Recoverability in Multilevel Systems, *IEEE Transactions on Software Engineering* **SE-4(6)**, 486–494.

Bernstein, P. A., Hadzilacos, V. and Goodman, N. (1987), *Concurrency Control and Recovery in Database Systems*, Addison-Wesley, Reading, MA.

Davies, C. T. (1973), Recovery Semantics for a DB/DC System, in *Proceedings of the ACM Annual Conference*, 136–141.

Davies, C. T. (1978), Data Processing Spheres of Control, *IBM Systems Journal* **17(2)**.

Eppinger, J. L., Mummert, L. B. and Spector, A. Z. (1991), *Camelot and Avalon: a distributed transaction facility*, Morgan Kaufmann.

Eswaran, K. P., Gray, J. N., Lorie, R. A. and Traiger, I. L. (1976), The Notions of Consistency and Predicate Locks in a Database System, *Communications of the ACM* **19(11)**, 624–633.

Gray, J. and Reuter, A. (1992), *Transaction Processing: Techniques and Concepts*, Morgan Kaufmann.

Gray, J. N., McJones, P., Blasgen, M., Lindsay, B., Lorie, L., Price, T., Putzolu, F. and Traiger, I. (1981), The Recovery Manager of the System R Database Manager, *ACM Computing Surveys* **13(2)**, 223–242.

Haerder, T. and Reuter, A. (1983), Principles of Transaction-Oriented Database Recovery, *ACM Computing Surveys* **15(4)**, 287–317.

Haskin, R., Malachi, Y., Sawdon, W. and Chan, C. (1987), Recovery Management in QuickSilver, *Proceedings of the Eleventh Symposium on Operating Systems Principles*, Austin, TX, 107–108, In *ACM Operating Systems Review* **21(5)**.

Herlihy, M. P. (1990), Apologizing versus asking permission: optimistic concurrency control for abstract data types, *ACM Transactions on Database Systems* **15(1)**, 96–124.

Herlihy, M. P. and Moss, J. E. B. (1992), Transactional Memory: Architectural Support for Lock-Free Data, Digital Equipment Corporation, Cambridge Research Laboratory, CRL 92/07.

---

[2]The views and conclusions contained here are those of the author and should not be interpreted as representing the official policies, either expressed or implied, of the U.S. government.

Herlihy, M. P. and Weihl, W. E. (1991), Hybrid Concurrency Control for Abstract Data Types, *Journal of Computer and System Sciences* **43**(1), 25–61.

Herlihy, M. P. and Wing, J. M. (1987), Avalon: Language Support for Reliable Distributed Systems, *Proceedings of the 17th International Symposium on Fault-Tolerant Computing*, Cristian, F. and Goldberg, J., eds., Pittsburgh, PA, IEEE Computer Society Press, 89–95, Also published as CMU-CSD Technical Report CMU-CSD-86-167.

Lampson, B. W. (1981), Atomic Transactions, in *Distributed Systems — Architecture and Implementation:*, Lampson, B., Paul, M. and Siegert, H., eds., Lecture Notes in Computer Science, vol. **105**, Springer-Verlag, 246–265.

Lindsay, B. G., Haas, L. M., Mohan, C. K., Wilms, P. F. and Yost, R. A. (1984), Computation and Communication in R*: A Distributed Database Manager, *ACM Transactions on Computer Systems* **2**(1), 24–38.

Liskov, B. (1988), Distributed Computing in Argus, *Communications of the ACM* **31**(3), 300–312.

Liskov, B. and Scheifler, R. (1983), Guardians and Actions: Linguistic Support for Robust, Distributed Programs, *ACM Transactions on Programming Languages and Systems* **5**(3), 381–404.

Lomet, D. B. (1990), Recovery for Shared Disk Systems Using Multiple Redo Logs, Digital Equipment Corporation, Cambridge Research Lab, CRL 90/4.

Lomet, D. B. (1992), MLR: A Recovery Method for Multi-Level Systems, in *Proceedings of the ACM SIGMOD Conference on Management of Data*, 185–194.

Lynch, N. A., Merritt, M., Weihl, W. E. and Fekete, A. (1993), *Atomic Transactions*, Morgan Kaufmann.

McKendry, M. S. (1984), Clouds: A Fault-Tolerant Distributed Operating Systems, *IEEE Tech. Com. Distributed Processing Newsletter* **2**(6).

Mohan, C. K., Haderle, D., Lindsay, B., Pirahesh, H. and Schwarz, P. (1992), ARIES: A Transaction Recovery Method Supporting Fine-Grained Locking and Partial Rollbacks Using Write-Ahead Logging, *ACM Transactions on Database Systems* **17**(1), 94–162.

Mohan, C. K. and Lindsay, B. (1983), Efficient Commit Protocols for the Tree of Processes Model of Distributed Transactions, in *Proceedings of the Second ACM Annual Symposium on Principles of Distributed Computing*, Lynch, N. A., ed., Montreal, Canada, 76–88.

352   William E. Weihl

Moss, J. E. B. (1981), Nested Transactions: An Approach to Reliable Distributed Computing, MIT Laboratory for Computer Science, Ph.D. Dissertation, Cambridge, MA, Available as Technical Report MIT/LCS/TR-260 and published by MIT Press, March 1985.

Randell, B. (1975), System Structure for Software Fault Tolerance, *IEEE Transactions on Software Engineering* **1(2)**, 220–232.

Reed, D. P. (1978), Naming and Synchronization in a Decentralized Computer System, MIT, Ph.D. Dissertation, Available as Technical Report MIT/LCS/TR-205.

Rosenblum, M. and Ousterhout, J. (1991), The Design and Implementation of a Log-Structured File System, *Proceedings of the 13th Symposium on Operating Systems Principles*, Pacific Grove, CA, 1–15 , In *ACM Operating Systems Review* **25(5)**.

Spector, A. Z., Butcher, J., Daniels, D., *et al.* (1985), Support for distributed transactions in the TABS prototype, *IEEE Transactions on Software Engineering* **SE-11(6)**, 520–530.

Weihl, W. E. (1987), Distributed Version Management for Read-Only Actions, *IEEE Transactions on Software Engineering* **SE-13(1)**, 55–64.

Weihl, W. E. (1989), Local Atomicity Properties: Modular Concurrency Control for Abstract Data Types, *ACM Transactions on Programming Languages and Systems* **11(2)**, 249–282.

Weihl, W. E. (1993), The Impact of Recovery on Concurrency Control, *Journal of Computer and Systems Sciences*, Also available as MIT/LCS/TM-382.b, August 1989.

Weihl, W. E., Lampson, B. W. and Brewer, E. (1992), 6.826 — Principles of Computer Systems: Lecture Notes and Handouts, MIT Laboratory for Computer Science, MIT/LCS/RSS 19, Cambridge, MA, Collected notes for the Fall 1991 course.

Weikum, G. (1986), A Theoretical Foundation of Multi-Level Concurrency Control, in *Proceedings of the Fifth ACM Symposium on Principles of Database Systems*, 31–42.

Weikum, G. and Schek, H. J. (1984), Architectural Issues of Transaction Management in Multi-Layered Systems, in *Proceedings of the Tenth International Conference on Very Large Data Bases*, Singapore, 454–465.

Chapter 14

Distributed File Systems

M. Satyanarayanan

14.1 Introduction

The sharing of data in distributed systems is already common and will become pervasive as these systems grow in scale and importance. Each user in a distributed system is potentially a creator as well as a consumer of data. A user may wish to make his actions contingent upon information from a remote site, or may wish to update remote information. Sometimes the physical movement of a user may require his data to be accessible elsewhere. In both scenarios, ease of data sharing considerably enhances the value of a distributed system to its community of users. The challenge is to provide this functionality in a secure, reliable, efficient and usable manner that is independent of the size and complexity of the distributed system.

We begin this chapter by examining the fundamental problems facing a distributed file system designer, and surveying the known techniques for addressing these problems. This overview is followed by in-depth descriptions of two distributed file systems, *Andrew* and *Coda*. The choice of these systems is primarily motivated by my personal involvement with both of them. But personal bias notwithstanding, their designs are widely recognized as good solutions to some of the most important problems in distributed file system design. To provide balanced treatment, the chapter ends with a brief overview of a number of other contemporary file system designs.

14.2 Background

14.2.1 Taxonomy

Permanent storage is a fundamental abstraction in computing. It consists of a named set of objects that come into existence by explicit creation, are immune to temporary failures of the system, and persist until explicitly destroyed. The naming structure, the characteristics of the objects, and the set of operations associated with them characterize a specific refinement of the basic abstraction. A file system is one such refinement. Databases and object-oriented repositories are other examples of refinements.

From the perspective of file system design, computing models can be classified into four levels. The set of design issues at any level subsumes those at lower levels. Consequently, the implementation of a file system for a higher level will have to be more sophisticated than one that is adequate for a lower level.

At the lowest level, exemplified by IBM PC-DOS (IBM [1983]) and Apple Macintosh (Apple Computer [1985]), one user at a single site performs computations via a single process. A file system for this model must address four key issues. These include the *naming structure* of the file system, the application *programming interface*, the *mapping* of the file system abstraction on to physical storage media, and the *integrity* of the file system across power, hardware, media and software failures.

The next level, exemplified by OS/2 (Letwin [1988]), involves a single user computing with multiple processes at one site. *Concurrency control* is now an important consideration at the programming interface and in the implementation of the file system. The survey by Bernstein and Goodman [1981] treats this issue in depth.

The classic time-sharing model, where multiple users share data and resources, constitutes the third level of the taxonomy. Mechanisms to specify and enforce *security* now become important. UNIX (Ritchie and Thompson [1974]) is the archetype of a timesharing file system.

Distributed file systems constitute the highest level of the taxonomy. Here multiple users who are physically dispersed in a network of autonomous computers share in the use of a common file system. A useful way to view such a system is to think of it as a distributed implementation of the timesharing file system abstraction. The challenge is in realizing this abstraction in an efficient, secure and robust manner. In addition, the issues of *file location* and *availability* assume significance.

The simplest approach to file location is to embed location information in names. Examples of this approach can be found in the Newcastle Connection (Brownbridge, Marshall and Randell [1982]), Cedar (Schroeder, Gifford and Needham [1985]), and Vax/VMS (DEC [1985]). But the static binding of name to location makes it inconvenient to move files between sites. It also requires users to remember machine names, a difficult feat in a large distributed environment. A better approach is to use *location transparency*, where the name of a file is devoid of location information. An explicit file location mechanism dynamically maps file names to storage sites.

Availability is of special significance because the usage site of data can be different from its storage site. Hence failure modes are substantially more complex in a distributed environment. *Replication*, the basic technique used to achieve high availability, introduces complications of its own. Since multiple copies of a file are present, changes have to be propagated to all the replicas. Such propagation has to be done in a consistent and efficient manner.

14.2.2   File Systems versus Databases

As refinements of the same abstraction, file systems and databases have much in common. Yet even a cursory glance at the designs of current file systems and databases will reveal extensive differences. Is this dichotomy intrinsic, or is it merely an accident of history?

Encapsulation is one area where databases conceptually differ from file systems. A file system views the data in a file as an uninterpreted byte sequence. A database, in contrast, encapsulates substantial information about the types and logical relationships of data items stored in it. Since the data is typed, the database can enforce constraints on values. As a result, databases can subsume some of the functionality supplied by individual applications that are built on a file system. The price paid for this functionality is some loss of flexibility as well as the greater effort involved in setting up a database.

Another fundamental distinction between file systems and databases is in the area of *naming*. File systems provides access to files by name, while databases allow associative access. Human cognitive ability limits the number of objects that users can effectively deal with by name. A hierarchical name space helps enlarge this number, but does not help when the working set of names is large.

The *ratio of search time to usage time* is the key factor that determines whether access by name is adequate. When the ratio is low, a file system is adequate; when it is high a database is preferable. Low search to usage ratio translates to *temporal locality*. Not surprisingly, usage patterns in a file system exhibit considerable temporal locality, while those in a database exhibit very little locality As a consequence, distributed file systems and databases use very different strategies. Distributed file systems use *data shipping*, where data is brought to the point of use. Distributed databases use *function shipping*, where computation is shipped to the site of data storage.

Neither the difference in encapsulation nor naming makes it *a priori* more difficult to build large-scale distributed databases. However, the circumstances under which databases are typically used are precisely those that make distribution difficult. The most demanding applications involve concurrent read and write sharing of data at fine granularity by large numbers of users, combined with requirements for strict consistency of data and atomicity of groups of operations. It is this combination of application characteristics that makes the implementation of distributed databases substantially harder than the implementation of distributed file systems.

14.2.3   Empirical Observations

A substantial amount of empirical investigation in the classic scientific mold has been done on file systems. The results of this work have been used to guide high-level design as well as to determine values of system parameters. For example, data on file sizes has been used in the efficient mapping of files to disk storage blocks. Information on the frequency of different file operations and the degree of read- and write-sharing of files has influenced the design of caching algorithms.

Type-specific file reference information has been useful in file placement and in the design of replication mechanisms.

Empirical work on file systems involves many practical difficulties. The instrumentation usually requires modifications to the operating system. In addition, it has to impact system performance minimally. The total volume of data generated is usually large, and needs to be stored and processed efficiently.

In addition to the difficulty of collecting data, there are two basic concerns about its interpretation. *Generality* is one of these concerns. How specific are the observations to the system being observed? Data of widespread applicability is obviously of most value. Independent investigations have been made of a variety of academic and research environments. The systems examined include IBM MVS (Revelle [1975]; Smith [1981]; Stritter [1977]), DEC PDP-10 (Satyanarayanan [1981]; Satyanarayanan [1984]), and UNIX (Floyd [1986a]; Floyd [1986b]; Majumdar and Bunt [1986]; Ousterhout *et al.* [1985]). Although these studies differ in their details, there is substantial overlap in the set of issues they investigate. Further, their results do not exhibit any serious contradictions. We thus have confidence in our understanding of file system characteristics in academic and research environments. Unfortunately, except for the recent paper by Ramakrishnan, Biswas and Karedla [1992], there is little publicly available information from other kinds of environments.

The second concern relates to the *interdependency* of design and empirical observations. Are the observed properties an artifact of existing system design or are they intrinsic? Little is known about the influence of system design on file properties, although the existence of such influence is undeniable. For example, in a design that uses whole-file transfer, there is substantial disincentive to the creation of very large files. In the long run this may affect the observed file size distribution. It is therefore important to revalidate our understanding of file properties as new systems are built and existing systems mature.

Studies of file systems fall into two broad categories. Early studies (Revelle [1975]; Satyanarayanan [1981]; Smith [1981]; Stritter [1977]) were based on *static* analysis, using one or more snapshots of a file system. The data from these studies is unweighted. Later studies (Floyd [1986a]; Floyd [1986b]; Majumdar and Bunt [1986]; Ousterhout *et al.* [1985]; Satyanarayanan [1984]) are based on *dynamic* analysis, using continuous monitoring of a file system. These data are weighted by frequency of file usage.

Although these studies have all been done on timesharing file systems their results have hitherto been assumed to hold for distributed file systems. This is based on the premise that user behavior and programming environment characteristics are the primary factors influencing file properties. A further assumption is that neither of these factors changes significantly in moving to a distributed environment. The recent work by Baker *et al.* [1991] and by Mummert and Satyanarayanan [1992] are the first to measure distributed environments.

The most consistent observation in all the studies is the skewing of file sizes toward the low end. In other words, most files are small, typically a few tens of kilobytes. The absolute value of average file size has increased over time, but it continues to remain small relative to contemporary disk sizes. Another common observation is that read operations on files are much more frequent than write operations. Random accessing of a file is rare. A typical application program sequentially reads an entire file into its address space and then performs nonsequential processing on the in-memory data. A related observation is that a file is usually read in its entirety once it has been opened.

Averaged over all the files in a system, data appears to be highly mutable. The *functional lifetime* of a file, defined as the time interval between the most recent read and the most recent write, is skewed toward the low end. In other words, data in files tends to be overwritten often. Although the mean functional lifetime is small, the tail of the distribution is long, indicating the existence of files with long-lived data.

Most files are read and written by one user. When users share a file, it is usually the case that only one of them modifies it. Fine granularity read-write sharing of files is rare. It is important to emphasize that these are observations derived from research or academic environments. An environment with large collaborative projects or one that makes extensive use of databases may show substantially greater write-sharing of data.

File references show substantial temporal locality of reference, corroborating the observation made in Section 14.2.2. If a file is referenced, there is a high probability it will be referenced again in the near future. Over short periods of time, the set of referenced files is a very small subset of all files.

The characteristics described above apply to the file population as a whole. If one were to focus on files of a specific type their properties may differ significantly. For example, system programs tend to be stable and rarely modified. Consequently the average functional lifetime of system programs is much larger than the average over all files. Temporary files on the other hand show substantially shorter lifetimes. More fine-grained classification of files is also possible, as demonstrated by some of the investigations mentioned earlier (Floyd [1986a]; Floyd [1986b]; Satyanarayanan [1981]).

14.3   Commonly-Used Mechanisms and Techniques

14.3.1   Caching at Clients

The caching of data at clients is undoubtedly the architectural feature that contributes most to performance in a distributed file system. Every distributed file system in serious use today uses some form of caching. Even AT&T's RFS (Rifkin *et al.* [1986]), which initially avoided caching in the interests of strict UNIX emulation, now uses it.

Caching exploits temporal locality of reference. There is a high probability that file data will be reused soon after its first use. By obtaining a local copy of the data a client can avoid many further interactions with the server. Metadata, such as directories, protection and file status information, and file location information also exhibit locality of reference and are thus good candidates for caching.

A key issue in caching is the size of the cached units of data. Most distributed file systems cache individual pages of files. The Coda file system (Satyanarayanan *et al.* [1990]) and early versions of the Andrew file system (Satyanarayanan *et al.* [1985]) cache entire files. Although this simplifies cache management and offers simpler failure semantics, it does suffer from the inability to access files that are larger than the client's cache. More recent versions of Andrew cache large portions (typically 64KB) of files. The unit of caching is closely related to the use of bulk transfer protocols, as discussed in Section 14.3.2.

In most systems clients maintain the cache in their main memory. Andrew and Coda are exceptions in that they cache on local disks, with a further level of caching in main memory. Besides providing larger cache sizes, disk caching preserves cache contents across system reboots. The non-volatility offered by disk caching is critical to disconnected operation in Coda.

The validation of cache contents can be done in two fundamentally different ways. One approach, used by most systems, is for the client to contact the server for validation. An alternative approach is to have the server notify clients when cached data is about to be rendered stale. Although more complex to implement, the latter approach can produce substantial reductions in client-server traffic.

A wide spectrum of approaches can be used in propagating modifications from client to server. Andrew propagates changes when a file is closed after writing. Sprite (Nelson, Welch and Ousterhout [1988]) delays propagation until dirty cache pages have to be reclaimed or for a maximum of 30 seconds. Deferred propagation improves performance since data is often overwritten, but increases the possibility of server data being stale due to a client crash. Disconnected operation in Coda represents an extreme case of propagation being deferred until network connectivity is restored.

File references also exhibit *spatial locality*. If a page of a file is read, there is substantial likelihood that succeeding pages will also be read. This property is exploited in many systems by using *read-ahead* of file data. The client can overlap the processing of one page with the fetching of the next page or set of pages from the server.

14.3.2   Transferring Data in Bulk

Network communication overheads typically account for a major portion of the latency in a distributed file system. Although the transit time of small amounts of data across a local area network is insignificant, the delays caused by protocol processing can be substantial. Transferring data in bulk reduces this overhead at both the source and sink of the data. At the source, multiple packets are formatted and transmitted with one context switch. At the sink, an acknowledgement is avoided for each packet. Some bulk transfer protocols also make better use of the disks at the source and sink. Multiple blocks of data may often be obtained at the source with a single seek. Similarly, packets can be buffered and written *en masse* to the disk at the sink. In effect, the use of bulk transfer amortizes fixed protocol overheads over many consecutive pages of a file.

Bulk transfer protocols depend on spatial locality of reference within files for effectiveness. There is a very high probability that succeeding pages of a file will soon be referenced at the client if an earlier page is referenced. As mentioned in

Section 14.2.3, there is substantial empirical evidence to indicate that files are read in their entirety once they are opened.

The degree to which bulk transfer is exploited varies from system to system. Andrew, for instance, is critically dependent on it for good performance. Early versions of the system transferred entire files, and the current version transfers files in 64KB chunks. Systems such as NFS (Sandberg *et al.* [1985]) and Sprite exploit bulk transfer by using very large packet sizes, typically 8KB. The latter systems depend on the link level protocol to fragment and reassemble smaller packets at the media access level. Bulk transfer protocols will increase in importance as distributed file systems spread across networks of wider geographic area and thus have greater inherent latency.

14.3.3   Hints

In the context of distributed systems, a *hint* (Lampson [1983]) is a piece of information that can substantially improve performance if correct but has no semantically negative consequence if erroneous. For maximum performance benefit a hint should nearly always be correct. Terry [1987] discusses the use of hints in detail and provides many examples of how they may be used in distributed systems.

By caching hints one can obtain substantial performance benefits without incurring the cost of maintaining cache consistency. Only information that is self-validating upon use is amenable to this strategy. One cannot, for instance, treat file data as a hint because the use of a cached copy of the data will not reveal whether it is current or stale.

Hints are most often used for file location information in distributed file systems. Sprite, for instance, caches mappings of path-name prefixes to servers. Similarly, Andrew and Coda cache individual entries from the volume location database. In these systems a client will use cached location information until a server rejects a request because it no longer stores the file referred to in the request. The client then obtains the new location of the file, and caches this information as a fresh hint. A more elaborate location scheme, incorporating a hint manager, is used by Apollo Domain (Levine [1987]).

14.3.4   Encryption

Encryption is an indispensable building block for enforcing security in a distributed system. Voydock and Kent [1983] classify threats to security as actions that cause unauthorized *release* of information, unauthorized *modification* of information, or unauthorized *denial of resources*. Encryption is primarily of value in preventing unauthorized release and modification of information. Because it is a national standard, DES (Meyer and Matyas [1982]) is the most commonly used form of private-key encryption.

The seminal work of Needham and Schroeder [1978] on the use of encryption for authentication is the basis of all current security mechanisms in distributed file systems. At the heart of these mechanisms is a handshake protocol in which each party challenges the other to prove its identity. Possession of a secret encryption key, known only to a legitimate client and server, is assumed to be *prima facie* evidence of authenticity. Thus two communicating entities that are mutually suspicious at the beginning end up confident of each other's identity, without ever transmitting their shared secret key in the clear.

This basic scheme is used in two distinct ways in current systems. The difference lies in the way user passwords are stored and used on servers. In the private key scheme used by Andrew, an authentication server that is physically secure maintains a list of user passwords in the clear. In contrast, the public key scheme used by Sun NFS maintains a publicly readable database of authentication keys that are encrypted with user passwords. The latter approach has the attractive characteristic that physical security of the authentication server is unnecessary. Unfortunately, public key encryption tends to be substantially slower than private key encryption.

Encryption is usually implemented end-to-end, at the RPC level. In some systems, such as Andrew, encryption can be used to protect the data and headers of all packets exchanged after authentication. Other systems, such as Sun NFS, do not provide this capability. A difficult nontechnical problem is justifying the cost of encryption hardware to management and users. Unlike extra memory, processor speed, or graphics capability, encryption devices do not provide tangible benefits to users. The importance of security is often perceived only after it is too late. At present, encryption hardware is viewed as an expensive frill. Hopefully, the emerging awareness that encryption is indispensable for security will make rapid, cheap encryption a universally available capability.

14.3.5 Mount Points

The *mount* mechanism in UNIX enables the glueing together of file name spaces to provide applications with a single, seamless, hierarchically structured, name space. On startup, the UNIX file name space consists of a single *root file system*. Individual mount commands may then be issued to bind the root of an external file system to an internal or leaf node of the local name space. A mount on an internal node hides the original subtree beneath that node. To simplify the implementation, UNIX imposes certain restrictions such as the inability to place hard links across mount points.

Mount was originally conceived as a mechanism to allow self-contained file systems on removable storage media to be added to or removed without reinitializing UNIX. When performing a name lookup, the kernel uses an internal data structure called the *mount table* to direct its search to the appropriate storage device. A single lookup may span many devices if multiple mounts are in effect. In a distributed file system, the mount mechanism provides a natural hook on which to hang a remote subtree. There are two fundamentally different ways to use the mechanism, with numerous variants of each.

The simpler approach is used by systems such as NFS, where each client individually mounts subtrees from servers. There is no centralized management of mount information. Servers are unaware of where the subtrees exported by them have been mounted. Although this approach is easier to implement, it has the disadvantage that the shared name space is not guaranteed to be identical at all clients. Further, movement of files from one server to another requires each client to unmount and remount the affected subtree. In practice, systems that use this approach have usually had to provide auxiliary mechanisms (such as the Yellow Pages and Automounter in NFS) to automate and centralize mounts.

The alternative approach is to embed mount information in the data stored in the file servers. Andrew, for example, uses mount points embedded in volumes. Sprite uses remote links for a similar purpose. Using this approach, it is trivial to ensure that all clients see precisely the same shared file name space. Further, operational tasks such as moving files from one server to another only involve updating the mount information on the servers.

14.4   The Andrew File System

The design of the Andrew File System began in 1983, in the context of a joint project between Carnegie Mellon University and IBM to develop a state-of-the-art computing environment for educational and research use. The project envisioned a dramatic increase in computing power made possible by the widespread deployment of powerful personal workstations. It was clear to us, from the outset, that a distributed file system for such an environment had to possess two critical attributes. It had to *scale* well, so that the system could grow to its anticipated final size of over 5000 workstations. It also had to be *secure*, so that users could be confident of the privacy of their data. The design of the Andrew File System has evolved over time, resulting in three distinct versions called AFS-1, AFS-2 and AFS-3. In the rest of this chapter, the term 'Andrew' will be used as a collective term referring to all three versions.

14.4.1   Architecture

The Andrew computing paradigm is a synthesis of the best features of personal computing and timesharing. It incorporates the flexible and visually rich user interface available in personal computing, with the ease of information exchange typical of timesharing. A conceptual view of this model is shown in Figure 14.1.

The large amoeba-like structure in the middle, called *Vice*, is the information sharing backbone of the system. Although represented as a single entity, it actually consists of a collection of dedicated file servers and a complex local area network. User computing cycles are provided by workstations running the UNIX operating system.

Data sharing in Andrew is supported by a distributed file system that appears as a single large subtree of the local file system on each workstation. The only files outside the shared subtree are temporary files, and files essential for workstation initialization. A process called *Venus* that runs on each workstation mediates shared file access. Venus finds files in Vice, caches them locally, and performs emulation of UNIX file system semantics. Both Vice and Venus are invisible to workstation processes. The latter just see a UNIX file system, one subtree of which

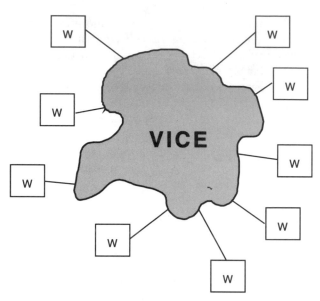

Figure 14.1. The Andrew Architecture. This is a high-level view of Andrew. The shaded structure labelled 'Vice' is a collection of trusted file servers and untrusted networks. The nodes labelled 'W' are private or public workstations, or timesharing systems. Software in each such node makes the shared files in Vice appear as an integral part of that node's file system

happens to be identical on all workstations. Processes on two different workstations can read and write files in this subtree just as if they were running on a single timesharing system. Figure 14.2 depicts the file system view seen by a workstation user.

Our experience with the Andrew architecture over the past eight years has been positive. It is simple, easily understood by naive users, and permits efficient implementation. It also offers a number of benefits that are particularly valuable on a large scale:

- *Data sharing is simplified.*
  A workstation with a small disk can potentially access any file in Andrew by name. Since the file system is location transparent, users do not have to remember the machines on which files are currently located or where they were created. System administrators can move files from one server to another without inconveniencing users. The users are completely unaware of such a move.
- *User mobility is supported.*
  A user can walk to any workstation in the system and access any file in the shared name space. A user's workstation is 'personal' only in the sense that he owns it.
- *System administration is easier.*

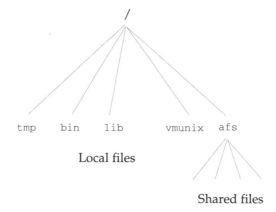

Local files

Shared files

Figure 14.2. File System View at a Workstation. This figure shows how the shared files in Vice appear to the user of a workstation. The subtree under the directory labelled 'afs' is identical at all workstations. The other directories are local to each workstation. Symbolic links can be used to make local directories correspond to directories in Vice

Operations staff can focus on the relatively small number of servers, ignoring the more numerous and physically dispersed clients. Adding a new workstation merely involves connecting it to the network and assigning it an address.

- *Better security is possible.*
  The servers in Vice are physically secure and run trusted system software. No user programs are executed on servers. Encryption-based authentication and transmission are used to enforce the security of server-workstation communication. Although individuals may tamper with the hardware and software on their workstations, their malicious actions cannot affect users at other workstations.

- *Client autonomy is improved.*
  Workstations can be turned off or physically relocated at any time without fear of inconveniencing other users. Backup is needed only on the servers, since workstation disks are merely used as caches.

14.4.2 Scalability

A *scalable* distributed system is one that can easily cope with the addition of users and sites, and whose growth involves minimal expense, performance degradation, and administrative complexity. We have achieved these goals in Andrew by reducing static bindings to a bare minimum, and by maximizing the number of active clients that can be supported by a server. In the rest of this section, we describe the evolution of our design strategies for scalability over the history of Andrew.

AFS-1

AFS-1 was a prototype whose primary function was to validate the Andrew file system architecture and to obtain rapid feedback on key design decisions. Each server contained a local file system mirroring the structure of the shared file system. Vice file status information, such as an access list, was stored in *shadow* directories. If a file were not on a server, the search for its name would end in a *stub* directory which identified the server containing that file. Since servers processes could not share memory, their only means of sharing data structures was via the local file system.

Clients cached *path-name-prefix* information and used it to direct file requests to appropriate servers. The Vice-Venus interface named files by their full path name. There was no notion of a low-level name, such as the *inode* in UNIX.

Venus used a pessimistic approach to maintaining cache coherence. All cached copies of files were considered suspect. Before using a cached file, Venus would contact Vice to verify that it had the latest version. Each open of a file thus resulted in at least one interaction with a server, even if the file were already in the cache and up to date.

Our experience with AFS-1 was quite positive. Almost every application was able to use Vice files without recompilation or relinking. There were minor areas of incompatibility with standard UNIX semantics, but these were never serious enough to discourage users.

AFS-1 was in use for about a year, from late 1984 to late 1985. At the peak of its usage, there were about 100 workstations and six servers. Performance was usually acceptable to about 20 active users per server. But there were occasions when a few intense users caused performance to degrade intolerably. The system turned out to be difficult to operate and maintain, especially since there were few tools to help system administrators. The embedding of file location information in stub directories made it hard to move user files between servers.

AFS-2

The design of AFS-2 was based on experience with AFS-1 as well as on extensive performance analysis (Howard *et al.* [1988]). We retained the strategy of workstations caching entire files from a collection of dedicated autonomous servers. But we made many changes in the realization of this architecture, especially in the areas of *cache management, name resolution, communication,* and *server process structure*.

A fundamental change in AFS-2 was the manner in which cache coherence was maintained. Instead of checking with a server on each open, Venus now assumed that cache entries were valid unless otherwise notified. When a workstation cached a file or directory, the server promised to notify it before allowing a modification by any other workstation. This promise, called a *callback*, resulted in a considerable reduction in cache validation traffic.

Callback made it feasible for clients to cache directories and to translate path names locally. Without callbacks, the lookup of every component of a path name would have generated a cache validation request. For reasons of integrity, directory modifications were made directly on servers, as in AFS-1. Each Vice file or directory in AFS-2 was identified by a unique fixed-length *fid*. Location information was contained in a slowly-changing *volume location database* replicated on each server.

AFS-2 used a single process to service all clients of a server, thus reducing the context switching and paging overheads observed in AFS-1. A nonpreemptive *lightweight process* mechanism supported concurrency and provided a convenient programming abstraction on servers and clients. The RPC mechanism in AFS-2 was integrated with the lightweight process mechanism, supported a very large number of active clients, and used an optimized bulk transfer protocol for file transfer.

Besides changes for performance, AFS-2 also eliminated the inflexible mapping of Vice files to server disk storage in AFS-1. This change was the basis of a number of mechanisms that improved the operability of the system. Vice data in AFS-2 was organized in terms of a data structuring primitive called a *volume*. A volume was a collection of files forming a partial subtree of the Vice name space. Volumes were glued together at *mount points* to form the complete name space. Venus transparently recognized and crossed mount points during name resolution.

Volume sizes were usually small enough to allow many volumes per server disk partition. Volumes formed the basis of disk quotas. Each user of the system was typically assigned a volume and each volume was assigned a quota. Volumes could be easily moved between servers by system administrators. A volume could be used, even for update, while it was being moved.

Read-only replication of volumes made it possible to provide increased availability for frequently-read but rarely-updated files, such as system programs. The backup and restoration mechanism in AFS-2 also made use of volume primitives. To backup a volume, a read-only clone was first made. An asynchronous mechanism then transfered this frozen snapshot to a staging machine from where it was dumped to tape. To handle the common case of accidental deletion by users, the cloned backup volume of each user's files was made available as a read-only subtree of that user's home directory. Restoration of files within a 24-hour period could thus be performed by users themselves using normal file operations.

AFS-2 was in use at CMU from late 1985 until mid-1989. Our experience with it confirmed that it was indeed a usable system at large scale. The results of controlled experiments (Howard *et al.* [1988]; Nelson, Welch and Ousterhout [1988]) established that it performed better under load than other contemporary file systems. Figure 14.3 presents the results of one such experiment.

AFS-3

In 1988, work began on a new version of the Andrew file system called AFS-3.[1] The revision was initiated at CMU, and was completed at *Transarc Corporation*, a commercial venture involving many of the original implementors of AFS-3. At the time of writing this chapter, AFS-3 is in use at many tens of sites in the United States, Europe, Japan and Australia, and links them together with a single unified file name space.

---

[1]For ease of exposition we have grouped all changes made after the AFS-2 release described in Howard *et al.* [1988] as pertaining to AFS-3. In reality, the transition from AFS-2 to AFS-3 was gradual.

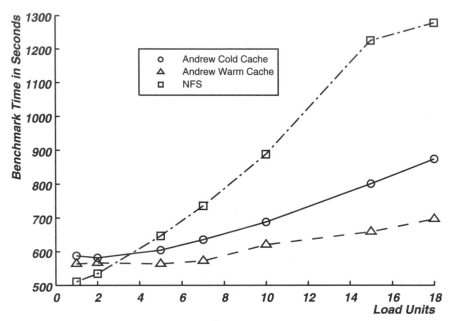

Figure 14.3. AFS-2 versus Sun NFS Performance under Load. This graph, reproduced from an earlier paper (Howard *et al.* [1988]), compares the behavior under load of AFS-2 and Sun NFS on identical client, server and network hardware. A load unit consists of one client workstation running an instance of the benchmark. Full details of the benchmark and experimental configuration can be found in the original paper. As the graph clearly indicates, the performance of AFS-2, even with a cold cache, degrades much more slowly than that of NFS

AFS-3 supports multiple administrative *cells*, each with its own servers, workstations, system administrators and users. Each cell is a completely autonomous Andrew environment. But a federation of cells can cooperate in presenting users with a uniform, seamless file name space. The ability to decompose a distributed system into cells is important at large scale, because it allows administrative responsibility to be delegated along lines that parallel institutional boundaries. This, in turn, makes for smooth and efficient system operation.

The RPC protocol used in AFS-3 is capable of providing good performance across local- and wide-area networks. Venus has been moved into the UNIX kernel in order to use the *vnode* file intercept mechanism from Sun Microsystems, a *de facto* industry standard. The change also makes it possible for Venus to cache files in large chunks (currently 64KB) rather than in their entirety. This, in turn, reduces file open latency and allows a workstation to access files that are too large to fit on its local disk cache.

14.4.3 Security

A consequence of large scale is that the casual attitude towards security typical of closely-knit distributed environments is no longer viable. Andrew provides mechanisms to enforce security, taking care to ensure that these mechanisms do not inhibit legitimate use of the system. Mechanisms alone cannot, of course, guarantee security; an installation will also have to follow proper administrative and operational procedures.

A fundamental assumption pertains to the question of who enforces security. Rather than trusting thousands of workstations, security in Andrew is predicated on the integrity of the much smaller number of Vice servers. No user software is ever run on servers. Workstations may be owned privately or located in public areas. Andrew assumes that the hardware and software on workstations may be modified in arbitrary ways.

In this section we summarize the main aspects of security in Andrew, pointing out the changes that have occurred as the system has evolved. These changes have been relatively small compared to the changes for scalability. More details on this aspect of Andrew can be found in an earlier paper (Satyanarayanan [1989]).

Protection Domain

The protection domain in Andrew is composed of *users* and *groups*. A user is an entity, usually a human, that can authenticate itself to Vice, be held responsible for its actions, and be charged for resource consumption. A group is a set of other groups and users, associated with a user called its *owner*.

AFS-1 and AFS-2 supported *group inheritance*, with a user's privileges being the cumulative privileges of all the groups he belonged to, either directly or indirectly. Modifications to the protection domain were made off-line by system administrators and were typically reflected in the system once a day. In AFS-3 modifications are made directly by users to a *protection server* that immediately reflects the changes in the system. To simplify the implementation of the protection server, the initial release of AFS-3 does not support group inheritance. This may change in future since group inheritance conceptually simplifies the management of the protection domain.

A group named 'System:Administrators' is distinguished. Membership in this group endows special administrative privileges, including unrestricted access to any file in the system. The use of a group 'System:Administrators' rather than a pseudo-user (such as 'root' in UNIX systems) has the advantage that the actual identity of the user exercising special privileges is available for use in audit trails.

Authentication

In AFS-1 and AFS-2, the RPC mechanism provided support for secure, authenticated communication between mutually suspicious clients and servers, using a variant of the Needham and Schroeder [1978] private key algorithm. When a user logged in to a workstation, his password was used to obtain *tokens* from an *authentication server*. These tokens were saved by Venus and used as needed to establish secure RPC connections on behalf of the user to file servers.

For reasons of standardization, AFS-3 adopted the Kerberos authentication system (Steiner, Neuman and Schiller [1988]). Kerberos provides the functionality of the original Andrew authentication mechanism, and resembles it in many ways.

File System Protection

Andrew uses an *access list* mechanism for file protection. The total rights specified for a user are the union of the rights specified for him and the groups he belongs to. Access lists are associated with directories rather than individual files. The reduction in state obtained by this design decision provides conceptual simplicity that is valuable at large scale. An access list can specify *negative rights*. An entry in a negative rights list indicates *denial* of the specified rights, with denial overriding possession in case of conflict. Negative rights decouple the problems of rapid revocation and propagation of group membership information, and are particularly valuable in a large distributed system.

Although the real enforcement of protection is done on the basis of access lists, Venus superimposes an emulation of UNIX protection semantics. The owner component of the UNIX *mode bits* on a file indicate readability, writability or executability. These bits, which now indicate what can be done to the file rather than who can do it, are set and examined by Venus but ignored by Vice. The combination of access lists on directories and mode bits on files has proved to be an excellent compromise between protection at fine granularity, conceptual simplicity, and UNIX compatibility.

Resource Usage

Security violations in a distributed system manifest themselves as unauthorized release or modification of information, or as denial of resources to legitimate users. The authentication and protection mechanisms of Andrew guard against unauthorized release and modification of information. Although Andrew controls server disk usage through a per-volume *quota* mechanism, it does not control resources such as network bandwidth and server CPU cycles. In our experience, the absence of such controls has not proved to be a problem. What has been an occasional problem is the inconvenience caused to the owner of a workstation by remote use of CPU cycles on his workstation.

14.5   The Coda File System

The Coda file system (Kistler and Satyanarayanan [1992]; Kumar and Satyanarayanan [1991]; Satyanarayanan *et al.* [1990]; Satyanarayanan *et al.* [1990]) is a descendant of AFS-2 that is substantially more resilient to server and network failures. The ideal that Coda strives for is *constant data availability*, allowing a user to continue working regardless of failures elsewhere in the system. Coda provides users with the benefits of a shared data repository, but allows them to rely entirely on local resources when that repository is partially or totally inaccessible.

A related goal of Coda is to gracefully integrate the use of *portable computers*. At present, users manually copy relevant files from Vice, use the machine while isolated from the network, and manually copy updated files back to Vice upon reconnection. These users are effectively performing manual caching of files with write-back on reconnection. If one views the disconnection from Vice as a deliberately-induced failure, it is clear that a mechanism for supporting portable machines in isolation is also a mechanism for fault tolerance.

By providing the ability to move seamlessly between zones of normal and disconnected operation, Coda may be able to simplify the use of cordless network technologies such as cellular telephone, packet radio, or infra-red communication in distributed file systems. Although such technologies provide client mobility, they often have intrinsic limitations such as short range, inability to operate inside buildings with steel frames, or line-of-sight constraints. These shortcomings are reduced in significance if clients are capable of temporary autonomous operation.

14.5.1   Architecture

The design of Coda retains key features of AFS-2 that contribute to scalability and security

- Clients cache entire files on their local disks. From the perspective of Coda, whole-file transfer also offers a degree of intrinsic resiliency. Once a file is cached and open at a client, it is immune to server and network failures. Caching on local disks is also consistent with our goal of supporting portable machines.
- Cache coherence is maintained by the use of callbacks.
- Clients dynamically find files on servers and cache location information.
- Token-based authentication and end-to-end encryption is used as the basis of security.

Failure resiliency is provided through the use of two distinct mechanisms. Coda uses *server replication*, or the storing of copies of files at multiple servers, to provide a highly available shared storage repository. When no server can be contacted the client resorts to *disconnected operation*, a mode of execution in which the client relies solely on cached data.

From a user's perspective, transitions between use of these complementary mechanisms are seamless. A client relies on server replication as long as it remains in contact with at least one server. It treats disconnected operation as a measure of last resort and reverts to normal operation at the earliest opportunity. A portable client that is isolated from the network is effectively operating disconnected

The need to handle network failures meant that we had to address the difficult issue of consistency guarantees across partitions. In the terminology of Davidson, Garcia and Skeen [1985], we had to decide whether to use a *pessimistic* replication strategy, providing strict consistency, or an *optimistic* strategy, providing higher availability. The former class of strategies avoid update conflicts by restricting modifications to at most one partition. The latter allows updates in every partition, but detects and resolves conflicting updates after they occur.

We chose to use an optimistic strategy for three reasons. First, and most important, such an approach provides higher availability. Second, we saw no clean way of supporting portable workstations using a pessimistic strategy. Third, it is widely believed that write sharing between users is relatively infrequent in academic UNIX environments. Consequently, conflicting updates are likely to be rare. We guarantee detection and confinement of these conflicts, and try to do this as soon after their occurrence as possible.

To summarize, Coda enhances availability both by the replication of files across servers, as well as by the ability of clients to operate entirely out of their caches. Both mechanisms depend upon an optimistic strategy for detection of update conflicts in the presence of network partitions. Although these mechanisms are complementary, they can be used independently of each other. For example, a Coda installation might choose to exploit the benefits of disconnected operation without incurring the CPU and disk storage overhead of server replication.

14.5.2 Server Replication

The unit of replication in Coda is a volume. A replicated volume consists of several physical volumes or *replicas* that are managed as one logical volume by the system. Individual replicas are not normally visible to users. The set of servers with replicas of a volume constitute its *volume storage group* (VSG). The degree of replication and the identity of the replication sites are specified when a volume is created. Although these parameters can be changed later, we do not anticipate such changes to be frequent. For every volume from which it has cached data, Venus keeps track of the subset of the VSG that is currently accessible. This subset is called the *accessible volume storage group* (AVSG). Different clients may have different AVSGs for the same volume at a given instant. Venus performs periodic *probes* to detect shrinking or enlargement of the AVSGs from which it has cached data. These probes are relatively infrequent, occurring once every ten minutes in our current implementation.

Access Protocol

Coda integrates server replication with caching using a variant of the *read-one, write-all* strategy. This variant can be characterized as *read-one-data, read-all-status, write-all*. In the common case of a cache hit on valid data, Venus avoids contacting the servers altogether. When servicing a cache miss, Venus obtains data from one member of its AVSG known as the *preferred server* (PS). The PS can be chosen at random or on the basis of performance criteria such as physical proximity, server load, or server CPU power. Although data is transferred only from one server, the other servers are contacted by Venus to collect their version and other status information. Venus uses this information to check whether the accessible replicas are equivalent. If the replicas are in conflict the system call which triggered the cache miss is aborted. If the replicas are not in conflict but some replicas are stale, the AVSG is notified asynchronously that a refresh is necessary. In the special case where the data on the PS is stale, a new PS is also selected and the fetch is repeated.

Callbacks are established with the AVSG as a side-effect of successfully fetching the data.

Update Protocol

When a file is closed after modification it is transferred to all members of the AVSG. This approach is simple to implement and maximizes the probability that every replication site has current data at all times. Server CPU load is minimized because the burden of data propagation is on the client rather than the servers. This in turn improves scalability, since the server CPU is the bottleneck in many distributed file systems. Operations which update directories, such as creating a new directory or removing a file, are also written through to all AVSG members.

Since its replication scheme is optimistic, Coda checks for existing conflicts on each server operation. The update protocol also guarantees eventual detection of new conflicts caused by the update. This protocol consists of two phases, COP1 and COP2, where COP stands for *Coda Optimistic Protocol*. The first phase performs the semantic part of the operation, such as transferring file contents, making a directory entry, or changing an access list. Each server verifies that its copy does not conflict with the client's copy before performing the update. The second phase distributes a data structure called the *update set*, which summarizes the client's knowledge of who performed the COP1 operation, to the servers. The update set is used to maintain the version information used in conflict detection.

Two protocol optimizations are used to improve performance. First, latency is reduced by Venus' returning control to the user after completion of COP1 and performing the COP2 asynchronously. Second, network and server CPU load are reduced by piggybacking the asynchronous COP2 messages on subsequent COP1 calls to the same VSG.

At present, a server performs no explicit remote actions upon recovery from a crash. Rather, it depends upon clients to notify it of stale or conflicting data. Although this lazy strategy does not violate Coda's consistency guarantees, it does increase the chances of a future conflict. An alternative approach, which we may adopt if warranted by usage experience, is for a recovering server to contact other servers to bring itself up to date.

Each server operation in Coda typically involves multiple servers. If the operation were done sequentially, latency would increase significantly. Venus therefore communicates with replication sites in parallel, using a parallel remote procedure call mechanism. This mechanism has been extended to use hardware multicast support, if available, to reduce the latency and network load caused by shipping large files to multiple sites. Shipping a large file to three servers in our current implementation typically takes about 10% longer than shipping it to one server.

14.5.3 Disconnected Operation

Logically, Venus operates in one of three states: *hoarding*, *emulation*, and *reintegration*. Figure 14.4 depicts these states and the transitions between them. Since all volumes may not be replicated across the same set of servers, Venus can be in

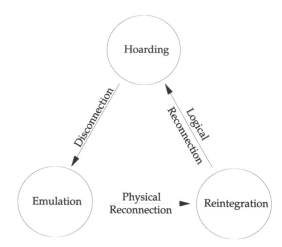

Figure 14.4. Venus States and Transitions. When disconnected, Venus is in the emulation state. It transits to reintegration upon successful reconnection to an AVSG member, and thence to hoarding, where it resumes connected operation

different states with respect to different volumes, depending on failure conditions in the system.

Hoarding

The hoarding state is so named because a key responsibility of Venus in this state is to hoard useful data in anticipation of disconnection. Venus combines implicit and explicit sources of information in a *priority-based cache management algorithm* that balances the needs of connected and disconnected operation. It periodically reevaluates which objects merit retention in the cache via a process known as *hoard walking*. The implicit information consists of recent reference history, as in traditional caching algorithms. Explicit information takes the form of a per-workstation *hoard database* (HDB), whose entries are path names identifying objects of interest to the user at that workstation.

A simple front-end program allows a user to update the HDB using command scripts called *hoard profiles*. Since hoard profiles are just files, it is simple for an application maintainer to provide a common profile for his users, or for users collaborating on a project to maintain a common profile. To facilitate construction of hoard profiles, Venus can record all file references observed between a pair of start and stop events indicated by a user.

Emulation

In the emulation state, Venus performs many actions normally handled by servers. For example, Venus now assumes full responsibility for access and semantic checks. It is also responsible for generating temporary *file identifiers* (*fids*) for new objects, pending the assignment of permanent *fids* at reintegration. But although Venus is functioning as a *pseudo-server*, updates accepted by it have to be revalidated with respect to integrity and protection by real servers. This follows from the Coda policy of trusting only servers, not clients.

Cache management during emulation is done with the same priority algorithm used during hoarding. Mutating operations directly update the cache entries of the objects involved. Cache entries of deleted objects are freed immediately, but those of other modified objects assume infinite priority so that they are not purged before reintegration. On a cache miss, the default behavior of Venus is to return an error code. A user may optionally request Venus to block his processes until cache misses can be serviced.

During emulation, Venus records sufficient information to replay update activity when it reintegrates. It maintains this information in a per-volume log of mutating operations called a *replay log*. Venus uses a number of optimizations to reduce the length of the replay log, resulting in a log size that is typically a few percent of cache size.

Metadata, consisting of cached directory and symbolic link contents, status blocks for cached objects of all types, replay logs, and the HDB, is mapped into Venus' address space as *recoverable virtual memory* (RVM). Transactional access to this memory is supported by the RVM library (Mashburn and Satyanarayanan [1992]) linked into Venus. The actual contents of cached files are not in RVM, but are stored as local UNIX files.

Reintegration

Reintegration is a transitory state through which Venus passes in changing roles from pseudo-server to cache manager. In this state, Venus propagates changes made during emulation, and updates its cache to reflect current server state. Reintegration is performed a volume at a time, with all update activity in the volume suspended until completion. The replay log is shipped in parallel to the AVSG, and executed independently at each member. Each server performs the replay within a single transaction, which is aborted if any error is detected.

14.5.4 Conflict Resolution

Since UNIX files are untyped byte streams there is, in general, no information to automate their resolution. Coda marks all accessible replicas of the file inconsistent. This ensures damage containment since normal operations on these replicas will fail until explicitly repaired by a user.

A directory, on the other hand, is an object whose semantics is completely known and whose resolution can often be automated. For example, partitioned creation of uniquely-named files in the same directory can be handled automatically by selectively replaying the missing creates. Coda uses a *log-based* strategy (Kumar and Satyanarayanan [1991]) to resolve directories. Each server maintains a per-volume history of directory operations. When the servicing of a cache miss on a directory indicates replica inequality amongst servers, Venus invokes the *resolution subsystem* on the servers. With one server acting as coordinator, a four-phase resolution protocol is executed by the AVSG. During the course of this protocol, each server replays the updates it missed. If no conflicts are detected, Venus continues normal operation. Otherwise all accessible replicas are marked in conflict, just as in the case of file conflict.

Coda provides a repair tool to assist users in manually resolving file and directory conflicts. It uses a special interface to Venus so that requests from the tool are distinguishable from normal file system requests. Venus, in conjunction with the tool, presents the illusion of an in-place 'explosion' of inconsistent objects into their distinct versions. Inconsistent objects appear as read-only directories with the same name as the original. Normal UNIX applications can be used in these directories to assist the user.

Failed resolution is handled in a different way if it occurs during reintegration. In keeping with our view that second-class replicas are inferior to first-class replicas, we do not mark the server replicas in conflict. Rather, we preserve the replay log in a local *replay file* whose format is a superset of the UNIX *tar* format. The log and all corresponding cache entries are then purged, so that subsequent references will cause refetch of the current contents at the AVSG. A manual replay tool is provided which allows the user to inspect the contents of a replay file, compare it to the state at the AVSG, and replay it selectively or in its entirety.

14.5.5 Status and Experience

Today, Coda runs on IBM RTs, Decstation 3100s and 5000s, and 386-based laptops such as the Toshiba 5200 and IBM PS2-L40. A small user community has been using Coda on a daily basis as its primary data repository since April 1990. All development work on Coda is done in Coda itself. As of May 1992 there was nearly 1GB of triply-replicated data in Coda. We regularly operate disconnected for periods lasting two to three days.

Latency of operations is usually a major concern with replication schemes. Our experience with server replication in Coda is quite positive. Controlled experiments on identical client and server hardware show that under light loads the performance of Coda is within 5% of the performance of the current release of Andrew. Thus the cost of replication is primarily the storage cost for additional replicas at the servers.

In our experience, typical disconnected sessions of editing and program development lasting a few hours require less than a minute for reintegration. A local disk capacity of 60MB on our clients has proved adequate for our sessions of disconnected operation. To obtain a better understanding of the cache size requirements for disconnected operation, we analyzed file reference traces from our environment. The analysis confirms that a disk of 50-60MB should be adequate for operating disconnected for a typical workday. Of course, user activity that is drastically different from what was recorded in our traces could produce significantly different results.

In our use of optimistic server replication in Coda for nearly a year, we have seen virtually no conflicts due to multiple users updating an object in different network partitions. To obtain data on the likelihood of conflicts at larger scale, we instrumented the Andrew servers in our environment. Since Coda is descended from AFS and makes the same kind of usage assumptions, we can use this data to estimate how frequent conflicts would be if Coda were to replace AFS in our environment. The data shows that more than 99.5% of all mutations are by the previous writer, and the chances of two different users modifying the same object within a week are less than 0.4%! This data is highly encouraging from the point of view of optimistic replication.

Our measurements of log-based directory resolution show that that the time for resolution is typically less than 10% of the time for performing the original set of partitioned updates. Trace-driven analysis shows that a log size of 20KB per volume per hour of partition should be ample for our environment. For a 100-volume server, this translates to a log size of 2MB per hour of partition.

14.6   Design Principles from Andrew and Coda

The essence of the Andrew and Coda strategy is to decompose a large distributed system into a small nucleus that changes relatively slowly, and a much larger and less static periphery. From the perspectives of security and operability, the scale of the system appears to be that of the nucleus. But from the perspectives of performance and availability, a user at the periphery receives almost stand-alone service.

A consequence of this strategy is that clients and servers need to be *physically distinct* machines. This seemingly minor detail turns out to be critical. Without this dichotomy, one cannot make different security and administrative decisions about clients and servers, nor can one optimize their hardware and software configurations independently. Although the need to have physically distinct clients and servers is not a problem at large scale, it is an expensive proposition at small scale. It is therefore tempting to make the client versus server distinction only a *logical* one, so that the start-up cost of a small installation is low. Unfortunately, systems such as NFS and Locus that have chosen this approach have foundered on the rock of scalability. Growth in these systems is unwieldy, and none of them appears capable of growth to thousands of sites. One is therefore forced to conclude that the client-server distinction is a fundamental one from the perspective of scalability, and that a higher initial cost is the price one pays for a system that can grow gracefully.

Besides this high-level principle, we have also acquired more detailed insights about scalability in the course of building Andrew and Coda. We present these insights here as a collection of design principles:

- *Clients have the cycles to burn.*
  Whenever there is a choice between performing an operation on a client and performing it on a server, it is preferable to pick the client. This will enhance the scalability of the design, since it lessens the need to increase central resources as clients are added.

  The only functions performed by servers in Andrew and Coda are those critical to security, integrity or location of data. Further, there is very little inter-server traffic. Pathname translation is done on clients rather than on servers in AFS-2, AFS-3, and Coda. The parallel update protocol in Coda depends on the client to directly update all accessible servers, rather than updating one of them and letting it relay the update.

- *Cache whenever possible.*
Scalability, user mobility and site autonomy motivate this principle. Caching reduces contention on centralized resources and transparently makes data available wherever it is being currently used.

AFS-1 cached files and location information. AFS-2 also cached directories, as do AFS-3 and Coda. Caching is the basis of disconnected operation in Coda.

- *Exploit usage properties.*
Knowledge about the use of real systems allows better design choices to be made. For example, files can often be grouped into a small number of easily-identifiable classes that reflect their access and modification patterns. These class-specific properties provide an opportunity for independent optimization, and hence improved performance, in a distributed file system design.

Almost one-third of file references in a typical UNIX system are to temporary files. Since such files are seldom shared, Andrew and Coda make them part of the local name space. The executable files of system programs are often read but rarely written. AFS-2, AFS-3 and Coda therefore support read-only replication of these files to improve performance and availability. Coda's use of an optimistic replication strategy is based on the premise that sequential write-sharing of user files is rare.

- *Minimize system-wide knowledge and change.*
In a large distributed system it is difficult to be aware, at all times, of the entire state of the system. It is also difficult to update distributed or replicated data structures in a consistent manner. The scalability of a design is enhanced if it rarely requires global information to be monitored or atomically updated.

Clients in Andrew and Coda only monitor the status of servers from which they have cached data. They do not require any knowledge of the rest of the system. File location information on Andrew and Coda servers changes relatively rarely. Caching by Venus, rather than file location changes in Vice, is used to deal with movement of users.

Coda integrates server replication (a relatively heavyweight mechanism) with caching to improve availability without losing scalability. Knowledge of a caching site is confined to those servers with callbacks for the caching site. Coda does not depend on knowledge of system-wide topology nor does it incorporate any algorithms requiring system-wide election or commitment.

Another instance of the application of this principle is the use of negative rights. More rapid revocation is possible by modifications to an access list at a single site rather than by system-wide change to a replicated protection database.

- *Trust the fewest possible entities.*
A system whose security depends on the integrity of the fewest possible entities is more likely to remain secure as it grows.

Rather than trusting thousands of clients, security in Andrew and Coda is predicated on the integrity of the much smaller number of Vice servers. The administrators of Vice need only ensure the physical security of these servers and the software they run. Responsibility for client integrity is delegated to the owner of each client. Andrew and Coda rely on end-to-end encryption rather than physical link security.

- *Batch if possible*
Grouping operations together can improve throughput (and hence scalability), although it is often at the cost of latency.

The transfer of files in large chunks in AFS-3, and in their entirety in AFS-1, AFS-2 and Coda is an instance of the application of this principle. More efficient network protocols can be used when data is transferred *en masse* rather than as individual pages. In Coda, the second phase of the update protocol is deferred and batched. Latency is not increased in this case, because control can be returned to application programs before the completion of the second phase.

14.7   A Glimpse of Other Distributed File Systems

In this section we examine three distributed file systems whose designs differ significantly from Andrew and Coda. Due to constraints of space, we only provide enough detail to compare and contrast their designs. Full descriptions of these systems can be found in the cited references.

14.7.1   Sun Network File System

Since its introduction in 1985, the Sun Microsystems *Network File System* (NFS) has been widely used in industry and academia. Portability and heterogeneity are two considerations that have played a dominant role in the design of NFS. Although the original file system model was based on UNIX, NFS has been ported to to non-UNIX operating systems such as PC-DOS. A high-level overview of NFS is presented by Walsh *et al.* [1985]. Details of its design and implementation are given by Sandberg *et al.* [1985], while Rosen, Wilde and Fraser-Campbell [1986] comment on the portability of NFS.

Design details such as caching, replication, naming, and consistency guarantees may vary considerably in different NFS implementations. In order to focus our discussion, we restrict our attention to the implementation of NFS provided by Sun for its workstations that run the SunOS flavor of UNIX.

With a view to simplifying crash recovery on servers, the NFS protocol is designed to be *stateless*. Consequently, servers are not required to maintain contextual information about their clients. Each RPC request from a client contains all the information needed to satisfy the request. To some degree functionality and UNIX compatibility have been sacrificed to meet this goal. Locking, for instance, is not supported by the NFS protocol, since locks would constitute state information on a server. SunOS does, however, provide a separate lock server to perform this function.

The NFS paradigm treats workstations as peers, with no fundamental distinction between clients and servers. A workstation may be a server, exporting some of its files. NFS clients are usually configured so that each sees a UNIX file name space with a private root. Each workstation is free to configure its own name space, and there is hence no guarantee that all workstations at an installation have a common view of shared files. But collaborating groups of users usually configure their workstations to have the same name space.

NFS clients cache individual pages of remote files and directories in their main memory. When a client caches any block of a file, it also caches a timestamp indicating when the file was last modified on the server. To validate cached blocks of a file, the client compares its cached timestamp with the timestamp on the server. If the server timestamp is more recent, the client invalidates all cached blocks of the file and refetches them on demand. A validation check is always performed when a file is opened, and when the server is contacted to satisfy a cache miss. After a check, cached blocks are assumed valid for a finite interval of time, specified by the client when a remote file system is mounted. The first reference to any block of the file after this interval forces a validation check.

If a cached page is modified, it is marked as dirty and scheduled to be flushed to the server. The actual flushing is performed by an asynchronous kernel activity and will occur after some unspecified delay. However, the kernel does provide a guarantee that all dirty pages of a file will be flushed to the server before a close operation on the file completes.

Directories are cached for reading in a manner similar to files. Modifications to directories, however, are performed directly on the server. When a file is opened, a cache validation check is also performed on its parent directory. Files and directories can have different revalidation intervals, typical values being 3 seconds for files and 30 seconds for directories.

NFS performs network data transfers in large block sizes, typically 8 Kbytes, to improve performance. Read-ahead is employed to improve sequential access performance. Files corresponding to executable binaries are fetched in their entirety if they are smaller than a certain threshold.

14.7.2   Apollo Domain File System

The DOMAIN system, built by Apollo Computers Inc., is a distributed workstation environment whose development began in the early 1980s. Levine [1987] presents the design and rationale of the DOMAIN file system. All nodes in a DOMAIN installation are viewed as peers. The DOMAIN software provides support for the distribution of typed files via an *Object Storage System (OSS)*. A system-wide *Single Level Store (SLS)* that provides a mapped virtual-memory interface to objects is built on top of the OSS. The DOMAIN distributed file system is layered on the SLS and presents a UNIX-like file interface to application programs.

At any instant of time an object has a *home* node associated with it. The OSS maps objects to their homes by using a *hint server*. As its name implies, the hint server performs the mapping using a number of heuristics. It is updated in normal system operation by many diverse components of the DOMAIN software as they discover the location of objects. Every object in the system is uniquely named by a 64-bit identifier called its *UID*. A distributed *naming server* that maps string names to UIDs is built on top of the OSS. This server provides a hierarchical, UNIX-like, location transparent name space for all files and directories in the system.

The DOMAIN system transparently caches data and attributes of objects at the usage node. Mapped virtual-memory accesses via the SLS interface and file accesses via the file system interface are both translated into object references at the OSS level. The latter manages a cache of individual pages of objects using a write-back scheme with periodic flushing of data to the home of the objects. The consistency of locally cached data pages is verified by comparing their timestamps with the timestamp of the object at the home node. Missing pages are obtained by demand paging across the network to the home node. Fetch-ahead (typically 8KB) is used to improve sequential access performance.

Cache management in DOMAIN is integrated with its concurrency control mechanisms. Each node runs a *lock manager* that synchronizes accesses to all objects which have their home at that node. Two modes of locking are supported. One mode allows multiple distributed readers or a single writer to access the object. The other mode allows access to multiple readers and writers co-located at a single node. Lock managers do not queue requests. If a lock for an object cannot be granted immediately, the requesting node must periodically retry its request.

Cache validation is performed when an object is locked. When a write-lock on an object is released, an implicit *purify* operation is performed. This operation atomically flushes updated pages of an object to its home node. Application software is responsible for ensuring that objects are locked before being mapped into virtual memory or opened for file access. It is also responsible for releasing locks when appropriate.

14.7.3   Sprite Network File System

Sprite is an operating system for networked uniprocessor and multiprocessor workstations, designed at the University of California at Berkeley. The goals of Sprite include efficient use of large main memories, support for multiprocessor workstations, efficient network communication, and diskless operation. Besides a distributed file system, Sprite provides other distributed system facilities such as process migration. Ousterhout *et al.* [1988] provide an overview of Sprite. Welch and Ousterhout [1986] describe the prefix mechanism used for file location. A detailed performance analysis of caching in Sprite is presented by Nelson, Welch and Ousterhout [1988].

Most workstations in a Sprite network are diskless. Although the design of Sprite does not make a rigid distinction between clients and servers, a few machines with disks are usually dedicated as file servers. These servers jointly present a location-transparent UNIX file system interface to clients. Clients do not have to explicitly import files from individual servers. Each server can respond to location queries, using *remote links* embedded in the file system at each server. Remote links are effectively pointers to files at other servers. Each client maintains a local *prefix table*, which maps path-name prefixes to servers. Substantial performance improvement is achieved by using the cached information in the prefix table for locating files.

Sprite is intended for use by a collection of collaborating users who are either incapable of subverting the kernels on workstations, or who trust each other. Consequently Sprite kernels trust each other, and communication between them is neither authenticated nor encrypted.

Exact emulation of UNIX file system semantics is an important goal of Sprite. Whenever a client opens or closes a file for reading or writing, it notifies the server that stores the file. A Sprite client usually caches pages of a file, validating these pages each time the file is opened. Caching is disabled when multiple clients have a file open, and one or more of these clients have it open for writing. Once caching is disabled, it is re-enabled only after all clients concurrently using the file have closed it. This strategy enables Sprite to provide consistency at the granularity of individual read and write operations.

Sprite provides location-transparent remote access to devices as well as files. To provide good performance under a wide variety of workloads, physical memory on a Sprite workstation is dynamically partitioned between the virtual memory subsystem and the file cache. Sprite uses ordinary file in the shared name space for paging. This simplifies process migration, since the backing files are visible at all other Sprite workstations in the environment.

14.8   Conclusion

Since the earliest days of distributed computing, file systems have been the most important and widely-used form of shared permanent storage. The continuing interest in distributed file systems bears testimony to the robustness of this model of data sharing. We now understand how to implement distributed file systems that span a few hundred to a few thousand nodes, although scaling beyond that will be a formidable challenge. Security continues to be a serious concern, and may turn out to be the Achilles heel of large distributed systems. Availability, especially in large systems and in the context of portable clients, is an important problem for which we now have some initial experience. Many other challenges also await us: mobility, heterogeneity, efficient search, and support for diverse types of data such as full-motion video and large stored images. Regardless of the specific technical direction taken by distributed file systems in the next decade, there is little doubt that it will be an area of considerable ferment in industry and academia.

Acknowledgements

M. Satyanarayanan's work on this book was supported in part by the the Advanced Research Projects Agency (Wright-Patterson AFB under Contract F33615-90-C-1465, Arpa Order No. 7597), the IBM Corporation, Digital Equipment Corporation, and Bellcore.[2]

---

[2]The views and conclusion expressed in this paper are those of the author, and should not be interpreted as those of the funding organizations.

14.9 References

Apple Computer (1985), *Inside Macintosh*, vol. **II**, Addison-Wesley, Reading, MA.

Baker, M. G., Hartman, J. H., Kupfer, M. D., Shirriff, K. W. and Ousterhout, J. K. (1991), Measurements of a Distributed File System , *Proceedings of the 13th Symposium on Operating Systems Principles*, Pacific Grove, CA, In *ACM Operating Systems Review* **25**(5).

Bernstein, P. A. and Goodman, N. (1981), Concurrency Control in Distributed Database Systems, *ACM Computing Surveys* **13**(2), 185–222.

Brownbridge, D. R., Marshall, L. F. and Randell, B. (1982), The Newcastle Connection, *Software—Practice & Experience* **12**, 1147–1162.

DEC (1985), *VMS System Software Handbook*, Digital Equipment Corporation, Maynard, MA.

Davidson, S. B., Garcia, H. and Skeen, D. (1985), Consistency in Partitioned Networks, *ACM Computing Surveys* **17**(3), 341–370.

Floyd, R. (1986a), Directory Reference Patterns in a Unix Environment, Department of Computer Science, University of Rochester, Technical Report TR-179.

Floyd, R. (1986b), Short-Term File Reference Patterns in a Unix Environment, Department of Computer Science, University of Rochester, Technical Report TR-177.

Howard, J. H., Kazar, M. J., Menees, S. G., Nichols, D. A., Satyanarayanan, M., Sidebotham, R. N. and West, M. J. (1988), Scale and Performance in a Distributed File System, *ACM Transactions on Computer Systems* **6**(1).

IBM (1983), Disk Operating System, Version 2.1, IBM Corporation, 1502343.

Kistler, J. J. and Satyanarayanan, M. (1992), Disconnected Operation in the Coda File System, *ACM Transactions on Computer Systems* **10**(1).

Kumar, P. and Satyanarayanan, M. (1991), Log-Based Directory Resolution in the Coda File System, School of Computer Science, Carnegie Mellon University, Technical Report CMU-CS-91-164.

Lampson, B. W. (1983), Hints for Computer System Design, *Proceedings of the Ninth Symposium on Operating Systems Principles*, Bretton Woods, NH, 33–48, In *ACM Operating Systems Review* **17**(5).

Letwin, G. (1988), *Inside OS/2*, Microsoft Press.

Levine, P. H. (1987), The Apollo Domain Distributed File System, in *Theory and Practice of Distributed Operating Systems*, NATO ASI, Springer Verlag.

Majumdar, S. and Bunt, R. B. (1986), Measurement and Analysis of Locality Phases in File Referencing Behaviour, *Proceedings of the Performance '86 and ACM Sigmetrics Conference*, Raleigh.

Mashburn, H. and Satyanarayanan, M. (1992), *RVM: Recoverable Virtual Memory User Manual*, School of Computer Science, Carnegie Mellon University.

Meyer, C. H. and Matyas, S. M. (1982), *Cryptography: A New Dimension in Computer Data Security*, John Wiley & Sons, NYC.

Mummert, L. B. and Satyanarayanan, M. (1992), Efficient File Reference Tracing in a Distributed Workstation Environment, School of Computer Science, Carnegie Mellon University, Technical Report (in preparation).

Needham, R. M. and Schroeder, M. D. (1978), Using Encryption for Authentication in Large Networks of Computers, *Communications of the ACM* **21**(12), 993–999.

Nelson, M. N., Welch, B. B. and Ousterhout, J. K. (1988), Caching in the Sprite Network File System, *ACM Transactions on Computer Systems* **6**(1).

Ousterhout, J. K., Cherenson, A. R., Douglis, F., Nelson, M. N. and Welch, B. B. (1988), The Sprite Network Operating System, *IEEE Computer* **21**(2), 23–35.

Ousterhout, J. K., Costa, H. D., Harrison, D., Kunze, J., Kupfer, M. and Thompson, J. (1985), A Trace-Driven Analysis of the Unix 4.2 BSD File System, *Proceedings of the Tenth Symposium on Operating Systems Principles*, Orcas Island, WA, In *ACM Operating Systems Review* **19**(5).

Ramakrishnan, K. K., Biswas, P. and Karedla, R. (1992), Analysis of File I/O Traces in Commercial Computing Environments, *Proceedings of the 1992 ACM SIGMETRICS Conference*, Newport, RI.

Revelle, R. (1975), An Empirical Study of File Reference Patterns, IBM Research Division, RJ 1557.

Rifkin, A. P., Forbes, M. P., Hamilton, R. L., Sabrio, M., Shah, S. and Yueh, K. (1986), RFS Architectural Overview, *Usenix Conference PROC, Atlanta, Georgia*.

Ritchie, D. M. and Thompson, K. (1974), The Unix Time Sharing System, *Communications of the ACM* **17**(7).

Rosen, M. B., Wilde, M. J. and Fraser-Campbell, B. (1986), NFS Portability, *Proceedings of the Summer Usenix Conference*, Atlanta, GA.

Sandberg, R., Goldberg, D., Kleiman, S., Walsh, D. and Lyon, B. (1985), Design and Implementation of the SUN Network File System, *Proceedings of the Summer Usenix Conference*.

Satyanarayanan, M. (1981), A Study of File Sizes and Functional Lifetimes, *Proceedings of the Eighth Symposium on Operating Systems Principles*, In *ACM Operating Systems Review* **15**(5).

Satyanarayanan, M. (1984), A Synthetic Driver for File System Simulations, *Proceedings of the International Conference on Modelling Techniques*.

Satyanarayanan, M. (1989), Integrating Security in Large Distributed Systems, *ACM Transactions on Computer Systems* **7**(3).

Satyanarayanan, M., Howard, J. H., Nichols, D. N., Sidebotham, R. N., Spector, A. Z. and West, M. J. (1985), The ITC Distributed File System: Principles and Design, *Proceedings of the Tenth Symposium on Operating Systems Principles*, Orcas Island, WA, In *ACM Operating Systems Review* **19**(5).

Satyanarayanan, M., Kistler, J. J., Kumar, P., Okasaki, M. E., Siegel, E. H. and Steere, D. C. (1990), Coda: A Highly Available File System for a Distributed Workstation, *IEEE Transactions on Computers* **39**(4), 447–459.

Schroeder, M. D., Gifford, D. and Needham, R. M. (1985), A Caching File System for a Programmer's Workstation, *Proceedings of the Tenth Symposium on Operating Systems Principles*, Orcas Island, WA, 25–34, In *ACM Operating Systems Review* **19**(5).

Smith, A. J. (1981), Analysis of Long Term File Reference Patterns for Application to File Migration Algorithms, *IEEE Transactions on Software Engineering* **7**(4).

Steiner, J. G., Neuman, C. and Schiller, J. I. (1988), Kerberos: An Authentication Service for Open Network Systems, *Proceedings of the Usenix Winter Conference*, 191–201.

Stritter, E. P. (1977), File Migration, Stanford University, Ph.D. Dissertation.

Terry, D. B. (1987), Caching Hints in Distributed Systems, *IEEE Transactions on Software Engineering* **SE-13**(1).

Voydock, V. L. and Kent, S. T. (1983), *ACM Computing Surveys* **15**(2), 135–171.

Walsh, D., Lyon, B., Sager, G., Chang, J. M., Goldberg, D., Kleiman, S., Lyon, T., Sandberg, R. and Weiss, P. (1985), Overview of the SUN Network File System, *Proceedings of the Winter Usenix Conference*, Dallas, TX.

Welch, B. B. and Ousterhout, J. K. (1986), Prefix Tables: A Simple Mechanism for locating Files in a Distributed System, *Proceedings of the Sixth International Conference on Distributed Computing Systems*, Cambridge, MA, IEEE Computer Society Press.

Chapter 15

Kernel Support for Distributed Systems

Sape J. Mullender

The operating system provides an environment in which application programs can run. An application, in the most general case, consists of a number of processes, possibly running on different nodes, and each process consists of an address space and one or more computations (*threads of control*).

Although address spaces, threads and processes are not always directly visible to the application programmer, most programming environments do make use of them at a lower level.

In this chapter, we shall examine what facilities operating systems provide to allow distributed applications to run. Section 15.2 examines address-space and memory management; Section 15.3 looks at process management and Section 15.4 discusses management of threads within a process.

15.1 The Kernel

All but the most primitive operating systems protect the operating system from being damaged by applications, by placing the operating system functions in a separate address space (or several separate address spaces) from the applications and by letting the applications run in an unprivileged mode of the processor.

Designers of multi-user operating systems usually assume a hostile user environment: one user's application must be protected from malicious interference from another's. This is achieved by letting each application run in a separate domain, with the memory-management unit set up so that one application cannot access another application's data in any way. Naturally, these applications must not be allowed access to the memory-management unit, or to peripheral devices. Applications are run in an unprivileged mode of the processor which is referred to as *user mode*.

The part of the operating system that has access to the memory-management hardware and switches between the application's protection domains is referred to as the *kernel*. The kernel's code runs in a special, privileged mode called *supervisor mode* or *kernel mode*.

Until quite recently, the operating system *was* the kernel, because all of the operating system ran in supervisor mode. This is now changing because of two reasons.

1. Operating system are becoming very large which makes them increasingly hard to maintain as a single monolithic entity running in supervisor mode where bugs can create so much damage.
2. Distributed systems place different functions on different machines, so not all operating system functions are needed in every copy of the operating system.

The result has been a shift towards *microkernels*, operating systems in which only functions that need access to privileged instructions, the MMU, or peripherals are placed in the kernel. All other operating system functions are carried out by processes running in user mode.

A microkernel usually contains the memory manager, process scheduler and device drivers. User-space operating services usually encompass file server, window system and terminal handling. Services for interprocess communication are sometimes placed in the kernel and sometimes in user space.

Note that the difference between structuring an operating system as a microkernel plus user-space services and structuring it as a monolithic kernel is purely one of modularization. Microkernels with user-space services are, in general, easier to test, debug and maintain than monolithic kernels, but monolithic kernels have potentially better performance because there are fewer context switches.

Microkernel-based operating systems seem to be widely regarded by the research community and the industry as a panacea, whereas, if monolithic operating systems are not quite treated with contempt, they are certainly regarded as old-fashioned. As a result, systems like Amoeba (Mullender *et al.* [1990]), Chorus (Rozier and Martins [1986]) and Mach (Accetta *et al.* [1986]) have suddenly become very popular. NT from MicroSoft was raved about before anyone had seen how it works.

A ready explanation for the popularity of microkernel-based systems in the operating-systems-research community is that they are easy to modify and to experiment with. Monolithic versions of UNIX, for instance, are so large today, that it takes students a long time before they even find the place where modifications for experimentation with research prototypes can be made.

Mach is an example of an operating system that has recently been turned from a monolithic system into a microkernel-plus-services one. The Mach microkernel designers chose to implement process management, thread management, address-space management, and local interprocess communication in the kernel, while implementing intermachine communication, the file system, window system, and pagers in user space.

Amoeba (Mullender *et al.* [1990]) is an example of a distributed operating system that was conceived and implemented as a microkernel-plus-services. In Amoeba, multithreaded processes are managed by the kernel, memory management is done by the kernel and all interprocess communication is handled by the kernel. As in Mach, file system and window system are under control of user-space services. Assignment of processes to processors, migration of processes, and interactive debugging are done by user-space processes with minimal kernel support. Most devices are accessed through minimal kernel-space 'microservers' with the bulk of device-handling code in user-space servers.

Plan 9 from Bell Labs (Pike *et al.* [1990]; Pike *et al.* [1993]; Presotto *et al.* [1991]) has a hybrid design. The kernel contains most of the functionality necessary to run applications, but many user-space services or remote services improve both functionality and performance. The kernel carries out process management and memory management, it implements a screen driver with a bit-blit interface for user-space window servers, it implements name-space management and it implements a minimal file system. Normally, however, file service is provided by a separate file server (implemented as a special-purpose application that runs in user mode). A user-space pager is needed when the sum of the sizes of the virtual address spaces exceeds the available physical memory.

Plan 9, although not a microkernel, is considerably smaller than the Mach microkernel. It has been observed that this is because the Mach microkernel has to support the weight of OSF/1 and Motif.

An important concern in the design of microkernel-based operating systems is the realization of a very efficient context switching mechanism. This is because the number of context switches is larger in such systems. Achieving this is made more difficult by the fact that faster (RISC) processors invest heavily in a context by collecting state in their cache; on a context switch, much of the cache contents becomes obsolete. We shall return to this issue in Sections 15.2.1 and 15.2.6.

15.2   Address-Space and Memory Management

Modern memory management units allow an operating system designer a large amount of flexibility in defining what constitutes a process' address space, how data can be shared in memory between processes, how virtual memory is backed by physical memory and disk, and so on.

Memory management is complicated because it affects both performance and ease of programming in radical ways. Therefore, the design of a system's memory-management system must be done with a great deal of thought and care. In this section, we explore a number of memory-management design issues for distributed systems and discuss their repercussions on performance and the design of other parts of the system. First, we examine the hardware support for memory management that is used in today's computers.

15.2.1   Hardware Support for Memory-Management

A memory-management unit (MMU) is a piece of hardware that maps virtual *pages*, sequences of virtual memory locations, to physical pages. In modern computer architectures, the function of the memory-management unit is made faster by implementing an on-CPU-chip cache of recently used virtual-to-physical address mappings. Such a cache is called a *translation look-aside buffer*, or TLB.

Usually, upon a TLB miss, the memory-management unit is consulted to provide the virtual-to-physical mapping and, if it cannot provide the mapping either, an interrupt is generated and operating system software has to deal with the page fault.

In some systems, mostly high-speed RISC machines, there is no memory-management unit at all. When a mapping cannot be provided by the TLB, an interrupt happens immediately. The machine architecture has instructions for replacing entries in the TLB. Using these instructions, the missing TLB entry can be provided.

When the virtual-to-physical address mapping is changed, in a context switch, for instance, or when a process maps a segment in or out, the TLB must also be updated. If this is not done, processes may use mappings that are no longer valid. Usually this is done by flushing the TLB. TLB flushes contribute significantly to the time it takes to do a context switch.

15.2.2   Address Spaces

An *address space* is the view a process has of its memory. It includes the set of usable addresses in the virtual address space and what operations (read, write, execute) are allowed at those addresses. An address space is made up of *segments*; each segment is further divided into *pages*.

Pages are the smallest units of memory that the memory management hardware can manipulate, usually four or eight kilobytes in size. Segments are the unit of allocation used by the operating system. Because segments must be manipulated using the memory-management hardware, segments must be an integral number of pages in size.

Operating systems usually provide address spaces with a standard structure to their processes. In UNIX, for instance, an address space typically consists of a *text segment*, a *data segment*, a *bss segment*, and a *stack segment*. Each segment serves a separate purpose: the text segment contains the executable code and is usually made read- or execute-only. The data segment contains the initialized data of the process. The *bss* segment is used for uninitialized data (so does not have to be initialized from the file containing the binary); the bss segment can grow to accommodate a heap structure. Finally, the stack segment contains the process' stack and can also grow as the stack grows. UNIX processes are single-threaded, so there is only one stack segment.

15.2.3   Shared Memory

When multiple instances of the same program are running concurrently, memory space can be saved by letting them all share the (non-writeable) code segment. A finer granularity of sharing can be offered by allowing processes to share code on a per-library basis by allocating different segments for the code of different libraries. System V UNIX is an example of a system with shared libraries.

Code sharing is fairly easy to realize, since the shared code is immutable. As long as there is sufficient memory to hold a process' code, data and stack, processes can be allocated to any suitable machine in a distributed system.

Sharing of mutable segments is much more complicated, because the processes sharing the data must be able to observe the modifications made by others immediately. The easiest way to guarantee this is to assign all processes sharing a segment to the same processor, or possibly to the same shared-memory multiprocessor.

But in so-called *firmly coupled* multiprocessors, or *non-uniform memory access* (NUMA) multiprocessors where there is no shared physical memory and processors communicate via a fast interconnection fabric, virtual shared memory is sometimes realized by sending pages or segments over the network on demand.

In the next sections, we shall look into the issues of shared-memory multiprocessors and firmly coupled multiprocessors.

15.2.4   Shared-Memory Multiprocessors

At present, the CPU chip of a workstation costs considerably less than all of the memory chips. It is therefore attractive to let several CPUs share the same memory. This has several advantages. First, a single workstation can become much more powerful without increasing its cost too much. Second, since the memory of a set of CPUs is pooled, it can be more productively used. Third, processes sharing memory do not have to run on the same processor and can thus run in parallel.

But sharing memory among a number of CPUs presents problems too, which require relatively expensive solutions. The biggest problem is that of bus contention. The more processors there are in a shared-memory multiprocessor, the more traffic there will be between processors and memory. A single, shared bus will become a bottleneck. For this reason, the number of processors in a shared-memory multiprocessor is limited (e.g., to 16 or 32).

Shared-memory multiprocessors reduce bus traffic through the use of a per-processor cache. This brings with it the problem of maintaining cache consistency.

Figure 15.1 shows the structure of a shared-memory multiprocessor. A bus interconnects the four caches and main memory. A *cache-coherency protocol* is executed over this bus for purposes of maintaining consistency.

Cache consistency dictates that every processor reading a memory location should always observe the latest value written. This suggests that every write operation should update every cached value as well as main memory; in other words, it suggests the use of a *write-through* cache.

But write operations occur quite frequently, so write-through caching could never bring a dramatic reduction in bus traffic. Fortunately, there are other ways of maintaining sufficient coherency among cached copies that the requirement that every read observes the latest write is satisfied. They come in three classes.

- **Software cache consistency** can roughly work in two ways. It either prevents shared data from being cached, for instance, by putting shared data in special, non-cacheable, parts of memory. Or it makes use of the fact that parallel applications prevent concurrent access to shared data with *critical sections*.

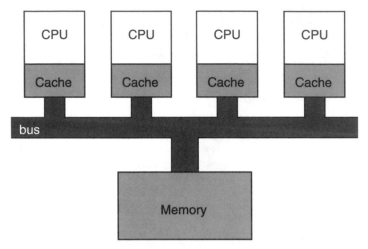

Figure 15.1. Structure of a shared-memory multiprocessor with four processors

The idea is that at the beginning of a critical section one makes sure that the cache is brought up to date and that, when the critical section is left, modified shared data is flushed to memory.

- **Snoopy caches** are caches that monitor the shared bus for read and write operations of data they have cached. For every cache line, a state variable indicates how the cache line is shared. In the Firefly multiprocessor (Thacker, Stewart and Satterthwaite Jr. [1988]), for example, a cache line can be in the states *valid-exclusive* (it is the only cached copy and it is consistent with main memory), *shared* (it is consistent with main memory and there are other consistent copies), or *dirty* (it is the only cached copy and it is not consistent with main memory) (Archibald and Baer [1986]; Stenström [1989]).

    Snoopy caches reduce bus traffic by an order of magnitude, but nonetheless allow single-bus multiprocessors to be scaled only to a moderate number of processors. Snoopy caches are also used in multiple-bus architectures, further complicating the cache-coherency protocols (Goodman and Woest [1988]; Wilson Jr. [1987])

- **Directory-based cache coherency** is used when there is no shared medium that can be 'snooped' to keep caches consistent. Directory-based schemes can be used in arbitrary network topologies — a directory in each main-memory module keeps track of which caches contain copies of data (Agarwal [1988]); alternatively, caches can also keep directories keeping track of other directories that cache the same data (Stenström [1989]). Directory-based schemes have been designed to scale to very large numbers of processors.

An excellent overview of a variety of cache consistency schemes can be found in a special issue on the subject of IEEE Computer Magazine, Vol. 23(6), June 1990.

15.2.5   Distributed Shared Memory

The scalability of shared-memory multiprocessors is limited to dozens of processors at most. If one wants to build systems with a larger number of processors, the interconnection must be made using a network. Processors do not share any physical memory; each processor has its own, private memory. As a consequence, a processor needs to exchange messages with another to access its memory. This makes memory access times non-uniform: local memory access is efficient, while remote memory access is inefficient. Such machines are called *Non-Uniform Memory Access* machines or NUMA machines.

Shared virtual memory can be implemented on NUMA machines, even though there is no shared physical memory (Li and Hudak [1989]). The protocols for maintaining consistency are similar in principle to those for cache consistency in shared-memory multiprocessors (Bolosky, Fitzgerald and Scott [1989]; Fleisch and Popek [1989]). Any inefficiencies caused by a coherency protocol, however, are enlarged enormously on NUMA machines, because communication over a computer network takes time. Many systems that implement shared virtual memory distinguish between different kinds of sharing so that consistency protocols can be optimized for a particular kind of sharing.

15.2.6   Wide-Address Spaces

Most processor architectures today make use of an address space of 32 bits, which can be used to address four gigabytes. For some applications this is no longer enough; some files are larger than that and some applications use arrays and matrices that do not fit in four gigabytes.

Processors are now beginning to emerge with 64-bit-wide addresses.[1] These *wide-address space* architectures are interesting, not merely because they allow applications to use almost arbitrarily large files and data structures, but because they may fundamentally change the way operating systems are structured.

An address space of 64 bits is extremely large. Koldinger *et al.* [1991] remarked that, if one allocates memory at a rate of 500 megabytes per second and never deallocates it, the address space will last more than a thousand years before it is used up. It is more than large enough to be shared by all processes on one machine and this gives an interesting performance advantage.

When all processes on a machine share a single address space, the translation look-aside buffer need not be flushed on a context switch — only the memory-protection map may need adjusting. Fortunately, memory-protection checks can be made largely in parallel with instruction execution. Koldinger *et al.* [1991] suggest a 64-bit architecture using a protection-look-aside buffer that does just this.

But another advantage, that will probably be much more significant, is that, in a 64-bit address space, an object can be assigned an address range for its lifetime, when it is created. This includes objects containing pointers and executable code, such as libraries. Thus, objects containing internal pointers and pointers into

---

[1]The HP-9000 series 700, the MIPS R-4000 and DEC's Alpha processor are examples.

other objects, moving out of memory to secondary storage and back in again, do not require any marshalling (or dynamic linking). Persistency no longer has to be achieved by *write* operations to files, it can be realized solely by secondary memory backing up primary memory using paging hardware.

Wide-address spaces can be shared among tightly or loosely coupled machines using the same techniques as conventional-address-space sharing. An interesting question here is whether it would be possible to use one 64-bit shared address space world wide. The answer is no, for several reasons.

In the first place, 64-bit address spaces are not wide enough for world-wide sharing: for considerations of scalability such sharing should continue to work for a few billion machines storing hundreds of gigabytes each. To address these, 64 bits of address are not enough. If this were the only reason, one could claim that one should then use a 128-bit address space instead. That many bits would surely be enough for any conceivable amount of world-wide sharing.

In the second place, address-space sharing is not very useful between machines with different data representations and instruction sets. There is no point in assigning an object the same address on machines of different type, since the data, including pointers, must be marshalled anyway.

And in the third place, a 64-bit or 128-bit address is not a very convenient thing to have when attempting to find a *physical* instance of an object. In the mapping of virtual addresses to physical data in a computer's main memory or disk somewhere on the planet, virtual addresses behave like *pure* names (see Chapter 12).

In the fourth place, sharing an address space with a machine that cannot be trusted to obey allocation and protection rules is likely to cause all sorts of problems.

We believe that address-space sharing is entirely useful within a group of like-architecture machines in, for instance, a local network. Within a local network, the number of machines is small enough for 64-bits of address to be sufficient. Address-space sharing is useful here, because the data representation is the same on all machines and objects can straightforwardly be copied from one machine's memory to another's. And in a reasonably small group of machines, tables can easily be maintained for mapping virtual address ranges to physical storage devices. The Pegasus distributed multimedia system uses this approach (Leslie, McAuley and Mullender [1993]).

15.3 Process Management

A process has always been the abstraction of a program being executed. The state of a process would include the contents of its address space, its registers, including program counter and stack pointer, and its state with respect to the operating system and file system — system-call state and open-file state.

With the advent of multiprocessors and parallelism, the process abstraction has become confused. Within a single address space, we now have several threads of control and thus several program counters and stack pointers and the state of several system calls. The confusion resulted in different research groups using different and sometimes conflicting names for address spaces and threads of control.

In Mach (Accetta *et al.* [1986]), the address space with all of its threads is called a *task* and the threads of control are *threads*. In Topaz (McJones and Swart [1987]), the address space is called *address space* and the threads of control are *threads* — in Topaz, the use of the word *process* is avoided. In Amoeba (Mullender *et al.* [1990]), originally, an address space with its threads was a *cluster*, while a thread of control was a *task*. This led to considerable confusion with the terminology of Mach, of course, so in Amoeba an address space with its threads is now a *process* and a thread of control is a *thread*.

We shall use the new terminology of Amoeba here. A *process*, therefore, is an address space, plus all the threads executing in it. In this section, we shall examine issues of process management, and focus on deciding where to run processes, how to control their execution, and how to deal with hardware and software failures.

15.3.1   Mechanisms for Process Management

Executing processes in distributed systems requires the collaboration of several entities in the system. First, there is the entity issuing the request to create and run a process. This can be a user or system process. In a UNIX system, this process is referred to as the *parent* process; we will use the same term here.

Next, there is, of course, the process to be created, which, as in UNIX, we shall refer to as the *child* process

Then, there is the child process' operating-system kernel which will have to carry out the creation and execution of the child process. We will refer to this as the *child kernel*.

Finally, there is some system entity that either selects a target node to run the process, or merely checks that the target node indicated by the parent is an appropriate one. Typically, this entity is a distributed system service that assigns processes to processors. This service may also do load balancing by migrating processes from one processor to another. We shall refer to it as the *process-management* service. In the most general case, it will be implemented as a distributed service that collaborates with the operating-system kernels in the nodes to gather the information it needs to make process-allocation decisions. But it could also simply be the operating system kernel in the parent process.

Between these entities a number of protocols must exist for the control and management of the child process.

- The *operating-system interface* is the familiar interface between a process and its kernel. The system calls issued by a process go across this interface. Any interprocess communication carried out by the child process, for instance, will use this interface.
- The *process-control interface* is the interface that the parent process uses to exercise control over the child. Requests to create, suspend, resume, and kill a child process use this interface as well as requests to query the status of a child process. The process-control interface is between parent and process-management service. The child operating system can be part of the

process-management service, so, in some cases, the interface can go directly from parent to child operating system.

• The *process-management interface* is the interface used by the process-management service to control child processes. Through this interface, processes are created at specific hosts, queries can be sent to inquire of process status, processes can be made to migrate from one host to another, and events, such as process exit or crash can be reported. The process-management interface will be used to implement the process-control interface.

These interfaces must be used in combination for such things as creation and destruction of processes, process migration, making checkpoints and debugging them.

Process migration usually requires the most complex machinery, because the state of an running process must be described by the old host and communicated to the new one in such a manner that the process can be recreated on the new machine in exactly the same state as it had on the previous host.

In the most general case, a process-to-be-migrated is multithreaded and any number of these threads can be engaged in the execution of a system call when the migration operation takes place. Therefore, in addition to describing and communicating the memory contents of the process and the registers associated with each thread — program counter,stack pointer, processor status word, and other registers — it is necessary to describe the status of active system calls. This obviously requires the operating system kernels of hosts between which processes migrate to be very similar. Migration leaves very little room for heterogeneity.

If the mechanisms for migration exist, mechanisms for process creation and destruction, checkpointing and even debugging can be created with very little additional effort. Creating a process can be made to look like 'migrating' a process from the file system to a host; checkpointing is like migrating a process from a host to a file, but without removing the process from its host; and debugging can be made to look like migrating a process from a host to a debugger and migrating it back in a — possibly — modified state.

In the Amoeba system (Mullender *et al.* [1990]) this is exactly what was done (Mullender [1987]). The next section describes how.

15.3.2   Process Management in Amoeba

In Amoeba, any process can be a client, a server, or both. Objects are identified by capabilities and the server that manages them is identified by a field in the capability. Thus, different file services can co-exist and clients can have capabilities for files managed by different file servers. If the servers provide the same interface, clients do not have to know that the services are, in fact, different. This property of Amoeba is used in the mechanisms for process management. For a more complete description of Amoeba, see Mullender *et al.* [1990], or Tanenbaum *et al.* [1990].

The key element of Amoeba's process-management mechanisms is the *process descriptor*. It is a portable data structure that describes the state of a running process, except for the contents of the process' memory.

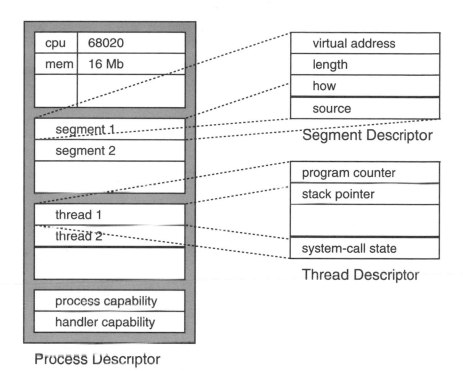

Process Descriptor

Figure 15.2. Structure of a Process Descriptor

A process descriptor consists of four parts, as illustrated in Figure 15.2. The first part is the *host descriptor*. It describes the properties of the host on which the process must run. These properties are encoded as a set of attribute-value pairs, for instance hostname=xor, or maxmem=10000 to indicate that the process must run on a specific host (named *Xor*), or that it needs a host with at least 10,000 kilobytes of memory (the maximum amount used by the process). Usually, specific hosts are not indicated; instead, the *instruction set* is defined, along with instruction-set options such as floating point. A process can only run on a host that has properties matching those in its process descriptor.

The next part, the *memory descriptor*, describes the layout — but not the contents — of a process' virtual address space. Virtual memory is segmented and, for each segment, a segment descriptor gives *virtual address*, *length*, *how*, and *source*. The *virtual address* indicates where the segment is mapped into the address space, the *length* how long the segment is; the *how* field describes what access the process has to the segment (e.g., read-only, execute-only), whether the segment can grow and in which direction; and the *source* field is a capability for a file-like object that provides the segment's memory contents.

The third part of the process descriptor is the *thread descriptor*. Amoeba has kernel-space threads (see Section 15.4), that is, the kernel manages the individual threads of a process. For each thread, the thread descriptor contains program counter, stack pointer, processor status word, registers and system-call state. The only system calls whose state need description here are the *blocking* ones. System calls that do not block a thread in the kernel are finished before a process is stopped and migrated. Fortunately, there are only a few system calls in Amoeba that can block. They are the system calls for communication (the ones that wait for an incoming message) and the ones for thread synchronization (the ones that block on mutexes or semaphores). Each of these blocking calls have some kernel state associated with them (e.g., ports on which messages are expected and memory addresses of receive buffers), but this state is straightforwardly described.

The last part of the process descriptor is the *capability descriptor*. It contains the capabilities needed for managing the process. There are two. The first is the capability for the process. A process is viewed as an object which is managed by the kernel of the host on which it runs. Requests for operations on the object (e.g., suspend, migrate, kill) are sent to the managing server, the kernel. Thus, when a process arrives at a host, the kernel needs to have the capability to which requests for operations are addressed. The second capability is a capability for the exception handler of the process. Usually, this is the parent process, but sometimes it is a debugger. When an exception occurs, the kernel builds a process descriptor for the process and sends it to the exception handler. As a special case, termination of a process is also treated as an exception.

In Amoeba, the *process-control* interface and the *process-management interface* are identical. Thus, the interface used by a parent process to control a child process is identical to the one used by a process-management service to schedule a process. This allows two styles of process management. In one, every parent process directly manages child processes subject to process-create rights on the various hosts in the system. In the other, parent processes manage child processes through the services of a process-management service. In the former case, parents have to select the host on which a child runs, in the latter, the process-management service does this; from the viewpoint of a parent process, there is one virtual host in the system, the process-management service. When the process-management service is used, it relays requests from parents to children and exceptions from children to parents.

From the viewpoint of the target host of a process, migration and creation of a process are the same. Creating a process is more or less migrating an executable file to a host. An executable, therefore, consists of a process descriptor and a number of segments. The process descriptor and the segments can be stored as separate files. The segment descriptor contains in the *source* fields of each of the entries the capability of a file containing a segment. A special capability is used to indicate a segment that needs no initialization (cf., UNIX' *bss* segment).

Unfortunately, sending a process descriptor and a number of segments to a process' future host does not produce the desired result. A process, when it is started up needs to be supplied with parameters and an environment. Amoeba processes have environment variables just like UNIX processes and, in addition, a *capability environment* — a set of named capabilities — as well. These, as well as the command-line arguments must be passed to a process when it is started up.

In UNIX, the environment and the command-line arguments are passed to a

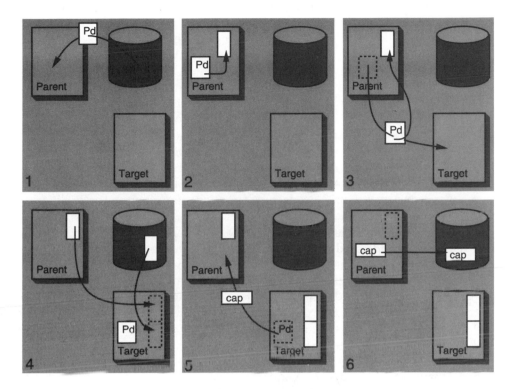

Figure 15.3. Process creation in six easy steps

process on the stack. This could have been done in Amoeba, but, since stacks have a machine-dependent representation, this was not attractive. Instead, Amoeba processes have a special *environment segment* which, after the process has begun execution can be turned into a stack segment by the *runtime start-off*[2].

A process is created in six easy steps, as illustrated in Figure 15.3.

1. The parent process — usually the command interpreter — reads the process descriptor from its file. One segment entry in the segment descriptor is already reserved for an environment segment.

2. The parent process creates a (local) segment and puts environment variables, capability environment and command-line arguments into it. Command interpreters re-use a segment for this purpose.

3. The parent process puts the capability of this local segment in the segment entry reserved for this purpose, fills in an appropriate exception-handler capability, and sends the process descriptor to the target machine's kernel with a request to create a process.

4. The target kernel allocates memory based on segment information in the process descriptor and uses the capabilities in the *source* fields to initialize

---

[2]The runtime start-off is a piece of code supplied by a compiler which does some initialization before calling the main body of a program.

the segments. This is where the importance of using the same interface for reading from segments and from files is important. The code and data segments will be read from the file system and the environment segment will be read from the parent process' memory (with the parent kernel acting as a file server).

5. The target kernel creates the threads according to the specification in the process descriptor and starts them. It then invents a capability for the newly created process and returns that to the parent process.

6. The parent stores the capability so that it can manage the child process and discards the environment segment it created earlier.

There is room for several optimizations in the protocol. First, processes creating lots of offspring, such as the command interpreter, can use a local environment segment over and over. It only needs minor modification between use for different child processes. Command interpreters can cache whole process descriptors to save reading them from the file system and hosts can cache code segments.

In the stepwise description above, a parent process selects a target host. Usually, a system-wide distributed service is made responsible for process allocation. 'Ordinary' parent processes do not have the required capabilities then to create processes on specific hosts directly. With the use of a process-management service, the protocol does not change from the viewpoint of either the parent process or the target host. The process-management service merely passes on requests, with some capability translation.

Migration is done with the same set of mechanisms as process creation. One extra mechanism is needed, however. When a process is to be migrated, a process descriptor needs to be made first. This is done by a so-called *stun* operation. When a stun request is sent to the controlling capability of a process, its host kernel stops the threads of the process and creates a process descriptor describing the process' state. The *source* fields in the segment entries of the new process descriptor are made to refer to the local segments. The process is not killed; it remains in a state where it can be revived.

The process descriptor is sent to the exception handler of the process, which forwards it to the new host. The new host allocates memory and fetches the segment contents (using file-read operations that are carried out by the old host). The process is then restarted on the new host and a capability is sent to the requestor.

Now, the stunned process at the old host can be cleaned up, by sending a *kill* operation.

It is important for two reasons that stunned processes are not removed immediately. First, of course, the memory contents have to be read out by the new host before the process is removed. But the process must also be kept around so that other processes that communicate with the migrating process do not declare the migrating process crashed. A stunned process reacts to incoming messages by returning a *try-again-later* response. When it is killed, after the new process has started, these processes will automatically find its new address, using Amoeba's *locate* mechanisms.

We have mentioned one externally induced exception already, the *stun* operation. When other exceptions occur, the process is also stunned, a process descriptor is made and sent to a handler. The handler can then kill the process, it can pass the process descriptor to a debugger, or it can have the execution resumed.

Debuggers make extensive use of the exception mechanism in order to generate process descriptors. Using a process descriptor, and reading (parts of) the segments as if they are files, a debugger can see all of a process's state. Memory contents can be modified by *writing* into the segments, and other state information can be changed by modifying the process descriptor itself. Every time a kernel receives a new or (potentially) modified process descriptor it runs a sanity check on it.

It is easily imagined how this mechanism can also be used to make checkpoints of a process. One stuns it, stores the process descriptor plus the segment contents on disk and resumes the process again. The Amoeba process-management mechanisms are, we believe, among the most flexible in distributed operating systems today.

15.3.3   Load Balancing and Migration

When processes can be allocated to one or several of a larger set of processors, it is possible by judicious allocation to try and optimize the overall performance of the system. This process is known as load balancing.

Load balancing can be done by processor allocation when processes are created, and also by re-allocating processes to processors when processes are already running — load balancing through process migration.

What optimal system performance is depends strongly on what the system is used for. One can optimize *throughput, response times, fairness,* or some combination of the three.

Throughput is measured as the amount of useful work carried out by the system in unit time. Useful work means executing programs. So throughput is maximized by minimizing *overhead, communication time* and *waiting time.* Overhead is the time spent allocating and re-allocating processes and the processor time used to make scheduling decisions. Communication time is the time processes spend waiting for data to be delivered to them or waiting for buffers of output data to be emptied. Waiting time is the time processors spend idle waiting for work while there are processes waiting for a processor elsewhere in the system.

Response time is the elapsed time between the creation of a process, or the delivery of input and its termination or production of output. Interactive users invariably like good response times. A scheduler that minimizes response times will attempt to minimize the sum of the response times of all the processes in the system.

Fairness is a somewhat more esoteric concept. If one optimizes throughput or response times, it is very possible that some process is never run at all. A *fair* scheduler will give processes equal access to processing resources.

It is easy to see that maximizing throughput, minimizing response time and ensuring absolute fairness are not simultaneously possible. Throughput is maximized by minimizing context switches, so longer jobs are always preferred over shorter ones. Response time, in contrast, is minimized by running the shortest jobs first. Fairness is obtained by lots of context switching which is neither good for throughput nor for response time.

Good schedulers aim to achieve a balance between the three scheduling criteria presented above. But good schedulers have to do much more. Processor allocation directly influences communication time as well: When two intensively communicating processes are placed far apart, processors may often be idle waiting for messages to travel over the network. When a process that produces data for other processes is not run, the other processes will be kept waiting which affects response times badly.

Practical experience shows that the amount of primary memory available to a process is often a key factor in overall system performance. If more (runnable) processes occupy a host than fit in its memory, performance can degrade very badly as a consequence of thrashing in the paging system. Balancing the memory needs of the processes over the available memory in the distributed system turns out to be a more important strategy than trying to balance processing load.

Another important consideration in scheduling and load-balancing decisions is the cost of the scheduling operations themselves. Migrating a process using ten megabytes of memory over a 10 Mbps Ethernet, for example, costs at least ten seconds, just for the transfer of the memory contents. The benefit of a migration must outweigh the costs. If the cost of migrating a process is ten seconds, it must have had at the very least a remaining execution time of another ten seconds at its previous host. In most cases, however, process migration can only be justified if the remaining execution time is an order of magnitude more than the cost of migration.

Most processes in general-purpose operating systems only run for between a fraction of a second and a few seconds. The few processes that run for much longer are not usually identified to a load-balancing scheduler beforehand, so, by the time a scheduler discovers that a process has a very long run time, a very long run time must already have been observed. Measurement of the observed run time between I/O operations on a UNIX system have, in fact, shown that the elapsed run time is a very good estimator of the remaining run time of a process (Mullender [1985]).

Migration times should be as short as possible if migration has to be useful as a tool for load balancing. It has already been mentioned that the overhead of transmitting the memory contents of a process across the network forms a major contribution to its migration time, so, if somehow memory could be transmitted while the migrating process is executing, an important speedup can be achieved.

This was observed by researchers at CMU and Stanford who developed two different ways of achieving this. At CMU, Zayas [1987] constructed a migration mechanism in Mach (Accetta et al. [1986]) where the state of a process is transmitted to a new host, plus, at most, the pages in the working set of the process' memory. The process is started again on its new host and pages are demand-paged in over the network. Theimer, Lantz and Cheriton [1985] essentially did it the other way round: In V (Cheriton [1988]), the process continues to run on the old host, while its pages are copied to the new host. As pages are copied, they are marked 'clean'. When the running process modifies a page, it is marked 'dirty'. When the copying is complete, another round is made over the dirty pages to copy them across. Then the process is stopped and its state is sent to the new host. Finally, all pages that became dirty after the second round of copying are copied. The effect is that the migrating process is only suspended for the time it takes to copy its working set of pages.

The migration strategies of Zayas and Theimer are quite different, but the effect is very similar. A process is only suspended for the time it takes to migrate the working set. Zayas' method has the advantage that pages that are no longer used by a process never need to be sent over the network, but the disadvantage that a process' state can remain distributed over several machines long after migration has completed. This makes Zayas' method more sensitive to processor and operating-system crashes.

Theimer's method has the disadvantage that all of a process' memory has to be copied and some of it up to three times. But it does not leave memory distributed over several hosts and is thus less sensitive to crashes. Memory shortage on a host is one of the important reasons for migrating a process away. Theimer's method frees memory at the source host much more quickly than that of Zayas.

Process migration remains an expensive operation, however — so expensive, apparently, that I do not know of distributed systems that use it for load-balancing purposes. Load balancing is almost exclusively achieved by carefully selecting a suitable host when a process is started.

Process migration can be useful, however, when processes have to be removed from a particular host, for instance, when it has to be serviced, or when it is a workstation whose owner wants to use it again.

15.4 Thread Management

Traditionally, a process is a program being executed. A process consists of an *address space*, and an *execution state*. The execution state typically consisted of the values of program counter, stack pointer, processor status word, a number of registers, and *system-call state*.

The traditional process model can be extended for parallel processing in two ways. One is to use several processes simultaneously that share memory; the other is to extend the execution state to incorporate more than one execution. The first model is referred to as the *shared-memory model*, the second as the *thread model*.

In functionality the two models are not very different; the main difference between the two models is the efficiency of the implementation. The overhead of context switching in the traditional process model is high. The virtual-to-physical address mapping has to be changed (whereby the contents of the TLB are usually lost) and the protection domain has to be changed.

The thread model does not have these overheads. Context switching from one thread to another within the same address space essentially consists of saving one thread's registers (including program counter, stack pointer and processor status word) and restoring those of another.

The earliest thread models were built on top of the traditional process model of UNIX (Doeppner [1987]). Since there is no knowledge of threads in the kernel, we shall refer to these as *user-space threads*. Later, operating systems started to provide kernel support for threads (Accetta *et al.* [1986]; Mullender *et al.* [1990]). These are referred to as *kernel-space threads*. In the next sections, we shall look into the difference between the two types and describe a hybrid user/kernel thread model that combines the advantages of the two models. First, however, we shall investigate the issues of thread scheduling.

15.4.1   Thread Scheduling

Threads form the structuring tool for parallel activities within an address space. Determining which thread or threads run when is the task of a thread scheduler. The scheduler has to select threads to run from a collection of *runnable* threads.

Threads can be *blocked*, *runnable*, or *running*. Blocking can be viewed as the mechanism that synchronizes a thread with some event outside it. Threads can wait for events in other threads — the release of a mutex, a *V* operation on a semaphore, or all other threads in a group reaching some point in their execution (a *barrier* synchronization event) — or they can wait for some completely external event which is almost invariably modelled as the completion of a *system call*.

Thread scheduling on a uniprocessors is not a particularly difficult task, especially if most of the blocking is of threads waiting for other threads. It is only on multiprocessors that thread scheduling becomes an interesting problem.

On multiprocessors the possibility exists to choose groups of threads to run concurrently on different processors. A producer/consumer pair of threads, for instance, never blocks as long as the queue of items produced and still to be consumed remains approximately half full. As long as these threads do not block, no context switches are needed, so throughput is increased. As another example, consider an parallelized computation where a number of threads independently compute for a while, then synchronize to exchange new values before proceeding independently until the next synchronization point. Suppose nine out of ten threads are allocated to processors and one remains on the runnable queue. When the nine threads reach the *barrier*, they all have to wait for the tenth thread which still has to be started. If the ten threads could be scheduled together, the application would finish in half the time.

This scheduling strategy that allocate threads together in order to make the ensemble of threads run faster is called *gang scheduling* (Ousterhout [1982]). Optimal — or even good — gang scheduling requires knowledge of the application, so its exploitation often depends on giving the application programmer access to the scheduling algorithms.

In many applications, threads block only for very short periods. If the blocking period is short enough, the cost of a context switch to another thread can be greater than the blocking time so that time is saved by letting the thread wait until the unblocking event occurs. Typically, a thread, instead of blocking, will execute a tight loop in which it waits until the blocking condition has gone away. We call this *spinning*.

On uniprocessors, spinning is only useful, of course, when waiting for external events, such as the completion of I/O. It is, therefore, only really used by kernel threads. On multiprocessors, spinning is also useful for waiting for synchronization events by other threads. Spinning is always useful when there are no other runnable threads.

If one had perfect advance knowledge of blocking times, one could decide in advance whether to block or to spin. Lacking predictive powers, one must resort to heuristics to determine the optimal spinning times under the circumstances. The extreme possibilities are *never spin* or *always spin*. Other possibilities are spinning some fixed time before blocking, or spinning some empirically determined time. A well-known algorithm is to spin for a fixed time that is equal to the time to do a context switch. Karlin *et al.* [1991] give an excellent comparison of spinning algorithms with references to further reading.

Selecting *which* threads to run is not the only issue on multiprocessors, selecting *where* to run them is also an issue. When a thread has run on a particular processor, that processor's cache tends to fill up with information relevant to that thread. If another thread is then assigned to that processor, the cached information is gradually replaced. If the new process runs only for a short time and the original thread is scheduled again, assigning it to its original processor has the advantage of providing that thread with a cache that is still 'warm.' We call this *cache affinity*.

The effects of cache affinity have been studied by Vaswani and Zahorjan [1991]. They concluded that exploiting cache affinity does not carry much benefit. However, they used a rescheduling frequency of once per 25 ms or less, so the rescheduling time was only a very small fraction of the total execution time. It may well be the case that cache affinity becomes an important factor when threads are rescheduled with a frequency of once per millisecond or more.

15.4.2   User-Space Threads

A user-space thread system is one where the operating-system kernel has no information about the number of threads and their states. User-space threads can be realized within a conventional process, or a set of processing sharing memory. Thread management is done by the run-time system and data structures for thread scheduling are maintained in shared memory.

A thread is created by allocating memory for a stack and per-thread data and registering the new thread in the thread-management data structures. This can probably be achieved in hundreds rather than thousands of instructions. Threads can be destroyed using the reverse process, but they can also be put on a special queue for later re-use. This possibility of recycling threads can make thread creation and destruction very efficient.

System calls have to be non-blocking for efficient user-space thread management. If they were blocking, an address space would be deprived of a processor while a system call is in progress, even if there are runnable threads. Unfortunately, non-blocking system calls introduce extra overhead — an extra system call is needed to wait for the results of extant asynchronous calls. Most modern versions of UNIX now have non-blocking versions of blocking system calls and the *select* system call to wait for one that finishes. Page faults are an even bigger problem, because a kernel that does not know of the existence of other threads cannot transfer control to them.

Synchronization between threads can be done to a large extent using user-space mechanisms. Most shared-memory multiprocessors have interlocked instructions, such as *test-and-set* or *compare-and-swap*. Using these, mutexes or semaphores can be implemented. If a mutex (or semaphore) cannot be obtained, one option is to *spin-wait* until it is released. This can lead to deadlock if the mutex must be released by another thread that is denied a processor because of the spinning thread. A second option is to mark the thread as waiting on a mutex and to select another thread to be run. But when there are no other threads left to run, a system call is necessary to relinquish the processor.

On multiprocessors, or on uniprocessors using multiple processes sharing memory to implement threads, some kernel support for synchronization is required. UNIX systems that offer shared memory usually offer system calls for process synchronization (e.g., semaphores) as well.

The best strategy for thread synchronization is one that uses a combination of spinning, user-space thread switching and synchronizing system calls: First, a thread can spin for a short while to see if the mutex or semaphore is released quickly. This is only useful on a multiprocessor, of course — on a uniprocessor there could be no other thread to do the release. Second, the queue of runnable threads can be searched in quest of another runnable thread. Third, when there are nu runnable threads left, a system call can be used to relinquish the processor blocking on a mutex or semaphore.

With such complicated procedures for obtaining a mutex or semaphore, releasing one becomes equally complicated. Releasing one for which another thread is spinning requires no extra work whatsoever — the spinning thread detects the release. Otherwise, threads waiting for the mutex or semaphore can be put back on the runnable queue, but when the processor has been relinquished, a releasing system call is needed too.

The implementation of synchronization mechanisms for threads, therefore, is something that needs to be done with great care. There is enormous potential for race conditions here which can lead to incorrect actions or deadlock.

The great advantage of user-space threads is that thread-scheduling mechanisms are part of the application so that the application programmer has control over them. The disadvantage is that page faults cause dealy for all threads in an address space and that clumsy, non-blocking system calls must be used. Examples of user-space thread-management systems are Brown threads (Doeppner [1987]), Presto (Bershad, Lazowska and Levy [1988]), and FastThreads (Anderson, Lazowska and Levy [1989]).

15.4.3 Kernel-Space Threads

Threads are such an important structuring mechanism for distributed applications and user-space servers that distributed operating system kernels often provide support for it.

Kernel threads are managed by the operating system kernel. The data structures for thread management — records containing thread states, queues of runnable threads, etc. — are all maintained in kernel space. An application creates a thread using a system call for that purpose. In some systems, the kernel allocates a stack segment for a thread, in others, the application has to allocate a stack. Thread destruction is done via another system call, usually one that is invoked by the exiting thread.

Threads can be recycled, either by a user-space system (instead of exiting, threads put themselves to sleep on some idle-thread queue, and instead of creating them, they are taken off that queue again and pit to work on the appropriate code), or in the kernel (by re-using thread data structures). User-space recycling is more efficient, of course, because more of the thread is re-used (e.g., its stack). System calls are not really saved, though, because threads must put themselves to sleep and be woken up again.

Many of the thread-synchronization techniques used by user-space threads can also be used by kernel-space threads. When a thread blocks on a mutex, for instance, it can spin in user space for a while before making a system call to release the processor. But, since the runnable-thread queue is not observable from user space, it is not possible to take into account when choosing between spinning and blocking whether or not other threads are waiting for a processor.

Normally, however, all synchronization between threads has to be done via the kernel. Compared to user-space threads, extra overhead is introduced by this. However, fewer system calls are needed to do I/O, because system call can be blocking (so there is only one user-to-kernel and kernel-to-user transition per I/O operation rather than two). Also, page faults do not cause other threads in the same address space to be held up.

Kernel-space and user-space threads both have their own advantages and disadvantages. Kernel threads perform better in I/O-intensive applications, user-space threads do much better in fine-grained parallel compute-intensive applications.

15.4.4   User/Kernel-Space Threads

A hybrid kernel/user-space thread-management system that combines most of the advantages of kernel-space and user-space threads is *scheduler activations*. Scheduler activations were invented by Anderson *et al.* [1991] — we briefly describe how they work here.

The guiding principles behind the design of scheduler activations were that there should be no unnecessary transitions between user and kernel space, a kernel-based scheduler should allocate processors to address spaces, and the run-time system of an address space should allocate threads to the available processors.

The run-time system schedules threads. To do this properly, it needs to know what state each thread is in. Threads can be running, runnable or blocked. Threads can be blocked in user space (on a semaphore, for instance), or in kernel space (on a system call, or page fault). The run-time system also needs to know how many processors are currently allocated to its address space. Whenever the state of a thread changes, or the number of allocated processors changes, the run-time system should be notified.

The kernel-based scheduler schedules processors. To do this properly, it needs to know what processors are allocated to what address spaces and how many processors each address space wants. There is little point, after all, in giving a single-threaded process five processors. Naturally, it is not always possible to give each address space as many processors as it wants; an address space may get fewer or even none.

Scheduler activations are pending notifications for the user-space scheduler (the run-time system) of threads blocked in the kernel. Whenever a thread makes a system call that blocks in the kernel, the processor is returned to the address space at a predefined entry point in the user-space scheduler. On the stack is information about the blocked thread (program counter, stack pointer, reason for blocking, etc.). The user-space scheduler can then select another thread for running and transfer control to it.

When a hardware interrupt occurs, the interrupt mechanism may transfer a processor from user space to kernel space. There are two ways in which a return from interrupt can occur. One is to return to the exact state of the interrupted thread (the conventional way). The other is to return the processor in a scheduler activation with the state of the interrupted thread on the stack. This second way is used when the user-space scheduler needs to be told about a state change of another thread or a change in the number of processors as well.

Generally, a scheduler activation is an invocation of the user-space scheduler with the message, 'Here is a processor and here is a description of events that are of interest.' A frequently occurring event is that a processor is taken away from the address space (with a description of the state of the processor at that time). And quite often it will be the same processor that is returned in the activation.

When a processor is taken away from an address space, one of the remaining processors is 'borrowed' for the scheduler activation that informs the user-space scheduler of the fact. The processors can then be reallocated to threads. When a processor is added to an address space, it is simply offered as a scheduler activation.

An initial implementation on the Firefly (Thacker, Stewart and Satterthwaite Jr. [1988]) showed that scheduler activations indeed give better performance than either kernel threads or user-space threads.

15.5   References

Accetta, M., Baron, R., Bolosky, W., Golub, D., Rashid, R., Tevanian, A. and Young, M. (1986), Mach: A New Kernel Foundation for UNIX Development, *Proceedings of the Summer Usenix Conference*, Atlanta, GA.

Agarwal, A. (1988), An Evaluation of Directory Schemes for Cache Coherence, *Proceedings of the 15th Annual International Symposium on Computer Architectures*, Los Alamitos, CA, Computer Society Press, 280–289.

Anderson, T., Lazowska, E. D. and Levy, H. M. (1989), The Performance Implications of Thread Management Alternatives for Shared-Memory Multiprocessors, *IEEE Transactions on Computers* **38(12)**, 1631–1644.

Anderson, T. E., Bershad, B. N., Lazowska, E. D. and Levy, H. M. (1992), Scheduler activations: Effective kernel support for the user-level management of parallelism, *ACM Transactions on Computer Systems* **10**(1), 53–79.

Archibald, J. and Baer, J. -L. (1986), Cache Coherence Protocols: Evaluation Using a Multiprocessor Simulation Model, *ACM Transactions on Computer Systems* **4**(4), 273–298.

Bershad, B. N., Lazowska, E. D. and Levy, H. M. (1988), PRESTO: A System for Object-Oriented Parallel Programming, *Software—Practice & Experience* **18**, 713–732.

Bolosky, W. J., Fitzgerald, R. P. and Scott, M. L. (1989), Simple But Effective Techniques for NUMA Memory Management, *Proceedings of the Twelfth Symposium on Operating Systems Principles* **23**(5), 19–31, In *ACM Operating Systems Review* **23**(5).

Cheriton, D. R. (1988), The V Distributed System, *Communications of the ACM* **31**, 314–333.

Doeppner, T. W. (1987), Threads: A System for the Support of Concurrent Programming, Brown University, Computer Science Technical Report CS-87-11.

Fleisch, B. D. and Popek, G. J. (1989), Mirage: A Coherent Distributed Shared Memory Design, *Proceedings of the Twelfth Symposium on Operating Systems Principles* **23**(5), 211–223, In *ACM Operating Systems Review* **23**(5).

Goodman, J. and Woest, P. (1988), A New Large-Scale Cache-Coherent Multiprocessor, *Proceedings of the 15th Annual International Symposium on Computer Architectures*, Los Alamitos, CA, Computer Society Press, 422–431.

Karlin, A. R., Li, K., Manasse, M. S. and Owicki, S. (1991), Empirical Studies of Competitive Spinning for Shared-Memory Multiprocessors, *Proceedings of the 13th Symposium on Operating Systems Principles*, Pacific Grove, CA, In *ACM Operating Systems Review* **25**(5).

Koldinger, E. J., Levy, H. M., Chase, J. S. and Eggers, S. J. (1991), The Protection Lookaside Buffer: Efficient Protection for Single-Address-Space Computers, Dept. of Computer Science and Engineering, University of Washington, Technical Report 91-11-05, Seattle, WA 98195.

Leslie, I. M., McAuley, D. and Mullender, S. J. (1993), Pegasus — Operating System Support for Distributed Multimedia Systems, *ACM Operating System Review* **27**(1), 69–78.

Li, K. and Hudak, P. (1989), Memory coherence in shared virtual memory systems, *ACM Transactions on Computer Systems* **7**(4), 321–359.

McJones, P. R. and Swart, G. F. (1987), Evolving the UNIX System Interface to Support Multithreaded Programs, DEC Systems Research Center, DEC SRC Report 21, 130 Lytton Ave., Palo Alto, CA 94301.

Mullender, S. J. (1985), Principles of Distributed Operating System Design, Vrije Universiteit, Ph. D. Thesis, Amsterdam.

Mullender, S. J. (1987), Process Management in Distributed Operating Systems, in *Experiences with Distributed Systems*, Nehmer, J., ed., Computer Science Lecture Notes nr. 309, Springer Verlag, Berlin.

Mullender, S. J., van Rossum, G., Tanenbaum, A. S., van Renesse, R. and van Staveren, J. M. (1990), Amoeba — A Distributed Operating System for the 1990s, *IEEE Computer* **23(5)**.

Ousterhout, J. K. (1982), Scheduling Techniques for Concurrent Systems, *Proceedings of the Third International Conference on Distributed Computing Systems*, Fort Lauderdale, FL, IEEE Computer Society Press, 22–30.

Pike, R., Presotto, D., Thompson, K. and Trickey, H. (1990), Plan 9 from Bell Labs, *Proceedings of the Summer 1990 UKUUG Conference*, London, 1–9.

Pike, R., Presotto, D., Thompson, K., Trickey, H. and Winterbottom, P. (1993), The Use of Name Spaces in Plan 9, *ACM Operating System Review* **27(2)**, 72–76, Reprint from Proceedings of the Fifth ACM SIGOPS European Workshop, Mont Saint-Michel.

Presotto, D., Pike, R., Thompson, K. and Trickey, H. (1991), Plan 9, A Distributed System, *Proceedings of the Spring 1991 EurOpen Conference*, Tromsø, Norway, 43–50.

Rozier, M. and Martins, J. L. (1986), The Chorus distributed operating system: Some design issues, in *Distributed operating systems*, Paker, Y., Banatre, J-P. and Bozyigit, M., eds., Springer-Verlag, 261–287.

Stenström, P. (1989), A Cache Consistency Protocol for Processors with Multistage Networks, *Proceedings of the 16th Annual International Symposium on Computer Architectures*, Los Alamitos, CA, Computer Society Press, 407–415.

Tanenbaum, A. S., van Renesse, R., van Staveren, J. M., Sharp, G. J., Mullender, S. J., Jansen, A. J. and van Rossum, G. (1990), Experiences with the Amoeba Distributed Operating System, *Communications of the ACM*.

Thacker, C., Stewart, L. and Satterthwaite Jr., E. (1988), Firefly: A Multiprocessor Workstation, *IEEE Transactions on Computers* **38(8)**, 909–920.

Theimer, M. M., Lantz, K. A. and Cheriton, D. R. (1985), Preemptable Remote Execution Facilities for the V-System, *Proceedings of the Tenth Symposium on Operating Systems Principles*, Orcas Island, WA, 2–12, In *ACM Operating Systems Review* **19**(5).

Vaswani, R. and Zahorjan, J. (1991), The Implications of Cache Affinity on Processor Scheduling for Multiprogrammed, Shared Memory Multiprocessors, *Proceedings of the 13th Symposium on Operating Systems Principles*, Pacific Grove, CA, In *ACM Operating Systems Review* **25**(5).

Wilson Jr., A. W. (1987), Hierarchical Cache/Bus Architecture for Shared-Memory Multiprocessors, *Proceedings of the 14th Annual International Symposium on Computer Architectures*, Los Alamitos, CA, Computer Society Press, 422–433.

Zayas, E. (1987), Attacking the Process Migration Bottleneck, *Proceedings of the Eleventh Symposium on Operating Systems Principles*, Austin, TX, 13–24, In *ACM Operating Systems Review* **21**(5).

Chapter 16

Real Time and Dependability Concepts

Hermann Kopetz and Paulo Veríssimo

The notion of time is fundamental to our existence. Although we do not have any sense of time — we always live in the present — we can reflect on past events and possible future occurrences and thus reason about events in the domain of time. In ancient history, the length of durations between events was mainly registered on the basis of subjective judgement. With the advent of the modern sciences, objective methods for the measurement of the progression of time have been devised and constantly improved. Figure 16.1 gives an overview on the progress of the accuracy of time measurement in the last four centuries (Whitrow [1988]).

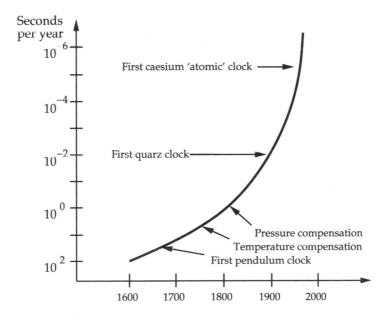

Figure 16.1. Progress in time measurement

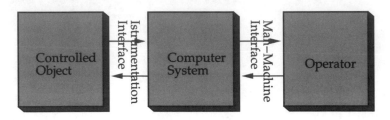

Figure 16.2. A real-time system

In many models of natural phenomena (for instance, Newtonian mechanics), time is considered as an independent variable which determines the sequence of states of the considered system. The basic constants of physics are defined in relation to a standard of time, the physical second. If we intend to control the behaviour of a natural system, we have to act on the system at precise moments in time.

We define a *real-time system* as a system that changes its state as a function of (real) time. Our interest focuses on real-time systems that contain embedded computer systems. It is sensible to decompose such a real-time system into a set of *clusters*, for instance, the *controlled object*, the *computer system* and a *human operator* (Figure 16.2). We call the controlled object and the operator the *environment* of the computer system. The computer system must react to stimuli from the controlled object (or the operator) within time intervals dictated by its environment. Such a computer system is called a *real-time* computer system.

Since the real-time computer system is only a part of the total real time system, there must be interfaces between the real-time computer system and its environment. We call the interface between the real-time computer and the controlled object the *instrumentation* interface, consisting of sensors and actuators, and the interface between the real-time computer system and the operator the *man-machine* or *operator* interface (Figure 16.2).

Nowadays, most real-time computer systems are distributed. They consist of a set of nodes interconnected by a real-time communication system. Access to this real-time communication system must be controlled by a *real-time protocol*; that is, a protocol that has a known small maximum execution time.

Based on the above definition of a real-time computer system it follows that the duration between a stimulus from the environment and the response to the environment is time constrained. We call the sequence of all communication and processing steps between such a stimulus and response a *real-time (RT) transaction*. A RT transaction must deliver the correct result at the intended point in time. Otherwise, the real-time computer system has failed.

Any real-time computer system has a finite processing capacity. If we intend to guarantee by design that the given temporal requirements of all critical real-time transactions can be satisfied then we have to postulate a set of assumptions about the behaviour of the environment. The *load hypothesis* and the *fault hypothesis* are two of these important assumptions.

Load Hypothesis. The load hypothesis defines the *peak load* that is assumed to be generated by the environment. It can be expressed by specifying the minimum time interval between — or the maximum rate of — each real-time transaction. Peak load implies that all specified transactions will occur with their maximum rate. In many applications the utility of the real-time system is highest in a *rare event situation* that leads to a peak load scenario. Consider the case of a nuclear power station monitoring and shutdown system. It is probable that in case of the rare event of a reactor incident — for instance, the rupture of a pipe — many alarms will be activated simultaneously and will thus generate a correlated load. Statistical arguments about the low probability for the occurrence of peak load, based on the argument that the tail of a load distribution of independent events is very small are not valid in such a situation. If a real-time system is not designed to handle the peak load it can happen that the system will fail when it is needed most urgently.

Fault Hypothesis. The fault hypothesis defines the types and frequency of faults that a fault-tolerant system must be capable of handling. If the identified fault scenario develops, the system must still provide a specified level of service. If the environment generates more faults than specified in the fault-hypothesis, then even a fault tolerant system may fail. The worst scenario that a fault-tolerant real-time system must be capable of handling exists if the peak-load and the maximum number of faults occur at the same time.

Even a perfect fault-tolerant real-time system will fail if the load-hypothesis or the fault hypothesis are unrealistic; that is, they do not properly capture the behaviour of the environment. The concept of *assumption coverage* defines the probability that the fault and load hypothesis — and all other assumptions made about the behaviour of the environment — are in agreement with reality.

16.1   Classification of Real-Time Systems

It is reasonable to classify real-time computer systems on the basis of their dependability requirements.

Soft real-time versus hard real-time system

We call a real-time system as *soft*, if the consequences of a timing failure are in the same order of magnitude as the utility of the operational system. Consider, for example, a letter-sorting machine. If a letter is placed in the wrong bin because of a timing failure, the consequences are not very serious — the letter will have to be sorted again.

Another example of a soft real-time system is a telephone switching system. The availability requirement of a telephone switching system is challenging: only a few hours of total outage time are allowed within the operational lifetime of a

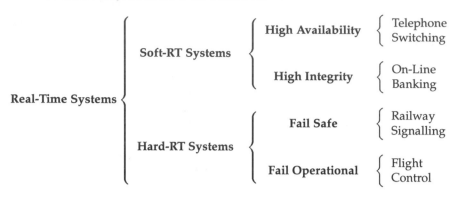

Figure 16.3. Classification of Real-Time Systems

telephone switch, that is, a period of thirty years. However, from the point of view of a single connection establishment, the correctness requirement is not very high — the specification states that one out of ten thousand calls can be misrouted.

An on-line transaction processing system of a bank is another real-time application. In this application the maintenance of data integrity, even in the case of system failure, is of utmost concern.

If the consequences of a timing failure can be catastrophic, that is, the cost of such a failure can be orders of magnitude higher that the normal utility of the system, then we call the system a *hard real-time system*. A railway signalling system is a good example of a hard real-time system.

Fail-safe versus fail-operational hard real-time system

For some hard real-time systems one or more safe states can be identified that can be accessed in case of a system failure. Consider the example of the railway signalling system. In case a failure is detected it is possible to stop all trains and set all signals to red to avoid a catastrophe. If such a safe state can be identified, than we call the system a *fail-safe system*. Note, that fail-safeness is a characteristic of the control object, not the computer system. In fail safe applications the computer system must have a high error detection coverage, that is, the probability that an error is detected, provided it has occurred, must be close to one.

There are, however, applications where such a safe state cannot be identified, for instance, a flight control system aboard an airplane. In such an application the computer system must provide a minimal level of service even in the case of failure in order to avoid a catastrophe. This is why these applications are called *fail operational*.

Guaranteed-response versus best-effort systems

Another classification of real-time computer systems is based on the approach taken during system implementation.

If we start out from the specified fault and load hypothesis and deliver a design that makes it possible to reason about the adequacy of the design without reference to probabilistic arguments, even in the case of the extreme load and fault scenario, then we speak of a system with a *guaranteed response*. The probability of failure of a perfect system with guaranteed response is reduced to the probability that the assumptions will hold in practice, that is, the assumption coverage. Guaranteed response systems are based on the principle of resource adequacy, that is, there are enough computing resources available to handle the specified peak load and the fault scenario (Lawson [1992]).

Many real-time system designs are based on the principle of resource inadequacy. It is assumed that the provision of sufficient resources to handle every possible situation is economically not viable and that a dynamic resource allocation strategy based on resource sharing and probabilistic arguments about the expected load and fault scenarios are acceptable. We call such systems *best effort systems*. These systems do not require a rigorous specification of the load and fault hypothesis. The design proceeds according to the principle 'best effort taken' and the sufficiency of the design is established during the test and integration phase. It is difficult to systematically validate the adequacy of a best effort design, particularly for rare event situations.

At present, the majority of real-time systems is designed according to the best effort paradigm. It is expected that this will change radically in the future. The use of computers in safety critical applications, for instance, in the field of flight control, will raise the public awareness and concern about computer related incidents and force the designer to provide convincing arguments that the design will function properly under all stated conditions. Hard real-time systems have to be designed according to the guaranteed response paradigm.

16.2 Typical Real-Time Applications

In this section we look at some typical application areas of real-time computer systems. We begin with the field of plant automation.

16.2.1 Plant Automation

Historically, plant automation was the first field for the application of real-time digital computer control. This is understandable since the benefits that can be realized by the computerization of a sizable plant are much larger than the cost of an even expensive process control computer of the late 1960s.

In the early days, industrial plants were controlled by human operators who where placed in close vicinity to the process. With the refinement of the plant instrumentation and the availability of remote automatic controllers plant monitoring and command facilities where concentrated into a central control room, thus reducing the number of operators required to run a particular plant. The next logical step was the introduction of at that time — in the late 1960s — central process control computers to monitor the plant and assist the operator in his routine functions, for instance, data logging, operator guidance, etc. At first the computer was considered an 'add-on' facility that was not fully trusted. It was the duty of the operator to judge whether a set point calculated by a computer makes sense and can be applied to the process (*open loop control*). With the improvement of the process models and the growth of the reliability of the computer, more and more control functions have been allocated to the computer and gradually the operator has been taken out of the control loop (*closed loop control*). Sophisticated control technique that have response time requirements beyond the human capabilities have been implemented.

Additional benefits have been realized with the introduction of distributed computer control systems since the end of the 1970s:

- Enhancement of the cost/performance by the utilization of mass produced microprocessors.
- The reduction of cabling costs by the introduction of bus systems and the installation of intelligent instrumentation.
- Improvement in the reliability and maintainability by the deployment of many identical standard components.
- Reduction in the design and development cost of an application.

These last benefits can only be realized if the additional complexity introduced by the communication between the distributed nodes is properly controlled. Up to today, these issues are not fully resolved.

A typical example of a complex plant automation system is the computer control of a rolling mill. In this application a slab of steel (or some other material, such as paper) is rolled to a strip and coiled. The rolling mill of Figure 16.4 has three drives and some instrumentation to measure the quality of the rolled product. The distributed computer control system of this rolling mill consists of eight nodes.

The sensor node observes the quality of the rolled product and generates periodically a message containing this *observation*. This message is distributed to the model node and the operator node. Based on the parameters selected by the operator, the observed quality of the rolled product and the position of the drives, the process model node calculates new *set points* for the drives. There are three nodes associated with the three drives, one for each drive. These three nodes receive the set points from the process model and activate the drives accordingly. The many analog and digital sensors in each drive to measure the speed of the rolls, temperature, pressure, electric currents, etc. are observed, preprocessed, and a message containing the momentary state of the drive is output to the rest of the system.

The real-time transaction between the sensor node and the drive nodes (dotted line) determines the quality of control. The shorter the delay of this transaction, the better the control quality since, from the point of view of control, this transaction contributes to the *dead time* of the critical control loop. The other important term of the dead time is the time it takes for the strip to travel from the drive to the sensor.

Note that the communication pattern between the nodes of this control system is *multicast*, not *point to point*. This is typical for most distributed real time control systems. Furthermore the communication between the model node and the drive nodes has an *atomicity requirement*. Either all drives are changed according to the

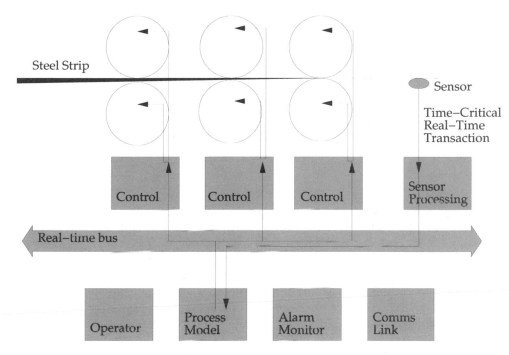

Figure 16.4. The rolling mill example

model result or none is changed. The loss of a message, which may result in the change of only one drive, can be critical.

16.2.2   Telephone Switching

Another mature application of distributed computer control is telephone switching. This application is characterized by rigid availability and maintainability requirements.

Consider the example of the ATT Nr. 4 ESS which is capable of handling 700 000 calls an hour. It consists of a powerful fault-tolerant central processor and hundreds of microprocessors in the switching network and the digital terminals. The switching network for a typical 72 000 trunk office consists of eight bays of logic equipment and the digital terminal for 72 000 trunks require 126 bays of equipment. The total system must be operational 24 hours a day. Maintenance activities have to be carried out on the operational system.

In addition to the standard call-processing software, the system software contains extensive audit programs to detect and correct data inconsistencies. Defensive programming techniques are used to locate anomalies during execution. In case of severe disturbances, an automatic reinitialization of the whole switch is performed with a minimal effect on switched connections. Table 16.1 gives some data on the dependability of the ESS 4 measured on more than 130 installed systems over a one-year period (Clement and Giloth [1987]).

Software audits	< 20 per day
Automatic initializations	< 0.5 per month
Manual initializations	< 1 per 50 months
Mean time to restore system	32 seconds
Cut-off calls	< 5 per million
Denied calls	< 4 per million
Trunk out of service	9 minutes per trunk year
System downtime (major outage)	< 1.7 hours per 40 years

Table 16.1. Dependability of the ESS 4 telephone switch

16.2.3   Automotive Control

The availability of powerful low-cost microelectronic devices makes it feasible to start the implementation of advanced distributed control systems in products for the mass markets, such as the automobile. At present the pattern of computerization of the automobile resembles the early stages of the installation of plant automation equipment. The computer is mostly used for comfort functions or non-safety critical guidance of the driver. It is expected, however, that within the next ten years complex distributed fault-tolerant computer systems will replace many mechanical and hydraulic control systems in the average car, making the *'drive-by-wire'* fantasy a reality. The 'computerization of the car' is driven by substantial expected benefits, such as

- Fuel economy: Computer controlled engines provide better fuel economy and have lower emissions than conventional engines.
- Safety: At present about 95% of all car accidents are due to human failure. A computer controlled car can assist the driver in the avoidance of critical situations and thus help to reduce the number of accidents.
- Comfort: New functionality, such as intelligent cruise control or traffic information systems can increase the driver's comfort.
- Reduced manufacturing costs: The introduction of multiplexed buses in the car will reduce the cabling costs. A total 'drive-by-wire' will have fewer mechanical parts and will be lighter than a conventional car, thus requiring less raw material for its production.

From the point of view of the computer engineer the field of automotive electronics is most challenging. This application field is characterized by demanding reliability, maintainability, and safety requirements in a hard real-time control context that has to be implemented under rigid cost constraints. Since it is projected that in the year 2000 about 20% of a car's manufacturing cost will be allocated to automotive electronics, this field will become one of the major application areas of distributed computer control systems.

Table 16.2 gives a list of some typical functions that will be supported by automotive electronics in the coming years.

Vehicle dynamic control	Driver information systems
Engine control	Traffic information
Transmission control	Navigation systems with
Brakes (antilock brakes)	route guidance
Autonomous intelligent	Active traffic signs
cruise control	Electronic dashboard
Suspension control	*Comfort functions*
Traction control	Climate Control
Steering	Central locking
Sight utilities	Device control (windows,
Lighting	seats, mirror, etc.)
Vision enhancement	Theft avoidance systems
by UV light	
Short range radar	

Table 16.2. Functions of automotive electronics in the coming years

16.2.4 Intelligent Products

An *intelligent product* is an autonomous real-time system that performs a specified service for its users. It generally consists of a mechanical subsystem, some sensors and actuators, a control subsystem and a simple user interface. An automatic scale with an integrated microcontroller to perform the calibration, the weighing, and some record keeping is a good example for an intelligent product. It is a tangible product that provides a service to untrained users and can be marketed on its own.

An intelligent product can be characterized by the following properties (Kopetz [1990]):

- *Focus on genuine user needs*: The ultimate success of any such product depends on the relevance and quality of service it can provide to its users.
- *Simple to operate*: Ideally, the use of an intelligent product should be self-explanatory and not require any training or reference to an operating manual.
- *Minimization of the mechanical subsystem*: in order to reduce the manufacturing cost and to increase the reliability, the complexity of the mechanical subsystem has to be minimized.
- *Functionality determined by software*: The functionality of an intelligent product is determined by the integrated software. Since there is hardly any possibility to modify the software after its release, the quality standards for this software are extremely high.
- *Mass production*: Successful intelligent products are designed for a mass market and consequently for mass production in highly automated assembly plants.
- *Ability to communicate*: Although most intelligent products can provide the specified service autonomously, an intelligent product is often required to interconnect with some larger system. The protocol controlling the data transfer should be simple and robust. Generally, an optimization of transmission speed is not required.

Depending on the production volume, the control system of an intelligent product will be based on a programmable microcontroller, a gate array or a custom designed VLSI chip. A substantial fraction of the development effort of an intelligent product is related to software development.

16.3   Dependability Concepts

The notion of dependability covers the nonfunctional attributes of a computer system that relate to the quality of service a system delivers over an extended period of time. The quality of service relates to the behaviour of a system as seen by a user. The following four measures of dependability attributes are of particular importance:

- *Reliability*: Measure of continuous service delivery, measured by the probability $R(t)$ that the system is still providing the correct service after a time interval t, if it has been functioning correctly at $t = 0$.
- *Safety*: Probability $S(t)$ that a system will not fail in a catastrophic failure mode within a time interval t.
- *Availability*: Measure of correct service delivery with respect to the alternation of correct and incorrect service, measured by the probability $A(t)$ that the system is ready to provide the service at a point in time t.
- *Maintainability*: Measure of the time to restoration from the last experienced failure, measured by the probability $M(t)$ that the system is restored at time t if it has failed at time $t = 0$.

There is a fifth important attribute of dependability — the *security attribute* — that cannot be measured easily: the ability of a system to prevent unauthorized access or handling of information.

16.3.1   Failures and Faults

Whenever the service of a system, as seen by the user of the system (the user can be human or another artificial system), deviates from the agreed specification of the system, the system has failed. A *failure* is thus an event occurring at a particular point in real time. Depending on the failure characteristics the classifications shown in Figure 16.5 can be made.

Most computer system failures can be traced back to an incorrect internal state of the computer, for instance, a wrong data element in the memory or a register. We call such an incorrect internal state an *error*. An error is thus an unintended state that lasts for a given interval of time. The cause of an error, and thus indirectly of a failure, is called a *fault*. Faults can be classified as shown in Figure 16.6.

A detailed description of the different types of failures and faults can be found in (Laprie [1992]). It is the goal of the fault-tolerant computing effort to detect and mask or repair errors before they show up as failures at the system — user service interface. The key to the design of fault-tolerant systems is the provision of redundancy.

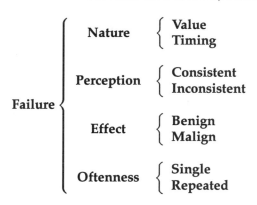

Figure 16.5. Classification of failures

16.3.2 Redundancy

The term *redundancy* refers to those extra resources in a system that are not needed in a perfect world. Redundancy is required to detect errors and to mask failures in the real world. We distinguish between three types of redundancy:

* *physical resource redundancy,*
* *time redundancy* and
* *information redundancy.*

Physical resource redundancy refers to the replication of physical resources. For example, if we provide three computers instead of one, compare the results of each computation, and select the result that is in the majority, then we can mask a single computer failure.

Time redundancy refers to the repetition of a computation or communication action in the domain of time. For example, it is an established technique in com-

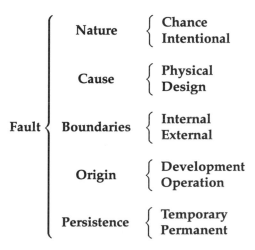

Figure 16.6. Classification of faults

munication systems to resend a message (at a different time) if the receipt of the first message is not acknowledged by the receiver. The implicit assumption that justifies such a procedure is that the a temporary disturbance will have disappeared and will not mutilate the second message transmission.

Information redundancy refers to a specific encoding technique. A source text is encoded into an object text such that the object text has a larger code space than the source text, thus deliberately increasing the redundancy of the object text to enable the detection and the correction of errors introduced into the object text. The addition of a check digit to a credit card number is a good example of information redundancy. All three forms of redundancy are used in the design of fault-tolerant systems. Information redundancy is used to protect state information (for instance, error detecting and correcting codes in computer memory) and to protect the transport of messages (cyclic redundancy check fields in a message). Time redundancy is employed to detect and possibly tolerate the occurrence of temporary faults. Resource redundancy is needed if permanent hardware or software faults have to be tolerated. Two types of resource redundancies are distinguished, passive redundancy and active redundancy

Passive redundancy

Passive redundancy (sometimes called *standby* or *cold* redundancy) refers to a redundancy organization that activates the redundant physical resources only after the primary resource has failed. It is implicitly assumed that the primary resource contains error detection mechanisms to detect errors in its internal state before an incorrect output is delivered to the user.

We call a subsystem that delivers either correct results or no result at all a *fail-silent* subsystem. If a fail-silent subsystem fails, it is either an *omission failure* (this is a special timing failure where sometimes no output is generated) or a *crash failure* (Cristian [1985]) (this is a special omission failure where no output is produced after the first omission failure, that is, the system terminates its operation after the first omission failure). From an architectural point of view, crash failures are the simplest type of failures to handle.

The standby system has to be informed somehow that the primary system has failed. In a passive redundancy organisation a subsystem that exhibits crash failures and has the additional property to inform the other subsystems that it has failed is called a *failstop* system (Schlichting and Schneider [1983]). For example, the failstop property can be realized by requiring the subsystems to transmit watchdog signals periodically.

Software exception handling can be considered as a special type of standby redundancy. When the processor detects an exception during the execution of a program, then control is transferred to an exception handler that either terminates the operation of the program (termination model) or replaces the failed program by some other program (resume model). *Rollback recovery* is another example for standby redundancy using time redundancy. After an error is detected, control is transferred to a recovery point to restart the program from a previously stored checkpoint state.

In real-time systems the scope for the implementation of standby redundancy is limited. In most cases the time needed to restart another subsystem from a fault-free state after an error has been detected is not available. There are only few hard-real time applications, where the deadlines are far enough in the future that all activities required for rollback recovery or exception handling can be executed before the deadline has expired.

Active redundancy

Active redundancy (sometimes called hot redundancy) refers to a redundancy organization that activates all redundant physical resources simultaneously. Depending on the failure characteristics of the redundant subsystems two (fail-silent failures) three (consistent failures masked by voting in a Triple Modular Redundancy configuration) or four (inconsistent or Byzantine failures) subsystems are grouped into a fault-tolerant unit (FTU) to tolerate the failure of a single subsystem.

Active redundancy requires that the replicated subsystems visit the same states at about the same time. This property is called *replica determinism*. If replica determinism is not maintained, the ability to tolerate failures is lost.

16.4   Models of Distributed Real-Time Computing

Real-time systems are in essence *responsive*: they interact with the environment, reacting to stimuli of external events and producing results, within specified time constraints. To guarantee this responsiveness in the presence of failures, fault-tolerance is necessary. Distribution is not only useful — for example, to achieve fault-tolerance — but inevitable — for example, in control, acquisition and supervision in large settings, flexible manufacturing, train or flight control, etc.

It is appealing to apply the theory of distributed computing developed in the past years to solving problems in responsive systems. There is no fundamental reason why algorithms, orderings, synchronization paradigms, clocks, may not be of help in the decentralised operation of a chemical process plant, a data acquisition/supervision system, a flexible manufacturing system.

Still, unlike commercial or scientific non real-time systems that have inspired a lot of research in distributed computing, responsive systems deal with the environment. They have attached 'things' like fluid level sensors, motor actuators. They have to act on 'variables' which are physical magnitudes, rather than computer registers, and which evolve with real time. So, before anything, one has to have a suitable way of mapping that physical reality into the computer world. That done successfully, one can abstract from the physical world and apply known concepts about distribution, timeliness, replication management and so forth, to solving — still very real — problems.

16.4.1   Real-time Objects and Observations

A simple macroscopic model is all we need for a start. It is represented in Figure 16.7. Three kinds of entities are relevant: real-time entities, representatives

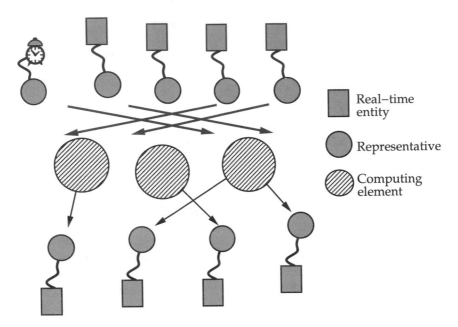

Figure 16.7. Distributed Real-time System Model

and computing elements.

A *real-time (RT) entity* is an element of the environment, which has a state the system is supposed to acquire or modify. Examples: fluid valve (position); fluid (level, flow); oven (temperature); piston (position); detector (motion, presence); plane (position, vector).

A *representative* of an RT entity is a computational entity which *observes* or *acts* on the RT entity. Representatives hide the complexity of the physical reality, transforming it into representations tractable by computers. Examples: an intelligent temperature sensor reader; a stepping motor driver; an A/D acquisition module.

A *computing element* is a computational entity which processes observations of RT entities, and eventually triggers actions on other RT entities. Examples: the control program of a temperature control loop; a process supervisor; a radar antenna control program; a real-time database server.

For the system designer, the real-time entities form the environment part of the requirements specification. There are two very distinct objectives in his job, made clear by this model:

- the reliable and timely perception of, and actuation on, the state of RT entities;
- the reliable and timely processing of the information acquired and production of responses.

The first concerns the path between RT entities and representatives. It includes the design of the interface between real-time entities and their representatives: this is input/output. Once solved the first problem, physical reality has been converted into a representation computers can understand. From then on, the designer may address the computational part reasoning exclusively in terms of distributed computing abstractions. For the sake of generality, let us call **real-time objects** to whatever computational entities are involved in a distributed real-time computation. So, the second problem consists in performing computations and interactions among real-time objects (representatives and computing elements).

This made our view of system design steps *simpler*, but it does not mean it made the design *simple*! In fact, there are a few questions to be solved in order to understand the process of designing responsive systems (i.e., systems combining distribution, real-time and fault-tolerance).

For example, note that the state of a real-time entity is not accurately reflected in its representative at all times during system evolution: the temperature of an oven and its measure at a sensor representative differ with sensor precision and, more importantly, with *time*; a valve actuator representative may command it to shut, but the valve may remain open because it is stuck, if no *reliability* measures were foreseen.

The problem gets worse with distribution and replication. Readings of the same event by different nodes should not be different, but they are bound to be, especially in the case of an analog variable. Readings of two events by different nodes should not be perceived in different orders, but different distances to the entity being observed and variable delays in communication may cause this anomaly. Replicated outputs to the same actuator, from different nodes, must occur 'at the same time'. Deferred outputs commanded by one node on another node may be difficult to ensure, without access to a global time base. We are going to spend the rest of the chapter pointing solutions to these problems.

16.4.2   Event-Triggered versus Time-Triggered Systems

There have been two main approaches to the design of real-time systems. Both have their merits:

- An **Event-triggered (ET)** system is one that reacts to significant external events directly and immediately.
- A **Time-triggered (TT)** system is one that reacts to significant external events at pre-specified instants.

Event-triggered systems, as shown in Figure 16.8, are, so to speak, 'idle': waiting for something to happen. When an event occurs (e.g., an object passing under a detector beam), a message is sent to the interior of the system, where one or several computing elements process it and eventually produce outputs. This is strict ET behaviour.

The definition of the operational envelope of ET systems (the set of assumptions about the behaviour of the environment to control) is by nature not rigid. A beneficial consequence is that they can admit situations where they are stressed beyond the design-time worst-case workload without falling apart. Obviously, if pure hard real-time behaviour is the goal, this must not happen: the system is designed to meet the worst-case assumptions for event arrival, etc. On the other

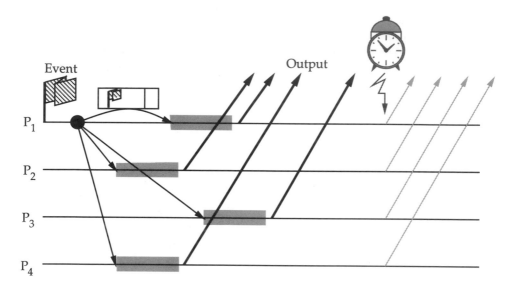

Figure 16.8. Timing of an Event-triggered (ET) system

hand, ET systems are best suited for mixed — say hard real-time and best-effort — requirements.

ET systems are prone to what are called *event showers* (Kopetz [1991]). These may occur in situations of exception (fire, leakage, explosion, crash, etc.), where the most probable outcome is that a number of system nodes start providing alarm information, some of it redundant or repeated, some of it multiplied by propagation, although concerning a same cause. In a pure ET system, this may flood and completely thrash the computing elements. So, how bad is this?

No system can treat a load that is completely random. *Aperiodic* events (i.e., events whose inter-event spacing — also called interarrival time — is undetermined) are not tractable under a deterministic perspective, not even by TT systems. *Sporadic* events, on the other hand, are a way of modelling the environment faithfully enough. They are tractable because rate and spacing are defined, and this assumption is adequate to accurately represent the environment encountered in most real-time problems (Burns [1989]).

Furthermore, when an alarm occurs, the subsequent event production can be predicted to a significant extent. That is, most events following a first alarm are *predictable* rather than *chance* events (Kopetz [1991]). The system designer can thus create rules: to *compact* successive instantiations of the same alarm at the representatives; to *discard* redundant events, either at the representative or upon arrival at the computing element (by a pre-processor); to *prepare* communication and computing resources for the forthcoming shower.

Additional engineering measures can further improve the event handling capability. These have to do with load or *flow* control, concerned with regulating the flow of information from the periphery (representatives) to the nucleus of the system (computing elements). Window-based schemes have been used in traditional communication protocols such as TCP/IP. For real-time — namely ET — operation, other schemes are more advisable, such as credit-based or rate-based flow control.

Real world events are sometimes bursty. The sporadic event class imposes a bound on the number of events that can arrive in an integral of time, and their separation. The transmission of such events to the computing elements can be *smoothened*, by spacing them by the equivalent of an average rate. These issues concern rate-based flow control, and will be discussed with detail in Chapter 17.

Observe that flow-control could be done at the computing element, but doing it at the source is preferred for two reasons: it also smoothens communications; it balances the arrival of event messages from several sources.

So, we see that ET systems need not be random. The 'event shower' effect can be predicted and neutralised, by the combination of the measures described above. Note that the front-end rôle played by the *representatives* in our model is crucial. They protagonize practically all the corrective measures responsible for transforming undisciplined environment stimuli into sporadic (or even periodic!) messages complying with the design assumptions.

Concerning communications, ET systems can combine event- and time-triggered protocols. As a matter of fact, one can superimpose time-triggered behaviour on top of an event-triggered communications system. This will be discussed in Chapter 17.

A system that has to treat several tasks simultaneously has to have some form of scheduling. Responsive systems are a typical example, and scheduling is important enough in real-time to deserve a separate chapter in this book (Chapter 18). Given their dynamic characteristics, the scheduling of ET systems cannot be decided *a priori*: it must be done *on-line* and will be *preemptive* in most cases. This way, a sporadic event of extreme importance can be given the processing resources it needs immediately it arrives (Jensen and Northcutt [1990]; Veríssimo *et al.* [1991]).

Active replication is the most used replication scheme for dependability of real-time systems. However, preemption complicates replica determinism (cf. 16.5), and this problem motivated the development of a new replication control model, called the leader-follower (Powell [1991]). It is sort of a semi-active replication model, with a number of virtues among which solving the determinism problem.

Now is the time to talk about *time-triggered* systems. TT systems are based on a very simple philosophy: the environment and its evolution are subject to a number of well defined assumptions; event patterns, and in consequence, the worst-case load, are perfectly determined *a priori*. Systems are built as periodic automata following the evolution of these events and acting accordingly. Activity is triggered at environment-independent instants (Figure 16.9). The period is short enough to match the rate of evolution of the environment and long enough for the duration of processing.

By assumption, there is no such thing as overload in TT systems. This would of course be a dangerous assumption if the environment would not be thoroughly described: a requirement of TT system design. Take the (unfortunate but realistic) example of a weapons-control system: a TT system designed for a maximum of 50

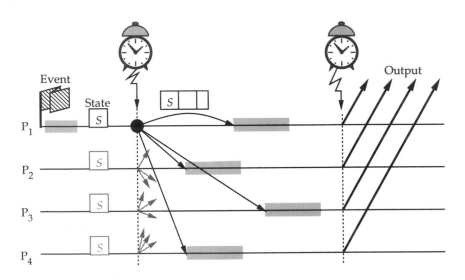

Figure 16.9. Timing of a Time-triggered (TT) system

incoming enemies will be blind or puzzled when a 51st enemy arrives. Reaction time is also important: the period cannot be made as small as one wishes, since it depends on technological and system-sizing issues. In consequence, when a very urgent alarm arrives, it may have to wait as long as a whole period to be served. This is only relevant, however, when the period duration is large enough to be of the order of magnitude of the expected service delay for these urgent sporadic events.

TT systems are the perfect match for a third class of events (besides aperiodic and sporadic): *periodic* events, mostly generated by artificial processes, but that is the case in a lot of process control settings (discrete or continuous). TT systems have other advantages. Given their cyclical and lock-step (in pulses) evolution they are simpler to test and show correct in the case of, for example, critical applications. They are excellent for small closed systems controlling static environments and repetitive processes, like some manufacturing cells, fly-by-wire control, automotive control networks, etc. On the other hand, they may be harder to commission for large-scale or often-varying settings.

There is no event-shower in TT systems. To comply with the cyclical operation style, events are collected and pre-processed in the periphery of the system, between periods (Figure 16.9). At given moments, this state information is disseminated to the computing elements, which then perform the necessary transformations and eventually produce outputs, also at a pre-determined instant. Either when the environment is 'quiet', or in worst-case alarm situations, the information flowing is the same.

Flow control would then seem to be a non-problem. Note two things however: (1) the system is always working as in full load; and (2) showers of alarm situations and maximum rate of event arrival must be handled by the representative.

The messages transactioned between the latter and the computing elements must always carry enough octets to represent the maximum I/O information that can be generated in a period in any situation. The efficiency of use of resources is thus compromised in favour of determinacy of operation.

Time-triggered communication is mandatory for TT systems. In fact, the whole architecture, including the network, works in pulses. For example, the MARS system, a pure TT system (Kopetz *et al.* [1989]), accesses the network through a TDMA[1] policy, a slotted access method where each node knows exactly when and for how long to transmit.

Scheduling is calculated *off-line* and it is *static*. The system still has to treat several tasks, so the automaton we mentioned before is a multi-tasking one. However, since we know the evolution of the system *a priori*, we can also determine how long the processing steps last, and combine their interleaving in order that all tasks perform their work by the end of a period. Once this schedulability exercise is done (Chapter 18), the schedule may be cast into the system executive.

Active replication is the scheme used in TT systems. It is rather easy to replicate deterministically a cyclical execution whose schedule is static and time-triggered.

16.4.3 Event-State Duality

One conclusion to draw from the previous section is that none of the fundamental problems disappear just because the system is time- or event-triggered:

- information flow control
- responsiveness
- predictability and assumption coverage
- efficiency and versatility
- extensibility

This prompts us to claim that the two approaches are not drastically different after all. Put in other words, there is a duality between the two: an *event-state* duality. Figures 16.10 and 16.11 illustrate this idea.

In ET systems, the *information flow* must be mastered up to the centre of the system. In essence, an external event or burst of events is transformed into a *message interrupt*, which retains an event-like nature while travelling inside the system (Figure 16.10). This approach adapts better to overload and unexpected events, either from the same or different representatives. On the other hand, event showers may cause the system to capsize if proper measures are not taken.

In TT systems, the information flow is throttled in the periphery of the system (Figure 16.11). However, one cannot exert 'flow-control' on the environment! This is universally true, that is, the situation is no different from ET systems in this respect. Flow control in TT systems is performed between the environment and the representative, which only accommodates the information it is prepared to recognise and transform in one period. So, in order that no overflow occurs at

---

[1] Time Division Multiple Access.

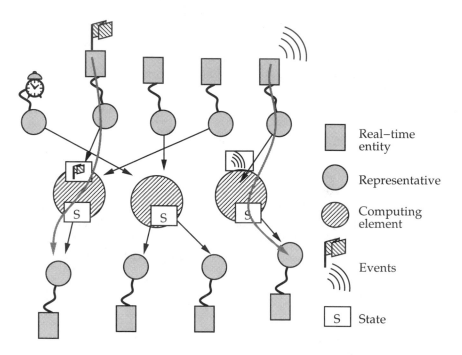

Figure 16.10. Flow of information in an ET system

the representative, the event arrival distribution must be well known. Otherwise, unexpected but important events may be filtered out.

On the other hand, the problem is solved from then on. If we look at Figure 16.9, we see that events are transformed into state at the representatives. As a matter of fact, it is as if the set of representatives holds the global state in pieces, which are disseminated to all the computing elements when the start-of-period ticks, in the form of *state messages*. These messages contain structured data, the whole of which forms the global state or system context. In consequence, they are not consumed; instead, each overwrites its previous instantiation in the global state, like a piece in a puzzle. Going back to Figure 16.11, the flow between representatives and computing elements pictured there is periodic and static, and it is always the same amount of information: the objective is the cooperative refreshment of the global state. In consequence, *resource reservation* rather than flow-control is necessary.

Average *responsiveness* of ET systems is the best possible in general, since an urgent event gets through and is processed just depending on preemption speed and communications transmission time. This is especially true if fast clock-less communication protocols are used (cf. Chapter 17). Note, however, the special case of the arrival of a burst of events: only the first one will deserve immediate response, while the others suffer a delay, which is $B.t_{treat}$ for the last one, B the burst length in messages, t_{treat} the treatment delay of a message. Priorities play an important role in ET systems, to let urgent events get through ahead of others. This

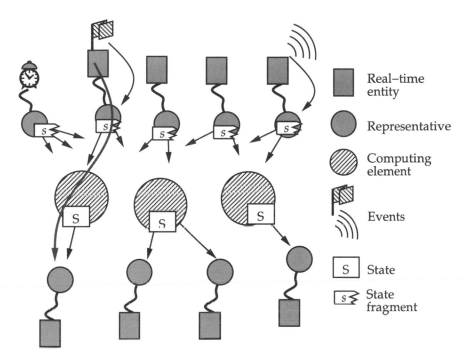

Figure 16.11. Flow of information in a TT system

way, the treatment delay of critical events is reduced to $B_{crit}.t_{treat}$, B_{crit} the critical burst length, hopefully much shorter than B.

Time-triggered-system response is cyclical, occurring at pre-specified instants in time. Given that the environment is asynchronous with regard to the system, an event may have a waiting time of one cycle in the worst-case, half-cycle on average. This is not a disadvantage for many systems, when the cycle is short enough for the evolution of the environment. Take continuous process control, for example: sampling may be synchronised with the system cycles. A second special case, in favour of TT systems, concerns data sampling. Since the sampling instants are controlled by the system, the equivalent events have zero waiting time. On the other hand, worst-case response of TT systems is optimal.

Combinations of ET and TT can produce good results. In an ET system we can play a little trick if we have a clock available at all nodes: the response, instead of taking effect immediately, can be produced at a pre-specified later instant, and perhaps in synchrony at several nodes, as shown in the right corner of Figure 16.8. This is a combination with TT behaviour. Thus, the truth is always in the middle.

ET systems dynamics and allowed event distributions (sporadics) make *predictability* a harder task to ensure than in TT counterparts. This is a very important factor of choice when reliability and safety figures have to be very high. In consequence, it is not surprising to see critical problems (nuclear, fly-by-wire, train control, etc.) be addressed by TT systems. Pure ET systems, on the other hand, are justifiable when system complexity and lack of environment knowledge would make predictability hard to achieve anyway: the so-called best-effort operation. The crux of the TT approach is to create the conditions to make the system appear well-behaved enough that events occur in synchrony with the system clock, and simple enough that only the assumed event distributions occur. In fact, when the environment does behave like this, why make matters more complicated?

Of course, there are additional issues that compound the argument: efficiency, versatility and extensibility. TT system resources are always allocated to their full extent, even if the system is idle. The TT systems we know are typically cyclical systems devoted to solving hard-real-time-only problems. There is no room for coexistence with soft or even non real-time. ET systems are *versatile* enough to accommodate several types of behaviour. To understand why in a few words, imagine that such a system is processing background soft real-time tasks in the idle periods of hard real-time ones and there comes a burst of high importance events: the scheduler sweeps out the low importance tasks and initiates treatment of the newcomers.

The ET approach is useful even under the perspective of more critical applications. Imagine that such a system is processing critical hard real-time tasks, but sometimes enters overload periods: an ET system can be designed in order to withstand this extra load, exhibiting what is called *graceful degradation*. These systems are called *best-effort* systems. They are not soft real-time systems, since they still aim at fulfilling hard timeliness requirements. In the impossibility of meeting them all, they will attempt at reducing the cost involved in failing to meet some, for example by selecting those that would, if not met, lead to catastrophic failure. Best-effort is not a field of preference for TT systems, which can only address the problem *a priori*, by means of several predefined *operating modes*. This means as many pre-tested schedules, and still leaves open the problem of falling outside the 'outer' operating mode.

Extension of TT systems is not trivial. Remember that scheduling in TT systems is about making the several tasks fit in one period of the lock-step execution. Obviously, increasing the number of nodes, or adding new tasks will require a total redesign of the node slots, communications, schedule, etc. On the other hand, they are based on state broadcast: this is an approach that runs into problems when number of nodes and state complexity increase.

The extra complexity put into the design principles of ET systems, a disadvantage already pointed out, becomes an advantage once the system is designed and it is necessary to extend it. Due to the provisions to support dynamic operation, this turns out to be easier. The event-based approach allows selective dissemination of information and allocation of resources. Compared to the TT approach, this means multicast instead of broadcast. In short, in the ET systems using groups that we know of (e.g., Veríssimo *et al.* [1991] and Audsley *et al.* [1991]), overall system scale and complexity (number of nodes, tasks and groups) can remain largely independent of group scale and complexity, because group size does not grow, at least proportionally.

A word of caution to finalise: inasmuch as extension of ET systems is easier than the extension of TT ones, testing of the latter is easier than testing of the former. In

Channel 1	speed < limit	abort	decelerate
Channel 2	speed > limit	takeoff	accelerate
Channel 3	speed > limit	takeoff	decelerate (erroneous)
Majority		takeoff	decelerate (erroneous)

Figure 16.12. A triplicated flight-control system

consequence, the overall task of re-commissioning either system may turn out to be equally complex, mainly in critical systems, where the importance of testing is paramount.

16.5 Replica Determinism

Replication is the foundation for fault-tolerance. Real-time systems normally need active replication, since the replicated responses are immediately present, be it for voting or merely to mask omission failures of replicas. In fact, passive replication schemes have a glitch when the primary replica fails: the time from when a response should have been issued, to when the backup, after taking over, is capable of providing it.

Managing active replication requires *replica determinism*: the ability of replicas to produce the same results, upon receiving the same inputs. The state machine is one way of achieving it. When the replicas are distributed, the situation gets slightly complicated, in that the inputs must be delivered in the same order to all replicas, for example through an ordered multicast protocol. See Chapter 7 for a better understanding of the state machine approach.

There are a number of causes for indeterminism, and some of them may be inadvertently introduced by designers: inconsistent input from sensors; uncoordinated access to clocks; inconsistent order of inputs to the state machine; nondeterministic language constructs (e.g., the Ada SELECT statement); absence of correct membership management; preemptive scheduling.

Let us give a simple example to motivate the need for replica determinism: a three channel (triplicated) flight control system in an airplane. At a given point before takeoff the system has to check whether the plane speed has reached a predetermined threshold and decide for takeoff, or abort, if otherwise. Consider the scenario of Figure 16.12.

Although the decisions of Channel 1 and Channel 2 are both correct, they are not consistent; that is, replica determinism is not maintained between Channel 1 and Channel 2. A single fault in Channel 3 cannot be tolerated anymore, since the majority voter will select the result of the incorrect channel. The problem will not disappear by increasing the number of replicas: when there is indeterminism the voting can always be balanced to the wrong side.

After this brief introduction, it should be obvious that active replication in TT systems (static in scheduling) presents no requirements further to the ones pointed out above: deterministic programs; reliable and ordered multicast. It will also behave well in ET systems without preemptive scheduling (Cristian, Dancey and

Dehn [1990]).   In consequence, replica determinism is a non-problem in these systems.

Imagine now an ET system with dynamic scheduling: scheduling must be preemptive since the evolution of the execution cannot be predicted beforehand. When the execution is replicated, the question is: *how to guarantee that preemption does not hinder replica determinism?*

A second problem with determinism is that certain entities also involved in replicated processing, such as clocks, analogue sensors, or random-number generators, if made redundant cannot, due to their nature, generate bit-for-bit identical values. For example, note that the analogue readings of two replicated temperature sensors of the same object will seldom be identical. We call them *pseudo-replicas*[2]. The question is: *how to guarantee that outputs from distributed pseudo-replicas are used consistently?*

Both questions will be addressed in the next sections.

Determinism with preemptive scheduling

To be useful, preemption must be allowed in the whole distributed processing path:

- *Message preemption*: Urgent messages must be allowed to overtake less urgent ones.
- *Process preemption*: Current processing must be allowed to be interrupted in order to process a more important event.

Process preemption is in fact complemental to the message preemption facility: it is of little use for hard real-time that an urgent message be simply put at the head of a queue, if it must then wait for the end of the (possibly long, low priority) current message processing, be it in the same or in a different address space. Furthermore, to be correct, preemption must be done *deterministically*, and occur in *bounded time*. Let us analyse the problems posed by preemption, to later discuss their solution:

- *An urgent message must be put ahead of all less urgent ones in the message queue of the destination process replicas.* But this is not enough, since in active replication, for example, the queues may not be in the same state (some replicas being slightly ahead of others in consuming messages).
- *A process is preempted by the local executive, to schedule another one of higher urgency.* This is *not* the preemption that poses problems: this low-level preemption concerns local operation of a real-time kernel and affects different addressing spaces. There is no problem with determinism of the interrupted process, since it merely freezes until resuming execution. This happens when the urgent message concerns another process than the one executing.
- *A process execution is preempted, to execute a higher urgency message coming to that process.* The difficulty arises here, since the higher urgency message must be treated in the context of the interrupted message, that is, in the same address space. There is no kernel support to do this. Furthermore, if the process is replicated, it is difficult to ensure that preemption occurs at the same point

---

[2]Denoted *rivals* in (Seaton and Chereque [1991]).

of the computation in all replicas, in order that the overall result does not become potentially non-deterministic.

- *Intra-process preemption must occur at the same 'point' in all replicas*. Here, the concept of *preemption point* is introduced: points in the execution of a process where preemption can occur inside its context, without damaging execution correctness. Each time the execution reaches a preemption point, the message queue is inspected for a higher urgency message at its head. If that is the case, the ongoing execution is preempted in favour of executing that urgent message. After executing it, processing of the previous message may be resumed if, again, no message of higher urgency is at the head of the queue.

- *Preemption must occur in bounded time*. To fulfil this aim, message preemption, as well as inter-process preemption, require a preemptive real-time kernel. Intra-process preemption, as just described, requires measurement of the time between preemption points in the software, so that they do not exceed a latency bound. Further reading about preemption point insertion techniques can be found in Veríssimo *et al.* [1991].

Semi-active replication management techniques, such as the *leader-follower* (Powell [1991]) are one way of solving the problem of non-determinism. They are called semi-active in the sense that they fall between active and passive replication. All replicas process the input messages, although the leader is always ahead of the followers by at least one message, and not in phase like in active replication. This leads to a slight glitch when the leader fails, although not comparable with the one of passive replication. Only the leader replica outputs results, obviating the need for collating replies. This reliance on the leader requires that components are fail-silent.

The replica group receives all messages (reliable multicast), though not necessarily in order (Figure 16.13a). The *leader* selects the order in which to execute. It picks one message from the queue and after processing it and sometimes producing an output, it notifies all *followers* to process that message. This hierarchy between leader and followers is the key to support deterministic preemption. With the L/F model, the problem of the insertion point of the urgent message is solved by the leader, who will dictate its execution order and propagate it to the followers, which will execute it at the same point.

Each time the leader reaches a preemption point (say, P_i, when executing m_2 in figure 16.13b), it increments a preemption counter and checks the head of the queue. Let us suppose an urgent message m_u is there: it preempts the current processing (m_2) in favour of executing m_u, and ensures that the followers are instructed to consume m_2 up to P_i, and from then on, to consume m_u.

Further to guaranteeing bounded preemption latency, the follower *takeover* glitch must also have a bounded duration. When the leader fails the time it takes for execution to resume normally must be bounded. The L/F protocol has to ensure that: followers detect leader failure and elect a leader in bounded time; desynchronization (the amount of lag) between leader and follower is bounded. The reader is referred to the Chapter 19, for details about the leader-follower mechanism in action.

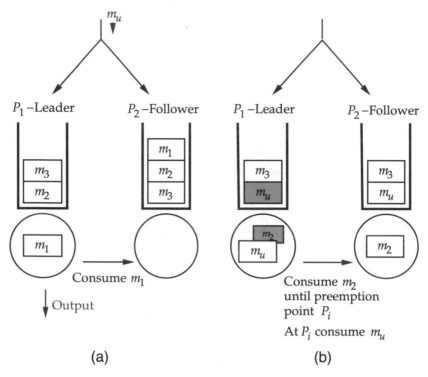

Figure 16.13. Leader-Follower Model

Determinism of pseudo-replicas

Pseudo-replicas are entities which, although being a redundant observation of a real-time entity, cannot, due to their nature, be bit-for-bit identical. The analogue readings of two replicated temperature sensors of the same object, when digitized, cannot be guaranteed to yield identical values. A more sophisticated example is when different methods are used, like measuring liquid flow through one flow sensor and one level sensor. Two 'replicated' random-number generators, if they are working properly, will provide two different numbers in response to a replicated request! A more common example is the global real time clock abstraction built with local synchronized clocks which aim at providing redundant observations of the same real-time entity: *the* real time. If a replicated program contains a *get_time* instruction for performing a time-dependent computation (e.g., logging of the time of an event; conditional statement depending on some elapsed period), replicas should not use their local clock reading and rely on a bit-by-bit identity. Care must be taken in these cases, in order to obtain deterministic results from the pseudo-replicas.

One possible approach is *pre-processing*: running a distributed consensus protocol to harmonise the readings. The pre-processing can be done either at the source

— among the entities providing pseudo-replica readings — or at the destination — among the recipients of the readings. It uses pseudo-replica-specific information — different measuring methods, admissible range of correct values,etc. — to arrive at a single value. In source-based pre-processing, this value will be given by one or all pseudo-replicas in response to the original request. In destination-based pre-processing, the requester receives the different pseudo-replica values and performs itself the pseudo-replica-specific consensus function. This approach should be used with sensor readings, and also to achieve a fault-tolerant clock reading.

In other situations, like for example a random number generator or a clock, the information is already in digital form and locally available to each computation. Besides, the value provided by a single component is often reliable (e.g., clock time) or significant enough (e.g., random number). Still, if each replicated computation grabs a local value, the results will diverge, hindering replica determinism. In this case, a *single-server* approach may be followed:

- Somewhere from within a replicated computation, a request must be made to a pseudo-replica.
- Pseudo-replicas must not be accessed directly (e.g., a *get_time* system call), they must be encapsulated in a pseudo-replica server.
- The first replica arriving to the request point addresses the local server and gets a reply.
- It must be ensured that the reply gets to *all* replicas: either the first replica sends it, or the server replies to all replicas.
- When the other replicas arrive at the requesting point, they use the first server reply in response to their call, and thus produce a mutually consistent result.

The support environment, namely the replication management protocol, must handle the dissemination of responses through the slower replicas: the responses must be kept awaiting and later bound to the request. This method matches semi-active replication very well (Veríssimo *et al.* [1991]). Active replication protocols must be modified to mutually sychronise the replicas and handle these messages coming before the requests.

16.6 Input/Output

Input/output is concerned with all that passes the computational border of a system. Recall however that there are more than sensors and actuators in I/O. Consider a system A, connected to system B via an application gateway, in order to deposit information in B or vice-versa. This is I/O, and all the mechanisms to ensure timeliness and fault-tolerance that we will discuss below apply to it, if we imagine each gateway as a sensor/actuator pair.

There is generally a problem in industrial (real-time) systems with making I/O reliable. A typical example of a 'trusted' valve is the quad represented in Figure 16.14, which tolerates a single failure. Distribution for fault-tolerance is as desirable for I/O as it is for computation. We are going to discuss a few principles for dependable distributed I/O. Most of these concepts are influenced by the

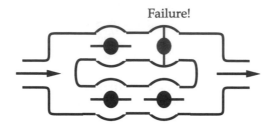

Figure 16.14. A classical mechanical quad valve

results of the DELTA-4 project (Seaton and Chereque [1991]), where the issue is further detailed.

16.6.1   Actuators

Simplex single drive

This is the simplest form. It is used when actuators are considered 'trustworthy' (e.g., outstanding mechanical reliability) and when the computer part is considered not to fail, or when the loss of the actuator is not crucial for system operation. Otherwise, it is an unreliable combination.

Simplex multiple drive

It is used when, although the actuator is trusted, its loss due to failure of the computer part (the representative) is undesirable. In consequence, only the representative is replicated. However, this poses some interface multiplexing problems, which are handled either by connecting the outputs of the representative replicas to the actuator in parallel, or in a changeover dual representative configuration whereby, upon detecting a failure, there is a switch to the standby representative. This mode works under the assumption that the unreliability of representatives is reduced to fail-silence, that is, while they work, they do not issue wrong outputs. Still, it is prone to common mode failures, since the representatives, while they may reside in different nodes, are electrically connected. For example, a 'stuck-at' failure of one representative's driver may block the actuator for good.

Fully redundant

This is the most general, expensive and dependable configuration (Figure 16.15). There are n actuators, 4 in the example of the figure, one representative per actuator, residing in different nodes. At least three are required for majority voting thus tolerating arbitrary modes of failure, either of the representative or the actuator. Synchronisation of outputs is most important. Active replication with tight synchronization is normally required, although semi-active replication is also allowed when the inherent glitches are acceptable[3].

---

[3]The mechanical valve is such an example, since the time constants involved are normally large with regard to computation times.

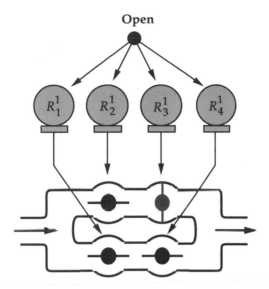

Figure 16.15. A very reliable actuator

16.6.2 Sensors

Simplex single access

This is the simplest form. It is used when the path from a sensor to the computing elements is considered reliable. Thus acquisition, conversion, preprocessing, and so forth, are performed by a single chain of elements, and finally conveyed to the system by the sensor representative.

Simplex multiple access

Note that in the configuration above, the sensor is connected to a single host. Should the host fail, the sensor is lost. In case the sensor is expensive, we may not want to replicate it just for availability reasons. In consequence, it is common in this situation to provide sensors with multiple access to representatives in different hosts. Note that this demultiplexing is done at the physical (analogue) level. Due to this electrical connection, there is a possibility of common-mode failure, although this is much less probable than for outputs.

The real problem is that the inputs received, after being digitised, are pseudo-replicas, rather than replicas: it is almost impossible to obtain bit-for-bit identity of two reads of the same sensor performed by different components, even if done at approximately the same time. In consequence, a passive replication technique, or one of the techniques described in Section 16.5 should be used, according to the application needs.

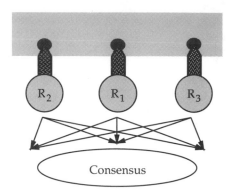

Figure 16.16. A very reliable sensor combination

Fully redundant

It may be desirable to replicate the sensor, either for reliability reasons, or to cross-check variable measurements performed by different methods. In that case, we have each sensor connected to a different representative, in a different node. This is a genuine *pseudo-replicas* case and again, the techniques of Section 16.5 apply. Figure 16.16 depicts an actively replicated sensor/representative set configuration, which will disseminate their values through an equally replicated set of computing elements. These receive the same set of values. In consequence, upon applying a deterministic consensus function they will arrive at the same result.

16.6.3   Distribution and Reliability

Since input/output is distributed, some of the techniques for replication and for communication presented in this chapter and in Chapter 17 are concerned with perception and actuation as much as they are with computation.

The role of time (cf. Section 17.7.1) is paramount. In a distributed system it goes far beyond supplying a time base for delayed or periodic actions: clock-driven perception allows synchronising the acquisition of data from different sensors. This way one can determine the order of external events, even if acquired in different nodes. Clock-driven actuation serves the purpose of aligning actions on the environment with a time grid, so that it may be possible to trigger outputs in relation with events occurring in other nodes: inputs, results of computations, other outputs.

When reliability is of concern, redundancy comes into play. In that case, one can use time to trigger a synchronised acquisition from replicated sensors (or an acquisition from a simplex sensor by replicated representatives), in order that the replicated data refer to approximately the same state of the RT-entity being sensed. A global clock can also synchronise the individual replicas of an actuator.

There is more to redundancy than the configurations of sensors and actuators discussed in the two previous sections: we should talk about how to properly interface and operate them. We will confine our discussion to the domain defined by one sensor or one actuator and its representative, at a time. That is, an 'open-loop' approach. In many settings, such as control loops, the feedback provided through the physical process back to the sensor can provide error detection. It may be useful, namely when the technique for reliability is time redundancy or switch-over to a stand-by (e.g., a piezoelectric oven lighter, triggered several times until a sensor detects that the oven lights).

The *semantics* of an actuator concerns, among other things, what it does when failures occur. Should it ensure that the action is done *at least once*? Should it force it to occur *exactly once*? Or should it perform it *at most once*? The answer depends on the needs of the entity being acted upon and on the good use of the end-to-end argument, that is, always use the weakest semantics possible.

At-least-once is the weakest and simplest semantics, it is achievable with any replication scheme, and should be used whenever possible. Namely, when the actuation is idempotent (e.g., *open valve*). The only remark goes for non-active replication management protocols, which have a window of uncertainty when the primary replica fails: in case of doubt, an output must be reissued upon take-over of the secondary.

Exactly-once has the strongest semantics. It fulfills any need, and is achieved by active replication with synchronised outputs. It is tricky to obtain with semi-active replication, requiring atomicity between output and notification to follower(s) (Veríssimo *et al.* [1991]).

At most-once is referred here for completeness. Normally, it is not a design approach for reliable actuation. When the requirement is such that the semantics cannot be at-least-once, but cannot be enforced to be exactly-once, the design uses exactly-once techniques, admitting certain 'omission' failures, that is, it falls into 'one or none' behaviour. A good example is a cash dispenser. One cannot triplicate the actual dispenser, otherwise users would get thrice the money. However, to make its operation reliable, it is driven by actively replicated representatives. They ensure exactly-once on their side, but if the physical unit fails, no money comes out. Overall, this falls into at-most-once.

The *synchrony* of distributed actuation is another important issue[4]. The steadiness of a distributed actuation command measures the stability with which one can cycle a remotely operated actuator. The tightness of a replicated and distributed actuation command is a critical parameter. It can transform an exactly-once actuation into at-least-once, and that is obviously undesirable. Consider *actuator granularity*, γ_a, the interval from command input to completion of the action or until the actuator is ready for a new command, whichever is longer (cf. Section 17.7.2). During that interval, the actuator does not respond to further commands (e.g., a discharge laser is unable to fire again until it recharges). If the actuation points of the replicas are separated by γ_a or more, they will be perceived as more than one actuation: the exactly-once semantics is lost. In consequence: *the tightness of actuation must be better than actuator granularity*, $\tau < \gamma_a$.

However, it need not be much tighter than γ_a, so, on the other hand, this condition

---

[4]See Chapter 17 for a definition of steadiness and tightness.

removes the general belief that replicated output must be tightly synchronised. In fact, some actuators have large enough a granularity to be driven by synchronous clock-less protocols, which can exhibit non-negligible untightness (cf. Section 17.8). Take the example of the valve quad in Figure 16.15: many valves have actuation times in the order of the hundred milliseconds, well within range of those protocols.

Last but not least, there is the issue of *interfacing*. There are three basic *operations* we need to be concerned about when interfacing to input-output:

Request – a down-call to the I/O subsystem, either explicit or implicit (e.g., by the passage of time);
Response – the response of the I/O subsystem to the request, either in the form of an action or returned data;
Notification – an (unsolicited) up-call from the I/O subsystem.

Confirmation, a fourth operation, is the physical feedback that 'closes the loop' between an actuation request and a related sensor. As mentioned before, we will not address the implications of physical feedback.

This said, let us have a look at interface timing. One might expect to review the event- and time-triggered duality in what follows. It so happens that timing in input/output is to a great extent decoupled from the approach followed in computation. Two good examples why: (i) in an ET system, one may wish to sample a set of continuous variables periodically ('TT'), and issue a message interrupt only when one of them deviates from an interval of confidence; (ii) in a TT system, a representative observing sporadic, discrete events, must act on an interrupt basis to handle them ('ET'), and later transform them into state. There are three *modes* whereby perception and actuation can be triggered:

Immediate – immediately upon reception.
Deferred – after a specified delay or at a specified time.
Periodic – every T units of time.

Let us discuss how they affect the operations we enumerated above. For a better understanding of the fundamental issues, we urge the reader to try and picture the inter-relations between the three modes in a very simple way: the response to immediate actuation occurs right after an *act* command request; deferred actuation, for instance, *act-at*(5:00) or *act-after*(100ms) is equivalent to an immediate command request, which is triggered by clock alarm or a timeout, instead of directly; periodic actuation, *act-every*(T ms), is a deferred actuation of delay T, always rearmed right after each timeout. Very similar to actuation, perception has two main mechanisms: the I/O takes a *snapshot* of the environment, subsequent to a *read* request, or it may otherwise *watch* the environment for significant events (e.g., pipe ruptures, intrusions), upon which a notification is generated.

In a same system, be it ET or TT, the interface to the several RT-entities can follow several styles, depending on the nature of the entity, and of the application controlling it. Immediate or deferred request operations are issued explicitly. Periodic requests are implicitly issued by the passage of time. Both are followed by an explicit response in the case of perception. If up-calls are allowed, notification generates an up-call immediately it is generated. Otherwise (strict TT behaviour) it is packed in the *read* information for the next cycle, with a waiting time of at most one period.

16.7   Concluding Remarks

In this chapter, we addressed the main issues relevant to the understanding of distributed, fault-tolerant real-time systems.

Divide-and-conquer

System design can be broken in two parts, concerning input/output and computation. There are correspondingly two objectives to attain, in the job of the designer: the reliable and timely perception of, and actuation on, the state of RT entities; the reliable and timely processing of the information acquired and production of responses. The first concerns the path between RT entities and representatives. The second concerns computations and interactions among real-time objects (representatives and computing elements).

Event-state duality

We have shown that there is a duality between time-triggered and event-triggered approaches to build responsive systems. This duality can and should be used to better understand the potential of both approaches, and to help designers build systems combining the best of each of them.

Flow control

When the entity to control, as happens in many real-time systems, is not fully in the sphere of control of the computer system, there is no possibility of limiting the occurrence of events, which may exceed the computer's capacity. Several engineering techniques exist to restrict the flow of events at this interface. However, it is still one of the difficult design problems to devise a flow control schema for a real-time system that: protects the computer from overload situations caused, for example, by a faulty sensor or by event showers; makes sure that no important events are filtered out by the flow control mechanism.

Scheduling

In general, the problem of deciding whether a set of real-time tasks whose execution is constrained by some dependency relation (e.g., mutual exclusion) is schedulable, belongs to the class of NP-complete problems (Mok [1983]). Finding a feasible schedule, if one exists, is another difficult problem. Chapter 18 will delve into these issues.

Execution time analysis

The interval between a stimulus from the environment and a computer response back to it can only be guaranteed if the execution time of all tasks and communication protocols within this real-time transaction is lower than a known upper bound. This implies that the worst case values of these times are known during system design, and that the operating system and hardware ensure that they are low enough for the desired service.

Testing for timeliness

In many real-time system projects, more than 50% of the resources are spent on testing. It is very difficult to design a constructive test suite to validate the timeliness of a best-effort system. Testing for timeliness is thus a difficult issue in hard real-time system design.

Error processing

In a real-time computer system we have to process errors (value and timing) before an erroneous output is delivered to the environment. Error detection, for example, is based on redundant information concerning the system operation. The provision of an error detection scheme that will detect all errors foreseen in the fault assumptions is a difficult design problem.

Replica determinism

Active redundancy requires replica determinism, i.e. the active replicas must take the same decisions, given the same ordered set of inputs. If replica determinism is secured, fault-tolerance can be implemented easily by duplex fail-silent self-checking nodes, or by Triple Modular Redundancy (TMR) for non fail-silent nodes. Determinism is difficult to achieve in systems based on dynamic preemptive scheduling strategies.

Acknowledgements

We are grateful to Carlos Almeida for his comments on an early draft of this chapter.

16.8   References

Audsley, N., Tindell, K., Burns, A., Richardson, M. and Wellind, A. (1991), The drtee architecture for distributed hard real-time systems, *Proceedings of the Tenth IFAC Workshop on Distributed Computer Control Systems*, Semmering, Austria, IFAC.

Burns, A. (1989), Distributed Hard Real-Time Systems: What Restrictions are Necessary?, *Proceedings of the 1989 Real-Time Symposium*, Zedan, H., ed., Elsevier Scientific.

Clement, G. F. and Giloth, P. K. (1987), Evolution of Fault Tolerant Switching System in AT&T, in *The Evolution of Faul-Tolerant Computing*, Avizienis, A., Kopetz, H. and Laprie, J. C., eds., Springer Verlag, Wien.

Cristian, F. (1985), A Rigorous Approach to Fault-Tolerant Programming, *IEEE Transactions on Software Engineering* **SE-11**(1).

Cristian, F., Dancey, R. D. and Dehn, J. (1990), Fault Tolerance in the Advanced Automation System, *Proceedings of the 20th Annual Symposium on Fault-Tolerant Computing*, Newcastle-Upon-Tyne, UK, IEEE, 1–12.

Jensen, E. D. and Northcutt, J. D. (1990), Alpha: a non-proprietary operating system for large, complex, distributed real-time systems, *Proceedings of the IEEE Workshop on Experimental Distributed Systems*, Huntsville, AL, IEEE, 35–41.

Kopetz, H. (1990), The production of intelligent products in developing countries, *Microelectronics Monitor* **29**, 63–71.

Kopetz, H. (1991), Event-Triggered versus Time Triggered Real-time Systems, Technische Universität Wien, Technical Report 8/91, Vienna, Austria.

Kopetz, H., Damm, A., Koza, C., Mulazzani, M., Schwabl, W., Senft, C. and Zainlinger, R. (1989), Distributed Fault-Tolerant Real-Time Systems: The Mars Approach, *IEEE Micro*, 25–41.

Laprie, J-C. (1992), Dependability: Basic Concepts and Terminolgy, in *Dependable Computing and Fault Tolerant Systems*, vol. 5, Springer Verlag, Wien, New York.

Lawson, H. W. (1992), Cy-Clone: An approach to the engineering of resource-adequate cyclic real-time systems, *Journal of Real-Time System* **4**, 55–83.

Mok, A. K. (1983), Fundamental Design Problems of Distributed Systems for the Hard Real-time Environment, MIT, Ph.D. Dissertation, Cambridge, MA.

Powell, D., ed. (1991), *Delta-4 — A Generic Architecture for Dependable Distributed Computing*, ESPRIT Research Reports, Springer Verlag.

Rodrigues, L. and Veríssimo, P. (1991), *x*AMp: a Multi-primitive Group Communications Service, *Proceedings of the Eleventh Symposium on Reliable Distributed Systems*, Houston, TX, Also available as INESC Technical Report AR/66-92.

Rodrigues, L. and Veríssimo, P. (1993), MESSAGE SLOTTING: Ensuring Replica Determinism in Preemptive Real-Time Systems, IST — INESC, Technical Report, Lisboa, Portugal.

Schlichting, R. D. and Schneider, F. B. (1983), Fail-Stop Processors: an Approach to Designing Fault-Tolerant Computing Systems, *ACM Transactions on Computer Systems* **1**(3), 222–238.

Seaton, D. and Chereque, M. (1991), Input/Output: Interfacing the Real World, in *Delta-4 — A Generic Architecture for Dependable Distributed Computing*, Powell, D., ed., Springer Verlag.

Veríssimo, P., Barrett, P., Bond, P., Hilborne, A., Rodrigues, L. and Seaton, D. (1991), The extra performance architecture (xpa), in *Delta-4 — A Generic Architecture for Dependable Distributed Computing*, Powell, D., ed., Springer Verlag.

Whitrow, G. J. (1988), *Time in History*, Oxford University Press.

Chapter 17

Real-Time Communication

Paulo Veríssimo

To achieve real-time communication, two things are necessary: real-time protocols and real-time networks. A real-time network is very simply one that displays timely and reliable behaviour. These fundamental characteristics materialise into several functional attributes:

- known and bounded message delivery delay;
- deterministic behaviour in the presence of disturbing factors (e.g., overload, failures);
- recognition of urgency, that is, of low-latency classes among overall traffic;
- connectivity, since the real world does not wait during communication blackouts.

When speaking of real-time networks, there are mainly two current fields of interest: the LAN (local-area network) and field-bus[1] settings; and the MAN (metropolitan-area network) and wider-area settings.

The first will be the focus of this chapter, and concerns control and automation applications, where hard real-time and a certain degree of criticality are normally implied. A number of proprietary and dedicated solutions exist here, although the trend is to use standard components when possible. These networks are normally small-scale, reliable to very-reliable, span a few thousand meter at most, and display round-trip times in the order of 10^{-5} to 10^{-1} seconds.

In wider area networks, real-time operation is also relevant, given the requirements of emerging distributed applications such as multimedia teleconferencing and other cooperative activities, or the pressure for improvement of the quality of service of on-line transactional systems, such as flight reservation, information servers, etc.

The latter environments are by definition not so well controlled from the point of view of the two fundamental attributes: timeliness and reliability. These networks are normally large-scale, unreliable, can span geographically broad regions

---

[1]Real-time instrumentation bus, mainly for sensing and actuating.

yielding round-trip times of the order of seconds or more. The best that can be achieved is best-effort or soft real-time operation, and that normally satisfies the non-time-critical uses of these networks. They lack technological support to do better, although the prospects are good, with the recent developments in high-speed fibre-optic and ATM technology, and the foreseen evolution of wide area networking to a scenario of MANs interconnected by very high capacity links.

17.1   Reliability Strategies

Communication protocols progress straightforwardly in absence of faults. When faults occur, things get complicated: lost messages, delays, corrupted contents, partition, etc. One may argue about the best way to cope with that undesirable facet of communication and computing systems.

In the domain of hard real-time distributed systems one often finds proprietary approaches with replicated hardware. In fact, from a dependability viewpoint, *space redundancy* is mandatory for critical systems (e.g., flight control, nuclear, military). One finds point-to-point graphs (Lamport, Shostak and Pease [1982]), survivable ring bundles for military applications (Talbott [1987]), or redundant rings or buses with multiple adapters, such as the MARS automation system (Kopetz *et al.* [1989]), with a duplicated Ethernet LAN, or the AAS air traffic control system, which uses multiplicated token-rings (Cristian [1990]), or the SIFT flight control system, which has a private unidirectional broadcast bus for each node (Wensley *et al.* [1978]). Non-replicated networks, from a cost and system complexity viewpoint, would be a preferable solution: hardware saving, and bound to use standard, off-the-shelf components. *Time redundancy*, meaning message repetition, applies in this case. The problem is that communication reliability is too low for most real-time applications. Even for *money-critical* applications, the cost of loss of connectivity may be high: think of a stopped manufacturing network which would otherwise debit a car module per minute.

Designers should nevertheless be able to build reliable real-time systems using existing technology and VLSI, for example standard LANs, because they lead to a simpler system and to a cost-effective network infra-structure. So, when thinking about which methods and techniques to use, two questions have to be asked: whether one can reliably obtain real-time behaviour out of simplex (non-replicated) LANs; and if yes, which protocols and quality of service to use.

One solution for the first question consists of a combination of simplex standard LANs using protocol time redundancy, with space redundancy in the physical layer[2]. It has been explored for example in the DELTA-4 system (Powell [1991]). Space redundancy is used exclusively in the physical layer to maintain connectivity, that is, in the electrical signalling part (modems, transformers, transceivers, cables), which is the most stressed one, with regard to permanent or transient failures. Since the protocols see only one LAN controller (thus, one network), they use time redundancy. It is satisfactory in all cases but those which require glitch-

---

[2]In ISO terminology, this layer, including the medium, makes-up the electrical and cabling part of a network.

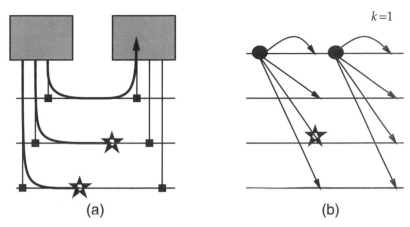

Figure 17.1. Error masking: (a) space redundancy; (b) time redundancy

free continuity of service provision, or which have very narrow timeliness and synchronism specifications.

The second question concerns protocols and quality of service. There is a large choice, from real-time datagrams to clock-driven atomic multicast. Its selection should obey a good use of the end-to-end argument, as discussed in Section 17.7.3. With regard to reliability of communication, one may use:

- error masking;
- error detection and forward recovery;
- error detection and backward recovery.

Error masking is much used in real-time networks, since it does not suffer from delays or message loss. It is the technique of diffusion protocols. Space-redundant networks transmit through several channels (Cristian [1990]). Their reliability stands on bounded network delay and number of failed components (Figure 17.1a). Simplex networks perform repeated message transmissions (Figure 17.1b). They further assume a bounded number of consecutive failures from a component. The key is to have respectively more than k channels or do more than k transmissions, to mask k failures. As we have been assuming, failures are understood to be *omissive*, that is, solely in the time (not in the value) domain: crash, omissions, or late timing. For failures in the value domain — or even arbitrary failures — space redundancy is mandatory. The criteria for the amount of redundancy are more demanding and the protocol has to introduce value checking mechanisms, like signatures, voting, etc. For examples of this kind of protocols, see Cristian *et al.* [1986], Lamport, Shostak and Pease [1982].

Remaining in the omissive failure world, error detection and recovery is another form of achieving reliability. *Forward recovery* is a common technique in periodic real-time communication, such as polling of continuous variable sensors. Note that there is a relationship between consecutive measurements, so it is possible to

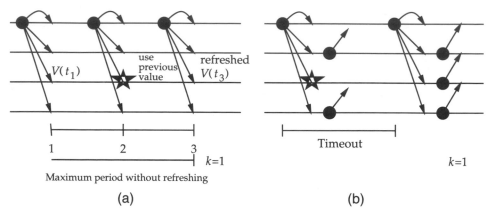

Figure 17.2. Error detection/recovery: (a) forward recovery; (b) backward recovery

skip a lost message and simply wait for the next, provided that the sampling period times the omission degree is a small duration compared with the time constant of the variable being sampled (Figure 17.2a).

Error detection with *backward recovery* is the technique of an acknowledgement-based protocol such as the one depicted in Figure 17.2b. It restarts when an error is detected and is appropriate when messages cannot be lost. The worst-case execution time may be significantly larger than the best-case one, especially on a LAN. Given that a variable reading is a representation of the state of a real-time entity at a given instant, it is time sensitive (cf. Chapter 16). In consequence, for certain cases, variable readings disseminated through a backward recovery protocol may no longer be very accurate after a worst-case execution. If this is relevant, it is preferable to use a diffusion or a forward recovery protocol.

When reading discrete variables or communicating sporadic events to other nodes, the idea is *not* to lose any message. Likewise when communicating inside the system, between computing elements: communication is supposed to be reliable, and many often directed to groups of nodes. In that case, masking or backward recovery are more appropriate. In Section 17.2, we will give concrete examples of how to build reliable low-level protocols giving these guarantees.

17.2   Making Real-Time LANs Reliable

Local area networks form the basis of a number of distributed real-time systems. It is mandatory that they display real-time behaviour — in essence, bounded and known message delivery delays — and an interesting fact is that structure alone does not determine real-time behaviour of a LAN. A number of factors like load patterns, priority allocation or failures, have to be taken into account.

Standard LANs, such as ISO 8802/4 Token-Bus, ISO 8802/5 Token-Ring, or ISO 9314 FDDI, and field-buses, such as Mil-Std-1553B, FIP, PROFIBUS, BITBUS[3], have been used in control and automation, but ad-hoc, 'plug-in' approaches have, not seldom, failed to meet the desired timeliness and reliability goals. Real-time behaviour of LAN-based systems is obtained through a systemic approach, that is, by establishing a model (traffic patterns, reliability and timeliness requirements, failure assumptions, etc.), a service and interface definition, and dressing the elementary LAN with the necessary hardware and software in order to comply with those requirements.

17.2.1   The Abstract LAN Model

If we settle with LANs as the basis for our reliable real-time network, one important point is how not to get tied to a particular LAN. For example, whatever protocols, mechanisms, systems, we build over a token-bus, should be usable over an FDDI. The question is more important than it may seem at first glance, since there are in fact standards harmonising the different LANs. However, these standards are too general: LANs display specific attributes necessary for real-time operation which are different from LAN to LAN.

Standardisation bodies have made an effort to render LAN interfacing LAN-independent, through the ISO-8802 *Logical Link Control (LLC)* sublayer (Pimentel [1990]). This protocol is LAN independent and supports a set of mechanisms for information transfer and control between peer entities, through several types of operation:

1. *unacknowledged connectionless*: protocol data units (PDUs) exchanged between peer entities without connection establishment;
2. *connection-oriented*: a data link connection must be established between peer entities prior to any exchange of information PDUs;
3. *acknowledged connectionless*: adds the reliability features provided by acknowledgement to type 1 operation;
4. *high speed transfer*: proposed as standard for general use over high-speed LANs and MANs.

Abstracting from physical particularities of each network allows one to obtain a LAN-independent interface. But hiding useful attributes does not help building protocols: neither of the services specified in LLC aims at real-time, reliability or groups (multicast), nor its interface reveals interesting properties of LANs (e.g., order). Now, suppose we devise a more complete model, overcoming these problems. In fact, there are a number of such properties, some of them known intuitively to designers, but never stated, which may be very useful to implement protocols. We describe a set of those properties in Table 17.1. They are defined in terms of a broadcast network delivering each frame, transmitted at a source, to all desti-

---

[3]The interested reader will find details about the operation of the token-bus in Pimentel [1990], the token-ring in Strole [1983], the FDDI in Ross [1989]. Likewise, details about field-buses may be found in MIL-STD [1988] for Mil-Std-1553B, Norme Française [1987] for FIP, Profibus [1987] for PROFIBUS, and Bitbus [1988] for BITBUS.

Abstract LAN Properties

An1 – *Broadcast*: Destinations receiving an uncorrupted frame transmission, receive the same frame.

An2 – *Error Detection*: Destinations detect any corruption by the network in a locally received frame.

An3 – *Network Order*: Any two frames indicated in two different destination access points, are indicated in the same order.

An4 – *Full Duplex*: Indication, at a destination access point, of reception of the frames transmitted by the local source access point, may be provided on request.

An5 – *Tightness*: Destinations receiving an uncorrupted message transmission, receive it at real time values that differ, at most, by a known interval T_{tight}.

An6 – *Bounded Transmission Delay*: Every frame queued at a source access point, is transmitted by the network within a bounded delay $T_{td} + T_{ina}$.

An7 – *Bounded Omission Degree*: In a known interval T_{rd}, omission errors may affect at most k transmissions.

An8 – *Bounded Inaccessibility*: In a known interval T_{rd}, the network may be inaccessible at most i times, with a total duration of at most T_{ina}.

Table 17.1. Abstract LAN Properties

nations. They are satisfied by the most relevant LANs in a real-time context: ISO 8802/4 Token-Bus, ISO 8802/5 Token-Ring, and ISO 9314 FDDI[4].

Properties **An1** and **An2** impose detection of errors in the value domain, in a broadcast. This derives directly from the CRC protection mechanism used in LANs. Frames not passing the authentication test are simply discarded, usually by the MAC VLSI.

An3 and **An4** are also common in LANs. The *Order* property is imposed by the communication medium within each single LAN segment; it is not ensured in interconnected LANs. The *Full Duplex* property implies that the sender itself be also included in that ordering property, as a recipient. For example, it is directly supported by the most popular chip set implementing the ISO 8802/5 Token-Ring standard. In LANs featuring bus topologies it is not usually supported: low-level firmware algorithms or specialised hardware are needed to secure the property.

Behaviour in the time domain, crucial for real-time, is described by the remaining properties. The property given by **An5** — *Tightness* — measures the maximum interval between reception instants in different nodes. T_{tight} is essentially a function of the variances of the end-to-end propagation delay and the interrupt processing time for a frame. In real-time systems, it is expected that this latter variance can be made not only deterministic but very small. In consequence, given that typical end-to-end propagation delays amount to a few dozens of microseconds, T_{tight} can

---

[4]A deterministic variant of the 8802/3 CSMA/CD (LeLann [1987]), though not a standard, is also covered.

be very small. This property is particularly important for the implementation of synchronisation services.

Property **An6** — *Bounded Transmission Delay* — specifies a maximum transmission delay, which is T_{td} in the absence of faults. It depends on the particular network, its sizing, parameterising and loading conditions. T_{ina} is added to account for the *inaccessibility* time, yielding the worst-case figure. Let us accept at this point that inaccessibility is a period when the network does not provide service, although remaining operational (take the example of the period from token loss to recovery in a token-based LAN). This problem will be discussed in Section 17.5. T_{ina}, the maximum duration of a burst of inaccessibility periods, depends on the network alone, and can be predicted for a set of local area networks (Rufino and Veríssimo [1992a]). Property **An8** ensures that the occurrences of these glitches are bounded.

The broadcast channel of a LAN is formed by several components: active physical layer entities (receivers and transmitters) and the passive medium. The channel may omit to deliver frames (omission errors) due to failures in those components. Omission errors may have many origins: mechanical defects in the cable, EMI corruption of a passing frame, modem synchrony loss, receiver overrun, transmitter underrun, etc. If it is possible to make assumptions about the number of components with failures during a protocol execution (an arbitrary interval of concern T_{rd}), and the number of consecutive omission errors produced (omission degree), property **An7** can be justifiably defined. This property is useful to implement protocols, as we will see later in the text.

Using LAN terminology, the implementation of this *abstract LAN* will comprise functions of the *Physical* (PHY) and *Medium Access Control* (MAC) layers, complemented with the necessary hardware and/or software. Simply speaking, it will be a driver, slightly more sophisticated than usual, sometimes together with some hardware. In the next sections we explain how to build a reliable real-time communication system, relying on the abstract LAN.

17.2.2   Real-Time Communication Requirements

As stated earlier, when designing the communication service we must create a model and state our requirements prior to anything else. Let us assume that LAN components may display the following failures (Powell [1992]): timing failures (delays) due to overload; omission failures (lost frames) due to transmission errors, overruns, etc.; network partitions (e.g., due to medium failure). It is an acceptable framework for non-replicated networks. As said before, admitting arbitrary failures would lead us anyway into space-redundant architectures.

The general requirement for reliable real-time operation of a communications subsystem is:

> **RT** – *A reliable real-time network displays bounded and known message delivery delay, in the presence of disturbing factors such as overload or faults.*

Additionally, in some architectures the subsystem should recognise *urgency*, a parameter that allows some messages to get through ahead of others. This is one mechanism for propagation or inheritance of priorities in a distributed setting. Practical systems will actually provide two or three urgency classes at this level, for example: critical or hard real-time; best-effort or soft real-time; and background or non real-time. Most LANs provide this distinction through priorities.

The next step consists in satisfying this requirement, in the presence of the failures just enumerated, with a non-replicated architecture. Notice that a very prosaic consequence of this latter fact is that transmission errors are unavoidable. Let us use a divide-and-conquer strategy, breaking down our solution as follows:

1. enforce bounded delay from request to transmission of a frame[5], given the worst case load conditions assumed (avoid timing failures);
2. ensure that a message[6] is delivered despite the occurrence of omissions (tolerate omission failures);
3. maintain connectivity (*control* partitions).

The conditions presented above are sufficient to achieve requirement **RT**: condition 1 makes sure that any frame is sent within a known time bound, even if it does not arrive. Condition 2 ensures that a message is delivered, even if that implies, for example, the transmission of several frames to tolerate omissions. When the network partitions without warning, it is as if it does more omission errors than assumed. Condition 3 may seem enigmatic. It is a folkloristic notion that real-time systems, needing to make progress within more-or-less rigid time constraints, do not tolerate partitions. In fact, through a technique described later in text, this problem can be and should be controlled, so that reliable real-time operation of non-replicated LANs is achieved.

17.3   Enforcing a Bounded Transmission Delay

Enforcing a bounded and known transmission time bound, T_{td} (**An6**), is not guaranteed per se by a LAN. To achieve it, a few points must be taken into account:

- traffic patterns;
- latency classes;
- LAN sizing and parameterising;
- user-level load/flow control.

The designer must be able to model the traffic offered to the network by each individual node. For example, if the traffic is aperiodic, no guarantees can be given about transmission delays from that node, and even the operation of other nodes may be jeopardised. The case is different with cyclic traffic, defined by a *period*, or with sporadic traffic, which is bursty, but can be completely defined by the *interarrival time* of requests, the *burst length* and *burst separation*. A comprehensive study of LAN traffic patterns is presented in the European COST project report (IITB [1984]).

---

[5]LAN-level information packet.
[6]User-level information packet.

The next step is to perform some traffic separation in latency classes, corresponding to the classes of urgency in the system. That is, a range of successively higher transmission time bounds, where the smallest corresponds to the highest-criticality traffic, and which may even be unbounded in the other end, for non real-time traffic sharing the network. The highest urgency traffic is thus guaranteed a certain amount of the channel bandwidth to fulfill its latency requirements, in detriment of lower urgency traffic. The latter may use the channel during idle periods, improving bandwidth efficiency of the communication system. We will get back to the definition of latency classes later in this section.

Let us focus on the lowest latency class, which normally corresponds to the critical, hard real-time part of the system operation. At this point, the designer is capable of computing the overall load offered by peer senders in this class. Knowing the individual traffic pattern of each node, he/she can go on to the next step, which is to enforce a given transmission time bound for every sender.

Remember that these bounds derive from requirements of the distributed real-time tasks of the system, which concern the whole execution path, including communication (Stankovic [1988]). Likewise, latency classes are a mapping of system-level task types on communications. For example, critical or hard real-time, best-effort or soft real-time, and background or non real-time tasks may be assigned to different latency classes.

The LAN must be sized and parameterised to comply with the aimed bound or vice-versa, that is, it may sometimes be discovered at this point that the aimed latency is not achievable with the amount of load offered. In consequence, either the latency goes up, the number of nodes and/or their offered load go down, or the node for which we were trying to obtain a given latency reduces its traffic demands (larger cycle for periodic, larger interarrival time or burst lengths for sporadic). This is thus an iterative procedure. It is also LAN dependent and should not be minimised for a successful design. For example, priority assignment and setting of the respective timers is most relevant for the correct operation of a token-bus (Gorur and Weaver [1988]; Janetzky and Watson [1986]) or an FDDI (Jain [1990]; Johnson [1987]). Incorrect designs have been one of the causes of unsuccessful MAP installations with Token-bus.

There are other methods to obtain deterministic access to a shared medium which are not standardised. The 802.3D is one of the deterministic variants of the ISO8802/3 CSMA/CD standard (LeLann [1987]). Unlike the latter, which has probabilistic access, the 802.3D enforces deterministic collision resolution, by establishing an order on the network nodes and performing a binary search algorithm to determine who transmits next, when there are collisions. The worst-case network access time is always known. On the other hand, there is a VLSI controller from a major manufacturer. Time division multiple access (TDMA) is another example of a non-standardised deterministic access method. It is slotted and slots are synchronised with a clock: each node has its time slot to transmit, in a fixed duration period, at a fixed instant. The result is a completely deterministic communication, where global priorities are no longer needed, because each node has a fixed allocation which cannot be preempted by another node. It is a communication scheme that fits pure time-triggered systems. Its bandwidth efficiency is affected by factors

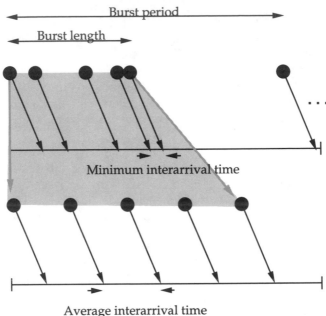

Figure 17.3. Timing pattern of sporadic events

like: safety interval in the end of the slot due to clock skew; overhead of message time redundancy for reliability; slots permanently allocated, even when idle.

The last step is to enforce user-level load control, which can be *flow-*, *rate-* or *credit*-based. Note however that in a real-time design, such control is of little use if the average load was misadjusted in the previous step. Flow control mechanisms, normally used in non real-time communication, like the sliding-window scheme used in TCP, can delay transmissions for long periods or even arbitrarily. Besides, they are not appropriate for multicast communication. The role of real-time load control is to regulate the global offered load, and to throttle individual traffic, in terms of the *request_rate* × *frame_length* product.

Sporadic, event-triggered traffic is the more demanding one vis-a-vis flow control, so we will have a close look at it. By definition, a sporadic event class has a bound for *interarrival time, burst length* and *burst rate*, as depicted in Figure 17.3. The first two are of primary importance for the design of the representatives (intelligent sensors, etc.): they must catch back-to-back events, and catch a whole burst. The second and third, combined, allow deriving a bound for average event arrival rate and they are relevant to the design of the communications and processing path: we can manipulate the rate at which we send data to the computing elements (servers, state machines, etc.), with the objective of smoothening their bursty nature, as long as it does not become smaller than the derived average event arrival rate (Figure 17.3). This is called rate-based flow control, and will help balance system load.

Rate control implements a rhythmic operation that is equally suited for periodic and sporadic traffic. It is harmonious in the sense that it aims at matching the sender's average debit with the recipient's capabilities, without discontinuities in traffic flow. The Express Transfer Protocol (XTP) (Sanders [1990]), a protocol under standardisation which follows the GAM-T real-time communication model (GAMT [1987]) (it integrates layers 3 and 4 of the ISO model), uses rate control. The user can manipulate a set of variables to tune it up: the maximum burst size a sender can transmit is set by 'burst[octets]'; the rate control interval is set by 'rtimer[µs]', and it specifies the interval between two burst starts; 'separation[µs]', present in an early version and later withdrawn, accounted for the minimum spacing between transmitted packets[7]. Note that 'burst' is in octets: the units of the request_rate × frame_length product mentioned above.

Credit control is a load control scheme based in allocating the recipients a certain amount of credit units (for example octets) per flow of information, coming from a sender or a group of senders. When the credit is over, the recipient refuses to accept more information. The scheme may be improved with look ahead credit request (by the recipient) or supply (by the sender), when it goes below a low-tide mark. On the other hand, high urgency flows (e.g., hard real-time traffic) may disregard the credit mechanism, in detriment of lower urgency ones. Credit-based control is used in the DELTA-4 communication system (Powell [1991]) and in the XTP. In the latter, credit and rate control may be combined: there is an extra variable, 'alloc[octets]', which specifies the n th octet that will be accepted by a receiver. Credit is well suited for 'abrupt' real-time operation, where it is necessary to perform resource reservation for significant amounts of information of bursty nature.

Allocating latency classes

Lowest latency classes have privilege in access to the network, thus achieving lower transmission delay bounds. LAN MAC-level priorities work differently from LAN to LAN. They allow in principle to let high priority frames to overtake low priority ones on the network, like a priority-based scheduler. Assignment and validation of LAN priorities have been studied by Janetzky and Watson [1986], Gorur and Weaver [1988], Johnson [1987], Dykeman and Bux [1987], Jain [1990] and Rzehak, Elnakhal and Jaeger [1989]. It would thus seem that priorities should be used generously. Priority-based ordering in standard LANs has some difficulties worthwhile pointing out though:

- One cannot order transmissions on a LAN based on a global knowledge about urgency of requests[8]. The sequence obtained varies from LAN to LAN.
- The LAN which best approximates that behaviour (8802/5 Token-ring) uses an approach in two rounds: it assesses the requests in the current token rotation, and gives access to the highest priority level waiting for transmission in the next round. However, the token-ring may display frame priority

---

[7]It can still be tuned, but not independently, by playing with 'rtimer' and 'burst'.

[8]The LAN does not stop each time a request arrives to a MAC queue. The decision (scheduling) time unit is one maximum transmission time (for priority reservation LANs) or one token rotation time (timed token LANs).

inversion in a number of conditions (Peden and Weaver [1988]), the most prosaic of which is due to the chip-set architecture: there is one request queue for all priorities, it is inside the chip set private bus, and it is FIFO. A very urgent frame may be appended after a long queue of low priority frames.

- Other LANs (8802/4 Token-bus, FDDI) have priority classes which are based on bandwidth sharing so they sequence access locally, per priority queue. Globally, there may be priority inversion, i.e. a station which has not high priority frames to transmit will allocate its bandwidth share to a lower priority frame, eventually long. A downstream station[9] with a high priority frame may have to wait for a stream of low priority transmissions of upstream stations until the token gets to it. The latency bound is not necessarily violated, but there is priority inversion.

- The number of priority levels is limited, eg. eight in the token-ring, four in the token-bus. There will certainly be frames of different *system* priorities which will be mapped onto the same MAC priority and treated as equal, so message priority inversion can happen.

In conclusion, good sense dictates that: (i) priorities should not be used to enforce transmission order; (ii) transmission order does not guarantee delay bounds anyway; (iii) latency classes based on traffic analysis and LAN sizing and parameterising should be the goal. All real-time LANs guarantee one deterministic latency class and a few others with at least high probability. In dynamic real-time systems one needs to support two or three urgency classes, corresponding typically to: hard real-time, best-effort or soft real-time, and background or non real-time. In consequence, the abstract LAN must map the *user urgency classes* into *LAN latency classes*, by translating user priorities into the appropriate LAN priorities, which are dependent on each particular network. As a general rule, urgent data (critical) and protocol control frames should be mapped into the highest LAN priority. The remaining traffic should be distributed by the remaining classes (1 or 2), according to their relative urgency and/or importance.

17.4   Handling Omission Failures

The *bounded omission degree*[10] assumption introduced in **An7** is very helpful as the foundation of basic error processing protocols with deterministic termination — crucial for real-time operation. Other properties of higher-level reliable broadcast/multicast protocols are easily implemented above the omission-free abstract LAN equipped with these protocols.

The assumption is realistic and it is based on the observation that omission errors are rare in LANs but may occur in bursts. Additionally, it is reasonable, for the limited interval of a protocol execution, to make the single failure assumption. In consequence, when omission bursts occur, they derive from the failure of a single

---

[9] A station to which the token will be passed.

[10] Recall that *omission degree (Od)* is the number of consecutive omissions produced by a component.

(a) transmission-with-reply   **(b) diffusion**

```
50  tries := 0;   Resp := empty              50  tries := 0;
51  do tries < nrTries ∧ Resp ≠ full →       51  do tries < nrTries →
52     Resp := empty;
53     Tx(data,id_tries);                     53     Tx(data,id_tries);
54     waitRepliesPutInBag(TwaitReply, Resp);
55     tries := tries +1                      55     tries := tries+1
56  od                                        56  od
```

Figure 17.4. K-omission tolerant protocol: (a) acknowledge-based;
(b) diffusion-based

component (a modem, a transmitter, the medium, etc.). A number of ways of handling omission failures are possible. Two alternative ways, based respectively on detection/recovery and on masking of omission errors (cf. Section 17.1), are presented in Figure 17.4. If k is the maximum omission degree as per **An7**, then $NrTries = k + 1$.

The detection/recovery algorithm is implemented through transmission-with-reply series[11]. Since error rate is expected to be low, this is optimal for the average case. After transmission, replies from a number of recipients are awaited for; replies are put in a bag *Resp*, which becomes full when it has all expected replies. In absence of errors there is only one try. The *waitRepliesPutIn* function waits at most during *TwaitReply*, after which it returns with the replies it got. Note that the several tries to send message with reference *id* are identified by an index $_{tries}$ (l.53). Reference *id* allows detection of duplicates. An interesting feature of protocol (a) of the figure is that it seeks a completely correct series, i.e. one where all recipients receive a given try and all replies are got. This way, besides transmission reliability, one obtains total order among competing LAN transmissions. Such low-level protocols may be used to build more complex ones very efficiently (eg. atomic multicast (Veríssimo, Rodrigues and Baptista [1989])). With a minor variation that consists of deleting line 52, the protocol falls into a more classic acknowledgement-based non-ordered multicast protocol.

The masking algorithm — (b) in the figure — is diffusion-based. It systematically repeats the transmission of the message $k + 1$ times. Given **An7**, after its execution at least one instance id_j of the message arrives at every recipient.

Anyway, if bounded transmission delay T_{td} is ensured, either of these mechanisms implementing **An7** satisfies the second condition to attain real-time behaviour: message delivery in bounded time despite omission failures. The main feature of the bounded omission degree technique, whichever transmission method used, is that it has deterministic termination; that is, it executes within a bounded and known time, in absence of partitions.

---

[11] This is different from the LLC type 3 service, namely because it is multipoint and because *replies* are not mere acknowledgements, they can convey semantically useful information.

17.5   Controlling Partitions: Inaccessibility

The third condition is to maintain connectivity. Let a network be partitioned when there are subsets of the nodes such that nodes from different subsets cannot communicate with each other[12]. Remember that the LAN is not replicated, so there are a number of causes for partition, even if temporary: bus medium failure (cable or tap defect), ring disruption, transmitter or receiver defects, token loss, etc.

Some LANs can recover from some of the situations described above (e.g., token regeneration for token-based LANs, medium reconfiguration in dual rings), but they will be out of operation for some time, that is, they will have glitches.

The solution for 'partition control' is based on a very simple idea: if one knows how long a partition lasts, then synchronous, real-time operation of the system is possible, provided that that glitch period is acceptably short for the service required. Let us call these periods *inaccessibility*, to differentiate from classical partitions (Veríssimo and Marques [1990]), and characterise them in the following way:

- a component temporarily *refrains* from providing service — without that being a failure — and its users can perceive that state;
- inaccessibility limits (duration, rate) are specified, and violation of those limits implies permanent failure of the component.

All that is necessary to implement inaccessibility control is: (i) to instrument the LAN to recover from all conditions leading to partition in a given failure scenario, that is, reestablish connectivity among affected nodes; (ii) ensure that the number of inaccessibility periods and their duration have a bound and that it is suitably low for the service requirements; (iii) accommodate inaccessibility in the protocols and in the timeliness calculations. This way, all partitions are *controlled*, and **An8** is attained. A network exhibiting **An8** satisfies the third and last condition to achieve reliable real-time behaviour enumerated in Section 17.2.2.

17.5.1   Implementing Inaccessibility Control

Inaccessibility control is the trickiest problem to solve, so its implementation will be discussed at some length. First, one must recover from all conditions leading to partition, show that all the recovery glitches are time-bounded and determine the upper bound. Some of them are operating situations typical to each LAN (e.g., reestablishment of the logical ring after loss of token or station insertion), or recovery actions resulting from failures (e.g., physical reconfiguration subsequent to ring breakage). For the sake of example, inaccessibility figures for the ISO8802/4 token-bus (Rufino and Veríssimo [1992a]) are presented in Table 17.2. Multiple station joins account for the maximum duration of an isolated occurrence. Note that this means that at least some nodes may lose connectivity for 140*ms*! If the network is properly managed and parameterised, the inaccessibility figures can be drastically reduced, to the numbers between parenthesis (Rufino and Veríssimo [1992b]). In

---

[12]The subsets may have a single element. When the network is completely down, *all* partitions have a single element, since each node can communicate with no one else.

Rate Mbps	t_{dl} μs	t_{SD} μs	t_{SI} μs	Scenario	t_{ina} (ms)	
				Station join	4.61	(0.85)
				Multiple joins	140.0	(25.8)
				Multiple station leaves	1.67	(1.67)
5	36	11	27	Token loss	5.79	(2.72)
				Group of adjacent station failures	5.18	(1.23)

Table 17.2. Inaccessibility Times For Token Bus. t_{dl}: delimiter (header/trailer) duration; t_{SD}: station delay; t_{SI}: slot-time; t_{ina}: inaccessibility periods

that case we have a bound for inaccessibility of 26*ms*. Medium failure has not been accounted for, and will be discussed in Section 17.5.2.

Finally, inaccessibility must be included in the timeliness model. Let us consider local clocks (timers) to implement timeouts, as used in a number of systems. Timeouts detect timing, omission and crash failures. They are used either by the abstract LAN protocols or by upper-layer protocols to perform surveillance of remote parties during a pending request (e.g., RPC). Inaccessibility must be accounted for in two things: calculation of real *worst-case execution times* and dimensioning of *timeouts*.

According to **An8**, in an interval of concern, T_{rd}, there may be at most l inaccessibility periods adding-up to at most T_{ina}. Let us assume that T_{rd} is the longest protocol execution duration. Calculation of real worst-case execution times of any protocol simply implies that T_{ina} be added to the worst-case protocol execution time expression computed as normal (without inaccessibility).

Timeout values are set in function of execution times. Protocol timers must in general include T_{ina}, or else they timeout too early should inaccessibility occur, which may even cause the protocol to fail[13].

At this point, note that incorporating T_{ina} in the timeout values is a sufficient condition for running synchronous (real-time) protocols over the abstract LAN, using the transmission-with-reply protocol. This confirms the statement we have made initially: 'if one knows how long a partition lasts, then synchronous, real-time operation of the system is possible'. However, T_{ina} may be much greater than T_{td}, causing the timeouts to be undesirably long. A solution taking away inaccessibility from the timeouts would be welcome, with two obvious advantages: giving the programmer the simple and elegant abstraction of a distributed environment which is always connected; yielding shorter timeouts.

There are two engineering techniques that make it possible (Veríssimo, Rufino and Rodrigues [1991]). The first is *timer freezing*, consisting in suspending all timers used for the timeouts when inaccessibility is detected and while it lasts,

---

[13]Consider the example of the protocol of Figure 17.4a: since T_{ina} is normally greater than *TwaitReply*, if this timer does not include inaccessibility, it may timeout all the $k + 1$ times during an inaccessibility period, and a failure is wrongly detected. In the same situation, the protocol in Figure 17.4b would make the higher-level user believe the message was indeed delivered after some estimated delay; but in reality, it may still be waiting in some queue long after.

and restarting them when the network becomes accessible again. All protocols can then be constructed as if the network were always accessible. Freezing cannot always be implemented because it implies manipulation of system software and hardware. An alternative method is *inaccessibility trapping*, consisting in trapping each inaccessibility period inside two consecutive *transmission(request;confirmation)* signals from the LAN, to avoid more than one timeout per inaccessibility period. Each inaccessibility occurrence counts as one 'omission', so it is a question of incorporating these extra omissions in the retry count of the low-level protocols.

17.5.2   LAN Redundancy

In more demanding real-time settings, enforcement of a bounded omission degree and bounded inaccessibility with acceptable coverage, must be obtained through redundancy in the physical and 'medium' layers. For example, standard FDDI has a dual-reconfiguring ring capable of surviving one interruption, but *just* one (Johnson [1986]; Peha [1988]). Similar measures have to be custom implemented in the Token-bus or the Ethernet, since they have no standardised redundancy. However, it is easy to implement dual-media or *multi-media* to survive multiple failures, so we will illustrate the technique for dual media, using the Token-bus (Veríssimo [1988]).

This LAN, featuring a bus topology and independent clocking information, allows real-time switch-over between media, avoiding logical ring disruption in case of medium failure. The idea, as depicted in Figure 17.5, is to duplicate all logic below the VLSI controller, to create a dual bus. Then, transmit on both buses at all times, but listen from the one that offers more reliability, according to some pre-defined rules (Veríssimo [1988]), which need no consensus among the nodes: each receiver chooses to listen from the medium its rules select locally. The only limitation is that switch over can neither be made abruptly nor in the middle of a frame. If independent cable layout is done, this method masks not only permanent failures but also bursts in one medium.

17.6   Low-Level Protocols

We already presented *reliable* communication among *sets* of nodes as a need in responsive systems. Reliable group communication protocols serve both purposes: they address groups and normally encapsulate a range of error processing mechanisms. Low-level protocols can confer reliability to group communication, or for the matter, to any higher level protocol: as advanced in section 17.4, in the context of simplex LANs they present the higher communication layers with an omission-free and always connected LAN. The alternatives, diffusion or transmission-with-reply, are compared in Figure 17.6.

In principle diffusion obtains the lowest worst-case delivery delay, given that it systematically repeats a transmission $k + 1$ times, without waiting for any replies or error-detecting timeouts. However, note that if $T_{waitReply} \approx T_{td}$, both expressions for worst-case delivery delay will yield similar values. On the other hand, it

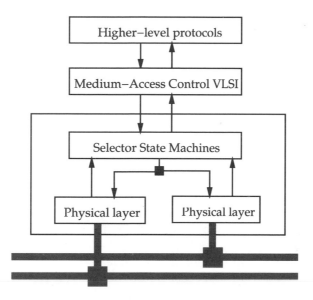

Figure 17.5. Dual Media Token Bus LAN

introduces a fixed overhead in processing, increases network load, and total order is not ensured.

The transmission-with-reply method allows detection of failure, that is, absence of reply after $k + 1$ tries. This also works as a robustness feature, in the case of coverage failure of the bounded omission degree assumption: a node does more than k omissions; the abstract LAN detects the fact, signalling the higher-level protocol; the latter can then handle it, for example forcing the faulty node to shut down. In this sense, transmission-with-reply is safer than diffusion, with regard to coverage of **An7**. This is very important in real-life networks, where despite

Features	Tx-with-reply	diffusion
execution time	lowest w/ no faults	lowest w/ w-case faults
worst-case delivery delay	$k.T_{waitReply} + T_{td}$	$(k + 1).T_{td}$
no-fault delivery delay	equal	equal
processing overhead		highest
directionality	bi- (tight coupling)	uni- (loose coupling)
scalability (overall)	equal	equal
(of groups)		highest
network load		highest
total order	possible	not possible
failure detection	yes	no
upper-layer inform. in reply frame	possible	not applicable
resilience to lack of coverage	high (detects violation of omission degree)	none

Figure 17.6. Comparison between transmission-with-reply and diffusion methods

realistic assumptions there is always the possibility of large noise bursts arising and causing problems even if the medium is thought to be fault-tolerant.

The transmission-with-reply method, being bi-directional, requires a tighter coupling between sender and recipients than its diffusion counterpart. Overall scalability is similar, if we consider that most applications are concerned with groups of tasks that interact through multicast. In real-time applications system size increase will lead to more of these groups, rather than to much larger groups. An additional feature of transmission-with-reply is that the replies can convey information from the recipients in a performance-efficient manner.

Group communication protocols built above the abstract LAN may benefit from these features (see (Veríssimo, Rodrigues and Rufino [1991]) for an example). Consider a channel with single failure assumption and an omission degree $Od \leq k$. Imagine we are trying to perform a reliable multicast to $M - 1$ recipients, using transmission-with-reply: to obtain a correct round we may thus need to perform several series of M transmissions. A faultless series is obtained at most after $t = k+1$ series, even if omission errors are not consecutive in the network[14]. The interval of concern T_{rd} to derive k is the worst-case time to perform the $M. (k+1)$ transmissions.

17.6.1   Addressing

Addressing is a low-level function that must be efficient and timely, and respond to the new requirements put by group communication and real-time. It should help support failure detection and group membership mechanisms, which are crucial for reliable real-time operation.

Frame addressing concerns: the construction of the address, on frame transmission; the interpretation of the address of a passing or received frame. The first step concerning address resolution is traffic discrimination, that is, the ability of the network to classify frames into different types. Frame types identify unambiguously the class of protocol(s) to which the frame belongs (e.g., AMp, TCP, XTP). This is not exclusive of real-time operation and is normally used in networked systems. For address generation/resolution to be straightforward and fast, it is best to have defined a set of *addressing modes*, and make protocol address formats correspond univocally to (*type;addressing mode*) combinations. Upon reception, '*type*' performs the first selection, when that protocol class exists in the node: it points to a set of possible filters, from which '*mode*' selects the appropriate one. Objective of address resolution: avoid reception of frames not addressed to anyone in that node. In practice, the more this is done by software, the farther we are from that aim: frames have to enter the station, and then be discarded. Necessary approach for efficiency: map '*modes*', as much as possible, into the hardware address filtering mechanisms of the VLSI LAN controllers.

This said, we now discuss types and modes themselves. To be efficient, type filtering should be implemented using the hardware mechanisms offered by the different LANs. The Ethernet provided a *type* field, no longer existent in the ISO8802/3 standard. But real-time LANs do supply special frame types one can

---

[14]In that case, they must originate in the same component, by the single fault assumption.

use for this purpose: *special frame control* in Token-Bus, or *implementor frame control* in FDDI.

In what concerns address modes, multicast (group addressing), a must in distributed systems (real-time or not), introduces a few new addressing modes. Given that they present a greater complexity to address recognition, they should rely as much as possible on the hardware. Here is a classification of the several addressing modes:

- *Individual* — This addressing mode enables the sender to address *only* a particular station by its physical address. It is the traditional point-to-point 48-bit LAN addressing.
- *Broadcast* — This addressing mode enables a frame to be accepted in all nodes. It is the traditional *all-ones* address in LANs.
- *Logical* — This addressing mode is intended to address a given group of nodes, identified by a *gate address*, independently of their location and number. An n-bit gate address may be an arbitrary number in the 2^n addressing space, for *pure* logical addresses, or a binary chain, where each of the n bits represents one or more groups[15].
- *Selective* — This addressing mode also consists of an n-bit binary chain, but now each of the bits represents a node. The association between a station and a bit can either be static or dynamic (via group membership). By setting bits as needed, the addressees are selected, transmission by transmission.

The idea behind logical and selective addressing is supporting requirements found in distributed and dependable real-time systems: allow location independence and thus efficient name-address translation; support migration; provide replication transparency; create group-oriented traffic confinement; improve performance and timeliness, by conserving LAN and adapter power.

The selective addressing mode is very powerful. We will stick to it in the next section, where we talk about group membership. Selective addressing may be used as the underlying mechanism to perform all addressing, even individual (a mask with only one bit set), and assist higher-layer logical group addressing, since pure logical addresses are not supported by standard LAN VLSI. For example, Figure 17.7 depicts the operation of logical addresses: a direct name (*alpha*) to address (50) translation is possible with a pure logical address; logical *gate* 50 is open at the relevant nodes belonging to group *alpha*; the message is only delivered at the nodes where the gate is open, which may include the sender node. Without hardware support, the frame must be received everywhere and then filtered in software, as occurs in the last node to the right.

17.6.2 Processor Group Membership Management

Group Membership (GM) management is a crucial function of group-oriented systems. As a system-level diagnostic tool, it has always been considered of great

---

[15] In which case part of the address hits in reception will be false, so the resolution must be completed by software.

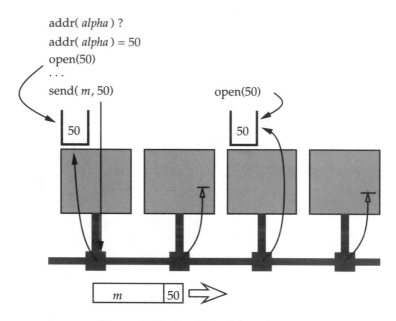

addr(*alpha*) ?
addr(*alpha*) = 50
open(50)
. . .
send(*m*, 50)   open(50)

50   50

m   50

Figure 17.7. Logical addressing

importance in distributed real-time systems. *Processor* group membership (PGM) is a low-level function that provides a map of the nodes belonging to a group. This is independent of higher-level groupings of processes, as a matter of fact, several of those processes belonging to the same *process group* may exist in one node. This prompts for the opportunity of cooperation between PGM and process group membership (pGM): a relevant processor group is the group of physical nodes where all the processes of a process group reside.

Going back to processors, a generalization of group is the whole real-time LAN, and in that case the objective of PGM is to obtain and maintain an *active stations table* (AST). When using selective address, the AST provides the station ordering, and a basic mask where stations are marked *'up'* or *'down'*, as shown in Figure 17.8. A logical group address *alpha* ≡ 50 is now represented by a selective address mask which contains all nodes where gate *alpha* is open. This way a frame is only received at the nodes concerned. Note that selective address further provides sub-group addressing capability: a message which should only get to a subset of *alpha* is addressed by a mask setting only the desired node positions.

Having discussed the addressing implications of PGM and ASTs, we now discuss PMG functions, which have to respond to three categories of events — *insert/delete*, *join/leave*, and *failure*:

- maintenance of the AST;
- provision of short-addresses;
- failure and group change handling;
- information about group members.

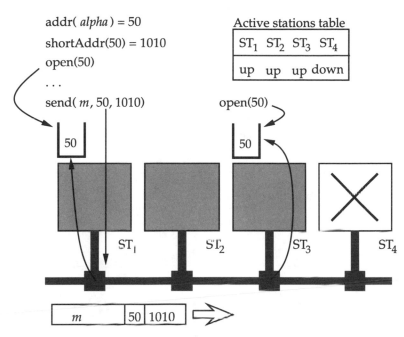

Figure 17.8. Logical addressing implemented with selective addressing; Active-Stations Table detail

The following discussion applies to a group of nodes, which can be all the nodes in the network. PGM responds to *insert* or *delete* requests by system administration, concerning the insertion of brand new machines or their permanent removal. This affects the length of the address and/or the order of stations. Short-addresses are supplied by referencing a node by its position in the AST, a number that can be much shorter and easier to manipulate than an individual address. Short-addresses are only guaranteed to be stable between *insert/delete* operations. Nodes already registered in the AST may leave or join again the group, by requesting a *leave* or *join* operation. Their position in the AST is kept, being marked *up* or *down* accordingly. A particular case of membership change is failure. The PGM protocol is prompted to act upon a suspicion of failure, that may come from a number of entities, such as the network driver, a group communication protocol, or a process group membership protocol. Finally, a PGM service can reply to a number of requests about the group members, depending on the implementation: their number, identity, location.

Figure 17.9 depicts a clockless real-time PGM protocol used the DELTA-4 system (Rodrigues, Veríssimo and Rufino [1993]). This protocol implements all the functions just described. A *GroupChangeEvent* triggers the protocol: join, leave or failure. In the latter case, some component detecting failure issues a *check* request, which can also be issued periodically by the passage of time. As shown in Figure 17.9a, the protocol execution is assumed by one node, which requests the members' state. If needed, this is done through a series of $k + 1$ tries, to overcome omissions

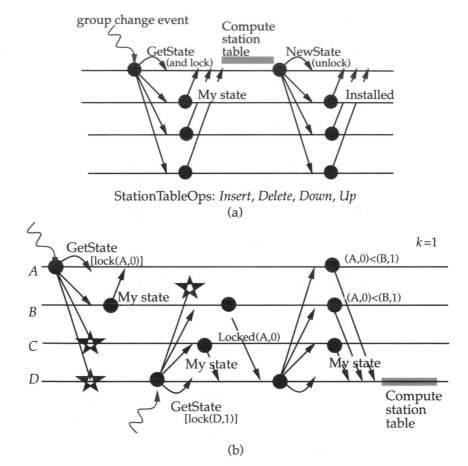

Figure 17.9. DELTA-4 XPA system clockless PGM protocol

or detect permanent failures (cf. Section 17.4). When it gets the replies it computes the new AST and disseminates it to the members, again through transmission-with-reply to make sure all members install the new table. The first message locks the table to ensure that competitors are left out. Still, with omissions, more than one competitor may lock subsets of the nodes (Figure 17.9b, in which case each of them retries incrementing a *lock_level* counter, until one of them locks all nodes successfully, and proceeds.

Figure 17.10 illustrates the clock-driven PGM protocol of the AAS system (Cristian [1988]). Membership management occurs either upon request (e.g., a join), or periodically, to ensure departures are detected in a bounded time. Since group communication in this system is by diffusion, without feedback, the only way to detect failures at this level is through such a protocol. The objectives of the PGM protocol are: all processors in a group to have the same view; join and departure to occur in bounded time; changes totally ordered with group communication. In essence, one of two events trigger the protocol: a join request, as in Figure 17.10a;

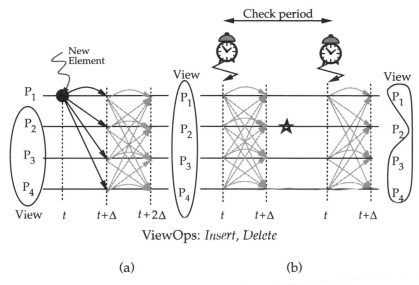

Figure 17.10. AAS system clock-driven PGM protocol

or the passage of time, for periodic checking of the membership, in order to detect failures in bounded time, such as the failure of P_2 in Figure 17.10b. When that happens, all processors diffuse an 'I'm alive' message, reliably and totally ordered, so that each and every one will build locally the same view, with the identifications of those that replied. The details of the clock-driven operation are the same as for the AAS group communication protocol, given in Section 17.8.

Finally, we show an example of PGM in time-triggered (TT) systems, the MARS system group membership protocol, illustrated in Figure 17.11. Membership is an integral part of the communication protocol, also exemplified in Section 17.8. TT

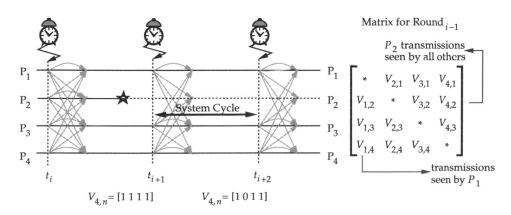

Figure 17.11. MARS system time-triggered PGM protocol

transmission is periodic: in each period, all nodes broadcast their message[16]. To overcome omissions, each message is sent twice and it is assumed that in absence of failures at least one copy of every message reaches all destinations. Membership management is performed every cycle, using information of the previous cycle. Each processor listens to all transmissions, and at the end of the cycle it builds a vector of dimension N, the number of nodes, similar to the active stations table, indicating the processors from whom it did or did not receive messages ($V_{u,v}$ is a boolean which is true when processor u saw a valid message from processor v). This vector is sent in the following period's transmission, in the message header. All processors receive then N vectors (including theirs) and build the matrix depicted in the figure. Each column u accounts for the messages P_u saw from all the others. Each row v accounts for the messages from P_v seen by all the others. The purpose of the membership protocol is to detect failures with one cycle delay, at most. Matrices may not be equal in all nodes, but they guarantee to have enough information to deterministically detect a failed processor, understood as one that: fails to transmit both copies of its message to all; fails to receive both copies of another node's message. Nodes are withdrawn at the end of the cycle where they are detected failed. Joining nodes start communicating and after a trial period, they are admitted as members.

17.7   Decentralised Control of Real-Time Systems

Traditional computer control is centralised. The philosophy is to organise the process in modules or *cells*, each composed of a supervisor controlling a set of machines performing a given task (e.g., car module manufacturing), or handling part of a continuous process (e.g., a chemical product).

This is the PLC (Programmable Logic Controller) world. It normally polls the sensors and issues commands to the actuators based on some control program. 'Distribution' in computerised control, when it exists, is mostly concerned with replacing point-to-point cabling, yielding the so-called *field buses*, which are a kind of digital system over a long wire: the central unit executes an automate which reads information from and sends commands to remote units on a polled, synchronised basis.

MAP, the Manufacturing Automation Protocol (MAP [1985]; Pimentel [1990]), despite its shortcomings, was a major cultural breakthrough, bringing networking into the *shop-floor*[17], vulgarising the idea of *cell networks*, composed of several cooperative nodes. Some added functionality appears with the MAP era, namely a closer integration between development and manufacture, through program download and supervision information up-load. For example, a program developed in a CAD/CAE station downloaded to a computer controlled printed circuit board drilling machine, or factory machine statistics up-loaded to workstations running control department programs.

---

[16]To simplify the figure, the detail of the access method, TDMA, is omitted, since it is irrelevant for the description. In reality, the processors transmit in slots, as depicted in Figure 17.18.

[17]Jargon to denote the manufacturing or process control areas of an industrial installation.

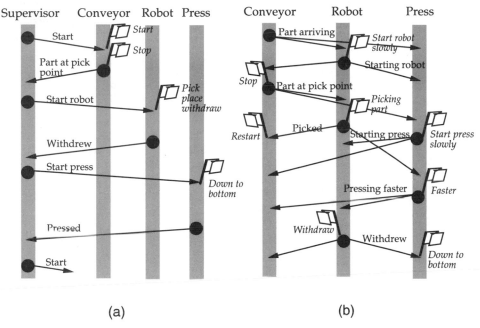

Supervisor   Conveyor   Robot   Press   Conveyor   Robot   Press

Figure 17.12. Example of a problem for decentralised control: (a)
ad hoc centralized solution; (b) decentralized solution

A few attempts in advanced distributed control with independent nodes rely
on the client-server model with RPC-type interaction. Again, the client being the
supervisor and the servers the cell nodes, some flavour of centralisation is still
retained. Servers are autonomous to perform background tasks (some advance
here), but they are tied to the client-imposed sequencing.

Looking at the example of a manufacturing process given in Figure 17.12a, it is
easy to understand why. The figure illustrates a cell composed of a conveyor belt
bringing pieces of raw material to be put by a pick-and-place robot under a 1 ton
press, which forms them into finished parts. For the traditional control engineer,
if this is handled by a single automaton, sequentially programmed, where things
happen one at a time, then no problem in 'distributing'. It can perfectly be done by
blocking RPCs issued by the supervisor: there is a global thread of control which
walks through the machines[18].

Let us imagine how it would be to handle this same task *without* a supervisor.
Figure 17.12b illustrates the idea. Nodes act in a decentralised fashion. They are
autonomous, and they work based on information they receive from other nodes.
This information is disseminated or *multicasted* to the group of nodes, so that every
node knows what the other is doing. It is a much more versatile and concurrent

---

[18]There is a new problem concerning the fail-safe state — how the system stops without doing silly
things if something fails seriously — which is no longer under the control of the supervisor at all times,
since a server may be in movement while the supervisor is blocked. But this is still much better than
having all the nodes in autonomous movement!

system, thus more performant. It reflects better the natural way an automation system operates. The best example to illustrate this is probably to picture a scenario where components are controlled by humans (e.g., with joysticks and levers) *in visible contact with one another*, acting in a *cause-effect* manner. However, if this is programmed ad-hoc, over ad-hoc operating and communication systems, it is most probable that the robot arm will once (and forever more …) be late getting from under the one-ton press while it goes down, confirming the fears of the control engineer about decentralisation.

Decentralised computer control, as a general application field for distributed real-time systems, needs to use concepts and tools that we have discussed and will continue discussing throughout this chapter. Recapitulating:

- real-time and reliability guarantees in communications and processing;
- a notion of time common to all nodes;
- temporal ordering of information;
- groups and group communication to encapsulate cooperating nodes from the timeliness, dependability and functionality viewpoints.

The fundamental real-time and dependability concepts have been discussed in Chapter 16. The last three points are extremely relevant, and will deserve particular attention in the following sections.

17.7.1   The Rôle of Time

Computing systems often use some notion of time, for example, for timeouts. These *relative time measurements* can be achieved by local *timers*, even in real-time systems. There is little to be said about the useful role of timers in distributed real-time systems, except that all timers at the several sites must have a bounded rate deviation from real-time, and thus from each other, during the execution of the longest distributed action or protocol. This attribute is normally considered acquired by programmers, although timer implementations are sometimes inaccurate and thus inadequate for real-time use.

Timers and clocks

Timers are unfortunately not enough for *absolute time measurements*, that is, the need to locate the position of events in the time line of a reference time base. A *clock* representing that time base is necessary. When talking about distributed real-time systems, clocks become also crucial for relative measurements, since they are the only way of measuring *distributed durations*: something that starts in a node and ends in another. In both cases, the notion of time, to be useful, must be global.

Agreement on time

Participant agreement on time, that is, on a *global time*, is best achieved through synchronised local clocks (cf. Chapter 5). It has two aspects:

- agreement on the time to trigger actions;
- agreement on the time at which events occurred.

The first is concerned with the *synchronisation of the concurrent process of a system*. For example, to disseminate the time to trigger both a change of points and a change of lights in a railway crossing, by a distributed group of actuator representatives. The specified time may be absolute, or it may be relative: the sender may specify 'change points within 1sec of change of lights'. This distributed duration is easily handled by global time, provided that the lights change instant is disseminated.

The second is concerned with the *distributed recording (logging) of events*. Such a distributed log is instrumental to determine (i) precedence relations through temporal order of sets of events (further discussed in Section 17.7.2). This is used, for example, for the study of alarm situations in power stations/networks or in process control plants, in order to determine causes, trace propagations, discover undue triggers.

Slightly different but important to mention is *replica agreement on time*. A replicated computation which reads time, for example to log the time of an event, should do so in a manner that all replicas get the same time. Take the example of leader-follower replication using the single-server approach (cf. Section 16.5): the leader would instruct the followers *'time of event e was T_e'*, after having read the time of e.

Time-stamps

Events may be ordered with time-stamps from a physical clock of granularity (tick) g_p. The latter is normally a small time interval, in consequence, we would end-up with a very fine-grained ordering. However, time-stamps must be allocated in a distributed way, so in reality one needs a global time-base formed by local virtual clocks. These are not exactly equal: they differ at most by the clock *precision*, π (cf. Chapter 5). If the physical granularity were maintained for the virtual real-time clocks, there would be tick overlaps and the same event might receive time-stamps distant more than one tick (Kopetz and Kim [1990]). While not incorrect per se, any granularity below precision is not significant. So the first remark, with regard to the use of clock time-stamps for temporal ordering is: *the granularity g_v of the global time-base should not be smaller than precision π, $g_v \geq \pi$.*

The Δ-protocols (e.g., Cristian, Dancey and Dehn [1990] and Chapter 5) are known to achieve total temporal order using a global time-base. However, since they are digital, and thus granular (g_p), they have a limitation that is sometimes overlooked: given two events a and b in different nodes, if $t_b - t_a \leq \pi + g_p$, we cannot tell which of a or b occurred first. (If $t_b - t_a < \pi$, there may even be order inversion.) This observation, together with the first remark, leads us to the second remark, with regard to the use of clock time-stamps for temporal ordering is: *the order discrimination of clock-driven protocols cannot be better than twice the granularity of the clocks, $2g_v$.* (The ordering condition becomes $\pi + g_v$, for which $2g_v$ is a suitable lower bound, since $g_v \geq \pi$.)

17.7.2   The Rôle of Order

Consider again the distributed system in Figure 17.12b: it is formed by processors with no shared memory, no centralised control or clock, communicating only by exchanging messages. It should be able to operate in a decentralised way, provided that it resists failures, and that *participants* acquire a consistent knowledge about system state, in order to coordinate their actions, namely the order, and sometimes the time, of event occurrence. Remembering the notions given in Chapter 4, participants are subject to an uncertainty in system observation: they perceive a *partial ordering* on events.

This is not disturbing though, since it is a fundamental characteristic of distributed systems. We will use a few examples in Figure 17.12b to explain very simply how order and timing of events and knowledge about the system can allow its components to operate autonomously. We just concentrate on the ordering and consistency issues, but it is obvious that such a system must also have reliability measures through fault-tolerance, if one does not wish to leave the robot arm under the press. The nodes in Figure 17.12b can operate autonomously if they know what caused what and when in the system, especially about events that concern their own activity. If nodes receive sequences of messages about system activity and timing in a cause-effect order, they are able to build a 'picture' of the controlled system state and determine their own actions on a per-message basis. Take these examples: if the robot in the figure receives an ordered and timely sequence of messages from the conveyor it can predict its movement and velocity and start moving concurrently; however, with this simple programming technique the press would be utterly confused should it receive the *'picked'* message before the *'part-at-pick-point'* message; on the other hand, the conveyor can receive the *'picked'* and the *'starting press'* messages interchangeably, without any disturbance. The reason for the different behaviour in the last two examples is because the reordered messages are causally related in the first, and not in the second.

We hope to have made clear that information exchange must be reliable, and must order any two messages such that one *could* have caused the another, that is, messages that are potentially-causally related. Let us call this relation *precedence*. There are two ways of guaranteeing precedence: through a *logical* order or through a *temporal* order (cf. Chapter 4).

Anomalous behaviour

Logical order is based on a simple observation: if participants only exchange information by sending and receiving messages, they can only define causality relations through those messages. Two situations where this principle is violated and an anomalous behaviour may occur:

- when participants exchange messages outside the ordering protocol;
- when the system interacts with the real world.

The reason is because there is information flowing between participants which is not controlled by the ordering discipline, so to speak, in a *clandestine* manner. The most common example is the mixed use of a protocol for logical order and another protocol, for example, RPC. It is shown in Figure 17.13a: m_2 is issued because of the RPC that the top sender executed, so it is preceded by m_1; nevertheless, for the protocol they are concurrent and m_2 is delivered before m_1; m_3 may carry

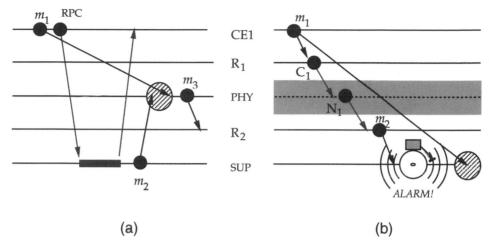

Figure 17.13. Anomalous behaviour examples: (a) RPC; (b) physical feedback

the undesirable effects of this violation. This already well-known anomaly was recalled here to illustrate its analogy to a less known but extremely common situation typical to real-time systems (Veríssimo *et al.* [1991]): it concerns interaction with the real world and can affect distributed real-time systems, prone to it because there are inevitably information paths through the environment. There is no way that logical order implementations know about them. Figure 17.13b presents such an example. R_1 and R_2 are representatives of some real-time entities residing in the physical process under control, PHY: for example, R_1 is a valve actuator, R_2 is an intelligent fluid sensor. CE and SUP are computing elements, SUP being a supervision unit which detects anomalies and handles alarms. CE issues an output command to R_1, which in turn issues the physical actuation. An event is generated in some other part of PHY in consequence. This event is read by R_2, which in response sends m_2 to notify SUP. Suppose the original message m_1 from CE meant *'open-valve'*. Since it arrives later than m_2 to SUP (the logical order protocol does not recognise any relationship between them), m_2 meaning *fluid-flowing*, SUP will most probably issue a *'leakage!'* alarm, whereas the system is functioning perfectly.

Temporal order

The solution for these situations consists in securing precedence through *temporal order*, for example with time-stamps of granularity $g_v \geq \pi$ as discussed in Section 17.7.1. However, given the precision achievable by clock synchronisation in real-time systems, which are normally LAN-based (order of milliseconds, can reach order of microseconds) in most of the settings one will be ordering too much, vis-a-vis the primary objective, which is to represent causality. In a distributed computer system or in a physical process, it takes a finite amount of time for an input event to *cause* an output event: the time for an information to travel from one node to the other; the response time of a computer process; the feedback time of a control loop in a physical process. Supposing δ_t is the minimum value of such a time for a given system, no two events separated by less than δ_t may be causally related in that system. In consequence, it is of no utility to order them. We introduce a definition to help us show how to take advantage of this fact in real settings.

Let us define the relation $\overset{\delta_t}{\rightarrow}$, called δ_t-*precedence* (Veríssimo and Rodrigues [1989]; Veríssimo, Rodrigues and Rufino [1991]), as:

For all events a and b, $a \overset{\delta_t}{\rightarrow} b$ if $t_b - t_a > \delta_t$.

Since δ_t is the minimum real time interval for causal relations to be generated, δ_t-*precedence* is the criterion for potential causality (which will not exist for smaller differences). The definition is helpful on the system-support and on the application-requirements side:

On the system support side it is a suitable definition of how fine-grained is the temporal order provided by a protocol. In fact, and recalling the discussion about temporal order in section 17.7.1, one can conclude:

Clock-driven protocols of granularity $g_v \geq \pi$ enforce $2g_v$-precedence, $(\overset{2g_v}{\rightarrow})$.

On the application side, it is a suitable definition of ordering requirements, given computer or physical *process granularity*, γ, the minimum time from input to response of a process. The granularity of computer processes is normally coarser than clock granularity. A practical consequence is the following: one can use a new virtual clock of granularity $g_g \approx \gamma/2$ (but $g_g < \gamma/2$), implementing $2g_g$-*precedence*, which is coarser than $2g_v$-precedence, thus improving the concurrency of the system. So, the next remark with regard to temporal ordering is:

The discrimination of temporal order protocols need not be better than process granularity, γ.

Whatever the granularity, such a system guarantees the following:
- any two events separated by more than $2g$ are correctly ordered;
- any two events separated by more than g but not more than $2g$, either receive the same time-stamp or are correctly ordered by consecutive time-stamps;
- two events separated by not more than g either receive the same time-stamp or are arbitrarily ordered by consecutive time-stamps.

With regard to our original order problem — respecting causality — the γ-*based* implementation of precedence has the following advantages: (i) it is a more faithful representation of precedence than clock-tick, g_p-based approaches, which order too much; (ii) it is free from anomalous behaviour, unlike logical order implementations (e.g., logical clocks, vector times).

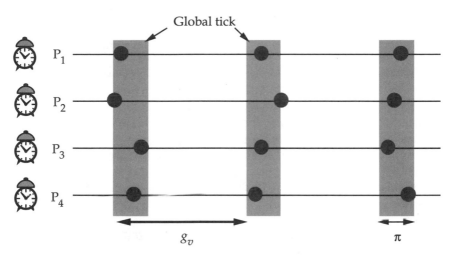

Figure 17.14. A sparse time-base lattice

Sparse time-bases

There are important consequences of applying the δ_t-precedence and process granularity concepts to time-triggered systems. In these systems, activity occurs in synchrony with *global ticks*. Suppose events are only produced at global time-base ticks. Seen microscopically, system activity only occurs at discrete points in time, that is, over the lattice of a *sparse time-base*, as opposed to the dense time-base of real time (Kopetz [1992]). The lattice points (Figure 17.14) correspond to global time-base ticks, which are in fact intervals of width π, due to the skew of the clocks. If the lattice has a period of g_v, a $\overset{2g_v}{\to}$ temporal order is secured.

Similarly, by taking γ into account, as above, we can enlarge the period of the lattice to g_g, aligned with clock ticks. The resulting temporal-order granularity $(2g)$ still satisfies any causal relations that may take place, since it is better than γ. However, one fundamental advantage is that, since $\pi \simeq g_v \ll g_g$, the skew of the global tick becomes much less significant in the overall period. That is, the time-base becomes sparser.

The time-triggered sparse time-base approach with large granularity is very useful: while temporal order is secured, tightness (i.e., simultaneity) of action is improved since the system acts at synchronised points with small skew. In terms of our model, all interactions concerning real-time objects (i.e., representatives and computing elements) can be controlled in this way. In applications where all the timing of the process is under control (e.g., a continuous process control loop), it can be also applied to input/output.

Relaxing ordering requirements

If to temporal order we add the fact that actively replicated processing requires total order by default, the general ordering requirement for dependable and decentralised real-time computing is *total temporal order* (see Chapter 7). This is an expensive requirement, both in performance and concurrency. How to relax it? In real settings, assumptions can sometimes be made about the distribution support environment and applications, which allow relaxing the order requirements:

- *specific knowledge about the application semantics* — for example: that senders are concurrent, reducing temporal order to FIFO order; that requests to a server are commutative, allowing no order;
- *particular computational model* — for example: single-thread, with interactions only via blocking RPC, imposes a sequential behaviour, where no concurrency exists; multi-threads with RPC create opportunities for trading-off concurrency with order;
- *particular replication model* — for example: when a privileged replica exists (the primary, coordinator or leader) it normally imposes its own processing order on the other replicas through a private replication management protocol, obviating the need to secure a total order in communication among processes;
- *several ordering paths to the same destination* — several temporal or FIFO order flows into the same receiver, for example for urgent messages that can overtake others freely, breaking an otherwise global order in *incomplete* orderings.

17.7.3   Group-Orientation

Building blocks for group activity have been a subject of ever-increasing interest throughout the past few years (API [1989]; Birman [1993]; Cheriton and Zwaenepoel [1985]; Cristian, Dancey and Dehn [1990]; Garcia-Molina and Spauster [1991]; Hughes [1988]; Mishra and Schlichting [1992]; Powell [1991]). Especially in the real-time arena, where activities tend to be concurrent, autonomous and group-oriented by nature, a few issues bring about the interest of paradigms oriented to message-passing and groups of processes or active objects:

- real-time — or *responsive* — systems deal with the environment, thus handling of events and event messages is inevitable;
- in highly concurrent interactive systems (e.g., distributed computer control) message-passing is a very useful and natural paradigm, reflecting the autonomy of the modules of the process under control;
- remote procedure call, being blocking, unilateral and asymmetric (client to server), presents shortcomings in such environments, and should be complemented with paradigms supporting multilateral, non-blocking and peer-to-peer interactions among groups of entities[19].

Since one encounters several or all of the conditions above in most distributed real-time settings, it is worthwhile to discuss the application of group-oriented programming and structuring principles to those systems.

---

[19]From an engineering perspective, some of these problems have of course been solved long ago one way or the other (replicated RPC, 'asynchronous' RPC or RSR, calling process fork, etc.). However, they should be properly addressed at the model level, if possible.

The good use of the end-to-end argument

Until recently, there has been a reluctance to accepting reliable group communication paradigms (e.g., reliable multicast). This can be traced back to the literal interpretation often made of the end-to-end argument (Saltzer, Reed and Clark [1984]). In essence, the argument is against providing more functionality than needed at a given layer of a system, because excess functionality can reduce efficiency, risks introducing redundant protocol actions like error recovery steps, clutters interfaces with infrequently used baggage, and ultimately, goes against good sense. Nevertheless, if a class of applications requires a certain functionality (or quality of service), there are advantages to having a lower layer, a tool box, or more generally the *operating system support*, provide it. It frees the user from programming this functionality, which may be rather complex. Moreover, it allows a higher degree of optimisation and testing than if programmed in an ad-hoc manner.

In fact, a number of classes of distributed applications can be defined whose requirements are solved by a set of distributed algorithms. In consequence, supplying a suite of the corresponding protocols is in essence a correct interpretation of the end-to-end argument, if done in a way such that the users not requiring them are not penalised by their existence. This reasoning applies to all levels of the architecture, from network hardware through communications to computing.

Group tools

There is a significant body of research in group-oriented protocols, but they seldom appear integrated in operating system technology, one reason for that being the lack of clear structuring guidelines, identifying the necessary building blocks and their interactions (mutual, and with the user and the system support).

A top-down approach is best to explain group-oriented programming. In essence, the first aim is to identify basic distributed group activities, such as *replication, cooperation and competition*[20], whose combination can structure the algorithmic part of any distributed application. The second is to provide support to control the way groups of participants perform them, that is, a set of protocols for managing those activities, to be used by application builders. Real-life experience has shown that this drastically simplifies the algorithmic and correctness problems of distributed application design (Birman [1993]; Kaashoek [1992]; Mishra and Schlichting [1992]; Powell [1991]). At this point it should be clear that merely having group communication protocols is not a complete solution.

For an efficient implementation, the notion of group should pervade all layers of a distributed architecture, from multipoint networking infrastructures, group communication and time services, to the protocols just mentioned, which are *group management* protocols. Figure 17.15 depicts such a scenario.

The network infrastructure is obviously the bottom layer. Most local enterprise, institution or factory settings run over LANs. This is specially true of real-time systems. A few key issues that may foster the efficiency of advanced distributed

---

[20]In LeLann [1979], under different designations.

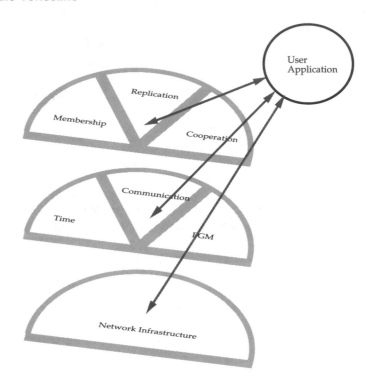

Figure 17.15. Structuring groups in distributed systems

systems have already been discussed in earlier sections: *abstract network classes* (e.g., LAN, MAN, etc.); *topology* for multipoint; *logical* group addressing; hardware *multicast* and *selective* addressing; efficient *address resolution*; active station lists, i.e. membership management; *reliability* and *availability*, specially for real-time applications.

The time service and *clock synchronisation* should be implemented as close to the network as possible: this improves quality of the global time-base. Besides, synchronisation protocols sometimes use group communication, and vice-versa, so they should have a close interaction, as suggested by Figure 17.15. *Group communication* services rely on the low-level network services. They ensure that groups of participants exchange or receive messages following a set of rules, without worrying about how they are secured: reliable group communication is the perfect encapsulation for the order and timing properties discussed in section 17.7.

While group communication is concerned with allowing participants of a group to exchange messages and establish rules for that exchange, *group management*, equally important, is concerned with defining and controlling the group objectives. To help the reader understand how to encapsulate the algorithmic part of a distributed application with group tools it is best to use a divide and conquer strategy, decomposing it in fundamental distributed activities — competition, replication and cooperation:

- *competition* in a group concerns rules for interaction of its members with a single entity (which may itself be a group), so these rules (e.g., ordering), may be satisfied by the group communication services alone;
- *replication* and *cooperation* concern activities performed *by* groups; to be useful, they normally require some management;
- when a group of processes exists, there is a fundamental problem requiring management: the *membership* of the process group, i.e. updated and consistent information about who are the participants or how many and if needed, what they do and where they are.

An example of cooperation management is a protocol to control a task performed concurrently by a group of processes, such as the manufacturing cell with a conveyor belt, a robot and a modelling press of our example in Figure 17.12. An example of replication management are protocols to control a set of replicated processes, in order that they perform fault-tolerant computations, ensuring whatever actions needed, like voting, collating, etc. (Powell [1991]). It would be applicable to our example, in case we wanted to replicate the robot and press controllers, to achieve safe behaviour. Membership protocols (Cristian [1988]; Kopetz, Grunsteidl and Reisinger [1989]; Ricciardi and Birmam [1991]) know who is in and who is out of the group, and control joins and leaves according to predefined rules. For example, they detect failures and re-establish the level of replication in a replica group, or ensure the necessary 'skills' are present in a group performing a functionally partitioned cooperative activity: the manufacturing cell would not start in case of a configuration error, or failure of a critical component.

This is a constructive approach to think about groups. Optimal solutions will lie somewhere between a collection of 'micro-protocols' (Mishra and Schlichting [1992]) for each of the activities above, and a hard-core implementation of the whole algorithmic part of each application, as in existing non-group-oriented applications.

17.8 Advanced Real-Time Communication

In this section we discuss a few advanced concepts concerning real-time communication, namely the real-time properties that can be achieved by reliable group communication protocols. The semantics of group communication services can be characterised by combinations of agreement, order and synchronism properties. Group communication would deserve a whole chapter, so we will just focus on the issues relevant to real-time. A few types of these protocols have nevertheless been described in Chapter 5. Other surveys can be found in Mishra and Schlichting [1992] and Veríssimo, Rodrigues and Rufino [1991].

There are essentially two ways of building group communication protocols, with regard to time domain properties: the *clock-driven* (Babaoğlu and Drummond [1985]; Cristian [1990]; Cristian *et al.* [1986]) and the *clockless* (Birman and Joseph [1987]; Kaashoek *et al.* [1989]; Veríssimo and Marques [1990]). The former rely on the existence of a global time-base (a clock), whereas the latter do not, using relative time references (timers). Clock-driven and clockless protocols have often

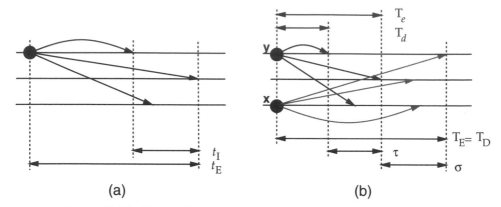

Figure 17.16. Protocol synchronism metrics — (a) execution (t_E) and inconsistency (t_I) times; (b) steadiness (σ) and tightness (τ)

been classified as 'synchronous' and 'asynchronous' respectively, but the former terminology is preferred, since there are synchronous clockless protocols (Veríssimo [1990]). Synchronous clockless protocols are an efficient alternative to clock-driven ones in a number of real-time settings. To understand why, let us introduce some metrics.

Given *execution time*, t_E, the interval between the *'send'* request and the last *'deliver'* indication[21], let **steadiness** of a protocol, σ, be the largest difference between the duration of any two executions, i.e. the difference between the maximum and the minimum execution times, $\sigma = T_E - T_e$. Given *inconsistency time*, t_I, the interval between *'deliver'* indications in one execution, let **tightness** of a protocol, τ, be the maximum inconsistency time[22], $\tau = T_I$. By definition, $T_i \leq T_e$.

These magnitudes are shown in Figure 17.16. They help defining temporal properties of protocols: if a protocol has bounded steadiness, it has a known bound for message delivery delay, $T_D = T_E$. They can also define temporal ordering properties. Observe Figure 17.16b: broadcast **y** executes in the minimum time, T_e, although having the maximum inconsistency time, $T_I = \tau$, whereas broadcast **x** executes in the maximum time, T_E. Now, suppose that, given "**x** before **y**", we wanted to guarantee that **x** was delivered before **y** to all destinations. In other words, **x** and **y** would be δ_t-precedent, and the question would be: how much should the separation $\delta_t = t_y - t_x$ be at the least, for this particular protocol to secure temporal order? Looking carefully at the figure, we obtain $\delta_t = \sigma + \tau$, that is, this protocol enforces $(\sigma+\tau)$-precedence[23]. This matches the discussion of section 17.7.2, but more than that, it puts synchronous clock-less and clock-driven protocols on the same grounds: (i) bounded delay; (ii) temporal order capability. In conclusion, σ and τ give the measure of the synchronism of a group protocol: an asynchronous

---

[21]It is usual in reliable communication, to differentiate between *'receive'*, the event of a message arriving at a node, and *'deliver'*, the event of it being delivered to the upper layer.

[22]For simplicity, it is assumed that $T_i = 0$, which is true of practically any protocol.

[23]Note that $T_E = T_D$, and $T_e - T_I = T_d$, the minimum delivery delay, thus $\sigma + \tau$ can also be formulated by $T_D - T_d$.

	CLOCK-DRIVEN	CLOCK-LESS
TIME-TRIGGERED	[MARS] Tx/Rx: lock-step periodic predictable reception tightly synchronous easy error detection	[—]
EVENT-TRIGGERED	[AAS] started by events Tx: any time Rx: after fixed delay tightly synchronous	[xAMp] started by events Tx: any time Rx: as soon as possible loosely synchronous

Figure 17.17. Classification and examples of real-time group communication protocols

protocol has unknown tightness and steadiness; a tightly-synchronous protocol is one where tightness and steadiness are very low figures, with regard to T_E; it is a loosely-synchronous protocol if otherwise. LAN-based clock-driven protocols normally yield tight-synchrony, whereas their clock-less counterparts yield loose-synchrony.

An orthogonal issue also related with time is whether the protocols are time- or event-triggered. The table in Figure 17.17 tries to systematise the issue a bit. We give below examples of the several types, concentrating on the synchronism and timing issues. The reader may refer to the Chapter 5 for further detail on the algorithmic issues.

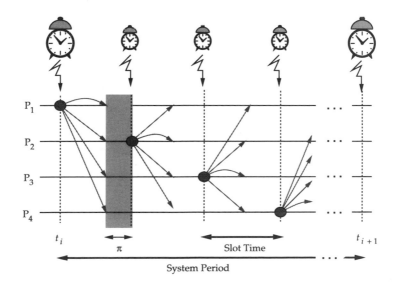

Figure 17.18. MARS system time-triggered TDMA protocol

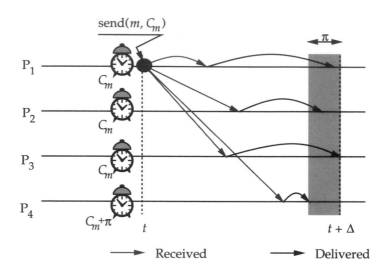

Figure 17.19. AAS system clock-driven atomic broadcast protocol

Time-triggered protocols transmit at prespecified periodic instants, they are clock-driven. The MARS system uses a TDMA protocol of this type (Kopetz *et al.* [1989]). As Figure 17.18 shows, each period is divided into slots, wherein each node transmits (the first 4 processors are shown). No sharing or collision problems exist this way. Slot times are controlled by a global clock of precision π. There must be a safety interval to account for precision: a fast clock may start its transmission π too soon. A message M_i may in reality be k frames in repetition, to perform masking of omission failures of degree k. These protocols can be used to work over sparse time-bases as discussed in Section 17.7.2.

Event-triggered protocols initiate a transmission the moment they receive a 'send' request. An example of a clock-driven ET protocol is the atomic broadcast of the AAS system (Cristian [1990]). As Figure 17.19 shows, at a real time t, which is measured as C_m in the sender's clock, a message m is transmitted, time-stamped C_m. Clocks are synchronised to a precision of π. The message has to arrive within a known and bounded time T_X to all nodes. Note that messages received are kept waiting to be delivered at $C_m + \Delta$ in each recipient's clock, where Δ is a protocol constant, $\Delta = T_X + \pi$. Due to the clock precision, the tightness of message delivery, as observed in the figure, is π. Due to the event-triggered nature, executions can be interleaved, protocol steadiness being π. The protocol enforces a π-precedent total temporal order.

The last example concerns clockless ET communication, the xAMp protocol used in the DELTA-4 XPA system (Rodrigues and Veríssimo [1991]). Figure 17.20 depicts the atomic multicast service: the protocol executes in two phases, each using transmit-with-reply rounds. In the first phase, a message is sent, and the sender waits for a predefined number of replies (it relies on group membership to have this information). In the example, an omission took place in the first round, so the sender waits for a timeout ($T_{waitResponses}$), and then repeats the message transmission.

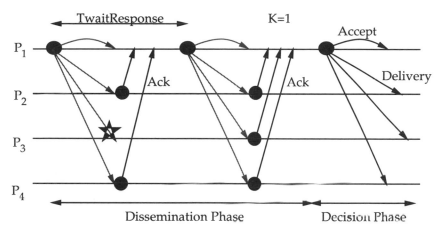

Figure 17.20. DELTA-4 XPA system clockless atomic multicast protocol

The messages arrive but are not delivered immediately. When all replies come, the sender enters the second phase, issuing a *decision* frame telling the recipients to deliver the message. If the sender fails before the decision reaching all recipients, a timeout, armed in all with the purpose of waiting for a decision, expires in one of them, who assumes a privileged (monitor) state and runs a termination protocol. In any case, the protocol ends in a known and bounded time, and enforces a $\sigma + \tau$-precedent total temporal order.

The idea behind clockless protocol synchrony, in the absence of a clock, is to connect protocol steps through a chain in time (coarser though this may be), such that the maximum length of that chain is known and bounded. Besides the normal requirements to build synchronous protocols, some guidelines must be followed. As an example, the steps to achieve xAMp synchrony are enumerated: (i) enforce bounds on frame delivery delays by the network, and on processing times of the protocol actions; (ii) structure the protocol so that any execution predictably has a bounded number of phases; (iii) structure phase error detection/recovery to contain failures, eg. structure each phase as a series of timed-out transmissions-with-response based on the bounded omission degree assumption (cf. Section 17.4).

17.9 Concluding Remarks

In this chapter, we addressed the main issues relevant to the understanding of real-time communication in distributed systems. We have discussed the several real-time networking and reliability policies, focusing thereafter on standard, non-redundant local area networks. These are obviously a cheap and available technology, but need some insight into the problem of being made reliable and timely. With this objective in mind, we addressed issues like bounded transmission delays, inaccessibility, media redundancy.

Low-level protocols may encapsulate a multitude of useful functions, from transmission-with-reply to powerful addressing and membership management schemes. They assist high-level protocols in providing transmission reliability, group support, selective and logical addressing, and short addresses. Group membership management, providing timely information about active stations and failures, is crucial to distributed real-time operation.

Real-time communication in distributed systems must preserve two fundamental notions: order and time. We have motivated, with concrete examples, the need to support these abstractions, and shown ways of programming them in a system. Likewise, we have suggested results that can be achieved in decentralised computer control, using these principles.

In conclusion, the reader will find it a useful exercise to try and combine the concepts learned in Chapter 16 with the communication techniques he was exposed to in the present chapter.

17.10   References

API (1989), *The ANSA Reference Manual*, vol. **Release 1.1**, Architecture Projects Management, Poseidon House, Castle Park, Cambridge CB3 0RD, UK.

Babaoğlu, Ö. and Drummond, R. (1985), Streets of Byzantium: Network Architectures for Fast Reliable Broadcasts., *IEEE Transactions on Software Engineering* **11**(6), 546–554.

Birman, K. P. (1993), The process group approach to reliable distributed computing, Department of Computer Science, Cornell University, Technical Report TR91-1216, To appear in Communications of the ACM.

Birman, K. P. and Joseph, T. A. (1987), Reliable Communication in the Presence of Failures, *ACM Transactions on Computer Systems* **5**(1), 47–76.

Bitbus (1988), *The BITBUS Interconnect Serial Control Bus*.

Cheriton, D. R. and Zwaenepoel, W. (1985), Distributed Process Groups in the V Kernel, *ACM Transactions on Computer Systems* **3**(2), 77–107.

Cristian, F. (1988), Agreeing on who is present and who is absent in a synchronous distributed system, *Digest of Papers of the 18th International Symposium on Fault-Tolerant Computing*, Tokyo, Japan, IEEE.

Cristian, F. (1990), Synchronous Atomic Broadcast for Redundant Broadcast Channels, IBM Almaden Research Center, Technical Report, San Jose, CA.

Cristian, F., Aghili, H., Strong, R. and Dolev, D. (1986), Atomic Broadcast: From Simple Message Diffusion to Byzantine Agreement, IBM Research Report RJ 5244 (54244).

Cristian, F., Dancey, R. D. and Dehn, J. (1990), Fault Tolerance in the Advanced Automation System, *Proceedings of the 20th Annual Symposium on Fault-Tolerant Computing*, Newcastle-Upon-Tyne, UK, IEEE, 1–12.

Dykeman, D. and Bux, W. (1987), An investigation of the FDDI media-access control protocol, *Proceedings of the EFOC/LAN Conference*, Basel, Switzerland.

GAMT (1987), GAM-T-103 Military Real Time Local Area Network — A Reference Model, Direction de L'Electronique et de l'Informatique, Technical Report.

Garcia-Molina, H. and Spauster, A. (1991), Ordered and Reliable Multicast Communication, *ACM Transactions on Computer Systems* **9**(3), 242–271.

Gorur, R. M. and Weaver, A. C. (1988), Setting target rotation times in an IEEE Token Bus network, *IEEE Transactions on Industrial Electronics* **35**(3).

Hughes, L. (1988), A multicast interface for Unix 4.3, *Software—Practice & Experience* **18**(1), 15–27.

IITB (1984), Performance Analysis of LANs for Real Time Environments, Final Report for COST 11 bis, Karlsruhe.

Jain, R. (1990), Performance analysis of FDDI token ring networks: effect of parameters and guidelines for setting TTRT, *Proceedings of the ACM-SIGCOM'90 Symposium*, Philadelphia, USA.

Janetzky, D. and Watson, K. S. (1986), Token bus performance in MAP and Proway, *Proceedings of the IFAC Workshop on Distributed Computer Protocol System*.

Johnson, M. J. (1986), Reliability mechanisms of the FDDI high bandwidth Token-ring protocol, *Computer Networks and ISDN Systems* **11**(2).

Johnson, M. J. (1987), Proof that timing requirements of the FDDI token ring protocol are satisfied, *IEEE Transactions on Computers* **35**(6).

Kaashoek, M. F. (1992), Group Communication in Distributed Computer Systems, Vrije Universiteit, Ph.D. Dissertation.

Kaashoek, M. F., Tanenbaum, A. S., Flynn Hummel, S. and Bal, H. E. (1989), An efficient reliable broadcast protocol, *Operating System Review* **2**, 5–11.

Kopetz, H. (1992), Sparse Time versus Dense Time in Distributed Real-Time Systems, *Proceedings of the Twelfth International Conference on Distributed Computing Systems*, Yokohama, Japan, IEEE Computer Society Press, 460–467.

Kopetz, H., Damm, A., Koza, C., Mulazzani, M., Schwabl, W., Senft, C. and Zainlinger, R. (1989), Distributed Fault-Tolerant Real-Time Systems: The Mars Approach, *IEEE Micro*, 25–41.

Kopetz, H., Grunsteidl, G. and Reisinger, J. (1989), Fault-tolerant membership service in a synchronous distributed real-time system, *Proceedings of the IFIP WG10.4 International Working Conference on Dependable Computing for Critical Applications*, Santa Barbara, CA.

Kopetz, H. and Kim, K. (1990), Real-time temporal uncertainties in interactions among real-time objects, *Proceedings of the Ninth IEEE Symposium on Reliable Distributed Systems*, Huntsville, AL.

Lamport, L., Shostak, R. and Pease, M. (1982), The Byzantine Generals Problem, *ACM Transactions on Programming Languages and Systems* **4(3)**, 382–401.

LeLann, G. (1979), An analysis of different approaches to distributed computing, *Proceedings of the First International Conference on Distributed Computing Systems*, Huntsvillle, Alabama, IEEE Computer Society Press.

LeLann, G. (1987), The 802.3D Protocol: A variation of the IEEE 802.3 Standard for Real-time LANs, INRIA, Technical Report, France.

MAP (1985), *Manufacturing Automation Protocol (MAP) specification V2.1*.

Mishra, S. and Schlichting, R. D. (1992), Abstractions for Constructing Dependable Distributed Systems, The University of Arizona, Department of Computer Science, Technical Report TR 92-19, Tucson, AZ.

Norme Française (1987), *FIP — Couche liaison de donnes* .

Peden, J. H. and Weaver, A. C. (1988), The utilization of priorities on token ring networks, *Proceedings of the 13th Conference on Local Computer Networks*, Minneapolis.

Peha, J. M. (1988), Station interconnection on dual rings and other multichannel networks, *Proceedings of the 13th Conference on Local Computer Networks*, Minneapolis.

Pimentel, J. (1990), *Communication Networks for Manufacturing*, Prentice-Hall, Englewood Cliffs, N.J. 07632.

Powell, D., ed. (1991), *Delta-4 — A Generic Architecture for Dependable Distributed Computing*, ESPRIT Research Reports, Springer Verlag.

Powell, D. (1992), Failure mode assumptions and assumption coverage, *Digest of Papers, The 22nd International Symposium on Fault-Tolerant Computing Systems*, IEEE, 386.

Profibus (1987), *Profibus Proposal to ISA SP50*.

Ricciardi, A. M. and Birmam, K. P. (1991), Using Process Groups to Implement Failure Detection in Asynchronous Environemnts, Cornell University, Department of Computer Science, Technical Report TR 91-118, Ithaca, NY.

Rodrigues, L. and Veríssimo, P. (1991), *x*AMp: a Multi-primitive Group Communications Service, *Proceedings of the Eleventh Symposium on Reliable Distributed Systems*, Houston, TX, Also available as INESC Technical Report AR/66-92.

Rodrigues, L., Veríssimo, P. and Rufino, J. (1993), A low-level processor group membership protocol for LANs, *Proceedings of the 13th International Conference on Distributed Computing Systems*, Pittsburgh, PA, IEEE Computer Society Press.

Ross, F. (1989), An Overview of FDDI: The Fiber Distributed Data Interface, *IEEE Journal on Selected Areas in Communication* 7(7).

Rufino, J. and Veríssimo, P. (1992a), A study on the inaccessibility characteristics of ISO 8802/4 Token-Bus LANs, *Proceedings of the IEEE INFOCOM'92 Conference on Computer Communications*, Florence, Italy, IEEE, Also available as INESC report AR 16-92.

Rufino, J. and Veríssimo, P. (1992b), Minimizing token bus inaccessibility through network planning and parameterizing, *Proceedings of the EFOC/LAN92 Conference*, Paris, France, IGI, Also available as INESC report AR 17-92.

Rzehak, H., Elnakhal, A. E. and Jaeger, R. (1989), Analysis of real-time properties and rules for setting protocol parameters of MAP networks, *Real-time Systems* 1(3).

MIL-STD (1988), *Field Bus Based on* MIL-STD-1553B — *Proposal to* ISA SP-50.

Saltzer, J. H., Reed, D. P. and Clark, D. D. (1984), End-to-End Arguments in System Design, *ACM Transactions on Computer Systems* 2, 277–278.

Sanders, R. M. (1990), The Xpress Transfer Protocol (XTP) —- A Tutorial, University of Virginia, Computer Science Report TR-89-1, Charlottesville, VA 2290.

Stankovic, J. A. (1988), Real-time Computing Systems: The Next Generation, University of Massachussetts, Technical Report TR-88-06, Amherst, MA.

Strole, N. (1983), A local communications network based on interconnected token-access rings: a tutorial, *IBM Journal of Research and Development* 27(5).

Talbott, R. R. (1987), Network survivability analysis, *Proceedings of the FOC/LAN'87 the Eleventh Annual International Fiber Optic Communication and Local Area Networks Expositions*, Anaheim, CA.

Veríssimo, P. (1988), Redundant media mechanisms for dependable communication in token-bus LANs, *Proceedings of the 13th Local Computer Network Conference*, Minneapolis, IEEE.

Veríssimo, P. (1990), Real-time data management with clock-less reliable broadcast protocols, *Proceedings of the Workshop on the Management of Replicated Data*, Houston, TX, IEEE, Also available as INESC report AR/25-90.

Veríssimo, P., Barrett, P., Bond, P., Hilborne, A., Rodrigues, L. and Seaton, D. (1991), The extra performance architecture (xpa), in *Delta-4 — A Generic Architecture for Dependable Distributed Computing*, Powell, D., ed., Springer Verlag.

Veríssimo, P. and Marques, J. A. (1990), Reliable broadcast for fault-tolerance on local computer networks, *Proceedings of the Ninth Symposium on Reliable Distributed Systems*, Huntsville, AL, IEEE, Also available as INESC report AR/24-90.

Veríssimo, P. and Rodrigues, L. (1989), Order and Synchronism Properties of Reliable Broadcast Protocols, INESC, Technical Report RT/66-89, Lisboa, Portugal.

Veríssimo, P., Rodrigues, L. and Baptista, M. (1989), AMp: a highly parallel atomic multicast protocol, *Proceedings of the SIGCOM'89 Symposium*, Austin, TX, ACM.

Veríssimo, P., Rodrigues, L. and Rufino, J. (1991), The Atomic Multicast protocol (AMp), in *Delta-4 — A Generic Architecture for Dependable Distributed Computing*, Powell, D., ed., Springer Verlag.

Veríssimo, P., Rufino, J. and Rodrigues, L. (1991), Enforcing real-time behaviour of LAN-based protocols, *Proceedings of the Tenth IFAC Workshop on Distributed Computer Control Systems*, Semmering, Austria, IFAC.

Wensley, J. H., Lamport, L., Goldberg, J., Green, M. W., Levitt, K. N., Melliar-Smith, P. M., Shostak, R. E., Weinstock, C. B. and Bersow, D. (1978), SIFT: Design and analysis of a fault-tolerant computer for aircraft control, *Proceedings of the IEEE* **10(6)**, 1240–1255.

Chapter 18

Scheduling

Hermann Kopetz

18.1 The Scheduling Problem

A distributed hard real-time system has to execute a set of concurrent real-time (RT) transactions in such a way that all time-critical transactions meet their specified deadline. Every transaction needs computational, communication, and data resources to proceed. The scheduling problem is concerned with the allocation of these resources to satisfy all timing requirements.

A RT-transaction can be decomposed into a set of tasks and a set of protocol executions. The tasks within a node compete for the available processors. The communication controllers compete for access to the communication network. The scheduling problem can thus be decomposed into two interrelated subproblems, scheduling the tasks within a node and scheduling the communication resources.

18.1.1 Classification of Scheduling Algorithms

Figure 18.1 presents a taxonomy of real-time scheduling algorithms (Cheng, Stankovic and Ramamritham [1988])

- **Real-Time Scheduling**
  - **Soft**
  - **Hard**
    - **Dynamic**
      - **Preemptive**
      - **Non-preemptive**
    - **Static**
      - **Preemptive**
      - **Non-preemptive**

Figure 18.1. Taxonomy of real-time scheduling algorithms

Hard real-time versus soft real-time scheduling

In a hard real-time system the deadlines of all critical tasks must be guaranteed *a priori* in all anticipated execution scenarios. This requires a resource adequate (Lawson [1992]) design. Since the reliance on stochastic simulations to 'verify' the timeliness of a complex safety-critical application (Xu, Jia and Parnas [1991]) is not acceptable, either sufficient off-line schedulability tests for all anticipated task scenarios must be performed or a constructive methodology to design feasible static schedules has to be followed.

In soft real-time applications the violation of a timing constraint is not critical. Therefore cheaper resource-inadequate solutions can be considered. In a soft real-time context it is tolerated that under adverse circumstances it is not possible to complete all real-time tasks on time.

Dynamic versus static scheduling

A scheduler is called dynamic (on-line) if it makes its scheduling decisions at run time on the basis of the current requests for service. Dynamic schedulers are flexible to adapt to an evolving task scenario and have to consider only the actual task requests and execution time parameters. However the run-time effort involved in finding a schedule can be substantial.

A scheduler is called static (or pre-run-time) if it makes its scheduling decisions off-line and generates a dispatching table for the run-time dispatcher at compile time. For this purpose it needs complete prior knowledge about the task set characteristics, for example, maximum execution times, precedence constraints, mutual exclusion constraints, deadlines, etc. The dispatching table contains all the information the dispatcher needs at run time to decide at every point of a discrete time base which task is to be scheduled next. The run-time overhead of the dispatcher is small.

Preemptive versus nonpreemptive scheduling

In a preemptive scenario the currently executing task may be preempted, that is, interrupted, if a more urgent task requests service. However preemption is only allowed to take place if given safety assertions (e.g., mutual exclusion constraints) are not violated.

In a nonpreemptive scenario the currently executing task will not be interrupted until it decides on its own to release the allocated resources — normally after completion. The shortest guaranteed responsiveness of single processor systems based on nonpreemptive scheduling is the sum of the longest and the shortest task execution time. Nonpreemptive scheduling is reasonable in a task scenario where many short tasks (as measured in relation to the time it takes for a context switch) have to be executed.

Central versus Distributed Scheduling

In dynamic distributed real-time system it is possible to make all scheduling decisions at one central site or to devise cooperative distributed algorithms for the

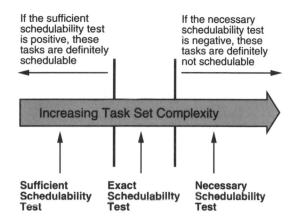

Figure 18.2. Necessary and sufficient schedulability test

solution of the scheduling problem. The central scheduler in a distributed system is a critical point of failure. Since it requires up-to-date information on the load situations in all nodes it can also contribute to a communication bottle-neck.

18.1.2   Schedulability test

The test to determine whether a schedule exists is called a *schedulability test*. We distinguish between exact, necessary and sufficient schedulability tests (Figure 18.2).

A scheduler is optimal if it will always find a schedule if an exact schedulability test indicates there is one. Garey and Johnson [1975] have shown that in nearly all cases of task dependency, even if there is only one common resource, the complexity of an exact schedulability test algorithm belongs to the class of NP-complete problems and is thus computationally intractable.

Sufficient schedulability test algorithms can be simpler at the expense of giving a negative result for some task sets that in fact are schedulable. The passage of a sufficient schedulability test is a sufficient but not necessary criterion for schedulability. On the other side, the passage of a necessary schedulability test is necessary but not sufficient for schedulability. For example, a simple necessary schedulability test requires that the laxity of a task; that is, the difference between deadline d_i and computation time c_i, must be nonnegative.

The adversary argument

The point in time, when a request for a task execution is made is called the task request time. Based on the request times it is useful to distinguish between two different task types: periodic and sporadic tasks. This distinction is important from the point of view of schedulability.

Starting with an initial request, all future request times of a periodic task are known *a priori* by adding multiples of the known period to the initial request time.

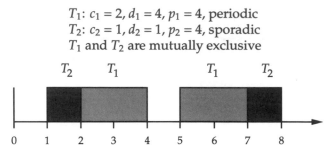

T_1: $c_1 = 2$, $d_1 = 4$, $p_1 = 4$, periodic
T_2: $c_2 = 1$, $d_2 = 1$, $p_2 = 4$, sporadic
T_1 and T_2 are mutually exclusive

Figure 18.3. The adversary argument

Let us assume there is a task set $\{T_i\}$ of periodic tasks with periods p_i, deadline d_i and processing requirements c_i. It is then sufficient to examine schedules of length on the order of the least common multiples of the periods of these tasks to determine schedulability. A necessary schedulability test for a set of periodic tasks states that the sum of the utilization factors μ_i

$$\mu = \sum \frac{c_i}{p_i} \leq n$$

must be less than, or equal to n, where n is the number of available processors. This is evident since μ_i denotes the percentage of time the task T_i requires service of a CPU.

The request times of sporadic tasks are not known *a priori*. However, in order to be schedulable, there must be a minimum interval p_i between any two request times of sporadic tasks. Otherwise the necessary schedulability test introduced above will fail. If there is no constraint on the request times of task activations, this task is sometimes called an aperiodic task.

Let us assume that a real-time computer system contains a dynamic scheduler with full knowledge of the past but without any knowledge about future request times of tasks. It determines on the basis of the current requests which task is to be scheduled next. In such a scenario an exact schedulability test is impossible, since we do not have enough information about future request times. Schedulability of the current task set may depend on when a sporadic task will request service in the future. We therefore need a new definition of optimality of a dynamic scheduler. A dynamic on-line scheduler is called optimal, if it can find a schedule whenever a clairvoyant scheduler; that is, a scheduler with complete knowledge of the future request times, can find a schedule.

The adversary argument (Mok [1983] p. 41) states that, whenever there are mutual exclusion constraints between a periodic and sporadic task, it is, in the general case, impossible to find an optimal totally on-line dynamic scheduler. The proof of the adversary argument is relatively simple:

Consider two mutually exclusive tasks, one periodic and the other sporadic, on a single processor system, with the parameters of Figure 18.3. The necessary schedulability test introduced above is satisfied, since $\mu = 2/4 + 1/4 = 3/4 \leq 1$.

Whenever the periodic task is started the adversary requests service for the sporadic task. Because of the mutual exclusion constraint the sporadic task has to wait until the periodic task is finished. Since the sporadic task has a laxity of 0 it will miss its deadline.

The clairvoyant scheduler knows all the future request times of the sporadic task and will at first schedule the sporadic task and afterwards schedule the periodic task in the gap between two sporadic task activations. Since the laxity of the periodic task is larger than the execution time of the sporadic task, the clairvoyant scheduler will always find a schedule which satisfies both tasks.

The adversary argument forcefully demonstrates the value of information about the future behavior of tasks in solving the scheduling problem. If the on-line scheduler does not have any further knowledge about the request times of the sporadic task, the scheduling problem is unsolvable, although the processor capacity is more than sufficient for the given task scenario. The design of predictable hard real-time systems is only feasible, if regularity assumption about the future scheduling requests can be made. This is the case in cyclic systems that restrain the points in time at which external requests are recognized by the computing system.

18.2   Dynamic Scheduling

A dynamic scheduling algorithm determines which task has to be serviced next after the occurrence of a significant event on the basis of the current task requests. The algorithms differ in the assumptions about the complexity of the task model and the future task behavior.

18.2.1   Scheduling independent tasks

The problem of scheduling a set of independent tasks on single and multiprocessor systems has been studied in great detail.

Rate Monotonic Algorithm

The classic scheduling algorithm for hard real time systems with a single CPU, the rate monotonic algorithm, has been published some time ago by Liu and Layland [1973]. The rate monotonic algorithm is a dynamic preemptive algorithm based on static task priorities. It makes the following assumptions about the task set:

1. The request for all tasks of the task set $\{T_i\}$ for which hard deadlines exist are periodic.
2. All tasks are independent of each other. There exist no precedence constraints or mutual exclusion constraints between any pair of tasks.
3. The deadline of every task T_i is equal to its period p_i.
4. The required maximum computation time of each task c_i is known a priori and is constant.
5. The time required for context switches can be ignored.
6. The sum of the utilization factors μ of the n tasks

$$\mu = \sum \frac{c_i}{p_i} \le n\,(2^{1/n} - 1)$$

The term $n\,(2^{1/n} - 1)$ approaches $\ln 2$, that is, about 0.7 as n goes to infinity.

The rate monotonic algorithm assigns the static priorities on the basis of the task periods. The task with the shortest period gets the highest static priority, the task with the longest period gets the lowest static priority. At run time the dispatcher always selects the task request with the highest static priority. If all the assumptions are satisfied, the rate monotonic algorithm guarantees that all tasks will meet their deadline. The algorithm is optimal for single processor systems. The proof of this algorithm is based on the analysis of the behavior of the task system at the critical instant. A critical instant for a task is the point in time at which the request of this task will have the largest response time. For the task system as a whole the critical instant occurs when request for all tasks are made simultaneously. Starting with the highest priority task it is shown that all tasks will meet their deadline, even in the case of the critical instant. For the details of the proof refer to Liu and Layland [1973].

It is also shown that assumption (6) above can be relaxed in case the task periods are multiples of the period of the highest priority task. In this case the utilization factor μ of the n tasks

$$\mu = \sum \frac{c_i}{p_i} \le 1$$

can approach 1, the theoretical maximum.

Earliest-Deadline-First Algorithm

The earliest-deadline-first algorithm is an optimal dynamic preemptive algorithm which is based on dynamic priorities. The assumptions (1) to (5) of the rate monotonic algorithm must hold. The processor utilization μ can go up to 1, even when the task periods are not multiples of the smallest period. After any significant event, the task with the earliest deadline is assigned the highest dynamic priority. The dispatcher operates in the same way as the dispatcher for the rate monotonic algorithm.

Least-Laxity Algorithm

In single-processor systems the least-laxity algorithm is another optimal algorithm. It makes the same assumptions as the earliest-deadline-first algorithm. At any scheduling decision point the task with the shortest laxity l, that is, the difference between the deadline d and the computation time c: $d - c = l$ is assigned the highest dynamic priority.

In multiprocessor systems neither the earliest-deadline-first nor the least-laxity algorithm is optimal, although the least-laxity algorithm can handle task scenarios which the earliest-deadline-first algorithm cannot handle.

18.2.2   Scheduling dependent tasks

From the practical point of view, results about the scheduling of tasks with precedence and mutual exclusion constraints are much more important than the analysis of the independent task model. With the availability of low priced microcontrollers it does not make sense to multiplex many independent tasks into a single computer at the cost of increased software complexity. Normally the concurrently executing tasks have to exchange information and access common data resources in order to cooperate in the achievement of the overall system objective. The observation of given precedence and mutual exclusion constraints is thus rather the norm than the exception in distributed real-time systems.

It has been mentioned already that the problem of deciding whether it is possible to schedule a set of periodic processes which use semaphores only to enforce mutual exclusion is a NP-complete problem. It is prohibitively expensive to look for an optimal schedule of a set of dependent tasks. The computational resources required for the solution of the dynamic scheduling problem are competing with those needed for the execution of the real-time tasks. The more resources are spent on scheduling, the fewer resources remain available to perform the actual work.

There are three possible ways out of this dilemma:

1. Providing extra resources, such that simpler sufficient schedulability tests and algorithms can be applied.
2. Dividing the scheduling problem in two parts, such that one part can be solved off-line at compile time and only the second (simpler) part has to be solved at run time.
3. Introducing restricting regularity assumptions about the behaviour of the task set.

The second and third alternative point into the direction of more static solutions to the scheduling problem.

The Kernelized Monitor

Let us assume a set of short critical sections such that the longest critical section of this set is smaller than a given duration q. The kernelized monitor algorithm (Mok [1983]p. 57) allocates the processor time in uninterruptible quantums of this duration q, assuming that all critical sections can be started and completed within this single uninterruptible. The only difference between this new scheduling problem and the previous scheduling problem is that a process may be interrupted only after it is been given an integral number of time quantums q. This little difference is already sufficient to cause problems, as the following example shows:

Assume two periodic tasks with a task T_1

$$T_1 : c_1 = 2, d_1 = 2, p_1 = 5$$

and a task T_2 with two scheduling blocks, where the second scheduling block (c_{22}) of T_2 is mutually exclusive to T_1

$$T_2 : c_{21} = 2, c_{22} = 2, d_2 = 10, p_2 = 10$$

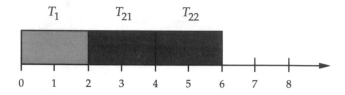

Figure 18.4. Schedule produced by the earliest-deadline algorithm

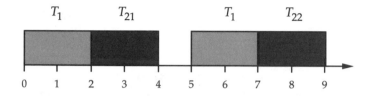

Figure 18.5. Schedule produced by the earliest-deadline algorithm

The preemption time quantum is 2.

Figure 18.4 shows what the earliest deadline first algorithm will do. At time 5 it has to schedule T_1 again, because otherwise T_1 will miss its second deadline. However, it cannot do so since T_{22} is blocking the critical section between T_1 and T_{22}.

A clairvoyant scheduler, or even a clever on-line scheduler that uses all available knowledge can find a solution to this scheduling problem. It will block the region before the second activation of T_1, as shown in Figure 18.5.

The region that has to be reserved in order to guarantee that the future request by T_1 can be serviced on-time is called a *forbidden region*. During compile time all forbidden regions have to be determined and handed to the dispatcher such that the dispatcher will not schedule any critical sections in the forbidden region.

Priority Ceiling Protocol

The priority ceiling protocol (Sha, Rajkumar and Lehoczky [1990]) can be used to schedule a set of periodic tasks that have exclusive access to common resources protected by semaphores. These common resources, for instance, common data structures, can be utilized to realize an interprocess communication.

If a set of 3 tasks T_1, T_2, and T_3 (T_1 has the highest priority and T_3 has the lowest priority), is scheduled with the rate-monotonic algorithm and T_1 and T_3 require exclusive access to a common resource protected by the semaphore S, it can happen that the low priority task T_3 has exclusive access to the common resource when the service of the high priority task T_1 is requested. T_1 has to wait until T_3 finishes its critical section and releases the semaphore S. If, during this time interval T_2 requests service, this will be granted and T_2, the medium-priority task, effectively delays T_3, the high priority task. This phenomenon is called *priority inversion*.

It has been proposed to elevate the priority of the low priority task T_3 during its blocking critical section to the high priority of the blocked task T_1 and thus eliminate

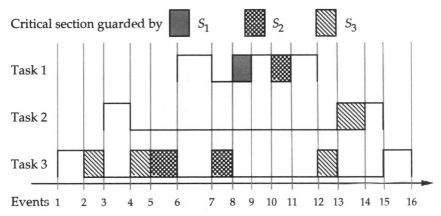

Figure 18.6. The priority-ceiling protocol (example taken from Sha, Rajkumar and Lehoczky [1990])

the possibility that the medium-priority task T_2 interferes during the critical section of the low priority task. This is the basic idea of the priority inheritance protocol. However, a rigorous analysis shows that this protocol can lead to chained blocking and deadlock.

To solve these problem, the *priority ceiling protocol* has been developed by Sha, Rajkumar and Lehoczky [1990].

The priority ceiling of a semaphore is defined as the priority of the highest priority task that may lock this semaphore.

A task T is allowed to enter a new critical section only if its assigned priority is higher than the priority ceilings of all the semaphores locked by tasks other than T. It runs at its assigned priority unless it is in a critical section and blocks higher priority tasks. In the latter case it inherits the highest priority of the tasks it blocks. When it exits the critical section it resumes the priority it had at the point of entry into the critical section.

The following example, taken from Sha, Rajkumar and Lehoczky [1990], illustrates the operation of the priority ceiling protocol:

Consider a system of 3 tasks, T_1, T_2 and T_3 with 3 critical sections R_1, R_2, and R_3 protected by the semaphores S_1, S_2 and S_3. The following command sequences are executed by T_1, T_2, and T_3:

Task	Priority	
T_1:	1	$\ldots, P(S_1), \ldots, V(S_1), \ldots, P(S_2), \ldots, V(S_2), \ldots$
T_2:	2	$\ldots, P(S_3), \ldots, V(S_3), \ldots$
T_3:	3	$\ldots, P(S_3), \ldots, P(S_2), \ldots, V(S_2), \ldots, V(S_3), \ldots$

Therefore the priority ceilings of the semaphores are: S_1: 1; S_2: 1; S_3: 2. As illustrated in Figure 18.6, the following (numbered) events and actions take place under the priority-ceiling protocol:

1. T_3 begins execution.
2. T_3 locks S_3.
3. T_2 is started and preempts T_3.
4. T_2 becomes blocked when trying to access S_3 locked by T_3. T_3 resumes the execution of its critical section at the inherited priority of T_2.
5. T_3 enters its nested critical section by locking S_2. T_3 is allowed to lock S_1.
6. T_1 is initiated and preempts T_3. This is possible because T_1 has a higher priority than the inherited priority of T_3.
7. T_1 is blocked when it tries to lock S_1, since the priority of T_1 is not higher than the priority ceiling of the locked semaphore S_2. T_3 resumes its operation.
8. T_3 unlocks S_2 and gets is assigned priority back. T_1 is awakened and preempts T_3. Now T_1 can lock S_1, since S_2 is unlocked.
9. T_1 unlocks S_1.
10. T_1 locks S_2.
11. T_1 unlocks S_2.
12. T_1 completes. T_3 resumes its operation at the inherited priority of T_2.
13. T_3 unlocks S_3 and returns to its assigned priority. T_2 preempts T_3 and locks S_3.
14. T_2 unlocks S_3.
15. T_2 completes. T_3 resumes its operation.
16. T_3 completes.

Sha, Rajkumar and Lehoczky [1990] has developed a sufficient schedulability test for the priority ceiling protocol. Let us assume a set of periodic tasks, $\{T_i\}$ with periods p_i and computation times c_i. We denote the worst case blocking time of a task t_i by lower priority tasks by B_i. The set of n periodic tasks $\{T_i\}$ can be scheduled, if the following set of equations holds:

$$\forall i, 1 \leq i \leq n : \frac{c_1}{p_1} + \frac{c_2}{p_2} + \cdots + \frac{c_i}{p_i} + \frac{B_i}{p_i} \leq i\,(2^{1/i} - 1)$$

In these equations the effect of preemptions by higher-priority tasks is considered in the first i terms (in analogy to the rate monotonic protocol), whereas the worst case blocking time due to all lower priority tasks is represented in the term $\frac{B_i}{p_i}$. The blocking term $\frac{B_i}{p_i}$, which can become very significant if a task with a short period (i.e., small p_i) is blocked for a significant fraction of its time, effectively reduces the CPU utilization of the task system. In case this first sufficient schedulability test fails more complex sufficient tests can be found in Sha, Rajkumar and Lehoczky [1990].

The priority ceiling protocol is a good example of a predictable, but non- deterministic scheduling protocol.

18.2.3   Dynamic scheduling in distributed systems

It is difficult to guarantee deadlines by dynamic scheduling techniques in a single processor multi-tasking system if mutual exclusion and precedence constraints between the tasks have to be considered. The situation is considerably more complex in a multiprocessor system or a distributed system, where access to the communication medium has to be controlled.

In most distributed system applications it is required to tolerate transient faults, e.g. message losses, and to quickly detect permanent faults, e.g., a broken wire, in the communication system. Transient faults can be handled by communication protocols of the Positive Acknowledgement or Retransmission (PAR) class or by masking redundancy. PAR Protocols have the disadvantage of a large temporal uncertainty; that is, the difference between the shortest and the longest protocol execution time is large. In the worst case the longest protocol execution time has to be assumed, causing a poor responsiveness of the system (Kopetz and Kim [1990]). Masking protocols, for example, sending the same message $k + 1$ times in case the tolerance of k transient faults is required, do not have this delay problem but are not capable to detect permanent faults in a dynamic system since they are unidirectional.

At present, the author does not know of any solution to the problem of guaranteed timeliness in a distributed real-time system based on dynamic scheduling techniques. However, the problem of providing good temporal performance in a best-effort distributed real-time system is a fashionable research topic. The critical issue in the evaluation of the timeliness of a distributed best-effort architecture by probabilistic models is related to the assumptions about the input distribution. Rare event occurrences in the environment, for instance, a lightning strike into an electric power grid, will cause a highly correlated input load on the system (e.g., an alarm shower) that is very difficult to model adequately. Even an extended observation of a real-life system is not conclusive, since these rare events, by definition, cannot be observed frequently.

18.3   Static Scheduling

In static or pre-run-time scheduling a feasible schedule of a set of tasks that guarantees all deadlines, considering the resource, precedence, and synchronization requirements of all tasks, is calculated off-line. The construction of such a schedule can be considered as a constructive sufficient schedulability test.

18.3.1   Static scheduling viewed as a search

Static scheduling is based on strong regularity assumptions about the points in time when future service requests will be honoured. Although the occurrence of external events that demand service is not under the control of the computer system, the recurring points in time when these events will be serviced can be established *a priori* by selecting an appropriate polling cycle for each class for events. During system design it must be ascertained that the sum of the maximum delay time until a request is recognized by the system plus the maximum transaction response time is smaller than the specified service deadline.

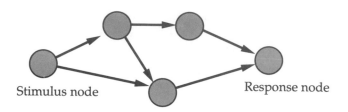

Stimulus node   Response node

Figure 18.7. Precedence graph of a task set

The role of time

In general, a static schedule is a periodic time-triggered schedule. The time line is partitioned into a sequence of basic granules, the basic cycle time. There is only one interrupt in the system: a periodic clock interrupt denoting the start of a new basic granule. In a distributed system, this clock interrupt must be globally synchronized to a precision that is much better than the duration of a basic granule.

Every transaction is periodic, its period being a multiple of the basic granule. The least common multiple of all transaction periods is the schedule period. At compile time, the scheduling decision for every point of the schedule period must be determined and stored in a dispatcher table for the operating system. At run time the preplanned decision is executed by the dispatcher after every clock interrupt.

Static scheduling can be applied to a single processor, to a multiple-processor and to a distributed system. In addition to preplanning the resource usage in all nodes, the access to the communication medium must also be preplanned in distributed systems. It is has been established that finding an optimal schedule in a distributed system is in almost all realistic scenarios NP-complete problem (Ullman [1976]), that is, computationally intractable.

In the general case, the solution to the scheduling problem can be seen as finding a path, a feasible schedule, in a search tree by applying a search strategy.

Given a set of tasks $\{T_i\}$ with known maximum execution times c_i and deadlines d_i, a set of mutual exclusion constraints and precedence relations between some tasks that specify which tasks must complete before another task may start. The precedence relation can be depicted in the form of an acyclic directed graph, known as the precedence graph of the task set. The tasks form the nodes of this graph and the directed edges describe the dependencies between the nodes (Figure 18.7). It is the function of the scheduling algorithm to determine whether a schedule for this task set $\{T_i\}$ exists, and if it exists, to calculate such a schedule.

The search tree

Every level of the search tree corresponds to one unit of time The depth of the search tree corresponds to the period of the schedule. The search starts with an empty schedule at the root node of this tree. The outward edges of a node point to the possible alternatives that exist at this point of the search. A path from the root node to a particular node records the sequence of scheduling decisions that have been made up to this moment. Each path to a leaf node describes a complete schedule. It is the goal of the search to find a complete schedule that observes all precedence and mutual exclusion constraints and completes before the deadline.

A heuristic function guiding the search

In order to improve the efficiency of the search it is necessary to guide the search by some heuristic function. Such an heuristic function can be composed of two terms, the actual cost of the path encountered until the present node in the search tree, that is, the present point in the schedule, and the estimated cost until a goal node. Fohler and Koza [1990] proposes a heuristic function that estimates the time needed to complete the precedence graph, called TUR (time until response). An necessary estimate of the TUR can be derived by summing up the maximum execution times of all tasks and message exchanges between the current task and the last task in the precedence graph, assuming true parallelism constrained by the competition for CPU resources of tasks that reside at the same node. If this necessary TUR is not short enough to complete the precedence graph on time, all branches from the current node can be pruned and the search has to backtrack.

18.3.2   Increasing the adaptability of static schedules

One of the weaknesses of static scheduling is the assumption of strictly periodic tasks. Although the majority of tasks in hard real time applications is periodic, there are also infrequent sporadic requests for service that have hard deadline requirements. An example of such a request is an emergency stop of a machine Hopefully it will never have to be executed. However, if it is requested it has to be serviced within a specified time interval.

In the following we will discuss three proposals to increase the flexibility of static scheduling, the transformation of sporadic requests into periodic requests, the sporadic server task and the execution of mode changes. We will see that some dynamic elements have to be introduced into the system to increase flexibility.

Transformation of sporadic requests to periodic requests

Scheduling a sporadic request is more demanding than scheduling a periodic request. While the future request times of a periodic task are defined *a priori*, only the minimum interarrival time of a sporadic task is known in advance. The actual points in time, when a sporadic task is to be serviced, are not accessible ahead of the request event.

The most difficult sporadic requests are those which demand a short response time — that is, the corresponding service task has a low latency — and those which require exclusive access to resources. The adversary argument has shown that it can be impossible to service such a request, even if a clairvoyant scheduler knows a solution.

It is possible to find solutions to the scheduling problem if an independent sporadic task has a laxity. One such solution, proposed by Mok [1983], p. 44, is the replacement of a sporadic task T by a quasiperiodic task T' with the following parameters:

		Sporadic T	Quasiperiodic T'
(1)	Computation Time	c	$c' = c$
(2)	Deadline	d	$d' = c$
(3)	Period	p	$p' = \min(p - d + 1, p)$

This transformation guarantees that the sporadic task will always meet its deadline if the quasiperiodic task can be scheduled. The quasiperiodic task can be scheduled statically. A sporadic task with a a short latency will continuously demand a substantial fraction of the processing resources to guarantee its deadline, although it might request service only very infrequently.

Sporadic Server Task

In order to overcome the significant resource requirements of a quasiperiodic task with a long interarrival time (period) but a short latency. Sprunt, Sha and Lehozky [1989] have proposed the implementation of sporadic server tasks.

To service a sporadic request, a periodic server task of high priority is created. This periodic server task maintains its execution time for the duration of the servers period, that is, whenever during this period the sporadic request arrives it will be serviced with the high priority of the service task. The service of a sporadic request exhausts the execution time of the sporadic server. The execution time will be replenished after the priority level of the server becomes active again. Thus the server task preserves its execution time until it is needed by a sporadic request by exchanging it for the execution time of a lower-priority periodic task. The sporadic service task is scheduled dynamically in response to a sporadic request event.

Mode Changes

During the operation of most real-time applications a number of distinctly different operating modes can be distinguished. Take the example of a flight control system in an airplane. When a plane is taxiing on the ground a different set of services is required then when the plane if flying.

It is evident that a significantly better resource utilization can be realized if only those tasks that are needed in a particular operating mode have to be scheduled. If the system leaves one operating mode and enters another one, then a corresponding change of schedules has to take place.

During system design it is required to identify all possible operating and emergency modes. For each mode a static schedule that will meet all deadlines is calculated off-line. Mode changes are analyzed and the appropriate mode change schedules are developed. Whenever a mode change is requested at run time the applicable mode change schedule will be activated immediately.

This topic of mode changes is an area of active research, see, for example, Sha *et al.* [1989] or Fohler [1992].

18.4   Comparison of Static and Dynamic Scheduling

The controversy whether a real-time system should be based on static or dynamic scheduling is going on in many disguised forms, for instance, *static* versus *dynamic*, *cyclic executives* versus *fixed-priority executives* (Locke [1992]), or *time triggered* versus *event triggered* (Kopetz [1991]). The decision, whether to follow one or the other route is a fundamental design decision for any real-time architecture that has far reaching consequences on all parts of the architecture, for instance, hardware, operating system, communication protocols, programming language, application software, and on all phases of the development process, for instance, the effort required in the design phase, the implementation phase and the testing phase.

In the following section we compare these two approaches to system design from the point of view of predictability, testability, resource utilization, and extensibility.

18.4.1   Predictability

Static scheduling

A system based on static scheduling requires careful planning during the design phase. First it is necessary to establish the granularities for the observation of the control objects. Then the maximum execution times of all time-critical tasks must be determined. After the allocation of the tasks to the nodes and the allocation of the communication slots on the LAN, appropriate execution schedules have to be constructed off-line. Because of this accurate planning effort, detailed plans for the temporal behavior of each task are available and the behavior of the system in the domain of time can be predicted precisely.

Dynamic scheduling

In a system based on dynamic scheduling it is not necessary to develop such a set of detailed plans during the design phase, since the execution schedules are created dynamically as a consequence of the actual demand. Analytical schedulability tests do not exist for distributed systems with mutual exclusion and precedence relations between tasks. Depending on the sequence and timing of the events which are presented to the system in a specific application scenario, different schedules unfold dynamically which may or may not meet the timeliness requirements.

18.4.2   Testability

Static scheduling

In a static system, the results of the performance test of every system task can be compared with the established detailed plans. Since the time-base is discrete and determined by the granularity of the scheduler, every input case can be observed and reproduced in the domains of time and value. Therefore testing of static systems is more systematic and constructive. To achieve the same test coverage, the effort to test a dynamic system is much greater than that required for the testing of the corresponding static system. The difference is also caused by the smaller number of possible execution scenarios that have to be considered in a static system, since in such a system the order of state changes within a granule of the scheduler is not relevant (Schutz [1990]).

Dynamic Scheduling

The confidence in the timeliness of a distributed system with dynamic scheduling can only be established by extensive system tests on simulated loads. Testing on real loads is not sufficient, because the rare events which the system has to handle (e.g., the occurrence of a serious fault in the controlled object), will not occur frequently enough in an operational environment to gain confidence in the peak load performance of the system. Since no detailed plans for the intended temporal behavior of the tasks of exist, it is not possible to perform 'constructive' performance testing at the task level. In a system where all scheduling decisions concerning the task execution and the access to the communication system are dynamic, no temporal firewalls for task encapsulation exist, that is, a variation in the timing of any one task can have consequences on the timing of many other tasks in different nodes. The critical issue during the evaluation of a dynamic system is thus reduced to the question, whether the simulated load patterns used in the system test are representative of the load patterns that will develop in the real application context. This question is very difficult to answer with confidence.

18.4.3   Resource Utilization

Static scheduling

In a static system all schedules are fixed and planned for the peak load demand in the specified operating mode. The time-slot assigned to a specific task must be at least as long as the maximum execution time of this task. If the difference between the average and the maximum execution time of a task is large, then in most cases only a small fraction of the allocated time slot will be needed by this task. If many different operating modes have to be considered, then there is the potential problem of combinatorial explosion of the number of static schedules.

Dynamic scheduling

In a dynamic system only those tasks that have been activated under the actual circumstances have to be scheduled. Since the scheduling decisions are made dynamically, the CPU will be available again after the actual (and not the maximum) task execution time. On the other hand, run-time resources are required for the execution of the dynamic scheduling algorithm and the synchronization and buffer management.

   If load conditions are low or average, then the resource utilization of a dynamic system will be much better than that of a comparable static system. In peak load scenarios the situation can reverse, since the time available for the execution of the application tasks is reduced by the increasing processing time required for executing the interrupt handling, buffer management, synchronization, and scheduling algorithms.

18.4.4   Extensibility

Every successful system must be modified and extended over its lifetime. The effort required to change existing functions and add new functions is captured by the notion of extensibility. There are two steps required to effect a change, the implementation of the new or modified task and the verification of the temporal properties of the modified system.

Static scheduling

From a temporal point of view, every task of a static system is encapsulated. As long as a modified task does not exceed the specified maximum execution time of the original task, the change has no temporal effect on the rest of the system. If the maximum execution time is extended, or a new task is added, then the static schedules have to be recalculated. The effort required to add a new node depends on the information flow to or from this new node. If the node is passive, that is, it does not send any information into the system (e.g., a display), then no modification of the existing system is required since the communication protocols are unidirectional and of the broadcast type. If the new node is active, that is, information is sent from the new node into the existing system, then a communication slot must be generated by recalculating the communication schedules.

If the number of tasks is required to change dynamically during system operation, then it is not possible to calculate static schedules.

Dynamic Scheduling

In dynamic systems it is easy to modify an operative task or to add a new task to an existing node, since all scheduling and synchronization decisions are deferred until the activation of these tasks at run time. Adding a new node requires the modification of some protocol parameters. Yet, a local change in the execution time of one task can impact the temporal properties of another task in a different node, for instance, by delaying its access to the LAN. Since the temporal effects of a change are not encapsulated to a task slot or a node, a local change can ripple through the entire system. Because no binding temporal parameters for the individual tasks are specified, a retesting of the temporal properties of the total system is required to assess the temporal consequences of a change in an individual task. Considering that both the probability of change and the system test-time are proportional to the number of tasks, the cost of assessing the consequences of a local change increases more than linearly with the number of tasks, that is, with system size. Such an architecture does not scale well to large applications.

Let us close this chapter with a recent comment by Xu, Jia and Parnas [1991], p. 134:

For satisfying timing constraints in hard real-time systems, predictability of the systems behavior is the most important concern; pre-run-time scheduling is often the only practical means of providing predictability in a complex system.

18.5 References

Cheng, S-C., Stankovic, J. A. and Ramamritham, K. (1988), Scheduling Algorithms for Hard Real-Time Systems — A Brief Survey, in *IEEE Tutorial on Hard Real-Time Systems*, Stan
-kovic, J. A. and Ramamritham, K., eds., IEEE Computer Society Press.

Fohler, G. (1992), Realizing changes of operational modes with a pre-run-time scheduled hard real-time system, *Proceedings of the Second Workshop on Responsive Computer Systems*, Kawagoe, Japan, 122–128.

Fohler, G. and Koza, C. (1990), Scheudling for Distributed Hard Real-Time Systems using Heuristic Search Strategies, Institut f"ur Technische Informatik, Technische Universität Wien, Research Report 12/90, Vienna, Austria.

Garey, M. R. and Johnson, D. S. (1975), Complexity results for multiprocessor scheduling under resource constraints, *Siam Journal of Computing* 4, 397–411.

Kopetz, H. (1991), Time-Triggered versus Event-Triggered Real-Time Systems, in *Proceedings of the Workshop: Operating Systems of the '90s and Beyond*, Springer Lecture Notes on Computer Science, Springer Verlag.

Kopetz, H. and Kim, K. (1990), Real-time temporal uncertainties in interactions among real-time objects, *Proceedings of the Ninth IEEE Symposium on Reliable Distributed Systems*, Huntsville, AL.

Lawson, H. W. (1992), Cy-Clone: An approach to the engineering of resource-adequate cyclic real-time systems, *Journal of Real-Time System* 4, 55–83.

Liu, C. L. and Layland, J. W. (1973), Scheduling Algorithms for Multiprogramming in a Hard Realtime Environment, *Journal of the ACM*, 46–61.

Locke, C. D. (1992), Software Architectures for Hard Real-Time Applications: Cyclic Executives versus Fixed Priority Executives, *Real-Time Systems Journal* 4(1), 37–54.

Mok, A. K. (1983), Fundamental Design Problems of Distributed Systems for the Hard Real-time Environment, MIT, Ph.D. Dissertation, Cambridge, MA.

Schutz, W. (1990), A Test Strategy for the Distributed Real-Time System MARS, *Proceedings of the IEEE Compeuro 90 'Computer Systems and Software Engineering'*, Tel Aviv, Israel, 20–27.

Sha, L., Rajkumar, R., Lehoczky, H. and Ramamritham, K. (1989), Mode Change Protocols for Priority-Driven Preemptive Scheudling, *Real-Time Systems Journal*, 243–265.

Sha, L., Rajkumar, R. and Lehoczky, J. P. (1990), Priority Inheritence Protocols: An Approach to Real-Time Synchronization, *IEEE Transactions on Computers* **39(9)**, 1175–1185.

Sprunt, B., Sha, L. and Lehozky, J. (1989), Aperiodic Task Scheduling for Hard Real Time Systems, *Journal of Real-Time Systems* **1(1)**, 27–60.

Ullman, J. D. (1976), Complexity of Sequence problems, in *Computer and Job-Shop Scheduling Theory*, Coffman, E. G., ed., J. Wiley, New York.

Xu, Jia and Parnas, D. L. (1991), On satisfying timing Constraints in Hard Real-Time Systems, *Proceedings of the ACM Sigsoft 91 Conference on Software for Critical Systems*, *Software Engineering Notes* **16(5)**, 132–145.

Chapter 19

Design of Distributed Real-Time Systems

Paulo Veríssimo and Hermann Kopetz

In this section the design of distributed real time system is treated by presenting the architectures of two well known distributed real-time systems — the first case study, MARS, covers the class of time-triggered distributed real-time systems, while the second case study, DELTA 4, covers the class of event-triggered real-time systems.

19.1 Case Study: MARS

19.1.1 Objectives

The MARS (MAintainable Real-time System) (Kopetz *et al.* [1989]) project is a research project that focuses on the topic of distributed fault-tolerant hard real-time computer systems in critical applications. The project has been ongoing for more than ten years and prototype implementations of the architecture have been completed and evaluated.

It is the objective of the MARS project to develop an architecture of a distributed fault-tolerant hard real-time system such that the proper operation of the system in the time and value domain can be analytically verified in the design phase. In our view such an analytical verification of the temporal properties is only possible if the architecture is time triggered. In particular the topics of guaranteed timeliness, testability, maintainability, fault-tolerance, and systematic software development are investigated in the MARS project.

Guaranteed Timeliness

Guaranteed timeliness is a fundamental requirement in any critical real-time application. Given a load- and fault hypothesis, it is a prime objective in the MARS project that the temporal behaviour of a given implementation is carefully planned in the design phase. In the MARS project it is felt that 'statistical' assurances about the timeliness of hard real-time systems are not sufficient, since in many applications the peak-load demand is highly correlated. Guaranteed timeliness is only possible if adequate resources are provided to handle the specified peak load. MARS is based on this principle of resource adequacy (Lawson [1992]).

Testability

Hard real-time systems that are to be deployed in critical applications must be carefully validated before they can be put into operation. At present, more than half of the development resources in a typical real-time system project is spent on testing, a substantial part thereof in the phase of integration testing.

Real-time systems must be tested in the value domain and in the time domain. Whereas a substantial body of literature exists about testing in the value domain, relatively little systematic work is known about testing the timeliness. Testability in the time domain can be supported by architectural properties (Schutz [1991]). If it is possible to decompose a system into a set of encapsulated subsystems the effort for integration tests can be reduced substantially.

It is one goal of the MARS project to develop an architecture that supports testability in the domain of time by design.

Maintainability

The effort required to restore the system service after a request for change has been issued is referred to as *maintainability*. Maintenance actions are needed to remedy permanent hardware faults, to eliminate design errors, and to modify the software to respond to change requests. A successful system changes its environment that again changes the requirements for this system. In order to keep a system in a state that is relevant to its users, it is mandatory to repeatedly modify and enhance the system functions. The ease with which such changes can be implemented is again dependent on the properties of the architecture. If the consequences of a change can be localized to well defined encapsulated architectural units, then the maintenance effort is minimized.

Since a system must be retested after every change, testability is an important issue in maintainability.

Fault Tolerance

Sooner or later, every man-made system will fail because of physical faults. If the inherent probability of failure of a given implementation technology cannot be accepted, redundancy must be provided in order to make the system fault-tolerant. If the mission time of a system is in the same order of magnitude as the MTTF (mean time to fail) of its components, then the on-line maintenance of the failed components must be supported by the architecture.

It is a goal of the MARS project to provide fault-tolerance in relation to the physical faults specified in the fault-hypothesis and to support the on-line maintainability of hardware and software. Fault-tolerance in relation to design faults is an issue of further research.

Systematic Software Development

At present, real-time software development resembles sometimes a 'black art'. Modules of conventionally designed software are integrated by 'real-time specialists' who tune the system parameters (e.g., task priorities, buffer sizes, etc.,) during an extensive trial and error testing period, consuming more than 50% of a projects resources. Why the system performs its functions at the end is sometimes a miracle, even to the 'real-time specialists'.

Temporal properties are system properties. They depend on the behaviour of all levels of an architecture, for instance, the hardware, the operating system, the communication protocols, and the application software. A systematic design of real-time software is only possible if the underlying hardware and operating system guarantee a predictable temporal behaviour. It is one goal of MARS to provide the architectural prerequisites for an engineering approach to the development of real-time systems, and to develop a systematic software design methodology (Kopetz *et al.* [1991]).

19.1.2   The State View as the Guiding Principle

MARS is an example of a pure time-triggered architecture. In such an architecture it is assumed that the behaviour of the world can be described by a sequence of equidistant observations of the states of the world.

Time Triggered Observation of States

The MARS architecture requires the time-triggered observation of the state of the control object. Depending on the dynamics of the control object an observation granule (sampling period) of a RT-entity is specified at compile time. At these predefined globally synchronized periodic points in time, the grid points of the observation grid, the states of the RT-entities are observed and transmitted to the computer system. The time-triggered observation of the states provides an implicit flow control between the control object and the computer system. In contrast to ET-systems, the input rate in a TT-system, such as in MARS, is always constant.

Intelligent State based Input Output

An intelligent sensor is a sensor with a capability to perform some preprocessing on the perceived raw data from the physical input device connected to the RT-entity before presenting its information to the receiving computer system. Similarly, an intelligent actuator is an actuator with a capability of postprocessing the data received from the computer system before transmitting it to the physical output device.

During the constant time interval between two successive points of a TT observation — the observation grid — a RT-entity can visit many different states. The

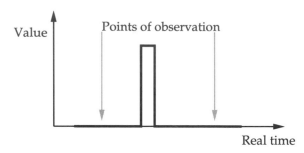

Figure 19.1. The intelligent sensor must store the relevant information about the input signal until the next point of observation

state that is occupied precisely at the point of observation may not be most relevant
for the purpose of the given control system. Therefore it may be necessary that
an intelligent sensor monitors the RT-entity with a finer granularity than the observation granularity. We call this finer granularity the *perception granularity* of the
sensor. The intelligent sensor will then form an abstract observation for the next
point of observation by executing a proper abstraction function over these many
fine grained perceptions. The concrete specification of this abstraction function
implemented in an intelligent sensor depends on the given application context.

In some application it may even be necessary to report to the computer system
the point in time, when a particular state of the RT entity occurred within the
observation granule, with a finer granularity than that of the observation grid.
We call such an observation that contains in addition to the value of the RT-entity
the point in time within an observation granule, measured with the perception
granularity of the intelligent sensor, a *timed observation*. This is illustrated in Figure
19.1.

In some scenarios, the time granularity of a periodic output action of a TT system
may not be sufficient for the given control purpose. In such a situation an intelligent
actuator will receive a *timed output message* that informs the actuator as to exactly
when, after the last output grid point, the data has to be released to the physical
device. An intelligent actuator is thus in the position to perform a finer control
than that given by the output grid of the computer system.

The Concept of State Messages

The most common message handling primitives in distributed systems are biased
toward event information, that is, a new message is queued at the receiver and
consumed on reading. In TT-systems a more appropriate message model for
handling state information is required. We call such a message model a *state
message model* and the corresponding message a state message (Kopetz and Merker
[1985]). The semantics of a state message is related to the semantics of a variable
in programming languages. A new version of a state message overwrites the
previous version. A state message is not consumed on reading. State messages are
produced periodically at predetermined points in real-time, the grid points of the
observation grid, known *a priori* to all communicating partners. They contain the

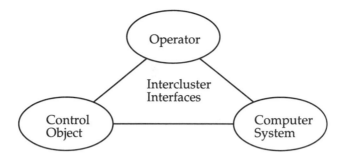

Figure 19.2. MARS system consisting of three clusters

information about the relevant state of the RT-entity at the last observation point.

A major advantage of the state message model is the minimal synchronization requirement between sender and receiver. There is no need for buffer management or tight synchronization between producer and consumer of state messages. Conceptually, reading a state message is very similar to reading a state sensor, for instance, a temperature, from the environment or a variable from computer memory.

The information flow of state-messages is unidirectional. It is the responsibility of the receiver to verify that all required state messages are available at the proper time. In such a system it is thus possible to add additional receivers without changing the message rate or the communication protocol.

19.1.3   Structure

In this section we describe the systematic decomposition of a MARS system into clusters, fault-tolerant units, components, and tasks.

System Viewpoint

A MARS application can be decomposed into a set of autonomous subsystems, the clusters. Different clusters have disjoint name spaces and can be implemented in different technologies. Name translation has to be performed in the intercluster interfaces which are realized solely by state message exchanges. A globally synchronized time is available in all clusters.

Even a small MARS application can be decomposed into three clusters, the controlled object, the operator, and the controlling computer. A large controlling computer system can itself be decomposed into a set of clusters (see Chapter 16). From a given computer cluster it cannot be decided if the adjacent cluster is another part of the computer system or the control object, since communication to either one of these clusters is realized by the same communication mechanism, the state message exchange. Interlinked clusters form a network, not a hierarchy.

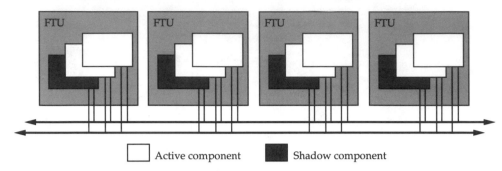

☐ Active component   ■ Shadow component

Figure 19.3. MARS Cluster consisting of four FTUs with three components (two active, one shadow) each

Cluster

A cluster can be decomposed into a set of Fault-Tolerant Units (FTUs) interconnected by a replicated real-time communication channel. The FTUs exchange information by state messages only. The media access to the real-time communication channel is controlled by the progression of the global time, that is, it is a time division multiple access (TDMA) protocol.

The problems of fault tolerance are addressed at the cluster level. A response membership protocol is implemented at this level to report consistently with a small awareness latency which FTU is active and which FTU has failed at its last membership point. This membership service establishes the basis for the implementation of atomic group communication services and distributed redundancy management (Grünsteidl [1993]).

Fault Tolerant Unit

A Fault Tolerant Unit is an aggregation of one or more replicated computational components operating in active redundancy in order to provide a dependable service to the cluster. As long as any one of the components of a FTU is operational, the FTU is considered operational.

As shown in Figure 19.3, a FTU can have two active components and a shadow component. Only the active components have a write slot on the TDMA bus. The shadow component updates its internal state and monitors the operation of the active components. In case one of the active components fails, the shadow component takes the write slot of the failed component in order to reestablish the redundancy (Reisinger *et al.* [1990]).

Component

A component is the smallest replaceable unit (SRU) of the MARS architecture, consisting of the computer hardware and the associated application software. Components have to be fail silent, that is, they either produce correct results or no results at all. In case an error is detected within a component, the operation of the component is terminated immediately.

Task

A task is the execution of a sequential program. The software inside a component can be decomposed into a set of communicating tasks. Intertask communication is achieved by state message exchanges. The task activation is cyclic and time-triggered. Since all communication in MARS is effected by state message exchanges before or after a task execution, there is no need for buffers and buffer management.

19.1.4 Operation

In many real-time application disjoint operational phases can be identified, for instance,in a batch process the startup phase, the processing phase, and the shutdown phase are three typical operational phases. In MARS an operational phase is mapped into a unique operational mode. A mode is characterized by a set of periodic task executions and messages exchanges. The changeover from one mode to another mode is controlled by a mode switch.

Task Execution

The execution of a MARS task begins at the predefined point in time with the reading of the specified input messages. It then proceeds without any external communication or synchronization until the production of the output messages. Since there is no synchronization point within a task that can lead to an arbitrary delay, the maximum execution time of every MARS task can be determined by an off-line analysis of the source code written in a restrictive programming language. For this purpose a set of development tools that help the programmer to design a task that will meet a given time budget are provided [Pus89,Pos92].

The progression of real time impacts the task execution in two different ways. The progression of real-time acts as a trigger that determines the transfer of control to the entry point of the task. In addition, the start time of a task is provided to the task as a data value. This data value can be accessed during the execution just as any other data value. In order to support replica determinism, it is not allowed to access the real-time clock during the execution of the task.

Communication

At the end of a task execution the results are diffused as broadcast state messages to the other tasks within the component or the cluster. Since the maximum execution time of the communication protocol is predictable — the communication resources are also prescheduled — it is known *a priori* when the results will arrive at the receivers and when the succeeding tasks can be started.

The regular pattern of the intercomponent communication facilitates the implementation of distributed consensus protocols to generate a consistent view of time and membership. A fault-tolerant clock synchronization service and a fault-tolerant membership service is provided as a low level service by the integrated real-time communication protocol TTP (Time Triggered Protocol) (Kopetz [1992a]).

Scheduling and Synchronization

MARS is based on static scheduling. A static schedule is a periodic time triggered schedule for all real-time transactions. A real-time (RT) transaction is a progression of processing and communication actions between a stimulus from and a response to the environment. The lowest common multiple of all transaction periods is the schedule period. At compile time, the scheduling decision for every point of the schedule period of every mode is determined and stored in a dispatcher table for the operating system. All synchronization constraints and task dependencies, e.g., precedence constraints or mutual exclusion constraints, are accommodated in the static schedule designed for each mode. At run time the preplanned decisions are executed by the dispatcher after every clock interrupt.

Mode Changes

One of the weaknesses of static scheduling is the assumption of strictly periodic tasks. Although the majority of tasks in hard real-time applications is periodic, there are also infrequent sporadic requests for service that have hard deadline requirements. An example of such a request is an emergency stop of a machine. Hopefully it will never have to be executed. However, if it is requested it has to be serviced within a specified time interval.

It is evident that a significantly better resource utilization can be realized if only those tasks that are needed in a particular operating mode have to be scheduled (Fohler [1992]). If the system leaves one operating mode and enters another one, then a corresponding change of schedules has to take place.

During design of the MARS software it is required to identify all possible operating and emergency modes. For each mode a static schedule that will meet all deadlines is calculated off-line. Mode changes are analyzed and the appropriate mode change schedules are developed at compile time. Whenever a mode change is requested at run time the applicable mode change schedule will be activated immediately.

19.1.5   Fault Tolerance

The MARS architecture supports the implementation of fault-tolerance by active redundancy. Active redundancy guarantees a timely service even in the presence of failures.

Fault Model

The fault model of MARS covers the occurrence of transient or permanent physical faults. If a physical fault effects the operation of a component, it is assumed that the component will detect the error and fail in a fail-silent mode, that is, it will terminate its operation without outputting any incorrect result. Since an FTU contains a number of replicated components, the FTU service will be provided as long as at least one of the replicated components is operational. After a repair action — in case of a permanent fault — or after a successful completion of a self test — in case the fault was transient — the failed component will attempt its reintegration at the next reintegration point.

We assume the following order of magnitude for the fault rates of the components:

permanent physical fault	10^2 ... 10^4 FITS
transient physical fault	10^4 ... 10^6 FITS
recovery from transient fault	10 seconds
repair of permanent fault	24 hours

Considering these failure rates, it is highly improbable that two failures will occur within a single recovery interval (1 FIT = 10^{-9} failures/hour).

Redundancy

In MARS redundancy is needed at two levels. At the component level, redundancy is introduced to achieve a high error detection coverage of the component. At the FTU level active redundancy is required to continue the FTU service in case a component of a FTU has failed.

A number of hardware and software mechanisms increase the error detection coverage of a MARS component. In addition to the standard hardware error detection mechanisms, such as parity or memory management hardware, a special microcomputer — the TDMA monitor — is introduced in each component to monitor the temporal behaviour of the component. The output port of a component can be activated only if the main processor and the TDMA monitor agree on the proper timing of the send request.

To increase the error detection probability in respect to short transient faults, time redundancy is introduced. Every task is executed twice and the signatures of the two results are compared. In case the signatures differ, the operation of the component is terminated.

The redundancy provided by the local real-time clocks in the components is used to establish a fault tolerant global time base. A distributed clock synchronization algorithm synchronizes the clocks even in the presence of failure (Kopetz and Ochsenreiter [1987]).

A distributed membership service is implemented in the distributed MARS operating system to detect transient failures of the input port or the output port. In order to avoid the formation of cliques, a quorum mechanism ensures that the majority view is winning (Kopetz [1992b]).

Replica Determinism

Active redundancy requires the maintenance of replica determinism among the replicated components. Replica determinism implies that all active replicated components perform the same state changes at about the same point in time. Two important reasons that lead to the destruction of replica determinism are the uncoordinated access to the local clocks and the dynamic scheduling decisions.

MARS prohibits reading of the local time during task execution. Only the start time of the task — it is identical at all replicated components — is made available to the application software. In case of a failure event — which is always unpredictable — a MARS component terminates its operation immediately.

If a component requests a dynamic mode change the integrated communication protocol TTP assures that all replicas and all FTUs agree on the point in time when such a mode change is activated. If — for instance, because of a fault — a component delays the mode change, the TTP protocol forces this component to terminate its operation.

Component Reintegration

For the purpose of component reintegration MARS distinguishes between two data structures that are contained in a component: the i-state (initialization state) and the h-state (history state). The i-state comprises all data elements that are static, that is, they are not modified during the operation of the component, for instance, the program code or the initialization data. The h-state, on the other side, is a dynamic data structure that is modified as the computation progresses. Certain well defined time points at which the size of the h-state is small, for instance, the LCM (lowest common multiple) of the task cycles, are designated as reintegration points of a component.

During the design of the static schedule it must be arranged that every component sends its h-state to the real-time bus at the statically defined reintegration points. It is then possible for the joining partner component to wait until the next reintegration point to recover the proper h-state. From this point onward state synchronism between the replicated components is reestablished.

Maintenance

Since a failure of a MARS component will not have any effect on the service of the corresponding FTU as long as at least one active component of this FTU is still operational, MARS tolerates hardware failures transparently. The reintegration of a repaired component can also be performed on-line to reestablish the desired level of redundancy.

If a change in the software is required it has to be checked whether the execution of the new version of the software will fit into the allocated time slot. If this is the case, no modification of the schedule is necessary. Otherwise a new schedule with an extended execution slot for the modified task must be generated off-line. This new schedule can be loaded as a new mode. At an appropriate point in time, for instance, at the end of the old schedule period, this new mode has to be activated.

To summarize, the MARS architecture is based on a strict separation of the concerns for functionality, timeliness, and dependability. It has been tried to keep the interdependence between these three properties as small as possible. The introduction of an approximate global time and a sparse time base simplifies the establishment of a consistent order and the maintenance of the temporal properties in the distributed context. All these design decisions help to make the architecture intelligible.

The experience during the implementation of the architecture and the commissioning of application software have shown that this understandability of the architecture is a powerful weapon against the complexity of the real-time software development process. Since detailed information about the expected temporal behaviour of every real-time task is specified at the time of software design, the testing phase of the real-time software significantly simplified.

19.2   Case study: DELTA-4 XPA

DELTA-4 is a fault-tolerant system based on distribution (Chereque *et al.* [1992]). The main issues about dependability achievement are: a reliable (fail-silent) networking infrastructure, hosting reliable group communication and replication management protocols, to which computers of different makes and failure behaviour can plug in; an object-oriented application support environment, which allows building applications with incremental levels of fault-tolerance, while hiding from the programmer the task of ensuring dependability. Additionally, black-box commercial applications can also be rendered fault-tolerant without change.

The problem of addressing applications in the real-time area, while maintaining the necessary distribution and dependability attributes, has required an overall approach, named XPA, Extra Performance Architecture (Veríssimo *et al.* [1991]). The main goal has been to depart from the DELTA-4 concepts and components, using them to the extent possible, and do a major rethinking with the aim of fulfilling the objectives established for DELTA-4 in the real-time area.

19.2.1   Objectives

Quoting Powell [1991]: 'If a real-time system is presented with circumstances outside the operational envelope, then it is not possible to assure that deadlines will be met. Two views can be taken on this [...] the bounded- and the unbounded-demand schools'. This is the fundamental thought underlying the XPA approach.

The bounded-demand school considers that the behaviour of the environment can be predicted. Let us call it the *operational envelope*: event types, rates and patterns; required computational complexity, output needs. The system is sized to this envelope and if properly designed to take computational constraints and failures into account, all tasks meet their deadlines and system generally responds as specified. Event classes are limited, to a great extent, to periodic.

The unbounded-demand school simply recognises that a number of problems exist where a complete definition of the operational envelope is not possible, or where the definition imposed by design has a limited coverage. The classes of events that must be handled are mainly sporadics, whose assumed distribution has only a known, non-unity coverage, and in extreme cases, aperiodic events that must be treated 'as well' as possible.

Bounded-demand is a classical approach to design hard real-time systems[1]. In the measure where the complexity of systems to be controlled grows, the assump-

---
[1]Considered for a long time in the real-time systems community, as the 'real' real-time.

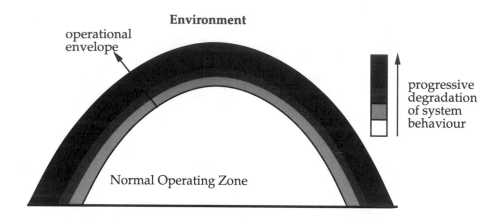

Figure 19.4. Operational envelope and graceful degradation

tions about predictability become less true. Finding feasible off-line schedules becomes a harder task, if possible at all. Bounds, while existent, may be unreachable or not discoverable. The system may become too complex to be proven correct. Interdependence of assumptions may prevent a piecewise or modular approach. Short of a better solution, such systems (take the example of on-board airplane computer systems) are broken into hermetical domains, simple enough to allow the classical design. These systems are not integrated and often do not have direct interaction.

One alternative approach would then be to admit that the behaviour of the system may fall outside the operational envelope, and thus provide it with some form of graceful degradation ability. This is depicted in Figure 19.4: while the system would normally act as a hard real-time one in the presence of the 'foreseen' environmental and computational constraints, it would adapt in a *best-effort* way, to 'unforeseen' situations — working in modes that are progressively less effective, precise, reliable, etc. — without abruptly falling apart.

The objective of XPA is thus to be capable of implementing hard real-time designs, while falling into a best-effort behaviour when circumstances posed by the environment so oblige. Moreover, it should improve efficiency of resource utilisation, that is, be able to allocate idle and/or unused resources, like computational power and communications bandwidth, to non-critical and even non real-time applications. This does not make XPA a soft real-time system. It is a hard real-time system with graceful degradation.

To this endeavour, it must decouple design-time timeliness objectives from run-time timeliness assurances, by introducing the notion of target timeliness or target line, and it must provide for preemptive scheduling based not only on some notion of deadline, but also of importance or criticality.

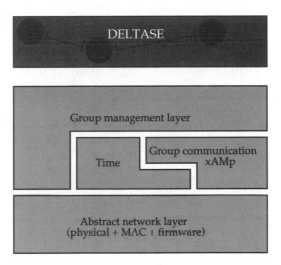

Figure 19.5. The XPA system architecture

19.2.2 Architecture

The architecture of XPA is outlined in Figure 19.5. The relevant blocks will be addressed below.

Network infrastructure

The communications sub-system comprises the Abstract Network layer[2]. The local area network to be used in the project's implementation of XPA may be one of the several standardised LANs, such as FDDI, a 100Mb/s high-speed, high-throughput fibre-optic Lan. FDDI provides up to 10 times the data rates of other standard LANs, speeding-up communication accordingly (Veríssimo and Rodrigues [1991]), provides support for the implementation of urgent traffic classes, and has built-in medium fault tolerance, so that expected availability is very high. Another alternative is the carrier band 5 or 10Mb/s Token-bus, equipped with media redundancy for availability, or even the Token-ring.

Time

In XPA, participant and replica agreement on time is obtained with the assistance of a distributed time service, which provides an abstraction of global time. Both an internal and an external time reference may need to be provided. The internal time is provided through a global clock approximation, maintained by a distributed time server. The clocks are synchronised through a novel algorithm for broadcast LANs (Veríssimo and Rodrigues [1992]) which, running on systems with real-time executives (as is the case) ensures precisions of the order of the low-level kernel interrupt latency variation, which can be made as small as several tens of

---

[2]'Network' is not taken in the sense of Layer 3 of OSI; it refers generically to the several communication infrastructures offering a common abstract interface on which xAMp runs.

microseconds. The external time consists of one of the standards of time, whichever is necessary for the particular use of a given XPA system, injected in the system through a privileged node or set of nodes (e.g., via radio receiver(s) or GPSs). This external time is used to achieve accuracy of the internal time.

Group communication

In XPA, distribution and fault-tolerance support heavily relies on the group communication layer, which has a set of communication services of varying quality, materialised by a multi-primitive group communication suite, the xAMp (Rodrigues and Veríssimo [1991]). Confidence on protocol reliability was increased by validation of the core of the protocol (Baptista *et al.* [1991]), and by fault injection on a real life implementation (Arlat *et al.* [1990]). Several services are offered, from atomic multicast to datagram. *Atomic* guarantees total order and unanimous delivery, for example to feed active replicas. A variation called *tight* implements the slotted-messages facility discussed in Chapter 16. Very fast non-ordered services of varying reliability are provided. These are instrumental for the efficient execution of the distributed replication management protocols of XPA: *bestEffortN* and *atLeastN* guarantee the delivery to N out of the group elements; *bestEffortTo* and *atLeastTo* guarantee the delivery to named group elements (e.g., the leader); unlike *bestEffort*, *atLeast* guarantees the service even when the sender fails; when N is all members, we have the *reliable* service, used to feed passive or leader-follower replica sets.

The services offered do not always permit a direct use by the distributed application, due sometimes to the complexity and algorithmic needs of the latter. This results in the introduction of an intermediate harmonising layer — the Group Management layer.

Group management

The Group Manager is actually a distributed object, represented locally on every node of an XPA system. In fact, the Group Management entities are pseudo-objects, since they present an object interface to the Deltase world, but interact with the group communications layer as another layer above. The Group Manager is concerned with the management of groups of objects, and with the support of the distribution of such groups. The Group Manager incorporates knowledge of the different modes of replication (active, passive, semi-active, etc.), and based on that view, it is able to provide, transparently to the objects themselves, the appropriate level of support, using the xAMp.

Application support environment

Deltase is an object-oriented application support environment, providing client-server and producer-consumer types of interactions. Its purpose is to provide a virtual machine concealing hardware and software details, namely, replication of components. Its computational model derives from the Open Distributed Processing (ODP) Reference Model (ISO [1987]). Applications are either written using Deltase or converted to it, through front-end preprocessors called *transformers*.

19.2.3 Design options

Achieving these goals implied a few innovative approaches, together with some good-sense engineering options, that we describe next.

Re-engineering of DELTA-4 OSA

DELTA-4 is quite effective at providing dependability in open and generic distributed applications. In order to use the mature and tested architecture guidelines of this open systems architecture of DELTA-4 (OSA), the approach taken was simplifying the system structure to an extent where the timeliness and performance goals of XPA might be achieved, while retaining the basic architecture.

In consequence, it was decided that the problems XPA is addressing are perfectly fit to less open solutions, with homogeneous hosts and network, avoiding the impact of the overhead of data conversion and the added complexity brought by heterogeneity, on the timeliness goals. With regard to failure assumptions, fail-silent hosts and network are assumed, and this, while enforced in a manner adequate to the coverage expected (Arlat *et al.* [1990]) (e.g., self-checking hardware) avoids the overhead of voting in the replication management protocols. The interactions between layers were simplified. This took three forms: layer elimination in the ISO-like structure of OSA; service simplification, concerned with skimming the protocols, getting them rid of unnecessary functionality; reorganisation. This latter task encapsulated the more creative aspects of interprocess communication in XPA. The group approach was used extensively, and it proved a very useful paradigm to reorganise the 'pieces' of protocols left from the two previous steps. As will be seen ahead, group communication and group management form the main blocks of this reorganisation.

Timeliness

Timeliness can only be guaranteed where the environment evolution falls within the predefined operational envelope. Still, when that does not occur, the designer must have tools to remedy this situation in the manner possible.

First of all, it must be able to choose what to do when the system enters overload. Static off-line scheduling does not directly support the idea of preferring some computations to others, in a set which cannot meet the timeliness criteria (deadlines). Several static scenarios are likely not to cover all the possibilities that may arise, or lead to an unmanageable combinatorial explosion. With on-line scheduling, while this is possible, the means to it are not obvious. Algorithms like earliest deadline or rate-monotonic (cf. Chapter 18) will find feasible schedules when one exists, *if* the system is not in overload. However, in overload, no feasible schedule exists, and those mechanisms are not as good as priority scheduling, which on the other hand gives poor results in the first case, when the system approaches overload.

It seems thus that there is a case for a scheduling policy that accommodates both the need to fulfill deadlines in normal conditions, and to reduce the consequence of missed deadlines in overload conditions. Let us call the measure used by such a policy *precedence*[3]. The mechanism (one of the possible) used in XPA to implement this policy is to refer precedence to a combined notion of *importance*, the measure of the consequences of a computation not meeting its deadline, and *urgency*, the notion of approaching deadline. In consequence, scheduling is a combined *priority* and *earliest-deadline* mechanism. It is performed on a priority basis first, among very few classes (two or three), to avoid as much as possible the unfairness problems that lead to unnecessary failure of deadlines but still represent high-level notions of computation: critical hard real-time, best effort, other. Then, inside each priority class, it is earliest-deadline-first.

Secondly, design-time timeliness expectations are decoupled from run-time timeliness achievement. The notion of *'targetline'*, the instant chosen by the designer for provision of the service, is introduced. It lies somewhere between a em 'liveline' and deadline, the earliest and latest opportunities at which that service may be provided. Using the cost-benefit curves (Jensen and Northcutt [1990]), targetline would be the instant of greatest benefit, whereas liveline and deadline would be the points of benefit inversion. Run-time support exists to process these parameters and detect their violation, for example, of a targetline or a deadline. This allows the designer some action before the deadline is violated or in consequence of it being violated, respectively, to avoid or minimise failure.

To end with, precedence in a distributed environment cannot be local, but instead subject to precedence inheritance throughout the path of a distributed computation. In communication, where LANs are used, a many-to-few mapping is made from precedence values into network (LAN) priorities.

Computation support

A computational view of objects responding to external events and interacting via RPC was used in the XPA prototype. Objects may either be unreplicated or replicated, in which case replication is handled by the system so that it remains transparent to the user. Active, semi-active and passive replication are supported, although semi-active, through the leader-follower technique, has been the workhorse of XPA. In order to focus on the timeliness and replica determinism aspects under dynamic operation, the computational model of the prototype was simplified to synchronous interactions under global threads of control. A primary implication was to reduce the temporal order relations inside the system to the path of those global threads, and cancel inter-thread relations (this does not apply to input-output). However, message preemption may violate this FIFO ordering: the XPA distribution support only guarantees ordering of message flows bearing the same precedence. On the other hand, all the issues related with ensuring replica determinism, among which total order in replicated executions and identity of replica preemption points, must still be tackled.

---

[3]We retain the terminology used in (Veríssimo *et al.* [1991]), although the word is used with a different meaning in Chapter 17.

Preemption and replica determinism

The leader-follower (L/F) model was used extensively in XPA (Barrett *et al.* [1990]). Since components are fail-silent, decisions can be made by one privileged replica, that imposes them on the others. Preemption points allow process and message preemption with the L/F model (cf. Section 16.5). To insert them, some tooling is necessary: measurement of software execution times to achieve bounds on preemption latency; preemption point insertion methodologies, which cannot be fully automated; testing of timeliness. Preemption points can be inserted as in-line assembly code in 'C', with a minimal overhead: in a Motorola MC68030 at 20MHz without caching, each preemption point test code takes 1.1 microsecond to execute (Powell [1991]). To assess overhead, this figure must be compared with the desired preemption latency, which we do not foresee to be lower than 100 microseconds, yielding an overhead always lower than 1%.

When a high precedence message arrives in a station, it may be directed to a process which does not have the processor, because its current precedence is lower than that of the running process. So the first step is to increase the destination process's precedence to the precedence of the incoming message which, being higher than that of the running process, will cause the local executive to schedule the destination process. Next, the *preemption flag* of the latter is set, so that when it performs the next preemption point test, it will select the highest precedence waiting message, performing the well-behaved intraprocess preemption needed to maintain execution correctness. This is done by launching a lightweight thread to execute the urgent message. All these actions are propagated to the followers, which will perform identical operations.

Another problem related to determinism is desynchronization. To bound the take-over glitch, followers must not be too much apart from leaders. When followers are too fast, they reach a preemption point or request a new message, without having received the relative notification from the leader. They remain blocked until that happens. When they are too slow, they detect the fact by a very simple mechanism using the global time service: the leader time-stamps notifications at the origin, marking the point where it just finished with executing the relevant action. The follower logs the time-stamp T, and if by $T + t_{desync}$ it did not execute that action, a *desynchronization* event is raised to both the leader and follower. System administration may handle this depending on the class of real-time. One example is to perform load-balancing alleviating the overloaded node. Prior to take-over, there must be failure detection. Detection of replica failure is performed by the group management protocol, which ensures that within a predefined detection latency interval, either there is a regular protocol message issued to (and thus replied by) the replica set, or else an 'I'm alive' message is sent. Followers are ranked (e.g., first follower, second follower, etc.) so from the moment failure is detected, take-over is immediate, and the new leader simply resumes executing from its queue.

Communication support

The communication support is structured around groups, and materialised by the group communication and group management modules. This structure offers all that is needed to the applications and provides a better performing support than OSI-like 7-layer alternatives, since it is compact, semantically rich, and oriented to distributed computing.

The Group Communication service offers a set of primitives aiming at solving the communication problems arising in XPA: several agreement attributes, from datagram or best-effort, to atomic delivery; order attributes, from FIFO to total order; timeliness properties, including bounded delay, tightness, and urgency recognition; reliability and availability, through several redundancy techniques, including media duplication.

The designer can perform different tradeoffs between quality of service and efficiency. For example, while the group manager will use atomic multicast to communicate with a set of actively replicated components, so that they receive the same inputs in the same order, the leader-follower will only require reliable, non-ordered delivery, a much simpler service.

Group management services reside in the Group Manager. Its rôle is to complement group communication in providing the final service to the application. In XPA its functions focus on managing the membership of the replica groups and on executing the replication management protocols, namely the leader-follower. It detects replica failure and takes steps to have it cloned at another node, to maintain the redundancy degree. It handles message precedence and preemption, and GM entities of a replica set cooperatively execute the leader-follower protocol we discussed earlier.

19.3   References

Arlat, J., Aguera, M., Crouzet, Y., Fabre, J., Martins, E. and Powell, D. (1990), Fault injection for dependability validation: a methodology and some applications, *IEEE Transactions on Software Engineering, Special Issue on Experimental Computer Science*.

Baptista, M., Rodrigues, L., Veríssimo, P., Graf, S., Richier, J. L., Rodriguez, C. and Voiron, J. (1991), Formal specification and verification of a network independent atomic multicast protocol, in *Formal Description Techniques*, Quemada, J., Mañas, J. and Vazques, E., eds., vol. **III**, North-Holland, 345–352.

Barrett, P., Bond, P., Hilborne, A., Rodrigues, L., Seaton, D., Speirs, N. and Veríssimo, P. (1990), The Delta-4 Extra performance architecture (XPA), *Digest of Papers, The 20th International Symposium on Fault-Tolerant Computing*, Newcastle-Upon-Tyne, UK, IEEE, Also available as INESC report AR/21-90.

Chereque, M., Powell, D., Reynier, P., Richier, J-L. and Voiron, J. (1992), Active Replication in Delta-4, *Digest of Papers, The 22nd International Symposium on Fault-Tolerant Computing Systems*, IEEE, 28.

Fohler, G. (1992), Realizing changes of operational modes with a pre-run-time scheduled hard real-time system, *Proceedings of the Second Workshop on Responsive Computer Systems*, Kawagoe, Japan, 122–128.

Grünsteidl, G. (1993), Dezentrales Redundanzmanagement in verteilten Echtzeitsystemen, TNF Fakultaet, TU Wien, Dissertation, Vienna.

ISO (1987), Proposed Revised Text for the NWI on Basic Reference Model of Open Distributed Processing, ISO TC97/SC21/WG1, N1889, Geneva.

Jensen, E. D. and Northcutt, J. D. (1990), Alpha: a non-proprietary operating system for large, complex, distributed real-time systems, *Proceedings of the IEEE Workshop on Experimental Distributed Systems*, Huntsville, AL, IEEE, 35–41.

Kopetz, H. (1992a), TTP — A Time Triggered Protocol for Fault-Tolerant Real-Time Systems, Institut für Technische Informatik, TU Wien, Mars Bericht 1992/16.

Kopetz, H. (1992b), Sparse Time versus Dense Time in Distributed Real-Time Systems, *Proceedings of the Twelfth International Conference on Distributed Computing Systems*, Yokohama, Japan, IEEE Computer Society Press, 460–467.

Kopetz, H., Damm, A., Koza, C., Mulazzani, M., Schwabl, W., Senft, C. and Zainlinger, R. (1989), Distributed Fault-Tolerant Real-Time Systems: The Mars Approach, *IEEE Micro*, 25–41.

Kopetz, H. and Merker, W. (1985), The Architecture of MARS, *Proceedings of the 15th FTCS*, Ann Arbor MI, IEEE Press, 274–279.

Kopetz, H. and Ochsenreiter, V. (1987), Clock Synchronization in Distributed Realtime Systems, *IEEE Transactions on Computers*, 933–940.

Kopetz, H., Zainlinger, R., Fohler, G., Kantz, H., Puschner, W. and Schutz, P. (1991), The design of real-time systems: from specification to implementation and verification, *Software Engineering Journal*, 72–82.

Lawson, H. W. (1992), Cy-Clone: An approach to the engineering of resource-adequate cyclic real-time systems, *Journal of Real-Time System* 4, 55–83.

Powell, D., ed. (1991), *Delta-4 — A Generic Architecture for Dependable Distributed Computing*, ESPRIT Research Reports, Springer Verlag.

Reisinger, J., Kopetz, H., Kantz, H., Grünsteidl, G. and Puschner, P. (1990), Tolerating Transient Faults in MARS, *Proceedings of the 20th FTCS*, Newcastle upon Tyne, UK, IEEE Press, 466–473 .

Rodrigues, L. and Veríssimo, P. (1991), xAMp: a Multi-primitive Group Communications Service, *Proceedings of the Eleventh Symposium on Reliable Distributed Systems*, Houston, TX, Also available as INESC Technical Report AR/66-92.

Schutz, W. (1991), On the Testability of Distributed Real-Time Systems, *Proceedings of the Tenth Symposium on Reliable Distributed Systems*, Pisa, Italy, 52–61.

Veríssimo, P., Barrett, P., Bond, P., Hilborne, A., Rodrigues, L. and Seaton, D. (1991), The extra performance architecture (xpa), in *Delta-4 — A Generic Architecture for Dependable Distributed Computing*, Powell, D., ed., Springer Verlag.

Veríssimo, P. and Rodrigues, L. (1991), Reliable multicasting in high-speed LANs, in *High-Capacity Local and Metropolitan Area Networks*, Pujolle, G., ed., NATO ASI Series, vol. **F72**, Springer Verlag, 397–412.

Veríssimo, P. and Rodrigues, L. (1992), A posteriori Agreement for Fault-tolerant Clock Synchronization on Broadcast Networks, *Digest of Papers, The 22th International Symposium on Fault-Tolerant Computing*, Boston, MA, Also available as INESC report AR/65-92.

Chapter 20

Cryptography and Secure Channels

Roger M. Needham

This section concerns the use of cryptography to implement secure channels between principals in a distributed system. We need to be able to pass data from A to B subject to a selection from the following constraints:

1. The data can't be altered without detection
2. The data can't be read by unintended recipients
3. The data is attributed to the correct originator, who can't disown it.

In centralised systems these are achieved by internal mechanisms of trusted operating systems, but those mechanisms have no direct analogues when communication is via an exposed network. Since the bits constituting a message over such a network will be subject to copying and alteration, the only way to proceed is to make use of cryptography. The methods of proceeding from cryptographic algorithms to systems solutions are not totally obvious, and form most of the subject matter of this chapter.

20.1 Cryptography

The forms of cryptography we consider are encompassed by the following. There are encryption and decryption functions E and D, each of which a function of two variables called a key and a text. The encryption operation is written $E(K, T)$, and the decryption operation $D(K, T)$. A pair of keys are called cognate if

$$D(K_2, E(K_1, T)) = T$$

If $K_1 = K_2$ the cryptosystem is called symmetric, and otherwise it is asymmetric. In asymmetric algorithms in current use it is the case that not only

$$D(K_2, E(K_1, T)) = T \quad \text{but} \quad E(K_2, D(K_1, T)) = T.$$

To emphasise the inverse relationship between K_1 and K_2 they are often written as K^{-1} and K. This convention is used in Chapter 21.

For any cryptosystem to be useful the functions must have some minimum properties. First, in the absence of knowledge of K_2 it must be very awkward ('computationally infeasible', it is often said) to recover T from $E(K_1, T)$. Of course it is always possible in principle to enumerate all possible K_2, but this space may be made impracticably large. (It is sometimes said that 2^{56} is rather a small key space. 2^{56} is actually a fairly substantial number, and one doesn't lightly set about trying 2^{56} possibilities in turn.) Second, given T and $E(K_1, T)$ it should, unless K_1 is to be used once only, be very awkward to recover K_1 (and similar statements). If the two keys are the same so that we have a symmetric system the statements simplify in the obvious way. For an asymmetric system to be useful the keys must be such that even if you know one is it is very awkward to compute the other.

Because various distinctions are clearer that way, we'll start with asymmetric cryptography, although the other way round is more usual. One attraction of asymmetric cryptography is that it is possible to avoid sharing secrets; indeed it is often known as public key cryptography. This name comes from the practice of a principal A keeping one of his two keys, say K_1, strictly to himself and publishing K_2 as it were in the phone book. We may now say that a message encrypted with K_1 has been *signed* by A. Given an encrypted message $E(K_1, M)$ (and presumably a hint that it might have been from A) an attempt to decrypt it using K_2 will yield M, and thus enable the decrypter to infer that A carried out the encryption in the first place.

> Let's go over that again slowly, because it will illustrate some important points. Call the decrypter B. B believes that A encrypted the message because B believes that only A knows K_1. B's belief relies on that assumption; B cannot know that this is justified. A might have told K_1 to his friend A'. In order to have the belief for any valid reason, B also needs to be sure that he has M. He could after all compute $D(K_2, X)$ for any X and produce a candidate M — which in general A will know nothing whatever of. B's inference relies on belief that M is 'good', which may come from several sources:
>
> – B knows M in advance
> – B knows parts of M in advance
> – B knows that M has certain structural redundancies, which will not arise by chance.

The first of these is straightforward. The latter two are less so. The second rests on the assumption that an adversary could not construct a message which when decrypted contained the parts expected by B and other random material. The third rests on the assumption that the structural redundancies (such as consisting of ASCII text) would be destroyed by any interference, or that if one decrypts an encrypted ASCII message with the 'wrong' key then it won't look like ASCII text at all. For these assumptions to be reasonable the system designer must keep his head quite carefully.

Note that the only way A can deny knowledge of M is to assert that K_1 is no longer secret. This will cast doubt on the value of A's signature in other circumstances too, of course.

A signed message such as M is certainly not confidential. Anyone can decrypt it using A's public key. If it is desired to make a message confidential to a particular recipient, it may be encrypted using the recipient's public key. So if B wants to send M confidentially to A, B sends $E(K_2, M)$, which may only be decrypted by A.

Again there are fine details. If B is to believe that M is confidential to A, then B should have reason to believe that K_2 is A's public key and not that of some other principal. How B obtains the evidence for this belief is not part of this discussion. If a confidential message is to be any good, it is also necessary to ensure that it has not been interfered with in the course of transmission.

Most confidential messages are also signed, though there is no logical requirement for this. If this is done, the proper order of encryption is as follows, using L_1 and L_2 for B's private and public keys:

$E(K_2, E(L_1, M))$.

One should not sign something one cannot read, as would be the case with the encryptions done in the other order.

If symmetric encryption is being used, signature and confidentiality are provided by encrypting once only with a suitable symmetric key. For the signature and confidentiality to carry conviction, A and B must believe that the key is a secret known only to themselves, or at worst to the two partners and an agency they trust not to disclose or use it. (This final point about use is not often mentioned.)

Since something simply signed is not confidential, and something signed and confidential is signed first and then made confidential, it may seem a little odd to encrypt the whole of the signed message. In this sort of discussion it is often assumed that one does; in real life a rather different procedure is adopted. It is possible (with some difficulty) to devise functions from the text of messages to quantities of a fixed size, known as *message digests* or *secure hashes* MD4 (Rivest [1991]) is a good example. The property of such functions is that given a message M and its digest D, it should be exceedingly awkward to find any other message M' whose digest is also D. The sender of the message signs the digest and not the whole message. The process of forming the digest is often quicker than encryption; further there are sometimes reasons extraneous to the system for wanting the text of the message to be transmitted in clear. (Fine point: a message digest differs greatly from a checksum or CRC. It is a requirement of a CRC that the messages which give rise to the same CRC value are sufficiently different. It's a requirement of a message digest that you can't find messages which give rise to the same digest value.)

20.2   Implementations

The system mainly used for public-key cryptography is the RSA algorithm (Rivest, Shamir and Adleman [1978]).

N is a large number with two prime factors p and q of comparable sizes. $\varphi(N)$ is defined as $(p - 1) \cdot (q - 1)$. We choose a number d such that d is coprime to $\varphi(N)$, and compute e such that

$$e \cdot d \equiv 1 \pmod{\varphi(N)}.$$

It turns out that a suitably sized message block may be encrypted by raising it to the power e (mod $\varphi(N)$) and decrypted by raising the ciphertext similarly to the power d. However, computing e from d (or vice versa) depends upon knowing p and q; the security of the RSA scheme rests upon the difficulty of factoring large numbers. If we consider N has having perhaps 600 (binary) digits, factoring N is far beyond the state of the art. There is no proof that factorisation is hard. Practical observation of the efforts of mathematicians over a long period suggests that it isn't easy.

The commonest system for symmetric cryptography is DES (National Bureau of Standards [1977]). DES is a block cipher which takes 64-bit blocks of cleartext and produces 64-bit blocks of ciphertext under the control of a 56-bit key. It is built by elaboration and iteration of a simple idea as follows. Suppose the 64-bit quantity to be encrypted to be divided into two 32-bit parts, L_0 and R_0. Let $G(K, X)$ be a one-way function from X and the key K to 32-bit quantities (i.e., given a value of G one can't easily determine X). We then set

$$L_1 = R_0, \text{ and } R_1 = \text{XOR}(L_0, G(K, R_0)).$$

From L_1, R_1 we may clearly recover L_0, R_0 if we know K, and we shall have some trouble otherwise. If this be iterated a few times the original material will be effectively concealed, but if we know K the whole business may be run backwards. To obtain good security this idea has to be decorated a great deal, and designing good one-way functions is very far from easy. That bit of structure, however, lies at the root of DES.

20.3   Comments

It has sometimes been remarked that good cryptography depends on a combination of mathematics and muddle. In the absence of muddle a mathematician may simply be able to solve whatever problem was presumed to be difficult. In the case of public-key systems the structural requirements are very strong, and this tends to mean that there can't be much muddle. Devising public-key systems is a knife-edge business. RSA has stayed at the top of the greasy pole for over a decade. Mathematicians have greatly improved factorisation techniques over this time, but one may always make the RSA numbers a little bigger (perhaps an odd expression for adding 100 bits in the exponent) and stay ahead.

Symmetric encryption and decryption are much faster than asymmetric. We are talking about factors of up to 1000 for hardware operations, and hundreds for software versions. Message digesting is faster than symmetric encryption. For these reasons it is not common to use public-key methods for encryption or signature of bulk data, but rather to use them for channel set-up, key distribution for symmetric cryptography, and for certificates of many sorts.

20.4   The Enemy

The usual assumption made in security for distributed systems is that an enemy is capable of reading and copying any message that passes between any pair of principals, and of injecting any bit-pattern of his choice into the network at any time. In many practical circumstances this would be sufficiently difficult to do that no likely enemy would consider it worth while, but one has to have a coherent set of assumptions about enemies, and this is the most appropriate. There is some debate about whether or not the enemy can prevent messages getting through at all; since there are no countermeasures it is not a very interesting debate.

20.5   What the Enemy can do

It is worth attempting a classification of attacks in order to separate out different logical concerns (Voydock and Kent [1983]).

Attacks on the cryptographic algorithm

Many cryptographic algorithms have yielded in the past to known-plaintext attacks or to chosen-plaintext attacks. That is to say, if the cryptanalyst has available to him the ciphertext corresponding to a known plaintext, or even better if he can provoke a principal to encrypt plaintext of the analyst's choice, he may be able to deduce useful properties of the encryption key used. The algorithms mentioned above are not generally believed to be susceptible to either of these attacks, and are often treated (particularly by people from a computing background as against a cryptographic one) as black boxes. Nevertheless a certain degree of caution is usually considered in order. The less one encrypts with long-term keys the better, and the less guessable the plaintext thus encrypted the better. Thus is it meritorious, if K is of long-term value, to transmit

$E(K, L)E(L, M)$

rather than just

$E(K, M).$

Here L is a new key which has not been used before. There is an evident connection between this trick and using a public-key system to transmit a symmetric key for use on bulk data for performance reasons.

This point is often glossed over, or tacitly assumed to be known, which is confusing for newcomers. Similarly some protocols for authentication make use of a 'challenge' — the dialogue is roughly 'If you're Joe, encrypt the following with Joe's key: 12ABFgXXX'. This is inviting Joe to encrypt chosen plaintext, and some writers believe that protocols should be so designed as to avoid this. Clearly, from the point of view of the challenger, the reply has to have known features or the whole business is no use. The response is usually for Joe to XOR the challenge with some random quantity Q of his own before encrypting, and to send Q separately. You may care to consider whether or not it is satisfactory to send Q in clear. This is OK for an honest verifier, but frustrating for one who is trying to persuade Joe to encrypt a very particular bit-pattern. In the public-key field, because of the multiplicative nature of RSA encryption, one is well advised to be cautious about using it to encrypt something formed by a multiplicative process — as for example a message digest function proposed for use in the CCITT standard X.509 (CCITT [1987]).

Attacks on the messages

The fact that a message has been encrypted does not necessarily mean that changes in transmission will be detected. Suppose for example we are using DES in what is known as 'electronic codebook mode' (ECB) . In this mode we arrange the source text in blocks of 64 bits, padding as necessary at the end, and replace each block by the result of encryption with the appropriate key. The resulting encrypted message would not have any means of detection of missing or reordered blocks, or of substitution of blocks from other messages encrypted using the same key. The defence is to include in a message, before encryption, a sum check which will be powerful enough to detect permutations, excisions, and so forth. When that has been done we have in addition ensured that the message is recognisable in the sense of having redundant structure, as mentioned above. It may be noted that one function which would certainly be adequate is a message digest — if it doesn't do for this then it's certainly no good for its primary purpose. It is prudent, if one uses an ordinary CRC as commonly employed in communications, to encrypt not in ECB mode but in Cipher Block Chaining mode (CBC). See Voydock and Kent [1983] for details of this, and for recommendations for good practice.

Attacks on keys based on guessing

In current circumstances many users of distributed systems do not have any sort of token with them which may be used to contain 'their' key. This is unsatisfactory, since people cannot remember 56-bit DES keys, let alone (say) 511-bit RSA keys. Systems often fall back on generating a key from a password, because people do have a limited capacity for remembering passwords. The potential attack here is for the enemy to copy a message and experiment, off-line, with decrypting it — for example by using all the words in a dictionary as trial keys. Careful protocol design can counter this problem by making sure that the content of messages protected by possibly weak keys cannot be predicted (Lomas *et al.* [1989]). Kerberos (Steiner,

Neuman and Schiller [1988]) is an example of a protocol which is potentially susceptible to this type of attack.

Attacks on the protocol being implemented by a set of messages

The attacks considered under this heading concern replay and misuse of messages. It is assumed that the enemy can copy and store away as much material as he likes by observation of passing traffic. In the ordinary course of business a good deal of traffic, especially traffic to do with dialogue initiation, is very similar from day to day. Consider by analogy how often I say 'Hello, Roger Needham here' or similar expressions. A good deal of the art of protocol design has to do with avoiding being confused by replays. If it matters that the content of a message is fresh, then this may be assured by requiring that a sufficiently current time-stamp be inserted (by an agent trusted to do it properly) or by means of a challenges and response where the challenger knows that the challenge is new. In the case mentioned above of the challenge to Joe, if the challenger has never before used 12ABFgXXX in this way, after a successful response he will know that Joe is there (near enough) now, not last week. It is possible to reason formally about trust and freshness (Burrows, Abadí and Needham [1989]). A different type of attack relies upon confusing messages which play different roles in a protocol. For example a protocol proposed as an international standard, which involved three messages, was broken because it was noticed that someone attempting to convince B that he was A when he was in fact C was able to do so by using as Message 3 the reply he got as Message 2 to an apparently innocent enquiry directed to A. The best defence here is labelling messages with their status, this is still a subject of active study.

20.6   Encryption Channels

To go back to where we began, the purpose of encryption in distributed systems is to be able to make assertions about the source or destination of messages. The set of messages encrypted with a certain key may be said to be an example of a channel, which is a very general notion to do with communication. All we really need here is to observe that a channel is a means of communication such that some properties may be quoted of all communications via the channel, because it is that channel. For example, a channel may be defined as the series of messages encrypted with A's private key K_1. It is true of anything that appears on that channel that there is good evidence that A said it. In Chapter 21 the terminology used is 'the channel speaks for A'. It is evidently necessary to give channels names (one cannot keep this discourse up for long without needing several of them), and in the public-key world the natural name to use is the public key, K_2. If symmetric encryption is used it is not plausible to name the channel by the key, because the name as well as the channel would then be secret as between the principals at its ends. It is possible to use as a name some hash function of the key, or the result of encrypting some well-known pattern (like zero) with the key. However the primary use of key-naming in the shared-key context is to tell the recipient of an encrypted message which key to use to decrypt it; names made by hashing are not especially apt for this purpose. Rather, following Lampson et al., we distinguish three types of *key reference* which may be used to identify a key to use. They differ in the amount of state presumed to exist in the recipient.

1. An offset into a table of keys maintained at the receiver. As a by-product of establishing the shared-key channel each participant notifies the other of the appropriate value.
2. The key itself, encrypted with a further key known only to the recipient. As a by-product of establishing the shared-key channel each participant encrypts the shared key with its own secret, and the result is passed out as necessary.
3. In effect a combination of the first two. The shared key is encrypted using some other key, a reference to which is attached.

Which of these techniques appears most suitable in a particular case will vary. For example, Method 1 will appeal where the receiver is going to maintain state about the channel anyway; Method 2 will appeal where the receiver is rendering some stateless service.

20.7   Establishing Secure Channels

As has already been said, channels which are to be used for passage of data in any bulk are likely to be implemented by means of symmetric encryption. The main feature of channel establishment is thus to arrange that there is a shared key accessible at both ends of the channel. There are two main approaches here, which appeal according to whether or not your brain is divided into layers.

An older tradition (Needham and Schroeder [1978] and similar work) saw the establishment of secure connections and the establishment of mutual authentication as two sides of the same coin. In this tradition, channel establishment consists of an exchange of messages at the conclusion of which, provided each of the players is who he says he is, there will be a shared secret which is suitable for use as a key. The Kerberos protocol (Steiner, Neuman and Schiller [1988]) is given below in a slightly simplified version, where A and B are the players, and S is a trusted authentication server with which A and B share symmetric keys K_{as} and K_{bs}, respectively. We denote by T_j the time as perceived by J, and K_{ab} a key made up by S to form a secure channel between A and B. We list the four messages:

1. $A \rightarrow S$ A, B
2. $S \rightarrow A$ $E(K_{as}, (T_s, K_{ab}, B, E(K_{bs}, (T_s, K_{ab}, A))))$
3. $A \rightarrow B$ $E(K_{bs}, (T_s, K_{ab}, A)), E(K_{ab}, (A, T_a))$
4. $B \rightarrow A$ $E(K_{ab}, (T_a + 1))$

Provided that A and B trust the server to put a correct time, and that they check the messages they receive for freshness, by the end of the dialogue each is satisfied that the other is present and authentic, and K_{ab} may be used as the basis of a secure channel. There is an exhaustive analysis of protocols of this type in Burrows, Abadí and Needham [1989].

In the papers on this type of approach a good deal of fine detail is omitted — for example the distinctions between the person using a workstation, the workstation itself, and the workstation as endowed with a particular piece of software. When one does make these distinctions (as Abadí *et al.* [1991] do) it may be less obvious that security and authenticity go hand in hand. For example it may be desirable to have a secure channel between two nodes in a network in circumstances where the identities of the nodes are not material; what will (later) be material are the identities of the principals on whose behalf the nodes operate today.

For two entities with some public-key competence to generate a secure channel is easy. The first step is for each to manufacture a public-private key pair. The second is for each to send the other its public key. The third is for each to generate a random quantity which it sends to the other encrypted with the recipient's public key. The fourth and last is for the recipient to decrypt the message just received, and to generate a shared key by hashing the two random quantities. Provided that either of the participants has maintained the secrecy of its private key, then the shared key will not be accessible to anyone else. This little algorithm is similar in spirit to the Diffie and Hellman [1976] key exchange protocol. If A and B are the players then A should believe that its random quantity is a suitable key, and B should believe similarly. The hash function should be such that these beliefs are carried forward; exclusive-or is quite a good one. If I believe that K is a good key to communicate with B, then I should believe the same of K XOR L for all L, provided only that I believe L to have been chosen independently of K.

It's evidently possible for the participants to make lots of keys at a go, which may be used in turn if it is desired to clear out old state, or to change key because a great deal of material has been transmitted.

In real life one would not proceed exactly as indicated. Some level of authentication is bound to be needed, so instead of starting with no authentication at all one starts with key-pairs that certify something useful — such as the identity of the machine.

20.8 Symmetric Encryption and Relays

If we look at the dialogue just mentioned for secure channel set-up, we see that it depends in a quite basic way on public-key cryptography. The players were able to convey their components of the nascent shared secret to each other in a confidential manner because of the two-way property of the public-key cryptosystem. In a symmetrical system, without a certain amount of help, it just can't be done.

20.8.1 Relays

A relay (the notion is due to Davis and Swick [1990], who devised it for a slightly different purpose) is a secure machine with no state other than its own (symmetric) key which it shares with no other machine except perhaps other instances of itself and with an authentication service. A particular application is to make a publicly handlable version of a symmetric key, simply by encrypting it with the relay's secret

— Version 2 of a key reference as discussed above. We may imagine that every principal has a key which in principle is shared with the relay service — although this is given effect by any number of people having copies of a reference for it in the above sense. We may now examine how the relay is used to communicate from A to B with integrity but not security. A first encrypts his message with the key shared with the relay, and passes the result to B, accompanied by a reference to A's key. B passes both to the relay, accompanied by a reference to B's key. The relay decrypts to find A's key, decrypts to find the message, re-encrypts with B's key found from its reference, and passes the result to B.

> We should be a little careful to understand the position of B after receiving his result. What the relay has told him is 'If the message was encrypted by the principal whose key-reference you passed me, this is what it was'. It is B's business, not the relay's, to judge whether the message is 'proper' or not.
>
> We should notice too that any other principal could have done likewise. By encrypting the original message and passing it on with his own key-reference, A has performed an operation very like signing it with A's private key in an asymmetric system.

It should now be obvious why the relay has that name! Can we use a relay to simulate the public-key encryption used in the algorithm given above for the establishment of a secure channel? The answer is clearly yes. A can pass to the relay its own key reference, B's key reference, and A's contribution to the eventual shared key encrypted using the key A 'shares' with the relay. The relay now has enough information to assemble a message to B giving A's contribution, A's name, and A's key-reference, all encrypted with the key B shares with the relay. The effect is identical (for practical purposes) to that of the message sent from A to B using B's public key in the earlier algorithm.

20.9 Conclusion

Cryptography, and its application to the creation and use of secure or authentic channels, constitute an enormous and very subtle subject. A brief chapter such as this can hope to do no more than suggest some main themes to be kept in mind when reading material about cryptography and distributed computing. Almost every point made here is subject to fine details and caveats; apparently simple solutions are almost always wrong. I do not know to whom should be credited the important truth "Whenever anyone says that a problem is easily solved by cryptography, it shows that he doesn't understand it". The treatment here is deliberately informal, since a theoretical structure is built up for some aspects of the subject in Chapter 21.

20.10   References

Abadí, M., Burrows, M., Lampson, B. W. and Wobber, E. (1991), Authentication in Distributed Systems: Theory and Practice , *Proceedings of the 13th Symposium on Operating Systems Principles*, Pacific Grove, CA, In *ACM Operating Systems Review* **25**(5).

Burrows, M., Abadí, M. and Needham, R. M. (1989), A Logic of Authentication, *Proceedings of the Twelfth Symposium on Operating Systems Principles*, Litchfield, AZ, 1–13, In *ACM Operating Systems Review* **23**(5).

CCITT (1987), The Directory-Authentication Framework Version 7, Draft Recommendation X.509.

Davis, D. and Swick, R. (1990), Network Security via Private-Key Ceryificates, *ACM Operating System Review* **24**(4), 64–67.

Diffie, W. and Hellman, M. E. (1976), New Directions in Cryptography, *IEEE Transactions on Information Theory* **IT-22**(6), 644–654.

Lomas, T. M. A., Gong, L., Saltzer, J. H. and Needham, R. M. (1989), Reducing Risks from Poorly Chosen Keys, *Proceedings of the Twelfth Symposium on Operating Systems Principles*, Litchfield, AZ, 14–18, In *ACM Operating Systems Review* **23**(5).

National Bureau of Standards (1977), Data Encryption Standard, *Federal Information Processing Standard Publication* **46**.

Needham, R. M. and Schroeder, M. D. (1978), Using Encryption for Authentication in Large Networks of Computers, *Communications of the ACM* **21**(12), 993–999.

Rivest, R. L. (1991), The MD4 Message Digest Algorithm, *Advances in Cryptology: Proceedings of the Crypto '90*, Springer Verlag, 303–311.

Rivest, R. L., Shamir, A. and Adleman, L. (1978), A Method for Obtaining Digital Signatures and Public-Key Cryptosystems, *Communications of the ACM* **21**(2), 120–126.

Steiner, J. G., Neuman, C. and Schiller, J. I. (1988), Kerberos: An Authentication Service for Open Network Systems, *Proceedings of the Usenix Winter Conference*, 191–201.

Voydock, V. L. and Kent, S. T. (1983), *ACM Computing Surveys* **15**(2), 135–171.

Chapter 21

Authentication in Distributed Systems

Butler W. Lampson

21.1 Introduction

Most computer security uses the access control model (Lampson [1984]) which provides a basis for secrecy and integrity security policies. Figure 21.1 shows the elements of the access control model:

- Principals: sources for requests.
- Requests to perform operations on objects.
- A reference monitor: a guard for each object that examines each request for the object and decides whether to grant it.
- Objects: resources such as files, devices, or processes.

The reference monitor bases its decision on the principal making the request, the operation in the request, and an access rule that controls which principals may perform that operation on the object.

The access control model is less useful for availability, which is not considered in this chapter. Information flow (Denning [1976]) is an alternative model which is also not considered, so we have nothing to say about mandatory security policies that can enforce nondisclosure of secrets.

This is joint work with Martín Abadi, Michael Burrows, and Edward Wobber. Much of it was presented at the Thirteenth ACM Symposium on Operating Systems Principles. A different version with considerable additional material has been published elsewhere (Lampson et al. [1992]).

543

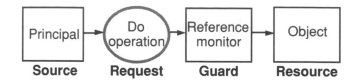

Figure 21.1. The access control model

To do its work the reference monitor needs a trustworthy way to know both the source of the request and the access rule. Obtaining the source of the request is called 'authentication'; interpreting the access rule is called 'authorization'. Thus authentication answers the question "Who said this?", and authorization answers the question "Who is trusted to access this?". Usually the access rule is attached to the object; such a rule is called an access control list or ACL. For each operation the ACL specifies a set of authorized principals, and the monitor grants a request if its principal is trusted at least as much as some principal that is authorized to do the operation in the request.

A request arrives on some channel, such as a wire from a terminal, a network connection, a pipe, a kernel call from a user process, or the successful decryption of an encrypted message. The monitor must deduce the principal responsible for the request from the channel it arrives on, that is, it must authenticate the channel. This is easy in a centralized system because the operating system implements all the channels and knows the principal responsible for each process. In a distributed system several things make it harder:

Autonomy: The path to the object from the principal ultimately responsible for the request may be long and may involve several machines that are not equally trusted. We might want the authentication to take account of this, say by reporting the principal as "Abadi working through a remote machine" rather than simply "Abadi".

Size: The system may be much larger than a centralized one, and there may be multiple sources of authority for such tasks as registering users.

Heterogeneity: The system may have different kinds of channels that are secured in different ways. Some examples are encrypted messages, physically secure wires, and interprocess communication done by the operating system.

Fault-tolerance: Some parts of the system may be broken, off line, or otherwise inaccessible, but the system is still expected to provide as much service as possible. This is more complicated than a system which is either working or completely broken.

This chapter describes both a theory of authentication in distributed systems and a practical system based on the theory. It also uses the theory to explain several other security mechanisms, both existing and proposed. What is the theory good for? In any security system there are assumptions about authority

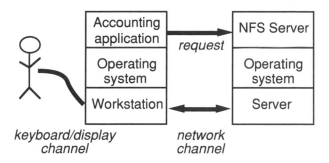

Figure 21.2. A request from a complex source

and trust. The theory tells you how to state them precisely and what the rules are for working out their consequences. Once you have done this, you can look at the assumptions, rules, and consequences and decide whether you like them. If so, you have a clear record of how you got to where you are. If not, you can figure out what went wrong and change it.

We use the theory to analyze the security of everything except the channels based on encryption and the hardware and local operating system on each node; we assume these are trusted. Of course we made many design choices for reasons of performance or scaling that are outside the scope of the theory; its job is to help us work out the implications for security.

We motivate our design throughout with a practical example of a request that has a complex source involving several different system components. Figure 21.2 shows the example, in which a user logs in to a workstation and runs an accounting application. The application makes a request to an object implemented by a server on a different machine, and the server must decide whether to grant the request. We can distinguish the user, two machines, two operating systems, two subsystems, and two channels, one between the user and the workstation and one between the workstation and the server machine. We shall see how to take account of all these components in granting access.

The next section introduces the major concepts that underlie this work and gives a number of informal examples. In Section 21.3 we explain the theory that is the basis of our system. Each of the later sections takes up one of the problems of distributed system security, presenting a general approach to the problem, a theoretical analysis, a description of how our system solves the problem, and comments on the major alternatives known to us. Sections 21.4 and 21.5 describe two essential building blocks: secure channels and names for principals. Section 21.6 deals with roles and program loading, and Section 21.7 with delegation. Section 21.8 treats the mechanics of efficient secure interprocess communication, and Section 21.9 sketches how access control uses authentication. A conclusion summarizes the new methods introduced, the new explanations of old methods, and the state of our implementation.

21.2   Concepts

Both the theory and the system get their power by abstracting from many special cases to a few basic concepts: principal, statement, and channel; trusted computing base; and caching. This section introduces these concepts informally and gives a number of examples to bring out the generality of the ideas. Later sections define the concepts precisely and treat them in detail.

If s is a *statement* (request, assertion, etc.) authentication answers the question "Who said s?" with a principal. Thus principals make statements; this is what they are for. Likewise if o is an object, authorization answers the question "Who is trusted to access o?" with a principal. We describe some different kinds of principals and then explain how they make statements.

Principals are either simple or compound. The simple ones in turn are named principals or channels. The most basic named principals have no structure that we care to analyze:

People	Lampson, Abadi
Machines	VaxSN12648, 4thFloorPrinter
Roles	Manager, Secretary, NFS-Server.

Other principals with names stand for sets of principals:

Services	SRC-NFS, X-server
Groups	SRC, DEC-Employees.

Channels are principals that can say things directly:

Wires or I/O ports	Terminal 14
Encrypted channels	DES encryption with key #574897
Network addresses	IP address 16.4.0.32.

A channel is the only kind of principal that can directly make statements to a computer. There is no direct path, for example, from a person to a program; communication must be over some channel, involving keystrokes, wires, terminal ports, networks, etc. Of course some of these channels, such as the IP address, are not very secure.

There are also compound principals, built up out of other principals by operators with suggestive names (whose exact meaning we explain later):

Principals in roles	Abadi **as** Manager.
Delegations	BurrowsWS **for** Burrows.
Conjunctions	Lampson∧ Wobber.

How do we know that a principal has made a statement? Our theory cannot answer this question for a channel; we simply take such facts as assumptions, though we discuss the basis for accepting them in Section 21.4. However, from statements made by channels and facts about the 'speaks for' relation described below, we can use our theory to deduce that a person, a machine, a delegation, or some other kind of principal made a statement.

Different kinds of channels make statements in different ways. A channel's statement may arrive on a wire from a terminal to serial port 14 of a computer. It may be obtained by successfully decrypting with DES key #574897, or by verifying a digital signature on a file stored two weeks ago. It may be delivered by a network with a certain source address, or as the result of a kernel call to the local operating system. Most of these channels are real-time, but some are not.

Often several channels are produced by multiplexing a single one. For instance, a network channel to the node with IP address 16.4.0.32 may carry UDP channels to ports 2, 75, and 443, or a channel implemented by a kernel call trap from a user process may carry interprocess communication channels to several other processes. Different kinds of multiplexing have much in common, and we handle them all uniformly. The subchannels are no more trustworthy than the main channel. Multiplexing can be repeated indefinitely; for example, an interprocess channel may carry many subchannels to various remote procedures.

Hierarchical names are closely related to multiplexed channels: a single name like /com/dec/src can give rise to many others (/com/dec/src/burrows, /com/dec/src/abadi, ...). Section 21.5.2 explores this connection.

There is a fundamental relation between principals that we call the 'speaks for' relation: A speaks for B if the fact that principal A says something means we can believe that principal B says the same thing. Thus the channel from a terminal speaks for the user at that terminal, and we may want to say that each member of a group speaks for the group.[1] Since only a channel can make a statement directly, a principal can make a statement only by making it on some channel that speaks for that principal.

We use 'speaks for' to formalize indirection; since any problem in computing can be solved by adding another level of indirection,[2] there are many uses of 'speaks for'. Often one principal has several others that speak for it: a person or machine and its encryption keys or names (which can change), a single long-term key and many short-term ones, the authority of a job position and the various people that may hold it at different times, an organization or other group of people and its changing membership. The same idea lets a short name stand for a long one; this pays if it's used often.

Another important concept is the 'trusted computing base' or TCB (Department of Defense [1985]), a small amount of software and hardware that security depends on and that we distinguish from a much larger amount that can misbehave without affecting security. Gathering information to justify an access control decision may require searching databases and communicating with far-flung servers. Once the information is gathered, however, a very simple algorithm can check that it does justify granting access. With the right organization only the

---

[1] Of course the notion of speaking for a group can have many other meanings. For instance, speaking for the U.S. Congress requires the agreement of a majority of both houses obtained according to well-defined procedures. We use only the simplest meaning in this chapter: every member speaks for the group.

[2] Roger Needham attributes this observation to David Wheeler of Cambridge University.

checking algorithm and the relevant encryption mechanism and keys are included in the TCB. Similarly, we can fetch a digitally signed message from an untrusted place without any loss of confidence that the signer actually sent it originally; thus the storage for the message and the channel on which it is transmitted are not part of the TCB. These are examples of an end-to-end argument (Saltzer, Reed, and Clark [1984]), which is closely related to the idea of a TCB.

It's not quite true that components outside the TCB can fail without affecting security. Rather, the system should be 'fail-secure': if an untrusted component fails, the system may deny access it should have granted, but it won't grant access it should have denied. Our system uses this idea when it invalidates caches, stores digitally signed certificates in untrusted places, or interprets an ACL that denies access to specific principals.

Finally, we use caching to make frequent operations fast. A cache usually needs a way of removing entries that become invalid. For example, when caching the fact that key #574897 speaks for Burrows we must know what to do if the key is compromised. We might remember every cache that may hold this information and notify them all when we discover the compromise. This means extra work whenever a cache entry is made, and it fails if we can't talk to the cache.

The alternative, which we adopt, is to limit the lifetime of the cache entry and refresh it from the source when it's used after it has expired, or perhaps when it's about to expire. This approach requires a tradeoff between the frequency (and therefore the cost) of refreshing and the time it takes for cached information to expire.

Like any revocation method, refreshing requires the source to be available. Unfortunately, it's very hard to make a source of information that is both highly secure and highly available. This conflict can be resolved by using two sources in conjunction. One is highly secure and uses a long lifetime, the other is highly available and uses a short one; both must agree to make the information valid. If the available source is compromised, the worst effect is to delay revocation.

A cache can discard an entry at any time because a miss can always be handled by reloading the cache from the original source. This means that we don't have to worry about deadlocks caused by a shortage of cache entries or about tying up too much memory with entries that are not in active use.

21.3   Theory

Our theory deals with principals and statements; all principals can do is to say things, and statements are the things they say. Here we present the essentials of the theory; there is a fuller description elsewhere (Abadi et al. [1992]). A reader who knows the authentication logic of Burrows, Abadi, and Needham [1990] will find some similarities here, but its scope is narrower and its treatment of the matters within that scope correspondingly more detailed. For instance, secrecy and timeliness are fundamental there, but neither appears in our theory.

To help readers who dislike formulas, we highlight the main results by putting them in boxes. These readers do need to learn the meanings of two symbols: $A \Rightarrow B$ (A speaks for B) and $A \mid B$ (A quoting B); both are explained below.

21.3.1 Statements

Statements are defined inductively as follows:

- There are some primitive statements (for example, "read file `foo`").[3]
- If s and s' are statements, then $s \wedge s'$ (s and s'), $s \supset s'$ (s implies s'), and $s \equiv s'$ (s is equivalent to s') are statements.
- If A is a principal and s is a statement, then A **says** s is a statement.
- If A and B are principals, then $A \Rightarrow B$ (A speaks for B) is a statement.

Throughout we write statements in a form intended to make their meaning clear. When processed by a program or transmitted on a channel they are encoded to save space or make it easier to manipulate them. It has been customary to write them in a style closer to the encoded form than the meaningful one. For example, a Needham-Schroeder authentication ticket [Needham and Schroeder [1978]) is usually written $\{K_{ab}, A\}_{K^{bs}}$. We write K_{bs} **says** $K_{ab} \Rightarrow A$ instead, viewing this as the abstract syntax of the statement and the various encodings as different concrete syntaxes. The choice of encoding does not affect the meaning as long as it can be parsed unambiguously.

We write $\vdash s$ to mean that s is an axiom of the theory or is provable from the axioms (we mark an axiom by underlining its number) . Here are the axioms for statements:

> If s is an instance of a theorem of propositional logic then $\vdash s$.   (S1)
> For instance, $\vdash s \wedge s' \supset s$.

> If $\vdash s$ and $\vdash s \supset s'$ then $\vdash s'$.   (S2)
> This is modus ponens, the rule for reasoning from premises to conclusions.

> $\vdash (A$ **says** $s \wedge A$ **says** $(s \supset s'))) \supset A$ **says** s'.   (S3)
> This is modus ponens for **says** instead of $\vdash$.

> If $\vdash s$ then $\vdash A$ **says** s for every principal A.   (S4)

It follows from (S1)–(S4) that **says** distributes over $\wedge$:

> $\vdash A$ **says** $(s \wedge s') \equiv (A$ **says** $s) \wedge (A$ **says** $s')$ (S5)

The intuitive meaning of $\vdash A$ **says** s is not quite that A has uttered the statement s, since in fact A may not be present and may never have seen s. Rather it means that we can proceed as though A has uttered s.

---

[3] We want all statements to have truth values, and we give a truth value to an imperative statement like "read file `foo`" by interpreting it as "it would be a good thing to read file `foo`".

Informally, we write that *A* *makes* the statement *s* when we mean that *A* does something to make it possible for another principal to infer *s*. For example, *A* can make *A* **says** *s* by sending *s* on a channel known to speak for *A*.

21.3.2 Principals

In our theory there is a set of principals; we gave many examples in Section 21.2. The symbols *A* and *B* denote arbitrary principals, and usually *C* denotes a channel. There are two basic operators on principals, $\land$ (and) and $|$ (quoting). The set of principals is closed under these operators. We can grasp their meaning from the axioms that relate them to statements:

$$\vdash (A \land B) \textbf{ says } s \equiv (A \textbf{ says } s) \land (B \textbf{ says } s) \tag{P1}$$

$(A \land B)$ says something if both *A* and *B* say it.

$$\vdash (A \mid B) \textbf{ says } s \equiv A \textbf{ says } B \textbf{ says } s \tag{P2}$$

$A \mid B$ says something if *A* quotes *B* as saying it. This does not mean *B* actually said it: *A* could be mistaken or lying.

We also have equality between principals, with the usual axioms such as reflexivity. Naturally, equal principals say the same things:

$$\vdash A = B \supset (A \textbf{ says } s \equiv B \textbf{ says } s) \tag{P3}$$

The $\land$ and $|$ operators satisfy certain equations:

$$\vdash \land \text{ is associative, commutative, and idempotent.} \tag{P4}$$

$$\vdash | \text{ is associative.} \tag{P5}$$

$$\vdash | \text{ distributes over } \land \text{ in both arguments.} \tag{P6}$$

Now we can define $\Rightarrow$, the 'speaks for' relation between principals, in terms of $\land$ and $=$:[4]

$$\vdash (A \Rightarrow B) \equiv (A = A \land B) \tag{P7}$$

and we get some desirable properties as theorems:

$$\vdash (A \Rightarrow B) \supset ((A \textbf{ says } s) \supset (B \textbf{ says } s)) \tag{P8}$$

This is the informal definition of 'speaks for' in Section 21.2.

$$\vdash (A = B) \equiv ((A \Rightarrow B) \land (B \Rightarrow A)) \tag{P9}$$

---

[4] Equation (P7) is a strong definition of 'speaks for'. It's possible to have a weaker, qualified version in which (P8) holds only for certain statements *s*. For instance, we could have "speaks for reads" which applies only to statements that request reading from a file, or "speaks for file foo" which applies only to statements about file foo. Neuman discusses various applications of this idea [1991]. Or we can use roles (see Section 6) to compensate for the strength of $\Rightarrow$, for instance by saying $A \Rightarrow (B$ **as** reader) instead of $A \Rightarrow B$.

Authentication in Distributed Systems   551

The operators $\land$ and $\Rightarrow$ satisfy the usual laws of the propositional calculus. In particular, $\land$ is *monotonic* with respect to $\Rightarrow$. This means that if $A \Rightarrow B$ then $A \land C \Rightarrow B \land C$. It is also easy to show that | is monotonic in both arguments and that $\Rightarrow$ is transitive. These properties are critical because $C \Rightarrow A$ is what authenticates that a channel C speaks for a principal A or that C is a member of the group A. If we have requests K_{abadi} **says** "read from foo" and $K_{burrows}$ **says** "read from foo", and file foo has the ACL SRC $\land$ Manager, we must get from $K_{abadi} \Rightarrow$ Abadi $\Rightarrow$ SRC and $K_{burrows} \Rightarrow$ Burrows $\Rightarrow$ Manager to $K_{abadi} \land K_{burrows} \Rightarrow$ SRC $\land$ Manager. Only then can we reason from the two requests to SRC $\land$ Manager **says** "read from foo", a request that the ACL obviously grants.

For the same reason, the **as** and **for** operators defined in Sections 21.6 and 21.7 are also monotonic.

21.3.2 Handoff and Credentials

The following *handoff* axiom makes it possible for a principal to introduce new facts about $\Rightarrow$:

$$\vdash (A \text{ says } (B \Rightarrow A)) \supset (B \Rightarrow A) \tag{P10}$$

In other words, A has the right to allow any other principal B to speak for it. There is a simple rule for applying (P10): when you see A **says** s you can conclude o if it has the form $B \Rightarrow A$. The same A must do the saying and appear on the right of the $\Rightarrow$, but B can be any principal.

What is the intuitive justification for (P10)? Since A can make A **says** $(B \Rightarrow A)$ whenever it likes, (P10) gives A the power to make us conclude that A **says** s whenever B **says** s. But B could just ask A to say s directly, which has the same effect provided A is competent and accessible.[5]

From (P10) we can derive a theorem asserting that it is enough for the principal doing the saying to speak for the one on the right of the $\Rightarrow$, rather than being the same:

$$\vdash ((A' \Rightarrow A) \land A' \text{ says } (B \Rightarrow A)) \supset (B \Rightarrow A) \tag{P11}$$

Proof: the premise implies A **says** $B \Rightarrow A$ by (P8), and this implies the conclusion by (P10). This theorem, called the handoff rule, is the basis of our methods for authentication. When we use it we say that A' hands off A to B.

A final theorem deals with the exercise of joint authority:

$$\vdash ((A' \land B \Rightarrow A) \land (B \Rightarrow A')) \supset (B \Rightarrow A)) \tag{P12}$$

From this and (P10) we can deduce $B \Rightarrow A$ given A **says** $(A' \land B \Rightarrow A)$ and A' **says**

---

[5] We take (P10) as an axiom for simplicity. However, it is preferable to assume only some instances of (P10)—the general axiom is too powerful, for example when A represents a group. If the conclusion uses a qualified form of $\Rightarrow$ it may be more acceptable.

$B \Rightarrow A'$. Thus A can let A' and B speak for it jointly, and A' can let B exercise this authority alone. One situation in which we might want both A and A' is when A is usually off line and therefore makes its statement with a much longer lifetime than A' does. We can think of the statement made by A' as a countersignature for A's statement. (P12) is the basis for revoking authentication certificates (Section 21.5) and ending a login session (Section 21.7).

The last two theorems show how we can prove $B \Rightarrow A$ from our axioms together with some premises of the form A' **says** $(B' \Rightarrow A')$. Such a proof together with the premises is called B's *credentials* for A. Each premise has a *lifetime,* and the lifetime of the conclusion, and thus of the credentials, is that of the shortest-lived premise. We could add lifetimes to our formalism by introducing a statement form s **until** t and changing (S2)–(S3) to apply the smallest t in the premises to the conclusion, but here we content ourselves with an informal treatment.

21.4   Channels and Encryption

As we have seen, the essential property of a channel is that its statements can be taken as assumptions: formulas like C **says** s are the raw material from which everything else must be derived. On the other hand, the channel by itself doesn't usually mean much—seeing a message from terminal port 14 or key #574897 isn't very interesting unless we can deduce something about who must have sent it. If we know the possible senders on C, we say that C has integrity. Similarly, if we know the possible receivers we say that C has secrecy, though we have little to say about secrecy here.

Knowing the possible senders on C means finding a meaningful A such that $C \Rightarrow A$; we call this authenticating the channel. Why should we believe that $C \Rightarrow A$? Only because A, or someone who speaks for A, tells us so. Then the handoff rule (P11) lets us conclude $C \Rightarrow A$. In the next section we study the most common way of authenticating C. Here we study why A might trust C enough to make A **says** $C \Rightarrow A$, or in other words, why A should believe that only A can send on C.

Our treatment is informal. Chapter 20 describes some methods of using encryption and some reasons why these methods justify statements of the form "a channel implemented by DES encryption and decryption using key #8340923 speaks for lampson". We do not, however, try to state precise assumptions about secrecy of keys and properties of algorithms, or to derive such facts about 'speaks for' from them.

The first thing to notice is that for A to assert $C \Rightarrow A$ it must be able to name C. A circumlocution like "the channel that carries this message speaks for A" won't do, because it can be subverted by copying the message to another channel. As we consider various channels, we discuss how to name them.

A sender on a channel C can always make C **says** X **says** s, where X is any identifier. We take this as the definition of multiplexing; different values of X establish different subchannels. By (P2), C **says** X **says** s is the same thing as $C \mid X$

says *s*. Thus if *C* names the channel, *C* | *X* names the subchannel. We will see many examples of this.

In what follows we concentrate on the flow of statements over secure channels and on the state that each principal must maintain. Except in Section 21.8, we gloss over many details that may be important for performance but are not directly relevant to security, such as the insecure messages that are sent to initiate some activity and the exact path traversed by the bits of an encrypted message.

21.4.1 Encryption

We are mainly interested in channels that depend on encryption for their security; as we shall see, they add less to the TCB than any others. Chapter 20 discusses encryption in detail; here we merely summarize our notation. An encryption channel consists of two functions *Encrypt* and *Decrypt* and two keys *K* and K^{-1}. By convention, we normally use *K* to receive (decrypt) and K^{-1} to send (encrypt). Another common notation for $Encrypt(K^{-1}, x)$ is $\{x\}_{K^{-1}}$.

There are two kinds of encryption, shared key and public key.

In shared key encryption $K = K^{-1}$. The most popular shared key encryption scheme is the Data Encryption Standard or DES. We denote an encryption channel with the DES key *K* by DES(*K*), or simply by *K* when the meaning is clear; the channel speaks for the set of principals that know *K*.

In public key encryption $K \neq K^{-1}$, and in fact it's infeasible to compute one from the other. Usually *K* is made public and K^{-1} kept private, so that the holder of K^{-1} can broadcast messages with integrity; of course they won't be secret.[6] Together, *K* and K^{-1} are called a key pair. The most popular public key encryption scheme is Rivest-Shamir-Adleman or RSA [1978]. We denote an encryption channel with the RSA public key *K* by RSA(*K*), or simply by *K* when the meaning is clear; the channel speaks for the principal that knows K^{-1}.

A public key channel is a broadcast channel: you can send a message without knowing who will receive it. As a result:

- You can generate a message before *anyone* knows who will receive it. In particular, an authority can make a single certificate asserting, for instance, that $RSA(K_a) \Rightarrow A$. This can be stored in any convenient place (secure or not), and anyone can receive it later, even if the authority is then off line.

- If you receive a message and forward it to someone else, he has the same assurance of its source that you have.

Table 21.1 shows that encryption need not slow down a system unduly. It also shows that shared key encryption is about 1000-5000 times faster than public key encryption when both are carefully implemented. Hence the latter is usually used only to encrypt small messages or to set up a shared key.

---

[6] Sometimes K^{-1} is used to denote the decryption key, but we prefer to associate encryption with sending and to use the simpler expression *K* for the public key.

	Hardware, bits/sec	Software, bits/sec/MIPS	Notes
RSA encrypt	220 K (Shand 1990)	.5 K (Comba 1990)	500 bit modulus
RSA decrypt	—	32 K (Comba 1990)	Exponent=3
MD4	—	1300 K (Rivest 1991)	
DES	1.2 G (Eberle 1992)	400 K (Comba 1990)	Software uses a 64 KB table/key

Table 21.1. Speeds of cryptographic operations[7]

From the existence of the bits $Encrypt(K^{-1}, s)$ anyone who knows K can infer K **says** s, so we tend to identify the bits and the statement; of course for the purposes of reasoning we use only the latter. We often call such a statement a *certificate*, because it is simply a sequence of bits that can be stored away and brought out when needed like a paper certificate. We say that K signs the certificate.

21.5   Principals with Names

When users refer to principals they must do so by names that make sense to people, since users can't understand alternatives like unique identifiers or keys. Thus an ACL must grant access to named principals.[8] But a request arrives on a channel, and it is granted only if the channel speaks for one of the principals on the ACL. In this section we study how to find a channel C that speaks for the named principal A.

There are two general methods, push and pull. Both produce the same credentials for A, a set of certificates and a proof that they establish $C \Rightarrow A$, but the two methods collect the certificates differently.

Push: The sender on the channel collects A's credentials and presents them when it needs to authenticate the channel to the receiver.

Pull: The receiver looks up A in some database to get credentials for A when it needs to authenticate the sender; we call this *name lookup*.

Our system uses the pull method, like DSSA (Gasser et al. [1989]) and unlike most other authentication protocols. But the credentials don't depend on the method. We describe them for the case we actually implement, where C is a public key.

---

[7] Many variables affect performance; consult the references for details, or believe these numbers only within a factor of two. The software numbers come from data in the references and assumed speeds of .5 MIPS for an 8 Mhz Intel 286 and 9 MIPS for a 20 MHz Sparc.

[8] Anonymous principals on ACLs are sometimes useful. For instance, a numbered bank account or highway toll account might grant its owner access by having on its ACL a public key negotiated when the account is established. But usually human review of the ACL must be possible.

21.5.1   A Single Certification Authority

The basic idea is that there is a *certification authority* that speaks for A and so is trusted when it says that C speaks for A, because of the handoff rule (P11). In the simplest system

- there is only one such authority CA,
- everyone trusts CA to speak for every named principal, and
- everyone knows CA's public key K_{ca}, that is, $K_{ca} \Rightarrow CA$.

So everyone can deduce $K_{ca} \Rightarrow A$ for every named A. At first this may seem too strong, but trusting CA to authenticate channels from A means that CA can speak for A, because it can authenticate as coming from A some channel that CA controls.

For each A that it speaks for, CA issues a certificate of the form K_{ca} **says** $K_a \Rightarrow A$ in which A is a name. The certificates are stored in a database and indexed by A. This database is usually called a name service; it is not part of the TCB because the certificates are digitally signed by K_{ca}. To get A's credentials you go to the database, look up A, get the certificate K_{ca} **says** $K_a \Rightarrow A$, verify that it is signed by the K_{ca} that you believe speaks for CA, and use the handoff rule to conclude $K_a \Rightarrow A$, just what you wanted to know. The right side of Figure 21.3 shows what B does, and the symmetric left side shows what A does to get two-way authentication.

The figure shows only the logical flow of secure messages. An actual implementation has extra insecure messages, and the bits of the secure ones may travel by circuitous paths. To push, the sender A calls the database to get K_{ca} **says** $K_a \Rightarrow A$ and sends it along with a message signed by K_a. To pull, the receiver B calls the database to get the same certificate when B gets a message that claims to be from A or finds A on an ACL. The Needham-Schroeder protocol [1978] combines push and pull: when A wants to talk to B it gets two certificates from CA, the familiar K_{ca} **says** $K_a \Rightarrow A$ which it pushes along to B, and K_{ca} **says** $K_b \Rightarrow B$ for A's channel from B.

As we have seen, with public key certificates it's not necessary to talk to CA directly; it suffices to talk to a database that stores CA's certificates. Thus CA itself can be normally off line, and hence much easier to make highly secure. Certificates from an off line CA, however, must have fairly long lifetimes. For rapid revocation we add an on line agent O and use the joint authority rule (P12). CA makes a weaker certificate K_{ca} **says** $(O \mid K_a \wedge K_a) \Rightarrow A$, and O countersigns this by making $O \mid K_a$ **says** $K_a \Rightarrow O \mid K_a$. From these two, $K_{ca} \Rightarrow A$, and (P12) we again get $K_a \Rightarrow A$, but now the lifetime is the minimum of those on CA's certificate and O's certificate. Since O is on line, its certificate can time out quickly and be refreshed often. Note that CA makes a separate certificate for each K_a it authenticates, and each such certificate makes it possible for O to convince a third party that $K_a \Rightarrow A$ only for specific values of K_a and A. Thus the TCB for granting access is just CA, because O acting on its own can't do anything, but CA speaks for A; the TCB for revocation is CA and O, since either one can prevent access from being revoked.

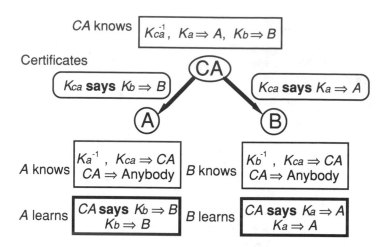

$$CA \text{ knows} \quad \boxed{Kca^{-1}, \; Ka \Rightarrow A, \; Kb \Rightarrow B}$$

Certificates

$$\boxed{Kca \textbf{ says } Kb \Rightarrow B} \qquad \text{(CA)} \qquad \boxed{Kca \textbf{ says } Ka \Rightarrow A}$$

(A)   (B)

$$A \text{ knows} \quad \boxed{\begin{matrix} Ka^{-1}, \; Kca \Rightarrow CA \\ CA \Rightarrow \text{Anybody} \end{matrix}} \quad B \text{ knows} \quad \boxed{\begin{matrix} Kb^{-1}, \; Kca \Rightarrow CA \\ CA \Rightarrow \text{Anybody} \end{matrix}}$$

$$A \text{ learns} \quad \boxed{\begin{matrix} CA \textbf{ says } Kb \Rightarrow B \\ Kb \Rightarrow B \end{matrix}} \quad B \text{ learns} \quad \boxed{\begin{matrix} CA \textbf{ says } Ka \Rightarrow A \\ Ka \Rightarrow A \end{matrix}}$$

Figure 21.3. Authenticating channels with one certification authority

Our system uses the pull method throughout; we discuss the implications in Sections 21.8 and 21.9. Hence we can use a cheap version of the joint authority scheme for revocation; in this version a certificate from CA is believed only if it comes from the server O that stores the database of certificates. To authenticate A we first authenticate a channel C_o from O. Then we interpret the presence of the certificate K_{ca} **says** $(O \mid K_a \wedge K_a) \Rightarrow A$ on the channel C_o as an encoding of the statement $C_o \mid K_a$ **says** $K_a \Rightarrow O \mid K_a$. Because $C_o \Rightarrow O$, this implies $O \mid K_a$ **says** $K_a \Rightarrow O \mid K_a$, which is the same statement as before, so we get the same conclusion. Note that O doesn't sign a public-key certificate for A, but we must authenticate the channel from O, presumably using the basic method. Or replace O by K_o everywhere. Either way, we can't revoke O's authority quickly; it's not turtles all the way down.

A straightforward alternative to an on line agent that asserts $O \mid K_a$ **says** $K_a \Rightarrow O \mid K_a$ is a 'black-list' agent or recent certificate that asserts "all of CA's certificates are valid except the ones for the following keys: $K_1, K_2, ...$" (CCITT [1988]). For obvious reasons this must be said in a single mouthful. Such revocation lists are used with Internet privacy-enhanced mail.

Changing a principal's key is easy. The principal chooses a new key pair and tells the certification authority its public key. The authority issues a new certificate and installs it in the database. If the key is being rolled over routinely rather than changed because of a suspected compromise, it may be desirable to leave the old certificate in the database for some time. Changing the authority's key is more difficult. First the authority chooses a new key pair. Then it writes a new certificate, signed by the new key, for each existing certificate, and installs the new certificates in the database. Next it distributes the new public key to all the clients; when a client gets the new key it stops trusting the old one. Finally, the old certificates can be removed from the database. While the new key is being distributed, certificates signed by both keys must stay in the database.

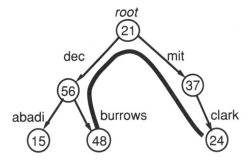

Figure 21.4. Authentication with a tree of authorities

The formalization of Figure 21.3 together with the relay scheme of Section 20.8.1 also describes the Kerberos protocol (Kohl, Neuman, and Steiner [1990], Steiner, Neuman, and Schiller [1988]), which differs in some details because it uses shared key rather than public key encryption.

21.5.2 Path Names and Multiple Authorities

In a large system there can't be just one certification authority—it's administratively impractical, and there may not be anyone who is trusted by everybody in the system. The authority to speak for names must be decentralized. There are many ways to do this, varying in how hard they are to manage and in which authorities a principal must trust in order to authenticate different parts of the name space.

If the name space is a tree, so that names are path names, it is natural to arrange the certification authorities in a corresponding tree. Because there is no global trust, a parent cannot unconditionally speak for its children; if it did, the root would speak for everyone. Instead when you want to authenticate a channel from $A = /A_1/A_2/.../A_n$ you start from an authority that you believe has the name $B = /B_1/B_2/.../B_m$ and traverse the authority tree along the shortest path from B to A, which runs up to the least common ancestor of B and A and back down to A. Figure 21.4 shows the path from /dec/burrows to /mit/clark; the numbers stand for public keys. The basic idea is described in Birrell et al. [1986]; it is also implemented in SPX (Tardo and Alagappan [1991]).

We can formalize this idea with a new kind of compound principal, written P **except** N, and some axioms that define its meaning. Here M or N is any simple name and P is any path name, that is, any sequence of simple names. We follow the usual convention and separate the simple names by '/' symbols.[9] Informally, P **except** N is a principal that speaks for any path name that is an extension of P as long as the first name after P isn't N, and for any prefix of P as long as N isn't '..'.

---

[9] We follow Unix conventions and write / for the root rather than the empty string that our axioms produce.

The purpose of **except** is to force a traversal of the authority tree to keep going outward, away from its starting point. If instead the traversal could retrace its steps, then a more distant authority would be authenticating a nearer one, contrary to our idea that trust should be as local as possible.

The axioms for **except** are:

$$\vdash P \text{ except } M \Rightarrow P \tag{N1}$$

So P **except** M is stronger than P; other axioms say how.

$$\vdash M \neq N \supset (P \text{ except } M) \mid N \Rightarrow P/N \text{ except } `..` \tag{N2}$$

P **except** M can speak for any path name P/N just by quoting N, as long as N isn't M. This lets us go down the tree (but not back up by (N3), because of the **except** `..`).

$$\vdash M \neq `..` \supset (P/N \text{ except } M) \mid `..` \Rightarrow P \text{ except } N \tag{N3}$$

P/N **except** M can speak for the shorter path name P just by quoting `..`, as long as M isn't `..`. This lets us go up the tree (but not back down the same path by (N2), because of the **except** N).

The quoting principals on the left side of $\Rightarrow$ prevent something asserted by P **except** M from automatically being asserted by all the longer path names. Note that usually both (N2) and (N3) apply. For instance, /dec **except** burrows speaks for /dec/abadi **except** `..` by (N2) and for / **except** dec by (N3).

Now we can describe the credentials that establish $C \Rightarrow A$. Suppose A is /mit/clark. To use the (N) rules we must start with a channel from some principal B that can authenticate path names; that is, we need to believe $C_b \Rightarrow B$ **except** N. This could be anyone, but it's simplest to let B be the authenticating party. In Figure 21.4 this is /dec/burrows, so initially we believe $C_{burrows} \Rightarrow$ /dec/burrows **except** nil, and this channel is trusted to authenticate both up and down. In other words, Burrows knows his name and his public key and trusts himself.[10] Then each principal on the path from B to A must provide a certificate for the next one. Thus we need

$C_{burrows}$	$\mid `..`$	**says** C_{dec}	$\Rightarrow$ /dec **except** burrows
C_{dec}	$\mid `..`$	**says** C_{root}	$\Rightarrow$ / **except** dec
C_{root}	$\mid$ mit	**says** C_{mit}	$\Rightarrow$ /mit **except** `..`
C_{mit}	$\mid$ clark	**says** C_{clark}	$\Rightarrow$ /mit/clark **except** `..`

The certificates quoting `..` can be thought of as 'parent' certificates pointing upward in the tree, those quoting mit and clark as 'child' certificates pointing downward. They are like the certificates specified by CCITT X.509 (CCITT [1988]).

From this and the assumption $C_{burrows} \Rightarrow$ /dec/burrows **except** nil, we deduce in turn the body of each certificate, because for each A' **says** $C' \Rightarrow B'$ we have $A' \Rightarrow B'$ by reasoning from the initial belief and the (N2-3) rules, and thus we can apply

---

[10] You may find it more natural to assume that Burrows knows the name and public key of his local certification authority. This corresponds to initially believing $C_{dec} \Rightarrow$ /dec **except** nil.

(P11) to get $C' \Rightarrow B'$. Then (N1) yields $C_{clark} \Rightarrow$ /mit/clark, which authenticates the channel C_{clark} from /mit/clark. In the most secure implementation each line represents a certificate signed by the public key of an off line certifier plus a message on some channel from an on line revocation agent; see Section 21.5.1. But any kind of channel will do.

If we start with a different assumption, we may not accept the bodies of all these certificates. Thus if /mit/clark is authenticating /dec/abadi, we start with $C_{clark} \Rightarrow$ /mit/clark **except**nil and believe the bodies of the certificates

C_{clark}	| '..'	**says** C_{mit}	$\Rightarrow$ /mit **except** clark
C_{mit}	| '..'	**says** C_{root}	$\Rightarrow$ / **except** mit
C_{root}	| dec	**says** C_{dec}	$\Rightarrow$ /dec **except** '..'
C_{dec}	| abadi	**says** C_{abadi}	$\Rightarrow$ /dec/abadi **except** '..'

Since this path is the reverse of the one we traversed before except for the last step, each principal that supplies a parent certificate on one path supplies a child certificate on the other. Note that clark would not accept the bodies of *any* of the certificates on the path from burrows. Also, the intermediate results of this authentication differ from those we saw before. For example, when B was /dec/burrows we got $C_{dec} \Rightarrow$ /dec **except** burrows, but if B is /mit/clark we get $C_{dec} \Rightarrow$ /dec **except** '..'. From either we can deduce $C_{dec} \Rightarrow$ /dec, but C_{dec}'s authority to authenticate other path names is different. This is because burrows and clark have different ideas about how much to trust dec.

Our method for authenticating path names using the (N) axioms requires B to trust each certification authority on the path from B up to the least common ancestor and back down to A. If the least common ancestor is lower in the tree then B needs to trust fewer authorities. We can make it lower by adding a 'cross-link' named mit from node 56 to node 37: C_{dec} **says** $C_{mit} \Rightarrow$ /dec/mit **except** '..'. Now /dec/mit/clark names A, and node 21 is no longer involved in the authentication. The price is more system management: the cross-link has to be installed, and it also has to be changed when mit's key changes. Note that although the tree of authorities is now a directed acyclic graph, the least-common-ancestor rule still applies, so it's still easy to explain who is being trusted.

The implementation obtains all these certificates by talking in turn to the databases that store certificates from the various authorities. This takes one RPC to each database in both pull and push models; the only difference is whether receiver or sender does the calls. If certificates from several authorities are stored in the same database, a single call can retrieve several of them. Either end can cache retrieved certificates; this is especially important for those from the higher reaches of the name space. The cache hit rate may differ between push and pull, depending on traffic patterns.

A principal doing a lookup might have channels from several other principals instead of the single channel C_b from itself that we described. Then it could start with the channel from the principal that is closest to the target A and thus reduce the number of intermediaries that must be trusted. This is essential if the entire name space is not connected, for instance if it is a forest with more than one root, since with only one starting point it is only possible to reach the names in one connected component of the name space. Each starting point means another built-in key, however, and maintaining these keys obviously makes it more complicated to manage the system.

When we use path names the names of principals are more likely to change, because they change when the directory tree is reorganized. This is familiar in file systems, where it is dealt with by adding either extra links or symbolic links to the renamed objects (usually directories) that allow old names to keep working. Our system works the same way; a link is a certificate asserting that some channel $C \Rightarrow P$, and a symbolic link is a certificate asserting $P' \Rightarrow P$. This makes pulling more attractive, because to push the sender must guess which name the receiver is using for the principal in order to provide the right certificates.

We can push without guessing if we add a level of indirection by giving each principal a unique identifier that remains the same in spite of name changes. Instead of $C \Rightarrow P$ we have $C \Rightarrow id$ and $id \Rightarrow P$. The sender pushes $C \Rightarrow id$ and the receiver pulls $id \Rightarrow P$. In general the receiver can't just use id, on an ACL for example, because it has to have a name so that people can understand the ACL. Of course it can cache $id \Rightarrow P$; this corresponds to storing both the name and the identifier on the ACL. There is one tricky point about this method: id can't simply be an integer, because there would be no way of knowing who can speak for it and therefore no way to establish $C \Rightarrow id$. Instead, it must have the form $A/integer$ for some other principal A, and we need a rule $A \Rightarrow A/integer$ so that A can speak for id. Now the problem has been lifted from arbitrary names like P to authorities like A, and maybe it is easier to handle.

21.5.3 Groups

A group is a principal that has no public key or other channel of its own. Instead, other principals speak for the group; they are its members. Looking up a group name G yields one or more group membership certificates K_{ca} **says** $P_1 \Rightarrow G$, K_{ca} **says** $P_2 \Rightarrow G$, ..., where $K_{ca} \Rightarrow G$, just as the result of looking up an ordinary principal name P is a certificate for its channel K_{ca} **says** $C \Rightarrow P$, where $K_{ca} \Rightarrow P$. A symbolic link can be viewed as a special case of a group.

This representation makes it impossible to prove that P is not a member of G. If there were just one membership certificate for the whole group, it would be possible to prove nonmembership, but that approach has severe drawbacks: the certificate for a large group is large, and it must be replaced completely every time the group loses or gains a member.

21.6   Roles and Programs

A principal often wants to limit its authority, in order to express the fact that it is acting according to a certain set of rules. For instance, a user may want to distinguish among playing an untrusted game program, doing normal work, and acting as system administrator. A node authorized to run several programs may want to distinguish running NFS from running an X server. To express such intentions we introduce the notion of *roles*.

If A is a principal and R is a role, we write A **as** R for A acting in role R. What do we want this to mean? Since a role is a way for a principal to limit its authority, A **as** R should be a weaker principal than A in some sense, because a principal should always be free to limit its own authority. One way for A to express the fact that it is acting in role R when it says s is for A to make A **says** R **says** s. This idea motivates us to treat a role as a kind of principal and to define A **as** R to be $A \mid R$, so that A **as** R **says** s is the same as A **says** R **says** s. Because $\mid$ is monotonic, **as** is also.

We capture the fact that A **as** R is weaker than A by assuming that A speaks for A **as** R. Because adopting a role implies behaving appropriately for that role, A must be careful that what it says on its own is appropriate for any role it may adopt. Note that we are not assuming $A \Rightarrow A \mid B$ in general, but only when B is a role. Formally, we introduce a subset *Roles* of the simple principals and axioms:

$$\vdash A \text{ as } R = A \mid R \quad \text{for all } R \in Roles \tag{R1}$$

$$\vdash A \Rightarrow A \text{ as } R \quad \text{for all } R \in Roles \tag{R2}$$

Acting in a certain way is much the same as executing a certain program. This suggests that we can equate a role with a program. Here by a program we mean something that obeys a specification—several different program texts may obey the same specification and hence be the same program in this sense. How can a principal know it is obeying a program?

If the principal is a person, it can just decide to do so; in this case we can't give any formal rule for when the principal should be willing to assume the role. Consider the example of a user acting as system manager for her workstation. Traditionally (in Unix) she does this by issuing a su command, which expresses her intention to issue further commands that are appropriate for the manager. In our system she assumes the role "user **as** manager". There is much more to be said about roles for users, enough to fill a paper.

If a machine is going to run the program, however, we can be more precise. One possibility that is instructive, though not at all practical, is to use the program text or image I as the role. So the node N can make N **as** I **says** s for a statement s made by a process running the program image I. But of course I is too big. A more practical method compresses I to a digest D small enough that it can be used directly as the role (see Chapter 20). Such a digest distinguishes one program from another as well as the entire program text does, so N can make N **as** D **says** s instead of N **as** I **says** s.

Digests are to roles in general much as encryption keys are to principals in general: they are unintelligible to people, and the same program specification may apply to several program texts (perhaps successive versions) and hence to several digests. In general we want the role to have a name, and we say that the digest speaks for the role. Now we can express the fact that digest D speaks for the program named P by writing $D \Rightarrow P$.[11] There are two ways to use this fact. The receiver of A **as** D **says** s can use $D \Rightarrow P$ to conclude that A **as** P **says** s because **as** is monotonic. Alternatively, A can use $D \Rightarrow P$ to justify making A **as** P **says** s whenever program D asserts s.

So far we have been discussing how a principal can decide what role to assume. The principal must also be able to convince others. Since we are encoding A **as** P as $A \mid P$, however, this is easy. To make A **as** P **says** s, A just makes A **says** P **says** s as we saw earlier, and to hand off A **as** P to some other channel C it makes A **as** P **says** $(C \Rightarrow A$ **as** $P)$.

21.6.1 Loading Programs

With these ideas we can explain exactly how to load a program securely. Suppose A is doing the loading. Usually A will be a node, that is, a machine running an operating system. Some principal B tells A to load program P; no special authority is needed for this except the authority to consume some of A's resources. In response, A makes a separate process pr to run the program, looks up P in the file system, copies the resulting program image into pr, and starts it up.

If A trusts the file system to speak for P, it hands off to pr the right to speak for A **as** P, using the mechanisms described in Section 21.8 or in the treatment of booting below; this is much like running a Unix `setuid` program. Now pr is a protected subsystem; it has an independent existence and authority consistent with the program it is running. Because pr can speak for A **as** P, it can issue requests to an object with A **as** P on its ACL, and the requests will be granted. Such an ACL entry should exist only if the owner of the object trusts A to run P. In some cases B might hand off to pr some of the principals it can speak for. For instance, if B is a shell it might hand off its right to speak for the user that is logged in to that shell.

If A doesn't trust the file system, it computes the digest D of the program text and looks up the name P to get credentials for $D \Rightarrow P$. Having checked these credentials it proceeds as before. There's no need for A to record the credentials, since no one else needs to see them; if you trust A to run P, you have to trust A not to lie to you when it says it is running P.

It is often useful to form a group of programs, for instance, `/com/dec/src-/trustedSW`. A principal speaking for this name, for example, the key K_{ca} of its certification authority, can issue the certificate K_{ca} **says** $P \Rightarrow$ `/com/dec/src-/trustedSW` for a trusted program P. If A **as** `/com/dec/src/trustedSW` appears on an ACL, any program P with such a certificate will get access when it runs on A because **as** is monotonic. Note that it's explicit in the name that `/com/dec/src` is certifying this particular set of trusted software.

---

[11] Connoisseurs of program specification will find this formula familiar—it looks like the implication relation between an implementation and its specification. This is certainly not an accident.

Virus control is one obvious application. To certify a program as virus-free we compute its digest D and issue a membership certificate K_{ca} **says** $D \Rightarrow$ trustedSW (from now on we elide /com/dec/src/). There are two ways to use this certificate:

- When A loads a program with digest D, it assigns the identity A **as** trustedSW to the loaded program if $D \Rightarrow$ trustedSW. Every object that should be protected from an untrusted program gets an ACL of the form (SomeNodes **as** trustedSW) $\wedge$ (...). Here SomeNodes is a group containing all the nodes that are trusted to access the object, and the ... gives the individuals that are trusted. Alternatively, if A sees no certificate for D it assigns the identity A **as** unknown to the loaded program; then the program will be able to access only objects whose ACLs explicitly grant access to SomeNodes **as** unknown.

- The node A has an ACL that controls the operation of loading a program into A, and trustedSW is on this ACL. No program is loaded unless its digest speaks for trustedSW. This method is appropriate when A cannot protect itself from a running program, for example, when A is a PC running MS-DOS.

There can also be groups of nodes. An ACL might contain DBServers **as** Ingres; then if $A \Rightarrow$ DBServers (A is a member of the group DBServers), A **as** Ingres gets access because **as** is monotonic. If we extend these ideas, DBSystems can be a principal that stands for a group of systems, with membership certificates such as DBServers**as** Ingres$\Rightarrow$ DBSystems, Mainframe**as** DB2 $\Rightarrow$ DBSystems, and so on.

21.6.2 Booting

Booting a machine is very much like loading a program. The result is a node that can speak for M **as** P, if M is the machine and P the name or digest of the program image that is booted. There are two interesting differences.

One is that the machine is the base case for authenticating a system, and it authenticates its messages by knowing a private key K_m^{-1} which is stored in non-volatile memory. Making and authenticating this key is part of installing M, that is, putting it into service when it arrives. In this process M constructs a public key pair (K_m, K_m^{-1}) and outputs the public key K_m. Then someone who can speak for the name M, presumably an administrator, makes a certificate K_{ca} **says** $K_m \Rightarrow M$. Alternatively, a certification authority constructs (K_m, K_m^{-1}), makes the certificate K_{ca} **says** $K_m \Rightarrow M$, and delivers K_m^{-1} to M in some suitably secure way. It is an interesting problem to devise a practical installation procedure.

The other difference is that when M (the boot code that gets control after the machine is reset) gives control to the program P that it boots (normally the operating system), M is handing over all the hardware resources of the machine, for instance any directly connected disks. This has three effects:

- Since M is no longer around, it can't multiplex messages from the node on its own channels. Instead, M invents a new public key pair (K_n, K_n^{-1}) at boot time, gives K_n^{-1} to P, and makes a certificate K_m **says** $K_n \Rightarrow M$ **as** P. The key K_n is the node key described in Section 21.4.

- M needs to know that P can be trusted with M's hardware resources. It's enough for M to know the digests of trustworthy programs, or the public key that is trusted to sign certificates for these digests. As with the second method of virus control, this amounts to an ACL for running on M.
- If we want to distinguish M itself from any of the programs it is willing to boot, then M needs a way to protect K_m^{-1} from these programs. This requires hardware that makes K_m^{-1} readable when the machine is reset, but can be told to hide it until the next reset. Otherwise one operating system that M loads could impersonate any other such system, and if any of them is compromised then M is compromised too.

The machine M also needs to know the name and public key of some principal that it can use to start the path name authentication described in Section 21.5; this principal can be M itself or its local certification authority. This information can be stored in M during installation, or it can be recorded in a certificate signed by K_m and supplied to M during booting along with P.

You might think that all this is too much to put into a boot ROM. Fortunately, it's enough if the boot ROM can compute the digest function and knows one digest (set at installation time) that it trusts completely. Then it can just load the program P_{boot} with that digest, and P_{boot} can act as part of M. In this case, of course, M gives K_m^{-1} to P_{boot} to express its complete trust.

21.7   Delegation

We have seen how a principal can hand off all of its authority to another, and how a principal can limit its authority using roles. We now consider a combination of these two methods that allows one principal to *delegate* some of its authority to another one. For example, a user on a workstation may wish to delegate to a compute server, much as she might `rlogin` to it in vanilla Unix. The server can then access files on her behalf as long as their ACLs allow this access. Or a user may delegate to a database system, which combines its authority with the delegation to access the files that store the database.

The intuitive idea of delegation is imprecise, but our formal treatment gives it a precise meaning. We express delegation with one more operator on principals, B **for** A. Intuitively this principal is B acting on behalf of A, who has delegated to B the right to do so. The basic axioms of **for** are:

$$\vdash A \wedge B|A \Rightarrow B \textbf{ for } A. \tag{D1}$$

$$\vdash \textbf{for is monotonic and distributes over } \wedge. \tag{D2}$$

To establish a delegation, A first delegates to B by making

$$A \textbf{ says } B|A \Rightarrow B \textbf{ for } A. \tag{1}$$

We use $B\,|\,A$ so that B won't speak for B **for** A by mistake. Then B accepts the delegation by making

$$B \mid A \text{ says } B \mid A \Rightarrow B \text{ for } A. \tag{2}$$

To put it another way, **for** equals delegation (1) plus quoting (2). We need this explicit action by B because when B **for** A says something, the intended meaning is that *both* A and B contribute, and hence both must consent. Now we can deduce

$(A \wedge B \mid A) \text{ says } B \mid A \Rightarrow B \text{ for } A$ using (P1), (1), (2);

$B \mid A \Rightarrow B \text{ for } A$ using (D1) and (P11).

In other words, given (1) and (2), B can speak for B **for** A by quoting A.

We use timeouts to revoke delegations. A gives (1) a fairly short lifetime, say 30 minutes, and B must ask A to refresh it whenever it's about to expire.

21.7.1 Login

A minor variation of the basic scheme handles delegation from the user U to the workstation W on which she logs in. The one difference arises from the assumption that the user's key K_u is available only while she is logging in. This seems reasonable, since getting access to the user's key will require her to type her password or insert her smart card and type a PIN; the details of login protocols are discussed elsewhere (Abadi et al. [1991], Steiner, Neuman, and Schiller [1988], Tardo and Alagappan [1991]). Hence the user's delegation to the workstation at login must have a rather long lifetime, so that it doesn't need to be refreshed very often. We therefore use the joint authority rule (P12) to make this delegation require a countersignature by a temporary public key K_l. This key is made at login time and called the login session key. When the user logs out, the workstation forgets K_l^{-1} so that it can no longer refresh any credentials that depend on the login delegation, and hence can no longer act for the user after the 30-minute lifetime of the delegation has expired. This protects the user in case the workstation is compromised after she logs out. If the workstation might be compromised within 30 minutes after a logout, then it should also discard its master key and node key at logout.

The credentials for login start with a long-term delegation from the user to $K_w \wedge K_l$ (here K_w is the workstation's node key), using K_u for A and K_w for the second B in (1):

$$K_u \text{ says } (K_w \wedge K_l) \mid K_u \Rightarrow K_w \text{ for } K_u.$$

K_w accepts the delegation in the usual way, so we know that

$$(K_w \wedge K_l) \mid K_u \Rightarrow K_w \text{ for } K_u,$$

and because | distributes over $\wedge$ we get

$$K_w \mid K_u \wedge K_l \mid K_u \Rightarrow K_w \text{ for } K_u.$$

Next K_l signs a short-term certificate

K_l **says** $K_w \Rightarrow K_l$.

This lets us conclude that $K_w | K_u \Rightarrow K_l | K_u$ by the handoff rule and the monotonicity of |. Now we can apply (P12) and reach the usual conclusion for delegation, but with a short lifetime:

$K_w | K_u \Rightarrow K_w$ **for** K_u.

21.7.2   Long-Running Computations

What about delegation to a process that needs to keep running after the user has logged out, such as a batch job? We would still like some control over the duration of the delegated authority, and some way to revoke it on demand. The basic idea is to introduce a level of indirection by having a single highly available agent for the user that replaces the login workstation and refreshes the credentials for long-running jobs. The user can tell this agent exactly which credentials should be refreshed. We have not worked out the details of this scheme; it is a tricky exercise in balancing the demands of convenience, availability, and security. Disconnected operation raises similar issues.

21.8   Authenticating Interprocess Communication

We have established the foundation for our authentication system: the theory of principals, encrypted secure channels, name lookup to find the channels or other principals that speak for a named principal, and compound principals for roles and delegation. This section explains the mechanics of authenticating messages from one process to another. In other words, we study how one process can make another accept a statement A **says** s. A single process must be able to speak for several A's; thus, a database server may need to speak for its client during normal operation and for itself during recovery.

   Figure 21.5 is an expanded version of the example in Figure 21.1. For each component it indicates the principals that the component speaks for and the channel it can send on (usually an encryption key). Thus the Taos node speaks for WS **as** Taos and has the key K_n^{-1} so it can send on channel K_n. The accounting application speaks for WS **as** Taos **as** Accounting **for** bw1; it runs as process pr, which means that the node will let it send on $K_n | pr$ or $C | pr$. Consider a request from the accounting application to read file foo. It has the form $C | pr$ **says** "read foo"; in other words, $C | pr$ is the channel carrying the request. This channel speaks for K_{ws} **as** Taos **as** Accounting **for** K_{bwl}. The credentials of $C | pr$ are:

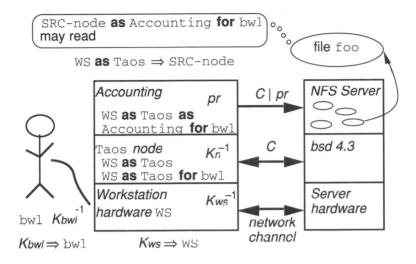

Figure 21.5. Principals and keys for the workstation-server example

K_{ws} **says** $K_n \Rightarrow K_{ws}$ **as** Taos From booting WS (Section 21.6).

K_{bwl} **says** $(K_n \wedge K_l) \mid K_{bwl} \Rightarrow K_n$ **for** K_{bwl} From bwl's login (Section 21.7).

K_l **says** $K_n \Rightarrow K_l$ Also from login.

$K_n \mid K_{bwl}$ **says** $C \mid pr \Rightarrow ((K_{ws}$ **as** Taos) Sent on $C \mid K_{bwl}$.

as Accounting**) for** K_{bwl}

The server gets certificates for the first three premises in the credentials. The last premise does not have a certificate. Instead, it follows directly from a message on the shared key channel C between the Taos node and the server, because this channel speaks for K_n as described in Section 21.4.

To turn these into credentials of $C \mid pr$ for WS **as** Taos **as** Accounting **for** bwl, the server must obtain the certificates that authenticate channels for the names bwl and WS from the certification database as described in Section 21.5. Finally, to complete the access check, the server must obtain the group membership certificate WS **as** Taos $\Rightarrow$ SRC-node. A system using the push model would substitute names for one or both of the keys K_{ws} and K_{bwl}. It would also get the name certificates for WS and bwl from the database and add them to the credentials.

The rest of this section explains in some detail how this scheme works in practice and extends it so that a single process can conveniently speak for a number of principals.

21.8.1 Interprocess Communication Channels

We describe the details of our authenticated interprocess communication mechanism in terms of messages from a sender to a receiver. The mechanism allows a message to be interpreted as one or more statements A **says** s. Our system

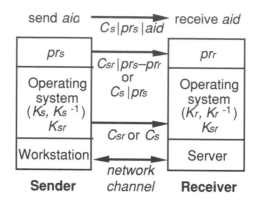

Figure 21.6. Multiplexing a node-to-node channel

implements remote procedure call, so it has call and return messages. For a call, statements are made by the caller (the client) and interpreted by the called procedure (the server); for a return, the reverse is true.

Most messages use a channel between a sending process on the sending node and a receiving process on the receiving node. As we saw in the example, this channel is made by multiplexing a channel C_{sr} between the two nodes, using the two process identifiers pr_s and pr_r as the multiplexing address, so it is $C_{sr} \mid pr_s\text{–}pr_r$; see Figure 21.6. A shared key K_{sr} defines the node-to-node channel $C_{sr} = \text{DES}(K_{sr})$.

Henceforth we concentrate on the integrity of the channels,[12] so we care only that the message comes from the sender, not that it goes to the receiver. Chapter 20 explains how to establish $\text{DES}(K_{sr}) \Rightarrow \text{RSA}(K_s)$, where K_s is the sending node's public key. So we can say that the message goes over $C_s \mid pr_s$ from the sending process, where $C_s = \text{RSA}(K_s)$. Some messages don't use $\text{DES}(K_{sr})$ but instead are certificates encrypted with K_s because they must be passed on to a third party that doesn't know K_{sr}; we indicate this informally by writing K_s **says** s instead of C_s **says** s.

The sender wants to communicate one or more statements A **says** s to the receiver, where A is some principal that the sender can speak for. A single process may speak for several principals, and we express this by multiplexing the channel from the process. Our strategy is to encode A as a number called an *authentication identifier* or *aid*, and to pass the *aid* as an ordinary integer. By convention, the receiver interprets a call like Read(aid, file, ...) as one or more statements C_{aid} **says** s, where $C_{aid} = C_s \mid pr_s \mid aid$; this is the channel $C_s \mid pr_s$ from the process multiplexed with *aid* as the subchannel address. The receiving node supplies $C_s \mid pr_s$ to the receiver on demand. Recall that C_s is obtained directly from the key used to decrypt the message and pr_s is supplied by the sending

---

[12] It is obvious that we also get secrecy, as a byproduct of using shared keys. We could show this by the dual of the arguments we make for integrity, paying attention to the receiver rather than the sender.

node. The *aid* is supplied by the sending process. An *aid* is chosen from a large enough space that it is never reused during the lifetime of the sending node (until the node is rebooted and its C_s changes); this ensures that a channel C_{aid} is never reused.

This design is good because the sending process doesn't need to tell the operating system about *aid* in order to send C_{aid} **says** *s* to the receiver, since *aid* is just an integer. The only role of the operating system is to implement the channel $C_s \mid pr_s$ securely by labelling each message with the process pr_s that sends it. Thus a principal is passed as cheaply as an integer, except for a one-time cost that we now consider.

The receiver doesn't actually care much about C_{aid}; it wants to interpret the message as *A* **says** *s* for some more meaningful principal *A* such as a user's name or public key. To do this, it needs to know $C_{aid} \Rightarrow A$; we call *A* the *meaning* of C_{aid}. There are two parts to this: finding out what *A* is, and getting a proof that $C_{aid} \Rightarrow A$ (that is, credentials for *A*). The receiver gets *A* and the credentials from the sender. Recall that the credentials consist of some premises *C* **says** $A' \Rightarrow B'$ plus the reasoning that derives $C_{aid} \Rightarrow A$ from the premises and the axioms.

The meaning *A* of C_{aid} is an expression whose operands are names or channels; in either case the credentials must prove that the sending channel C_s can speak for *A*. In our system all the operands of *A* are either roles or the public keys of nodes or of users; in the example of Figure 21.5 the keys are K_{ws} and K_{bwl}, and all the names are roles. Sections 21.6 and 21.7 explain how the sending system gets credentials for these keys as a result of booting or login. Section 21.5 explains how the receiving system pulls credentials that authenticate these keys as speaking for named principals.

21.8.2   The Authentication Agent

Thus the credentials are a collection of certificates and statements from the sender, together with the connective tissue that assembles them into a proof of $C_{aid} \Rightarrow A$. The receiver gets them from the sender, checks the proof, and caches the result. In our system a component of the receiver's operating system called the *authentication agent* does this work for the receiver.

The receiving process:

- gets a message containing *aid*, interpreted as *aid* **says** *s*;
- learns from its operating system that the message came on channel $C_s \mid pr_s$ (this is exactly like learning the source address of a message), so it believes $C_s \mid pr_s$ **says** *aid* **says** *s*, which is the same as $C_s \mid pr_s \mid aid$ **says** *s*;
- calls on its local agent to learn the principal *A* that $C_{aid} = C_s \mid pr_s \mid aid$ speaks for, so it believes *A* **says** *s*;
- and perhaps caches the fact that $C_{aid} \Rightarrow A$ to avoid calling the agent again if it gets another message from C_{aid}.

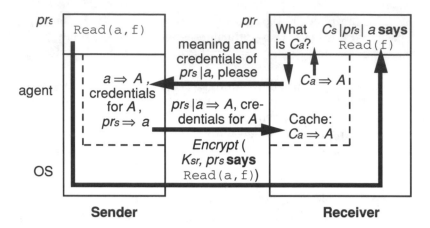

Figure 21.7. Messages to the agents for authenticating a channel

The process doesn't need to see the credentials, since it trusts its agent to check them just as it trusts its operating system for virtual memory and the other necessities of life. The process does need to know their lifetime, since the information $C_{aid} \Rightarrow A$ that it may want to cache must be refreshed after that time. Figure 21.7 shows communication through the agent.

The agent has three jobs: caching credentials, supplying credentials, and handing off authorities.

Its first job, acting for the receiver, is to maintain a cache of $C_{aid} \Rightarrow A$ facts and lifetimes like the cache maintained by its client processes. The agent answers queries out of the cache if it can. Because this is a cache, the agent can discard entries whenever it likes. If the information it needs isn't in the cache, the receiver's agent asks the sender's agent for the meaning and credentials of C_{aid}, checks the credentials it gets back, and caches the meaning.

The agent's second job, acting now for the sender, is to respond to these requests. To do this it keeps track of

- the meaning A of each *aid* a that it is responsible for (note that a is local to the node, not to a channel),
- the certificates it needs to make a's credentials, that is, to prove $C_s | a \Rightarrow A$, and
- the processes that are allowed to speak for a (that is, the processes pr such that the agent believes $pr | a \Rightarrow a$ and hence is willing to authenticate $C_s | pr | a$ as A).

An *authority* is an *aid* that a process speaks for. For a process to have an authority, its agent must have credentials to prove that some channel controlled by the agent speaks for the authority's meaning, and the agent must agree that the process speaks for the authority. Each process pr starts out with one authority, which it obtains by virtue of a user login or of the program P running in pr. In the latter case, for example, the node N loading P makes a new authority a, tells pr

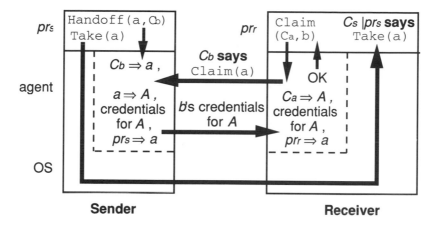

Figure 21.8. Messages to the agents for handing off an authority

what it is, and records $a \Rightarrow N$ **as** P and $pr \mid a \Rightarrow a$.

The process can get its initial authority by calling Self(). If it has authorities a and b, it can get the authorities $a \wedge b$ by calling And(a, b) and a **as** r by calling As(a, r). It can give up a by calling Discard(a). What the agent knows about an authority is original information, unlike the cached facts $C_{aid} \Rightarrow A$. Hence the agent must keep it until all the processes that speak for the authority discard it or disappear.

The agent's third job is to hand off authorities from one process to another, as shown in Figure 21.8. A sending process can hand off the authority a to another principal b by calling Handoff(a, C_b). This is a statement to its local agent: a **says** $C_b \Rightarrow a$, where $C_b = C_r \mid pr_r \mid b$. The agent believes it because of (P10). The process can then pass a to the receiving process by sending it a message in the usual way, say by calling Take(a). If pr_r has the authority b, it can obtain the authority a by calling Claim(C_a, b). This causes the receiving agent to call the sending agent requesting its credentials for the meaning A of a (proof that $K_s \mid a \Rightarrow A$) plus the certificate $K_s \mid a$ **says** $K_r \mid a \Rightarrow A$. These are credentials that allow the receiving agent to speak for A. The certificate lets $K_r \mid a$ speak for A rather than a because the receiver needs to be able to prove its right to speak for the meaningful principal A, not the authentication identifier a. The certificate is directly signed by K_s (the sender's public key), rather than simply sent on $DES(K_{sr})$ (the shared key channel between sender and receiver) because the receiver needs something that it can pass on to a third party.

Claiming an authority has no effect unless you use it by passing it on to another process. This means that the claiming can be automatic. Suppose that process pr passes on an authority a, the recipient asks for a's credentials, and pr hasn't claimed a. In this case pr's agent can claim a automatically as long as pr has the authority for b.

When is it appropriate to hand off an authority a? Doing this allows the recipient to speak for a as freely as you can, so you should do it only if you trust the recipient with *a* as much as you trust yourself. If you don't, you should hand off only a weaker authority, for instance one that corresponds to a delegation as described in Section 21.7. The login procedure of Section 21.7.1 is an example of this: the user hands off authority for "machine **for** user" rather than her entire authority.

Our system has two procedures for dealing with delegation, one for each of the certificates (1) and (2) in Section 21.7. A process calls For(a, C_b) to delegate the meaning *A* of *a* to the meaning *B* of the principal C_b; this corresponds to making (1), which in this context is *a* **says** $C_b | a \Rightarrow B$ **for** *A*. Before it calls For, the process normally checks C_b against some ACL that expresses the principals to which it is willing to delegate.

Now the process can pass *a* to a receiver that has an authority *b* corresponding to C_b, and the receiver calls Accept(a, b) to obtain an authority *result* that speaks for *B* **for** *A*. This call corresponds to claiming *B* **for** *A*, making (2), which in this context is $C_b | a$ **says** $b | a \Rightarrow B$ **for** *A*, and making $b | a$ **says** *result* $\Rightarrow B$ **for** *A*. The sending agent supplies a certificate signed by its public key, $K_s | a$ **says** $K_r | a \Rightarrow B$ **for** *A*, along with *a*'s credentials that prove $K_s | a \Rightarrow A$, just as in an ordinary handoff. The receiving agent can construct credentials for *B* **for** *A* based on the credentials it has for *B*, the claimed certificate and credentials, and the reasoning in Section 21.7. So the receiver can prove to others its right to speak for *B* **for** *A*.

You might feel that it's clumsy to require explicit action at both ends; after all, the ordinary handoff can be claimed automatically. But the two cases are not the same. In accepting the **for** and using the resulting authority, the receiver adds the weight of authority *b* to the authority from the sender. It should not do this accidentally.

What about revocation? The sending agent signs a handoff (or delegation) certificate that expires fairly soon, typically in about 30 minutes. This means that the handoff must be refreshed every 30 minutes by asking the sender for credentials again. If the sender's credentials in turn depend on a handoff from some other sender, the refresh will work its way up the chain of senders and back down. To keep the cost linear in the depth of handoff, we check all the certificates in a set of credentials whenever any one expires, and refresh those that are about to expire. This tends to synchronize the lifetimes.

Table 21.4 summarizes the state of the agent. Table 21.5 summarizes the interface from a process to its local agent.

There are many possible variations on the basic scheme described above. Here are some interesting ones:

- Each thread can have an authority that is passed automatically in every message it sends. This gets rid of most authority arguments, but it is less flexible and less explicit than the basic scheme in which each message specifies its authorities.

Key	(K_n, K_n^{-1}), the public key pair of this node.
Principal cache	A table mapping a channel $C_a = C_s \mid pr_s \mid a$ to A. An entry means the agent has seen credentials proving $C_a \Rightarrow A$; the entry also has a lifetime.
Authorities	A table mapping an *aid* a to A, the principal that a speaks for. Credentials to prove this agent can speak for A. A set of local processes that can speak for a. A set of C_b that can speak for a.

Table 21.4. The state of an agent

Procedure	**Meaning**
`Self() : A`	
`Discard(a: A)`	
`And(a: A, b: A): A`	$a \wedge b$ **says** *result* $\Rightarrow a \wedge b$
`As(a: A, r: Role): A`	$a \mid r$ **says** *result* $\Rightarrow a$ **as** r
`Handoff(a: A, b: C)`	a **says** $b \rightarrow a$
`Claim(a: C, b: A): A`	Retrieve a **says** $b \rightarrow a$; b **says** *result* $\Rightarrow a$
`For(a: A, b: C)`	a **says** $b \mid a \Rightarrow b$ **for** a
`Accept(a: C, b: A): A`	Retrieve a **says** $b \mid a \Rightarrow b$ **for** a ; $b \mid a$ **says** $b \mid a \Rightarrow b$ **for** a $\wedge$ *result* $\Rightarrow b \mid a$

`CheckAccess(acl: ACL, b: C,`
`            op: Operation )`
`            : Boolean`
	Does *acl* grant b the right to do *op*?

Types: A for authority, represented as *aid*.
            C for channel principal, which is $C_{aid} = C_s \mid pr_s \mid aid$.

Table 21.5. Programming interface from a process to its local agent

- In the basic scheme, authentication is symmetric between call and return; this means that each call can return the principal responsible for the result or hand off an authority. Often, however, the caller wants to authenticate the channel from the server only once. It can do this when it establishes the RPC binding if this operation returns an *aid* for the server's authority. This is called 'mutual authentication'.
- Instead of passing certificates for all the premises of the credentials, the

sending agent can pass the name of a place to find the certificates. This is especially interesting if that place is a trusted on line server which can authenticate a channel from itself, because that server can then just assert the premise rather than signing a certificate for it. For example, in a system with centralized management there might be a trusted database server to store group memberships. Here 'trusted' means that it speaks for these groups. This method can avoid a lot of public key encryption.

- It's possible to send the credentials with the first use of a; this saves a round trip. However, recognizing the first use of a may be difficult. The callback mechanism is still needed for refreshing the credentials.

21.8.3 Granting Access

Even a seemingly endless chain of remote calls will eventually result in an attempt to actually access an object. For instance, a call `Read(file f, authority a)` will be interpreted by the receiver as C_a **says** "read file f". The receiver obtains the ACL for f and wants to know whether C_a speaks for a principal that can have read access. To find this out the receiver calls `CheckAccess(f's acl, Ca, read)`, which returns true or false. Section 21.9 explains how this works.

21.8.4 Pragmatics

The performance of our interprocess authentication mechanism depends on the cache hit rates and the cost of loading the caches. Each time a receiving node sees C_a for the first time, there is a miss in its cache and a fairly expensive call to the sender for the meaning and credentials. This call takes one RPC time plus the time to check any certificates the receiver hasn't seen before (on an m-MIPS processor, about $40/m$ ms per certificate with 512-bit RSA keys). Each time a receiving process sees C_a for the first time, there is one operating system call time and a fast lookup in the agent's cache. Later the process finds C_a in its own cache, which it can access in a few dozen instructions.

When lifetimes expire, it's as though the cache was flushed. We typically use 30-minute lifetimes, so it costs less than 0.0001% to refresh one certificate on a 20 MIPS processor. If a node has 50 C_a's in constant use with two different certificates each, this is 0.01%.

The authentication agent could be local to a receiving process, so that the operating system wouldn't be involved and the process identifiers wouldn't be needed. We put the agent in the operating system for a number of reasons:

- When acting for a sender, the agent has to respond to asynchronous calls from receivers. Although the sending process could export the agent interface, this is a lot of machinery to have in every process.
- An agent in the operating system can optimize the common case of authentication between two processes on the same node. This is especially

important for handing off an authority a from a parent to a child process, which is very common in Unix. All the agent has to do is check that the parent speaks for a and add the child to the set of processes that speak for a. This can be implemented almost exactly like the standard Unix mechanism for handing off a file descriptor from a parent to a child.

- The agent must deal with encryption keys, and cryptographic religion says that key handling should be localized as much as possible. Of course we could have put just this service in the operating system, at some cost in complexity.

- Process-to-process encryption channels mean many more keys to establish and keep track of.

- The operating system must be trusted anyway, so we are not missing a chance to reduce the size of the trusted computing base.

21.9 Access control

Finally we have reached our goal: deciding whether to grant a request to access an object. We follow the conventional model of controlling access by means of an access control list or ACL attached to the object, as described in Section 21.1.

We take an ACL to be a set of principals, each with some rights to the ACL's object.[13] The ACL grants a request A **says** s if A speaks for B and B is a principal on the ACL that has all the rights the request needs. So the reference monitor needs an algorithm that will generate a proof of $A \Rightarrow B$ (then it grants access), or determine that no such proof exists (then it denies access). This is harder than the task of constructing the credentials for a request, because there we are building up a principal one step at a time and building the proof at the same time. And it is much harder than checking credentials, because theorem proving is much harder than proof checking. So it's not surprising that we have to restrict the form of ACLs to get an algorithm that is complete (that is, always finds a proof if there is one) and also runs reasonably fast.

There are many ways to do this. Our choice is described by the following grammar for the principal in an ACL entry or a request:

principal	::=	forList | principal $\wedge$ forList
forList	::=	asList | forList **for** asList
asList	::=	properPrincipal | asList **as** role
role	::=	pathName
properPrincipal	::=	pathName | channel

The roles and the properPrincipals must be disjoint.

In addition to A and a set of B's we also have as input a set of premises $P \Rightarrow Q$,

---

[13] A capability for an object can be viewed as a principal that is automatically on the ACL.

where P and Q are properPrincipals or roles. The premises arise from group membership certificates or from path name lookup; they are just like the premises in credentials.

Now there is an efficient algorithm to test $A \Rightarrow B$:

- Each forList in B must have one in A that speaks for it.
- One forList speaks for another if they have the same length and each asList in the first forList speaks for the corresponding asList in the second forList.
- A as R_1 as ... as $R_n \Rightarrow B$ as R_1' as ... as R_m' if $A \Rightarrow B$ and for each R_j there is an R_k' such that $R_j \Rightarrow R_k'$.
- One role or properPrincipal A speaks for another B if there is a chain of premises $A = P_0 \Rightarrow ... \Rightarrow P_n = B$.

The inputs to the algorithm are the ACL, the requesting principal, and the premises. We know how to get the ACL (attached to the object) and the principal (Section 21.8). Recall that because we use the pull model, the requesting principal is an expression in which every operand is either a role or a public key that is expected to speak for some named principal; Section 21.8 gives an example. What about the premises? As we have seen, they can be either pushed by the sender or pulled from a database by the receiver. Our system pulls all the premises needed to authenticate a channel from a name, by looking up the name as described in Section 21.5.

If there are many principals on the ACL or many members of a group, it will take too long to look up all their names. We deal with this by

- attaching an integer hint called a *tag* to every named principal on an ACL or in a group membership certificate,
- sending with the credentials a tag for each principal involved in the request, and
- looking up a name only if its tag appears in the request or if it is specially marked to be looked up unconditionally (for instance, the name of a group that is local to the receiver).

The tags don't have to be unique, just different enough to make it unlikely that two distinct named principals have the same tag. For instance, if the chance of this is less than .001 we will seldom do any extra lookups in a set of 500 names.

Note that a request with missing tags is denied. Hence a request must claim membership in all groups that aren't looked up unconditionally, by including their tags. In particular, it must claim any large groups; they are too expensive to look up unconditionally. This is a small step toward the push model, in which a request must claim all the names that it speaks for and present the proof of its claims as well.

What about denying access to a specific principal? This is tricky for two reasons:

- Principals can have more than one name or key.

- Certificates are stored insecurely, so we can't securely determine that a principal is *not* in a group because we can't count on finding the membership certificate if it is in the group.

The natural form of denial for us is an ACL modifier which means that the access checker should disbelieve a certificate for any principal that satisfies some property. For example, we can disbelieve certificates for a principal with a given name, or one with a given key, or one whose name starts with 'A', or one with a given tag (in which case the tags should be unique or we will sometimes deny access improperly). The idea behind this approach is that the system should be fail-secure: in case of doubt it should deny access. So it views positive premises like $A \Rightarrow B$ skeptically, negative ones like "deny Jim access" trustingly.

Instead, we can represent the entire membership of a group securely, either by entrusting it to a secure on line server or by using a single certificate that lists all the members. But these methods sacrifice availability or performance, so it is best to use them only when the extra information is really needed.

21.9.1 Auditing

Our theory yields a formal proof for every access control decision. The premises in the proof are statements made on channels or assumptions made by the reference monitor (for instance the premise that starts off a name lookup). Every step in the proof is justified by one of a small number of rules, all listed in the appendix. The proof can be written into the audit trail, and it gives a complete account of what access was granted and why. The theory thus provides a formal basis for auditing. Furthermore, we can treat intermediate results of the form $A \Rightarrow B$ as lemmas to be proved once and then referenced in other proofs. Thus the audit trail can use storage efficiently.

21.10 Conclusion

We have presented a theory that explains many known methods for authentication in distributed systems:

- the secure flow of information in the Needham-Schroeder and Kerberos protocols;
- authentication in a hierarchical name space;
- many variations in the paths along which bits are transmitted: from certification authority to sender to receiver, from certification authority directly to receiver, etc.;
- lifetimes and refreshing for revoking grants of authority;
- unique identifiers as partial substitutes for principal names.

The theory also explains a number of new methods used in our system for:

- treating certificates and online communication with authorities as logically equivalent mechanisms;
- revoking secure long-lived certificates rapidly by requiring them to be countersigned with refreshable short-lived ones;
- loading programs and booting machines securely;
- delegating authority in a way that combines and limits the power of both parties;
- passing RPC arguments or results that are principals as efficiently as passing integers (after an initial startup cost), and refreshing their authority automatically;
- taking account of roles and delegations in granting access.

The system has been implemented. The basic structure of agents, authentication identifiers, authorities, and ACLs is in place. Our operating system and distributed file system are both clients of our authentication and access control. This means that our ACLs appear on files, processes, and other operating system objects, not just on new objects like name service entries. Node-to-node channel setup, process-to-process authentication, roles, delegation, and secure loading are all working, and our implementation is the default authentication system for the 50 researchers at SRC.

Acknowledgements

This is joint work with Martín Abadi, Michael Burrows, and Edward Wobber. Many of the ideas discussed here were developed as part of the Digital Distributed System Security Architecture (Gasser et al. [1989], Gasser and McDermott [1990], Linn [1990]) or were greatly influenced by it. Morrie Gasser, Andy Goldstein, and Charlie Kaufman made major contributions to that work.

References

Abadi, M., Burrows, M., Kaufman, C., and Lampson, B. (1991), Authentication and Delegation with Smart-Cards. In *Theoretical Aspects of Computer Software*, LNCS 526, Springer, 326-345. Also Res. Rep. 67, Systems Research Center, Digital Equipment Corp., Palo Alto, Calif., Oct. 1990. To appear in *Science of Computer Programming*.

Abadi, M., Burrows, M., Lampson, B., and Plotkin, G. (1992), A Calculus for Access Control in Distributed Systems. In *Advances in Cryptology — Crypto '91*, LNCS 576, Springer, 1-23. Also Res. Rep. 70, Systems Research Center, Digital

Equipment Corp., Palo Alto, Calif., March 1991. To appear in *ACM Trans. Program. Lang. Syst.*

Birrell, A., Lampson, B., Needham, R., and Schroeder, M. (1986), Global Authentication Without Global Trust. In *Proceedings of the IEEE Symposium on Security and Privacy*, Oakland, Calif., 223-230.

Burrows, M., Abadi, M., and Needham, R. (1990), A Logic of Authentication. *ACM Trans. Comput. Syst.* **8** (1), 18-36. An expanded version appeared in *Proc. Royal Society* A *426* (1871), 233-271 and as Res. Rep. 39, Systems Research Center, Digital Equipment Corp., Palo Alto, Calif., Feb. 1989.

CCITT (1988), *Information Processing Systems — Open Systems Interconnection — The Directory Authentication Framework.* CCITT 1988 Recommendation X.509. Also ISO/IEC 9594-8:1989.

Comba, P. (1990), Exponentiation Cryptosystems on the IBM PC. *IBM Syst. J.* **28** (4), 526-538.

Davis, D. and Swick, R. (1990), Network Security via Private-Key Certificates. *ACM Oper. Syst. Rev.* **24** (4), 64-67.

Denning, D. (1976), A Lattice Model of Secure Information Flow. *Commun. ACM* **19** (5), 236-243.

Department of Defense. (1985), *Trusted Computer System Evaluation Criteria.* DOD 5200.28-STD.

Diffie, W. and Hellman, M. (1976), New Directions in Cryptography. *IEEE Trans. Inf. Theor.* **IT-22** (6), 644-654.

Eberle, H. and Thacker, C. (1992), A 1 Gbit/second GaAs DES Chip. In *Proceedings of the IEEE 1992 Custom Integrated Circuit Conference*, Boston, Mass., 19.7.1-19.7.4.

Gasser, M., Goldstein, A., Kaufman, C., and Lampson, B. (1989), The Digital Distributed System Security Architecture. In *Proceedings of the 12th National Computer Security Conference*, Baltimore, Md., 305-319.

Gasser, M., and McDermott, E. (1990), An Architecture for Practical Delegation in a Distributed System. In *Proceedings of the IEEE Symposium on Security and Privacy*, Oakland, Calif., 20-30.

Herbison, B. (1990), Low Cost Outboard Cryptographic Support for SILS and SP4. In *Proceedings of the 13th National Computer Security Conference*, Baltimore, Md., 286-295.

Kohl, J., Neuman, C., and Steiner, J. (1990), The Kerberos Network Authentication Service. Version 5, draft 3, Project Athena, MIT, Cambridge, Mass.

Lampson, B. (1974), Protection. *ACM Oper. Syst. Rev.* **8** (1), 18-24.

Lampson, B., Abadi, M., Burrows, M., and Wobber, E. (1992), Authentication in Distributed Systems: Theory and Practice. *ACM Trans. Comput. Syst.* **10** (4), 265-310.

Linn, J. (1990), Practical Authentication for Distributed Systems. *Proceedings of the IEEE Symposium on Security and Privacy*, Oakland, Calif., 31-40.

Needham, R. and Schroeder, M. (1978), Using Encryption for Authentication in Large Networks of Computers. *Commun. ACM* **21** (12), 993-999.

Neuman, C. (1991), Proxy-Based Authorization and Accounting for Distributed Systems. Tech. Rep. 91-02-01, University of Washington, Seattle, Wash.

Rivest, R., Shamir, A., and Adleman, L. (1978), A Method for Obtaining Digital Signatures and Public-Key Cryptosystems. *Commun. ACM* **21** (2), 120-126.

Rivest, R. (1991), The MD4 Message Digest Algorithm. In *Advances in Cryptology— Crypto '90*, Springer, 303-311.

Rivest, R. and Dusse, S. (1991), *The MD5 Message-Digest Algorithm.* Internet Draft [MD5-A]: draft-rsadsi-rivest-md5-01.txt.

Saltzer, J., Reed, D., and Clark, D. (1984), End-to-End Arguments in System Design. *ACM Trans. Comput. Syst.* **2** (4), 277-288.

Shand, M., Bertin, P., and Vuillemin, J. (1990), Resource Tradeoffs in Fast Long Integer Multiplication. In *2nd ACM Symposium on Parallel Algorithms and Architectures*, Crete.

Steiner, J., Neuman, C., and Schiller, J. (1988), Kerberos: An Authentication Service for Open Network Systems. In *Proceedings of the Usenix Winter Conference*, Berkeley, Calif., 191-202.

Tardo, J. and Alagappan, K. (1991), SPX: Global Authentication Using Public Key Certificates. *Proceedings of the IEEE Symposium on Security and Privacy*, Oakland, Calif., 232-244.

Voydock, V. and Kent, S. (1983), Security Mechanisms in High-Level Network Protocols. *ACM Comput. Surv.* **15** (2), 135-171.

Index

Authors' Biographies

Özalp Babaoğlu

Özalp Babaoğlu is Professor of Computer Science at the University of Bologna, Italy. He received a Ph.D. in 1981 from the University of California at Berkeley where he was one of the principal designers of BSD Unix. Before moving to Bologna in 1988, Babaoğlu was an Associate Professor in the Department of Computer Science at Cornell University. He is active in several European research projects exploring issues related to fault tolerance and large scale in distributed systems. Babaoğlu serves on the editorial boards for ACM *Transactions on Computer Systems* and Springer-Verlag *Distributed Computing*.

Navin Budhiraja

Navin Budhiraja received a B.Tech. in Computer Science from IIT Kanpur in 1988, and a M.S. and Ph.D. in Computer Science from Cornell University in 1991 and 1993 respectively. In 1993, he joined the IBM T.J. Watson Research Center where he is currently a Research Staff Member. He has published papers in the area of Fault-Tolerant Distributed Computing, Network Simulators and Natural Language Parsing.

Vassos Hadzilacos

Vassos Hadzilacos received a BSE from Princeton University in 1980 and a Ph.D. from Harvard University in 1984, both in Computer Science. In 1984 he joined the Department of Computer Science at the University of Toronto where he is currently an Associate Professor. In 1990–1991 he was visiting Associate Professor in the Department of Computer Science at Cornell University. His research interests are in the theory of distributed systems.

Hermann Kopetz

Hermann Kopetz received his Ph.D. degree in physics *'sub auspiciis praesidentis'* from the University of Vienna, Austria in 1968. He was a manager of a computer process control department at Vöst Alpine in Linz, Austria, before joining the

Technical University of Berlin as a Professor for Computer Process Control in 1978. Since 1982 he is Professor for Real-Time Systems at the Technical University of Vienna.

His research interests focus at the intersection of real-time systems, fault-tolerant systems, and distributed systems. Dr. Kopetz is the chief architect of the MARS project on distributed fault-tolerant real-time systems at the Technical University of Vienna. He has published more than 80 papers in these fields and has been active in the organisation of many international conferences. From 1990 to 1992 he was the chairman of the IEEE Technical Committee on Fault-Tolerant Computing. In 1993, Dr. Kopetz has been elected 'Fellow of the IEEE'.

Butler W. Lampson

Butler Lampson is a Senior Corporate Consulting Engineer at Digital Equipment Corporation. He has worked on computer architecture, local area networks, raster printers, page description languages, operating systems, remote procedure call, programming languages and their semantics, programming in the large, fault-tolerant computing, computer security, and WYSIWYG editors. He was one of the designers of the SDS 940 time-sharing system, the Alto personal distributed computing system, the Xerox 9700 laser printer, two-phase commit protocols, the Autonet LAN, and several programming languages.

He holds a Ph.D. in EECS from the University of California at Berkeley and an honorary ScD from the Eidgenoessische Techniche Hochschule, Zurich. He holds patents on networks, security, raster printing, and transaction processing. He is a member of the National Academy of Engineering and a fellow of the American Academy of Arts and Sciences. He received the ACM's Software Systems Award in 1984 for his work on the Alto, and the Turing Award in 1992.

Keith Marzullo

Dr. Keith Marzullo is an associate professor in the Computer Science and Engineering Department at the University of California in San Diego. Dr. Marzullo received his Ph.D. from Stanford University in 1986, and has subsequently worked at Xerox Corporation in Palo Alto, California, was on the Computer Science faculty at Cornell University, and was a principal member of ISIS Distributed Systems, Inc. He has also been a consultant, and is currently consulting for IBM FSD on the application design of the FAA Air Traffic Control System. His research interests are in the principles and the engineering of fault-tolerant distributed systems in both hard-real-time and asynchronous settings. He is currently leading a research team in the design and implementation of Corto, a group-based communication system that is portable across real-time Unix platforms and supports the development of hard-real-time, fault-tolerant systems.

Sape J. Mullender

Sape Mullender is professor of systems programming and architecture in the Faculty of Computer Science of the University of Twente in the Netherlands, where he leads the Huygens research project on fault-tolerance, real time, security and multimedia in distributed systems.

He received his Ph.D. from the Vrije Universiteit in Amsterdam and was a faculty member there until 1983. From 1984 to 1990 he has been the head of the distributed systems and computer networks research group at the Centre of Mathematics and Computer Science (CWI) in Amsterdam. He is a principal designer of the Amoeba distributed operating system.

Sape Mullender is particularly interested in high-performance distributed computing and the design of scalable fault-tolerant services. He is also concerned about organization and security of distributed systems that can span a continent.

He has published papers on file systems, high-performance RPC protocols, locating migratable objects in computer networks, and protection mechanisms, and has been the principal organizer of a series of advanced courses on distributed systems — Arctic'88, Fingerlakes'89, Bologna'90, Karuizawa'91, Lisboa'92 and Seattle'93. He is vice-chairman and conference coordinator of the ACM Special Interest Group on Operating Systems.

Roger M. Needham

Roger Needham is Professor of Computer Systems at the University of Cambridge, where he has been Head of the Computer Laboratory since 1980. He took his Ph.D. from Cambridge in 1961 and has worked there ever since. He was elected to the Royal Society in 1985 and the Royal Academy of Engineering in 1993.

Needham has contributed extensively to many aspects of distributed computing and has most recently been interested in computer protection and security.

Thomas L. Rodeheffer

Dr. Thomas L. Rodeheffer is a Research Engineer at Digital's Systems Research Center in Palo Alto, California. He received a Ph.D. in Computer Science from Carnegie Mellon in 1985. His primary interest is discovering efficient and elegant solutions in low-level systems such as compilers, operating systems, and computer networks.

Mahadev Satyanarayanan

Mahadev Satyanarayanan is an Associate Professor of Computer Science at Carnegie Mellon University. His research addresses the problem of information access in large distributed systems. He currently leads work on the Coda File System, whose mechanisms for high availability have proved to be a key enabling technology for mobile computing.

Prior to his work on Coda, Satyanarayanan was a principal architect and implementor of the Andrew File System, now a widely used commercial product. Satyanarayanan received the Ph.D. in Computer Science from CMU in 1983, after the B.Tech. and M.Tech. from the Indian Institute of Technology, Madras. He was named a Presidential Young Investigator by the National Science Foundation in 1987.

Fred B. Schneider

Fred B. Schneider is a Professor of Computer Science at Cornell University, where he has been on the faculty since 1978. His research is primarily concerned with methodologies for designing and reasoning about concurrent programs, particularly fault-tolerant and distributed ones. Schneider is author (along with D. Gries) of *A Logical Approach to Discrete Math*. He is the managing editor of *Distributed Computing*, co-managing editor of Springer-Verlag Texts and Monographs in Computer Science, as well as being a member of the editorial boards for *Information Processing Letters*, *IEEE Transactions on Software Engineering*, *High Integrity Systems*, and *Annals of Software Engineering*. In 1993, Schneider was elected a Fellow of the American Association for the Advancement of Sciences.

Michael D. Schroeder

Dr. Michael D. Schroeder is a Senior Consulting Engineer at Digital's Systems Research Center in Palo Alto, California. He received a Ph.D. in Computer Science from MIT in 1972, was a faculty member at MIT and was a member of the research staff at Xerox PARC before joining SRC in 1984. His particular interest is discovering practical structures for distributed systems. He has worked on time-sharing systems, computer protection and security, encryption-based authentication protocols, replicated transport systems for e-mail, e-mail user interfaces, global naming in large networks, remote-procedure-call performance, distributed file systems, structures for client-server computing, and switch-based local area networks.

Sam Toueg

Sam Toueg received a B.Sc. from the Technion in 1976 and a Ph.D. from Princeton University in 1979, both in Computer Science. In 1981 he joined the Department of Computer Science at Cornell University where he is currently a Professor. He has published papers in the area of Fault-Tolerant Distributed Computing, and is a past Program Committee Chairman of the ACM Symposium on Principles of Distributed Computing and of the International Workshop on Distributed Algorithms.

Paulo Veríssimo

Dr. Paulo Veríssimo is a professor at IST — in the Technical University of Lisboa. At INESC he leads the Distributed Systems and Industrial Automation Group. His group has been in several projects in distributed systems, the most prominent of which is the DELTA-4 project. His interests are: real-time and dependability in distributed systems and computer networks; group-oriented architectures and protocols; support for CSCW and distributed computer control. He is an editor for Baltzer Telecommunications Systems Journal.

William E. Weihl

William E. Weihl is an Associate Professor of Computer Science and Engineering at the Massachusetts Institute of Technology. His research addresses a wide range of issues in parallel and distributed systems, including high-performance communication and synchronization, programming languages, compilers, fault-tolerance, and scalability.

Dr. Weihl's recent work has focused on methodological issues related to parallel programming, and has included the design and implementation of the Prelude parallel programming system and the Proteus multiprocessor simulator. In earlier work, he was one of the principal designers of the Argus programming language and system and of the Mercury communications system. He also made significant contributions to the theory of atomic transactions. He is a co-author, with Nancy Lynch, Michael Merritt, and Alan Fekete, of a recent book that presents a comprehensive theoretical framework for describing, analyzing, and designing algorithms for transaction processing, particularly for nested transaction systems.

Dr. Weihl received the S.B. degree in Mathematics in 1979, the S.B. and S.M. degrees in Computer Science in 1980, and the Ph.D. degree in Computer Science in 1984, all from the Massachusetts Institute of Technology. He joined the MIT faculty in 1984. He is a member of the editorial board of the Journal of Programming Languages.